EVERY CATHOLIC AN APOSTLE

EVERY CATHOLIC AN APOSTLE

A Life of Thomas A. Judge, CM, 1868–1933

WILLIAM L. PORTIER

The Catholic University of America Press
Washington, D.C.

The paper used in this publication meets the minimum requirements of American National Standards for Information Science—Permanence of Paper for Printed Library Materials, ANSI Z39.48–1984.
∞

Image on page iii: Father Thomas A. Judge. Library of Congress, Prints & Photographs Division, photograph by Harris & Ewing.

LIBRARY OF CONGRESS CATALOGING-IN-PUBLICATION DATA
Names: Portier, William L., author.
Title: Every Catholic an apostle : a life of Thomas A. Judge, CM, 1868–1933 / William L. Portier.
Description: Washington, D.C. : The Catholic University of America Press, 2017. | Includes bibliographical references and index.
Identifiers: LCCN 2017014452 | ISBN 9780813229812 (pbk. : alk. paper)
Subjects: LCSH: Judge, Thomas Augustine, 1868–1933. | Catholic Church—United States—Clergy—Biography. | Priests—United States—Biography. | Missionary Cenacle Apostolate—History. | Missionary Servants of the Most Holy Trinity—History. | Missionary Servants of the Most Blessed Trinity—History.
Classification: LCC BX4705.J77 P67 2017 | DDC 271/.79 [B]—dc23
LC record available at https://lccn.loc.gov/2017014452

❖ In grateful remembrance of
Father Brendan Smith, ST (1928–2001)

CONTENTS

ILLUSTRATIONS

Illustrations appear between pages 11 and 16. Courtesy of the Archives of the Missionary Servants of the Most Holy Trinity, Silver Spring, Md.

ACKNOWLEDGMENTS

Back in 2001, the late Fr. Austin Walsh, Custodian General of the Missionary Servants of the Most Holy Trinity, approached me about writing Fr. Judge's biography. When I began working on it in 2002, neither he nor I realized how long it would take to finish. I am especially grateful to Fr. Austin for his confidence in me, his patience, and his kind support and encouragement, and to his successor, Father John Edmunds, for more of the same. Over the past fourteen years of research and writing, many people have been there with the help I needed. It is now my happy task to thank them.

The work began at the archives in Silver Spring in the fall of 2002. Thank you to Fr. Ralph Frisch, ST, the archivist, and to Bro. Hilary Mettes, ST, for their warm welcome and hospitality. I am also grateful to Sr. Theresa Ahern, MSBT, for welcoming me to the archives of the Missionary Servants of the Most Blessed Trinity in Philadelphia and her generous responses to my ongoing queries. A special thank you to Fr. John Carven, CM, not only for welcoming me to the Ducournau Archives in Philadelphia and guiding me through the world of St. Vincent de Paul, but also for the interest he has taken in this project over the years and for his help and support in many ways. In matters of St. Vincent, I am also grateful to Sr. Marie Poole, DC, editor in chief of the English edition of St. Vincent's works and our Emmitsburg neighbor.

Thank you to Richard Chastang, Archives of the Archdiocese of Mobile; Tricia Pyne, Associated Archives at St. Mary's Seminary and University, Baltimore; Phil Runkel, Marquette University's Special Collections and University Archives; John Shepherd and staff, American Catholic History Research Center at Catholic University; Joseph Casino, Philadelphia Archdiocesan Historical Research Center; Sr. Betty Ann McNeil, DC, Provincial Archives, Daughters of Charity, Emmitsburg; Phil Haas, Archives of the Diocese of Cleveland; Pat McNamara, Archives of the Diocese of Brooklyn; Fr. Walter

Gagne, SA, Atonement Archives and Records Center; and Sr. Angela Pikus, Carmelite Monastery, Elysburg, Pennsylvania.

By the nature of their work, historians rely on those who have gone before, painstakingly collecting and assembling sources and doing the groundbreaking work in them. Though I never met Sr. Mary James Collins, MSBT, or Fr. Lawrence Brediger, ST, I am acutely conscious of my debts to them and to those who have worked in the sources Collins and Brediger assembled, especially to Fr. Timothy Lynch, ST, and his associates on the six volumes of monographs related to Fr. Judge's life and work, and also to the scholars of what I refer to in the text as the "Cenacle *ressourcement*" that followed the Second Vatican Council: Sr. Joseph Miriam Blackwell, Sr. Mary Tonra, Fr. James P. O'Bryan, Sr. Marie Josepha McNutt, and my old friend, Fr. Dennis Berry.

My research and writing were supported by the Missionary Servants of the Most Holy Trinity in the academic year 2002–3 and by sabbatical leaves from the University of Dayton in the spring of 2009 and the academic year 2015–16, during which I enjoyed the hospitality of the Theology Department at Mount St. Mary's University. During the years of research, I was fortunate to have the help of many graduate assistants at the University of Dayton. Among them, I am especially grateful to Robert Parks, Dara Delgado, and Laurie Eloe. Two Dayton graduate students gave me special assistance. The outstanding 2006 MA thesis on the MSBT constitutions and Rule of Life by Sr. Deborah Wilson, MSBT, was a great help to me in navigating Fr. Judge's complex canonical situation. Before coming to the University of Dayton, Antonio Mari graduated from the Marianists' Colegio San José in Rio Piedras, Puerto Rico. I am grateful to Antonio for reading chapter 9 and for the gift of Bro. Joseph Jansen's *The First Seventy-Five Years*. Thank you to Sr. Deb and Antonio!

When the manuscript was completed in draft, seven Missionary Servants read and carefully commented on it. For their helpful, and in many cases indispensable, comments and suggestions, I am deeply grateful to Sr. Theresa Ahern, Fr. Gary Banks, Bro. Jordan Baxter, Fr. Dennis Berry, Sr. Sara Butler, the late Sr. Joseph Miriam Blackwell, and Fr. Sidney Griffith.

Over the course of many months, Fr. John Carven read and commented extensively and insightfully on every chapter of the final manuscript. His careful reading resulted in many clarifications and the avoidance of numerous mistakes. Thank you, Fr. Carven! After the manuscript was revised in response to previous readers, Bill Collinge went through it once more. More clarifications and corrections followed. Thank you, Bill! I am also extremely grateful to the two anonymous readers at the Catholic University of America Press, to Theresa Walker for her careful guidance, to Aldene Fredenburg for her copy editing, and to Trevor Lipscombe for his confidence in me and his longtime interest in this biography.

Over the past decade, my "handler," Fr. Gary Banks, ST, has worked closely with me on this book as liaison, adviser, researcher, translator, and trusted friend. Without Gary there would be no biography.

This book is dedicated to Fr. Brendan Smith, ST, beloved teacher and exemplary bearer of Fr. Judge's spirit. I met Fr. Brendan in September 1959 when I went to Holy Trinity, Alabama, as a high school seminarian. He taught first-year English. He was the assistant high school prefect and director extraordinaire of our plays. Brilliantly zany and unutterably kind, he taught us Sophocles and Shakespeare and Faulkner and Eliot in college. When I grew older, I realized that all those crazy movies he used to show us on Friday nights were the classics of the American film canon. Among many wonderful teachers, he was the most memorable. There are probably still a few hundred old guys out there who will testify to his lasting effects on us. How I wish he could read this book.

Once, in 2007, when I was particularly discouraged at my slow progress, Austin reminded me that Brendan, who always seemed late or behind, used to laugh at the title of the very sad 1982 film *I'm Dancing as Fast as I Can*. As the years went by, on an almost nightly basis, I asked for Brendan's prayers that I could get it done. As always, he came through.

Fr. Judge's youngest sister, Sr. Alice Judge, DC, died in 1950. She is buried in the old cemetery on the grounds of the Seton Shrine Basilica in Emmitsburg. Over the years, Sr. Alice gave me a kind of local and physical link to Fr. Judge. Often I would walk through the cemetery, stopping at her grave between the fifth and sixth Stations of the Cross on the stone wall around the old cemetery, asking for her prayers, as well. On most of these cemetery trips, my wife walked with me, as she has for these past forty-six years. Thank you, Bonnie!

In spite of all this prodigious help, the errors that no doubt remain are solely mine.

William L. Portier

ABBREVIATIONS

AAM	Archives, Archdiocese of Mobile
ACUA	American Catholic History Research Center and University Archives
ADC	Archives, Diocese of Cleveland
AMSBT	Archives of the Missionary Servants of the Most Blessed Trinity
AST	Archives of the Missionary Servants of the Most Holy Trinity
CM	Congregation of the Mission
CO	Congregation of the Oratory
CSJ	Sisters of St. Joseph
CSsR	Congregation of the Most Holy Redeemer
DA	Ducournau Archives, St. Vincent Seminary
DC	Sisters of Charity of St. Vincent De Paul
DD	Doctor of Divinity
FSC	Fratres Scholarum Christianarum (Brothers of the Christian Schools)
IHM	Sisters, Servants of the Immaculate Heart of Mary
MF	Microfilm number
Monographs 2	*Father Thomas A. Judge, C.M., Founder, The Missionary Cenacle Family, Early Days and Final Days*
Monographs 3	*Father Thomas A. Judge, C.M., Founder, The Missionary Cenacle Family, Father Judge Teaches Ministry*

Monographs 4	*Father Thomas A. Judge, C.M., Founder, the Missionary Cenacle Family, The Writings of Father Judge: Key Documents*
Monographs 5	*Father Thomas A. Judge, C.M., Founder, The Missionary Cenacle Family, The Grace of Our Founder*
Monographs 6	*Father Thomas A. Judge, C.M., Founder, The Missionary Cenacle Family, Father Judge and the Missionary Cenacle*
MSBT	Missionary Servants of the Most Blessed Trinity
MSSsT	Missionary Servants of the Most Holy Trinity
NCCC	National Conference of Catholic Charities
NCE	*New Catholic Encyclopedia*
NCWC	National Catholic War Council (1917); National Catholic Welfare Council (1919)
OFM Cap.	Order of Friars Minor Capuchin (Capuchins)
OSA	Order of St. Augustine
OSF	Order of St. Francis of Assisi
PAHRC	Philadephia Archdiocesan Historical Research Center
RSM	Sisters of Mercy
SA	Society of the Atonement
SJ	Society of Jesus
SM	Society of Mary
SS	Society of St. Sulpice
SSCM	Servants of the Holy Heart of Mary
ST	Missionary Servants of the Most Holy Trinity
USCCB	United States Conference of Catholic Bishops

EVERY CATHOLIC
AN APOSTLE

INTRODUCTION

Father Judge at Vatican II

> In view of the immensity of the suffering still afflicting the greater part of the human race, and with a view to the universal promotion of justice as well as the love of Christ for the poor, the council considers it most appropriate that an organization of the universal church should be set up to stimulate the catholic [*sic*] community to the promotion of progress in poor areas and social justice among nations.

This closing section of paragraph 90 of *Gaudium et spes*, the Second Vatican Council's Pastoral Constitution on the Church in the World of Today, led to the creation by Pope Paul VI in 1967 of the Pontifical Council on Justice and Peace.[1] This section found its way into *Gaudium et spes* through the intervention of "the only layman to participate in the debates of the Second Vatican Council."[2] His name was James Norris. He had spent the previous decades working with migrants and refugees in Europe for Catholic Relief Services and its forerunner agency, War Relief Services.

Between 1924 and 1934, however, he had been known as "Brother James," boy genius and heir apparent to Father Thomas A. Judge, founder of an early twentieth-century Catholic lay missionary movement and the two religious communities that grew from it. Father Judge deemed Norris

1. The text is cited here from Norman P. Tanner, SJ, ed., *Decrees of the Ecumenical Councils* (London: Sheed and Ward; Washington, D.C.: Georgetown University Press, 1990), 2:1134.

2. This designation is from Raymond J. Kupke, "An American Intervention at Rome: Father Judge and James Norris at Vatican II," in *Building the Church in America: Studies in Honor of Monsignor Robert F. Trisco on the Occasion of His Seventieth Birthday*, ed. Joseph C. Linck, CO, and Raymond J. Kupke (Washington, D.C.: The Catholic University of America Press, 1999), 247. Two other laymen addressed the council: Patrick Keegan of England on October 13 and Juan Vasquez of Argentina on November 10. Keegan spoke in English, Vasquez in Spanish. Norris spoke in Latin in the great aula; see Giuseppe Alberigo and Joseph Komonchak, eds., *History of Vatican II* (Maryknoll, N.Y.: Orbis; Leuven: Peeters, 2003), 4:27, 318.

so indispensable to the work that he never made a canonical novitiate. After Father Judge's death, Norris separated from the community and eventually went to work for the National Catholic Welfare Conference. By the time of the council he was president of the International Catholic Migration Commission and assistant to the executive director of Catholic Relief Services. Norris had urged a "dramatic intervention" on world poverty by a woman economist such as Lady Jackson (Barbara Ward). That proposal was rejected, and on the evening of November 4, Norris learned that he was to address the assembled bishops. He wrote his Latin text that night.

On November 5, 1964, in the great aula, Norris addressed a fourteen-minute Latin intervention to the assembled Council fathers. Its English title was, "World Poverty and the Christian Conscience." Norris saw the obliteration of world poverty as a long and arduous work. The churches alone, he thought, and especially the Catholic Church, had the staying power to undertake it. To wipe out world poverty, Norris called for "a strong, committed, well-informed, and courageous group of men of good will" in each wealthy country. After a gruesome look at the sheer human misery of the world's poor, he urged, "A loving human family does not permit its members to suffer in this way."

In concluding, he asked the fathers for "a clarion call for action" to create a structure that might "secure full Catholic participation in the world wide attack on poverty."

> This great gathering of bishops represents every continent and every country on earth. Since world poverty affects all humanity, the great contribution of our universal Church can be a world-encircling manifestation of brotherly love, bringing effectively to bear the social teaching of the Church.

He concluded with the words of his friend Pope Paul VI urging that, in the spirit of Christ who had compassion on the multitude, "We make our own the sufferings of the poor."[3]

As a result of Norris's intervention, there followed the proposal already cited from the conclusion of paragraph 90 of *Gaudium et spes* and eventually Paul VI's creation of the Pontifical Council on Justice and Peace in 1967. On November 13, eight days after Norris's intervention, Paul VI made the sym-

3. For a translation of Norris's Latin text, see Floyd Anderson, ed., *Council Daybook, Vatican II, Session 3, September 14–November 21, 1964* (1965; repr. Washington, D.C.: National Catholic Welfare Conference, 2005), 225. See the accounts of Norris's intervention in Xavier Rynne [Francis X. Murphy, CSsR], *Vatican Council II* (1968; repr. Maryknoll, N.Y.: Orbis, 1999), 376–78, and Alberigo and Komonchak, *History of Vatican II*, 4:25–27, 318–22, 372–74.

bolic gift of the papal tiara the people of Milan had given him upon his election. It now rests in the lower level of the Basilica of the Shrine of the Immaculate Conception in Washington, D.C. Nearby is a bust of James Norris, whose speech is thought to have influenced the pope's decision.[4]

In Norris's advocacy for the poor, and especially in his conciliar plea to the family of the church on behalf of the world's hungry, his biographer, Raymond Kupke, heard clear echoes of Norris's early mentor, Father Judge, who had died thirty-one years before. Norris himself died in 1976, twelve years after his historic participation at the Council. "Lest anyone doubt the enduring effect of Father Judge on James Norris," Kupke wrote, "among the personal effects found in Norris's wallet that day [November 15, 1976] were a prayer to the Holy Spirit, composed for him personally four decades earlier by Father Judge, as well as a lock of Judge's hair."[5]

His brief appearance and influence at Vatican II in the person of James Norris highlight Father Judge's signature emphasis on the apostolic role of the laity in the world and his care for the poor and abandoned. The two canonical religious communities he founded are still carrying on his work. But, as this opening story suggests, Father Judge's wider impact has to do with his prophetic instincts about the laity. *Lumen gentium*, chapter 4, on the Laity, and chapter 5, on the Universal Call to Holiness, along with the entirety of *Apostolicam actuositatem*, the Decree on the Apostolate of the Laity, testify to his far-sighted pastoral vision.

At the Council, James Norris stood in for the thousands of Catholics Father Judge and his followers inspired and formed as lay apostles. Now little known outside the circle of his own religious family, Father Judge was in his own day a powerful preacher and leading figure in the American church. Kupke's story of Norris leads back to Father Judge, underlines his significance, and points to the need to tell Judge's own story.

Father Judge in Brief

Born in Boston of Irish immigrant parents, Thomas A. Judge, CM (1868–1933) preached up and down the East Coast on the Vincentian mission band

4. Alberigo and Komonchak, *History of Vatican II*, 4:374.

5. Kupke, "An American Intervention at Rome," 251, 242. Two chapters of Kupke's doctoral dissertation are devoted to Norris's decade of association with the Missionary Servants of the Most Holy Trinity, the men's community founded by Father Judge; see Kupke, "James J. Norris: An American Catholic Life" (Ph.D. diss., The Catholic University of America, 1995), chaps. 2 and 3.

between 1903 and 1915. Disturbed by leakage of the immigrant poor from the church, he enlisted and organized lay women he met on the missions to work for "the preservation of the faith." His work anticipated papal teaching on the lay apostolate. When he was sent to the Vincentian Alabama mission in 1915, his superior urged him to invite the lay apostles to come south to help him. They came.

"This is the layman's hour," he wrote in 1919.[6] By then, however, many of his lay apostles had evolved in the direction of vowed communal life. This pioneer of the lay apostolate soon found himself the head of a missionary Cenacle family that included a religious community of women, the Missionary Servants of the Most Blessed Trinity, and a community of men, the Missionary Servants of the Most Holy Trinity. He spent the last decade of his life organizing these groups and trying to help them promote the lay apostolate. As he articulated it in 1922, they aimed "to train the work-a-day man and woman into an apostle, to cause each to be alert to the interests of the Church, to be the Church."[7]

The decade of Charles Lindbergh and Babe Ruth saw boundaries shift and possibilities expand. An ecclesial entrepreneur in an immigrant church, Father Judge exploited the increasing fluidity of women's roles in both national life and in the 1917 Code of Canon Law to capture the imaginations of a new kind of woman in the church and to address the needs of the immigrant poor they served. The roaring twenties saw the work grow beyond the Alabama missions as far as Puerto Rico, which Father Judge envisioned as a gateway to Latin America.

The Great Depression of 1929 ended the decade's expansive mood and put agonizing pressure on Father Judge and his work. In the year before Father Judge's death, the apostolic delegate Archbishop Pietro Fumasoni-Biondi, upon being apprised of Father Judge's financial straits, described his work as "the only organized movement of its kind in the Church today that so completely meets the wishes of the Holy Father with reference to the Lay Apostolate."[8] Father Judge's death on November 23, 1933, put this movement at risk.

At the time of Father Judge's death, the women's community, the Mis-

6. Thomas A. Judge, CM, "A Spiritual Militia," *Ecclesiastical Review* 61, no. 3 (September 1919): 277.

7. Judge to Mother Boniface Keasey, Brooklyn, September 28, 1922, Father Judge Papers, Archives of the Missionary Servants of the Most Holy Trinity (hereafter AST), Silver Spring, Md., Microfilm number (hereafter MF) 7545–46.

8. The delegate's description is cited in Monsignor Thomas Nummey to Bishop Thomas E. Molloy, March 19, 1932, Nummey Papers, Archives of the Roman Catholic Diocese of Brooklyn.

sionary Servants of the Most Blessed Trinity, were in relatively stable condition with more than two hundred members and some thirty foundations. His death plunged the much smaller and unstable men's community, the Missionary Servants of the Most Holy Trinity, into a period of turbulence from which it did not fully emerge until after the Second World War.

Plan and Sources of This Work

As the previous sketch suggests, Father Judge's life divides itself into three parts: (1) Beginnings, 1868–1915; (2) The Creative Center, 1915–26; (3) Times of Trial and Loss, 1926–33. The first three chapters treat the period of beginnings up to Father Judge's appointment to the Vincentian Alabama mission in 1915. Six chapters are devoted to the creative center of his life between 1915 and 1926. They include the beginnings of the sisters' community, with Mother Boniface Keasey as founding mother general; the founding of the Cenacle Bethlehem at Holy Trinity, Alabama; the building of the sisters' motherhouse there; and expansion into Puerto Rico.

The final period of trial and loss and its aftermath are treated in the last eight chapters. These chapters include the death of Bishop Edward P. Allen of Mobile and his replacement by Bishop Thomas Toolen, who came to view Father Judge as a fiscally irresponsible visionary; the effects of the Great Depression on the sisters' attempt to build a state-of-the-art hospital in Gadsden, Alabama; the destruction by fire of the sisters' motherhouse at Holy Trinity and the subsequent death of Mother Boniface at age forty-six in what appears to have been an outbreak of typhoid; and the death of Father Judge in 1933, the ensuing turmoil in the men's community leading to an apostolic visitation that lasted from 1937 to 1949, and the beginnings of the renewal of the Cenacle's family spirit in the late twentieth century.

Historical and biographical writing involves choices that are often a function of the extent and nature of the sources. Father Judge had neither a spiritual nor a theological system. He did, however, leave more than fifteen thousand pages of papers, mostly unpublished and chiefly in the form of letters. Based primarily on these sources, this book is more a chronological than a thematic study of Father Judge, his work, and his legacy. It seeks to show the reader his thoughts and beliefs over time rather than to summarize them systematically. Though not as prolific as St. Vincent de Paul, his patron and exemplar, the extent and often only indirectly personal nature of the sources are daunting.

Until near the end of his life, Father Judge rarely spoke directly about himself, telling his correspondents how he felt and what he thought. Writing about him has required quoting his own words freely and generously in hopes of conveying a faithful sense of his personality and his voice and how he inspired so many people to do extraordinary things. Near the end of Father Judge's life, the sources seem to increase exponentially; it took four lengthy chapters to narrate the last three years of his life. All of this has resulted in a long but, I pray, not tedious, book.

As mentioned, its primary unpublished sources are the more than fifteen thousand pages of Father Judge's papers, as well as related collections, housed at the Archives of the Missionary Servants of the Most Blessed Trinity in Philadelphia and the archives of the Missionary Servants of the Most Holy Trinity in Silver Spring, Maryland. These collections contain full runs of the *Holy Ghost* and *Preservation of the Faith* mission magazines. The archival collections listed in the bibliography contain further unpublished sources.

The aim of this biography is to tell the story of Father Judge's life and work from the documentary sources to contextualize him in the broad sweep of the history of the United States and more specifically in the history of U.S. Catholicism. To the extent possible, I hope to reconstruct the worlds in which Father Judge made sense and bring both him and his lasting significance to life in the present.

A note on terms: central to the drama of Father Judge's life was the attempt to squeeze his vision of the Cenacle as a religious family into the emerging canonical structures of religious life at the beginning of the twentieth century. This is the setting for his use of the terms *sister* and *brother.* In the beginning, these terms are used broadly, sometimes as an expedient, to refer to the early members, some of whom were in private vows, of what Father Judge might have called the "Cenacle movement." Until the two communities he founded received canonical recognition (the men in 1929, the women in 1932), none of these people were sisters and brothers in any canonical sense. The distinction between clerical and lay brothers or between student brothers and missionary brothers has more to do with canon law than with Father Judge's founding vision. In his eyes, every Missionary Servant, whether a candidate for the priesthood or not, had the same missionary vocation and spirituality.

The story of Father Judge's life is filled with references to the *Rule* or *constitutions* of the two communities. Church law distinguishes *rule,* a broader spiritual framework under which families of religious communities such as Benedictines or Augustinians can organize themselves, and *constitutions*, which are specific to particular communities. Father Judge often uses these terms interchangeably. In the technical sense, it was *constitutions* that he was writing.

Finally, Father Judge referred to the religious movement or family that he founded as the Cenacle or Missionary Cenacle. *Cenacle* includes both the religious communities of men and women and the lay apostles associated with them in what was at first called the "Outer Cenacle" and, after 1950, the Missionary Cenacle Apostolate. Individual houses of Missionary Servants, whether of women or of men, were also known as cenacles. When referring to the movement as a whole, I capitalize Cenacle. When referring to individual houses or foundations, unless they have a specific proper name—for example, Holy Trinity Missionary Cenacle—cenacle is not capitalized.

PART 1

BEGINNINGS, 1868–1915

Figure 1. Andrew Philips and Eugene Brennan arrive at Phenix City in July and live in St. Patrick's Rectory, 1916.

Figure 2. Move to the old Mott Plantation in Cottonton; seated (l. to r.): Lou Keasey, Ella Lonergan, Eugene Brennan, and Mary Weiskircher, 1917.

Figure 3. Old Negro cabin that was transformed into the first chapel on the plantation. Behind is the old smokehouse that was Fr. Judge's sacristy/bedroom, 1917. First Missionary Servants of the Most Holy Trinity surrounding Father Judge in front of the old chapel, 1926.

Figure 4. Children of Holy Trinity Academy, the plantation school. Fr. Judge and Bro. Augustine on left; Mother Boniface in middle of children, 1922.

Figure 5. Children of the plantation school with Sr. Zita Friedenburg, 1930. There was serious KKK opposition to this school.

Figure 6. Fr. Judge at retreat in Stirling, New Jersey. Dr. Barrett, his close associate, is on his left, 1924.

Figure 7. June 11 was the completion and dedication of the sisters' new motherhouse, 1924.

Figure 8. The sisters had more than 136 members, and the men's group clothed 26 in the habit, 1924.

Figure 9. Fr. Judge with the faculty, brothers, sisters, and cadets of St. Augustine's Military Academy, Río Piedras, Puerto Rico, 1932.

Figure 10. Fr. Judge, Mother Boniface, and the first sister graduates of Gadsden Nursing School. Seated (l. to r): Sr. Rose Francis, Sr. Marie Dolorosa, Sr. Mary Grace; standing: Sr. Mary Edward, Mother Boniface, Fr. Judge, Sr. Joseph Mary, 1928.

Figure 11. St. Joseph Apostolic School to form priests, in Holy Trinity, Alabama, 1928.

Figure 12. Mother Boniface, cofounder of the MSBT Sisters, 1928.

❖ I

YOUNG TOM JUDGE

Early Life

Irish Americans

"Once I thought to write a history of the immigrants in America," Oscar Handlin wrote. "Then I discovered that the immigrants were American history."[1] We are, to borrow the title of John Fitzgerald Kennedy's posthumously published book, *A Nation of Immigrants*. Immigration defines nineteenth-century American history. Immigration shaped the life and work of Thomas Judge, Boston-born son of Irish immigrant parents.

In the century between 1820 and 1920, 4.3 million Irish sailed across the Atlantic to the United States.[2] Historians divide the Irish exodus into three periods. The first wave of Irish came between 1820 and 1845. The second wave, the famine and post-famine emigration, lasted from 1846 to 1870. The fifty years between 1870 and 1920 saw the modern migration, or third wave.[3] People left Ireland for many reasons. The potato blight that began in 1846 and lasted for six years is the key event in the second wave of Irish emigration. With an agricultural economy and a growing population, Ireland simply could not deal with the social effects of potato rot. During that six-year period, from 1846 to 1851, a million people starved to death. Another million came to the United States. More than half of them wound up in Boston.

More Irish came to Boston during the 1850s than at any other time. By 1841,

1. Oscar Handlin, *The Uprooted* (Boston: Little, Brown, 1951), 3.

2. Jay P. Dolan, *The American Catholic Experience: A History from Colonial Times to the Present* (Garden City, N.Y.: Doubleday, 1985), 128–29.

3. Timothy J. Meagher, *Inventing Irish America: Generation, Class, and Ethnic Identity in a New England City, 1880–1928* (Notre Dame, Ind.: University of Notre Dame Press, 2001), 22.

the British Cunard Line had made Boston its main port between England and Canada. Most of the second wave of Irish emigrants sailed from Liverpool to Boston. Having spent all they had on the trans-Atlantic voyage, they often had little choice but to remain in Boston.[4] Most lived in "Southie," as the area of South Boston was known. By century's end, it would be known as "Irishtown."

Family

Thomas Judge, from County Sligo, and Mary Danahey, from County Derry, joined the post-famine exodus and landed in Boston sometime during the decade of the 1850s. Like the majority of their fellow exiles, they were unmarried when they arrived. City records indicate that they were married sometime in the second half of 1859, probably on June 6.[5] Their first child, Mary Elizabeth, was born on May 1, 1860.[6] Thomas and Mary Judge had seven more children. John Aloysius came along on June 19, 1861.[7] Then came Ann and Jane. Thomas was the fifth child, born August 23, 1868.[8] He was baptized a week later, on August 31, 1868, at St. Peter and Paul Church in South Boston, where they lived at 122 Sullivan Street.[9] His two older sisters,

4. Handlin, *Boston's Immigrants* (New York: Atheneum, 1971), 49, as cited in Joseph Miriam Blackwell, MSBT, *Ecclesial People: A Study of the Life and Times of Thomas Augustine Judge, CM* (Holy Trinity, Ala.: Missionary Cenacle Press, 1984), 30.

5. In this, as in many of the details of Judge's early life, I am relying upon Blackwell, *Ecclesial People*. Blackwell's second chapter, on Judge's "background and formative years," is the best-documented account of his early life. Blackwell cites city records "denoting their intention to marry as of May 13, 1859"; see 31 and 44n125. The June 6, 1859, date is reported by Thomas and Mary Judge's grandchildren, Alice and Winifred Ledwidge, and Grace Minten, the daughter of Ann Veronica Ledwidge, Father Judge's younger sister. Upon her husband's death, Mrs. Ledwidge became Sr. M. Gerard Majella, MSBT; see Sr. Mary Gerard Ledwidge, MSBT, and the Ledwidge Sisters, "Life with Father Judge," in *Father Thomas A. Judge, C.M., Founder, The Missionary Cenacle Family*, Monographs 2, *Early Days and Final Days*, ed. Timothy Lynch, ST (Silver Spring, Md.: The Archives, Missionary Servants of the Most Holy Trinity, 1983), 10–41. Written many years after the events it describes, this account tends to romanticize them. Nevertheless, used to supplement documentary evidence, it remains a valuable source, especially for the flavor of the Judges' family life that it provides. There is little reason, for example, to doubt the grandchildren's recollection of the counties of origin in Ireland of Thomas and Mary Judge; see 10–11.

6. Blackwell, *Ecclesial People*, 31, 44n126.

7. Ibid., 33, 45n139.

8. Thomas Judge's date of birth is recorded in the Vincentian *Catalogus Personarum in Congregatione Missionis in Provincia Statuum Foederatorum Americae Septentrionalis*, no. 94. After the division into Eastern and Western provinces in 1888 (Father Judge would belong to the Eastern Province), it became *Catalogus Personarum Provinciae Orientalis Statuum Foederatorum Americae*; Ducournau Archives, St. Vincent's Seminary, Philadelphia (hereafter DA).

9. Blackwell cites copies of Thomas Judge's birth records from both the city and Archdiocese of Boston preserved in the Archives of the Missionary Servants of the Most Blessed Trinity, Philadelphia (hereafter AMSBT); see Blackwell, *Ecclesial People*, 33, 45n140.

Ann and Jane, died during his early years, perhaps of lung disease. Thomas was followed by his younger sisters, Ann Veronica, Winifred, and Alice.

Most of the Judges' South Boston neighbors were unskilled laborers. But the elder Thomas Judge had a skill. He was a painter who could do detailed interior work. In 1850 Massachusetts had only 461 painters, 119 of them Irish. With his son John, Thomas Judge had his own painting business. On May 3, 1887, Thomas Judge died at age forty-five.[10] According to family lore, he died of lung disease, perhaps exacerbated by the lead content of his paints. His son Thomas was eighteen years old at the time of his father's death.

Education and Work

The Irish came to Boston as unwelcome outsiders. New England greeted them with nativist suspicion and resisted Catholic schools as "foreign." A mere two decades before Thomas and Mary Judge came to Boston, violent mobs, stoked by Lyman Beecher's anti-Catholic preaching, had burned the Ursuline convent in Charlestown, Massachusetts. Rather than fight the natives on the school question, Bishop John Williams of Boston (1866–1907) preferred to look on as outsider immigrants used public school education to begin their assimilation to American culture and gain a measure of insider status.[11] Cardinal William O'Connell, Boston's archbishop from 1907 to 1944, presided over the Irish ascendancy in Boston. "The Puritan has passed away," he would say, "the Catholic remains."[12] But in 1876, when the young Thomas Judge started elementary school, John Williams was still the bishop of Boston and Boston public schools were the chief route to middle-class respectability for the children of the immigrants.

When he was eight years old, Tom Judge went to John A. Andrew Public School. During this time he was active in St. Augustine's Parish, where Monsignor Denis O'Callaghan was the pastor. He made his first Holy Communion at St. Augustine's and took the name of Augustine for his confirmation name. He also sang in the cathedral choir. His sister Ann Veronica recalled that, due to their father's illness, Tom had to go to work when he finished elementary school. He finished high school at Boston High night

10. Blackwell, *Ecclesial People*, 35, 46n153. The figures on Massachusetts painters are cited at 33, 45n138.

11. James W. Sanders, "Catholics and the School Question in Boston: The Cardinal O'Connell Years," in *Catholic Boston: Studies in Religion and Community, 1870–1970*, ed. Robert E. Sullivan and James M. O'Toole (Boston: Roman Catholic Archbishop of Boston, 1985), 121–22.

12. James M. O'Toole, *Militant and Triumphant: William Henry O'Connell and the Catholic Church in Boston, 1859–1944* (Notre Dame, Ind.: University of Notre Dame Press, 1992), 5.

school.[13] At the time of his father's death, Tom was working in a place that made dental and surgical tools. Previously he had worked in a broom factory. Around 1888, he got a position in the post office.[14]

Shortly after her own husband's death, Mary Judge's sister and her husband died in Ireland, leaving five orphaned children. The strong kinship network among the Irish contributed to immigration, and Mary Judge sent for the five children. They arrived in 1889. She reluctantly sent the three oldest to live with her sister in California, who was in a better financial position to care for them. The death of his father and the presence of two additional mouths to feed made it necessary for Tom to work while completing high school.[15]

Seminary

Around the time he started working in the post office, Tom Judge began thinking about whether he had a vocation to the priesthood. In a pattern familiar to those who have spent time around Irish American men, he tended not to reveal much, at least in words, about what was going on inside him. His natural charm and wit not only made those around him comfortable, but also deflected queries about personal matters. When his younger sister asked him what he wanted to be, he told her a "horse doctor."

Early in November 1889, a Vincentian mission band came to St. Augustine's. It was shortly after this that Tom first talked to his mother about becoming a priest. She asked him if this were a sudden thing, and he told her that he had been looking into local orders. The parish mission had swung him in the direction of the Vincentians, founded in France by St. Vincent de Paul in the seventeenth century. She went to see the pastor, Monsignor O'Callaghan. By January 25, 1890, Thomas Judge was a college student at St. Vincent's Seminary in Germantown, Pennsylvania.[16]

In January 1890, Judge was twenty-one years old. He stayed at St. Vincent's for almost a decade, a decade that concluded with his ordination to the priesthood on May 27, 1899, a few months short of his thirty-first birthday.

13. Ledwidge, "Life with Father Judge," 2:19; see also Dennis Berry, ST, *God's Valiant Warrior* (Holy Trinity, Ala.: Missionary Cenacle Press, 1992), 8, 343n16. Berry prefers the Ledwidge memoir to Blackwell's suggestion that Judge went to night school only after his father's death; see Blackwell, *Ecclesial People*, 35.

14. Ledwidge, "Life with Father Judge," 2:20; Blackwell, *Ecclesial People*, 35.

15. Ledwidge, "Life with Father Judge," 2:16–17; Blackwell gives the more likely 1889 date, whereas the Ledwidge sisters give 1882; see *Ecclesial People*, 31.

16. Most of the information in this paragraph and the previous one is taken from the Ledwidge memoir "Life with Father Judge," 2:20–21.

The basic outline of his life during this decade is relatively easy to sketch. He spent three years, from January 1890 to January 1893, in the college division or apostolic school, which the Vincentians called Gentilly, after its Vincentian counterpart in France. On January 24, 1893, he was received into the novitiate and the Congregation of the Mission. On January 25, 1895, he made his perpetual vows. From 1895 until his ordination in 1899, he studied theology at St. Vincent's Seminary.[17]

As a brand-new college student at Gentilly, Tom Judge had the expected difficulties of homesickness and doubts about his vocation. His weekly letters home show how hard it was for him to separate himself from his family. He worried about their health and finances. In one of his first letters home to "Dear Mother and sisters," he told them that the previous night he had dreamed of his late father and his brother. He dreamed that he was home on vacation. "Imagine my feelings," he wrote, "when I was awakened in the morning by the bell and instead of finding myself in the kitchen at home, where I was talking to you, I found myself in the dormitory."[18]

A letter from his pastor, Monsignor O'Callaghan, reassured him on the day before his entrance into the novitiate. "You certainly have my good wishes and prayers," O'Callaghan wrote, "and if an expression of opinion will tend to give you confidence and also contentment of mind—allow me to say that I deem you a fit subject for the sacerdotal state ... I feel, indeed, that you will be a good Priest."[19] Though we don't have Judge's side of the correspondence, it is clear enough that O'Callaghan is responding to some expression of uncertainty or unworthiness from the twenty-four-year-old soon-to-be novice.

As students left Gentilly for the internal seminary, or novitiate, it was the custom to write a brief appreciation for them in the school diary. Judge's was entered on January 22, 1893.

> "Tom" was of an active and energetic disposition, and quite a favorite among the boys on account of his unselfishness and generous spirit. He belonged

17. Thomas Judge's official record as a Vincentian is found in the ledger-style *Catalogus personarum*, in DA; see note 8.

18. Judge to Mother and sisters, Germantown, February 9, 1890, in "With Love to All, Tom," in *Father Judge Anthology*, ed. Lawrence Brediger, ST (Silver Spring, Md.: Archives, Missionary Servants of the Most Holy Trinity, 1961), 17. The *Anthology* is a privately printed collection of articles that appeared originally in the *Missionary Servant* magazine between 1951 and 1961. This is popular writing that uses no notes to refer to its sources and sometimes relies on memories and oral testimony. For the early years, it is not always possible to corroborate.

19. O'Callaghan to Judge, Boston, January 23, 1893, AMSBT, as cited in Blackwell, *Ecclesial People*, 37, 47n166.

to the serious class but yet was head and heart in all entertainments for the common good. He was earnest in study and steadfast in following the rules of discipline. His preciseness in language and decorum indicated that he was a native of the "City of Culture"—Boston. . . . The Juniors liked him for his kindness and condescension. The Elders found in him an apt student. . . . He made Gentilly his home and did not look beyond it for pleasure or happiness.[20]

The summer of 1892 was the last in which he spent time at home. Tom Judge apparently overcame his difficulties and went on to the novitiate and then theology. One of his classmates recalled him as a seminary student:

> He had jet black hair and piercing eyes. Always very honorable and as good natured as honorable. He was very impulsive, quick tempered; but . . . in all the years I have known him I never saw him lose his head, even though he was at times terribly indignant, the indignation flashing from his eyes. He was always clean-mouthed. He had a very fine tenor voice. . . . He was even in those days a very dramatic elocutionist, and had a great penchant for writing, a good student, and a reader of good literature. And with all his other qualities he had a keen sense of humor. This attended him all through his life till maybe 1908. Then the seriousness of the work he was in seemed to drown all his humor, but not his good nature. I've always thought that he could have made one of the greatest humorists of the country had he taken to that kind of literature. Mark Twain had nothing on him. He was very active but did not take much to athletics. He never was a very good ball player. He was always of a very nervous constitution; anything he took up he held with greatest tenacity.[21]

Tom Judge spent ten years at St. Vincent's. There he completed college, studied philosophy and theology, and engaged in apostolic work. But he could have done these things at any seminary. Distinctive and decisive to his decade in Germantown was his deep exposure to and formation in the spirit of St. Vincent de Paul. The ideals of simplicity, charity, humility, and zeal seeped deep into his soul. Indeed, the effects of the spirit of St. Vincent on Thomas Judge would be difficult to exaggerate.[22]

20. Cited in Brediger, "True Son of St. Vincent," in *Father Judge Anthology*, 23–24. This appreciation does not appear in the "Gentilly Diary." Its source is not clear.

21. Joseph P. McKey, CM, as cited in Brediger, "Thomas Judge Seminarian," in *Father Judge Anthology*, 20.

22. See John W. Carven, CM, "Son of Saint Vincent," *Vincentian Heritage* 6, no. 2 (1985): 241–46. This is Father Carven's sermon on the fiftieth anniversary of Father Judge's death in 1983. See also Dennis M. Berry, ST, "A Comparative Study of the Spiritual Theologies of Saint Vincent de Paul and Father Thomas A. Judge, CM" (Ph.D. diss., Washington University, St. Louis, 1989). On July 19, 1921, Father Judge wrote a circular letter to the Missionary Cenacle on St. Vincent. It was reprinted for the tercentenary celebration of St. Vincent's death in 1961 and sums up

Becoming a Vincentian

St. Vincent's World: The Grand Siècle

The French often speak of the seventeenth century as the *Grand Siècle.* The reigns of Louis XIII (1601–1643) and the Sun King, Louis XIV (1643–1715), with their cardinal ministers Richelieu and Mazarin, spanned the century. It was the century of the Thirty Years' War, which ended in 1648, but also a time of unparalleled cultural and political ascendancy for France. It was the century of Versailles and of Molière and Pascal. One historian has named it the "century of spirituality."[23]

It was in the seventeenth century that the crown finally allowed all the decrees of the Council of Trent to be published in France and a tremendous religious renewal and reform, "an era of youthful bloom and dazzling revival," ensued.[24] This was not, however, a theological revival in any contemporary academic sense. Rather, it was a time when theologians were no longer saints and saints were not theologians. Ascetical and mystical theology separated from dogmatic and moral theology, theology in general from what came to be called "spirituality."[25]

Central to this early modern religious renewal was what historian Henri Bremond called the "French School" of spirituality, often associated with the name of Pierre de Bérulle (1575–1629). Bérulle died nearly a third of the way into the Grand Siècle, but, he remained at the heart of a network, continuing long after his death, of saints, missionaries, and religious founders, both male and female.[26]

Father Judge's sense of his spiritual master. "Plead with him," he wrote, "that in our hearts and the hearts of the Cenacle may be that great love of God that distinguished him; that we may hold our virtue in humility, that zeal may inflame our hearts, and that our discouragements and the strife with nature may be repelled by an ardent zeal for the poor and those desolate in all things spiritual"; "Monsieur Vincent Lives on," in Brediger, *Father Judge Anthology*, 155.

23. Henri Daniel-Rops, *Monsieur Vincent: The Story of St. Vincent de Paul*, trans. Julie Kernan (New York: Hawthorn, 1961), 88.

24. These are the words of historian Daniel-Rops, *The Church in the Seventeenth Century* (New York: E. P. Dutton, 1963), 6, as anthologized in Raymond Deville, *The French School of Spirituality: An Introduction and Reader*, trans. Agnes Cunningham, SSCM (Pittsburgh: Duquesne University Press, 1994), 6. Deville includes documents from and commentary on Pierre de Bérulle, Charles de Condren, Jean Jacques Olier, John Eudes, John Baptist de la Salle, Louis-Marie Grignion de Montfort, Louise de Marillac, Mère Marie de l'Incarnation Guyart, and others.

25. Hans Urs von Balthasar, "Theology and Sanctity," in *Word and Redemption: Essays in Theology*, trans. A. V. Littledale, in cooperation with Alexander Dru (Montreal: Palm, 1965), 2:49–86.

26. See William M. Thompson, ed., *Bérulle and the French School: Selected Writings*, trans. Lowell M. Glendon, SS, preface by Susan A. Muto, Classics of Western Spirituality (New York and

In a general way, the French School's distinctive characteristic is a "sense of God, that *religion* of loving adoration that characterizes the Bérulle School."[27] This leads to spiritual life focused on the central mysteries of the faith, especially the incarnation and the Trinity, and a deep interiorization of liturgical life.[28] The seventeenth century was also the century of the Jansenists. The "dark side" of the French School is a near-rigorist pessimism about human nature and an emphasis on the "self-annihilation" necessary for "total communion with Jesus."[29] Capturing both sides of Bérulle, Henri de Lubac found him "as magnificent as he was severe."[30]

St. Vincent de Paul was part of a loose network connected to Bérulle. Despite Bérulle's early influence, however, St. Vincent was not, strictly speaking, a disciple of Bérulle and the French School. He defies such easy categorization. Indeed, Henri Daniel-Rops describes him as standing astride the Grand Siècle.[31] Historian André Dodin begins his portrait of St. Vincent by locating him at the political center of life in France during the Grand Siècle:

> Vincent de Paul was born in 1581 in the village of Pouy in Landes of southern France during the reign of Henry III. He may have seen Henry IV, while living in Paris from 1608 to 1610. At any rate, he knew and associated with people of rank—Richelieu, Louis XIII (who asked for him when he was dying), Anne of Austria, Mazarin, Chancellor Seguier and those responsible for the education of Louis XIV. It was not until Louis XIV was ready to take charge of the destinies of France that Vincent died on September 27, 1660.[32]

Mahwah, N.J.: Paulist Press, 1989). In addition to Bérulle, Thompson includes selections from Madeleine de St. Joseph, Jean Jacques Olier, and John Eudes.

27. Deville, *French School of Spirituality*, 240, and the entire introduction to the final chapter, "The French School Today," 236–46; the introductory chapter with documents on "Definition of Terms"; and the introduction to chap. 7 on "Theology of the French School," 136–52. For a brief but authoritative account of the French School, see E. A. Walsh, "Spirituality, French School of," *New Catholic Encyclopedia* (hereafter *NCE*) (2003), 13:451–53.

28. Deville, *French School of Spirituality*, 238.

29. See ibid., appendix B, on "The Dark Side of the French School," 263.

30. Henri de Lubac, *The Mystery of the Supernatural*, trans. Rosemary Sheed, with an Introduction by David L. Schindler (1965; repr. New York: Crossroad Herder, 1998), 57.

31. As cited in Deville, *French School of Spirituality*, 6.

32. André Dodin, CM, *Vincent de Paul and Charity: A Contemporary Portrait of His Life and Apostolic Spirit*, trans. Jean Marie Smith and Dennis Saunders, ed. Hugh O'Donnell, CM, and Marjorie Gale Hornstein (New Rochelle, N.Y.: New City Press, 1993), 11. My sketch of St. Vincent relies heavily on Dodin, originally published in French in 1960. The standard biography remains Pierre Coste, CM, *Grand saint du grand siècle: Monsieur Vincent*, 3 vols. (Paris: Gabalda, 1932).

The Spirit of St. Vincent de Paul

Despite his association with people of rank, St. Vincent was born a peasant among the people to whom he would eventually be a "missionary." A priest but not an especially fervent one, he was at first more interested in benefices than in souls. But in 1608, when he was in his late twenties, Vincent met Pierre de Bérulle. Though they later grew apart, and, as a cardinal, Bérulle opposed canonical approval of the Congregation of the Mission at Rome, and though Dodin suggests that Bérulle didn't quite know what to make of Vincent, Bérulle did help change Vincent's life.[33]

Under Bérulle's influence, Vincent entered a long period of conversion that began around 1610 and was completed by around 1618. One of Vincent's benefices, acquired through Bérulle's encouragement, was the chaplaincy to Philippe Emmanuel de Gondi, general of the galleys of France. Over time the spiritual abandonment of the peasants on the Gondi estates overwhelmed Vincent. They were being deprived of the faith by the scarcity of pastors and the laxity of those who failed to instruct and minister to them.

A particular peasant's deathbed repentance had a strong effect on him, and, at Folleville on January 25, 1617, he began his first mission to the peasants. He left the Gondi estate for the last five months of 1617 and served as pastor at Châtillon-les-Dombes, a parish whose lax pastors left it open to Protestant missionizing. In order to help the laity continue what the mission had begun, he conceived and wrote a rule for the Confraternity of Charity, "an association founded for the purpose of helping sick and/or poor persons in the parishes."[34] By the end of 1617, he had returned to the Gondi estate, where his unexpected departure had caused much upheaval.

Between 1618 and 1625, Vincent's primary work was preaching missions to the peasants on the Gondi estates. He had found his deep calling. As Dodin describes it, Bérulle's theocentrism "took on flesh in a mystique of service to the poor."[35] By 1625, with royal approval, and eventually in 1626 with the approval of the archbishop of Paris, Madame de Gondi had endowed the Congregation of the Mission with Vincent at its head. Madame de Gondi died

33. Ibid., 20–21. On Vincent's relationship with Bérulle, see Vincent de Paul, *Correspondence, Conferences, Documents*, vol. 2, *Conferences*, ed., trans. Marie Poole, DC; *Conferences*, newly translated, edited, and annotated from the 1923 edition of Pierre Coste, CM (Hyde Park, N.Y.: New City Press, 2008), 11:51–52n1.

34. On the Confraternity of Charity, see St. Vincent de Paul, *Correspondence, Conferences, Documents*, vol. 2; *Conferences*, 11:94n1.

35. Dodin, *Vincent de Paul and Charity*, 23.

shortly thereafter. Her husband, who had joined Bérulle's Oratory, wished to withdraw the endowment. Saint-Cyran intervened, and Monsieur de Gondi relented. Nevertheless, Roman approval didn't come until 1633.

Between 1618 and 1625, St. Vincent found himself surrounded by a fascinating set of companions. Bérulle, who had only a few more years to live, faded from the picture. Through his frequenting of Bérulle's house, however, Vincent had met the latter's teacher and Sorbonne theologian André Duval, who introduced him to Benet of Canfield's *Rule of Perfection*, reduced by Canfield to doing the will of God. Through Bérulle he also met Jean du Vergier de Hauranne, abbot of Saint-Cyran, spiritual director and confessor to the nuns at the Abbey of Port Royal, and known to history as Saint-Cyran. Vincent had known Francis de Sales since 1618, and they became good friends. Francis made him superior of the Visitation convents in Paris. To Francis, Vincent confided "his worries about religious life and the sanctification of the laity in and through secular life." After Francis's death, he became spiritual director to Jeanne de Chantal and "quite unconsciously imbibed Salesian doctrines and practices."[36]

Dodin describes the mission and the charities as Vincent's "essential work."[37] The former involved him in addressing the poor state of the clergy that necessitated the missions. From this concern grew the retreats for ordinands begun in 1628, which in less than a decade developed unexpectedly into seminaries.[38] From these ordination retreats also developed the Tuesday conferences. The Conférences du Mardi for Parisian clergy began at St. Lazare in 1633. By the time of St. Vincent's death in 1660, 250 priests gathered at St. Lazare every Tuesday.[39]

St. Vincent's charities likewise evolved over the years. The lay confraternities of charity that Vincent had begun in 1617 at Châtillon spread through-

36. Ibid., 26–27. St. Francis de Sales's *Introduction to the Devout Life* was a staple of spiritual reading during Thomas Judge's novitiate; see Berry, *God's Valiant Warrior*, 11.

37. Dodin, *Vincent de Paul and Charity*, 27.

38. "The stimulus of his major work for the clergy came from his experience of the missions. Actual work among the people had shown him that the fruit of these exercises, although spectacular, was likely to be only temporary, unless the people were provided with zealous and trained priests who could conserve the good dispositions conceived during the mission. It was in order to save the people that Vincent de Paul started to work for the clergy"; Maurice A. Roche, CM, *St. Vincent de Paul and the Formation of Clerics* (Fribourg, Switzerland: University Press, 1964), 21. Chapter 2 covers the retreats for ordinands. Roche calls the retreats the "immediate parent" of modern French seminaries and Vincent's "chief contribution to the work of clerical formation," at 139, 141.

39. On the Tuesday conferences, see St. Vincent de Paul, *Correspondence, Conferences, Documents*, vol. 2; *Conferences*, 11:xvii, n11.

out France. Soon Vincent decided to "concentrate on perfecting the charities run by women" in preference to those involving men only or women and men together.[40] Eventually, he decided that even the women of the confraternities were not up to the task of physically caring for the poor. Some assigned the care of the poor to their servants. Not long after the first mission in 1617, Vincent met Louise de Marillac (1591–1660). By 1633 they had founded the Daughters of Charity to work with the poor, especially foundlings. In the words of Dodin, the Daughters "were to be religious without habits, veils, or solemn vows. Vincent combined the perspectives of religious life with the vocation of missionary servants."[41] Roman approval of the Congregation of the Mission in 1633 meant there would be one superior for both the Vincentians and the Daughters of Charity. Vincent also directed the Visitation Convent of Sainte-Marie in Paris in the spirit of Francis de Sales and in close cooperation with Jeanne de Chantal.[42]

In the administration of these works, St. Vincent wrote approximately ten letters a day. He is estimated to have written a total of 30,000 letters.[43] In considering the problems facing St. Vincent's biographers, Dodin emphasizes the difficulty in classifying him. He was neither speculative nor anyone's disciple. He had no spiritual doctrine in the sense of method or formulas. He learned from all the great souls with whom he associated, including the poor he served. He followed the "missionary Christ" on the "mysterious adventure of the Incarnate Word." His doctrine is in his life. Dodin sums up in words that recall the theology of the French School:

> Without doubt, this life in and through Christ remains hidden and mysterious. It asks for everything, for death to self. Without the detachment and humility which empties us of self, we cannot truly live in Christ nor can Christ act in us. It's in persons empty of self that Christ not only dwells, but acts and bears fruit. Jesus the Christ is the unique source of all our life and action.[44]

According to Dodin, St. Vincent personified the simplicity and purity of intention that characterizes true practical wisdom. He recommended five virtues to the missionaries: simplicity, humility, meekness, mortification, and zeal, and three virtues to the Daughters: humility, simplicity, and charity. As his meditation on "uniformity" suggests, however, he offered no easy formulas, method, or doctrine, only the company of the poor.[45]

40. Dodin, *Vincent de Paul and Charity*, 31.
41. Ibid., 33.
42. Ibid., 36.
43. Ibid., 39, 118.
44. Ibid., 48–57; the "missionary Christ" is at 56, the last full quote at 57.
45. Dodin, "De l'uniformité," 5 novembre 1657, in *Conférences de S. Vincent de Paul aux Filles*

"Charity at white heat" or the "white heat of charity" as specifying zeal is one of Father Judge's most recognizable and often-cited sayings.[46] It would not be too much of a stretch to read these specifications of zeal as a disciple's riff, whether conscious or not, on an equally well-known saying of St. Vincent: "If the love of God is fire, zeal is its flame."[47] This suggests an approach to understanding Father Judge. Begin with something like the previous sketch of St. Vincent. Instead of a French peasant, imagine a second-generation Irish-American from Southie. Instead of France during the Grand Siècle, imagine the early twentieth-century United States. Instead of the Confraternities of Charity, imagine the early Cenacle. Instead of Louise de Marillac and the Daughters of Charity, imagine Mother Boniface Keasey and the Missionary Servants. Before he soured on him in the late 1920s, Archbishop Michael Curley of Baltimore called Father Judge "an American St. Vincent de Paul."[48] The church has never declared Father Judge a saint. And to be sure, many factors, including his family and his country, helped to form him into the apostolic man he was. None was more important than the spirit of St. Vincent de Paul. That spirit first descended on Tom Judge during his years in Germantown.

Thomas Judge and the Spirit of St. Vincent de Paul

In the fall before Judge arrived at Germantown, on November 10, 1889, Pope Leo XIII beatified Jean-Gabriel Perboyre (1802–40). A Vincentian missionary, Perboyre was martyred in China on September 11, 1840, at the age of thirty-eight. On October 15, 1890, Judge wrote home an eight-page letter describing the "triduum," a three-day devotion that capped the year-long Vincentian celebration of Perboyre's beatification. He included a long account of the canonization process in which beatification is the penultimate step. He went on to recount in detail the story of Perboyre's martyrdom—his betrayal by one of his own converts, his trial, confinement, torture, death. "The most remarkable part of our martyr's suffering and death," Judge wrote, "was the resemblance to that of Our Lord's." He described the missionary as

de la Charité, ed. Jean-Baptiste Pémartin, CM (Paris: Pillet et DuMoulin, 1881), 2:295. On "Uniformity," see also May 23, 1659, in St. Vincent de Paul, *Correspondence, Conferences, Documents*, vol. 2; *Conferences* (2009), 12: 201–12.

46. In a January 1922 circular letter to the Cenacle, "charity at white heat, zeal invincible" describes the "apostolic spirit"; AST, MF 12138–40. In a Pentecost conference of May 31, 1924, "zeal is the white heat of charity"; AST, MF 8477.

47. Cited in Dodin, *Vincent de Paul and Charity*, 54.

48. Brediger, *Father Judge Anthology*, 152. No source is offered for this quotation.

"suspended on a cross on a Friday, in the midst of malefactors, and slowly strangled to death."[49] The story of this heroic martyr missionary appealed to young Judge's idealism. Perboyre embodied the total self-sacrifice in imitation of Christ honored and promoted by the French School. Judge was deeply attracted by Perboyre's example and would return to him throughout his life. The first meeting of what would become the Cenacle took place in the Perboyre Chapel at St. John the Baptist Church in Brooklyn. He wrote his last letter to the Cenacle on November 7, 1933, then the Feast of Blessed John Gabriel.[50]

"In Jan'y '90 came Thos. A. Judge." This was young Tom's first mention in the "Gentilly Diary," a day book that described seminary activities.[51] The diary goes on to list semester courses with their students. In his first semester, Tom Judge took reading, arithmetic, and spelling. He was in first German but dropped it. During his first semester, students began a publication known as "The Guide." Judge was listed, along with two other students, as rendering "valuable assistance in writing 'The Guide.'"[52] On May 4–6, a solemn triduum introduced Judge to the year-long celebration of Blessed John Gabriel Perboyre, about which he wrote at length the next fall.

His letters home during 1890 indicate that he had a hard time adjusting to his new status as a full-time student. But his grades steadily improved, and by June he could send home a summary of his marks for the semester and proudly report that he was "eighth best in the school."[53] His courses were Latin, rhetoric, ancient history, reading, spelling, declamation, arithmetic, and composition. After exams, on June 27, the students sailed down the Delaware to spend the summer in Bordentown, N.J.

When the students returned to classes on September 10, in addition to reading, arithmetic, and spelling, courses offered included algebra, geometry, various levels of Latin and Greek, natural philosophy, first and second French and first and second German, ancient history, rhetoric, elocution, and catechism. No list of students appears. The solemn Perboyre triduum

49. Judge to Dear Mother, and Sisters, Germantown, October 15, 1890, AST, Judge Papers, Letters to Family, 1890, MF 3213–18. On June 2, 1996, Pope John Paul II canonized Jean-Gabriel Perboyre. He is the patron of Vincentian missionaries, and his feast is on September 11.

50. For further exploration of the "hero martyr missionary" ideal, see William L. Portier, "*Père Just*'s Hero-Martyr Secularized: John R. Slattery's Passage from Self-Sacrifice to 'Honest Manhood,'" *U.S. Catholic Historian* 17, no.2 (Spring 1999): 32–41.

51. Gentilly Diary, September 7, 1889–June 18, 1907, 4, DA.

52. Ibid., 6.

53. Judge to Dear Mother, and Sisters, Bordentown, N.J., June 1890, AST, MF 3198, Letters to Family, 1890.

about which Judge wrote home took place from October 12 through October 14. From spring 1891 to fall 1892, it is difficult to tell which courses Judge took.

One of his notebooks from this period contains an entire set of weekly English essays for the fall 1892 semester. The essays include such standards as, "Why Should We Study English?" and "The Advantages of Reading." But they also draw from the expansive nationalism of the 1890s for such titles as, "The Beauty of America" and "American Freedom." A four-page essay from 1892, entitled "The United States of the Present Day," took this Americanism in a Catholic direction. In 1892 Bishop John Ireland of St. Paul was at the height of his influence as leader of the liberal or Americanist party among the American bishops. After lamenting "the spirit of irreligion" as the one threat to future national greatness, young Judge went on in tones that, but for the twinge of anti-Judaism, Bishop Ireland might have used:

> But in the past, in all her struggles, an unseen power greater than man has been manifested. God has assisted us in a special manner from the first struggles for independence to the present day. His designs upon this land have been marked in a special manner and he has destined it for some great end. Who knows but that it may become the repository of Catholic Faith? Rome is ungrateful like the Jews. She has turned her face from God and followed the way of iniquity, and like them, she must suffer the consequences. We can, therefore, but thank God for our many national blessings.[54]

Gentilly or the apostolic school was housed in a separate building (now home to the Ducournau Archives) across a courtyard from the main building where the internal seminary or novitiate was. A courtyard gate separated the two sides. The diary entry for January 22, 1893, says simply, "Geo Eckhardt and Thos Judge went over to the other side."[55] The "Gentilly Diary" goes on to record that, as a novice, Thomas Judge taught second elocution in both fall 1893 and fall 1895.

The future archbishop and president of the Extension Society, William O'Brien, was one of Tom Judge's thirty-five elocution students. He recalled the powerful impression that Judge made on them. O'Brien claimed that Judge made each student feel that he was especially interested in them:

> He seemed to have that particular interest in all of us.... With me as with all the students, he was the personification of patience, gentleness and forbear-

54. AST, MF 14448, Fr. Judge 1891–98. The notebook for fall semester 1892 is at 14453–89. For Berry's comments on these early essays, see *God's Valiant Warrior*, 132–33.

55. "Gentilly Diary," 7.

ance. We were all young students, in our teens, and these qualities of his made a deep impression on us. The spirit of piety seemed to envelop him at all times, whether in class or at any time we came in contact with him.[56]

The Internal Seminary (1893–95)

Tom Judge's deep immersion into St. Vincent began when he crossed over from Gentilly into the "internal seminary" (St. Vincent's term for the novitiate). The internal seminary was designed to form students in the spirituality of St. Vincent and give them a sense of Vincentian history. Novices studied the *Common Rules* of St. Vincent and the *Rule of the Internal Seminary of the Congregation of the Mission*.[57] They were required to copy out by hand in Latin the *Rule of the Internal Seminary* that guided their daily routine. They also had daily conferences and colloquies from the writings of St. Vincent. The "Novitiate Diary" for Judge's years as a novice from January 1893 to January 1895 offers a monthly record of the topics of the conferences and colloquies.[58]

One of the most striking aspects of Father Judge's devotion to the central mysteries of the faith and of Christ's life, as well as to the saints, is how closely it adheres to the church's liturgical calendar. The "Novitiate Diary" suggests a major source for this deep internalizing of liturgical time. The diary's calendar of conferences and colloquies closely follows the liturgical year and the dates in the life of St. Vincent.

The virtues Vincent commended to the missionaries and the Daughters are consistent topics of conferences and colloquies. Simplicity and humility recur, along with trust in God, mortification, meekness, poverty, silence, charity, and zeal for souls. St. Vincent's conferences on these topics are cited and sometimes read. Jean-Baptiste Pémartin's 1881 two-volume edition of *Conférences de S. Vincent de Paul aux Filles de la Charité* would have been available during Thomas Judge's novitiate years, perhaps accompanied by unofficial English translations.[59] Repetition of prayer, a practice according to which a novice or confrere is called upon to repeat their meditation to the

56. Brediger, "Ordained to Die," *Father Judge Anthology*, 32.

57. Berry, *God's Valiant Warrior*, 10–11.

58. "Novitiate Diary," vol. 1, 1864–1907, DA. Whoever was assigned to keep the diary during the two years of Thomas Judge's novitiate did a thorough job, leaving a complete calendar of conferences and colloquies between January 1893 and January 1895.

59. Vincent de Paul, *Correspondence, Conferences, Documents*, vol. 2; *Conferences*: on simplicity, 11:40–41; humility, 11:44–51; zeal, 11:62–63; trust in God, 11:31–32; human respect and purity of intention, 11:52–53; meditation and repetition of prayer, 11:76–83, 104; on repetition of prayer, 12:13–16, 24–25, 58–60, 61–62, 63–65, 352; on simplicity, 12:139–50; on humility, 12:161–72; on charity, 12:213–25.

group, recurs in the calendar. Father Judge taught this practice to the early Cenacle associates. St. Vincent's conference on "Uniformity" appears more than once.[60]

In addition to reading his conferences and marking the events of his life, novices were urged to study and imitate St. Vincent's life. To this end, *The Life of the Venerable Servant of God Vincent de Paul,* by Louis Abelly, was a staple at St. Vincent's Seminary. Published in three volumes in 1664, just four years after Vincent's death, it had gone through many French editions and translations. It was first translated into English in 1934.[61]

Tom Judge's surviving papers from his novitiate years indicate that he also translated and copied out extensive portions of Abelly's text. Judge's papers include a lined copy book from his seminary years, entitled "Spiritual Reading Notes." This forty-page notebook contains chapter by chapter summaries with extensive quotes from St. Vincent. There was another life of Vincent de Paul by Pierre Collet. It had been translated into English and would have been available in Judge's day. But a comparison of Tom Judge's notebook with Abelly's text indicates that Abelly, with its generous quotations from St. Vincent, was the text he worked with so closely during his novitiate years.[62]

During Judge's two years in the internal seminary, he asked for and received permission to receive daily Communion. Pius X's instruction on frequent Communion would not appear until 1905. Judge took some criticism from his confreres for his practice of daily Communion. He defended it with appeals to the fathers of the church, especially St. Augustine.[63] It was over the issue of frequent communion that St. Vincent split with Saint-Cyran and the Jansenists.[64]

60. For conferences on "Uniformity," see note 44.

61. On Abelly's biography, see Dodin's discussion in *Vincent de Paul and Charity,* 49–50; his discussion of Abelly in the "Bibliographic Essay" that concludes the book, 119–20; and his contrast, in the section on "Problems Facing Vincent's Biographers," of Abelly's chronological approach to Vincent's prodigious activity with the more thematic attempts at synthesis inspired by Coste and the documentary resources he had made available, 50–51.

62. "Spiritual Reading Notes," AST, MF 2576–2616. Compare, e.g., MF 2582–85 on poverty and trust in God with the text of Louis Abelly, *La vie du Vénérable Serviteur de Dieu, Vincent de Paul* (Paris: 1664, 1891), 3:23–35; see Abelly, *The Life of the Venerable Servant of God Vincent de Paul,* trans. William Quinn, FSC, introduction by Stafford Poole, CM (New Rochelle, N.Y.: New City Press, 1993); and Pierre Collet, *Life of St. Vincent De Paul, Founder of the Congregation of the Mission and of the Sisters of Charity,* trans. a Catholic clergyman (Baltimore: John Murphy, 1878).

63. Blackwell, *Ecclesial People,* 38, 47n168.

64. On St. Vincent on the condemnation of Jansen, see St. Vincent de Paul, *Correspondence,*

On January 25, 1895, Thomas Judge took perpetual vows as a member of the Congregation of the Mission. The date of January 25 was significant. On January 25, 1617, St. Vincent de Paul preached the sermon at Folleville that began his mission to the peasants. Vincentians remember this date as the beginning of the Congregation of the Mission. Tom Judge's novitiate years between 1893 and 1895 took him up into the story of St. Vincent de Paul. He came to dwell there. Eventually he would rewrite this story for the twentieth-century United States. Daughters and sons of immigrants would replace French nobility as the main characters. Immigrants would replace rural peasantry as the focus of his work. The mission to the poor, the preservation of the faith, the key role taken by women, involvement of lay people, collaborative ministry between men and women—nearly everything they do is prefigured in his novitiate notes from Abelly on the life of St. Vincent de Paul. In the conferences and the colloquies of the "Novitiate Diary," Tom Judge's extensive notes on Abelly's life of St. Vincent, and the practices of his novitiate such as daily Communion and repetition of prayer, it is not difficult to find the seed bed for the Cenacle spirit.[65]

Theological Studies

Spiritual and Intellectual Atmosphere

Between his profession in January 1895 and his ordination to the priesthood in May 1899, Thomas Judge studied theology at St. Vincent's Seminary. Maurice Roche's study of St. Vincent's ideas on the formation of students for the priesthood offers a general picture of how he envisioned seminary educa-

Conferences, Documents, vol. 2; *Conferences*, 11:149–50; on frequent Communion, 11:138–39; see also Dodin, *St. Vincent de Paul and Charity*, 44–45. Noting St. Vincent's friendship with Saint-Cyran, Stafford Poole concludes, "Vincent's opposition to Jansenism after 1644 seems to have arisen from the question of frequent communion and especially the impact that Jansenist teaching on this subject had on the parish missions"; Stafford Poole, "Louis Abelly, His Life and Works," in Abelly, *Life of the Venerable Servant of God, Vincent de Paul*, 15. For a discussion of the arguments surrounding the question of frequent Communion, see John A. Hardon, SJ, "Historical Antecedents of St. Pius X's Decree on Frequent Communion," *Theological Studies* 16 (1955): 493–532. At 510–12, Hardon chronicles St. Vincent's opposition to Antoine Arnauld's *De la fréquente communion* (1640), a work he places, along with Jansen's posthumous *Augustinus* (1640, 1652 in France), in the "arsenal of Jansenist theology for subsequent generations" (505). Hardon identifies St. Vincent as Arnauld's "outstanding opponent" (510).

65. Berry's chapter on "Father Judge's Spiritual Development" includes a substantive section on his "Vincentian Formation," noting both convergences and differences of emphasis in St. Vincent and Father Judge; see Berry, *God's Valiant Warrior*, 133–37.

tion. Roche portrays St. Vincent, who was well educated in theology, as taking a practical or pastoral approach that, while certainly not neglecting intellectual formation, subordinated it to the inculcation of zeal for souls.[66] The diary for those years was not well kept and yields little information about Judge's course of study.[67] It can at best be sketched lightly relying on his surviving notebooks. Following the general modern curriculum, Judge probably took courses in scripture, dogmatic and moral theology (using some variation of the tract system), and church history. He left evidence of outside reading in the fathers and doctors of the church and in contemporary journals.[68]

Seminary education generally in the 1890s may well have been intellectually mediocre. But the 1890s were also an exciting and vital period. The condemnation of modernism by Pope Pius X in 1907 and his imposition of the "Oath against Modernism" on seminary professors in 1910 cast a pall of fear and suspicion over seminary theology and biblical studies. It would not lift until the Second Vatican Council. The period of the 1890s, by contrast, was relatively open and eclectic.

During the 1890s, for example, we know that Judge read *American Ecclesiastical Review*, edited by Herman Heuser, an unimpeachably orthodox professor at St. Charles Seminary in Philadelphia. In its pages he could have found articles by Alfred Loisy and George Tyrrell. Loisy was a leading Catholic biblical scholar who would eventually be excommunicated as a modernist; Tyrrell was a Jesuit devotional writer and philosopher of religion who met the same fate. The fact that Thomas Judge was a student in the 1890s schooled him in a spirit of intellectual openness and confidence that many educated between 1907 and 1963 would find hard to appreciate.

Scripture

Judge's discussions on Romans and Hebrews in an 1895 scripture notebook are able for the time. Regarding Romans, he asks why there is no mention of Peter and about the "deaconesses" in chapter 16. Regarding Hebrews, his discussion of its authorship relies on patristic sources. On the name of God in Hebrews, he consults Fulcran Vigouroux's discussion of the Yahwist

66. Roche, *St. Vincent de Paul and the Formation of Clerics*, chap. 4. Roche treats extensively and with considerable nuance St. Vincent's views on the intellectual life in general and theological education in particular (78–136). Because he embodied both knowledge and virtue, Sorbonne theologian André Duval serves as an exemplar of Vincent's intellectual ideal.

67. "Diary, St. Vincent's Seminary, Gentilly, 1868–December 20, 1920," DA.

68. Blackwell compiles a list of patristic and later writers from whom Judge cites "snippets" in his seminary notes; ibid., 48n189.

and Elohist.[69] His brief exegetical notes on Matthew, the New Testament book that he will cite most frequently, focus on the symmetry of the number fourteen in Matthew's genealogy.

"Take the word literally if it will stand it," he writes as a general rule of interpretation. "St. Paul used words as they were used. A spiritual sense is sometimes applicable."[70] This represents a solid theological approach to the Bible in the years immediately after Leo XIII's 1893 encyclical *Providentissimus Deus*.

Theology

André Dodin's claim that St. Vincent "was not a speculative person" applies *mutatis mutandis* to Thomas Judge.[71] That the fewest of his notes survive in the area of dogmatic theology is not surprising.[72] Judge's moral theology notes are more extensive but not very revealing. They begin with pastorally oriented notes on casuistry, the art of applying general moral norms to particular cases. "The priest," he writes, "is the casuist of the people."[73] He has Latin notes on justice for the tract *De jure et justitia* and notes from Fr. Duane, SJ, on the morality of an act. *Moral Philosophy* by Fr. Rick, SJ, seems to have been one of his textbooks. There is another reference to Fr. Rick and his treatment of the cardinal virtues in his *Theologia naturalis.* P. Clarke's *Logic* provides definitions of habit and virtue.[74]

Judge punctuated his theology notes with meditations on such topics as the presence of God, the Eucharist, and Communion. In addition, he meditates frequently or takes notes on Butler's *Lives of the Saints*.[75] This alternation

69. In 1895 Vigouroux (1837–1915) was professor of scripture at the Institut catholique in Paris, where he was Loisy's rival and nemesis. Vigouroux took every opportunity to defend the Bible's historicity. He was appointed first secretary of the newly formed Pontifical Biblical Commission in 1902 and had a hand in the commission's controversial decrees of 1905 and 1912. Nevertheless, he was "one of the key figures in the Catholic Scripture revival." He edited *Dictionnaire de la Bible* (1895–1912). His book *Manuel biblique* (1879–80) on the Old Testament was a "classic in French seminaries." This is most likely the work of Vigouroux's that Judge consulted; see P. F. Chirico, "Vigouroux, Fulcran Grégoire," *NCE* 14 (2003): 512.

70. This comes at the end of the 1895 scripture notes; AST, MF 2558–69. The notes on Matthew are at 2806.

71. Dodin, *Vincent de Paul and Charity*, 52.

72. See, e.g., AST, MF 2825, 2813, 2830.

73. For the notes on casuistry, see AST, MF 2802–05, with the "casuist of the people" at 2802.

74. Notes on moral theology are at AST, MF 2823–40.

75. According to St. Vincent, along with the texts he used in the seminary, every priest's library should have, in addition to the New Testament and Roman Catechism (*Catechism of the Council of Trent*), a book of the lives of the saints; Roche, *St. Vincent de Paul and the Formation of Clerics*, 95.

between theology and meditation illustrates both Judge's personal inclinations and the fractured relationship between theology and spirituality since the late Middle Ages.

Periodical Reading

Blackwell has made the most thorough examination of Judge's notes from 1895–99 and offers perhaps the best sense we can have of what he was reading.[76] He organized his periodical reading according to a topical list that included the following topics: controversy, priest, church, scripture, and God. He cites articles on these topics from *Irish Ecclesiastical Review, North American Review, American Ecclesiastical Review, Catholic World,* and *American Catholic Quarterly Review.*[77] He read John Lancaster Spalding, champion of Catholic education and the leading intellectual among the bishops of the 1890s, Henry F. Brownson, who had just organized a lay Catholic congress in Baltimore, and John Zahm, Notre Dame physicist whose controversial *Evolution and Dogma* appeared in 1895. Pope Leo XIII published his encyclical on the Holy Spirit, *Divinum illud,* in 1897, during Judge's years at St. Vincent's. Given his devotion to the Holy Spirit, one might expect to find some reference to it in these notes. But there is no mention of it.

These fragmentary intellectual remains suggest that, for Thomas Judge, theology was in the service of devotion and pastoral practice. During his years of formation from 1890 to 1899, his two years as a novice (1893–95) no doubt had the deepest and longest-lasting impact, giving him a soaking in the spirit of St. Vincent that would last the rest of his life.

Apostolic Work

Those who remembered Thomas Judge from his last years in Germantown recalled his "merry laugh, his bright sparkling eyes, jet black hair and erect carriage."[78] He walked the neighborhoods around St. Vincent's talking to the Italian families who lived there. He met a young barber named James Matturro, who lamented the plight of the neighborhood's Italian children. The church was not catechizing them. Their families were struggling,

76. Blackwell, *Ecclesial People,* 41–42 and notes.

77. AST, MF 2853–61; see Blackwell, *Ecclesial People,* 41, 49n190.

78. Sr. Mary James Collins, MSBT, "A Voice from the Past," *Holy Ghost,* March 1949, 10. This is part of an important series of articles that ran for five years in the *Holy Ghost* magazine between 1949 and 1954. Sr. Mary James was a witness to much of what she wrote about in this series. She organized the archives of the Missionary Servants of the Most Blessed Trinity and based the articles on her own memories and a chronological review of her holdings.

in need of food and clothing. Their only pastoral and social care came from neighborhood workers, Protestant women, who started kindergartens for the children and offered help with food and clothing, with the expectation that the Italians would start going to their churches. Matturro asked Judge to help. Together they teamed up to organize and perform catechetical and social work among the Italian children and their families.[79]

This pattern repeated itself in East Orange and Newark, New Jersey, Brooklyn, New York, and in other places where the Missionary Cenacle would eventually work. The young Protestant women in Germantown and other places where large numbers of Italian immigrants lived were part of a late nineteenth-century campaign for "Americanization."[80] With the U.S. victory in the Spanish-American War of 1898, Americanization came to Puerto Rico, as well. Sr. Mary James Collins relates that it was the memory of the "non-Catholic women in the Italian district in Germantown" that inspired Father Judge to call upon young Catholic women to "help in parish work."[81] The reverend mother who asked Father Judge if he was trying to make "Salvation Army women" out of her sisters was not far from the truth. He wanted them to shift some of their emphasis from schoolwork to what he called "missionary" work—for instance, home visiting, the kind of settlement work that would make them present to a neighborhood.[82]

One way of understanding the beginnings and early stages of Father Judge's promotion of the lay apostolate and his commitment to the "preservation of the faith" is as a creative Vincentian-style response to "Americanization" policies. Such policies were embodied in a figure like Jane Addams (1860–1935) whose span of life coincides with Judge's own and whose settlement work in Chicago represents the kind of "Americanization" efforts he sought to counter with Catholic lay apostles.

79. Ibid., June 1949, 7. Matturro related this story to Sr. Mary James. With Judge's help, James Matturro eventually became a priest in Schenectady, New York; see Blackwell, *Ecclesial People*, 49n201, and Brediger, "The Young Priest's Apostolate," in *Father Judge Anthology*, 40–41.

80. On Americanization during this period, see John Higham, *Strangers in the Land: Patterns of American Nativism, 1860–1925* (New Brunswick, N.J.: Rutgers University Press, 1955), chap. 9, "Crusade for Americanization."

81. Mary James Collins, "Voice from the Past," *Holy Ghost*, June 1949, 9.

82. Ledwidge, "Life with Father Judge," 2:49–50. Father Judge himself in 1931 related the reverend mother's question in a rare personal reminiscence; see "Father Judge's Recollections of His Mission," Monographs 2:42–51, citing AST, Judge Papers, 11467–84.

Illness and Ordination

During his last year at Germantown, Thomas Judge became seriously ill and was diagnosed with pulmonary tuberculosis. Some feared that he would not live long enough to be ordained. His family had not seen him since the summer before he entered the novitiate. When they came to Philadelphia for his ordination, they were shocked at his frail and thin appearance.[83] Archbishop Patrick J. Ryan of Philadelphia ordained him on May 27, 1899, in the chapel of St. Charles Borromeo Seminary in Philadelphia. It is said that when he celebrated his first Mass the next day, Dr. Schenk, his physician, was sitting in the first pew "ready to rush to his aid should he collapse."[84]

"Yes, twenty-five years is a long time to look back," Father Judge wrote on the Silver Jubilee of his ordination. His cousin had sent her congratulations from South Africa. "Few people that day thought I would be living twenty-five years hence. You will remember how I was quite sick but it pleased God for some reason to extend my earthly pilgrimage."[85] After his first Mass, his superiors sent him home to Boston, hoping he would have a better chance to recover there. "He said Mass for the sisters at Carney Hospital, rested, and soaked up the sun at the old L Street Beach near his home. Later he would half jokingly say that it was 'L Street and Mrs. Kelly's eggs that had brought him through.'"[86] At the end of the summer, he returned to St. Vincent's Church, Price St., Germantown.

Father Judge really believed that God had given him back his life and that he would spend it in God's service.[87] "Let me narrate something that may help you," he wrote to a young sister in her illness:

> I know of a student when he was young who wished to do much for God but he was so sick, he was sicker than you. Everyone said he must die. This he was willing to do but he did wish to [do] something for God so he prayed this way: "Oh, God, whatever you wish for me, I wish also in life or in death. I am resigned to your holy will. If, Dear Lord, you wish me to work for you, I need health, this is very necessary, so please give it to me."

83. Ledwidge, "Life with Father Judge," 2:23. For the family's memories of this period, see 23–25.

84. Collins, "Voice from the Past," *Holy Ghost*, March 1949, 10.

85. Judge to My dear Cousin [Sr. Mary of the Resurrection], June 14, 1924, AST, MF 5648. He went on to urge her to devotion to the Holy Spirit to whom he attributed "whatever success I have had."

86. Brediger, "The Apostolic Priest Recovers," in *Father Judge Anthology*, 36.

87. Collins, "Voice from the Past," *Holy Ghost*, March 1949, 11.

> He was much comforted and strengthened by these words of Holy Scripture, "If Thou shalt see good days, do good." Therefore, he determined to do good so that he could see good days. He has lived for years a life of many labors and outlived many who thought he would live but a few days.[88]

In 1850 the Sisters of Charity founded by St. Elizabeth Ann Seton joined together with the Daughters of Charity. The Vincentian superior general was now their superior. At this time, the Vincentians took on St. Joseph's Church in Emmitsburg, Maryland, then the location of the Daughters of Charity mother house. Sometime in the fall of 1899 or early in 1900, Judge was sent to St. Joseph's in Emmitsburg. The country air, it was thought, would help him recover. He spent his months in Emmitsburg walking around talking to people, as he had done in the neighborhoods around Germantown. Finally, the pastor got him a buggy so he wouldn't have to walk.[89] He spent almost a year in Emmitsburg and returned much improved to Germantown. He did some parish work and some teaching at the seminary, but it was not until 1903 that he was deemed sufficiently healthy to be assigned to the Mission Band.

88. Judge to Sr. Thomas Marie, Rio Piedras, Puerto Rico, May 16, 1932, AST, MF 10770–71. The scripture quotation is most likely from Ps 33:13–14 in the Douay version: "Which of you desires life, and takes delight in prosperous days? Keep your tongue from evil and your lips from speaking guile"; see also 1 Pt 3:10, which cites this verse.

89. This is from the recollections of Fr. Hayden, CM, who was Judge's superior at St. Vincent's Church in Germantown. "After his ordination, Father Judge was sent to Emmitsburg because of his ill health for a rest. One of the Fathers told me that he had to get him a horse and buggy to take him around the country-side, as he would take these long walks, looking up the people, talking to them on religion, and doing missionary work. He was aflame with zeal just one month after his ordination, and although he was sick, he did not do what others would have, merely rested, but he immediately started his work for souls"; interview with Father Hayden, taken down in shorthand as given by him on May 13, 1937 by Sister Marie of the Precious Blood, MSBT, Box 1H.17A Fr. Thomas A. Judge, CM, Folder 1, DA; see also Brediger, "Father Judge Was Zealous for Souls," in *Father Judge Anthology*, 38–39, drawing on this interview with Father Hayden.

❖ 2

PARISH MISSIONS AND HOLY AGONY 1903–1909

From the spiritual revitalization of seventeenth-century France, described in chapter 1, emerged the parish mission.[1] St. Vincent employed the parish mission to revive the religious spirit of the French peasantry. "Parish missions in the rural districts of France were the original apostolate of the Congregation of the Mission and the work that gave rise to its existence."[2] Through most of the eighteenth century, the parish mission continued to flourish. For a variety of reasons, it fell into disfavor as that century ended. It made a comeback in the mid-nineteenth century.

Vincentians arrived in the United States in 1817 and immediately began preaching parish missions. Despite the mission's centrality to their purpose, however, Vincentians did not lead the way in this area. Commitments to parish work and especially to their seminaries and colleges limited the number of men available. Most of the mission preachers had other fulltime work. "Mission bands," teams of priests devoted full-time to parish missions, helped to organize their sporadic mission efforts. But they never came close to the number of missions given by the Jesuits, Redemptorists, and Paulists

1. On missions, catechetical instruction, and confraternities in early modern Catholicism, see Robert Bireley, *The Refashioning of Catholicism, 1450–1700: A Reassessment of the Counter-Reformation* (Washington, D.C.: The Catholic University of America Press, 1999), chap. 5; see also Jay P. Dolan, *Catholic Revivalism: The American Experience, 1830–1900* (Notre Dame, Ind., and London: University of Notre Dame Press, 1978), 13.

2. Douglas Slawson, "'To Bring Glad Tidings to the Poor': Vincentian Parish Missions in the United States, in *The American Vincentians: A Popular History of the Congregation of the Mission in the United States, 1815–1987*, ed. John E. Rybolt, CM (Brooklyn, N.Y.: New City Press, 1988), 163.

who feature in *Catholic Revivalism*, Jay Dolan's classic study of parish missions in the United States.[3]

During the 1890s, Thomas Judge's student years, Vincentian missions fell upon hard times. Tension between educational and mission work gave rise to a pattern of contention. In these disputes, he would eventually take the side of those who argued that extensive Vincentian educational commitments took resources away from the signature work of the congregation.

In 1888 the Vincentians in the United States split into Eastern and Western provinces. By the time of Father Judge's ordination in 1899, the mission had become an "invincible presence" in U.S. parish life,[4] and by 1903 the Eastern Province, to which Father Judge belonged, decided to expand its mission work. In October of that year, a new mission house in Springfield, Massachusetts, was added to the one in Germantown, Pennsylvania. Such a house served as a home base for traveling teams of fulltime mission priests. A band of six worked out of Springfield.

Also in 1903, Father Thomas Judge's superiors decided that he was sufficiently recuperated from the lung disease that had afflicted him at the time of his ordination and assigned him to a mission band of four priests who worked out of Germantown. Thirty-five years old, a priest for only four years, Judge would go on to spend twelve formative years as a member of an itinerant band of preachers. In the context of the parish mission, rich in the high-intensity devotional and sacramental practices of Catholicism, Thomas Judge came of age as a man and as a priest. Father Judge was a Vincentian, and the mission was the signature work of his congregation.

The Parish Mission

As we have seen in chapter 1, St. Vincent de Paul began the missions on the Gondi estates in 1617. Uninstructed in the faith and often without the sacraments, the country people's spiritual abandonment moved St. Vincent deeply. About six months later, at Châtillon, he started the first Confraternity of Charity to sustain and extend the good fruits of parish missions. Because the peasants were by and large ignorant of doctrine, St. Vincent regarded catechetical instruction as central to the mission. Catechetical instructions taught the people doctrine. Mission sermons aroused their affec-

3. Slawson provides comparative statistics on the number of missions during the last quarter of the nineteenth century; see "'To Bring Glad Tidings to the Poor,'" 175, 185.

4. Dolan, *Catholic Revivalism*, 24.

tions and moved them to act.[5] Centuries later, during Father Judge's years as a theology student, a Vincentian *Directory of the Missions* was published in France that specified the duties of the missionaries as twofold: to preach and to give catechetical instruction.[6]

Few of Father Judge's sermons from his time on the missions survive. One on "Frequent Holy Communion," given at the close of Forty Hours Devotion, illustrates the purpose of mission sermons in general. "Hence it will be my duty this evening to endeavor to foster in your minds a higher appreciation of the value and importance of Holy Communion, and to stir up in your hearts a desire to receive Holy Communion as frequently as you possibly can."[7]

As "relative newcomers to the mission field" in the United States, the Vincentians adapted their traditional missions to the new forms that had developed there. The typical mission that Father Judge would have participated in between 1903 and 1909 looked a lot like the missions Jay Dolan describes in chapter 3 of *Catholic Revivalism*, but might have differed from traditional missions in three ways.

First, St. Vincent had envisioned his rural French missions as preferably lasting for four weeks. In the second half of the nineteenth century, missions in the United States tended to last only two weeks and to focus heavily on repentance. Ordinarily, pastors who invited the missionaries determined the length of the mission, and they usually preferred the U.S. custom. Another development in the U.S. context was the division of men and women. This meant separate missions for married women, married men, single women, and single men. Instead of a two-week mission, such arrangements resulted in something more like "a series of back to back week-long retreats."[8]

5. Abelly's chapter on missions emphasizes the virtues of the missionary, especially humility, and the order to be observed. Instruction predominates, with preaching confined to the early morning and extensive catechesis in the evening; see Abelly, *The Life of the Venerable Servant of God Vincent de Paul*, vol. 2, chap 1. On the order of the missions, see 13–29; on topics of sermons and instructions, see 21–23.

6. *Directoire des missions*, 2nd ed. (Paris: D. Dumoulin, 1896), chap. 4 on duties of missionaries, 84–90.

7. This undated sermon in Father Judge's hand, along with one on "The Holy Eucharist as a Sacrament," is found in Box 1H.17A Fr. Thomas A. Judge, CM, Folder 3, DA. He preached it at a Forty Hours devotion sometime after the death of Pius X in 1914 and during the pontificate of Benedict XV, who died in 1922 and to whom he refers. The sermon's conclusion summarizes the 1905 teaching of Pius X.

8. This section follows Slawson, "'To Bring Glad Tidings to the Poor.'" The phrases in quotation marks appear at 175, 222.

Finally, American Vincentians had to reinterpret their traditional understanding of the poor. Rather than ministering to rural peasants, Vincentian missionaries like Father Judge evangelized urban immigrants. His mature commitments to the abandoned work and to the poor and abandoned as signature apostolates of the Missionary Servants were part of the process of reinterpreting and adapting St. Vincent for the United States. As missionaries to the poor, Vincentians, according to St. Vincent's direction, were not to accept money for their services. The custom in the United States, however, allowed for expenses such as travel and voluntary offerings.[9]

The agriculturally oriented mission season usually extended from the first Sunday of September to the end of June. In the United States, the season was eventually interrupted with a winter break during the coldest months, when travel was difficult. During this period, the missionaries gave retreats—often to religious—that required less travel.[10] The "exhausting pace" of the missions was a commonplace.[11] Father Judge's typical day on the mission band began around 4:00 a.m.; 5:00 a.m. Mass was followed by a twenty-minute instruction. By 7:00 a.m. laborers and other working people went off to work. The householders came in for Mass and instruction at 8:30 a.m. Priests were available for confessions during most of the day. The people returned around 7:30 p.m. for another brief instruction and the rosary. The highlight of the daily schedule was the hour-long mission sermon followed by benediction. After benediction the missionaries were again available for confessions. Despite this grueling schedule, mission priests were still obliged to complete the Divine Office or Prayer of the Church by midnight.

In the new two-week format, the mission's first week focused on repentance. Brief catechetical instructions, ranging from ten to twenty to thirty minutes, were offered Monday through Friday throughout the day. Topics by day included the sacrament of penance and general confession, examination of conscience, contrition and absolution, the Blessed Virgin Mary, and the passion of Jesus or his love, followed by heaven on Sunday. The content of evening sermons from Sunday through Friday included salvation, mortal sin, death and judgment, hell, delay of repentance, and the mercy of God.

The second week focused on fostering Catholic life. Instructions during the day covered the commandments of the Decalogue and of the church.

9. Ibid., 177–79.

10. Ibid., 199.

11. Ibid., 171.

Sunday-morning sermons dealt with the duties of parents, with an evening sermon offered on the church or the real presence. Monday through Friday sermons covered cursing, drunkenness, impurity, the Blessed Virgin Mary, and the passion or love of Jesus. Sunday morning concluded with a sermon on heaven.[12]

By Father Judge's time, these topics had been revised to fit what Slawson calls the "new style" of mission. Preachers substituted sermons on vocations in life and the power of the confessional for sermons on hell and delay of repentance. Sexual matters were largely avoided.[13] The "new style" also included new forms of sacred eloquence. Stories, examples, the sensational, and the spectacular gave way to new homiletic ideals. As one of Father Judge's contemporaries put it, "the missionary must spend all that he possesses in learning, understanding, and memory, and also make a great effort with his voice." Ornate preaching had to give way to the down-to-earth and practical. Another Vincentian contemporary put it in terms that aptly describe Father Judge's preaching style. Mission sermons:

> must be the product of hearts and souls filled with zeal, faith, love and self-sacrifice. One must consume himself and speak from the heart with a zeal that knows no bounds, if he is to reach the hearts of those to whom he speaks. He must be a lion in the pulpit and in the confessional a lamb, if he would reap a harvest of souls in the mission.[14]

Conversion of heart remained a central goal of the mission. A profound experience of a penitent's conversion of heart figured strongly in the mission's origin.[15] For Catholics after the Council of Trent, true repentance or conversion of heart was embodied in the practice of sacramental confession. As yet another of Father Judge's contemporaries put it, "the greatest good to be attained by the missions is to be found through the work of the priest in the confessional."[16] Throughout the mission, priests were available for con-

12. Ibid., 176–77.

13. Ibid., 201. A 1962 *Mission Manual for Vincentian Fathers* for the Eastern Province indicates that by this time a mission usually lasted a week (see 15–34 on the week's structure); from a copy in DA.

14. These quotations come from Slawson, "'To Bring Glad Tidings to the Poor,'" 200–202. The descriptions of the new style of preaching are from Thomas McDonald of the Eastern mission band and Francis X. McCabe of the Western band.

15. See the account of the peasant's general confession and conversion of heart that occasioned St. Vincent's first mission on January 29, 1617, in Abelly, *Life of the Venerable Servant of God, Vincent de Paul*, vol. 1, chap. 8, 59–62.

16. Slawson, "'To Bring Glad Tidings to the Poor,'" 200, citing Fr. Francis X. McCabe of the Western mission band.

fessions. Normally the mission team sought the help of local clergy. During his twelve years on the mission band, Father Judge would have heard thousands of confessions. It was through the sacrament that he identified potential lay apostles. He would ask them to come and see him outside of confession.

Despite its routine presence and nearly standard form, the mission was also an extraordinary event in the life of a neighborhood parish. In any given parish, missions were not annual events. They came around every four or five years at the pastor's discretion. For a people schooled in the highly formal liturgical tradition of early modern Catholicism, another of the mission's extraordinary aspects was what Jay Dolan calls its "evangelical" mood or style. Missionaries focused on touching the hearts of parishioners, arousing in them what Jonathan Edwards would have called the "religious affections." They aimed for a conversion of heart embodied in sacramental confession. Dolan calls their approach "sacramental evangelicalism."

As the sermon topics indicate, the content of their "preaching to the heart" was reminiscent of the First Week of the *Spiritual Exercises* of St. Ignatius Loyola, a modern Catholic classic, and well expressed in the structure of the Act of Contrition with which penitents concluded their confession.[17] From a sense of one's sin to the reality and consequences of God's judgment to hope in God's mercy and finally to love of God, mission sermons sought to bring parishioners to repentance.[18]

Local parishes billed missions far in advance as special times of grace. The mission was a time "when the central saving truths of Christianity were pressed upon the people like 'an irresistible steam engine of grace, which can grind a heart of quartz to dust.'"[19] Father Judge learned to drive this "irresistible steam engine of grace" with considerable skill. He was sought after as a preacher. To achieve the affective results they sought, missionaries turned to liturgical music and to the array of devotions that characterized nineteenth-century Catholicism. Father Judge was well known for his ability

17. The movement from sorrow for sin through fear of divine justice to love of God is well described in chap. VI of the Council of Trent's Decree on Justification, Session 6, January 13, 1547; see Norman P. Tanner, SJ, ed., *Decrees of the Ecumenical Councils*, 2:672–73.

18. See Dolan, *Catholic Revivalism*, 76–77. On "preaching to the heart," see ibid., 69. The phrase "sacramental evangelicalism" appears at xvii. In his use of the term *evangelical*, Dolan insists that American Catholic mission preachers were not simply imitating their Protestant counterparts. Rather, they were "following a centuries-old European tradition" (12).

19. Ibid., 224n5, from a description by Francis X. Weninger, SJ, a noted nineteenth-century mission preacher.

to lead congregational singing and for promoting the Holy Name Society. After 1908, the Holy Agony devotion, as we shall see, was a staple of his preaching.

From the huge mission crosses he planted from New Jersey to Puerto Rico to his confident demeanor and personal magnetism, it would be difficult to overstate the effects of his years on the missions. Long after he left the mission band, its itinerant form and evangelical style remained his hallmarks. Rarely confined to a city, neighborhood, or parish, Father Judge was constantly on the move. He was a powerful preacher. If he couldn't be there to preach, he sent conferences and sermons by mail. The missions helped to shape Father Judge's larger-than-life persona. Even after many decades, people still vividly recalled their first meetings with him, his eyes, his voice, what he dared to ask of them.

Apart from general knowledge of the parish mission and of the U.S. Vincentian mission in particular, the documentary sources for Father Judge's life during his first assignment to the mission band (1903–9) are rather scant. The best-documented period of this time in Father Judge's life extends from April 1908 to June 1909. Early in 1908, the Vincentian superior general in Paris, Antoine Fiat, appointed Father Judge "national coordinator" of the Archconfraternity of the Holy Agony.[20]

As we have seen, St. Vincent began the confraternities to extend the fruits of the missions. In Father Judge's day, Vincentians often used the Holy Name Society for this purpose. In 1894 Pope Leo XIII authorized the extension of the Archconfraternity of the Holy Agony beyond France. Fourteen years later, the superior general appointed Father Judge to promote the devotion. His replacement of the familiar Holy Name Society with the relatively recent Archconfraternity of the Holy Agony, as well as his association of the archconfraternity with the innovative practice of frequent Communion, brought him into conflict with his confreres. As we shall see, he did not always handle these conflicts as well as he could have.

20. The phrase "national coordinator" is Berry's. He cites Judge's October 1, 1908, letter to Fiat; AST, MF 14214. Unfortunately, we don't have Fiat's letter to Judge instructing him to promote the devotion in the United States. This letter and Fiat's intent would be central in the conflicts over Father Judge's attempts to propagate the devotion on his missions; see Berry, *God's Valiant Warrior*, 18–22. In a draft of a letter to Fiat from around November 1908, Judge wrote, "[Y]ou picked me out an unknown man and honored me with your honorable communications and you have just now confirmed your 1st kindness by your last letter"; AST, MF 4053.

The Holy Agony Devotion

The white stone figure of the angel of consolation (Lk 22:43) stands erect holding the chalice out to the kneeling figure of Jesus. This is the agony in the garden. In Mark 14:36, Jesus asks the Father to take away the cup. Luke compares the sweat of his agony to drops of blood (Lk 22:44). His soul, Jesus says, is sorrowful even unto death (Mk 14:34). In the background is a mosaic of the hill country around Jerusalem. In the foreground are the figures of Peter, James, and John strewn about the mosaic wall like sleeping students in a boring class. Jesus is alone with the angel and the chalice. The angel evokes the figure of a priest offering Communion. This is a description of the Shrine of the Holy Agony near the entrance to the Basilica of St. Elizabeth Ann Seton in Emmitsburg, Maryland. From here, in the days of Fr. Judge, the Daughters of Charity kept track of the archconfraternity's membership and dispensed Holy Agony medals and the red scapular, both staples of the devotion.

The Emmitsburg Shrine of the Holy Agony, built in 1964, embodies some of the basic principles of the seventeenth-century French School of spirituality discussed in chapter 1. When Thomas Judge was a student in the 1890s, historian Henri Bremond had yet to coin the name "French School." Nevertheless, its language and sensibility were like devotional fluoride in the religious waters from which Judge drank as a student.

Especially typical of the French School is the language of mystery so dear to Father Judge. Centered on the mystery of the incarnation, Christianity itself is a mystery. All the events of Christ's life, the agony in the garden, for example, are also mysteries. At the heart of each mystery is the inner state and disposition of Christ. His most fundamental interior disposition was his state of "infinite servitude" to God in the hypostatic union, the complete possession of humanity by divinity. The masters of the French School taught their disciples to live the life of Christ by participating in or entering into the mysteries of his life.[21]

In a conference on "Meditation," St. Vincent advised that, when a mystery is the subject of meditation, rather than dwelling on a particular virtue, it is "better to think about the story of the Mystery and to pay attention to all its details because there isn't a single one of them ... in which great treasure

21. The French masters sought a "deep and total renunciation of self that is at the same time total adherence to Christ and being possessed by him"; see E. A. Walsh, *NCE* (2003), 13:451.

might not be hidden."[22] When Father Judge told his own disciples that they were "coming into the very life of the Holy Family, into the secrets of the Incarnation," he was speaking the idiom of the French School.[23]

The Shrine of the Holy Agony dramatizes this mystery. Its structure allows one to enter the garden and kneel beside Jesus, consoling him in the garden. Alone in the garden, his closest friends lost in sleep, Jesus appears even more vulnerable than on the cross, where at least a few stayed with him. He is left completely alone to contemplate the chalice the angel offers. The devout can only imagine Jesus' interior state as he sorrows unto death. The images of the sleeping disciples underscore Jesus' seeming deep need for consolation. This is mental suffering of the deepest kind. Consoling the agonized Jesus is the work of the members of the Archconfraternity of the Holy Agony.

After preaching a mission sermon on the agony in the garden, Father Judge would urge the men to sign a pledge to join the archconfraternity. Speaking of his own ability to touch the hearts of men on the mission, Father Judge wrote, "The secret of my success is that I have appealed to them as Christ appealed to His Apostles. He spoke to them of his sufferings, His Agony. His sufferings always touch men, to induce them to most perfect dispositions."[24] What can save such devotion from mere sentiment is a strong sense of the Mystical Body. Christ and his members make up one living body. It is in his members that Christians console Jesus in his Holy Agony.

The Holy Agony devotion that Father Judge promoted as a missionary in the United States found its original home in post-revolutionary France. Its context is, more particularly, contemplation of the plight of the popes in the European political situation that followed on the revolutions of 1848 and gave impetus to new Catholic devotions. The Holy Agony devotion is an example of the kind of "counterrevolutionary mysticism" that Joseph Komonchak describes so well.[25]

A Vincentian priest, Antoine Nicolle, founded the confraternity at Val-

22. Vincent de Paul, *Correspondence, Conferences, Documents*, vol. 2; *Conferences*, 11:80.

23. Cited by Berry, *God's Valiant Warrior*, 235, from a Retreat Conference of September 14, 1917, AST, MF 8394; see also Judge to My dear Brothers, Gadsden, September 14, 1927, AST, MF 4202. "The mystery of the Incarnation means much to us.... How often have I said to you considering how the Triune God has favored us that it almost seemed as if we had been invited into the privacy of the Holy Family?" See also the section on "Devotionalism," in William L. Portier, "The Eminent Evangelist from Boston: Father Thomas A. Judge as an Evangelical Catholic," *Communio* 30 (Summer 2003): 311–13.

24. Judge to James McGill, CM, Carnegie, Pa., April 8, 1908, AST, MF 003011.

25. Joseph A. Komonchak, "The Enlightenment and the Construction of Modern Roman Catholicism," *Annual of the Catholic Commission on Intellectual and Cultural Affairs* (*CCICA*) (1985): 31–59.

fleury near Lyons late in the 1850s. Nicolle's religious imagination joined the interior agony of Jesus in the garden with the contemporary sufferings of the church at the hands of secular states and, in particular, the plight of Pope Pius IX as "prisoner of the Vatican." "As he thought of the consoling angel who ministered to Christ in his Agony in the Garden, he [Nicolle] was inspired with the desire to see the faithful in the Church assume the role of consoling angels to the Sovereign Pontiff in his trials." The confraternity Nicolle founded would be a "prayerful army" to console the beleaguered pope.[26]

In a brief of March 14, 1862, Pope Pius IX recognized Nicolle's new association, attached indulgences to its practices, and encouraged its spread. He entrusted this devotion to the care of the Vincentians. By 1873 it was declared an archconfraternity for all of France. Like many nineteenth-century devotions, the Holy Agony had a profoundly counter-revolutionary cast in its European context. In 1905 the French laws separating church and state secularized schools, hospitals, and other state-supported institutions. Many French Catholics regarded this as the latest episode in the ongoing apostasy of the church's eldest daughter.

In this context, and with the approval of Pope Pius X, the Vincentian superior general, Antoine Fiat, created the Association of Priestly Atonement. Father Judge took it upon himself to translate the superior general's circular on the association, which was dated January 22, 1908.[27] In 1892, Father Fiat had recommitted the Congregation of the Mission to promoting the Holy Agony devotion. He wrote, "I deem it a duty to exhort the priests of the Mission and the Daughters of Charity, to render to the Holy Agony of our Lord a special worship, and to make every effort to propagate it [*sic*] as widely, as possible, The Archconfraternity established in its honor."[28] In 1908, as we have seen, Father Fiat appointed Father Judge to promote the devotion in the United States.

Confraternities and devotions were central to early modern Catholicism and to the parish mission. Father Judge took seriously his new responsibility to promote the archconfraternity and made the devotion central to his mission preaching. He insisted on the traditional sermon on the Passion. Like all

26. This description of the devotion's origin is taken from the archconfraternity's *Quarterly Bulletin* 78, no. 3 (July 1965): 4, from a copy in the Daughters of Charity Archives, Emmitsburg, Md.

27. For Father Judge's translation of the letter on the "Sacerdotal Association of Reparation," see AST, MF 2952–60.

28. Cited by Father Judge in Judge to James McGill, Carnegie, Pa., April 8, 1908, AST, MF 3013.

the counterrevolutionary devotions that crossed the Atlantic, however, the Holy Agony was reinterpreted for a different political context. Father Judge took a leading role in this reinterpretation.

Practicing the Holy Agony

The stated object of the archconfraternity was to "honor the interior sufferings of Christ during his Holy Agony" and to obtain through his sufferings four aims: (1) peace for the church; (2) preservation of faith; (3) cessation of scourges for church and society; and (4) graces necessary for the dying, especially for hardened sinners on their deathbed. Nicolle had conceived the confraternity as "an army of prayer." The practices recommended to members primarily involved prayer.

First was daily recitation of the prayers of the archconfraternity. "Spare, O Lord, spare thy people, and be not angry with us forever! By thy Agony and Passion, deliver us, O Jesus! Our Lady of the Seven Dolors, pray for us." Members would have been familiar with the first part of this prayer from the Lenten liturgy. They had another prayer "for dying Associates and for the Agonizing throughout the world." "Deliver, O Lord, the souls of thy servants from all danger of damnation, from the penalties which they owe to Thy justice, and from all the tribulations of death. Amen." A brief litany called upon the prayers of St. Joseph, patron of a happy death, for "our last Agony"; the good thief (Lk 23:40–43), to pray for hardened sinners on their deathbed; and St Vincent de Paul to protect the archconfraternity.

Members of the archconfraternity were also urged to a number of other practices: (1) to offer the actions of Friday or some other day for the archconfraternity's intentions "in union with Jesus agonizing"; (2) to assist at Mass once a month for the same intentions; (3) to offer one Holy Communion each year for these intentions. Members were also urged to wear the medal of the Holy Agony and to distribute it, especially among sinners; to meditate for fifteen minutes each week on the Agony or the Passion of Our Lord or on the Seven Dolors of our Blessed Mother; to perform the exercise of the "hour of agonizing" that consists of ejaculatory prayers, offered during the work day, for the salvation of those who will die during the day; to make the way of the cross for deceased associates; and to wear the scapular of the Passion or red scapular.[29] Such practices were typical of early modern Catholic piety. In the

29. This description of the archconfraternity's practices is taken almost word for word from pamphlets and other literature found in the box of Holy Agony materials in the Daugh-

face of whatever difficulties might beset church and world, people could embody faith and hope through such practices.

To these inherited practices, Father Judge added two new dimensions: frequent Communion and apostolic work. To strengthen its appeal to men he called the members Christ's "body guards." He prefixed "Body Guards of" to "The Archconfraternity of the Holy Agony of Our Lord Jesus Christ."[30] Writing nearly twenty years later, Father Judge recalled to a young Vincentian his early experience with the archconfraternity: "I found it a powerful means of getting men to frequent reception of the Sacraments and of inspiring them with a particular devotion to the Passion."[31] In Father Judge's hands, the archconfraternity became a vehicle for encouraging frequent Communion. His coupling of frequent Communion with local confraternities was one of the chief causes of opposition among his confreres.

As a novice, Father Judge had received permission from his confessor to receive daily Communion. St. Vincent de Paul was well known for his opposition to the Jansenist Antoine Arnauld's lengthy 1643 treatise against frequent Communion.[32] Whether Father Judge followed St. Vincent in his view of the Eucharist as a strengthening in the spiritual life or reached his opinion on other grounds is not clear.[33]

At the time of Father Judge's work with the archconfraternity, Pius X's *Sacra Tridentina synodus* (1905) was already in effect. In proclaiming it "the desire of Jesus Christ and the Church that all the faithful should daily approach the sacred banquet," Pius X recovered the remedial or medicinal purpose of the Eucharist as an extension of Christ's redemptive work. He de-

---

ters of Charity Archives in Emmitsburg. In what follows, I shall refer to the international organization as the archconfraternity and its local branches as confraternities.

30. Father Judge had this designation "Body Guards of" preceding the name of the archconfraternity printed on holy cards. One is preserved in his papers; AST, MF 2932.

31. From a letter of August 20, 1925, as cited by Sister Collins, "Voice from the Past," *Holy Ghost*, June 1949, 8.

32. John A. Hardon, SJ, "Historical Antecedents," 508–13. Written on the fiftieth anniversary of Pius X's *Sacra Tridentina synodus* of December 20, 1905, Hardon's article is an excellent historical-theological treatment of the question of frequent Communion. He credits Pius X with restoring a balance upset by those such as Arnauld and the Jansenists, who overemphasized the Eucharist as an honor or a dignity of which Christians could never truly be worthy; see Hardon, "Historical Antecedents," 530–31.

33. We know that Father Judge read Abelly's *Life of the Venerable Servant of God Vincent de Paul* and took careful notes on it. Although Abelly devotes two chapters (vol. 2, chap. 12, and vol. 1, chap. 44) to St. Vincent's opposition to the Jansenists, the question of frequent Communion is alluded to only indirectly. The bulk of Abelly's treatment concerns St. Vincent's pastoral care for his friend Saint Cyran and for the priests of his own congregation.

finitively clarified the necessary dispositions for worthy reception of Communion. A right and devout intention did not include freedom from venial sin, as some had urged. Father Judge's mature position emphasizes that receiving Christ "in the sacrament of His Love" is "for our nourishment, our strength and our defence [*sic*]."[34]

In the context of the Mystical Body, the dimension of apostolic work that Father Judge added to the archconfraternity flowed naturally from the practices of prayer and frequent Communion. In founding the archconfraternity, Antoine Nicolle had urged its members to prayerful solidarity with a beleaguered pope. But more than in the pope, Father Judge came to see the agonized Christ who needed consolation in poor immigrant Catholics, especially the Italians. The people who didn't come to the missions were his special concern, and he sent archconfraternity members out to find them. It is the poor and abandoned Christ who is ministered to in these people.[35]

The "Italian question" agitated the church in the first decade of the twentieth century.[36] Father Judge became something of an expert on it. His concern for Italian immigrants occasioned his crucial relationship with the apostolic delegation in Washington, D.C. He reported to his superior general that Diomede Falconio, the apostolic delegate, had summoned him to Washington to consult on the "Italian question."[37] In the context of the Italian question, the archconfraternity marked the beginning of Father Judge's organized work for the lay apostolate. The pioneer women with whom Fa-

34. This phrase is taken from a handwritten transcript of a sermon on "Frequent Holy Communion" preserved in Father Judge's file, Bbox 1H.17A, Folder 4, DA.

35. See Berry, on "The Continuing Passion: The Mental Sorrows," in *God's Valiant Warrior*, 240–43.

36. See, for example, John T. McNicholas, OP, "The Need of American Priests for the Italian Missions," *Ecclesiastical Review* 39 (1908): 677–87. The future bishop of Cincinnati identified the "spiritual care of the vast army of Catholic emigrants [*sic*]" as an important, perhaps the most important, "duty incumbent on the Church in the United States." He focused his attention on the children of Italian immigrants and urged awakening in Catholic people "a missionary activity to cooperate with priests and bishops in instructing and keeping the faith alive in our millions of Catholic exiles."

37. Defending himself against charges of imprudence, Father Judge wrote, "Again it would seem strange that the Papal Legate Falconio would send a special messenger who happened to be a count of the Holy See to invite an imprudent man to a communication of views. His Excellency Mgr. Falconio summoned me to give him information and views on the Italian question in the U.S., a matter upon which he heard I was well informed"; Judge to Fiat, draft, ca. November 1908, AST, MF 4056. On Falconio, who served as apostolic delegate between 1901 and 1910, see Timothy M. Dolan, "'Hence We Cheerfully Sent One Who Should Represent Our Person': A Century of Papal Representation in the United States," *U.S. Catholic Historian* 12, no. 2 (Spring 1994): 8–9.

ther Judge began the Cenacle in 1909 or 1910 had all been "promoters" in the archconfraternity. An 1896 pamphlet on "Regulations for the Promoters" described their chief duties as increasing the number of members of the archconfraternity and exciting them in fervor.

Stumbling Promoter of the Holy Agony, April 1908–June 1909

Father Judge's promotion of the Holy Agony devotion as a member of the mission band brought him into conflict with both confreres and superiors. His consistent appeals in these conflicts from local superiors to the superior general indicate that, at least at this stage in his life, he lacked a sense of how to read and respond virtuously to opposition among his confreres. Between April 1908 and June 1909, Father Judge wrote nine lengthy letters to the Vincentian superior general, Antoine Fiat, then in Paris.[38]

While Father Judge's letters are more like diatribes against his local superiors and lamentation at the sad state of the American Vincentians, the two responses from Father Fiat that we have are brief and measured. In order to make his case to the superior general, Father Judge tried to establish his credibility as a prudent and well-respected man of the American church. He associated himself with Cardinal James Gibbons of Baltimore, with the apostolic delegate, the rector of Catholic University, Msgr. Denis J. O'Connell, and other U.S. Catholic luminaries. Father Judge's nine letters to the superior general, all save one written in French, provide the best documentary evidence we have for his activities between 1903 and 1908.

The record begins with an April 8, 1908, letter from Father Judge to his visitor or provincial, Father James McGill.[39] Appointed for life, McGill had served as visitor of the Eastern Province since its creation in 1888. By 1908 he was aging and in poor health. He relied heavily on one of his consultors, Father Patrick McHale. McHale (1853–1937) had recently served terms as president of both Niagara University (1894–1901) and St. John's College (1901–6). In addition to his role as McGill's consultor, McHale was also superior of St. Vincent's Seminary. On October 21, 1909, he succeeded McGill as visitor or

38. Father Fiat had an exceptionally long tenure as superior general, from September 4, 1878, to July 29, 1914; see the charts in Rybolt, *American Vincentians*, 470.

39. In the French of this correspondence, Irish or American names such as McGill and McHale are usually rendered with Mac instead of Mc. For consistency and to avoid confusion, I will use McGill and McHale.

provincial of the Eastern Province. In 1919 he was selected as one of the superior general's consultors in Paris, where he served until 1932. In this capacity, his support was crucial in Father Judge remaining a Vincentian and continuing his work with the Cenacle. It was with this highly respected confrere that Father Judge clashed in 1908 and 1909 over his role as promoter of the Archconfraternity of the Holy Agony.[40]

Father Judge's April 8, 1908, letter to Father McGill is most striking for the scolding and even imperious tone the forty-year-old Judge takes as he presumes to lecture McGill on his "duty" and attempts to direct his course of action. "Father McGill," he begins, "I hope and pray for your eternal glory, you will insist that our confreres take more pride and interest in community institutions and privileges. We have the greatest society in the Church for men in adapting for them, the principles of the Holy Agony."[41] To lend weight to his argument that "the Holy Agony is the society we must propagate for men," Judge presented himself as the "man's man," the one who has "had more success in dealing with men, in attracting men, than any man on the mission."

He went on to lament the lack of appreciation for the Holy Agony devotion among his fellow missioners. "How careless, how shiftless, how wanting" we are. "How cheap we have made the glorious community grace, the Archconfraternity of the Holy Agony." Instead of the archconfraternity, he complained, Vincentians promoted a Dominican devotion, the Holy Name Society. Judge denounced the "Holy Name frenzy," chiding Vincentians as content to be "a tail on the Dominican kite."[42] "Either the Archconfraternity is a community devotion, or not. If it is, we have reason to strike our breast and cry out *peccavimus*."

Strongly implying that McGill had been derelict in his duty, he cited to the visitor Father Fiat's 1892 letter, calling it his "duty" to exhort both Vincentians and Daughters of Charity to render a "special worship" to the Holy Agony and to propagate the archconfraternity "as widely as possible." In case McGill missed the reference to *duty*, Judge underscored it for him. "Analyze this passage from our Honored Father Fiat, he tells us it is his duty. He could

40. The dates of Father McHale's assignments come from his personnel record in DA.

41. Judge to James McGill, Carnegie, Pa., April 8, 1908, AST MF 003011–15. Hereafter this letter will simply be cited in the text.

42. Ironically, between 1905 and 1908, Father Judge himself had been known for his own promotion of the Holy Name Society on the missions; see Berry, *God's Valiant Warrior*, 16–17, citing a letter from Joseph P. McKey, CM, to Bro. Joachim V. Benson, MSSsT, May 14, 1934, at 345n56.

not make it more forcible." Fiat had urged missioners in particular to promote the devotion. But without even a sermon on the Passion, Judge concluded, "we have ignored him and his wish, almost to material contempt." Rejoicing that McGill "will command missioners after Easter, to make this their work," he pronounces it "a matter of shame and reproach that long since it has not been done."

He urged McGill to be strong in propagating the work. He hoped loyal Vincentians would not oppose it, but "should opposition arise," he warned, "*mark my words,* unrelentingly, I will fight it day and night" (emphasis in original). He cited a January 28, 1908, letter from Father Laux, subdirector of the archconfraternity, urging Judge to propagate the work, the red scapular, and the chaplet.[43] He reported Laux's request for frequent news and his hope that he would not have to report to Laux that the work is "neglected and opposed." "You will help me greatly," he concluded, "by giving the confreres to understand two things: the work must be done, and according to the plan which I have working at Dr. [John] Mullaney's, and communicated to France."[44]

After receiving Father Judge's letter, Father McGill presumably never sent the "command" Judge wanted. Judge believed that McGill had instructed Father Patrick McHale to write the letter, and McHale had never done it. So he next took his case to Father Fiat in Paris. In a long (twenty-three pages handwritten; seven single-spaced typed pages) bill of particulars, he took McHale to task for obstructing the visitor's (McGill's) wishes in the matter of the Holy Agony devotion and for subverting the wishes of the superior general and Father Laux in Paris.

He began by informing the superior general that his letters and circulars went largely unheeded in the United States. Judge "knew positively" that the superior general's letter on priestly reparation had never been read at Price St., the house where Judge lived. When he learned this, Judge reported, he translated the letter himself and gave copies to the pastor and to McHale, but the letter still remained largely unread.

43. A chaplet is a set of rosary-like beads, with varying numbers of beads, designed for particular devotions.

44. In a draft of a later letter to Fiat, Judge identified Dr. Mullaney as "one of the best known educators of the United States and the founder of the Catholic Summer School"; see Judge to Fiat, draft, ca. November 1908, AST, MF 4053. The Catholic Summer School was located on Lake Champlain near Plattsburg, New York. Judge had established a successful Holy Agony confraternity in the Syracuse parish where Mullaney was pastor and sent Fiat a testimonial from him.

He went on to claim that, for the last six months, Father McHale had tenaciously opposed the Holy Agony devotion "not openly" but through "diplomatic evasions." Father Judge believed Father McGill to be strongly in favor of promoting the devotion but claimed that McHale consistently obstructed the visitor's wishes. According to Judge, McGill had a constant tremor in his hands, and McHale had to write for him. Judge claimed that McGill himself had led him into McHale's room and, in Judge's presence, ordered him to write a letter to all local superiors to urge them to work for the spread of our devotion. McHale had never written the letter.[45]

Father Judge offered further examples of Father McHale's failures to use opportunities to promote the devotion. Neither the superior general's nor Father Laux's letters to Judge seemed to have any effect. In fact, Laux's letters, he claimed, made less of an impression than if they had been written by a novice. Judge's main purpose in writing to Father Fiat was to urge Fiat himself to write to McHale. "You can now understand why I so strongly want a word from you to reach Fr. McHale during the retreat."

Father Judge went on to rehearse his arguments with Father McHale, who found the devotion impractical and thought it would not appeal to men. In McHale's absence, Judge had reorganized the confraternity at the public chapel of the Immaculate Conception at St. Vincent's Seminary in Germantown and reported that he had attracted 3,000 members, including 900 men, 600 married women, and 1,200 young women. McHale, he claimed, had instead tried to direct the men into the Holy Name Society. With Laux's

45. Judge to Fiat, St. Vincent de Paul Rectory, Price St., Germantown, sometime after April 23, 1908: "il me conduisait lui-même dans la chambre de M. McHale et ordonnait à ce dernier d'écrire une lettre à tous les supérieurs locaux pour les inviter à travailler a la diffusion de notre dévotion. M. McHale n'a jamais écrit cette lettre." I am citing this and subsequent French letters from copies in Box 1H.17A, Fr. Thomas A. Judge, CM, Folder 4, DA. The Vincentian generalate moved from Paris to Rome in 1963. In 1964, when he was serving as postulator for Father Judge's cause for canonization, Father David O'Connor, ST, obtained certified copies from the Vincentian's General Archives in Rome of their material related to Father Judge. Included among the certified copies is this series of letters from 1908–9, along with copies of two of the superior general's responses. O'Connor then sent copies of the material he had received from the Vincentians in Rome to Father Sylvester A. Taggart, CM, at the Archives of the Vincentian Eastern Province. Taggart supplied O'Connor with certified copies of material on Father Judge from the Eastern Province; see O'Connor to Taggart, Silver Spring, Md., May 28, 1964 (included with the letters), and Taggart to O'Connor, Philadelphia, September 1, 1964. Compare the French letters in AST, MF 2980–3009. Judge drafted his letters to Fiat in English and had them translated. Some of the English drafts are preserved in AST with occasional notes to a translator identified only as "John." The translations from Judge's letters in the Vincentian's General Archives are my own. Where I thought it important for accuracy, I have, as in the present note, cited the French in the notes.

approval, Judge explained, he had organized the men into guards of eleven with a "promoter" whose task was to recruit eleven more members each year.

During a mission, Father Judge had also organized a confraternity in the cathedral parish at Baltimore. He enclosed a testimonial letter from Cardinal James Gibbons of Baltimore.[46] He assured Fiat that Cardinal Gibbons supported his work with the archconfraternity. "If Fr. McHale," he concluded, "can finally be persuaded that such is your will, and if he would just speak to a few confreres in this sense, all opposition will cease."[47]

On October 7, 1908, Father Judge wrote to thank Father Fiat for a letter that he described as "a great consolation and an immense encouragement" in his charge of reviving the moribund Holy Agony devotion in the Eastern Province. Unfortunately, we do not have Fiat's letter to which Judge is responding. The superior general had apparently asked why the American Vincentians neglected the devotion. Judge's explanation went over much of the same ground he covered in his previous letter. He emphasized that all his activities on behalf of the archconfraternity had been at the behest and with the approval of his superiors. But to his amazement the devotion was "so dead and buried" that missioners had never distributed Holy Agony medals, nor had they preached on the Passion, and had only established one confraternity before Judge took over the work. Instead, they argued that the devotion was impractical, not made for Americans, and that it was a new devotion.

Such critics were not happy with the letters Judge had received thanking him for establishing three new confraternities during the past year. Here he mentioned letters from Cardinal Gibbons, Dr. John Mullaney of Syracuse, and a pastor of one of the largest parishes in Boston. Mullaney, he reported, had opened his journal to Judge enabling him to bring the archconfraternity to the attention of the clergy.

46. A copy of a letter from Gibbons to McGill is preserved in AST, MF 3467, but it is dated December 8, 1908, well after the letter under consideration here. It has to do with mediation work that Judge did in a parish in the Archdiocese of Baltimore, probably Hagerstown. "Fr. Judge has done splendid work," Gibbons wrote, "in a country mission in this Diocese. He formed discussions where he went, and has left concord after him. He has been an angel of peace." Gibbons asked McGill to allow Judge to return and "confirm the work he has done. By granting this favor you will place me under great obligations to your Reverence. I am delighted with his work. Please write directly to Fr. Judge." Gibbons's name is on the Holy Agony literature as having approved the archconfraternity in the United States. The December date of this letter suggests that Gibbons may have written an earlier testimonial specifically about the Holy Agony that Father Judge included in his April letter to Father Fiat.

47. "Si M. McHale peut être enfin persuadé que telle est votre volonté et s'il veut bien parler dans ce sens à un peu de confrères, toute opposition cessera."

The campaign he began the previous January to promote the devotion, he informed Fiat, had resulted in requests (which he enclosed) for the establishment of at least six confraternities. These requests had been ignored. "In vain," he wrote, "I showed your own urgent communications on this subject, the statement of Fr. [J. B.] Étienne, the letters of Fr. Laux and the decree of the General Assembly." Rather than help or encouragement, he had encountered only apathy. Those most ardent in declaring the Holy Agony devotion impractical were the same ones who have no fear in declaring that the holy father's rules on frequent Communion were equally impractical. They accused Judge of a lack of wisdom for insisting on even monthly Communion for men.

Father Judge urged his superior general that nothing positive could be accomplished without a word from him. If God desired a victim, he would offer himself. Again he emphasized the need for a direct command from on high. A word from Fiat would put an end to the struggles that divide the province. He wanted to know if he should go forward with the approval of his major superiors or if he should resign himself to "seeing the treasure the Church has confided to us perish in our hands."[48]

Sometime in November 1908, Father Judge sent Father Fiat a newspaper article highlighting his presence at a ceremony at St. Matthew's Church in Washington, D.C., which included various national and ecclesiastical dignitaries. He presented it as evidence of the kind of important people interested in the propagation of the archconfraternity.[49] Judge had apparently raised money for St. Matthew's and helped to heal dissensions among its distinguished parishioners. In an English draft, written around this time, he gave Fiat a more detailed account.[50]

48. This ends the summary of Father Judge's October 7, 1908, letter to Father Fiat. The role of McHale is not highlighted in this letter as in the previous one. Here he seems to assume that McGill and McHale are at one.

49. Unfortunately the text is incomplete, and the newspaper article is not included. It appears on the letterhead of St. Vincent de Paul's Rectory, Price St., date and subject from Vincentian generalate stamp.

50. With reference to the clipping mentioned previously, he writes, "You, also, saw in the same account that I am responsible for the activity in this great international church which is destined to be the great church of the U.S. and where, Supreme Court judges, senators, diplomats and the very cream of Catholicity assembled in Washington from every part of the world [to] worship. Mgr. Lee, its rector, in a financial crisis in this parish called upon me and in an appeal for his Church I raised him 65,000 francs; I also destroyed at this time certain parochial dissensions that were the cause of much sorrow both to Cardinal Gibbons and Mgr. Lee. Certainly, a man able to face the corps d'elite of this parish, and induce them to forgive, forget and then disgorge 65,000 francs, is no imprudent, rash, or irresponsible man.... The work

On December 9, 1908, Father Judge wrote to Father Fiat again to furnish further evidence that the members of the province were, for the most part, indifferent to the promotion of the Holy Agony devotion. He enclosed a letter from Father John A. Garvin, professor of dogmatic theology and philosophy at St. Vincent's Seminary. Garvin was the vicar of the public chapel of the Immaculate Conception, and Judge intended Garvin's letter as testimony to the revitalization of the archconfraternity Judge had accomplished at the chapel. Lest Fiat believe those who said that the Germantown authorities always supported the archconfraternity, Judge bade him simply to check the registry in Paris to see that they had established only two confraternities, one in Brooklyn and one in Germantown; the latter, fifteen years old, was the one Judge claimed to have revived.

He went on to report that, six weeks previously, he had set up another confraternity in Baltimore, and he noted two confraternities outside the province, one in Reading, Pennsylvania, and one in Utica, New York, established by the Daughters of Charity. "And I say," he wrote, "the apathy and indifference of our friends is so profound that they don't even know that these two confraternities exist."

Father Judge appears to have believed that Father McHale wrote to Paris insisting that the province had always supported the archconfraternity and that there had been a confraternity at Germantown for fifteen years. Judge insisted that the confraternity at Germantown was moribund until his recent mission there. In careful language, with conditional clauses, he came close to calling McHale a liar and accusing the provincial authorities of negligence.

In closing, Father Judge urged his superior general to have someone "very familiar with the English language and with its peculiarities" read Father Garvin's letter. "He speaks of the ardor with which everyone, not only the parishioners, received the devotion—he speaks of the impetus given to the implementation of the Decree of the Holy Father to lead people to the Holy Table, 750 received Holy Communion the first month after the mission."

The day before Father Judge wrote this December 9, 1908, letter, Father Fiat had responded to his earlier letters of April and October. Rather than granting Judge's urgent request for a word commanding Father McHale's

done in this parish has gained for us the lifelong gratitude of Cardinal Gibbons for its debt has been to him an insistent burden and many times he has begged me since to return and nurse this parish back to a safe financial standing"; AST, MF 4054–55. The debt to which Judge referred probably had to do with the construction of St. Matthew's that took place between 1893 and 1913; see John Tracy Ellis, *The Life of James Cardinal Gibbons, Archbishop of Baltimore, 1834–1921* (1952; Westminster, Md.: Christian Classics, 1987), 2:450.

cooperation, however, Fiat directed Judge to reconcile with McHale. Less than a year later, on October 21, 1909, Fiat would appoint McHale to succeed Fr. McGill as visitor.[51] Fiat began his brief response by simply stating that he had read Judge's report and praised his zeal for the Holy Agony. But "to assure the success of your efforts," the superior general urged "a heartfelt overture to M. McHale, so that he will support you, because if the Superior is not for you, you will work in vain, I fear it at any rate."[52]

The second of the two paragraphs of this brief communiqué offered Father Judge some encouragement. Father Fiat mentioned that the publication of the life of Father Nicolle, now in press, would furnish him with new arguments (*de nouveaux arguments*). "Courage and confidence," Fiat concluded; "God's works suffer contradiction."[53] Despite the consolations of this conclusion, with its suggestion that Judge was doing the work of God, Fiat's message seemed clear. There would be no command from Paris. Judge would have to work it out with his local superior. That this message got through to Father Judge is not so clear.

Around the time Father Fiat's letter arrived, on December 19, 1908, Father Judge received from Father Laux in Paris a huge shipment of seventy-five gross (10,800) of chaplets of the way of the cross that he had ordered almost a year before. According to Judge, McHale refused to give him the promised funds to pay the tariff on the chaplets. At the very time Fiat instructed Judge to reconcile with McHale, relations between them were especially strained.[54]

On January 10, 1909, Father Judge did indeed write Father McHale on

51. Rybolt, *American Vincentians*, 471.

52. "[M]ais pour assurer le success de vos efforts je vous engage à avoir une bonne overture de coeur avec Monsieur MacHale, afin qu'il vous appuie car si le Supérieur n'est pas pour vous, vous travaillerez en vain, je le crains du moins"; Fiat to Judge, Paris, December 5, 1908, Registre du Grand Conseil 159, 151, from a copy in Box 1H.17A, Folder 4, DA.

53. "Courage et confiance, les oeuvres de Dieu souffrent contradiction"; Fiat to Judge, Paris, December 5, 1908.

54. Judge to Laux, St. John's College, Brooklyn, English draft, sometime after February 4, 1909, AST, MF 3148–53. The date of December 19 is mentioned at 3149. This draft goes over the chaplet episode and also contains revealing instructions to the translator. The money from the chaplets was to go to the construction of a church in Paris dedicated to the Holy Agony. Judge wrote to the translator, "I want to feed out this thought that I had a big idea to clear him of debt and that my idea is being realized. Respect on part of Paris for my word and judgment must follow. I promised to send him sums of money [Judge enclosed 200 francs in this letter], and I wish to justify his great confidence in me. I want to work in a nice way that I have been the pioneer in this big idea at least in America and that I have begun a big financial movement in his favor. My offering is original and first." See also Judge to Laux, St. Vincent de Paul's Rectory, Germantown, December 1908, English draft AST, MF 3055–64.

stationery from St. Augustine Rectory in South Boston. He began by explaining that Father McGill had told him to expect a letter from McHale. The letter had not come, but Judge assured McHale of his ardent hope that the letter would dispel the misunderstandings between them regarding the Holy Agony devotion. He reminded McHale of its sacramental effects and the recommendations of local bishops as a result of the great number of pastors who wanted confraternities. Finally, he told McHale that he was in possession of a very consoling letter from the superior general regarding the devotion.

Father Judge made the overture his superior general had asked of him but not without making his points. He told Father McHale that Father Fiat earnestly desired the archconfraternity to prosper but that he enjoined Judge at the same time to do everything possible to reestablish peace between McHale and himself. Judge promised to appear before McHale in person as soon as the retreat for collegians he was giving ended. At that time, he would show McHale the letter from Fiat.

> In the spirit of profound gratitude [*reconnaissance*] I owe the Superior General for the confidence he has seen fit to put in me and in the spirit of obedience I owe you as Superior, I am prepared to do all and to suffer all so that nothing stands in the way of the propagation of our special devotion.

He went on to say that he was prepared to "show himself submissive" to McHale's authority "even to complete self-annihilation" (*de l'anéantissement complet de moi-même*). He then pleaded with McHale, in the names of the Agonizing Christ and of their superior general, to support him in his efforts to promote the Holy Agony devotion.

Father Judge told Father McHale that he had a letter from Cardinal Gibbons urging him to continue the work of establishing the archconfraternity in his diocese. He found himself in the impossible position of not accepting the cardinal's urgent invitation without putting himself at odds with McHale's decision to remove him from the mission band. This is the first mention of such a decision. McHale had not ignored the visitor's (Father McGill's) support of the cardinal's request for Judge's services, but at the same time had removed Judge from the mission band and ordered him to return to St. Vincent's Seminary.

"What should I do?" Father Judge pleaded. "You can certainly see," he told McHale, "what an embarrassing position I find myself in and with what impatience I await your instructions." He asked McHale to respond by courier. He said he would wait until the following Monday, and "if by then I do not have your instructions in hand, I shall act according to the wishes and positive instructions of the visitor and I shall write to Cardinal Gibbons accepting his invitation." It was probably at this point that McHale decided to send Judge to Baltimore but with another priest in charge of the mission band.[55]

Father Judge then wrote back to Father Fiat. His letter, however, is dated January 9, 1909, the day before he wrote to McHale. In response to Fiat's letter, Judge began by assuring him that he had written to McHale "in the spirit of most perfect submission" and enclosed a copy. He thanked Fiat for his confidence in him and assured him that he was prepared to do all and suffer all to show his gratitude and to promote the Holy Agony devotion. For the past year, he explained, his chief activities had been the promotion of the devotion and encouragement of monthly Communion, especially among the men. Despite opposition, even within the Vincentians, he claimed some success.

His main point in this letter was to show that Father McHale took the side of the Baltimore Vincentian pastor, Father McKinney, in opposing Judge's campaign for frequent Communion and his effort to set up a confraternity in McKinney's parish. He added that this opposition had displeased Cardinal Gibbons and the apostolic delegate, Archbishop Diomede Falconio. He did not wish to accuse McKinney formally before the superior general but mentioned McKinney's name in connection with McHale so that Fiat could know the justice of the cause over which he and McHale differed. Such differences among the Vincentians on their own devotion would surely confuse the cardinal. While regretting having to burden Fiat with his long letters, Judge assured him of his certain belief that the introduction of the Holy Agony devotion among American Catholics would lead to a renewed devotion to the Blessed Sacrament that would well repay their efforts. Continuing their divisions would only damage the cause of religion.

Father Judge added a postscript informing Father Fiat that Father McHale's response had arrived and that McHale had agreed not to stand in the way of Cardinal Gibbons's request. At least he was pleased with this, Judge reported, implying that there were parts of McHale's response he was not pleased with. He added, "I will be employed in certain works dear to the

55. Judge to McHale, St. Augustine Rectory, South Boston, January 10, 1909, Box 1H.17A, Fr. Thomas A. Judge, CM, Folder 4, DA. In an interview with Sister Marie of the Holy Trinity, May 13, 1937, Fr. Hayden, CM, recalled that "at one time Cardinal Gibbons invited Fr. Judge to give a mission at the Cathedral in Baltimore. Again, [Hayden had told of a previous time this had happened in Hagerstown, Maryland] he was not put in charge of the mission but someone else was appointed superior of it. This time too, he never said a word, although it must have cut him to the quick. But Fr. Judge, as they say these days, could take a beating"; from a copy of the interview, taken down in shorthand by Sister Marie, in DA.

Cardinal."[56] By sending Judge to Baltimore, McHale avoided displeasing Cardinal Gibbons. By putting another man in charge, he disciplined Judge. Judge later alleged that the Vincentians had tried to deceive Gibbons in this matter.[57]

It was probably sometime after this mission assignment was complete that Father Judge was removed from the mission band and sent to Brooklyn. After February 1, 1909, Judge dated his letters from Brooklyn.[58] It is not clear whether Father McGill himself as visitor sent Judge to Brooklyn or whether Father McHale did so acting as one of the visitor's assistants. Despite his removal from the mission band, Judge believed, on the basis of previous letters from Fiat and Laux, that he was still in charge of promoting the Holy Agony devotion in the United States.

Sometime in the spring of 1909, Father Judge wrote to Father Fiat again. He sought to exploit what he saw as a division between Father McGill, who had publicly supported his work with the archconfraternity, and Father McHale, who had removed him from the mission band for refusing to cease his work to promote the devotion. "I lay special stress," he wrote, "on the public sanction that the Visitor [McGill] gave me on the work of the Holy Agony; and yet for carrying out his very ideas, I have been taken off the Missions. This inconsistency demands explanation."[59]

56. "Je serai employé à certaines oeuvres que le Cardinal a [illegible] à coeur." See also Gibbons to McGill, Baltimore, December 8, 1908, AST, MF 3467.

57. "I was to have left a Confraternity of the Holy Agony in this Cathedral [Baltimore]; the opponents of the Holy Agony devotion are responsible for undoing my work of four years in this city. The bitterest opponent of this movement of the Holy Agony, being a monthly communion for men, was made leader of the Cathedral Mission, and in his stupid attempt to deceive this great Prince of the Church, Cardinal Gibbons, he has involved himself and his associates in an unsavory complication. The Cardinal had his Rector demand an explanation for this deception—none could be given"; from an English draft of Judge to Fiat, ca. Spring 1909, AST, MF 3135. This seems to indicate that Father McHale put Father McKinney in charge of the Baltimore Cathedral mission. Interestingly, these and other details of Judge's involvement with Gibbons do not appear in his letters to Fiat from the Vincentian's General Archives.

58. See "Chronological Whereabouts—Father Judge, Itinerary of Father Judge, Compiled from his Collected Writings," March 22, 1973, Silver Spring, Md., by Bro. Hilary Mettes, ST, 1, AST.

59. This is from an undated eight-page draft or set of notes in English in Father Judge's papers. It is clearly a letter and contains a direct address to "Honored Father," the title with which Judge addressed Father Fiat in his letters to him. From its contents, this draft represents the state of the situation around winter or spring of 1909. There is no French letter in the Vincentian General Archives material that corresponds to this draft. But there is a copy of a letter to Judge that looks very much like a response to Judge's question in this letter. It is dated June 23, 1909; see AST, MF 3128–36. In what follows, I will treat this draft as representing the substance of a query Judge communicated to Fiat in the spring of 1909.

He gave a clear account of his side of the case, accusing his opponents—stirred up by "two or three of the Superiors of this Province"—of opposing Pius X's decree on frequent Communion and thwarting the desires of Cardinal Gibbons and the apostolic delegate for the expansion of the archconfraternity. It would not be difficult for the reader to see Father McHale beneath the text as Father Judge's chief antagonist. "Honored Father," this letter concludes, "if I am to continue this work, a special communication should reach the Superiors in Germantown, because they informed me there is nothing in the letters I have received from you justifying my continuance."

In the summer of 1909, Father Judge received a reply, dated June 23. The oblique reply was signed by the general's assistant, Father Léon Forestier. Forestier explained that the superior general was away for a few weeks. "It has seemed better to us," he wrote, "that you not pursue any further the project that you explained. It is a sacrifice for you at this time, but have confidence that God will bless it. He will also count in your favor your pious intentions."[60]

Thus Father Judge ended his brief tenure as chief advocate for the Holy Agony devotion in the United States. Before he received this communication from the Vincentian generalate in Paris, however, Judge found himself embroiled in another controversy that gave him new opportunities to communicate with Father Fiat about the Holy Agony devotion. His last letter to Fiat on the subject is dated June 30, 1909. By that date, he had probably yet to receive the June 23 communication from Forestier. After June 30, 1909, Judge is silent on the Holy Agony devotion.

DePaul University's Financial Crisis and Judge's Intervention

Strangely, the context for Father Judge's last two letters to Father Fiat concerning the Holy Agony devotion is the financial situation of DePaul University in Chicago, a work of the Vincentian Western Province. DePaul opened its doors in 1898 as St. Vincent's College. The college expanded rapidly under

60. "M. le Supérieur général est absent pour quelques semaines. Il nous a semblé qu'il vaut mieux de ne pas donner suite au projet que vous exposes. C'est un sacrifice pour vous en ce moment, mais ayez confiance que Dieu le bénira. Il vous tiendra compte aussi de vos pieuses intentions"; Forestier to Judge, Paris, June 23, 1909, General Archives of the Congregation of the Mission, Lettres des Supérieurs Généraux, registre no. 161 (Iere Série), 382, from a certified copy in DA.

its president, Father Peter V. Byrne. Byrne built a new administration building, instituted various engineering programs, and built a thousand-seat theatre he hoped would generate revenue. In 1907, the year the theater was completed, St. Vincent's College changed its name to DePaul University. By 1908 it had accumulated a debt of $574,112—an obligation that would not be completely paid off until after World War II.[61]

In February 1909, Father McHale, probably acting on behalf of Father McGill as visitor, had sent Father Judge to St. John the Baptist Church in Brooklyn. He was to do a parish census and help reduce the parish debt. The pastor of the parish was Father John Moore, president of St. John's College (1906–25). On Saturday, April 24, 1909, Judge wrote to Father Fiat from a speeding train. Breathless with drama, he explained that he was en route to Chicago, with forty-eight hours notice, to offer his services for a financial bailout of "our crippled college of St. Vincent."[62] Unless the institution met its obligations by the following Monday, April 26, he claimed, "the creditors will press their claims and we may lose one of the finest pieces of property in the entire community." He enclosed a copy of a letter from Father Moore to Father McHale "which explains everything."[63]

Why Judge's superiors called upon him in the DePaul situation is not clear. He had been involved in resolving financial difficulties before, in

61. On DePaul's financial crisis of 1908–9, see Stafford Poole, CM, "The Educational Apostolate: Colleges, Universities, and Secondary Schools," in Rybolt, *American Vincentians*, 318–23. Poole does not mention Judge, nor does his name appear in any of the provincial records of this episode. In a letter to me dated August 13, 2004, Morgen MacIntosh, archivist and librarian at DePaul's John T. Richardson Library, wrote, "In response to your inquiry, I reviewed the provincial files of Thomas O'N. Finney, CM (Visitor of the Western Province from 1906 to 1926), the Board of Trustee Minutes of DePaul University, and the Daniel McHugh, CM collection which contains much of DePaul's early history. I did not see any mention of Fr. Thomas Judge's name in any of the correspondence or documents from 1909." This would make sense if he was acting on a special commission from the superior general. In any case, documentary evidence for this account of Judge's involvement is limited to the Vincentian General Archives and the AST.

62. Judge to Fiat, en route, Pennsylvania Limited, Pullman vestibuled train, April 24, 1909, General Archives of the Congregation of the Mission, from a certified copy in Box 1H.17A, Folder 4, DA. This letter is written in English. For a very similar but incomplete version of this letter, see AST, MF 3083–87.

63. The enclosed letter from Moore to McHale, dated April 23, 1909, is very brief. It refers to another letter not in evidence, perhaps from William Zeh, mentioned later in the correspondence, promising financial assistance. Moore wrote, "I have with the approval of Germantown [presumably Father McGill] sent Fr. Judge to Chicago on the strength of the enclosed letter, in the hope of being able to do something for St. Vincent's College. I hope, we all hope, he may be able to succeed."

Washington, D.C., and later in New York.[64] One of his responsibilities in Brooklyn, where he worked under Moore, was to help reduce the parish debt. In this case, it probably had something to do with his personal acquaintance with William Zeh, a Chicago businessman, whose wife Judge knew from his days on the mission band.[65]

Father Judge told Father Fiat that he hesitated to accept this assignment because "prudently I did not wish to add any other complications with many already existing around this Holy Agony devotion." Fiat had already sent Father McHale to Chicago as a special emissary in this situation.[66] Judge assured Fiat that he would see McHale as soon as he got to Chicago and would not proceed without his approval "because for the sake of the Holy Agony devotion I do not wish any more misunderstanding."

> Some very unpleasant events have taken place here because of the Holy Agony propaganda for which at the proper time I will ask for an explanation and an adjustment, not on my own account, for the individual in a great work of God is nothing, and it seems to me, perhaps my humiliation and rejection or elimination may be of more benefit to the Holy Agony movements than anything else I can give it; but lest this great devotion be unjustly treated and checked. You will know from this why I want it understood that the authority of the Eastern province has sent me to Chicago.[67]

If McHale approved, Judge promised to contact some "moneyed men" and get their help in preventing Monday's crash. He took this occasion to tout

64. On the St. Matthew's Church episode, see Gibbons to McGill, Baltimore, December 8, 1908, copy, AST, MF 3467. In his account for Fiat of financial disarray at St. John's College, Judge mentions that he had been asked to help secure a loan for them; see Judge to Fiat, St. John's College, Brooklyn, N.Y., June 30, 1909, General Archives of the Congregation of the Mission, from a certified copy in Box 1H.17A, Folder 4, DA; compare AST, MF 2918–28.

65. Sr. Collins was the first to suggest this connection; see "Voice from the Past," *Holy Ghost*, June 1949, 9, referring to a letter of May 11, 1909.

66. Clearly, Judge's superiors placed great confidence in McHale and relied upon him. Why Judge failed to grasp that he could not succeed in the face of McHale's opposition remains a mystery. In his May 30 account of his trip to Chicago for Fr. Laux, Judge noted that McHale had been sent to Chicago as Fiat's "commissary"; AST, MF 3099.

67. I cite here from AST, MF 3084 because the copy is clearer. The final copy reads, "perhaps my humiliation or elimination." *Rejection* is omitted. Berry takes this passage to indicate "a shift in his own [Judge's] interior dealings with the whole difficult affair." This reading seems strained. The passage appears in the middle of a letter in which Judge still refuses to back down in the matter of the Holy Agony. He is still making his case to the superior general and doesn't stop until he receives the communiqué of June 23, 1909. He still clearly thinks McHale is in the wrong. Perhaps this thought represents a glance by Judge in the direction such a shift might take; see Berry, *God's Valiant Warrior*, 25.

to the superior general the progress he had made with the Holy Agony devotion. He concluded on an ominous note that indicated the approach he would take until he withdrew from the controversy at the end of June—that is, an emphasis on the financial mismanagement of those who opposed the Holy Agony devotion. "I am trusting and praying to our Good God to send me in this moment some Moses to lead us out of our financial troubles." And then he added, "for we are none too safe even in the Eastern province."

On April 30, 1909, the Friday after the deadline on DePaul's credit, Father Judge wrote from Philadelphia to Father Thomas Finney, the Western visitor, with a report on his trip to Chicago.[68] Judge reported to Finney that Father Byrne, DePaul's president, could have a loan of $500,000 "providing he will locate outstanding notes." He urged Finney to go to Chicago and meet with William Zeh of the White Oak Coal Co. "I have asked him to be a good friend and meet you anywhere you name." Judge urged Finney to sort out the finances. "I have the people who will avert this storm but you must insist that a number of notes be found." Judge reported that he was "not at all satisfied with the exposition given me. To be candid it seems to me that somebody or something is being covered." He summarized the financial situation in six points. Byrne resigned within a month of Judge's visit.[69]

After his return from Chicago, Father Judge seemed to be riding high. The missions were his primary vehicle for promoting the Holy Agony devotion and the confraternities, but McHale had removed him from the mission band. Judge still considered himself empowered by Fiat and Laux as the devotion's primary agent in the United States. Paris had yet to respond to his question about whether he should continue to promote the devotion. He no doubt felt his successful Chicago mission might raise his stock at Paris. On May 30, 1909, Judge wrote enthusiastically to Father Laux about an event that "will have important bearing on the status of the agitation [over the devotion]." "I have just returned," he wrote, "from a most remarkable mission."[70]

68. This letter is in French in the Vincentian's General Archives. An English version of it, on St. Joseph's Hospital, Philadelphia, stationery, is in AST, MF 3088–91. The latter is probably the original, since both Judge and Finney were Anglophones. Judge probably had it translated for enclosure.

69. See Poole, "The Educational Apostolate," in *American Vincentians*, 323. Poole reports that the Vincentian treasurer general, Emile Villette, made a "special visitation" of the U.S. Vincentian houses in the fall of 1909. He and Finney then arranged for "a short-term, unsecured loan of $100,000" from the Mercantile Trust Company in St. Louis. Poole identifies the university's debt in 1908 as $574,112, a figure consistent with Judge's.

70. Judge to Laux, Brooklyn, May 30, 1909. This is a four-page fragment of a letter, prob-

Father Judge interpreted his removal from the missions as an expression of "indifference and disloyalty to provincial interest that sought quiet by removing us from the missions in the hope that, I [being] hampered and discredited, the new born activity in favor of the Holy Agony devotion would soon die out." He emphasized to Laux his success in spite of this opposition. "It will please you to know I have the good will of the Province and all current events are favoring me." He went on to describe the enthusiasm of younger priests and students for the devotion.

Clearly he thought that his trip to Chicago had turned the tide of "current events" in his favor. His description of the trip emphasized McHale's cooperation. "I consented to proffer my good services only on the condition that Fr. McHale would declare my mission agreeable to him." McHale did this "most anxiously," Judge reported, and McHale even agreed "that he would push his verbal pleasure on paper." Judge told Laux that he planned to send the superior general McHale's letter, along with one from Finney, and letters "from the influential Superiors of both Provinces inviting my action."

His promised letter to Father Fiat is dated June 19, 1909. Father Judge's April 24 letter, written on the train, had already informed Fiat of his trip. The June 19 letter had two main purposes. First, Judge wanted to emphasize to Fiat that his Chicago mission was totally in keeping with the wishes of his superiors, especially McHale, whom Fiat himself had dispatched to Chicago as his own representative. To this end Judge enclosed letters from Moore to McHale, McHale to Judge, Finney to Judge, and Byrne to Judge. Moore was Judge's immediate superior, McHale consultor to Judge's provincial superior, the Eastern visitor. Finney was the Western visitor and Byrne the president of DePaul. He also enclosed a copy of his report to Finney.

Father Judge's second purpose in this letter was to draw his superior general's attention to the "entire lack of financial management" in both provinces. Financial mismanagement was so complete in the West that DePaul didn't even have enough credit to buy coal for the severe Chicago winter. In Judge's view, things were no better in the East, and he felt it his duty to call Father Fiat's attention to the financial state of the Eastern Province. He blamed it on a "passion for construction and the accumulation of debt."

ably a draft, in English. The pages are numbered through 6. Pages 1–2 are missing, and there is no conclusion; AST, MF 3095, 3097, 3099, 3101. His letters to Laux tend to be less formal and more revealing than those to the general; see previous English drafts of letters to Laux of December 1908 and February [probably] 1909 in AST, MF 3055–64 and MF 3148–53. This last draft comes with instructions to the translator.

He warned that what happened in the West will soon happen in the East. "Already certain banks regard us with suspicion [and] our houses at Germantown, Niagara, and Brooklyn have borrowed up to the last sou." He described himself as "drawn despite myself into the affairs of the West."

Since he felt it his duty to give Fiat a complete account of the whole affair, his exposition necessarily involved discussion of conditions in his own province.[71] While this is a straightforward enough explanation for the letter, Judge also clearly intended it to gain him credit in Paris, even while it reflected poorly on McHale and the others who opposed him in the matter of the Holy Agony.

By June 30, 1909, Father Forestier had already written his brief negative reply to Father Judge's question about whether he should still consider himself chief promoter of the Holy Agony devotion in the United States. But Judge had probably yet to receive Forestier's reply when he wrote his last letter to Father Fiat in the matter of the Holy Agony. Judge's letter of June 30 develops the last point of the June 19 letter—namely, that the superiors in the East rather than Judge are responsible for the discord of which the superior general disapproves. Financial mismanagement and not the Holy Agony devotion is the reason for discord and spiritual unrest in the province. To make his case, Judge provides many more details of the financial conditions at Germantown and at the Vincentian colleges at St. John's and Niagara.

The letter is cast as a warning. Financial conditions in the Western Province are only the tip of the American Vincentian iceberg. Father Judge took the West's shame and embarrassment as a warning for all to correct the congregation's financial administration. The income of four parishes, Judge charged, is used to support the three large institutions at Germantown, Brooklyn, and Niagara. The bulk of his criticism is directed to the superiors at Germantown. He accuses them of trying to raise money by "shabby and imprudent means," of making the annual retreat an occasion of pathetic appeals to missionaries, and risking the finances of the poor in a bank-like scheme that uses the savings of parishioners to pay the province's debts without having the surplus U.S. law required of a bank.

71. Judge to Fiat, St. John the Baptist Church, Brooklyn, N.Y., June 19, 1909, General Archives of the Congregation of the Mission, from a certified copy in Box 1H.17A, Folder 4, DA. Compare AST, MF 2900, 2894, 2896, 2898, 2902–3. Judge's introduction to the financial affairs of his own province probably took place after February 1909, when he started to work with Father Moore at St. John's.

> If they were as anxious to institute the Archconfraternity as they are to start a bank, if they were as anxious to save souls as they are to get money, we would have less dissension and we would no longer be in danger of having our affairs vetted in the newspapers and courts. These disastrous conditions clearly show you the spirit and politics of those who are opposed to the propagation of the Holy Agony.

Judge concluded his long account of Germantown's finances with the statement that they seemed, in effect, to "have forgotten the A-B-C—of prudence, precaution, and good sense." No doubt Judge hoped Fiat would notice that these were the very faults of which McHale had accused him.

His accounts of St. John's and Niagara are briefer. In the case of St. John's, he claims that he had been asked by "the functionaries of that institution" to negotiate a $15,000 loan. He had refused. He identified Niagara as the most compromised institution with a debt of $120,000 and a growing annual deficit of $10,000. The only justification for this is the "hope that if we build more comfortable buildings, we will get more students." Fifteen of Niagara's 120 collegians, he noted, were on athletic scholarships.

Again, one of Judge's clear rhetorical purposes in this letter is to associate in the mind of the superior general financial irresponsibility and mismanagement with opposition to the Holy Agony devotion. He sends his letter in the hope that "some project will be conceived to save our works and our future." The congregation's financial embarrassment left him with no doubts about why the Holy Agony devotion and the idea of frequent Communion had such a chilly and limited reception. Discord, dissension, institutions shaken to their foundations by foolishly contracted debts—"these are certainly not signs of the grace and favor of God."[72]

It must have been shortly after Father Judge mailed this letter that Father Forestier's reply of June 23 came crashing down on his hopes for the Holy Agony devotion. Never again would he promote it. Father Fiat did indeed, as we have seen, send the treasurer general, Father Villette, to the United States to examine financial conditions there. How much Judge's interventions had to do with this decision is not clear. As Fiat's own envoy to Chicago, Father McHale too must have submitted a financial report. Perhaps, at this point,

72. Judge to Fiat, St. John's College, Brooklyn, N.Y., June 30, 1909, General Archives of the Congregation of the Mission, from a certified copy in Box 1H.17A, Folder 4, DA. This handwritten letter is almost six single-spaced pages in transcription; compare the English draft in AST, MF 2918–28. I have found no corroboration for Judge's claims about the finances of Niagara.

Judge finally came to understand that it would have carried more weight than his own.

Taking Stock in the Matter of the Holy Agony Devotion

His response to conflicts arising from his manner of promoting the Holy Agony devotion serve as a baseline for Father Judge's spiritual growth and development. Even as he admitted Judge's genuine desire to promote the Holy Agony devotion and frequent Communion, a financially strapped superior might be inclined to describe Judge's behavior in this controversy as willful, petulant, self-righteous, and self-serving. Someone like St. Luke's centurion, who says to one, "come," and he comes, and to another, "go," and he goes (Lk 7:8) might read Judge's letters, despite his protestations of obedience, as calculated to come as close as possible to insubordination without going over the line.

This tale of transatlantic devotion, religious obedience, and near financial ruin brims with irony. In the years after the Great Depression, a young sister and the treasurer general of Father Judge's own community of women would go over the heads of their local superiors to Bishop Toolen of Mobile. They denounced Judge for the same kind of shabby dealings and financial mismanagement of which he accused McHale. The young sister was dismissed. The greatest irony is that Patrick McHale, who outlived Judge by four years, eventually became the staunchest Vincentian supporter of Judge's work. In his role as visitor and later as consultor to the superior general, McHale is the one most responsible for enabling Judge to remain a Vincentian until his death in 1933.

As the conflicts wore on, Father Judge's belligerent tone became more shrill, his criticisms of McHale less oblique. Despite Father Judge's well-reasoned attempts at self-justification, Father Fiat never sent the direct command Judge so desired. The superior general refused to demand provincial support for Judge's plans for the archconfraternity. Such a command would have undercut Father Fiat's trusted man in the field. One might suppose that it was naïve of Judge to think that his superior general would ever have issued such a command. The saddest part of this controversy was that Father Judge failed to gain the support of his fellow Vincentians for the Holy Agony devotion.

But Father Judge learned much from what he termed his "humiliation and rejection or elimination" in the matter of the archconfraternity of the Holy Agony.[73] In no future conflict, even the bitter struggles with Bishop Thomas Toolen of Mobile and Archbishop Michael Curley of Baltimore, both of whom wanted to put an end to Judge's leadership of the work he had founded, did the tone Judge took regarding the Holy Agony ever reappear. Nor would he tolerate it from members of his religious family.

After receiving Father Forestier's communiqué of June 23, 1909, Father Judge never spoke again of the Archconfraternity of the Holy Agony. At this time, the Holy Spirit began gradually to displace the Holy Agony in his talk. Nevertheless, the religious dynamic of the Holy Agony devotion, the idea of entering personally into the interior of the mysteries of Christ's life, remained central to his spirituality. The image of the abandoned Christ agonizing in the garden helped him to reinterpret for the twentieth-century United States the traditional Vincentian work of evangelizing the poor. He took the motto "for the preservation of the faith" directly from the aims of the archconfraternity. Most importantly, it was from the ranks of the archconfraternity's "promoters" that his first organized group of lay apostles came.

73. This phrase appears in Judge to Fiat, en route Pennsylvania Limited, Pullman vestibuled train, April 24, 1909, from an incomplete copy in AST, MF 3083–87.

❖ 3

NOT SO MUCH BY ANY PRECONCEIVED PLAN

1909/1910–1915

Making History in the Perboyre Chapel

By early summer, Father Forestier's June 23, 1909, letter from Paris reached Father Judge in Brooklyn. On behalf of the superior general, Forestier removed Judge from his role as promoter of the Archconfraternity of the Holy Agony to which Father Fiat had assigned him the previous year and that had consumed so much of his energy over the past year and a half. By September 1, 1909, he was assigned as parochial vicar at St. John the Baptist Church, Willoughby Avenue in Brooklyn, where he had been living since the previous February. After receiving Forestier's letter, he devoted all his time and energy to the parish census. In the neighborhoods of Brooklyn Judge rediscovered the poor and abandoned who needed the gospel preached to them and the faith that needed to be preserved. He knew, however, that he needed help.[1]

Either by the following April, after he had immersed himself in the parish census, or back in April 1909, while he was still preoccupied with the archconfraternity and the DePaul financial crisis, Father Judge had formulated a new plan of action. It was continuous with the archconfraternity but distinctly different in its emphasis on a more apostolic than devotional role for the laity. Either in April 1909 or a year later, probably on April 11, he invited five women to meet him in the evening in front of St. John the Baptist

1. See Brediger, "He Saw the Need for Lay Apostles," in *Father Judge Anthology*, 46–48.

Church in Brooklyn. All five had served as promoters in the archconfraternity. He trusted their discretion and heart for apostolic work.

The five women were Amy Marie Croke, Katherine V. Shelvy, Mary T. Seitz, Catherine A. Jacques, and Laura C. Sickles.[2] They found Father Judge inside the church, where he took them to the chapel of Blessed Jean-Gabriel Perboyre, the young missionary martyr in China who so inspired Tom Judge as a seminarian. In Perboyre Chapel he put before these women his vision for a group of lay apostles who would minister to the agonized Jesus in the poor all around them and all those who were slipping away from the church, especially the Italian immigrants and their children, whom Judge viewed as particularly abandoned and religiously at risk.

Father Judge laid before them that evening some of the cases his census had uncovered and urged them to strict confidentiality in dealing with these cases. Writing in 1944, as Sister Marie Baptista, Amy Croke recalled his message in these terms:

> He told us of the condition of many children who had never heard the name of God or the sweet name of Jesus, or of his Blessed Mother. He spoke of the terrific leakage from the Catholic Church, which not even the number of converts, though large, could balance. He told us that proselytizing was rampant

2. This account of the meeting follows James P. O'Bryan, ST, *Awake the Giant: A History of the Missionary Cenacle Apostolate* (Holy Trinity, Ala.: Missionary Cenacle Press, 1986), 30–35, citing Father Judge's own recollections in a conference of August 2, 1918, AST, MF 8408, and the "Recollections of Sr. Marie Baptista, MSBT" (Amy Croke). The first three of these five women eventually became Missionary Servants of the Most Blessed Trinity. Both Sr. Mary James Collins and Sr. Mary Tonra list six women as present at this meeting. The sixth is Agnes Mullane; see Sr. Mary Tonra, MSBT, *Led by the Spirit: A Biography of Mother Boniface Keasey, MSBT* (New York: Gardner Press, 1984), 21. Until O'Bryan published his book in 1986, the date for this meeting in Perboyre Chapel had been remembered and celebrated in the Missionary Cenacle as April 11, 1909. Berry provides a thorough discussion of the issue in *God's Valiant Warrior*, 348 n102, and comes down on the side of the 1909 date. O'Bryan argues for the 1910 date; see *Awake the Giant*, 28 and notes. Most decisively in favor of O'Bryan's date is the Holy Agony episode. A careful reading of the sources surrounding it shows that, until June 1909, it was at the center of Father Judge's attention, absorbing most of his emotional and spiritual energy. It is easier to imagine that a year later he would take archconfraternity members in this new direction than that he was already doing so in the heat of a controversy that consumed him so. The 1910 date, well after he was relieved of responsibility for promoting the archconfraternity, is more consistent with a new beginning. The 1909 date could mean that, as Brediger put it, the Perboyre Chapel meeting was "simply a special meeting of some of the promoters of the Archconfraternity of the Holy Agony"; Lawrence Brediger, "In the Name of the Father, and of the Son, and of the Holy Ghost," in *Father Thomas A. Judge, CM, Founder, The Missionary Cenacle Family*, Monographs 6, *Father Judge and the Missionary Cenacle*, ed. Timothy Lynch, ST (Silver Spring, Md.: Archives of the Missionary Servants of the Most Holy Trinity, 1985), 25–26.

among aliens, especially the Italians; that numbers of the unbaptized, of invalid marriages, and of those who never went to Mass or to the Sacraments were all around us.[3]

With this historic meeting in Perboyre Chapel, Father Judge began what would become the signature work of his life: the promotion of the lay apostolate. Though the five women had been members of the Archconfraternity of the Holy Agony, this was a work with a distinct emphasis. In addition to their personal devotion, they would console the agonized Jesus primarily through organized apostolic work. In this work of making apostles, Father Judge anticipated later developments in Pope Pius XI's teaching on the lay apostolate.[4] Significantly, all of these first lay apostles were women.

Work-a-Day Women

Writing of the years 1910 and 1911, Sister Mary James Collins drew attention to the key role women played in Father Judge's early success with lay apostles. Contrasting these pioneer women with a short-lived men's group, she wrote, "No wonder Father so often preached on the constancy of women to Our Lord during his Passion!" Wherever Judge gave missions, "through Massachusetts, Connecticut, New York and down in Baltimore," new "cenacles" sprang up. "Reports of these early years make interesting reading," Collins wrote, "for it shows interest and zeal on the part of these work-a-day women."[5]

By 1910 about 25 percent of American women were "work-a-day women," representing about 20 percent of the U.S. labor force. In industrialized New England and the mid-Atlantic states, where the Springfield Mission Band worked, the percentage of work-a-day women in the labor force was closer to 30 percent. This was part of a consistently upward trend that had begun

3. Cited in Brediger, "In the Name of the Father," 6:26, citing from Croke's April 1944 *Missionary Cenacle Review* article.

4. In 1922 Pope Pius XI applied the royal priesthood text from 1 Peter to lay participation in the works of the apostolate: "Tell your faithful children of the laity that when, united with their pastors and their bishops, they participate in the works of the apostolate, both individual and social, the end purpose of which is to make Jesus Christ better known and loved, then they are more than ever 'a chosen generation, a kingly priesthood, a holy nation, a purchased people,' of whom St. Peter spoke in such laudatory terms (1 Peter 2:9)"; Pius XI, *Ubi arcano Dei consilio*, December 23, 1922, paragraph 58, in Claudia Carlen, IHM, *The Papal Encyclicals* (Raleigh, N.C.: McGrath, 1981), 3:236.

5. Sister Mary James Collins, MSBT, "Voice from the Past," *Holy Ghost*, June 1949, 11.

with the 1870 census and the post–Civil War industrialization and urbanization of the United States.

Between the 1910 and 1920 censuses, daughters of immigrants were increasingly likely to work in offices as clerks, stenographers, and typists rather than in more traditional occupations such as seamstresses and launderers. The number of women bookkeepers, cashiers, and accountants also increased dramatically during this period. A significant rise in women teachers continued, as well.[6] It was from the ranks of such clerks, office workers, and teachers that Judge's first lay apostles tended to come. Writing to Cardinal William O'Connell of Boston in 1913, Judge described them as "simple, humble working people, as a rule workers in shops, factories, and stores.... I may include also many school teachers and nurses."[7]

In 1910 the typical work-a-day woman was "a working class daughter who lived in the parental home."[8] By 1920, 40 percent of female workers were under twenty-five years of age. Their wages were far below those of men, who were considered "breadwinners." Female workers had little hope of security outside a family home. "Women without men were by definition deviant; women who failed to marry were often ridiculed, the widowed and the deserted were pitied, and the divorced woman was stigmatized."[9] Without financial independence, most work-a-day women anticipated marriage and their own families as the normative future that awaited them. But there were exceptions.

As Collins suggested, Father Judge's first lay apostles were work-a-day women. But they did not necessarily fit the under-twenty-five census profile. A core group was a little older and less content with the life choices open to them. Marriage, traditional religious communities, and other alternatives, such as teaching and nursing, failed to attract them in a compelling way. Later, when the lay movement evolved into a religious community, it attracted women who were available for more conventional reasons. Some, like Father Judge's sister Ann Veronica, were widows. Others had never married because of caring for a sick or elderly parent. The pioneer lay apostles,

6. Joseph A. Hill, *Women in Gainful Occupations, 1870–1920*, Census Monographs 9 (1929; repr. Westport, Conn.: Greenwood Press, 1978), 8–11, 28. This work was originally published by the U.S. Government Printing Office.

7. Judge to William Cardinal O'Connell, Troy, N.Y., September 27, 1913, from a copy in AST, MF 3304.

8. Leslie Woodcock Tentler, *Wage-Earning Women, Industrial Work and Family Life in the United States, 1900–1930* (New York: Oxford University Press, 1979), 85.

9. Ibid., 16.

however, in addition to being a little bit older, were also a bit more independent, more willing to take risks, to do something new and different, something that might distance them from their families. Father Judge challenged them and appealed to their religious idealism. He invited them into the Holy Family. One such woman was Amy Marie Croke.

Amy Croke

Amy Croke was about thirty-four years old when she first heard Father Judge preach at a mission in Our Lady of Mercy Church in Brooklyn on December 18, 1904.[10] Croke lived at 221 Division Avenue in Brooklyn. Licensed by the State of New York in 1905 to teach stenography, Croke taught at a business school in the city. On January 26, 1905, Judge wrote to her from a train to thank her for an "excellent" copy of one of his sermons. He mentioned previous "ambitious stenographers" who "gave up in disgust."[11] She finally met Father Judge sometime in 1907. She became a promoter in the Archconfraternity of the Holy Agony and asked Father Judge to be her spiritual director.

In the latter half of 1909, as Father Judge undertook the parish census at St. John the Baptist, he was struck by the number of people, especially among immigrants and the urban poor, who fell through the cracks of parish ministrations. He regarded these people as in mortal danger of their eternal salvation, and this fed his sense of urgency about them. He remembered the Protestant women who worked among the Italian immigrants in Philadelphia during his student days. When he tried to recruit some Daughters of Charity to do home-visiting among the people his census had turned up, their superior suggested that he wanted to make "Salvation Army women" out of her sisters.[12]

The counter-example of Protestant evangelists and settlement workers among Italian immigrants in the urban Northeast helped Father Judge to imagine people like Amy Croke doing the kind of apostolic work he found so urgent and that priests in normal parish ministry did not seem able to do. This idea of reaching "abandoned" souls outside ordinary parish life is central to his original conception. Croke recalled that Judge's ideas for lay apostles crystallized during a stay in the hospital for a hand infection.[13]

10. On Croke's early life, see O'Bryan, *Awake the Giant*, 26ff. Croke is at the center of O'Bryan's story. His account includes her later published and unpublished recollections.

11. Judge to Miss Croak [*sic*], southbound train to Philadelphia, January 26, 1905, AST, MF 12.

12. O'Bryan, *Awake the Giant*, 23.

13. In a letter to Cardinal William O'Connell three years later, Father Judge explained his

Committed associates of the archconfraternity—namely, the promoters—were available. Judge began to give Amy Croke and others various apostolic works to do, primarily "spiritual works of mercy."[14] At the beginning such works often involved home-visiting with an eye to bringing people back to the sacraments. Such work was clearly in keeping with the archconfraternity's aim of preserving the faith. Eventually it would evolve into catechetical work with children and social work with families. Writing in 1913, Father Judge assured Cardinal O'Connell that he had engaged lay people in apostolic work with the approval of his superior.[15]

After eighteen months in Brooklyn (February 1909 to September 1910), Father Judge was assigned to the mission band based in Springfield, Massachusetts. He traveled up and down the Northeast region from Boston to New York with periodic stops in Baltimore. He traveled as far north as Bangor, Maine, and as far south as Norfolk, Virginia. His transfer to the mission band meant that his Brooklyn-born vision for a trained group of lay apostles would soon spread over the Northeast.

At this point, it was still clear that the new thing Father Judge was doing originated in the Archconfraternity of the Holy Agony. His original Brooklyn lay apostles were all serious associates in the archconfraternity. In his first letter to them as a group, he referred to them as "Consolers of the Agonized Jesus." He sent a meditation for the Feast of the Immaculate Conception in which he described them in terms of the Holy Agony devotion as "the loyal friends and consoling angels of her [Mary's] Jesus—whose mind is again agonized in the sorrows of His Vicar on earth." And then there is an undeveloped hint of the Holy Ghost as he urges them to persevere in their "unity of purpose and charity of spirit." "We *see* and *feel* God's presence when those who work for Him are in *peace* and *harmony*."[16]

From Holy Agony to Holy Ghost

The five years between April 1910 and August 1915 were formative for the lay movement that began to take shape that first night in the Perboyre

---

thinking in some detail; see Judge to O'Connell, Troy, N.Y., September 27, 1913, AST, MF 3301–6. This letter will be discussed in detail later.

14. See Croke's account of her first case in O'Bryan, *Awake the Giant*, 25.

15. Judge to O'Connell, September 27, 1913.

16. Judge to My Dear Consolers of the Agonized Jesus, December 6, 1910, as cited in Brediger, "In the Name of the Father," 6:32–33.

Chapel. In a series of letters, conferences, and other talks over those years, Father Judge described the shape and spirit of the religious movement he envisioned. Before considering these documents in detail, it is well to note their most striking characteristics—namely, the central role Judge gives to the third Person of the Blessed Trinity. Most intriguing is the question of the sources for Judge's newfound emphasis on the Holy Spirit. Father Judge never explicitly answers this question. The Holy Spirit is all but absent from his writing prior to 1911.[17] By the 1920s, the Holy Ghost was the "Father of the poor."[18]

Devotion to the Holy Ghost in the United States

During the period between the Civil War and the early twentieth century, devotion to the Holy Ghost was "one of the most creative, widespread, and indicative religious expressions of the era."[19] At this time, Catholics whose native language was English were a relatively small group. Catholics in the United States read English Catholic writers. The devotion's roots go back to the convert Cardinal Archbishop of Westminster Henry Edward Manning (1808–92). His *Temporal Mission of the Holy Ghost* appeared in 1865 and his *Internal Mission of the Holy Ghost* in 1875. *Temporal Mission* went through seven American editions before 1890; *Internal Mission* had five. Citing the Ignatian phrase *sentire cum ecclesia*, Manning concluded *Internal Mission* by identifying the true test of a spiritual person with conformity to the church. Manning promoted the Confraternity of the Servants of the Holy Ghost, founded at London in 1877.

Isaac Hecker (1819–88), founder of the Paulists, and John J. Keane (1838–1918), bishop of Richmond and Dubuque and founding rector of Catholic University, represented an alternative stream of the devotion. Manning emphasized the Holy Ghost as holding the church together in its worldly struggles. Conformity to authority was the surest sign of the Spirit's presence. By

17. Berry draws attention to Father Judge's new emphasis on the Holy Spirit, pointing out its simultaneity with the beginnings of his lay apostolic movement; see *God's Valiant Warrior*, 149–50, 252–55. Judge's eventual choice of the name *Cenacle* for this movement, and that term's close association with the Holy Spirit, lend support to Berry's suggestion that we need look no further than the New Testament and the Acts of the Apostles for the source of this new and defining emphasis; ibid., 252.

18. Judge to Sister Mary James, Philadelphia, July 12, 1922, AST, MF 5226.

19. Joseph P. Chinnici, OFM, ed., *Devotion to the Holy Spirit in American Catholicism* (New York and Mahwah, N.J.: Paulist Press, 1985), 15. Chinnici's ninety-page introduction traces the history of devotion to the Holy Spirit. On Manning, see ibid., 17–25, and on Hecker and Keane, see 25–48.

contrast, Hecker and Keane emphasized the Spirit's indwelling presence in the soul and urged the laity to pay more attention to their interior impulses for good. Neither would have denied the truth in the emphasis of the other.

While Father Judge did emphasize attention to interior impulses as possibly coming from the indwelling Spirit, there is no evidence that he learned this from Hecker.[20] Pope Leo XIII's encyclical on devotion to the Holy Ghost, *Divinum illud*, appeared in 1897, while Judge was a student. Leo recommended novenas to the Holy Ghost each year before Pentecost. But again Judge does not refer to *Divinum illud* in the period before 1911.[21] During Judge's years on the mission band, the chief promoter of Hecker's vision was the Paulist Joseph McSorley. Judge read *Catholic World* and could have seen McSorley's "Devotion to the Holy Spirit." In this 1900 article McSorley attempted to rescue Hecker's legacy, and specifically his teaching on the Holy Spirit, from the strictures of *Testem benevolentiae*, Pope Leo XIII's apostolic letter censuring "Americanism."[22] Though Judge later corresponded with McSorley, there is no evidence that he drew at this time from the Paulist's ideas on devotion to the Holy Spirit.

The Cenacle

In the summer of 1911, about a year after the Perboyre Chapel meeting, Father Judge began to use the term *cenacle* to refer to the groups of lay apostles he had planted all over the Northeast.

> The word *Cenacle* of all words is one of the most beautiful. It is just fragrant with the Holy Ghost, it is a prayerful word. The *Cenacle* was a chamber in which the devout went to pray. Into such a chamber went the Blessed Mother in preparation for the coming of the Holy Ghost. It was in the *Cenacle* the Lord instituted the Holy Eucharist. After Our Lord's resurrection, she remained in the Cenacle, and it was there the Apostles went to be encouraged. We cannot

20. Here is an early example, written at a time of trial, of Father Judge urging attention to interior impulses for good: "and let us be true to the impulses for good. The Spirit of God is going to move us for good. If we are responsive to the word of the Holy Ghost, He will shift us, draw us here and there for good. Sometimes the Holy Ghost will lead us through fragrantly scented meadows, through beautiful sun-checkered groves, or it may be He may lead us into rough places, on the brink of precipices, or into bleak desert places—but let us be responsive, let us be led by Him, let the Spirit of God find us"; minutes of an inner council meeting held Sunday, January 18, 1913 [1914?], AST, MF 3320.

21. For this reason, Berry finds *Divinum illud* an unlikely source for Judge's devotion to the Holy Spirit; see *God's Valiant Warrior*, 396n1168.

22. See Joseph McSorley, CSP, "Devotion to the Holy Spirit," *Catholic World* 71 (June 1900): 290–304.

> mention *Cenacle* without thinking of the Holy Ghost. Whenever we mention the word *Cenacle*, we should repeat it as a prayer, and train ourselves to think of the Holy Ghost. It should be a prayer to the Holy Ghost, an act of adoration, a prayer for the apostolic spirit.[23]

In the term *cenacle* we have perhaps the clearest indication of the source for Father Judge's new emphasis on the Holy Spirit—the New Testament. St. Jerome chose *coenaculum* to render "upper room" (Acts 1:13) in Acts 1 and 2. The church was born in the cenacle in the power of the Holy Spirit manifest in the wind and fire of Pentecost (Acts 2:1–4). Judge was forming an apostolic movement. He wanted apostles. The clear narrative sense of Acts 1 and 2 is that the Holy Spirit makes apostles. The major apostolic figures of Acts, from Peter to Stephen to Paul, are all described as filled with the Holy Spirit. It would not be surprising if the term *cenacle* came to Judge while he was preparing his sermon for Pentecost in 1911.

A letter dated October 1911 serves as an example of how Father Judge read the New Testament meditatively and taught his lay apostles to do the same. The gospel for the Seventeenth Sunday after Pentecost was Matthew 12:36–41 on the two great commandments. Judge called it "the Gospel of Charity." Referring to the associates, he writes, "Let them place themselves at His feet, look up into His Sacred Face and listen to His Words." Then he cites the gospel text. "I wish," he continues, "they would write down their thoughts and later let me see what The Holy Spirit gave them to ponder, the holy inspirations with which he may have inspired them."[24]

He encouraged them in the practice of "reading a few passages from the Bible at every meeting in the The Cenacle."

> I wish all to become familiar with Our Lord's life and teachings. This practice, surely, will be conformable to the spirit of the SERVANTS OF THE HOLY GHOST, for should they not be familiar with the Word of the Holy Ghost? The readings need not be long but they should be regular and continuous.... Many souls are returning to God through your dear sisters in New England and in our other Cenacles.[25]

23. Brediger, "In the Name of the Father," 6:36–37. In what follows, I shall use *Cenacle* to refer to Father Judge's lay apostolic movement as a whole and *cenacle* to refer to individual local branches of the movement

24. Judge to Dear Friend, St. Rose's, Meriden, Conn., October 1911, AST, MF 3310–12. This seems to be a long-distance form of the "repetition of prayer" recommended in the conferences of St. Vincent de Paul.

25. Judge to Dear Friend [Amy Croke], no place, May 30, 1912, AST, MF 0173. Interestingly, the name Servants of the Holy Ghost (in capital letters in the original) is the same as that of the

A letter conference on the Holy Spirit, written from Brattleboro, Vermont, in 1912, probably to the Cenacle in Brooklyn, suggests that Judge saw them as taken up into the story of Acts, reliving in twentieth-century Brooklyn the Spirit-filled apostolic moments in which the church began.

> You and your devoted associates are the first Apostolic Band. He gathered you first in the upper church and spoke to your hearts. He inflamed your wills after enlightening your minds that you might help Him; so instruct in His way those who eagerly assemble in new "Coenacula" to learn from you how they may love the Holy Ghost the more and sacrifice for Him. Never forget you are *communicating a spirit to others. Pray, pray that it may be the Spirit of God, His good influence.*[26]

From the Incarnation to the Most Blessed Trinity

In the absence of documentary evidence for the sources of Father Judge's newfound emphasis on the Holy Spirit around 1910 and 1911, his own meditative reading of the Acts of the Apostles emerges as a strong candidate for the main source. It is also possible that it was his role in the conflicts of 1909 surrounding the Archconfraternity of the Holy Agony that prepared Father Judge's ears to hear what Acts has to say about the Holy Spirit as the One who makes apostles. It is as if, in the aftermath of the heavily incarnational Holy Agony, Father Judge really discovers what he would call the Most Blessed Trinity. Perhaps his own prayerful self-examination showed him that the Spirit's gifts had been lacking to him during the Holy Agony controversy. "We *see* and *feel* God's presence," he wrote in 1910, "when those who work for Him are in *peace* and *harmony*."[27]

Whatever the cause, his writings in 1911 and 1912 convey a strong sense of the need for the vivifying and discerning powers that are the gifts of the Holy Spirit. By 1912 he had become convinced of the need for serious attention to the present activity of the Holy Spirit. Without the Holy Spirit there can be no real apostolic work. As did the ancient church in the years between the Council of Nicaea in 325 and the first Council of Constantinople in 381, we might say that Father Judge moved from putting a primary emphasis on the mystery of the incarnation in his promotion of the Holy Agony devotion

---

confraternity promoted by Manning and Keane, among others. Perhaps that is why it didn't last.

26. Judge to Dear Friends, St. Michael's Church, Brattleboro, Vt., 1912, AST, MF 212.

27. Judge to My Dear Consolers of the Agonized Jesus, December 6, 1910, as cited in Brediger, "In the Name of the Father," 6:32–33.

to putting a primary emphasis on the Holy Spirit and the Holy Trinity, without leaving the incarnation behind, in his approach to the apostolic life of the Cenacle.

Neither the Holy Spirit nor the Trinity replaced the incarnation. Like St. Vincent de Paul, Father Judge did not have a well-worked-out system of theology or spirituality. Contemporary theologians would be hard-pressed to find a systematic theology of the Trinity in his writings. This is not a bad thing. John Henry Newman's discussion of "belief in the Holy Trinity" illustrates how someone like Father Judge might hold together the mysteries of the incarnation, the Holy Trinity, and the Holy Spirit without the need always to advert to the complexities of trinitarian doctrine.

Writing in 1870, Newman distinguished between notional and real apprehension and assent. Notional apprehension or assent is abstract and impersonal, based primarily on appeals to reason, and generally does not affect conduct. Real apprehension and assent, on the other hand, are personal, based on appeals to our imagination and emotions, and can move us to action.[28] Theology and devotion, the theological and the religious, roughly correspond for Newman to notional and real. He doesn't play them off against one another. Both are needed in the church, and in some individuals they combine. "Theology, as such," he writes, "always is notional, as being scientific: religion, as being personal, should be real."[29]

Applying these categories to "belief in the Holy Trinity," Newman asks, "is it capable of being apprehended otherwise than notionally? . . . Does it admit of being held in the imagination and embraced with a real assent?"[30] Newman answers "yes" to both questions and distinguishes between a creedal or confessional account of the doctrine in terms such as *three, one, Father, Son, Spirit,* and a theological or dogmatic account using words such as *substance, essence, form, subsistence, circumincession*. The latter he describes as "doubtless addressed to the intellect, and can only command a notional assent."[31]

"Strictly speaking," he thinks, "the dogma of the Holy Trinity, as a complex whole, or as a mystery, is not the formal object of religious apprehension and assent; but as it is a number of propositions, taken one by one." Newman doesn't think real assent to the mystery as a whole is possible. We can imagine its propositions separately, but we cannot imagine them together.

28. John Henry Newman, *An Essay in Aid of a Grammar of Assent* (London: Longmans, Green, 1870), chap. 4, "Notional and Real Assent."

29. Ibid., 55.

30. Ibid., 126, 127.

31. Ibid., 128.

The Holy Spirit abides as in the ubiquitous salutation, "May the grace and peace of the Holy Ghost be with us forever." But the incarnation and the Holy Trinity remain, as well, their presence modulated by the church, as in the conferences of St. Vincent, through the rhythms of the liturgical year. Newman's summary is most salutary for approaching Father Judge on the Trinity. In his distinction between theology and religion, we find a suggestion in the latter of what Father Judge meant by "devotional knowledge":

> Religion has to do with the real and the real is particular; theology has to do with what is notional and the notional is the general and systematic. Hence theology has to do with the Dogma of the Holy Trinity as a whole made up of many propositions; but Religion has to do with each of those separate propositions that compose it, and lives and thrives in the contemplation of them. In them it finds the motives for devotion and faithful obedience; while theology on the other hand forms and protects them by virtue of its function of regarding them, not merely one by one, but as a system of truth.[32]

The Cenacle Expands

When Father Judge left Brooklyn for the Springfield mission band, leadership of the Brooklyn cenacle naturally fell to Amy Croke. He formalized this arrangement in a letter of February 2, 1911.[33] By this time, new cenacles started to appear in the cities where Judge was giving missions. He tried to convey to the pioneer associates a sense of being part of the great apostolic movement that was the history of the church begun at Pentecost. He started off the Brooklyn associates with a course in church history, beginning with the Acts of the Apostles. Each new cenacle, each conversion, each abandoned soul attended to would begin again and continue the Spirit-filled movement described in the opening chapters of Acts. Judge emphasized the role of the laity in the history of the early church and saw the history of the Cenacle as a recapitulation of that history in the twentieth century.[34]

Early in 1911 Father Judge gave a mission in Baltimore and established

32. Ibid., 140.

33. Brediger, "In the Name of the Father," 6:34.

34. On the church history course, see O'Bryan, *Awake the Giant*, 38. Early on the Brooklyn cenacle had a library. Judge's three lectures on church history were included along with books on the Reformation and Anglican orders by Abbot Gasquet. The library also included two books by Notre Dame physicist John Zahm, CSC, on the church and science, and *Progress in Education* and *The Victory of Love* by Bishop John Lancaster Spalding of Peoria. Judge expected the associates to be prepared to answer intelligently the objections they met in their case work. A list of the contents of the Brooklyn cenacle library is at AST, MF 3279–80.

the second cenacle there. In April he started a cenacle in the Bronx at St. Jerome's parish, where he met Ella Lonergan, a young student at the College of New Rochelle. In addition, 1911 saw the establishment of two cenacles in Boston and others in Brattleboro, Vermont; Andover, Massachusetts; and Meriden, Connecticut. One of the leaders of the Meriden cenacle was Mary Rahaley, who would eventually become the second mother general of the Missionary Servants of the Most Blessed Trinity. In 1912 cenacles began in Brockton, Randolph, and Malden, Massachusetts; Hartford and New Britain, Connecticut; Syracuse, New York; Wakeman, Ohio; and San Francisco, California. As the letter of May 30, 1912, indicates, by this time Father Judge was referring to all the cenacles together as the Servants of the Holy Ghost.[35]

Most of the Servants of the Holy Ghost were work-a-day women. Cenacle work, especially the secrecy strictly required by Judge, often led to difficulties and sometimes conflict with their families. Judge's correspondence with Ella Lonergan leading up to her leaving home in New York for Alabama in 1915 is a good example. Concluding a chapter on working women living "on their own," historian Leslie Tentler drew attention to the crucial place of family, usually the family of origin, in their emotional lives.

> For the working-class woman, then, life outside the family was apt to be economically precarious and very lonely. It was not a life of freedom and autonomy.... Ultimately, the family provided the only emotional world in which working-class women were secure and fully acceptable. The experience of most independent women taught this lesson both to women "on their own" and to a larger female audience.[36]

To such work-a-day women, Judge offered an alternative emotional world, a new family. The cost of such a commitment for single women in 1912 we can only imagine. Eventually this commitment would lead many of the core group to become vowed religious. Some seriously committed women, Margaret Healy and Mary Elizabeth Walsh, for example, never entered what came to be known as the "Inner Cenacle."[37]

35. In the listing of the Cenacles I am following Brediger, "In the Name of the Father," 6:38–39. He also includes an account from Mother Mary of the Incarnate Word (Mary Rahaley) on the long process Judge went through in founding the Meriden cenacle; see 39–42. She emphasizes the importance of confidentiality or "secrecy," even with respect to her family. For Servants of the Holy Ghost, see Judge to Dear friend [Amy Croke], no place, May 30, 1912, AST, MF 0173.

36. Tentler, *Wage-Earning Women*, 135.

37. On Healy, see Sr. Josepha McNutt, MSBT, *Margaret: Called and Chosen; A Life of Margaret Mary Healy, Ph.D., A Pioneer Cenacle Lay Missionary* (Holy Trinity, Ala.: Missionary Cenacle Press, 1989), 53, 56.

The conflicts surrounding such decisions highlight a question, just below the surface in relations between Inner (women and men religious) and Outer Cenacles (lay apostles) and vexingly embedded in the theology of the day and in Father Judge's approach to the lay apostolate: could one really live an evangelical life outside the religious state? Whether *Lumen gentium*'s "universal call to holiness in the church," in chapter 5 of that work, resolves this question for the contemporary church or merely flattens it out remains to be seen. In any case, no one could deny the eloquence of Father Judge's challenging appeal to religious idealism as he invited these young working women into a new family.

An annunciation novena offers an effective example. Adapting the idiom of the French School to St. Michael's Church in Brooklyn in 1912, Father Judge called the associates "into the very family of the Incarnation." In a meditation for the novena's seventh day entitled, "The Servants of the Holy Ghost," he wrote:

> This day of the Annunciation is one of our greatest feasts. Its mysteries and those connected with it are the subjects of our meditations, and constant prayer.... We honor the Angel Gabriel in love.... The great grace that God is giving us leads us Servants of the Holy Ghost into the very family of the Incarnation. We should be very grateful for the *grace* that God gives us by drawing and inspiring us with a special love. He *demands our service and influence* in the *battle* between *good and evil.*[38]

The first attempt to embody this new family in the practices of a common life took place in the fall of 1912 at the cenacle in Baltimore. The house at 209 West Madison St. in the neighborhood of Baltimore's Cathedral of the Assumption had from its beginning multiple purposes and serious financial obstacles. Both Cardinal Gibbons and the cathedral rector, Monsignor Fletcher, were pleased to have the cenacle house nearby. Gibbons gave them the unusual permission to have the Blessed Sacrament reserved in their house, but he gave little or no financial support.

After visiting the house at Christmas time in 1912, Father Judge was happy to report, "We have a place now to shelter poor girls who may come to us.... It will be a house of retreat, a house of study, a house of prayer; they

38. Judge, "The Annunciation Novena–March 1912," in *Father Thomas A. Judge, CM, Founder, The Missionary Cenacle Family*, Monographs 4, *The Writings of Father Judge: Key Documents*, ed. Timothy Lynch, ST, 9–17, and Monographs 5, *The Grace of Our Founder*, ed. Timothy Lynch, ST (both Silver Spring, Md.: Archives of the Missionary Servants of the Most Holy Trinity, 1984); the emphasized words are underlined in the original. See also AST, MF 9435.

will have a family life there."[39] Judge's references to sheltering poor girls and family life recall the socioeconomic situation of single working women at this time. One of the three permanent residents worked as a sales clerk in a store, another as a seamstress. In addition to taking in needy young women, their chief apostolic work was home-visiting and catechizing in an Italian neighborhood, work that drew the grateful approval of the cathedral rector and Cardinal Gibbons.

The Baltimore experiment in community living lasted for three years, from 1912 to the end of 1915. Overwhelmed by such material needs as a broken furnace and stove and no place to wash and hang their clothes, working and doing apostolic work at the same time, the Baltimore associates did not have the wherewithal to survive their financial and interpersonal difficulties. Neither Father Judge himself nor Amy Croke was free to spend much time there. The house closed shortly after Judge was reassigned to the Alabama Mission in the summer of 1915. A number of the women who lived at this house eventually joined the Missionary Servants of the Most Blessed Trinity. During Amy Croke's visit to the house, she went to see Cardinal Gibbons. He told her they were doing "the work of angels." "Father Judge, Father Judge," he said, "his feet just touch the earth and his heart is in heaven."[40]

1913: A Pivotal Year of Growth and Conflict

By 1913 the Servants of the Holy Ghost had grown sufficiently to have a national meeting at the cathedral in Hartford, Connecticut. They had taken on a certain practical shape that Father Judge began to solidify into a rule. At the same time, they had been around long enough to arouse controversy.

In March 1913, Father Judge produced a kind of preliminary rule or constitution. The name "Servants of the Holy Ghost" doesn't appear on it. It is entitled simply, "Inner Council Meetings," and dated March 23, 1913 (New York) and March 25, 1913 (Boston).[41] The document is eight pages long and divided into forty-eight numbered points. There were five national officers with Amy Croke listed by name as the "Servant of all the Cenacles" (no. 36).

39. From the Minutes of the Inner Council Meeting, Sunday, January 18, 1913, AST, MF 3321. O'Bryan, *Awake the Giant*, 69–75, gives the most complete account of the Baltimore house; see also Brediger, "In the Name of the Father," 6:51–53.

40. From a letter of Sr. Marie Baptista (Amy Croke) to Mother Mary of the Incarnate Word (Mary Rahaley) no date, as cited by O'Bryan, *Awake the Giant*, 75.

41. For the text, see Judge, "Annunciation Novena," 4:9–17; see also MF 12510–18. Lynch says that the document comes from Amy Croke's papers.

"Inner Councils" could apparently be national (presumably the national officers) or provincial (no. 15 refers to Inner Provincial Councils). The "Cenacle Council" (no. 13) "comprised of heads of different Cenacles and their secretaries" was to meet once a month. Inner Councils should meet every two weeks (no. 12).

This document, written on the move, partly in New York and partly in Boston, mixes constitutional and procedural matters as if designed to drive attorneys to distraction. It does clarify, however, that case work was at the heart of what associates did. The section on "Reports" (no. 34) calls for details about number of visits, baptisms, people brought back to the sacraments, conversions, and so on. Most of the hour-and-a-half cenacle meetings were devoted to discussing these cases.

A distinguishing feature of this document is its discussion of what Judge refers to as *council*. The word council does double duty for him. It refers both to meetings and to the gift of Holy Spirit usually spelled as *counsel*. He also uses it as a verb. The term embraces both meetings themselves and the spirit or "disposition necessary" for them (no. 14).

> It is necessary that *all* before coming to Council Meeting should individually and earnestly pray to the Holy Ghost for the Gift of Council [*sic*]. We should enter with prayerful minds free from bias and love of our own opinion. We should calmly state our views without tenaciously adhering to them, manifesting quietly and with holy indifference to our own interests and sentiments whatsoever the Holy Spirit may make manifest to us. We must avoid being wedded to our ideas, and be prepared to acquiesce to the best judgment of the Council (no. 14).

Essential to the disposition necessary for council is the desire to include the voices of all. The document includes directives for drawing out overly modest or diffident associates as well as the inactive and the negligent.

Rule no. 14 on council concludes with the admonition, "Never discuss on the outside Council matters; to violate this rule would be considered a grave indiscretion." There is also a rule that the associates charged with notifying others of meeting times (the Evangelists, "chosen for their prudence, tact, and devotion" [no. 38]) never do this by telephone. They are also directed not to discuss cases by name in letters, memoranda, or notes (nos. 41, 43). "Their apostolate is of a most professional character and grave injury may be done their clients by violations of this [telephone] rule" (no. 40). Their work has a "dignity, sacredness and almost priestly nature" that demands the "utmost caution not to write nor leave scattered about, notes, memoranda, letters concerning others or confidential communications with their officers" (no. 41). To ensure confidentiality, they often referred to Father Judge himself by the code name "Tillie Fisher," as in, "Tillie Fisher is in town."[42]

These forty-eight points make clear the nature of the commitment involved in being a Servant of the Holy Ghost or Cenacle associate. Recalling St. Vincent's admonition "to think about the story of the Mystery and pay attention to all its details," Father Judge's conferences at this time called the associates to insert themselves into the mysteries of Christ's life as portrayed in the gospel stories.[43] He also consistently reminds them of their own deathbeds and purgatory.

After referring to their work as "almost priestly," Judge is careful to insist on proper respect for "clergy and all ecclesiastical superiors" (no. 26). This juxtaposition reflects the ever present possibility of conflict with priests who may have felt that lay people were usurping their role and duties. This possibility was part of the reason for the strict secrecy or confidentiality insisted on by Judge. Before the end of the year 1913, such conflict would erupt in the Archdiocese of Boston.

"It is the Same Story"

On September 27, 1913, Father Judge wrote to Cardinal William O'Connell of Boston in response to his three questions about the nature of the work. Judge's letter, in response to O'Connell's dated September 20, gives his own account of the beginnings of the Cenacle, its methods, and purpose. O'Connell wanted to know: (1) "How the Society started"; (2) "Who are the members?"; and (3) "How are the members secured?"[44]

Responding to the first question, Father Judge told the story of his assignment to St. John the Baptist Church in Brooklyn and the "disheartening conditions" he found there due "partly, to want of system, partly, to a shifting New York population." He described how, with his superior's ap-

42. See Lynch's introduction to this document in "Annunciation Novena," 4:9, citing the recollections of Katherine Shelvy (Sister Michael).

43. St. Vincent de Paul, *Correspondence, Conferences, Documents*, vol. 2; *Conferences*, 11:80.

44. A July 16, 2014, email communication to me from Robert Johnson-Lally, archivist/records manager for the Archdiocese of Boston, indicates that he has not found "any Judge correspondence in the O'Connell records" in the Boston Archdiocesan Archives. We do not have O'Connell's letter of September 20 or any Boston correspondence related to this episode. Without this correspondence it is hard to tell with certainty what concerns or complaints might lie behind Cardinal O'Connell's questions.

proval, and "after careful thought and experiment," he came to ask the help of "good souls" in the parish. At first he thought of them as "guardians" who would tell the pastors about "the negligent" and "newcomers." They would discover "abuses and danger spots" and public schoolchildren to be safeguarded. Before long his "good souls" were "visiting, instructing, preparing for the Sacraments many that never would otherwise come under the influence of our ministrations." He told the cardinal that in the first year alone they made "about 1,000 visits and had a multitude of good works in Baptisms, etc." Judge emphasized that some of their deathbed conversions "obstinately had resisted the ministry of our most zealous priests so determinedly so as to be abandoned to their fate." This convinced him "still more the tremendous power for good latent in the lives of our people if they could be encouraged and spiritualized."

He went on to explain that, after his reappointment to the mission band, he had interested the pastors he met on the missions "in the wonderful possibilities for good of the devout of their flocks." He assured O'Connell that "these gentlemen, almost to a man have wished that such a spirit would be made possible in their parish." He reported that after each mission he had left behind "a little silent band of quiet workers who try to be an influence for good in the little circle in which God's Providence has placed them." He concluded with examples.

To O'Connell's second question about the members, he used the term *associates*. Associates may be:

> Any good hearted or good willed souls who can be persuaded to sacrifice for the sake of personal service their time and feelings offering up prayers & good works to the Holy Ghost for sinners & that they may become a greater influence for good they strive to sanctify themselves by constant prayer & very frequent reception of the Sacraments.

He went on to describe them by their occupations. Into their "shops, factories, and stores" they "carry a blessed influence that reclaims many to forgotten duties, preventing sin and the working of impious principles and practices." He provided O'Connell with a list of the Boston pastors in whose parishes the associates lived and then described their services to children, poor women, and older girls "exposed to the danger of street seduction." The cardinal must have asked about the funding behind all this activity. Judge assured him that there was "no treasure save their generous hearts and zeal for God's interests."

In response to O'Connell's third question about how members were secured, Father Judge didn't really describe his recruiting tactics. Rather, he claimed that every locality had "hidden saints" and even some "frail" people with "good hearts and generous dispositions." They can be persuaded "to sanctify themselves in the cause of Religion" with "remarkable conversions" as the result. Rather than describe recruiting strategies, Judge concluded with one of his earliest detailed statements of the kind of spirit he tried to inculcate in the first associates. In 1913 the language of "lay apostles" had yet to gain currency. He described this spirit as "a great personal devotion to the Holy Ghost."

> All are directed to a certain spirit that the apostolic may be formed in them, urged to work quietly and hide under the charity of silence good done that God may reward them the more. They pray much to the Holy Ghost being taught of His Divine Activity, in the Church and in their souls, that He is promised to those who ask for Him [Judge cites Luke 11:13 and 2 Corinthians 12:7 from the Latin Vulgate]. Continually they ask for His Gifts and Fruits, Wisdom and Fortitude, especially and to please Him the more they are encouraged to pray and sacrifice constantly for the coming back of the Greek Church and the reunion of Christianity. This develops a great personal devotion to the Holy Ghost which they are spreading amongst their companions and hold it as a rarest privilege and duty to substitute in the workroom or assembly edification of word & work for what is sinful. They never cease praying and suffering for the Church beseeching the Holy Spirit that She be victorious over her enemies and that He may encourage, guide and sustain our Holy Father, Bishops and Priests.[45]

Cardinal O'Connell must have responded by October's end. "I have never been so prayerful as since the last of October," Father Judge told an inner council meeting on January 18, 1914. "In regard to our Boston Cenacle, the Vicar General of the diocese is opposed to our work. The Bishop and the Vicar General are one. At the command of the Vicar General of the diocese I have stopped this work."[46] Around the same time, Judge wrote to John Farrell, one of the Boston priests who had been supporting the work. He told Farrell that he had "withdrawn from the work in Boston since last October, having dropped all extension and direction." He added a sentence that reflected his state of mind on Cardinal O'Connell's suppression of the Cenacle in the Archdiocese of Boston. Echoing the words of the Pharisee Gamaliel in

45. Judge to William Cardinal O'Connell, St. Francis Church, Troy, N.Y., September 27, 1913, AST, MF 3301–6. All the sentences and phrases in quotation marks are from this letter.

46. Minutes of an Inner Council Meeting Held Sunday, January 18, 1913, AST, MF 3320-21.

Acts 5, Judge wrote to Farrell, "Either it is—or is not God's work, if it is, then, it cannot be overthrown; if it is not, then, the quicker it is destroyed, the better."[47]

"I think the Acts of the Apostles are beautiful," he told the inner council in January. "I wish you would make it a practice to read them. I read today where honorable men, good men, were inclined to crush the disciples; you know they threw St. Paul out." Clearly, Father Judge was reading the plight of the Cenacle in Boston as a renarration of the history of the early church in Acts. At the beginning of 1914, he urged the members of the inner council to enter into the gospel mystery of the Epiphany, to bring their gifts to Christ and welcome him who was turned away at every door in Bethlehem. In the face of rejection in Boston, he told the inner council that they were "the heart and brains of the whole movement."

> The work is going to last as long as you last; the work is going to last as long as you have the spirit; the work will be as big as you are. You have the Divine Fire; it may die out; it may be knocked to pieces; great men may jump on it and try to smother it. It will never die out as long as you are here and transmit the spirit to others.

He urged them to be "big-hearted women." "The Spirit of God must find that in storm, in trial, in sacrifice, He can purge you; that you ring true; that you are only solicitous about two things—am I right with God and am I responsive to the inspirations of the Holy Spirit."

"There is a problem today," he continued. "Honorable men have decided they are going to wipe out the Cenacle." Then his biblical imagination kicked in. The weak confound the strong. Strength is made perfect in weakness. "Poor girls" face "honorable men." He ran the rejection of Christ in the Christmas story together with the rejection of the early church in the opening chapters of Acts. Without explicitly drawing out the parallels with the situation in Boston, he made them more than clear. Then he turned this complex of New Testament images into an exhortation to the women at the meeting, urging them not to shut Christ out. He left unspoken the clear implication that certain "honorable men" in Boston were doing just that. "It is the same story," he insisted.

47. Judge to Father John Farrell, Brooklyn, N.Y., January 10, 1914, AST, MF 4219. At St. Peter's hearing before the Sanhedrin, Gamaliel warned his fellow Pharisees to leave Peter and the others alone. "If their purpose or activity is human in its origins, it will destroy itself. If, on the other hand, it comes from God, you will not be able to destroy them without fighting God himself" (Acts 5:38–39).

I am just waiting to see what God is going to do with these poor girls and these honorable men. Apparently the thing is smothered, yet it isn't; the Divine spark is there. Let us pray. It seems peculiar at this time of year, when the poor Infant Christ is lying in the crib to teach us a lesson. Let us think of the Blessed Mother and St. Joseph, how they knocked at every door and no one had any room for them. If they had only let her in! Those poor foolish women, if they had only let her in! . . . Look at these poor people in the homes of wickedness. One could imagine they would be glad to think there were women to help these homeless people. It is the same story. Why didn't they let Christ in?

At this point, he exclaims, "I think the Acts of the Apostles are beautiful." The whole emphasis in his conclusion is on the openness and responsiveness to the Holy Spirit embodied in the narrative of Acts:

May the Spirit of God find us responsive . . . the Spirit of God may find the right kind of metal, the right kind of a soul to work on. . . . Let us be charitable; let us be kind to the homeless, to the negro, and we won't criticize anybody. . . . Trial is a good thing; if we suffer for Christ's sake that will be a good thing. Let us have the Spirit of Christ. Can we show the Spirit of the Holy Ghost in our lives? How do we know we have the Spirit of the Holy Ghost? Let us pray for the gifts of the Holy Ghost. If you have the seven gifts, you shall have the twelve fruits.

This talk to the inner council in January 1914, at a time when the Cenacle was banned in Boston, is one of Father Judge's most powerful rhetorical performances. Its contrast with the whining tone of his letters to Father Fiat in 1909 regarding the Holy Agony devotion is striking. And yet it is continuous. He still thinks he is right, and he is not going to stop until he is told to. The measure of the difference is a heartfelt attempt, rooted in a meditative appropriation of the New Testament, to be open to the Holy Spirit. The Holy Spirit is the difference between 1909 and 1914. In 1909 he tried to resolve a conflict with authority externally by appeal to a higher authority. By 1914 he had spiritualized or personalized the conflict by an appeal to the authority of the Holy Spirit.

At the end of his talk at the inner council meeting of January 18, Father Judge called for a series of novenas amounting to a "continuous" novena to the Holy Ghost. The chief purpose of the novena was to ask the Holy Ghost "to spread devotion to the Holy Agony of Jesus and that there may be a more personal and more direct devotion to the Holy Ghost."[48]

48. Minutes of an Inner Council Meeting Held Sunday, January 18, 1914, AST, MF 3320–21.

Boundary Issues

From the beginning, Father Judge's attempts to enlist the laity in pastoral work courted the danger that pastors would perceive his lay apostles as transgressing the boundaries between clergy and laity. At this time, those boundaries were rather tight. The fact that these lay apostles were women lent added complexity. "Almost priestly" was the phrase Judge used to describe the nature of their work in his 1913 Rules for Cenacle Meetings (no. 41). But the rule (no. 26) on "Priests and our Associates," with its emphasis on distance and respect, maintained a clear sense of the boundaries between priest and people.

This built-in tension between Father Judge's high view of the priesthood, typical of the time, and his genuine desire to have lay women do "almost priestly" pastoral work came into painful view when Cardinal O'Connell forbade Cenacle work in his archdiocese. As Brediger explained it, writing in the years after World War II, large numbers of confessions and Communions led many priests to doubt the significant "leakage" from the church that so troubled Father Judge. They didn't share his urgency and thought he was "making a lot of needless disturbance by stirring up young women to do work which 'didn't concern them.'"[49] For having "lay people doing the work that is the work of priests," one Vincentian confrere denounced Judge as "a Martin Luther."[50]

In addition, the heavy emphasis on secrecy, extending even to code names, seemed to exceed the ordinary confidentiality required of pastoral workers. This perhaps troubled some pastors. Though we don't know the exact nature of the concerns or complaints that drew Cardinal O'Connell's attention to Cenacle work in his archdiocese, he seemed to speak for those priests who thought, in Brediger's words, that Father Judge was "making a lot of needless disturbance."

After he ordered Cenacle work in Boston to stop in October of 1913, but before he publicly addressed the issue in January of 1914, Father Judge gave a conference to a group of associates gathered in the basement of St. Andrew's Church in New York City. Coming on the heels of Cardinal O'Connell's action in Boston, this conference, given to a group of young women willing to

49. Brediger, "In the Name of the Father," 6:49. Brediger claims that some of the clergy labeled Judge "queer" and "a troublemaker." To settle the question about "leakage" was the point of Gerald Shaughnessy's classic *Has the Immigrant Kept the Faith?* (New York: Macmillan, 1925).

50. Blackwell, *Ecclesial People*, 87.

brave the Bowery, is striking for its emphasis on the "priestly" character of their work.

"You are doing a great work," he began. "You are doing things that priests cannot do today; you are doing something that demands the highest kind of courage and the profoundest kind of wisdom—saving souls." He urged them to pray for fortitude, courage, and strength. Again, he repeated, "You are doing work that we priests simply cannot do. We priests need help, and be it to your glory and honor to know you are called to do that work." Why they were called, he went on to say, he did not know. He suspected the "remote cause" had to do with "the respect women have for Christ." He could not say more than that. But "you are doing the work of priests and you must have a priest's spirit." They had to have the "heroism of a priest." "Your Communion," he assured them, "is not the Communion of an ordinary woman, it is not, it is more." "Soul-savers," he called them. Very carefully he even suggested that, in some cases, they might be doing more than priests. "You are the ones who are lifting the cross of Jesus. You are doing more, maybe, in a certain sense, than some priests." He urged them to be brave.

He then offered examples of clergy, one priest from Boston, who appreciated and urged the help of the laity. He cited one bishop urging the laity to "compete" with Protestant workers. If they persevered in the work, he promised them "a special paradise," "a special eternity."[51]

Clearly, Father Judge envisioned these women as lay apostles involved in the "care of souls." The reigning theology of baptism in the church, however, had not yet developed to the point where "priesthood"—for example, as in the "holy priesthood" of 1 Peter 2:5—could be attributed to them in any proper sense. The only theological account Judge could offer for their calling was a kind of argument from fittingness based on the "respect women have for Christ." Yet, from his own observation, from the testimony of other priests, he believed that their work was a vocation. The unavailability of a theological account of "almost priestly" tended to make the apostolic vocation of the laity inherently unstable. Religious life would provide an obvious resolution for this instability.

51. General Meeting Held at St. Andrew's Church, New York City, November 30, 1913, AST, MF 3327–28.

Turning Point

In the first weeks of November 1914, Father Judge received a brief communication from his provincial superior, the Eastern visitor Father Patrick McHale, with whom he had clashed a few years earlier over the Holy Agony. Judge had given a mission in Baltimore for three weeks in July 1914. He and McHale must have talked about his situation. A fulltime missioner who also directed the activities of what was now referred to as the Cenacle, Judge had no doubt requested that McHale free him for greater involvement with the Cenacle. "After serious thought concerning the subject which you broached to me in Baltimore," McHale had concluded that "you should give it up entirely, for the present at least."[52] Judge's subsequent correspondence with Amy Croke makes clear that McHale had told Judge to give up entirely his work as reverend director of the Cenacle. McHale reached his decision "in view of the difficulties which attract your attention to that work, on account of your present labors, and for other reasons of same weight."

In February of 1915, Judge wrote a long letter to Amy Croke. He must withdraw from the work, and she "must assume complete charge." "You see," he wrote, "I have been informed by my Superior that he thinks: 'for, the present, because of certain difficulties,' it would be best to give it up; now I am acting on this." He would pray "night and day" that "our Dear Lord may remove these obstacles and when it pleases him call me back to this work." She could communicate with him about "personal affairs," but in matters of "apostolate work," she was to be on her own.[53]

By July of 1915, Father Judge had informed the Cenacle associates of his transfer to the Alabama mission, headquartered at Opelika, near what is now Auburn University. He wrote to Amy Croke that he was convinced "that Our Dear Lord is sending me South for community purposes, to help the Cenacle and through this I have a hope that our complete intentions will be generously and fully answered."[54] At their yearly retreat during August 4–9 at St. Regis Cenacle Retreat in New York, Judge again reached into Acts and

52. McHale to Judge, St. Vincent's Seminary, Germantown, November 5, 1914, AST, MF 11498. It is not clear whether Father McHale's decision concerned issues such as recruitment that led to Cardinal O'Connell's letter of the previous year or whether O'Connell had anything to do with the decision.

53. Judge to Dear Friend [Amy Croke], Springfield, Massachusetts, February 5, 1915, AST, MF 4311.

54. Judge to Dear Friend [Amy Croke], Springfield, Massachusetts, July 22, 1915, AST, MF 439–40

related to two hundred sorrowful associates the tearful story of St. Paul's departure from Ephesus in Acts 21:32–38. On the train to Alabama, he stopped at the Baltimore cenacle and then was gone.[55]

On May 30, 1934, after his retirement as third assistant to the Vincentian superior general in Paris, Father McHale sat down for an interview with Brother Joachim Benson at St. Vincent's Church in Germantown. In regard to the assignment to Opelika, he explained that he thought Father Judge would have "more freedom in the South." In Benson's summary, "He said to Father Judge, 'Now go down there and take your social service workers with you. There is a greater field of action.' Father McHale thought there would be upset if Father Judge kept on with his work in his various parishes. He was neglecting the mission work."[56]

Father Judge's move to Alabama had tremendous consequences for his apostolic movement. It meant that, rather than in houses like Baltimore and Orange in the urban Northeast, much of the Cenacle's further growth and development would take place in the South. Boundary issues would be reshaped. The new location added momentum to the move in the direction of their becoming religious. The "heart and brains of the movement" would no longer be found among the laity. The Brooklyn stenographer Amy Croke eventually gave way as the movement's leader to a farm girl and teacher from rural Pennsylvania named Lou Keasey. As the Southern Express pulled out of Pennsylvania Station in Baltimore on August 10, 1915, all of this was in the future.

55. See the account in O'Bryan, *Awake the Giant*, 139–43.

56. Summary of interview with Patrick McHale, CM, by Brother Joachim Benson, May 30, 1934, copy in AST.

PART 2

CREATIVE CENTER, 1915–1926

❖ 4

LAY APOSTLES IN THE SOUTH 1915–1916

Vincentian Alabama Mission

The Chattahoochee River divides Georgia and Alabama, Eastern from Central time. Columbus, the largest city in southwestern Georgia, sits on the Chattahoochee just across from Phenix City, Alabama. From Baltimore, the Southern Express carried Father Judge to Columbus. By August 15, 1915, he had reached Opelika, Alabama, a mill town and railroad junction just west of Columbus in the southeastern part of the state.

St. Mary's Mission House in Opelika was the center for the Vincentian Alabama mission. The Vincentians had come to Alabama five years before in 1910 at the invitation of Edward P. Allen (1853–1926), bishop of Mobile. After nearly twelve years as president of Mount St. Mary's College in Emmitsburg, Maryland, Allen was named the fifth bishop of Mobile in January 1897. He was forty-four years old. He knew the Vincentians from his years in Emmitsburg, where they have had St. Joseph's parish since 1850.[1] Until his death in 1926, Bishop Allen consistently encouraged and supported Father Judge's wide-ranging initiatives.

Disconsolate was the word Father Judge used to describe southeastern Alabama. The superior of the Alabama missions was Fr. John Paul Molyneaux, who had been serving there since 1911. When Judge arrived at St. Mary's, he

1. John E. Rybolt, CM, "Parish Apostolate: New Opportunities in the Local Church," in *The American Vincentians: A Popular History of the Congregation of the Mission in the United States, 1815–1987*, ed. John E. Rybolt, CM (Brooklyn, N.Y.: New City Press, 1988), 260. On Bishop Allen, see O. H. Lipscomb in *NCE* (2003), 1:295.

found "poor old Fr. Molyneaux in collapse." Molyneaux was suffering from cancer and kidney disease and would soon be a patient at the Hotel Dieu Sanitarium in New Orleans. "I never can describe the depression I felt the first month," Judge wrote a decade later to the priest he had replaced at Opelika, "the whole experience was so new to me and everything looked so disconsolate." He felt that "in no way could I follow the resourceful and zealous confreres preceding me."[2]

In five years, sixteen Vincentians had preceded Father Judge to St. Mary's. In the chronicle kept in every mission house, he would have read about their work. In a fundraising letter written less than a year after his arrival, he catalogued their woes in Pauline fashion: "Our priests have been assaulted, a price has even been set upon the heads of some the Fathers, and slander, villification [*sic*], suspicion and innuendo are ordinary." He went on to say that "one Father after another has broken under the strain and terrible depression."[3] He did not exaggerate. A local minister warned that "the priests were devils in disguise and to look for their horns and tails." Storekeepers had refused to sell food to them. The post office withheld their mail until a Catholic postal inspector intervened. A local woman turned a garden hose on Fr. Molyneaux on his way to the train station. Late in 1915, Father James Halligan, CM, was called during the night for a sick call in Phenix City. As he walked across the bridge from Columbus to Phenix City, he was mugged and beaten so severely that he was hospitalized.[4]

After a few weeks in Opelika, in a letter of encouragement to Cenacle associates on retreat in the North, Father Judge wrote, "It gives me joy to tell you that our Lord has sent me to the poorest house in our province." He described the condition of the place as one "of irreligion and impiety that is a constant trial and agonizing cross, and that is not far removed from persecution."[5] To the priests of the Alabama mission was entrusted "the entire eastern part of Alabama to evangelize." He described the Alabama mission as "a country larger than the square content of Connecticut, yet in this great area there are not 200 Catholics. It is really the heart of protestantism [*sic*]." With only a trace of fundraising hyperbole, he continued:

2. Judge to Joseph McKey, CM, Orange, N.J., June 15, 1925, AST, MF 9801–3.

3. Judge to Dear Friends, Opelika, c. May 1916, AST, MF 4345.

4. Sr. Miriam Lonergan, MSBT, "The Alabama Adventure," Monographs 2:55–58. On the Halligan episode, see Vincent O'Malley, CM, "Centennial Celebration of the Vincentian Mission in East Central Alabama, 1910–2010," booklet, 27.

5. Judge to Dear Friends, Opelika, September 3, 1915, AST, MF 11493.

> We are struggling against a malignant bigotry that is a blood condition, because from babyhood these unfortunates are fed with a hatred of all that is good and holy in our Church. Illiteracy, superstition, provincialism and deep rooted bad will make our approach to them almost impossible, then, too, unprincipled teachers, ministers, unspeakable papers and Tom Watson as our neighbour, keep this unfortunate people in constant frenzy and fanatical hate of the Church and the Priesthood.[6]

Tom Watson as Our Neighbor

The "unspeakable papers" were Wilbur Franklin Phelps's "The Menace" and "Watson's Magazine."[7] In 1915 Tom Watson was a national political figure, and Father Judge mentioned him without explanation or elaboration. Watson was not always the anti-Catholic bigot he had become by 1915 when Father Judge referred to him as "our neighbour."

The roots of the unremitting hostility to Catholicism voiced by Watson and Phelps at this time went deep into the cultural inheritance of the English Reformation. Its more immediate context was what C. Vann Woodward called the "age-long, and eternally losing struggle" of Southern farmers "against a hostile industrial economy."[8] Elected to the U.S. House of Representatives in 1890 as a Democrat, Edward Thomas Watson (1856–1922) rose to national prominence as an agrarian populist champion. William Jennings Bryan was elected to his first term in the House the following year.

In 1892 Watson renounced the Democrats and embraced the People's Party or Populists. He failed to win reelection to the House in 1892 and again in 1894. In the 1896 presidential election, the Democrats nominated the Populist Bryan. The Populists named Tom Watson as their own candidate for vice president. After Republican William F. McKinley's victory in the election of 1896, Watson temporarily withdrew from national politics and devoted his time to publishing popular histories, including biographies of Thomas Jefferson and Andrew Jackson and a history of France.

6. Judge to Dear Friends, Opelika, c. May 1916, AST, MF 4345.

7. On Wilbur Phelps and Tom Watson, see Justin Nordstrom, *Danger on the Doorstep: Anti-Catholicism and American Print Culture in the Progressive Era* (Notre Dame, Ind.: University of Notre Dame Press, 2006), 86–89.

8. C. Vann Woodward, *Tom Watson, Agrarian Rebel* (New York: Oxford University Press, 1963), 418. First published in 1938, Woodward's remains the authoritative biography of Watson. This quotation appears near the beginning of a chapter entitled, "The Shadow of the Pope." See also Ferald Bryan's entry on Watson in *American National Biography*, ed. John A. Garraty and Mark C. Carnes (New York: Oxford University Press, 1999), 800–802.

When Watson returned to national politics and ran for president as a Populist in 1904, he received barely more than 100,000 votes. The Populist cause had long since peaked, and it was clear that Watson's racially inclusive efforts to unite Southern and Midwestern farmers against Northern banking and business interests had failed. He founded *Tom Watson's Magazine* in 1905 and shortened its title to *Watson's Magazine* the following year.[9]

About the time the Vincentians came to southeast Alabama in 1910, Watson centralized his publishing business at his Hickory Hill plantation across the Georgia border, and "Watson's Magazine" began a withering nativist campaign against socialists, African Americans, Jews, and Catholics, blaming them for Southern woes and Populist failures. Watson's anti-Catholic crusade began in August 1910 with a series on "The Roman Catholic Hierarchy: The Deadliest Menace to our Liberties and Civilization." It ran for twenty-seven months, to be followed by another series on "The History of the Papacy and the Popes."

Watson also wrote a series of letters to Cardinal James Gibbons denouncing "that stupid, degrading faith of yours." He reserved some of his choicest words for priests, whom he called "chemise-wearing bachelors," "bull-necked convent keepers," "shad-bellies," and "foot-kissers." Catholicism was a "jackassical faith." By 1915 the "anti-Catholic genre" of newspapers enjoyed the height of its popularity.[10] At this time, "Tom Watson became almost as closely identified in the public mind with the anti-Catholic crusade as he had once been with the Populist movement."[11]

In 1912 one of Watson's articles on the Catholic hierarchy led to a federal case against him for sending obscene literature through the U.S. mail. At the time Father Judge's train arrived in Columbus in August 1915, Watson's trial was still in progress.[12] Earlier in 1915, Watson had engineered what was popularly known as Georgia's "convent inspection act." The Veazy Inspection Law, chapter 59-4 of the Georgia Code, was an early twentieth-century legislative performance of classic Protestant convent captivity narratives such as Maria Monk's *Awful Disclosures of the Hotel Dieu Nunnery* (1836). It required county grand juries to appoint committees "to visit, inspect, and carefully

9. For *Watson's Magazine*, see https://archive.org/details/tomwatsonsmagazinei24wats.

10. Nordstrom, *Danger on the Doorstep*, 9–10

11. Woodward, *Tom Watson*, 419. Watson's denunciations of the priesthood are cited at 421. Considering the question of Watson's personal motivation, Woodward concluded that "the personal motivation of a Martin Luther would not be sufficient to explain Tom Watson's onslaught upon the Pope" (420).

12. Ibid., 425.

inquire into every orphanage, sanitarium, sanitorium, hospital, asylum, House of Good Shepherd, convent, monastery, house of correction, reformatory, penitentiary, school, and college, for the purpose of ascertaining what persons are confined within said institutions and by what authority such persons are held within the same."

In a 1918 article, Father Judge referred to the Veazy Bill as illustrating the "horrible conceptions" of sisters in the South. "By law," he lamented, "the grand jury of a neighboring State, Georgia, is empowered to enter a convent at any time on the resumption [*sic*] that public decency demands such visitation." Though Prior Gardner Veazy's name was on the convent inspection law, Tom Watson was the "power behind its passage." The law withstood various legal challenges and was not repealed until 1966 on the grounds that it was impractical to enforce.[13] Until 2013 a twelve-foot bronze statue of Tom Watson towered over the grounds in front of the Georgia State Capitol.[14]

One of the first Cenacle pioneers in Alabama invoked the name of Tom Watson to describe the situation in Opelika to a former teacher in New York

> In Opelika previous to our coming, this congregation consisted of one Catholic white woman, one old blind man and a Negro family. No Protestant dared enter the Church, for they were fully imbued with Tom Watson's definitions of all things Catholic. One woman frankly confessed to me that they had really believed priests had horns, and had been looking for them constantly during the five years in which these zealous missionaries have been working here.[15]

Lay Apostles: Father Judge's Answer to Anti-Catholics

Thomas Judge had a certain reputation in the Vincentian Eastern Province. In a personal reminiscence two years before he died, he recalled the kinds of reports his provincial, Father McHale, was hearing about him: "that I was kind of a free lance, a dangerous man, upsetting and getting priests

13. Felicitas Powers, RSM, "Prejudice, Journalism, and the Catholic Laymen's Association," *U.S. Catholic Historian* 8, no. 3 (Fall 1989): 204. The text of the Veazy Bill appears at 203–4. Veazy testified that the "main purpose of the bill is to get at Roman Catholic institutions, to get into them and to see what is going on there; to investigate them. Of course to do that we had to put in a lot of other things too"; 204n13. Judge's comments are in "The Lay Apostolate in the South," *Catholic Convert*, September 1918, 5, from a copy in AST, MF 4946–50.

14. Alan Blinder, "Bid to Move Statue Opens Window to Past," *New York Times*, October 23, 2013, A22.

15. Ella Lonergan to Mother Ignatius, Phenix City, Ala., August 1916, in Monographs 6:67.

worried and generally that I was some kind of a nut."[16] In the matter of the Alabama missions, the Vincentians didn't have many options left. Some wanted to abandon the work. While Father Judge's energy, creativity, initiative, and obvious zeal may have grated on some of his confreres, who was to say that he wasn't just the man the Alabama mission needed at the time?

"When you missioned me south in 1915," Father Judge recalled to Father McHale years later, "I fell heir to a condition of desolation. Lord rest poor Fr. Moyneaux, he said, 'Start something. You have been starting things in the North. Go ahead.'"[17] What Judge had been starting in the North was, of course, the Cenacle movement. As Joachim Benson's account of his 1934 interview with Father McHale indicates, during the summer of 1915, Father Judge discussed bringing the Cenacle to the South with his superior.[18] His immediate response to Tom Watson and local resistance to priests and sisters was, as Father McHale had urged, to call in the lay apostles. He began within days of his arrival.

On August 16, the day after his arrival, Judge wrote to his sister Winifred, hospitalized in Troy, New York. He told her that he had received permission to start Cenacle work. He always thought big. "If we can get them, they can exercise every department of the work, nursing, social service, manual training, and as catechists." He went on to say that "Bishop Allen I am told by my superior will sanction all these plans. I am certain that our Cenacle associates will by their methods do much for the conversion of the South."[19]

A week later he wrote to ask Amy Croke, then working at a Cenacle house in Bridgeport, Connecticut, "Would it be possible for you to open a Cenacle here?" He went on to assure her, "I have some very large permissions to do any amount of good and amongst other things I have been asked to start the Cenacle." He was now in full swing. "A couple of nurses" would mean "a beginning of a little private hospital." There would be work for a dressmaker, a hairdresser. He went on to suggest possible names.[20]

This August 23 letter was not the first Miss Croke had heard of the Cena-

16. "Father Judge's Recollections of His Mission," an "impromptu talk" given at the close of the First General Cenacle of the Missionary Servants of the Most Blessed Trinity, December 1931, Monographs 2:47.

17. Judge to McHale, ca. March 1929, AST, MF 1404; see Judge, "Lay Apostolate in the South," 5, for a more contemporary account of lay apostles as the answer to anti-Catholic bigotry in the South.

18. Summary of interview with Patrick McHale, CM, by Brother Joachim Benson, May 30, 1934, copy in AST.

19. Judge to Dearest Winnie, Opelika, August 16, 1915, AST, MF 449.

20. Judge to Amy Croke, Opelika, August 23, 1915, AST, MF 451.

cle in the South. Before he made the general announcement at the beginning of August of his move to Opelika, he had been in correspondence with Croke about the possibilities it would open for the Cenacle. "God has sent me a great grace in sending me to Opelika," he wrote her on July 12. "This is a mission for which I have long been craving and God grant that it may mean the introduction of the Cenacle in the South."[21] Despite his efforts to portray Opelika as a grace, Croke was not convinced. "It may be in part his Good Pleasure to show that you and your work need but Him," he wrote back to her on July 22.

> You may have seen the wisdom in my teaching you to become more and more detached even from my direction. I am convinced that our Saviour is sending me South for community purposes to help the Cenacle and through this I have hope that our complete intention will be generously and fully answered.[22]

In September, a few weeks after his arrival in Opelika, he wrote to Ella Lonergan, "There are great opportunities here for the lay apostolate and the more I view conditions, the surer I am that God has sent me here to prepare for this great work." "It seemed to me," he continued, "if we opened a nursery and kindred works of charitable visiting among the poor cotton factory workers, it would be an opening wedge: with evening classes for the grown-up children."

As he did in all his appeals for volunteers, Judge held out the prospect of "associates directly under my direction." "Suppose we get it started," he asked, "could you come down here. . . . If you are free to come and would like to if we open there is none who would be more welcome."[23] By January both Croke and Lonergan would be in Opelika.

Mission Pastor

The Cenacle, however, was not Father Judge's chief concern at this time. By September, Fr. Molyneaux was in the Hotel Dieu Sanitarium in New Orleans. In his absence, Judge had to administer, in addition to Opelika, the four other Vincentian mission churches at Phenix City, Salem, Lanett, and Auburn.[24] "Everything is so different from the north," he told his younger sister Winifred. "I am to open a revival Sunday a week announced as the

21. Judge to Croke, Naugatuck, Conn., July 12, 1915, AST, MF 435.
22. Ibid., Springfield, Mass., July 22, 1915, AST, MF 440.
23. Judge to Ella Lonergan, Opelika or Phenix City, ca. September 1915, AST, MF 4396.
24. Rybolt, "Parish Apostolate," 260 and the accompanying map.

Eminent Evangelist from Boston. Is it not awful! But they would not know what a mission meant and would pay little heed to the call of a missioner." He saw "apologetic work" for the Cenacle here and added after his signature, "I am gladder every minute that I came here."[25]

Father Judge wrote this long and upbeat letter to Winnie on the day after his arrival in Opelika knowing that she was seriously ill. In late October, while he was in Wheeling, West Virginia, giving a retreat at the newly founded Wheeling Carmel, he learned from his sister Alice, a Daughter of Charity in Troy, New York, that Winnie had died in Troy. He returned her body to Boston, where he sang her funeral Mass on Tuesday, October 26, and his aunt's funeral the next day. He started back, but his older sister Mary Elizabeth, Melize, died on Friday in Troy. He brought her back to Boston and sang her funeral on All Souls Day, November 2.[26] Fr. Molyneaux died six days later, on November 8, 1915.[27]

In the meantime, Father Judge was still a missioner. In addition to ministering to Opelika and the four churches attached to it, Judge gave missions in the South. He also had to schedule missions in the North in order to raise funds for the Alabama missions. Among other places, his travels brought him to Montgomery. He reported to the Northern Cenacle associates that "six lovely colored girls are now your sisters." "It will please you to know," he wrote, "we have started in the Josephite Church in Montgomery, a Cenacle amongst the Negroes."[28] Judge had been acting superior at St. Mary's Mission House almost since his arrival in August. Fr. Molyneaux's death in November left the Alabama missions without a superior. The minutes of the Vincentian Provincial Council for January 29, 1916, state that "Fr. Visitor [Patrick McHale] announced that, after having made his Visitation of Opelika and its Missions, he had directed Fr. Judge to take charge."[29]

25. Judge to Dearest Winnie, Opelika, August 15, 1915, AST, MF 449. Berry chronicles his mission work in September 1915 in *God's Valiant Warrior*, 36–37.

26. Collins, "Voice from the Past," *Holy Ghost*, September 1949, 7, citing a November 15, 1915, letter from Sister Alice Judge, DC.

27. "Several months ago he went to the Gulf Coast to do some mission work and while thus engaged, was taken ill. After treatment in Mobile he was removed to a hospital in New Orleans, where it was found he was suffering from cancer of the liver and Bright's disease"; *Opelika Daily News*, Tuesday, November 9, 1915.

28. Judge to Dear Friends, Opelika, September 3, 1915, AST, MF 11495.

29. "Due to the conditions existing in Europe during the First World War, no catalogue of the personnel was printed in 1915. . . . It is therefore impossible to establish from the personnel the date on which Fr. Judge became superior in Opelika"; John J. Cloonan, CM, to Sylvester A. Taggart, CM, Northampton, Pa., October 16, 1958; see Thomas A. Judge, CM, Box 1H.17A, Folder 4, DA.

Ella Lonergan and the Invincible Evidence of a Perfect Catholic Life

During fall 1915, two formidable tasks taxed Father Judge's ingenuity and powers of persuasion. First, he had to find a project for the Cenacle to take on in Opelika, a project that would provide the kind of access to the community that the priests had so far failed to gain. Looking back two years later, he made his assessment of the situation sound a bit more clinical than the providential scramble it was. "We found in the impregnable defenses shutting out our entrance two weak spots: One was their school system and the other a lack of charity to the poor and to the sick."[30] Both a school and a hospital had been suggested. Judge's second task was to find Cenacle associates from the North willing to come to Alabama for more than a few weeks.

On the first score, he reported to Amy Croke in September that a local doctor just called on him and "went over the possibilities of starting in a humble and small way a hospital." He invited Miss Susan Downs and Miss Lavinia Copeland "to come here and open the hospital."[31] By October a more concrete proposal had come Father Judge's way, and he attributed it directly to God. "He inspired," Judge wrote to Amy Croke, "a prominent Protestant and freemason to plead with me to open a private school." He went on to explain that the local schools were "wretched," and the people knew it. Their potential benefactor had come to Judge "urged by self-protection for his children." Judge reported that this "prominent Protestant" had "promised to furnish, gratis, a house for two years, we merely paying the taxes."[32]

In 1915 Amy Croke was Father Judge's most trusted associate. He would later address her as "the eldest daughter of the Cenacle, its first born."[33] Ella Lonergan was an unemployed graduate of the College of New Rochelle and trained as a teacher. With the school proposal seemingly a live option, Judge worked hard during the fall to bring both of them to Opelika to start the proposed school. At this time Amy Croke was working at the cenacle in Bridgeport and in the midst of conflicts with the pastor there. These conflicts took up much of her correspondence with Judge at this time. In the same letter in

30. Rev. Thomas A. Judge, CM, "Lay Apostolate in the South," 18, from a copy in AST, MF 4950.

31. Judge to Croke, Opelika, September 1915, AST, MF 462–65.

32. Judge to Croke, Carmelite Convent, Wheeling, October 8, 18, 1915, AST, MF 466–68, 469–74.

33. Judge to Sr. Marie Baptista [Amy Croke], So. Meriden, Conn., June 2, 1919, AST, MF 563–64.

which he told her of the school proposal, Judge wrote to Croke, "I would like you to come and open the school, if possible, to give it a good start. Should our Dear Lord preserve us here, I hope that you may be able to make Opelika your headquarters—if things go well."[34]

Ella Lonergan was already under Father Judge's spiritual direction and had accompanied him to Baltimore in August, but then probably returned home to New York. Judge wrote to her on October 8, told her about the possibility of a school in Opelika, and asked her to come south. God, he told her, "has been conditioning things so that you may leave home and here he has been preparing things and work for your coming." Since leaving the North, he continued, he had had "at heart placing you in some school: but all are closed." A school in Opelika seemed impossible. Then with reference to the recent proposal he had just written about to Amy Croke, he wrote that "God has worked a miracle for you, my dear Child, he wants you to help open a private school here."

He went on to tell her of the offer from "a prominent gentleman of the city." When Father Judge told him that it would be impossible to compete with the public schools, his new benefactor replied that "because of the wretched school conditions and morals of the public school children, he and many other parents would gladly send their children to a school that I would start." So, he told Ella Lonergan, "prepare then to come":

> You can tell your parents that you have a chance to teach, in fact to help start a private school and gently but firmly insist upon coming. I will expedite arrangements on this side just as soon as I hear from you. When can you come? Thank God, I will be able to help you in some way and I will have near me one of my most cherished daughters; one who has given to me so much consolation.[35]

Ella Lonergan's father was a New York City policeman.[36] Her parents were understandably reluctant to send her off to Opelika, Alabama. The knowledge that the formidable Miss Amy Croke would accompany their daughter to Alabama and be in charge of the school gave them some reassurance. Ella Lonergan was to meet Miss Croke in Wheeling, where Croke was scheduled to give a talk and where Father Judge had arranged for Ella to observe Mount de Chantal Academy.

Under twenty-five, single, and unemployed, Ella Lonergan had neither

34. Judge to Croke, Carmelite Convent, Wheeling, October 18, 1915, AST, MF 469–74.

35. Judge to Lonergan, Wheeling, W.Va., October 8, 1915, AST, MF 4262–64.

36. From typescript of an interview with Brother Augustine Philips by Father Lawrence Brediger, September 6, 1945, AST.

prospects nor plans for marriage. Her family home in New York was the only secure and socially acceptable place for a woman in her position. Her worried parents might easily have construed Father Judge's vision and trust in providence as the idle dreams and empty promises of someone who clearly had no solid teaching prospects for their daughter. The story of Ella Lonergan's departure for Opelika, with its frustrating delays and false starts, and her first months in the South reveals much about the social space occupied by the Cenacle women and later by the Missionary Servants of the Most Blessed Trinity and about the kind of religious motivation required to establish and sustain such a space.

Unfortunately, we have only Father Judge's side of the correspondence with Ella Lonergan, carefully preserved by her. Miss Lonergan finally reached Opelika but only after a delay of nearly three months. The rendezvous with Amy Croke in Wheeling that Judge had arranged failed to materialize. Instead of Croke, Mary Howard, from the Baltimore cenacle, accompanied the young woman on the train south as they began what she later recalled as "the Alabama Adventure."

Around October 21, while he was traveling for his sisters' funerals, Father Judge wrote Ella Lonergan a detailed set of instructions for her trip to Wheeling, where she was supposed to meet Amy Croke and then proceed to Opelika. He presented the Wheeling trip as educational, an opportunity to prepare further for teaching. She was to study the private schools in Wheeling, especially Mount de Chantal, the Visitation Academy there, and also to publicize the proposed Opelika school project wherever it was prudent to do so. "Local circumstances and present inspiration of the Holy Spirit" would guide her. He gave her the names of two sisters at the Wheeling Carmel, Mother Mary Magdalen Potts and Mother Teresa, whom she could consult about education.[37] He had arranged for her to stay with the Beattys, a local Catholic family from Elm Grove. One of their daughters was a student at Mount de Chantal Academy.[38]

37. Mother Mary Magdalen Potts came from the Baltimore Carmel in July 1913, along with her sister, Mother Teresa Potts, and two other Carmelites to found the Wheeling Carmel. At Cardinal Gibbons's request, Father Judge accompanied the Carmelite sisters on the train to Wheeling in 1913 and, according to Mother Magdalen's letter at the time of his death, they remained close friends; see Brediger, "In the Name of the Father," 6:16–17. A long excerpt from Mother Magdalen's 1933 letter is at 17. She moved the Wheeling Carmel to Morristown, N.J., in 1926. Its archives, presently at the Carmelite Monastery in Elysburg, Pa., have no record of his accompanying the founders to Wheeling.

38. Visitation Sisters from Baltimore founded Mount de Chantal in 1848. Originally

Much more than a coordinator for young volunteers, however, Father Judge was Ella's spiritual director. This long letter illustrates the care he took to train her to be a missionary, someone who could show forth what he would later call the "invincible evidence of a perfect Catholic life."[39] He warned Mrs. Beatty that Ella did not wish to be "entertained except spiritually." He gave Ella detailed instructions on how to behave with the young people she might meet, including young men who might offer "notice or unnecessary service," how to avoid "merely 'good times,'" how to be an example of modesty and purity, how to be a help and example to the young Beatty children, "to fan their generous hearts into more love for the poor, more love for God."[40]

Amy Croke's speaking engagement in Wheeling was apparently delayed by her work at the Bridgeport cenacle and by family responsibilities in the North. When the Lonergans heard that Miss Croke might not be accompanying their daughter to Opelika, they balked. Father Judge wrote to Amy Croke, "Mrs. Lonergan is trying to recall Ella because some young lady reported that she understood you were not going down because of your sister." "It was so difficult for Ella to get away," he continued. "These people would do almost anything to prevent her from giving herself to God." He explained to Croke what he had instructed Ella to tell her parents and asked Croke to write Ella Lonergan assuring her that she would join her in Wheeling and accompany her south.[41]

To Ella he wrote, "Answer quietly and calmly that you will be a teacher in a high class private school . . . you are going to Wheeling to study private school work." He emphasized that she should reassure her parents that Miss Croke would definitely accompany her to Opelika and would take care of her expenses. "You are of age," he concluded; "you cannot be coerced, but do not take an extreme stand unless necessary." Speaking as her spiritual director, he added, "You cannot be forced to do in a life work what neither you nor God will. Be cheerful, hopeful, brave, and calm, it will all pass."[42]

---

located next to St. James Cathedral, by 1915 the academy had moved outside the city; see Tricia T. Pyne, *Faith in the Mountains: A History of the Diocese of Wheeling-Charleston, 1850–2000* (Strasbourg: Éditions du Signe, 2000), 10–11.

39. This phrase appears in a letter to Edith Collins (later Sister Mary James), a recent convert whose aunt had ridiculed her for her inability to give a coherent account of her faith; Judge to Collins, Phenix City, August 18, 1918, AST, MF 4612–14.

40. Judge to Lonergan, train letter en route to Opelika, [October] 1915, AST, MF 4383–86.

41. Judge to Croke, no date, 1915, AST, MF 484–85.

42. Judge to Lonergan, Opelika, no date, c. early November 1915, AST, MF 4394–95.

Amy Croke was further delayed, and by late November, neither she nor Ella Lonergan had reached Wheeling. The Lonergans softened a bit, and on November 22, Father Judge could write, "God certainly has moved the hearts of your parents and this is a marvel almost to a miracle." By this time, Father Judge had to report that he didn't think the school building would be open until September, almost a year away. He instructed Ella to wait in Baltimore until she heard from Mrs. Beatty.[43] By November 30, Lonergan was still waiting. Judge enclosed a note—probably from Amy Croke—to explain the delay. He now entrusted her to the care of Mary Weiskircher, a music teacher working at the Traveler's Aid Office in Wheeling. He described her as wanting to "enter the Cenacle."[44]

By December, Ella Lonergan finally reached Wheeling. On December 15, Father Judge reported that he was expecting his provincial, Father McHale. He reiterated that the beginning of the school would be delayed. Christmas was approaching, but Judge advised Ella against returning home to New York. "If I were you," he wrote, "I would hesitate about going home. It will not be so easy to get away the next time." Instead of going to New York, he advised her to spend Christmas at the cenacle in Baltimore.[45]

In early November, by the time Judge returned to Opelika from his sisters' funerals in the North, he learned that, as Amy Croke would later put it, "those freemasons had disappointed him." Some thirty years later, Ella Lonergan recalled it this way:

> Shortly after he arrived in the South he obtained a promise of a house suitable for a school, and three of the northern Associates prepared to leave for Opelika. But while these preparations were being made, one of Father's sisters died in Boston and within a week two other members of his family died too. During that time of sorrow, while he was in the North for the funerals, word reached Fr. Judge from his confreres on the mission that the school plans were upset. The man who had promised them a house was forced to withdraw his offer under threat of violence from a few local bigots.[46]

43. Ibid., November 22, 1915, AST, MF 4388–89.

44. Ibid., November 30, 1915, AST, MF 4377–78.

45. Ibid., December 15, 1915, AST, MF 4328–29.

46. Lonergan, "Alabama Adventure," 55. The article originally appeared in the *Missionary Servant* magazine, November 1948. She concluded her reminiscence of more youthful years by assuring the reader that the joys far outnumbered the trials and sorrows that seemed to predominate. "The joys by far the more numerous, were mostly the little, indescribable joys of peace, the overflow of united, simple, merry hearts. And after the privilege of serving God, we had no greater joy than the privilege of saying 'Father' and of being children to a man who lived only for God—Father Judge."

At this point, with the school project seemingly in jeopardy, Father Judge might have postponed the arrival of those who were coming to Alabama specifically to work in the proposed school. But he was not to be deterred. Father McHale was in Opelika, and Judge wanted him to meet the associates, especially Amy Croke, who Judge hoped would lead the Cenacle's Southern initiative. "Do come south at once, please," he wrote to Croke just two days before Christmas. "I have promised Fr. McHale our visitor and chief Superior, that he will have the opportunity of seeing you and talking things over with you here."[47] Mary Howard from the Baltimore Cenacle accompanied Ella Lonergan on the train to Columbus. They arrived as the New Year began. Amy Croke arrived a few days later. Ella Lonergan left two firsthand accounts of their Alabama beginnings, one a letter, written in the summer of 1916, to one of her former teachers at the College of New Rochelle, the other a memoir written as Sister Miriam in 1948 and entitled "The Alabama Adventure."

At first the three young women stayed in Columbus, where "Mrs. Mary K. Walker and the Misses Degnan, Catholics of nearby Columbus, offered the hospitality of their homes."[48] The three associates lived in a single room at the Degnans. Mrs. Walker offered mealtime hospitality at her home, where Father Judge often joined them for lunch and a conference. Amy Croke recalled, "It was about a month before we got a place to stay. In the meanwhile we lived in one room and we surely were nearly frozen."[49] From the beginning they had a common life of prayer that included St. Vincent de Paul's practice of "repetition of prayer," which Judge had learned as a novice in Germantown.[50]

On January 6, they started a Sunday school for Opelika-Auburn and managed to recruit ten students. Joseph P. McKey, CM, one of the first two Vincentians to work on the Alabama missions, enthused over this modest beginning. McKey wrote to Father Judge at the end of January, "One who is familiar with Opelika knows that twelve children at Sunday School is a

47. Judge to Amy Croke, Opelika, December 23, 1915, AST, MF 480–82.

48. Lonergan, "Alabama Adventure," 55.

49. Unpublished recollections of Sr. Marie Baptista, as cited in O'Bryan, *Awake the Giant*, 158n458.

50. They were to spend an hour in morning meditation, with twenty-five minutes toward the end spent in "repetition of prayer." "This is the order," Judge wrote to Ella Lonergan; "morning prayers, read subject of meditation [these were often supplied by Judge's letters] ... about 5 o'clock call Miss Croke and Miss Howard for their thoughts received in med. Any good thoughts given them by the Holy Ghost: then give yours. You could continue this until time to leave for Mass"; Judge to Lonergan, Pinehurst, N.C., February 22, 1916, AST, MF 4424. On St. Vincent and the practice of "repetition of prayer," see St. Vincent de Paul, *Correspondence, Conferences, Documents*, vol. 2; *Conferences*, 11:xiii, n. 3.

miracle—Your parochial school scheme is another miracle. . . . Who knows what your initial efforts will lead to?" McKey went on to compare the Alabama missions unfavorably with China. "God," he continued, "may have been preparing you all these years for this work. Those women will do more good than a dozen priests would do." But McKey raised the question of how Judge would support the lay women. "It is a bold stroke," McKey concluded. "But nothing for God was ever gained without boldness."[51]

Holy Name Academy, Opelika

After a month or so, they found a house at 509 North 8th St. in Opelika.[52] Mary Weiskircher, who arrived on February 17, described the house as "large and spacious, one story high" with "seven rooms and bath with a large porch across the front and down one side." In the spring months, this porch served as the school. *Scanty* was the word Miss Weiskircher used to describe both their furnishings and the meals, provided by a small vegetable garden.[53]

They went ahead with what Father McKey had called the "parochial school scheme." Publicity leaflets announced that the new Catholic school was "now prepared to offer complete courses, based according to standard and most approved up-to-date methods ... in kindergarten, Languages, Music, Art, English, Mathematics and a Commercial Course."[54] The school's name, more ambitious than its overinflated prospectus, was Holy Name Academy. News of the academy brought a ruling from Opelika's superintendent of schools that "no credit would be given for any work done in the Catholic school." After this ruling, even the parents who had invited Father Judge to begin the school failed to send their children.[55]

Father Judge's widowed sister from Boston, Ann Veronica Ledwidge—

51. Joseph P. McKey, CM, to Judge, Bangor, Pa., January 31, 1916, AST, MF 13112. On the Sunday school, see Ella Lonergan to Mother Ignatius, Phenix City, August 1916: "In January we opened our Sunday School, which was attended by four or five families of wretchedly poor people with whom the good Fathers had shared their crusts. Eleven children from these families were baptized one Sunday in March. The parents were held over for further instruction, and will be baptized soon."

52. Brediger gives the date of January 21, but provides no source; see Brediger, "Leaving All Things: A History of the Beginnings of the Cenacle in the South," originally published in *Missionary Cenacle Review* (September–October, 1944), AST, typescript, ca. 1948, 9.

53. Mary Weiskircher's description is from Collins, "Voice from the Past," *Holy Ghost*, September 1949, 7–8.

54. The text of the "attractive prospectus" appears in Brediger, "Leaving All Things," 10.

55. Lonergan, "Alabama Adventure," 57.

Annie, as she was called—arrived with Mary Weiskircher on February 17 and brought her three youngest children, Joseph, Grace, and Alice. When Judge wrote to Ella Lonergan about repetition of prayer from Pinehurst, North Carolina, on February 22, he also asked if she had yet arranged hours of class for his nephew and nieces. Joseph, Grace, and Alice Ledwidge would be Holy Name Academy's only students. In this letter, Judge also told Lonergan that he was asking Amy Croke to meet him in Baltimore, "if you can spare her."[56]

Summer provided Ella Lonergan a chance to look back on Holy Name Academy's brief history. In a letter to Mother Ignatius, who had taught her at New Rochelle, she described the opposition to Catholicism they met in Opelika and gave this account of the school:

> With this condition confronting us, it seemed an almost hopeless task to open any kind of school; yet trusting in God to help us, we attempted the Academy. We started in the mid-term and seemed to have everything against us. We were, therefore, very grateful to have two or three pupils to serve, as an excuse for staying in the town. Our real purpose, as you can realize, was not so much to found a second New Rochelle College, but rather first to work our way into the confidence of the people, and thereby give them some true conception of what Catholicity means. That they permitted us to remain in the town or even rented a house to us was a great cause for thanksgiving.[57]

In Ella Lonergan Judge had found a capable and willing lay apostle. He would have nodded in approval at her articulation of what she and her companions were doing in Opelika. But Lonergan did not tell Mother Ignatius how hard that first semester had been on her. On February 23, the day after he told Ella he was asking Amy Croke to meet him in Baltimore, Judge wrote that he was sorry to hear that Ella was sick. He promised that Mary Jankowski would be there soon. "She will be of great help in housekeeping. I gathered this is the matter." He urged her to be patient and strong. "God will remedy all things."[58]

By the beginning of March, Amy Croke had returned to Bridgeport at the urging of the pastor there.[59] Around the same time, Mary Howard returned

56. Judge to Ella Lonergan, Pinehurst, N.C, February 22, 1916, AST, MF 4419–22.

57. Ella Lonergan to Mother Ignatius, Phenix City, Alabama, August 1916; the text is given in Monographs 6:68.

58. Judge to Ella Lonergan, Southern Pines, N.C., February 23, 1916, AST, MF 4419–22.

59. O'Bryan, *Awake the Giant*, 167. Shortly after Croke's departure for the North, Judge announced in early April that he had appointed Miss Mary McMahon general superior of the Cenacle and moved the general headquarters to Opelika, where Mary McMahon would be custodian or superior. In O'Bryan's estimate, these moves meant that Amy Croke "ceased to be a

to Baltimore, probably to help close down the house there. Mary Weiskircher taught music. That left the burden of instructing the Ledwidge children on Ella Lonergan. Father Judge was much on the road in both South and North in the winter and spring of 1916. He moved from North Carolina in February to New Jersey in March, Louisiana in April, and back to New Jersey in May. While on the road he was constantly working to recruit new Cenacle volunteers for the work in the South and to provide long-distance support to Ella Lonergan, to whom he had promised personal spiritual direction. With new responsibilities and three children constantly around, she tended to fret about "order."

On March 3, Father Judge wrote from New Jersey promising that he would return to Opelika soon. He also promised to bring reinforcements, as many as five. "Miss Sarah O'Donnell will assume general charge and God willing we will have things assume the order you desire." He urged her to "let every prayer and thought and action bear the imprint of Christlike meekness and charity."[60]

Father Judge's letter of April 8 from New Orleans contained a mild reprimand: "I may be mistaken, My dear Child, but there seems to me just the least strain of impatient complaining in your note." He encouraged her to "try more for the virtues of great amiability and graciousness." He also advised her on possible courses, probably summer school courses, in history and literature that she was considering at Auburn.[61]

From Newark, New Jersey, Judge reported that he had had a "most enjoyable day" with the Lonergans. "If your dear parents are not bounding with joy," he assured her, "at least, they are resigned and content, in fact, they seem well satisfied." Judge concluded, "I am charmed with your good father and mother and I will not stop until I get them down with you."[62]

The school year, however, had taken its toll. In June Ella Lonergan took

---

major influence upon the evolution of the Cenacle movement that was occurring in the South. Though she continued to occupy a prominent position even for some years ... circumstances no longer permitted her to play a decisive role in the evolution of the Cenacle movement. This would be within the hands of those who shared the early Alabama experience"; ibid., 167–68.

60. Judge to Ella Lonergan, Harrison, N.J., March 3, 1916, AST, MF 4409–11. Sarah O'Donnell and Mary Dolan had both lived and worked at the Baltimore Cenacle. Its closing freed them to come to Opelika.

61. Judge to Ella Lonergan, New Orleans, April 8, 1916, AST, MF 4400–405. It is not clear whether she took these courses. On May 31, Judge congratulated her on her "splendid report"; MF 4376.

62. Ibid., Newark, N.J., May 16, 1916, AST, MF 4377–78.

the Ledwidge children to Birmingham, and Father Judge wrote to her from Opelika that "you evidently needed very much the rest you are getting."[63] This much-needed rest proved insufficient, and early July found Lonergan in St. Vincent's Hospital in Birmingham for her eyes. Her doctor ordered rest. Judge recommended an auto ride "as a medicine"—"if you can modestly and prudently and with the permission of Sr. Chrysostom."[64] A week later, he reported from New York that he was about to return and that Agnes Gore and Susan Downs would soon be on their way to Opelika.[65]

By August Lonergan had recovered sufficiently to teach in the summer school in Phenix City. It was from Phenix City that she wrote to Mother Ignatius the account of her first months as a missionary. As his correspondence with Ella Lonergan makes clear, Father Judge asked much of the women who sought to give themselves to God under his direction. As he concluded his own account of their first years as lay apostles in the South, he referred to them as "these valiant warriors of the Church."[66]

63. Ibid., Opelika, June 21, 1916, AST, MF 4372–73.
64. Ibid., Roselle Park, N.J., July 5, 1916, AST, MF 4368–71.
65. Ibid., New York City, July 13, 1916, AST, MF 4365–67.
66. Judge, "Lay Apostolate in the South," 18.

❖ 5

PHENIX CITY

Missionary Servants of the Most Blessed Trinity, 1916–1918

Phenix City and the Mills

In 1916 the Eagle and Phenix cotton mill across the Chattahoochee River in Columbus, Georgia, employed many of the inhabitants of Phenix City and the neighboring village of Girard in Russell County, Alabama. By 1920 the average millworker made about $450 annually, but Phenix City's economy had other resources. The village of Girard, absorbed into Phenix City in 1923, had a long history of lawlessness and violence. It produced both illegal corn liquor and bonded whiskey that was shipped as far north as Boston. Alabama's 1915 Prohibition law threatened to strangle the economy of Girard. Its violent resistance to Prohibition brought a trainload of forty deputies from the Alabama capital in Montgomery into Russell County. On May 17, 1916, they seized more than a million dollars' worth of illegal liquor.

The state of Alabama disqualified Russell County courts and appointed a special judge and prosecutor to try illegal liquor dealers and complicit law enforcement officials for bribery and other crimes. A young Hugo Black, future justice of the U.S. Supreme Court, was appointed special prosecutor. The trials took place during the summer in 1916, about the time the "Catholic ladies" were arriving to attempt a new school venture in Phenix City.[1]

1. Margaret Anne Barnes, *The Tragedy and Triumph of Phenix City, Alabama* (Macon, Ga.: Mercer University Press, 2005), chap. 1, esp. 5–8, 12.

Father Judge's lay apostles had a rough time of it in Opelika. Despite Phenix City's reputation for lawlessness and violence, their Catholic friends in Columbus had suggested they might be better received in Phenix City. It was closer to Columbus, and there were more Catholics. In 1911, the Vincentians took on St. Patrick's Church there as an extension or mission church of St. Mary's in Opelika. The superior of St. Mary's was technically the pastor of each of the five mission churches. The priests of the Alabama mission officially resided at St. Mary's. The records for baptisms and marriages also remained at Opelika, but St. Patrick's had Mass every Sunday. With a congregation of about seventy people, it was the largest Vincentian mission church in Alabama. In 1916 it had a small, recently completed church.[2]

By July Father Judge had rented a house in Phenix City for the Cenacle associates. When he returned from the North on July 12, he brought with him two young men from New Jersey, Andrew Philips and Eugene Brennan. Miss Mary Elizabeth Walsh of Harrison, New Jersey, whom Father Judge referred to as "that angel of zeal and charity," had introduced them to him and recruited them for Cenacle work.[3] Philips and Brennan helped to move the "Catholic ladies" from Opelika to Phenix City. At this time, Father Judge was still superior of the Alabama mission with his residence at St. Mary's in Opelika. Soon, however, he made St. Patrick's his permanent address.[4] His work with the Cenacle, authorized by Father McHale, would bring him into conflict with fellow Vincentians.

Phenix City was less well off than Opelika. Father Judge described the "poor mill people and farm workers" of Phenix City as "destitute in every way; poorly paid for their labor; illiterate and deceived by the slanders repeated continuously against the Christ sent friend of the poor, the Catholic Church." Their condition was "sad beyond all picturing; ill fed, ill clothed, ignorant and bigoted . . . a most difficult problem for Religion and Charity."[5]

Judge's description hit the mark. The house he had rented in Phenix City

2. See Rybolt, *American Vincentians*, 260. On the move from Opelika to Phenix City, see Collins, "Voice from the Past," *Holy Ghost*, September 1949, 8–10; Brediger, "Leaving All Things, A History of the Beginnings of the Cenacle in the South," Unpublished ms., 1948, 15–25, AST; and O'Bryan, *Awake the Giant*, 169–78.

3. "Do pray for that angel of zeal and charity, Miss Mary Walsh. She is dangerously ill with pneumonia"; Judge to Ella Lonergan, Newark, N.J., January 29, 1917, AST, MF 4358.

4. Judge to Revd. and Dear Father, St. Vincent's Hospital, Birmingham, Ala., November 22, 1916, AST, MF 4437.

5. Judge to Joseph F. McGlinchey, DD, Phenix City, December 22, 1916, AST, MF 4433–34. Father McGlinchey was the head of the Society for the Propagation of the Faith in Boston.

was at a spot called Flat Crossing, "the only place on Railroad St. where there was a street crossing at the railroad, the others were crossed by trestles."[6] In mill towns such as Phenix City, the railroad tracks often separated the "mill people" Judge described from the "town people." It was largely among the mill people that the Cenacle began its work in Phenix City.[7]

Alabama textile mills turned bales of Southern cotton into pieces of cloth. In earlier days most cotton had been shipped to manufacturing centers in the North or overseas. But even before the Civil War, Columbus had been a Southern center of textile manufacturing. By the early twentieth century, the industry had spread from Columbus through the Chattahoochee Valley. Phenix City's mill people worked across the river at Georgia Mills, Muscogee Mills, or the Eagle and Phenix Mill.

The growth of the Southern textile industry was just the kind of cultural shift that fueled Tom Watson's agrarian fires. Most of the mill people were poor Appalachian whites who had once picked cotton and chopped tobacco. The long hours and low wages of the Southern labor force made the South more attractive to Northern businesses than traditional manufacturing centers such as Massachusetts. By the time the Vincentians arrived in Alabama in 1910, the textile industry was on the rise.

When the "Catholic ladies" came to Phenix City in 1916, textile workers represented about one- fifth of the manufacturing jobs in Alabama. In 1910 Alabama had more than 12,000 textile workers. A little less than half were women. Among semi-skilled workers, women predominated. Approximately 8 percent of millworkers were children, often called "helpers," between the ages of ten and thirteen. Mill people worked a twelve-and-a-half-hour day for an average annual salary of $453 in 1920. Though economically preferable to tenant farming and sharecropping, the mills were noisy and full of cotton dust. The dust caused "brown lung" and gave rise to the name "lint heads" that "town people" used to distance themselves from "mill people." In addition to brown lung, mill people often suffered skin and intestinal diseases resulting from a diet too heavy on salt pork and cornmeal.[8]

6. Collins, "Voice from the Past," *Holy Ghost*, September 1949, 8.

7. John Lyles, *Images of America: Phenix City* (Charleston, S.C.: Arcadia, 2010), chap. 4, "Emergence of the New South," features photographs and sketches of the Eagle and Phenix Mill and Muscogee Mills, the two largest mills in the area at this time, and photographs of dinner toters and child helpers from these mills.

8. Wayne Flynt, *Poor but Proud: Alabama's Poor Whites* (Tuscaloosa and London: University of Alabama Press, 1989), 92–112. The information in the previous paragraphs is taken from

Alabama schools were substandard in 1916. A 1918 survey that resulted in modest legislation to limit child labor showed that only 376,000 of the state's 455,000 white children of school age were actually in school. Among the forty-eight states, Alabama ranked forty-sixth in "local tax revenue expended for education." Rural schools were especially poor. "Of 4,570 rural Alabama schools for whites in 1913, 3,401 were one-teacher rural schools where grades one through twelve were taught by the same person. Only 277 of the state's public schools had three or more teachers."[9]

St. Patrick's School

What the mill people of Phenix City needed was a school. The "Catholic ladies" were not the first to recognize this need. A local woman known as Miss Lizzie had tried to start a school for mill children at 16th and Broad streets in Phenix City, but she was the only teacher and in poor health.[10] In August 1916, Ella Lonergan returned from Birmingham. Susan Downes, a nurse from Hartford, Connecticut, arrived on August 4. On August 16, Mary Weiskircher returned. She brought with her Lulu Keasey, a teacher from Butler County, Pennsylvania. They began with a summer school. Ella Lonergan helped to start it but then went to stay with Marie Mott Burr, a Catholic widow who lived alone on a 1,300-acre plantation at Mott's Landing on the Chattahoochee about twenty miles south of Phenix City. They began with only four students, but the summer school quickly expanded to more than twenty. From the summer school's success grew the proposal for a school in Phenix City.

As Ella Lonergan explained in the August letter, a letter she probably hoped would result in some financial contributions to their work, the seventy-some Catholics in Phenix City

> are truly Catholic and have done their best to alleviate our difficulties. However, mill salaries do not enable them to help us very much, so that at times we find it very difficult to "make ends meet." They have begged us to conduct our

chap. 4, which is devoted to Alabama's textile workers. See also chap. 9, on "Poor Folks' Culture," which treats both race relations and religion.

9. Ibid., 274, 193. "Where schools existed in rural areas, they were often remote from sharecroppers' cabins. Tales told by children of walking miles to school were true. And when they arrived, the schools were taught by poorly paid teachers not much older than many of them and in some cases not much better educated"; 193.

10. From a personal conversation between Sylvia Grant and Fr. Gary Banks, August 3, 2013.

> school here this fall, instead of Opelika, and we have considered it a very good plan, for we can reach many here, while in Opelika we could reach only a few.

She went on to say that they planned to open the school on September 11 and already had more than fifty applications. Each student was supposed to pay 25 cents per week, but they didn't expect to collect this half of the time. "We are forced, therefore, to depend upon contributions sent to us by kind friends in the North, and so far with the help of God, we have been able to keep the wolf from the door." She described their school furnishings. The desks were "long pine-wood tables," the benches "a promiscuous lot of chairs which have been donated," and the blackboards "simply painted walls." "This," she concluded, "we are forced to call an Academy in order to distinguish it from the public and private schools, of very poor repute, about us."[11]

St. Patrick's opened in September 1916 with twenty-five students.[12] Lulu Keasey and Ella Lonergan did most of the teaching. Initially classes were held in the house at Flat Crossing, "a tiny house with four rooms and a large front yard."[13] Each morning the associates rearranged their sleeping rooms to serve as classrooms. Phenix City "dinner toters" were a big reason for the school's success. "Dinner toters" were children charged with bringing food to their parents working in the mills. As Ella Lonergan explained, "It was a long walk to the mills and the children had to be there on time since the mill hands had only 30 minutes for lunch. The public school would not tolerate their leaving class in mid-morning."[14] St. Patrick's excused the dinner toters from 10:30 to noon. Teachers filled that time with auxiliary subjects such as sewing and drawing. Regular classes continued from 1:00 to 4:00 p.m.

Susan Downes was a nurse and, at some point in September, the Catholic ladies started a "hospital" in a six-room apartment over Blake's department store. More like a clinic, it offered medical care to the poor. Two surgeries were reportedly performed there. But the clinic was short-lived, probably because of lack of support from local physicians. Its "comet-like existence" could not have lasted more than a month.[15] Closing the clinic freed Susan

11. Ella Lonergan to Mother Ignatius, August 1916, Monographs 6:69–70.

12. Judge to Revd. Agatho, OFM Cap., Roselle Park, N.J., September 15, 1916, AST, MF 4937–41.

13. Collins, "Voice from the Past," *Holy Ghost*, September 1949, 8, citing a contemporary description.

14. Lonergan, "Alabama Adventure," 2:59; see the photographs of dinner toters in Lyles, *Phenix City*, 60–65.

15. On the "hospital," see Lonergan, "Alabama Adventure," 2:8–9. The "comet-like" designation is O'Bryan's, *Awake the Giant*, 176.

Downes to earn some money as a nurse in Columbus and the whole group to move from Flat Crossing to the six-room second-floor apartment. A photo shows ten of them together for Thanksgiving dinner in 1916.[16]

In keeping with Father Judge's sense of institutions as missions, St. Patrick's served as an outreach center for night courses, home visiting, care for the sick, and other forms of charity. In addition, it was home to the "only library in town."[17] On September 15, 1916, Judge wrote a long appeal letter describing the work done by the "band of apostolic ladies" since their arrival in the South nine months ago. With reference to St. Patrick's School, he wrote, "We have established contact with the public in this—that they have a concrete Catholicity in our co-workers whom they meet and question."

This was an appeal letter, and Judge went on to describe the school as "a tumbledown place. Our desks are planks and rough seats but we have splendid teachers." One of the teachers was Mary Weiskircher, and this letter was addressed to Fr. Agatho, her spiritual director at the Capuchin monastery in Herman Township, Pennsylvania. Judge assured him that "anything that man, woman, or child can wear will be of great service to us."[18]

The Guardians of Liberty

However kind and charming they may have been, Judge's "band of apostolic ladies" didn't work without arousing resistance and opposition. Tom Watson had helped to organize the Guardians of Liberty in 1911. By 1912 he had steered them toward "a predominantly anti-Catholic complexion." From Baltimore Cardinal Gibbons dismissed Watson's Guardians as "nothing more than an attempt to revive the bigotry of the A.P.A. [American Protective Association], which was presumed to have died of inanition." But Gibbons didn't live in Phenix City, Alabama, and his "foreign ruled crowd," as Watson called them, would not be received there without a fight.[19] "The Guardians of Liberty have organized against us," Ella Lonergan reported in August 1916 as they prepared for the opening of the new school:

16. Berry, *God's Valiant Warrior*, 214.

17. O'Bryan, *Awake the Giant*, 183, citing from an unpublished 1923 article, "Missionary Efforts in the South"; see 349n511.

18. Judge to Revd. Agatho, OFM Cap., Roselle Park, N.J., September 15, 1916 AST, MF 4937–41.

19. Woodward, *Tom Watson*, 422–23. Woodward cites Cardinal Gibbons from Michael Williams, *The Shadow of the Pope* (New York: Whittlesey House and McGraw Hill, 1932), 114; Woodward borrows his chapter title from Williams's book. Watson responded to Gibbons in his magazine in April 1912 and again in 1914.

> Every Wednesday evening they have a man (who has a criminal record) get up and speak in the public square in front of the Church. His stand is not one hundred feet from the Church door, and here with the aid of a most ear-splitting brass band, he does his best to malign the Church, the Blessed Virgin, the priests, and everything Catholic. The louder he bawls outside the Church, the more heartily do our good people sing the hymns within the Church.[20]

According to the *Opelika Mission Chronicle*, the man Lonergan described was "Captain Jeff Marchant." Organizer of a local "Court" of the Guardians, Marchant denounced the teachers at St. Patrick's as "tainted women who were driven out of Opelika." Men from the parish had to escort the teachers from the church building back to Flat Crossing. Some of them had to be dissuaded from trying to shoot Marchant. For his part, Marchant promised to shoot the first priest he could. "The ignorance, bigotry and prejudice here," Ella Lonergan wrote, "are well fed by Tom Watson and 'The Menace.'" This harassment ended, according to the *Chronicle*, when "no notice being taken of the gentleman other than to storm heaven with prayers, the meetings of 'guardians' soon began to dwindle and finally ceased."[21]

In August 1917 they had an opportunity to buy a two-story house with fourteen rooms at 432 Broad St. "in the best part of town." Father Judge described it as "one of the finest pieces of real estate" in the city. The Catholic ladies used their own money to pay cash for the house.[22] To the Guardian types such Catholic aggression was unacceptable.

On August 17, 1917, "a body of the citizens of Phoenix City, Alabama" sent a threatening letter to Father Judge. They addressed it to "Sir Priest." They threatened "foul play to your person" if "Yankee women" didn't stop bringing in Protestant students to St. Patrick's. As "patriotic citizens of this beautiful southern town," they meant "peaceably if possible, but otherwise if necessary, to prevent the Roman Catholic Church from being instrumental in the destruction of our progressive city."

The "rough boys of Phoenix City" added a postscript with more dire threats. "To make for your church Roman Catholics we don't want any more of it and don't you dare to proceed. If you do, you will be sure to hear from

20. Ella Lonergan to Mother Ignatius, August 1916, cited in Brediger, "In the Name of the Father," 6:70.

21. Brediger, "In the Name of the Father," 6:71–72, citing the *Opelika Chronicle*, 2–4, no date.

22. Judge to Patrick McHale, CM, Phenix City, August 14, 1917, AST, MF 4484–85. The purchase of the new house and its role in moving the "Catholic ladies" in the direction of religious life will be treated in more detail in a later chapter.

us rough boys some dark night." Reflecting the public mood that gave birth to Georgia's "convent inspection bill," they added, "We have heard enough about your nuns in your convents, jails is a better name we think."[23]

On August 22, 1917, the "Christian citizens of this our hometown not to be duped by Roman Catholic priests" addressed Father John Ewens, the priest in residence at St. Patrick's. Addressing him as "Sir Priest," they reminded Ewens "that we intend to hold you physically responsible if any member of your church attempts to lead away or persuade our protestant children in any way to attend your school or to enter your church." They accused him of targeting "soft protestants," luring them "from their own Christian homes." "No honest person," they were convinced, "would ever embrace Romanism if they really knew it as it is." Those who do "do not know the vile wickedness of its teaching until too late."[24]

In the face of these threats, St. Patrick's School reopened in September as scheduled. The Guardians of Liberty sponsored a series of public speeches, featuring a "sensational" declamation on convents. For two days, St. Patrick's Church was pelted with stones, rotten eggs, and tomatoes. Threats were made to tar and feather the teachers. "All of us at this time," the mission chronicler records, "priests and Cenacle, were very near to violent treatment. God's kindly providence spared us."

Each day at St. Patrick's, the teachers raised the American flag, "the only one floating in town during war time." One night after a storm, they left it on the pole to dry. They found the flag the next morning "torn to shreds, braided and knotted." "The miscreants," the mission chronicle reports, "tore it and then raised it aloft." The people of Phenix City responded to this insult "in apathy."[25]

Andrew Philips had been in Alabama since July 1916. In May 1917 he and Eugene Brennan moved to a cabin on the edge of the Mott Plantation. Brennan had spent the previous semester studying at the Vincentians' Niagara University. To Mrs. Burr, Judge presented the move to the farm as "patriotism," calling Brennan and Philips from their studies. They would be no trouble, he assured Mrs. Burr; "they are coming to you as soldiers." "I am

23. Vincent O'Malley, CM, "Centennial Celebration of the Vincentian Mission in East Central Alabama," booklet, 28; see also AST, MF 704.

24. O'Malley, "Centennial Celebration, 27–28. Brediger also cites this letter in "In the Name of the Father," 6:73–74.

25. These two paragraphs follow the *Mission Chronicle*, probably written by Father Judge, as cited in Brediger, "In the Name of the Father," 6:74–75.

anxious," he wrote, "and they are eager to continue their schooling but, nevertheless, they and myself hear the call of their country and are willing to make any sacrifice for their flag."[26]

When Philips heard of the flag incident at Phenix City the following September, he contacted a military friend at Fort Benning:

> In the middle of a busy afternoon, the officer marched a platoon of soldiers up Broad Street in full equipment and with bayonets fixed. They halted smartly before St. Patrick's School and presented arms while a new flag was solemnly raised. It was not molested again during the war.[27]

Catholics, as they would have to do many times in the "tribal twenties" that followed the war, had made martial and national symbols their own to show that they were Americans, too.[28] As Ella Lonergan later recalled, these "petty and violent persecutions" never represented "the sentiment of all the townspeople." She mentioned editors and public officials who spoke out against the anti-Catholic demonstrations as a disgrace to Phenix City. She recalled the "courage and charity" of a local Protestant minister who "risked injury to dispel a violent mob outside St. Patrick's Church one night, and for his courage and charity was forced to leave town."[29]

The Spanish Influenza of 1918

Despite the cultural resistance of the Guardians of Liberty and their supporters, St. Patrick's School continued to grow. On September 9, 1918, it opened with an enrollment of one hundred students. But that very fall, at the height of the Great War, the Spanish Flu pandemic of 1918 hit Phenix City. The pandemic peaked between mid-September and early December. By October 10, all churches and schools were ordered closed "due to the epidemic of Spanish influenza." Schools did not reopen until November 4.[30]

The mysterious flu of 1918 first appeared in the spring. It brought the

26. Judge to My dear Child (Marie Mott Burr), St. Vincent's Hospital, Birmingham, Ala., April 30, 1917, AST, MF 4533.

27. Brediger, "Leaving All Things: A History of the Beginnings of the Cenacle in the South," unpublished ms., 1948 28, AST.

28. On this dynamic, see Lynn Dumenil, "The Tribal Twenties: 'Assimilated' Catholics' Response to Anti-Catholicism in the 1920s," *Journal of American Ethnic History* 11, no. 1 (Fall 1991): 21–49. "Tribal Twenties" is the title of chap. 10 of John Higham, *Strangers in the Land.*

29. Lonergan, "Alabama Adventure," 63.

30. Collins, "Voice from the Past," *Holy Ghost*, December 1949, 9; see also, Brediger, "Leaving All Things," 29.

usual three days of chills and fever but killed few. But like a biblical plague, it roared back in the fall. A world engulfed in the Great War offered little resistance. To this day, researchers don't know what made this 1918 flu so deadly.[31] Nor do they know for sure where it started.[32] It infected 25 percent of the U.S. population and left half a million Americans dead.[33] The influenza pandemic "killed more people in a year than the Black Death of the Middle Ages killed in a century; it killed more people in twenty-four weeks than AIDS has killed in twenty-four years."[34]

Because of the 1918 flu's scope and a national shortage of nurses, volunteers, especially women, played key roles in the collective response to it.[35] As a nurse, Susan Downes led the Cenacle volunteer efforts in Phenix City. Lulu Keasey, Mary Howard, and Agnes Gore were her chief assistants. Each day they took soup to the homes of flu victims. "The Flu rages in the South," Lulu Keasey wrote, "claiming many victims. Our schools were closed for seven weeks in all, but no rest. We all went out to nurse, and I was on night duty."[36] When the flu hit one of the doctors, Susan Downes visited him each day and picked up medications to bring with them on their soup runs.[37]

As a result of this volunteer work, "Homes that had been closed against us for three years were now open wide."[38] "Your Sisters here are nursing night and day," Father Judge wrote to an associate in the North. "This is a Divinely sent opportunity to move the Church into the homes of bigotry; doors now on all sides have been thrown wide open to them as to so many ministering angels."[39] The pandemic did not spare the volunteers. Eight members of the Cenacle group came down with the flu. "Thank God, all were spared," Lulu Keasey wrote. "I think the flu did a lot of good here," she continued. "Many have visited our church. Others ask for books explaining our religion. I really think it did more good than our three years of teaching, at least it achieved quicker results."[40]

31. Gina Kolata, *Flu: The Story of the Great Influenza Pandemic of 1918 and the Search for the Virus That Caused It* (1999; New York: Touchstone and Simon and Schuster, 2001), 28.

32. John M. Barry, *The Great Influenza: The Story of the Deadliest Pandemic in History* (New York: Penguin, 2005), 5.

33. Kolata, *Flu*, 6, 5. On the worldwide death toll, see Barry, *Great Influenza*, 396–98.

34. Barry, *Great Influenza*, 456–58.

35. On the shortage of nurses, see ibid., 141–43, 319–20.

36. See the account in Mary Tonra, MSBT, *Led By the Spirit: A Biography of Mother Boniface Keasey, MSBT* (New York: Gardner, 1984), 50.

37. Brediger, "Leaving All Things," 29.

38. Collins, "Voice from the Past," *Holy Ghost*, December 1949, 9.

39. Judge to Frances O'Driscoll, Opelika, October 27, 1918, AST, MF 4578.

40. Cited in Tonra, *Led by the Spirit*, 50.

With their works of mercy during the flu epidemic, the "band of apostolic ladies" offered in concentrated form the kind of witness Judge had hoped for. They embodied the "concrete Catholicity," the "invincible evidence of a perfect Catholic life" that he wrote about. Their care of the sick, as Ella Lonergan recalled, "gave an unanswerable reply to the voice of bigotry."[41]

What the Catholic ladies had done during the influenza pandemic did much to solidify the position of St. Patrick's and the Cenacle in Phenix City. In 1917 Tom Watson had denounced conscription and opposed the United States' entry into the Great War. As the war dragged on, his Guardians became less of a force. Keasey's suggestion that the flu accomplished more than their three years of teaching was typically modest and understated. More than the flu or the decline of the Guardians, it was Keasey's inspiring leadership that, from a human point of view, accounted for St. Patrick's success and the strong beginnings of the Cenacle in the South.

Lulu Keasey: "She Came Full of Life and Energy"

When Mary Weiskircher went North in the summer of 1916 to arrange for her piano to be shipped from Wheeling to Opelika, she went to Herman Township, Pennsylvania, to visit her cousin, Fr. Felix, and her spiritual director, Fr. Agatho. Both belonged to the Capuchin community in Herman. As Miss Weiskircher related her own Alabama adventures, another Capuchin, Fr. Boniface, thought of Lulu Keasey, a young teacher under his direction who was seriously thinking about volunteering on an Indian mission in the West. Fr. Boniface arranged for Mary to meet Miss Keasey at the Fourth of July picnic in Herman. Here is Mary Weiskircher's first impression:

> She came full of life and energy, radiant in a lovely summer dress and a big picture hat because she had a date at the July Fourth dance in the evening. I looked at her and doubted that she would make the grade in our poor little "shanty" with its meager meals and limited household effects.[42]

Fun is the word most frequently used to describe Miss Keasey. But Lulu Keasey came from a hardworking farm family, and she did much more than make the grade in Alabama. "To the associates she was a joy," wrote the Cenacle's first historian, "because of her fun and the happiness she diffused

41. Lonergan, "Alabama Adventure," 2:63.

42. Cited in Tonra, *Led by the Spirit*, 38.

about the very room she was in." Sister Mary James Collins went on to attribute "the success of the early years at Flat Crossing School" largely to Lulu Keasey.[43] Lawrence Brediger, who as a schoolboy knew her in the late 1920s, recalled her knack for "turning hardships into fun."[44] Under her leadership, St. Patrick's "became a need for the little mill town of Phenix City and 'Miss Keasey' was a name familiar to children and grownups alike":

> Her presence in a classroom made her pupils forget the drab surroundings, the lack of classroom facilities, and even the uncomfortable, handed-down desks at which they sat. They loved her as everyone who ever came within the pale of her compelling personality loved her. There was nothing sentimental or weak in the feeling she inspired. She brought out the noblest and the best in the poor little barefoot lads of Phenix and the little girls in their patched gingham frocks and sunbonnets.[45]

Joy is one of the fruits of the Holy Spirit, and it didn't take Father Judge long to realize that in Lulu Keasey the Cenacle had been sent an extraordinary gift. One Sunday shortly after school began in fall 1916, he called her in for a talk. "Suppose we were to say that Miss Keasey is the principal of St. Patrick's School," Judge asked. She thought he was joking. Despite her characteristic protests of unworthiness, Judge appointed her principal right there "on the spot."[46]

Missionary Servants of the Most Blessed Trinity

According to Father Judge's vision and under Miss Keasey's direction as principal, the school became a center of missionary outreach. St. Patrick's School continued to prosper under Keasey's leadership. Mary McMahon,

43. Collins, "Voice from the Past," *Holy Ghost*, September 1949, 9. Collins cites a letter of recommendation from Frank McClurg, the superintendent of schools in Butler County, Pennsylvania, where Miss Keasey taught: "I am glad to recommend Miss Lulu Keasey to any school board. She has been teaching in our county and I have been able to observe her work. She is tactful, positive, and interested in her work. She is very successful in her work and much above the average in teaching."

44. "Her hard work and easy, unassuming charm of manner made her someone whom others instinctively watched for example"; Brediger, "In the Name of the Father," 6:71.

45. Mother Mary of the Incarnate Word (Mae Rahaley of Meriden, Conn.), "Mother Boniface, MSBT," privately published article, AMSBT, as cited by O'Bryan, *Awake the Giant*, 185, 350n534. Rahaley succeeded Keasey as Mother General in 1931.

46. The phrase "on the spot" is Brediger's from "In the Name of the Father," Monographs 6:71, based on the account of Sister Mary Francis (Mary Taylor of Brooklyn), in "Mother Boniface," *Missionary Cenacle Review 3: 133–34;* see also Tonra, *Led by the Spirit*, 42–43.

Mother McMahon, as she was called, was in charge of their common household. In March 1917, the bank almost sold the Flat Crossing house out from under the associates. That would have meant the end of the school. But Mary McMahon's quick-witted response to the bank and a completely unexpected gift of $1,000 from Father McHale kept them afloat. Then in August 1917 they bought the large house at 432 Broad St. and moved there from the apartment over Blake's store. It was this purchase and the move uptown that so exercised the Guardians of Liberty. As Father Judge explained to McHale, they pooled their money and bought the Broad Street "Castle" themselves.[47]

In November 1917, Bishop Allen donated fourteen used double desks to the ever-growing school. At the same time, he wrote to encourage the teachers: "I commend very highly the excellent work done by Miss Lulu Keasey and her associates in their school. As they are doing the work of a religious community, I believe they are entitled to all the Church can give them." He gave Father Judge permission for the Blessed Sacrament to be reserved "for the present at least" in the chapel of the house at Broad Street. By Christmas they began perpetual adoration. "Our Blessed Lord," wrote Mary McMahon, "has at least one adorer through the long hours of each and every night."[48]

They now owned the house at Flat Crossing, which served as the school, as well as the larger house at 432 Broad St. On January 28, 1918, attorneys Dickinson and Dickinson informed Mary McMahon that a formal corporate decision was needed on the purchase of the Broad Street house. This led to the formation of a religious and charitable corporation on February 2, 1918, "the decree filed in the court house in Opelika on May 21, 1918."[49] On February 2, 1918, the day of incorporation, Father Judge wrote north, "Your Sisters

47. "A very large house fourteen very large rooms, two stories, an eight-foot porch up and down stairs around two sides of the house. This will be of great value for so many reasons, ½ ac. of ground, barn and other things and all in the best part of town. The amount to be paid is $1,200; the remainder $1,800 on easy terms. At 8 percent they could borrow a sum and the interest will only be equivalent to the rent that now they are paying. They can easily get a mortgage on the property for this amount in fact this will not be needed since some of them delighted with the grace of possessing such an institution will put up enough money for a cash sale and thus save the banks the usurious money rate they demand"; Judge to McHale, Phenix City, Ala., August 14, 1917, AST, MF 4484–86.

48. Bishop Allen's letter of November 2, 1917, to Judge is cited in Collins, "Voice from the Past," *Holy Ghost*, December 1949, 5. I found no copy of it in Bishop Allen's papers in the Archives at the Catholic Center, Archdiocese of Mobile. Mary McMahon's January 28, 1918, letter is cited at ibid., 6.

49. Ibid., 7. O'Bryan lists the trustees as Mary J. McMahon, Mary E. Howard, Catherine Gray, Marie Burr, Sarah J. O'Donnell, and Lulu Margaret Keasey; see O'Bryan, *Awake the Giant*, 186.

are now incorporated as Missionary Servants of the Most Blessed Trinity." He went on to describe this as "more legal advantage than a spiritual blessing, but, nevertheless, it touches the spiritual for it will relieve your Sisters of many anxieties regarding the tranquil possession of their temporalities."[50]

Father Judge's remark points to the role of their joint "possession of their temporalities," along with his inspiration and their common work, in moving the group in the direction of what in the church would be recognized as a religious community. It was holding their property in common that occasioned their incorporation. The decision to own property together was momentous. Cenacle houses such as Bridgeport, Connecticut, and Orange, New Jersey, were usually attached in some way to a parish. Ownership of property in common set the Southern Cenacle apart and gave it a solidity the North did not have.

From this time, the Catholic ladies evolved further in the direction of a religious community. They began internally to call each other "Sister." Already in October 1917 they had discussed in a council, described as "so American and democratic" as a New England town meeting, the name the corporation would take and noted the various experimental forms of garb developed in the North at the mission houses in Roselle Park and Orange, New Jersey. Private vows dated from 1918.[51]

The Cenacle in the North

Mention of mission houses in Roselle Park and Orange, New Jersey, recalls that Cenacle work continued to grow in the North at the same time as the new work was developing in the South. As superior of the Alabama missions, Father Judge had to travel frequently. Giving missions in the North helped him financially support the work of the Vincentian Alabama missions. He also used these trips as occasions to give inspiration and support to Cenacle associates in the North.

On August 4, 1918, for example, Father Judge was able to address a large general meeting of the Cenacle in the basement of St. Andrew's Church in

50. Judge's February 2, 1918, letter is cited in Collins, "Voice from the Past," *Holy Ghost*, December 1949, 7–8.

51. Ibid., 6; see also the discussion in Berry, *God's Valiant Warrior*, 44–48. Reference to an annual private "vow of chastity" is at 45. Berry cites an April 18, 1918, letter of Father Judge to Katherine Champion, AST, MF 13720. Tonra says that Keasey had taken private vows on April 19, 1917; see *Led by the Spirit*, 44.

lower Manhattan's Bowery. He recalled meetings of three or four years ago when they and their work were dismissed and they were being told to mind their own business. Now that their work was attracting "at present a very widespread notice," he wondered what effect such notice would have on them.

He urged them to "keep within the spirit of the Cenacle." "You are trained," he continued, "in simplicity, charity, humility, sacrifice, and patience." He recalled their characteristic devotions: "You are, sleeping and waking, devoting yourselves to the interests of the Blessed Trinity, the Holy Spirit, the Passion and Death of our Lord, exalting His Holy Name, praying for sinners." Even in the face of seeming success, practicing these virtues and being faithful to these devotions would preserve them in the Cenacle spirit.[52]

Sometimes Father Judge's efforts to support the Cenacle in the North conflicted with the missions in the North he gave in his role as superior of the Alabama mission. In a letter of March 15, 1917, Father McHale reprimanded Father Judge for his "underhand 'recruiting' in Lakewood," New Jersey. He had "made use of the mission as an occasion of carrying out a plan." McHale warned Judge that he was alienating pastors and jeopardizing the possibility of future missions in parishes such as Lakewood, where he promoted the Cenacle during his missions.

While Father McHale found Father Judge's zeal commendable, he found him often lacking in prudence. The visitor came down hard on Judge: "Unless you absolutely refrain from trying to induce women to associate themselves with the lay Apostolate during your Missions, I cannot conscientiously appoint you to Mission work." In the interests of the missions, he urged Judge to "limit your activity during them to our traditional methods and practice." Then McHale softened the blow a bit. "I have no desire to quench your zeal for good. I am writing both in your own interest and in that of our chief work." He instructed Judge to try to repair the damage he had done with the pastor at Lakewood.[53]

Previous complaints from another New Jersey pastor gave Father Judge the opportunity to explain in detail the work to "stem some of the leakage from the Faith" among Italian immigrants living in the vicinity of Newark.

52. Brediger gives a long excerpt from Father Judge's talk in New York on August 4, 1918; see "In the Name of the Father," 6:83–86. These remarks on Cenacle virtues and devotions are at 86. See also Berry, *God's Valiant Warrior*, 52, on the "Spirit and Virtue of the Cenacle."

53. McHale to Judge, Baltimore, March 15, 1917, AST, MF 11506–8. This letter suggests that recruiting may have played a key part in Cardinal O'Connell's banishing the Cenacle from Boston in the fall of 1913.

He described the mission in Orange, New Jersey, of "four poor working girls in a leaky house." He linked their work with that of the "band of apostolic women" in Alabama. Such lay apostles he compared to St. Paul: "they work during the day that they be a burden to no one and evangelize and catechize at night."[54]

But Father Judge was spending less and less time in the North. His lay apostles soldiered on in his absence. Mary Walsh continued her work with Italians in Orange, but her ties with the Cenacle would not last. In Brooklyn, Margaret Healy, at this time a young teacher just beginning graduate school, continued her heavy involvement with the Cenacle. Her close friend Mary Taylor had gone to Alabama in August 1918, and Miss Healy "became very conscious that there was a difference between Mary Taylor and herself."[55]

In March 1918, Father LoVecchio, the pastor in Roselle Park, New Jersey, was forced to sell the house that had served as Assumption Mission House. Under pressure to relocate and unable to reach Father Judge in the South, Katherine Shelvy and the other lay women at the house consulted as best they could, made a novena to St. Joseph, and decided on their own to accept an offer to work at what would become the Dr. White Memorial Settlement House at Gold Street in Brooklyn and a center of Cenacle work for many years to come.[56]

The Cenacle's center had shifted to the South. By 1919, the year after the flu pandemic, St. Patrick's School had two hundred students. The rather stable community oriented around its work became the Cenacle's institutional center. Ever on the road, Father Judge remained the charismatic glue uniting "the 'Cenacle' movement" in the North to the work in the South. In 1918 Father Judge was fifty years old and beginning to feel the strain. He was hospitalized in Montgomery, Alabama, in September 1917 for approximately three weeks and again in April 1919 at Providence Hospital in Washington.[57]

> Up and down the Eastern seaboard from Maine to Florida we see his words in letters to and from those writing for information, advice, and help. Backs of telegram blanks, an unused side of a letter, stationery from unexpected places

54. Judge to Rev. and Dear Father, St. Vincent's Hospital, Birmingham, Ala., November 22, 1916, AST, MF 4437–42.

55. McNutt, *Margaret*, 42.

56. On Assumption Mission House and the decision to move from Roselle Park to Brooklyn, see the recollections of Sister Michael (Katherine Shelvy) written in 1945, as cited by Brediger, "In the Name of the Father," 6:90–97.

57. Berry, *God's Valiant Warrior*, 41, 50.

served his purpose as he moved from place to place and used the odd moment at his disposal.[58]

"Cottonton is the Place"

On August 14, 1917, while the associates in Phenix City were getting ready to move to Broad Street and the Guardians of Liberty were working on their first "Sir Priest" letter, Father Judge wrote to Father McHale, "We have added another mission center to our local springs of activity. Cottonton is the place." He went on to explain that Mrs. Burr was "giving over" her plantation "for Cenacle purposes." Only Father Judge could have envisioned Marie Burr's heavily mortgaged, overgrown, weevil-ridden acreage as "a villa and a Mother House" for "our Ladies."[59] That is what it became.

Little did the associates in places like Orange, Brooklyn, and Meriden suspect that a rundown excuse for a plantation at Mott's Landing in faraway Cottonton, Alabama, was becoming the center of their Cenacle world. This land along the banks of the Chattahoochee, some twenty miles south of Phenix City, would become the Cenacle Bethlehem, a tiny Catholic outpost in the cotton and Klan country of Russell County, Alabama. Father Judge named it Holy Trinity Cenacle. Soon even the U.S. Post Office would recognize it as simply Holy Trinity, Alabama.

58. Thus Sister James describes the "tempo of his life during these formative years of the apostolate"; see Collins, "Voice from the Past," *Holy Ghost*, December 1949, 6. The phrase "the 'Cenacle' movement" is hers, at 7.

59. Judge to McHale, St. Patrick's Church, Phenix City, Ala., August 14, 1917, AST, MF 4484.

6

THE CENACLE IS THE WORK OF GOD

Holy Trinity, 1917–1920

Mrs. Burr's Donation

In 1915, when Father Thomas Judge first came to the Alabama mission, Marie Mott Burr was a widow living alone on acreage she had inherited at Mott's Landing on the Chattahoochee River in Cottonton, Russell County, Alabama. As one of the few Catholics in the area, she had to travel twenty miles north to the Vincentian church at St. Patrick's in Phenix City to go to Sunday Mass. When she went up to Phenix City, Mrs. Burr arranged to stay for more than one day. It was probably on one of these Sunday trips that she first met Father Judge. She also attended one of the missions he preached, perhaps the week-long mission at Opelika in September 1915, where he was billed as "the eminent evangelist from Boston."[1] In any case, by the beginning of 1916, she was arranging for her trip to Phenix City to coincide with Judge's and was probably by then under his spiritual direction.[2]

Years later Father Judge recalled Mrs. Burr as "a jaunty, up to date, striking young lady."[3] In May 1915, he told her as "your Father in God" that he found her "dramatic, emotional, easily disturbed by small things, heedless and wanting tact." And this, he added, "I must correct."[4] Two weeks later, he

1. Judge to Dearest Winnie, Opelika, August 16, 1915, AST, MF 449.

2. Judge to Burr, St. Mary's Mission House, Opelika, January 12, 1916, AST, MF 4328.

3. Post General Cenacle Notes, December 31, 1931, AST, MF 12497–502.

4. "[I]f you will not pay attention to gentle hints and counsels," he continued, "then you must not be surprised if I do show some surprise at your lack of progress, and remember, if I had no interest in you I would be merely polite and good natured when I met you"; Judge to Burr, no place, May 12, 1916, AST, MF 4476.

was commending her on "what a deep religious nature you have or are developing." In a P.S., he advised her to keep an eye out for a "good but second hand cotton compress" and not to give up her "Phenix City accommodation for Sunday Mass." It was planting season, and Mrs. Burr was hoping for rain. "If your poor parched land is crying for water, your soul is certainly being well watered by the grace of God."[5]

In addition to the plantation at Mott's Landing, Mrs. Burr also owned "timber and mine property in Kentucky" as well as family jewelry and even a prize-winning shawl that Judge believed to be from the Paris Exposition of 1876.[6] But she was short of the cash she needed to pay the mortgage on the plantation and to run the farm there. Father Judge's correspondence with her, during the fall of 1916, indicates that on his trips to the North he was trying to help her liquidate some of her holdings.[7] She had even considered laying railroad track into the plantation (probably from Fort Mitchell), but a contact in Boston told Judge that it would cost $8,000 per mile. He advised her that, if there were a prospective buyer, she should consider selling the plantation. By November, however, he told her that property was about as low as it was likely to be for a while.[8]

When Mrs. Burr appeared at St. Patrick's in Phenix City one day in early 1917, she already had a history with Father Judge. But she brought him up short when she offered on the spot to donate her 1,300-acre plantation to the group of lay volunteers in Phenix City. Ella Lonergan had spent part of August at Mott's Landing with Marie Burr recuperating and getting ready for the next school year. Burr had been touched by the witness of the Cenacle in Phenix City and told Judge that she had been admiring their work. Burr and Judge went back and forth, one more single-minded than the other. Burr was determined to donate her plantation. Judge found her decision precipitous. He proposed a novena, and then, when she refused, a triduum. Burr finally agreed to the latter. After the three days, she returned still determined. She told him she had already decided eight months ago.[9]

5. Judge to Burr, Opelika, May 21, 1916, AST, MF 4473–75.

6. Judge to Edith Collins, Phenix City, November 7, 1918, AST MF 4625–27.

7. See Judge to Burr, Wheeling, September 9, 1916; no place, September 25, 1916; en route, September 29, 1916, AST, MF 4456–59; 4454–55; 4449–51. This correspondence also indicates that Judge had already come to Cottonton for Mass and told Burr that it could either be at her place or at Mrs. Patterson's, a neighbor; see Judge to Burr, Opelika[?], September 26, 1916, AST, MF 4435–36.

8. Judge to Burr, S. Boston, October 3, 1916; Birmingham, Ala., November 21, 1916, AST, MF 4445–48; 4443–44.

9. See O'Bryan, *Awake the Giant*, 187–89, citing AST, MF 12497–502.

Father Judge called the Cenacle ladies to council and asked Burr to attend. They were apprehensive about the inaccessibility of Burr's property and its lack of facilities. They knew nothing of farming, and the plantation had a $15,000 mortgage.[10] But Father Judge argued in favor of accepting Burr's donation. "If you do not grow you are going to perish," he told them. "[B]ut you must have a place where you can expand; that place must be out of town and it must be in the nature of a villa." He regarded such a property as "an absolute necessity." "[T]here is a need," he concluded, "therefore, this thing enters your act of confidence in God."[11]

They took the plantation. It marked the first of the great financial obligations that would stalk Father Judge into the Great Depression. When the Cenacle ladies in Phenix City bought the house on Broad Street, it had been momentous in their development as a body. But they made a large cash down payment and quickly paid off the house. The plantation came with a staggering mortgage. Judge's confidence in providence was boundless and remarkable. But the various moneymaking schemes into which he entered to meet subsequent financial obligations would cause both Bishop Toolen of Mobile and Archbishop Curley of Baltimore to lose confidence in him.

Holy Trinity's Pre-History: Apalachucla and the Spanish Franciscans

Mott's Landing became Blessed Trinity Cenacle Plantation. Eventually it would be known simply as Holy Trinity. But this Chattahoochee land had been holy ground long before the Cenacle took possession in 1917. Holy Trinity, at the present site of the Blessed Trinity Shrine Retreat, was once called Apalachucla, the eighteenth-century "esteemed mother town or capital of the Creek or Muscogulge confederacy." This was the description of King George III's botanist, William Bartram, an English artist and naturalist, who visited Apalachucla in 1775–76. Bartram had crossed into Alabama north of this spot and traveled south along the river, making scientific notes on local plants and animals. A mile and a half down the river, the Creeks showed Bartram the ruins of an earlier settlement inhabited by mound builders who inhabited this area centuries before the Creeks. Apalachucla was described

10. Ibid., 188. For a description of the 1,300-acre "plantation" at this time, see Collins, "Voice from the Past," *Holy Ghost*, September 1949, 12–13.

11. O'Bryan, *Awake the Giant*, 188.

to Bartram as "sacred to peace; no captives are put to death or human blood spilt there."[12]

Burr's family and the members of the Cenacle were not the first Catholics to live on this land next to the Chattahoochee. In the seventeenth century, Spanish Franciscans had come from North Florida to evangelize the Creeks. In 1689 the Spanish governor of Florida, Diego de Quiroga y Lasada, ordered construction of a fort with a small garrison of soldiers to protect the Franciscan missionaries. The fort proved short-lived. By the 1690s, English colonists had driven the Spanish from this area. By the 1830s, their descendants did the same to the Creeks. The Spanish fort's ruins still stand near the Chattahoochee next to Blessed Trinity Shrine Retreat.

About ten miles north of Mott's Landing on Eufaula Road, now Alabama 165, was Fort Mitchell. Built in 1813 as an outpost in the Creek War of 1813–14, it was manned by Georgia Militia troops. At the end of the Creek War of 1836, the Georgia Militia helped to detain the remaining Creeks for their forced removal to Oklahoma. The notorious "Trail of Tears" began at Fort Mitchell. The Georgia Militia left in 1837, and only the name remained. In Judge's day, Fort Mitchell was the end of the line on a local railroad spur.[13]

Blessed Trinity Cenacle Plantation

When Marie Mott Burr gave her plantation to the Cenacle in 1917, Father Judge knew nothing of the Creeks and the Franciscan missionaries who had preceded the Cenacle in this place. *Plantation* belied its primitive conditions. Edith Collins first came to Holy Trinity as a young woman late in 1918. Writing years later as Sr. Mary James, she left a long firsthand description of the plantation's layout and its "few scattered whitewashed cabins of two rooms with a couple of them boasting three rooms."[14]

12. John Bartram, *Travels through North and South Carolina, Georgia, East and West Florida, the Cherokee Country, the Extensive Territories of the Muscogulges or Creek Confederacy, and the Country of the Chactaws* (Philadelphia: 1791), 386–90, as cited in John Reed Swanton, *Early History of the Creek Indians and Their Neighbors*, Smithsonian Institution, Bureau of American Ethnology, Bulletin 73 (Washington, D.C.: Government Printing Office, 1922), 132. In 1928 Mark Van Doren edited an unabridged version of *The Travels of William Bartram*, reprinted in 1955 by Dover. These quotations from Bartram appear at 313 in the 1955 edition.

13. On the Spanish fort or Appalachicola Fort, as well as Fort Mitchell, see Lyles, *Images of America: Phenix City*, 10–11. Lyles includes a photo of the original plans for the Spanish fort and a sketch of Fort Mitchell ca. 1813–37.

14. Collins, "Voice from the Past," *Holy Ghost*, September 1949, 12

After accepting Mrs. Burr's donation of the plantation in the early months of 1917, Judge and the Cenacle moved slowly in taking full possession of it.[15] In the spring, Eugene Brennan returned from a semester at Niagara University. Judge sent him and Andrew Philips to the plantation to help with the spring farmwork.[16] Judge presented their farmwork to Mrs. Burr as a patriotic contribution to the war effort and assured her that they would be no trouble.[17] Philips and his free-spirited sidekick were a long way from their New Jersey homes. With some donated cows, they started Clover Leaf Dairy and sold their products in Columbus, Georgia. But they were working with a strong and capable female "farm boss," and it didn't take long for sparks to fly. The correspondence on the partnership of Philips and Brennan with Mrs. Burr is, as Sr. Mary James put it, "a story in itself."[18]

Father Judge's long response to Burr's complaints about Philips and Brennan included a copy of his instructions to them to "seek Mrs. Burr daily and be advised by her regarding farm operation, control of negroes [*sic*], and general disposition of work." He told them he had "a supreme confidence and respect for her word when it is a question of farm management or negro [*sic*] control." Failure to honor his request to "submit your plans and work to her every evening" would "grieve and offend [him] very much."

Having fully backed Marie Burr in the face of Philips and Brennan, Father Judge then admonished her to guard against "speaking in a bossy way."[19] A week later, he repeated this admonition about being "bossy." "Don't show by your manner, by shaking and tossing your head, that you know more than they do, otherwise I will be writing you letters and you will be the obstruction to the farm progress and not they."[20]

Father Judge wrote again at the end of 1918 placing Burr, now Sr. Angel Guardian, in complete charge of repairing the roads on the plantation, with Mr. Philips to "help and assist her." "If she wishes," Judge wrote, "she will give orders directly to the negroes [*sic*] or if she prefers through Mr. Phil-

15. Following the "Post-General Cenacle Notes" of December 31, 1931, O'Bryan attributes this to caution and the hope not to alarm the neighbors with something of a Catholic invasion into rural Russell County; see O'Bryan, *Awake the Giant*, 189.

16. In 1950, Brother Augustine (Andrew Philips) gave an account of how he had come to Alabama and how he and Eugene Brennan wound up on the Mott Plantation; see "Brother Augustine in Missionary Class," September 30, 1950, typescript, 5 pp.

17. Judge to Burr, Birmingham, Ala., April 30, 1917.

18. Collins, "Voice from the Past," *Holy Ghost*, September 1949, 11.

19. Judge to Burr, St. Philip Neri Church, Newark, N.J., January 20, 1918, AST, MF 4593–4601.

20. Judge to Burr, no place, January 27, 1918, AST, MF 4943.

ips."[21] This story would end only when Father Judge sent both Philips and Burr to missions in the North.

Philips and Brennan had come to the plantation in early May 1917. At this point, the farm produced primarily cotton and some lumber. They added cows and the grain necessary to feed the animals. By July 17, Judge announced that "this place will be the Motherhouse of the Cenacle where souls are to be trained in a special love of the Holy Trinity." Furniture, cots, and lanterns had to be carted, sometimes by mule, sometimes by truck or car down the dark and bumpy Eufaula Road. They whitewashed one of the two-room cabins for the chapel. The neighboring Patterson family, who had once been observant Catholics and hosted traveling priests for Mass at their house, supplied the altar stone.

On August 12, 1917, in a grotto built by Philips and Brennan from local clay called "marl," the first annual pilgrimage took place at the plantation. Mary's statue, donated by friends in the North, arrived in Columbus by train the day before the pilgrimage and made it to the plantation just in time. About one hundred people attended the first pilgrimage.[22] Two days after the pilgrimage, Father Judge sent an enthusiastic account of it to his provincial superior describing the newly acquired plantation to Fr. McHale as "indeed a gift of Heaven."[23]

Father Judge's Missionary Challenge

The pilgrimage was followed by a retreat at which eighteen women of the Cenacle slept on cots in the "mule barn." During the previous May, about the time Philips and Brennan began their farming careers in Alabama, Father Judge was in New York City. He spoke to a small group of local custodians and secretaries of the Northern cenacles. He led them in a *lectio divina* or scriptural meditation that brought them inside one of his favorite biblical texts, Matthew 28:19. While hesitating to distinguish among the words of Jesus, Father Judge had to admit that some of his sayings stand out more than others.

One such saying "launched His Church into existence. 'Going, therefore, teach all nations, baptizing them in the name of the Father and of the Son and of the Holy Ghost.' 'Teach all things, whatsoever have been commanded

21. Judge to My dear Children, St. John's Rectory, Newark, N.J., December 7, 1918, AST, MF 4668.

22. Collins, "Voice from the Past," *Holy Ghost*, September 1949, 12–13.

23. Judge to McHale, Phenix City, August 14, 1917, AST, MF 4484.

you.'" Father Judge proposed that they ask "reverently ... what was in Our Lord's mind when he said that." He went through salvation history to review a memorable series of God's words: creation, Mount Sinai, various mysteries of Christ's life. He concluded with "the word of Jesus as He gathered the apostles around." "'All power is given to me in heaven and on earth. As the Father has sent me, I send you. Going, therefore, teach all nations.'" "To us," Judge told the pioneer leaders of the Cenacle, "it is a command."

He told them that they formed "the very heart of the Cenacle. The future of the work lies with you. It does not lie with me." The Cenacle was now "an approved work," "a movement that has its works and its records." He reviewed the work they knew so well and then turned to the South:

> We know what has transpired in the south. Two years ago we would have been considered insane to open a school there. We now have a cross lifted fifty feet in the air, capping a flag pole. Thousands look upon it. The south is a land without the cross and without the Blessed Sacrament.

What, Father Judge asked these workaday women of the Cenacle, do these facts show us? They show, he concluded, "that you were very much in the mind of Jesus when he spoke these words." Jesus, Father Judge urged, was speaking the command of Matthew 28:19 directly to them as leaders of the Cenacle. The fact that they were in the mind of Jesus when he spoke these words, he continued, "should make you very, very happy, very, very anxious, and very terrified lest you lose this grace."

With this reference to terror, we enter the "harsh and dreadful" dimension of the love that Father Judge preached.[24] He had come to believe that the Cenacle was the work of God and spent himself for it without measuring the cost, stretching himself very thin. Though he was now in Alabama, the work in the North had to continue. "Do you know," he said, "it would be a very serious thing for you now if you ever left the Cenacle":

> You could not leave the Cenacle now without hurting the interests of the Church. This could be said of anybody in the Cenacle but if the Cenacle is going to exist it is going to be through you. It can be said now if the Cenacle disappears that harm will be done to the work of Jesus that will never be righted. As humbled, as mean, as crippled, as unworthy as we are, yet God in his mercy

24. "[L]ove in practice is a harsh and dreadful thing compared to love in dreams," says Dostoevsky's Father Zossima in *The Brothers Karamazov.* This was a favorite saying of Dorothy Day's, and, as he explains in his 1982 biography of Day, William D. Miller took *A Harsh and Dreadful Love* as the title for his history of the *Catholic Worker,* see Miller, *Dorothy Day: A Biography* (San Francisco: Harper and Row, 1982), 284.

seems to be pleased to do something through us. It seems that he is choosing you to right impossible conditions.[25]

The Southern successes amidst the adversity of 1915–17 convinced Father Judge more than ever that the Cenacle was God's work. Encouragement from ecclesiastical superiors, especially Father McHale, emboldened him over the next two years to make a public appeal on behalf of his vision of lay missionaries as a pastoral necessity for the church in the United States. But that would be in the future years of 1918 and 1919.

Back at Holy Trinity in August 1917, eighteen retreatants rose at 4:00 a.m. from their cots in the mule barn. They feasted on plantation fare, and Father Judge preached to them. It's not hard to imagine that in this Southern setting he told them, as three months before he had told the women in Elmhurst, New York, that Jesus was thinking of them when he spoke the words of commission in Matthew 28:19. It's not hard to imagine that here too he evoked the terror of God's call as he had done in New York.

The terror of God's call, as Father Judge well knew, is as eminently biblical as the consolation of God's presence. He dared to challenge these mostly young and single American women with the complete biblical package as he had received it.[26] The women of the Cenacle rarely shrank before this challenge. The drama of their responses led them deeper into their lives as missionaries, "the invincible evidence of a perfect Catholic life," as Father Judge called it. Of such lives, he said, "The Church has no greater proof than this of the divinity of Her mission."[27] His missionary challenge would lead many of these women into the vowed religious life.

25. A record of this talk is preserved in Minutes of the General Council, May 4, 1917, Elmhurst, N.Y., AST, MF 11996–98.

26. To a reluctant prospective lay missionary who claimed to have heard a rumor that the Southern mission was about to close, Father Judge addressed these questions. They are cited at length because they give a sense of what it might have felt like when he told them that Jesus had addressed the words of the great apostolic commission directly to them. Clearly Judge had asked these questions of himself in prayer. "The questions I wished you to deliberate on were these. How much do you love God? Have you a love of God and a zeal for His interests that lead you to sacrifice all? How much can you offer up for God? Have you a zeal to work for the glory of His Church, to help tear down prejudice and ignorance? Can you suffer inconvenience and hardship? Can you be obedient? Can you leave tomorrow and the day after to God's goodness? Can you serve Him without looking for any return from Him except the spread of His Kingdom and His greater honor and glory? These questions make manifest the souls of your Sisters, and what is the spirit of their vocation. If their sacrifices should discourage you, it may be by prayer the Holy Spirit will give it to you, for it is from Him they have received it"; Judge to My dear Child, Phenix City, March 11, 1918, AST, MF 4605.

27. Judge to Edith Collins, Phenix City, August 18, 1918, AST, MF 4612–14. This letter, in

Tensions and Growth

On February 2, 1918, as seen in chapter 5, with the approval of Bishop Allen of Mobile, the group of women who purchased the house at 432 Broad St. in Phenix City legally incorporated in the state of Alabama as a religious and charitable corporation called the Missionary Servants of the Most Blessed Trinity. Lulu Keasey, already in private vows, was one of the trustees of the corporation, as was Marie Burr. Presumably, this new corporation also held the title to the Mott plantation. Writing north, Father Judge had referred to the members of the corporation as "your Sisters." Even capitalized, the term *Sisters* could only be used of them in a loose or non-canonical sense. They had begun to call each other "sister." Judge's correspondence with Marie Burr and Ella Lonergan, for example, indicates that during 1918 they began to take "religious" names.[28] By the end of 1918, as we shall see, other Catholics in Maryland and Pennsylvania had begun to call them "sisters."

These developments came with a certain irony and tension. When at the end of 1918, Father Judge began to explain the work of these women to a wider Catholic public from whom he hoped to gain financial and spiritual support, he presented them as engaged in what a growing body of papal encyclical literature called the "lay apostolate." Their effectiveness in the deeply anti-Catholic South depended precisely, he would claim, on the fact that they were not sisters. But when, in the fall and winter of 1918, they undertook missions in Ridge, Maryland, and Pensacola, Florida, and fund-raising in Pennsylvania, Catholics naturally looked upon them as sisters and expected to see them in some sort of a garb. To women such as Amy Croke who had been lay apostles for many years, this would be a new and perhaps unsettling development.

Father Judge was not a trustee of the Missionary Servants of the Most Blessed Trinity in 1918 and, for his part, remained a Vincentian and superior of the Alabama mission.[29] Though his official residence remained St. Mary's Mission House in Opelika, he had by 1916 described St. Patrick's in Phenix

which Judge contrasts the "missionary" and the "apologist" for the future Sr. Mary James, conveys effectively what he thought a "missionary" was and why the witness of the missionary's life is the best apologetic for the church.

28. From a reference in the *Vincentian Chronicle* referring to the women as "Sisters," Brediger speculates that "They had probably taken religious names in the South by Christmas 1917"; see "In the Name of the Father," 6:97.

29. Vincentian Catalogues for 1917, 1918, and 1920 at the Ducournau Archives list Father Judge as superior of the Alabama mission.

City as his "permanent residence."[30] The members of the new corporation were not canonical religious in any sense that would be recognized by the newly promulgated 1917 Code of Canon Law, and yet they seemed to the Catholics with whom they worked to be more like sisters than lay people.

Their common commitments and financial obligations, as well as the theology and canonical forms of the church of their day, also pushed these lay apostles in the direction of being sisters in a more technical sense. Father Judge's Vincentian superiors viewed them as a desperate measure, the last and only hope of the beleaguered Alabama mission. This is how Father Judge presented them in his publications of 1918 and 1919.

But through 1917 and 1918, they had clearly become a more stable and independent body than was envisioned when the first volunteers came in January 1916 or than would be recognized by many of the individual members of the Cenacles in the North. Pope Pius XII's apostolic constitution on secular institutes, *Provida mater ecclesia*, February 2, 1947, made it possible for Margaret Healy and other Cenacle lay apostles to organize Blessed Trinity Missionary Institute. After the Second Vatican Council, the 1983 Code of Canon Law, and Pope John Paul II's Apostolic Exhortation *Vita consecrata*, March 25, 1996, more complex forms such as the new religious movements began to emerge. In 1918, however, Father Judge found himself not only in the middle between the North and the South but also between the Vincentians and this newly emerging body that was something more than a loose group of lay apostles and something less than a canonical religious community.

Father Judge's correspondence with Father McHale during 1918 indicates these tensions. At this point, St. Patrick's School in Phenix City, close by a Vincentian mission, was the institutional heart of the Cenacle in the South. With a stable group of Cenacle members living at the plantation from December 1917, Judge's attention and the institutional center began to shift from St. Patrick's to what he had described in 1917 as the motherhouse of the Cenacle at Holy Trinity.

In early January, Father McHale wrote to Father Judge about tensions with the other Vincentians at Phenix City. "It appears that there is great objection to the maintaining of those boys at Phoenix [*sic*]." They did not constitute "a school in the proper sense," nor were they likely to become lay apostles or Vincentians. Their presence—presumably they were staying in

30. Judge to Revd. and Dear Father, St. Vincent's Hospital, Birmingham, Ala., November 22, 1916, AST, MF 4437.

the rectory—violated the rights of the priests on a difficult mission. "I am sure," McHale concluded, "that you are quite unconscious of causing any dissatisfaction among them."[31] These boys were most likely the small group, including Fr. Judge's nephew Joseph Ledwidge, who had been living at Holy Trinity since sometime in 1917 and for whom Ella Lonergan held outdoor classes, "with the boys taking turns at watching the cows."[32] Perhaps they were brought to Phenix City when the weather turned cold.

Opelika, thirty miles from Phenix City, remained the formal center of the Alabama mission. Though he was the superior of the mission, Father Judge spent more time at St. Patrick's in Phenix City than at St. Mary's Mission House in Opelika, where the other Vincentians had their primary residence. This added to the tensions that concerned Father McHale. He wrote again in March. Apparently the boys were gone by now from St. Patrick's, but "Mr. Donnagan" remained.[33] McHale asked Judge to find some other place for "Donnagan" so that Judge and Father [William A.] O'Neill would each have his own space.[34]

Father McHale noted the "unsatisfactory condition" that the superior of this mission "is separated from a portion of his community," but saw no remedy at hand. Reflecting the unmet need for a resident chaplain at Holy Trinity, he advised Father Judge as superior against sending any of the other Vincentians "to *stay* for a very long period, such as a week, unless one of them should be perfectly willing to do so" (McHale underlined "stay"). Send-

31. McHale to Judge, Germantown, January 7, 1918, AST, MF 11515.

32. Brediger, "In the Name of the Father," 6:75–76 describes the boys: "some had outgrown the Sisters of Charity orphanage in Birmingham, one was Sr. Gerard's son [Joseph Ledwidge], a few were boys from around Phenix." He provides some names of the boys at 107.

33. The Mr. Donnagan to whom McHale referred was Jerome Patrick Donegan. According to the Vincentian Vow Book for the Eastern Province, Donegan was born in Glasgow, Scotland, on September 30, 1880, entered the Vincentians in 1918, at age 38, and made his vows in 1920. He was dispensed from his vows on June 30, 1923. According to the Registres du Grand Conseils for January 29, 1923, the Vincentian General Council permitted Donegan to devote himself to Judge's work on the condition that he ask to be dispensed from his vows: "On a permet à M. Jérôme Doneghan de se consacrer aux oeuvres de M. Judge mais à condition qu'il demande la dispense des voeux"; from a copy of an extract from the Registres du Grand Conseil, Reg. IX, 541, authenticated at Rome, November 13, 1963, by Vincentian superior general William M. Slattery, from a copy in Fr. Judge's file in DA. Timothy Lynch identifies Donegan as "the third male to join the Cenacle after Bro. Augustine [Philips] and Fr. Eugene Brennan." According to Lynch, Donegan eventually felt called to be a lay apostle rather than a religious. He returned to Scotland and died there, as Lynch says, "a lay apostle to the last and very much a Missionary Servant at heart"; Monographs 4:47.

34. Father William Aloysius O'Neill was a young Vincentian, who, according the Vow Book in Ducournau Archives, entered in 1913 and made his vows in 1915. He died in 1927.

ing a priest for the "weekly Mass" would be "perfectly proper," but McHale reminded Judge that "everyone is not so ready to deny himself as you are for the cause you have at heart. Even priests and missionaries are not all perfect."[35]

Father McHale's letters indicate both his recognition of the tensions created by Father Judge's dual responsibilities as Vincentian superior and director of this new religious body and his basic support of Judge and both these works. Two days after McHale's March 9 letter, Judge wrote to assure an inquirer that the Cenacle's work in the South enjoyed ecclesiastical approval from both Bishop Allen and Father McHale. With reference to McHale, he wrote, "Through him this work was begun, and he is behind it, and but the other day he told me that this work must go on, as it is the only hope our mission has had in six years."[36] Noteworthy is the fact that, three years after the first Cenacle volunteers had arrived in Alabama, Father Judge recognized that his provincial superior still understood the Cenacle's work in the South in terms of the Vincentian Alabama mission. This too is how Judge presented the Cenacle lay apostles when he wrote about them later in the year.

Presenting the Lay Apostolate to a Wider Audience

Father Judge published "The Lay Apostolate in the South" in the *Catholic Convert* in September 1918. After years of confidentiality and even secrecy about Cenacle work in the North, Judge decided late in 1918 that it was time to go public about his lay missionaries in the South. A year after the "rough boys of Phenix City" had threatened St. Patrick's School and its teachers, Judge presented lay apostles as the only way to overcome Southern prejudice against the church and its priests and sisters.

During August 1918, probably while he was working on "The Lay Apostolate in the South," Father Judge wrote to Edith Collins, a recent convert, who was disturbed at her inability to respond more effectively to her aunt's hostility to Catholicism. He distinguished the missionary from the apologist, the gift of teaching from the gift of faith, and appealed to "the invincible evidence of a perfect Catholic life" as the greatest proof of the Church's divine mission. "If, therefore," he told Collins, "you meet her intolerance with the

35. McHale to Judge, Opelika, Ala., March 9, 1918, AST, MF 11518.

36. Judge to My dear Child, Phenix City, March 11, 1918, AST, MF 4604.

breadth of a Catholic spirit, if you meet her petulance with a generous spirit of forbearance, ... at the same time saying a prayer to the Holy Spirit, there would be a greater heart change in your aunt than you can imagine."[37] Thus he explained the witness of the Cenacle lay apostles in a hostile South.

Lay apostles were everyday people, "recruited from those who may be found in every parish." Explaining their role, Father Judge returned to the church's "divine commission—'To teach all nations.'" "Fear and dread of our holy religion, and the fierce hatred entertained toward its priesthood," had prevented the Vincentian missionaries in Alabama from fulfilling the church's divine commission. "The one thing untried" was "a force that has been a tremendous evangelizing power since the days of Our Lord Himself." This untried force was "the life and the example, the cooperation and good will of a highly spiritualized laity,—in other words, the lay apostolate."

Lay apostles demonstrated Catholicity "as a merchant does his goods." Many, Father Judge speculated, would owe their eternal salvation to God's grace and "these quiet and devoted apostles." In such an unfriendly environment, "our good works were our only defense." Two openings presented themselves, a weak school system and "lack of charity to the poor and to the poor sick." The lay apostles began to meet these needs with "merely elemental Christianity." In the face of the Guardians of Liberty, the "rough boys of Phenix City," and the Great Influenza, Christian ladies witnessed "by their charm and grace and modesty ... that the Catholic Church is the mother of all that is sweet, refined, gracious and lovable." Judge closed with an appeal to readers of the *Catholic Convert* for financial support for these apostolic ladies and their work.[38]

The Mission to Ridge, Maryland

But events were running ahead of Father Judge. Even as his apologia for the lay apostolate was going to press, the new charitable and religious corporation of the Missionary Servants of the Most Blessed Trinity was making plans to send small groups of missionaries to Ridge, Maryland, and Pensacola, Florida. On September 28, 1918, Ella Lonergan, now known as Sister Miriam, left Holy Trinity with two companions, Stella Rivers (Sister Anthony) and Teresa Harrigan (Sister Teresa Marie), to teach at St. Michael's Mission School at Ridge in historic St. Mary's County on Maryland's rural Eastern Shore.

37. Judge to Collins, Phenix City, August 18, 1918, AST, MF 4614.
38. Judge, "Lay Apostolate in the South," 4–5, 18.

An emergency request for teachers had come from John LaFarge, SJ (1880–1963), who spent fifteen years on the Jesuit Maryland missions before moving to the staff of *America* in 1926, where he became a well-known advocate for "interracial justice." On October 7, 1918, three more women left Holy Trinity for Pensacola, where, at the request of Bishop Allen, they would work with Father Hartkoff in setting up a home for Creole boys. Cenacle associates in the North had long discussed the possible adoption of a common garb. All six women left Holy Trinity for their missions dressed in a "black garb," a dress that resembled a nurse's uniform with a white collar.[39]

Father LaFarge included in his autobiography a chapter on "The Ridge Schools," describing the mission at the Church of St. Michael. "September 20, 1918," he wrote, "we opened a white school at St. Michael's conducted by the Missionary Servants of the Blessed Trinity, a group of four ladies who were not as yet strictly members of a religious community but were devoted to a missionary life. They started in utmost poverty."[40] It was at Ridge that Father LaFarge first called these Missionary Servants of the Most Blessed Trinity "Sisters."

Sister Miriam must have written immediately to Father Judge about this development. He began his response on October 1 and anticipated later distinctions between "garb Sisters" and "habit Sisters." "In a section where Catholicity has a hold," he thought, calling them "Sisters" might not cause too much of a surprise. On the other hand, they would look like unusual "Sisters." And "such a large departure from the conventionally garmented guardians of the School Room" might indeed cause surprise. He decided to have council. On October 10, he resumed his response and reported that councils at both St. Patrick's and Holy Trinity had favored "taking the name Sister." He favored this, he said, but had not made his preference known prior to council. He was grateful that somebody else, the Jesuits in this case, had settled the question, "as it makes God's will more apparent."[41]

The Great Influenza of 1918 complicated the mission to Ridge. In his October 10, 1918, letter to Sister Miriam, Father Judge mentioned that "the schools are closed and many of the Sisters are nursing." By October 27, he reported that "the plague is upon us and we have put ourselves under the protection of the Queen of Angels and her Angelic host."[42] The sisters had

39. Collins, "Voice from the Past," *Holy Ghost*, December 1949, 9. Collins describes the garb; see also Tonra, *Led by the Spirit*, 49–50.

40. John LaFarge, SJ, *The Manner Is Ordinary* (New York: Harcourt, Brace, 1954), 199.

41. Judge to Lonergan, Phenix City, October 1, 10, 1918, AST, MF 4972–73.

42. Judge to Frances O'Driscoll, Opelika, October 27, 1918, AST, MF 4577.

not been long at Ridge when Sister Anthony came down with the flu. She was sent to Georgetown Hospital in Washington. Her extended hospitalization and recovery time meant that they were short-handed. They also had to decide whether to move Sister Anthony.

In November Father Judge sent Sister Mary Francis (Mary Taylor) from Holy Trinity "as substitute teacher and visitor." He instructed Sister Miriam to "go to her for charity" or fraternal correction. In addition, it was a "lonely mission" with the "danger of isolation." LaFarge reassured Judge with a kind note. On January 24, 1919, Judge reported from Brooklyn that he had visited Sister Anthony's parents in New York and that she wanted to stay at Ridge. He encouraged Sister Miriam, in the midst of a difficult situation, not to hesitate to act. "If you must act, pray to the Holy Spirit for council; weigh well the matter as you have been taught, then do not hesitate. Should you have time to get word to your superiors, all right do so."[43]

Finally, at the beginning of February 1919, Father Judge visited Ridge himself. "Good news from Ridge, thank God," he wrote to Katherine Shelvy (Sister Mary Michael), "I have been there."[44] He noted that the Jesuits had been unsuccessful in their repeated attempts to bring teaching sisters to Ridge. He found "wonderful possibilities here, providing we can live under Cenacle conditions." St. Mary's County had been the site of the first Jesuit missions in Maryland. Judge was moved by the thought of living in a place "sanctified by three hundred years, nearly, of these holy men who have done so much to save the whites and blacks in this portion of the world." Ridge gave him "a very spiritual soothing."[45]

Though it was "the first outside mission of the Cenacle Sisters," the mission to Ridge didn't last.[46] Perhaps living "under Cenacle conditions" proved too difficult there. In any case, at the end of the school year, Judge wrote to Sr. Miriam that "the question of returning is being ventilated between Fr. LaFarge and Sr. Boniface (Lulu Keasey). I believe the decision now rests with

43. Judge to Lonergan, Phenix City, November 18, 1918; Phenix City, November 27, 1918; Brooklyn, January 24, 1919, AST, MF 4693. Later in the year, he would correct Sr. Miriam for showing at times "an irritated and self-assertive manner"; Judge to Lonergan, Phenix City, May 5, 1919, AST, MF 4737.

44. Judge to Shelvy, en route to Brooklyn, February 10, 1919, AST, MF 4700–01.

45. Brediger, "In the Name of the Father," 6:103. The race-specific reference to "whites and blacks" indicates that LaFarge conveyed to Judge the "interracial" concerns that took root during his years on the Maryland Eastern Shore.

46. This is the description from the *Vincentian Chronicle* for September 1918 as cited in ibid., 98–99.

Fr." "No doubt the letter came regarding our status of the Ridge question," he wrote a few weeks later. He cautioned Sr. Miriam, "Do not give the Fathers any hope of our return."[47] As LaFarge put it, the sisters "were the soul of zeal and charity, but their work was more social service than educational."[48]

Further Developments at Holy Trinity, Fall/Winter 1918–1919

"The plantation is voracious in its needs so you can send anything usable," Father Judge wrote to Edith Collins in the fall of 1918.[49] In addition to the plantation, the flu epidemic, which no doubt limited travel, as well as Judge's duties as superior and Father McHale's concerns about the mission, all combined to keep him, with the exception of brief trips north in August and December, in the South for most of the period from March through December 1918. One of those trips found him in Brooklyn for a week at the beginning of August.

On August 4, 1918, Father Judge returned to the basement of St. Andrew's Church, where Monsignor Luke Evers had given a home to the Cenacle.[50] His talk that day recalled the parable of the Pharisee and the publican and warned the Cenacle general meeting against pride, self-complacency, and the need to make an impression. Their work was now attracting "a very widespread notice." This made him uneasy. "What a change in three or four years," he remarked, looking around at the basement. It had been "all piled up with boxes," and they were grateful for it. Now it had "painting and electric fixtures." "There has been such a tremendous change in three years by the grace of God which is a comfort to all of us. But I do not know what effect it is going to have on us." He reminded them of when they went around and people "were slamming the doors in your face." "Oh, that was glorious," he exclaimed. "Now when they say, 'Sit down and have a cup of tea,' I am afraid."[51]

47. Judge to Lonergan, Phenix City, May 25, 1919; So. Meriden, Conn., June 15, 1919, AST, MF 4744–50.

48. LaFarge, *Manner Is Ordinary*, 200.

49. Judge to Collins, Phenix City, November 7, AST, MF 4626.

50. On Evers's devotion to the poor and his relationship with Judge, see Lynch's introduction to Document 3, "Conference Given by Father Judge, Nov. 30, 1913 at St. Andrew's Church, New York City," Monographs 4:18–19.

51. On this talk and for the quotations from Father Judge, see Brediger, "In the Name of the Father," 6:83–86.

At Holy Trinity on October 4, 1918, around the time the sisters were leaving for Ridge and Pensacola and the Great Influenza was hitting Phenix City, Father Judge dedicated an abandoned "negro cabin" with a cross on its roof as Blessed Trinity Academy. Anne McCormick, who would become Sister Ignatius, had been teaching eight students, five boys and three girls, in the cow pasture. Blessed Trinity Academy permanently solved the problem of what to do with the boys when the weather turned cold. Two weeks later, on October 18, in another cabin, Nora Griffin, who would become Sister Mary Clare, opened a school on the plantation. In the afternoon, the school doubled as a store.[52] In its different incarnations, this would come to be known as St. Peter Claver School and later, until 1997, St. Joseph's School.

Father Judge spent an increasing amount of time at the plantation. Writing to the North on November 4, 1918, he returned to the theme of his August 4 talk in Brooklyn. He praised God for the prosperity of the cenacles at St. Patrick's and Holy Trinity but warned that "too much prosperity is a dangerous thing and I pray that our people will never forget the goodness of God to them." In this context, he spoke of "debt in the Blessed Trinity Cenacle." "You can just merrily roll it up, sheet after sheet, trusting that God will help us out and not fail us in the hour of need. What a thrilling pleasure it is, through confidence, to provoke the goodness of God."

As he described the plantation's "prosperity," he shifted to the more lighthearted tone of a "backwoods pastor." "Dusty as a miller," he spent the days picking "the cockle-burrs from my very much frayed garments." They now had a grist mill, a tractor, and even a "beautiful car" that looked like "an ambulance or a sightseeing bus." The mule barn was now the cow barn. They called it "Bethlehem," and Judge likened it to Noah's Ark. "All kinds of things seek its shelter." Its inhabitants included "a family of turkeys, many different kinds of rats, snakes and innumerable insects." Sisters who lived in such conditions would have no fear. "Surely they are being trained to missionary sacrifices after this summer and autumn's experiences, they will be daunted by nothing."[53]

52. Collins, "Voice from the Past," *Holy Ghost*, December 1949, 10. Brediger mentions that when the school was first opened, it included more than just plantation children, and the Klan threatened to burn it down. The teachers had to scale back the school and then expand it again. Brediger dates the name St. Peter Claver School to 1925; Brediger, "In the Name of the Father," 6:117.

53. Brediger, "In the Name of the Father," 6:78–80, citing a letter of November 4, 1918, AST, MF 4560–61.

Apart from his growing attachment to it, another reason Father Judge spent so much time at the plantation was that the growing number of people living there needed a priest for daily Mass, confession, and spiritual direction. On December 8, 1918, returning from Newark, Father Judge took the train from Columbus to Ft. Mitchell and started walking the remaining ten miles to Holy Trinity. A neighbor picked him up on the way, and he arrived in time for Mass for the Immaculate Conception but then had to be back in Phenix City later in the day.[54]

Father McHale had forbidden him to send Vincentians to Cottonton for any extended periods. As Holy Trinity grew, he became increasingly preoccupied with trying to find a resident priest. This led to a string of priests who passed through Holy Trinity in the 1920s. They were all men of good will but mostly ill-suited for the work. Eugene Brennan was already taking courses, and Judge's thoughts turned eventually to home-grown Cenacle priests.

Father Judge spent Christmas 1918 at the plantation. Earlier in the year, just after the Feast of the Annunciation on March 25, 1918, he had written a letter north, highlighting the centrality to the Cenacle of the mystery of the incarnation. "In the great Christian mystery that we commemorate today began all that has come to us through Our Lord's life." He prayed that they would come to appreciate "all the love and power and goodness of His in the Incarnation." Meditating on the incarnation, he told them, is "the greatest pleasure that we can get out of life."[55]

When Christmas came, he wrote a "Preparation for Christmas Eve" for the Southern cenacles. Looking back over the past three years in the South, he placed the Cenacle story inside the story of Christmas. Three years ago, in 1915, the first two sisters had come "as the wild birds without home or shelter. More than that, they came as the Christ Child came." From the ministrations of God's providence over the past three years, he urged them to take confidence.[56]

A General Superior for the Sisters

In addition to the cenacles at St. Patrick's and Holy Trinity in Alabama and the missions at Ridge and Pensacola, there were also cenacles at the Dr.

54. Collins, "Voice from the Past," *Holy Ghost*, December 1949, 10–11.

55. Judge to My dear Child, Phenix City, March 27, 1918, as cited in Brediger, "In the Name of the Father," 6:81.

56. "Preparation for Christmas Eve," December 1918, AST, MF 11464.

White Memorial Center on Gold Street in Brooklyn and at Tomkins Street in Orange, New Jersey. The number of sisters was growing, perhaps approaching fifty. Just before Christmas in 1918, Father Judge wrote to the cenacles at Brooklyn, Orange, Ridge, and Pensacola. "For a long time," he told them, "I have been praying that God the Holy Ghost would work out for us in His own good way the perfection of the Cenacle organization." Then he wrote simply, "A general superior is needed."[57]

On New Year's Day 1919, Father Judge gathered the sisters in their chapel at St. Patrick's. He told them that, after much prayer and consideration, he had decided that they needed a superior for themselves. There was silence and then the announcement that he was appointing Sister Mary Boniface as general superior. Most of the sisters had expected the appointment of one who had been longer in the Cenacle, Amy Croke, perhaps. But by all accounts, those present were happy and relieved. Lu Keasey was shocked. "She buried her face in her hands and would not appear for sometime either to be consoled or congratulated." The next day, Judge sent out a letter to the other cenacles announcing his appointment of Lu Keasey, Sr. Boniface, as the "Arch Custodian of all the Inner Cenacles."[58] Then he left for the North.

Lu Keasey eventually came to terms with her appointment and fully accepted the role of Mother Boniface. Her initial discomfort with her new rank was genuine. She was only thirty-four. Public speaking and the thought of meeting formidable bishops such as Philadelphia's Dennis Dougherty intimidated her. She also felt unworthy at being chosen over older women who had been with Father Judge and the work of the Cenacle from the beginning. "I felt like a thief," she told Judge.[59] In addition, she had to bear the resentment of some of the older women.[60] But over the years she grew gracefully into her office, as apparently she did just about everything. Eventually she signed her letters "Mother." Perhaps she came to know that she could charm the likes of the archbishop of Philadelphia simply by showing up.

The distance and formality that characterized Father Judge's relations with the women under his direction made it possible for him to make this decision. Sister Boniface would have known that it was not personal. Like

57. Collins, "Voice from the Past," *Holy Ghost*, December 1949, 11.

58. Ibid., 11–12; Tonra, *Led by the Spirit*, 52–53.

59. Tonra, *Led by the Spirit*, 60, 66. Chaps. 6 and 7, citing generously from Keasey's own words and from the witness of contemporaries, convey a thick sense of her response to her appointment as mother general.

60. Ibid., 53–54.

all the others under his direction, she too was "My dear Child." However amazed she might have been that he chose her, she would also have known that he was thinking about the work and about God and really thought she was the best one for the job. The natural gifts, not least his warm humor, of a man who had grown up with four sisters would let her know that he cared about her even if she were not the best person for the job. And then he had the grace and good sense to get out of town. Father Judge's choice of Lu Keasey as mother general was inspired in every possible way.

Until the end of the school year in 1919, the new mother general continued as principal and teacher for the seventh and eighth grades at St. Patrick's in Phenix City. By September of 1919, however, she was living permanently at the plantation or Blessed Trinity Cenacle in Cottonton. With her move, the Cenacle center clearly made a decisive shift. The new needs created by this move—for example, for a new principal at St. Patrick's—factored into the decision not to return to Ridge.[61] Father Judge wrote to Father LaFarge in September, closing the book on the sisters' work at Ridge. "Our Sisters came back, thank God, safely, speaking gratefully of your many kindnesses to them, and regretting that they could not do more for you." He noted that St. Patrick's had "opened very prominently . . . having the largest September enrollment to date."[62]

Taking the Cenacle Public in a Postwar American Church

The end of the Great War began a period of both national consolidation and expansion for the Catholic Church in the United States. In 1917 the Paulist John J. Burke (1875–1936), then editor of the *Catholic World*, had, with the support of Cardinal Farley of New York, founded the National Catholic War Council. The council coordinated Catholic efforts during the war, especially providing Catholic military chaplains. The war council brought together a talented group of priest professionals clustered around Catholic University in Washington. After the war, it continued as the National Catholic Welfare Council and eventually evolved into the present United States Conference of Catholic Bishops. Many of the schools, hospitals, and other institutions that characterized the immigrant Catholic subculture of the first half of the

61. Ibid., 57.
62. Judge to LaFarge, Phenix City, September 23, 1919, AST, MF 47933.

twentieth century took shape at this time. There was also, however, a sense of the importance of engagement with American culture, especially in areas of social reform that had an impact on the lives of Catholic Americans.

In 1919 John A. Ryan (1869–1945) drafted the "Bishops' Program of Social Reconstruction," which included such proposals as minimum wage legislation and various forms of insurance for health, unemployment, and old age. In 1920 he became director of the NCWC's Social Action Department. In 1921 Burke and William Kerby, chair of the Sociology Department at Catholic University, who back in 1905 had invited Father Judge to speak in his class, founded the National Catholic School of Social Work where Ryan also lectured.[63] The work of the Cenacle, especially with Italian immigrants in Orange, New Jersey, and at the Dr. White Center in Brooklyn, converged with many of these efforts and concerns. In the near future, Cardinal Dougherty and other bishops would ask the sisters to make further commitments to "social work."[64]

From the Dr. White Memorial in Brooklyn, Father Judge wrote to John A. Ryan in January. Ryan edited the *Catholic Charities Review*, which he had founded in 1917. Judge asked him for permission to reprint as a pamphlet an article that the Dr. White director, Fr. John B. Gorman, had brought to his attention, presumably because "I have been concerned and associated with just such work as the article mentions for some years." At the bottom of Judge's letter, Ryan wrote, "By all means republish the article."[65]

Early in 1919, Father Judge was also in touch with Paulist John J. Burke, one of the leading forces behind the National Catholic War Council. On March 5, 1919, Judge wrote to Bishop Allen about an invitation from Burke "to take over the work of colonization." Burke had apparently read or heard about Judge's efforts in Alabama, perhaps from the *Catholic Convert* article. He had proposed Holy Trinity as a site where soldiers returning from the Great War might start a Catholic colony. Judge described Burke as "urgent

63. On all of these developments, see Elizabeth McKeown, *War and Welfare: American Catholics and World War I* (New York: Garland, 1988). On Kerby and Judge, see Timothy Lynch's introduction to Document 9, Father Judge's 1923 "Address before the National Conference of Catholic Charities in Philadelphia," Monographs 4:75.

64. On the sisters and social work, see Margaret Alacoque Gallaher, MSBT, "The Social Work of the Missionary Servants of the Most Blessed Trinity, from the Year 1909 Up to and Including the Year 1940" (master's thesis, Fordham University School of Social Service, 1942).

65. Judge to Ryan, Brooklyn, January 17, 1919, AST, MF 4685. The article in question was probably Margaret Tucker, "Catholic Settlement Work: An Analysis," *Catholic Charities Review* 2, no. 10 (December 1918): 304–8; *Catholic Charities Review* 3, no. 1 (January 1919): 18–21.

that we accept a colony of returning soldiers." Judge was all for Catholic colonization in Alabama. Two families, the Ryckleys and the Searles, came to the plantation around 1919, to be joined later by a few others.[66] But he didn't think returning Catholic soldiers would be likely to succeed as colonists at Holy Trinity. He explained in detail to Bishop Allen his case that single men, familiar neither with the "Satanic bigotry" in the "sub-South" nor with the hardships of farm life, would be more likely to lose their faith than to build a successful Catholic colony. He begged Allen "to excuse us for the time being" from Burke's invitation.[67] Allen replied on March 11, 1919, and apparently granted Judge's request, but noted the great benefit to the church "if neglected farms could be purchased and placed in the hands of practical farmers."[68]

Another of Father Judge's Catholic University connections was the biblical scholar Charles P. Grannan (1864–1924). At the end of his life, Grannan retired to Pensacola for health reasons. He was working on his last book, *A General Introduction to the Bible*, published in four volumes from Herder in 1921. At the end of 1919, Judge sent Katherine Shelvy, Sister Mary Michael, from Brooklyn, where she was working at the Dr. White Memorial, on "a short sea trip to Mobile." Sister Michael needed a rest, and he wanted her to spend six weeks to two months at the cenacle in Pensacola. At the same time, he told her, "You will be able to help Dr. Grannan the eminet [*sic*] Scripture Scholar who is publishing a work." "This will be a very small tax on you," he added. "Something to engage you a little." Grannan apparently paid for the trip.[69]

By February 1920, Sister Michael was worried that Grannan might not be able to finish his book. Father Judge promised to try to get someone to help him. In May 1920, Sister Michael was still at Pensacola. Sending her to Holy Trinity, Judge assured Sister Michael that "Dr. Grannan is evidently much pleased with your work. You may be consoled in knowing that you have made a substantial contribution to the Church at least by cooperation."[70] Grannan did indeed finish his book, but his acknowledgments failed to mention Sister Michael.

66. On the colonizers at Holy Trinity, see Brediger, "In the Name of the Father," 6:117–18.

67. Judge to Allen, Phenix City, March 5, 1919, AST, MF 4709–11.

68. Collins, "Voice from the Past," *Holy Ghost*, March 1950, 9, cites from Bishop Allen's March 11, 1919, reply but I didn't see it in the Allen papers; Archives of the Archdiocese of Mobile.

69. Judge to Shelvy, Montgomery, Alabama, November 24, 1919, AST, MF 3942.

70. Judge to Shelvy, Phenix City, February 25, 1920, AST, MF 4932; Judge to Shelvy, New Haven, Conn., ca. May 1920, AST, MF 4895. Judge's connection to Grannan is not clear. It is likely that Grannan promised some or all of the proceeds from the sale of his book to the Cenacle.

A Spiritual Militia

The *Catholic Convert* article of 1918 and its reprinting in the Brooklyn *Tablet* had given Father Judge and the Cenacle some limited exposure.[71] At Easter 1919, after meeting in Washington with the apostolic delegate, Archbishop John Bonzano, Father Judge sent out a mailing to select U.S. clergy and bishops. It included the text of the *Catholic Convert* article and a letter asking them to encourage the laity to volunteer as lay apostles. In the aftermath of this mailing, Judge received written support from the apostolic delegate and Cardinal James Gibbons of Baltimore.

At this time, Bonzano, who had been delegate since 1911, was trying unsuccessfully to solicit American support for Pope Benedict XV's inclusion at the Paris peace conference, which ended with the Treaty of Versailles on June 28, 1919.[72] Bonzano's May 14 reply enthused about Judge's success and the need for the lay apostolate. Regarding Judge's account of Southern mission work," he wrote, "What struck me most in that narrative is the success obtained by the lay apostolate in breaking down the barriers of prejudice and ignorance, from which those difficulties chiefly arise." He concluded his letter by stating his personal approval "of your efforts to obtain, not only sufficient means to carry on and extend the work, but also young men and women who are willing to labor, if only for a few years, in those fields."[73]

Gibbons affirmed his familiarity with the work of Father Judge and his fellow Vincentians in the Alabama missions and promised his "cordial approbation" for "any new effort which you may undertake to increase results." He thought an appeal to priests such as Judge proposed would "meet with hearty response." To Gibbons Judge's six years in Alabama "proves conclusively that only a Lay Apostolate can break down the barrier raised by ignorance and prejudice." He pronounced the record of his work "truly marvelous."[74] Encouraged by ecclesiastical authorities beyond the Vincentians and

71. A copy of the *Tablet* article is found in AST, MF 4933–34.

72. On the social and political background for Bonzano's work in the United States, see Peter D'Agostino, *Rome in America: Transnational Catholic Ideology from the Resorgimento to Fascism* (Chapel Hill and London: University of North Carolina Press, 2004), 118–23, 132–57.

73. Bonzano to Judge, Washington, D.C., May 14, 1919, in Thomas A Judge, CM, Box 1H.17A, DA; see also Brediger, "In the Name of the Father," 6:111–12. Recognition of the significance of Father Judge's promoting the lay apostolate was a major reason for the apostolic delegation's consistent support for him and his work. The work to preserve the Italian diaspora's ties to the church in the face of Protestant proselytizing drew Bonzano's strong support.

74. Gibbons to Judge, Baltimore, June 28, 1919, as cited in Brediger, "In the Name of the

the Diocese of Mobile, Father Judge decided to bring the Cenacle's localized works into the postwar national mix. His voice reached a national Catholic audience with a September article in the *Ecclesiastical Review*.

The *Ecclesiastical Review* was the premier clerical journal of its day.[75] It was published in Philadelphia, the home both of Father Judge's provincial superiors and of Archbishop Dennis Dougherty. The body of the article reproduced "The Lay Apostolate in the South" from the *Catholic Convert*. Judge bookended this with new material and added a new title.[76] The title "A Spiritual Militia" sought to tap into the postwar mood and "supernaturalize" the "spontaneous and generous response of the youth of our country to the call to the colors" (276).

"This," he declared, "is the layman's hour" (277). For Father Judge this was simple. Christ, "Our Divine Lord," divides the human race into "those who work for Him and those who do not." If young people understood this—and presumably it was the job of priests to help them understand—"then the Fifth and Sixth Stations of the Cross on the walls of our churches would mean more . . . and every parish would have many Saint Simons of Cyrene and Saint Veronicas."[77]

> If our people did but realize that in the little circle where Divine Providence has placed them, they may become an invincible power for good; that they may stand for their Church, alert for its interests, zealous to reclaim the wayward, to strengthen the weak, to hinder the perverse and save little ones from scandal, what allies we would have in our priestly care for souls (277).

Without "priestly encouragement and enlightenment," the "good will and spirit of sacrifice" of the laity will not bear fruit. In urging each priest "to open his ministry to others," he put before them the "terrifyingly plain" words of the Holy Ghost in Proverbs 3:27: "Do not withhold him from doing

Father," 6:110. It would not have been uncharacteristic of Gibbons to have waited for Bonzano's reply before writing his own.

75. See Timothy Lynch's introduction to Document 5, "A Spiritual Militia," in Monographs 4:25–27.

76. Judge, "Spiritual Militia," *Ecclesiastical Review* 61, no. 3 (September 1919): 276–85. The *Catholic Convert* material begins at the bottom of page 279 and continues to the bottom of page 283. Hereafter page numbers will be cited in the text.

77. He had used this image of St. Veronica at a retreat at Orange, New Jersey, in July1919. In his third conference, speaking on Ps 29:10, "What profit is there in my blood," he dwelt on the "mental sorrow of our dear Christ." "You are the Veronicas of today," he told the women of the Cenacle, "that is your vocation, to do Jesus a personal service. It is your vocation to go amidst horrible conditions, impossible conditions, to do something for the image of the Blessed Trinity"; AST, MF 573–74.

good who is able, if thou art able do good thyself also" (278). "A priestly life barren of good works," he warned, "and wanting in encouragement to others to do good, will be an unsightly thing in God's eyes" (279).

He noted the "cordial approbation" of both the papal delegate and Cardinal Gibbons for "the plan of encouraging young men and young women to offer two or three years of their life to the service of God." He transitioned into the *Catholic Convert* text as offering "concrete examples" of the service he was proposing. The pages he added after this material (283–85) talked explicitly about "the millions of negroes [*sic*] to be evangelized" in the "one vast mission field" of the South (283) and the "home missions," in which he singled out "the Italian child" in the urban North. Priests and religious needed help to do this work. He urged "Hallowed be Thy Name, Thy Kingdom come" as a "personal obligation" (283). In his concluding appeal for priests to encourage the spiritual militia he proposed, Judge acknowledged recent developments in the Cenacle and distinguished between those who "carry on the work from their homes" and those "who are free to do so" who "live in community, wearing a modest civilian garb" (284).

It did not take long for responses to come in. On September 4, in a letter to the apostolic delegate, Father Judge drew Archbishop Bonzano's attention to the September *Ecclesiastical Review* article and identified it as "substantially the letter submitted to you some weeks ago, but changed and developed into a magazine article." In this letter, Judge makes reference to a previous conversation with Bonzano. Judge met with Bonzano, perhaps twice, near the end of April or the beginning of May 1919.[78] Bonzano's May 14 letter, written after the Easter mailing and cited previously, was the result.

Father Judge's conversations with Archbishop Bonzano in the spring of 1919 were pivotal in gaining widespread national support for the Cenacle. In his September 4 letter to Bonzano, Judge recalls that the archbishop had "mentioned you would have to keep in mind what might be the sentiment of the Bishops." So Judge was happy to report to him that "several of our prel-

78. O'Bryan cites "Minutes of Council Meeting," April 29, 1919, Gold Street, Brooklyn, from the Archives of the Missionary Cenacle Apostolate, uncatalogued: "Father explained that he had an interview with the Papal Delegate on the previous Saturday, and was to see him again the following week." The minutes go on to record that Bonzano was "much pleased with the work being done by the Cenacle." He even asked for the names of those working in the Cenacle's houses because he wanted to write to them. He asked how the work would be supported, and Judge said it was "God's work." It was at this meeting that Bonzano agreed to write his May 14 letter of support. According to the minutes, "One point which his Excellency remarked upon particularly was the fact that we are free to do work which those who are restricted by the rules of their order cannot undertake"; see O'Bryan, *Awake the Giant*, 204, 351n578.

ates, amongst others, Cardinal Gibbons and Archbishop Dougherty, with a very large number of priests, have given their encouraging words." He added that "since seeing you," he had met Bishop Curley of Baltimore and "spent several days" with him. He described Curley, too, as "very much interested and encouraging." Bonzano had apparently asked him how he would financially support the work he was directing.

> You may remember, you asked me how the work would be maintained. I answered that I left that to Divine Providence, feeling that as He would inspire the workers He would provide their sustenance. Thank God, not from the beginning have they ever wanted for the necessities of life, and now, as their numbers are increasing, their means of support are increasing also.[79]

Father Judge would soon have additional support from ecclesiastical authority in unexpected quarters. A few days after writing to Bonzano, Judge contacted the offices of the *Ecclesiastical Review* and asked them to send a copy of the September issue to Father McHale in Paris.[80] On November 7, 1916, the Vincentian superior general, Emile Villette, had died.[81] Since the Great War made a general assembly impossible, Villette was succeeded by two vicar generals. The Treaty of Versailles made it possible for the Congregation of the Mission to hold at Paris their twenty-eighth general assembly. The assembly met in Paris from September 27 to October 9, 1919. On September 30, word came from the secretary general in Paris that Father François Verdier, who had been serving as vicar general since February 18, 1918, had been elected superior general. He would serve in that office until his death on January 26, 1933.[82]

79. Judge to Bonzano, Phenix City, September 4, 1919, AST, MF 4777. Years later, in 1931, Judge recalled the pivotal role of this meeting with Bonzano as beginning the strong support for the Cenacle from four apostolic delegates. Here is Judge's 1931 recollection of his reply to Bonzano's question: "Your Excellency, you have asked me a question that I cannot answer. I do not know. I have only one answer and that is, when the time comes, God will send the maintenance. We leave that in the Hands of God." According to Judge, Bonzano replied, "You have given me the answer I wanted to hear." Judge went on to recall the subsequent constant support of the apostolic delegation in Washington. Around 1927, he recalled, the present delegate [Archbishop Pietro Fumasoni-Biondi] reminded him, "Father, I want you to understand that there are three Papal Delegates on record declaring that this work is very necessary and I am the fourth. If you have any trouble with Bishops, come to me"; "Post General Cenacle Notes," December 31, 1931, AST, MF 12497, as cited by O'Bryan, *Awake the Giant*, 206, 351n582. If this is what Fumasoni-Biondi said, he was mistaken. He was the third delegate, following Diomede Falconio (1902–11) and Giovanni Bonzano (1911–22). Fumasoni-Biondi served from 1922 to 1933.

80. Judge to Edward Galvally, Phenix City, September 7, 1919, AST, MF 4784.

81. Catalogue of Personnel (1917), DA.

82. See appendix C, listing Vincentian superiors and vicars general, and assemblies in Rybolt, *American Vincentians*, 469–70, 474.

Elected as Verdier's third assistant in Paris was the visitor or provincial superior of the Eastern Province, Father Patrick McHale. During the years Father Judge was assigned to promote the Holy Agony devotion in the United States, he found himself at odds with McHale. But after McHale assigned Judge to the Alabama Mission and visited Phenix City and Holy Trinity, the witness of the women who had volunteered on the Alabama mission won McHale over, and he became Judge's staunchest Vincentian ally and most significant supporter. Over the next fourteen years until Father Judge's death, Father Patrick McHale, from his new post in Paris, would have even more influence on the future development of the Cenacle.

Collections, Archbishop Dougherty, and Father Judge's New Assignment

When the 1919 school year ended in the spring, Mother Boniface and the sisters from St. Patrick's School went down to the plantation. Much to their surprise, Father Judge announced that he was sending Mother Boniface to Pittsburgh to see Bishop Regis Canevin and begin what came to be known as the "collection band." Bishop Canevin had given permission to "collect" in his diocese. But the collection band still had to call on pastors individually and get their permission to stand outside the church doors at Sunday masses begging for contributions.

In Pennsylvania the sisters ran directly into the problem of how to present themselves to Catholic people in "a section where Catholicity has a hold," as Father Judge had put it to Sr. Miriam when this question came up at Ridge. Instead of veils, they wore "broad-brimmed hats." "With their black dresses, long and tailored, set off by severe white collars and cuffs," they looked to local Catholics more like "visiting nurses" than nuns. But Bishop Canevin introduced them to the diocese as sisters and, in spite of "some 'uneasiness' in the North," Mother Boniface was adamant that they be called "sisters." They spent six months from the summer through Christmas collecting in the various cities of the Diocese of Pittsburgh. In addition to organizing the collection band, Mother Boniface also had to supervise the work at St. Patrick's and Holy Trinity through the mail. They returned to Holy Trinity for Christmas 1919.[83]

83. On the collection band and the various phrases in quotations marks above, see Collins, "Voice from the Past," *Holy Ghost*, March 1950, 7–8; see also Tonra, *Led by the Spirit*, 57–60.

As 1920 began, Mother Boniface and her collection band were back on the road, going now to parishes in the Diocese of Scranton and eventually Philadelphia. She had to ask Archbishop Dennis Dougherty (1865–1951) for permission to collect in the Archdiocese of Philadelphia. Dougherty had been appointed archbishop of Philadelphia two years before at age fifty-three. Educated in Montreal and Rome, in addition to St. Charles Seminary in Philadelphia, he taught at St. Charles and then spent twelve years as a bishop in the Philippines and three years in Buffalo. Dougherty and the Great Influenza arrived in Philadelphia the same year. He acquitted himself and the church well during this crisis.[84] By 1920 he was just beginning his thirty-year tenure as archbishop of Philadelphia. As Judge reported to Bonzano the previous September, Dougherty had responded to "A Spiritual Militia" with "encouraging words." Judge wrote to Dougherty in May to take him up on an offer to help. He discussed "A Spiritual Militia" and prepared the way for Mother Boniface's visit by asking if the sisters could collect in the archdiocese.[85]

Sometime in July Mother Boniface appeared at the archbishop's residence. Archbishop Dougherty was a large and imposing figure. Lu Keasey was just learning the ropes as Mother Boniface. Dougherty granted her request to collect in Philadelphia parishes. In return, he asked for the reverend mother's address. He had something important to talk to her about. Mother Boniface was embarrassed to tell him that she was the mother general. Instead she gave the archbishop her Alabama address. Eventually she returned, and Dougherty asked her for sisters to work at the Catholic Children's Bureau.

In October 1920 she sent four sisters to work in the home visiting department of the bureau. At this time, Dougherty made the first of his invitations for the sisters to move their motherhouse to Philadelphia.[86] In 1920 they declined his offer. But Dougherty would become a major supporter of the sisters and their work. By decade's end, he did welcome their motherhouse to Philadelphia. When Mother Boniface died, Dougherty insisted that her funeral Mass be held in his cathedral. He celebrated the Mass himself.

After Mother Boniface's second meeting with the archbishop, Father Judge wrote immediately to Father McHale telling him that Dougherty had

84. Barry, *Great Influenza*, 327, 329.
85. Judge to Dougherty, New Haven, Conn., May 19, 1920, AST, MF 4896.
86. Tonra, *Led by the Spirit*, 72–73.

invited the sisters to work in the Archdiocese of Philadelphia, where the Eastern Province of the Vincentians and their seminary happened to be located. He also asked if he could serve as the ecclesiastical superior of the sisters.[87] The Vincentian *Registres du Grand Conseil* for November 22, 1920, records that "M. Judge Thomas who has founded a flourishing congregation will be relieved as Superior of Opelika in order to devote himself entirely to this work."[88] On the same day, Patrick McHale wrote Judge from Paris to tell him of this decision:

> The Council has decided to leave you free to direct the "Missionary Sisters," and in consequence to leave you free from the office of Superior. The Visitor will make you a formal announcement to that effect. You will, of course, be under his jurisdiction, and consult him concerning their affairs. No doubt you will arrange with him about your residence, which had best be apart from the Sisters. Your reports are very interesting and encouraging. I hope that Opelika will soon profit by the Sisters' Apostolate.[89]

In response to the latest of Father Judge's reports, Father McHale wrote again two weeks later and commended Judge's work in strong terms. "The Lord seems to be 'Building the City,'" McHale wrote, "and He never fails." "It took some time to see the development," he continued, "and patience to await it, but the Holy Ghost was all the time at work." As he had in January, McHale again attributed the Cenacle's success to providence: "The Cenacle seems to be the work of Providence, and its members have proved their worth in a thousand ways. They have my unqualified esteem, and I commend myself to their prayers." McHale promised to "tell the General of your success" when he returned to Paris and referred to his former letter (November 22, 1920) "in which you are left free to devote yourself exclusively to the Cenacle and its works."[90]

87. Judge to McHale, Orange, N.J., July 21, 1920, AST, MF 4967.

88. "M. Judge Thomas qui a fondé une congregation florissante sera déchargé de la supériorité d'Opelika pour pouvoir se consacrer entièrement à cette oeuvre"; my translation of an extract from the Registres du Grand Conseil, Reg. IX, 342, authenticated at Rome November 13, 1963 by Vincentian superior general William M. Slattery, from a copy in Box 1H.17A, Folder 4, DA.

89. McHale to Judge, Paris, November 22, 1920, AST, MF 628; also at 11526; see also McHale to Judge, Barcelona, January 27, 1920, AST, MF 11524–25. McHale wrote in response to one of Judge's reports, "The development of your work down there reveals a direct intervention of Providence for the conversion of the South.... You are on the right track; but the devil is going to raise a big row before he gives in. I am very glad to have been even a feeble helper in the work." McHale had a high estimate of the sisters and never failed to ask Judge, as he did in this letter, to ask for their prayers.

90. McHale to Judge, Dublin, December 10, 1920, AST, MF 628.

In response to his own request, and no doubt with the strong recommendation of Father McHale, the Vincentian General Council freed Father Judge to work exclusively with the Cenacle. This, it would soon become clear, would not have been the decision of Father Judge's own provincial council. He remained technically attached to St. Mary's mission house at Opelika until his death but did not live there.[91] Judge's residence, mentioned by McHale, continued to be a sticking point. When he was in Alabama and not on the road, Judge spent most of his time at the plantation.

The Cenacle was growing fast in Alabama. The U.S. Census for 1920 records twenty women, the profession of most listed as teacher, living at the house in Phenix City, with Amy M. Croke as the head of the household. In addition to Brennan and Phillips [*sic*], the census lists five young men ranging in ages from eighteen to twelve as living at the plantation.[92] In a September report to Bishop Allen, Judge mentioned the "heavy registration" at St. Patrick's, where "the Sisters are making preparation to handle five hundred children."

To a visionary such as Father Judge small initiatives could be movements and repainted shacks could be academies and even agricultural institutes. In reporting on the progress at Cottonton, Judge wrote, "We open this year a High School and Normal School for our Novices." This was "but a beginning." "Our Plantation school we hope is making towards an Agricultural Institute." He hoped to attract the children of the surrounding farms. "We have about thirty children living on the plantation," he told the bishop, "all little missionaries." He even reported "two remarkable cures" that took place at the annual pilgrimage on August 15. An invalid woman with "a very pronounced and long standing case of neurasthenia" had "gone home completely cured."[93]

On November 21, 1920, Bishop Allen administered the sacrament of confirmation to groups of children at St. Patrick's in Phenix City and on the

91. "The personnels continue to list Father Judge as attached to the house at Opelika year after year until his death, but I do not think that Opelika saw much of Father Judge during the last ten years of his life, as during that period he was busily engrossed in promoting the two Trinitarian communities which he founded"; John J. Cloonan, CM, to Sylvester A Taggart, CM, Northampton, Pa., October 16, 1958. Cloonan was responding to a request from Taggart, then the Eastern Province visitor, to gather information on Judge's life from Vincentian records; from a copy in Box 1H.17A, Folder 4, DA.

92. U.S. Federal Census 1920, Russell County, Alabama Precinct 10, Phoenix City, Ward 14327, Sheet 8, Lee County, January 10, 1920; U.S. Federal Census 1920, Russell County, Alabama, Beat 8, Oswichee, 249–50.

93. Judge to Allen, Cottonton, September 18, 1920, AST, MF 4961–63.

Burr Plantation. On Christmas Eve, Father Joseph Koury arrived from North Dakota. He was the first resident chaplain at Holy Trinity. He stayed for two years and then moved on to Gillette, N.J. With his arrival, daily Mass was offered at the plantation.[94]

Eleven days after Father Judge wrote this report to Bishop Allen, on September 29, 1920, Andrew Philips, now Brother Augustine, went to the First National Bank in Columbus, Georgia, and finalized the purchase from Mrs. Emma Bradley Nuckolls of 1,347.5 acres of land. Her father, Forbes Bradley, had purchased this land in pieces during the nineteenth century. Located across what is now Alabama State Route 165 from the Burr Plantation, this tract of land was known as the Bradley Plantation. Despite the name, it was, like the Burr Plantation, a run-down farm.

The idea of a separate place for the men and boys at the plantation had come from Eugene Brennan earlier in the year. Philips and Brennan, in addition to about a dozen boys, moved across the road to the main house of the Bradley Plantation. They turned one of the large rooms in the house into a chapel, and, on Christmas Eve 1920, Fr. Judge celebrated the first Mass at St. Joseph's Missionary Cenacle. Joined together, the Mott and Bradley plantations would come to be known as Holy Trinity.[95]

As 1920 drew to a close, Father Judge wrote a general letter announcing to the Cenacle his appointment as the sisters' "Ecclesiastical Superior." He enclosed with it copies of Father McHale's November 22 and December 10 letters to him. He described these letters as "of the greatest importance to all." He protested his unworthiness and asked for their prayers. He recalled the "hard and sad days in our early Cenacle history, when the infant and tender Cenacle was terrifically shaken and threatened." He professed his "tender and particularly prayerful affection," surely both "natural and supernatural," for those early "fire-tried" followers "who, in those days of trial, were faithful to the cause and movement of the Cenacle Lay Apostolate, especially when their fidelity in almost every case meant to them hardship, misrepresentation and abuse." Father Judge now found his vision and work vindicated by some of the church's highest authorities. "What a joy it is to me now to quote to them the words of the chief pastors of the flock and those in authority in the Church that the Cenacle Apostolate is the work of God."[96]

94. On Father Koury, see Tonra, *Led by the Spirit*, 76.

95. On the acquisition of the Bradley Plantation, see Brediger, "Leaving All Things: A History of the Cenacle in the South," 1948, 33–55, and Brediger, "In the Name of the Father," 6:123–26.

96. See Brediger, "In the Name of the Father," 6:125–26, where this letter is cited in full.

7

ON THE NATIONAL STAGE

1921–1923

The decision of the Vincentian General Council in November 1920 to free Father Judge to devote himself exclusively to work with the "Missionary Sisters," as Father McHale called them, coincided with the final ratification the previous August of the Nineteenth Amendment to the U.S. Constitution guaranteeing women the right to vote. Of course, no direct connection existed between these two events, but the passage of the Nineteenth Amendment, opposed by most Catholics of the day, reflected the social conditions that helped make the work of the sisters possible. The volatile 1920s, in many ways a time of cultural experimentation and change, gave Father Judge the room to exercise the new freedom with which the Vincentians had entrusted him.

But the 1920s would also confine him. Father Judge was in his fifties now. Part Irish clan chieftain, part religious entrepreneur, he was in a sense a throwback to an earlier, more freewheeling time. It was later in the 1920s that Babe Ruth hit an unprecedented sixty home runs and Charles Lindbergh made his history-making transatlantic solo flight. Such larger-than-life cultural exploits match the scale of Judge's impact and his dreams for the Missionary Servants. The 1920s, however, also saw the end of Progressivism and a new degree of consolidation, also reflected in the church and in economic and social life.[1] A universal Code of Canon Law was promulgated in 1917, and,

1. On the 1920s, see Frederick Lewis Allen, *Only Yesterday: An Informal History of the 1920s* (1931; San Francisco: Harper and Row, 1964); Lucy Moore, *Anything Goes: A Biography of the Roaring Twenties* (New York: Overlook Press, 2010); and Warren I. Sussman, *Culture as History: The Transformation of American Society in the Twentieth Century* (New York: Pantheon, 1973), chap. 7, "Culture and Civilization: The Nineteen-Twenties."

in the aftermath of the Great War, the Catholic Church in the United States began to organize itself on a national scale with the beginnings of the bishops' conference and other national organizations.

The Cenacle was also consolidating. Between 1920 and 1924, the twenty-fifth anniversary of Father Judge's ordination to the priesthood, the movement he founded grew from a lay organization with volunteer associates to something more like a structured religious community. Though this development occurred in response to the needs of the day, it also tended to limit or at least discipline Father Judge's expansive spirit, whose first inclination was to respond generously, and often originally, to whatever religious needs he encountered. In addition to the tensions involved in the process of trying to give organizational shape and direction to his pastoral vision, there was a deeper tension built into this vision. From the beginning, Judge's movement had been about promoting an apostolic laity for the preservation of the faith. Though Pope Pius XI would continue throughout the 1920s to advocate the lay apostolate, the church's canonical structures never made it easy for clergy and religious to work together with lay apostles. As the Missionary Servants, both women and men, came closer to the form of religious communities, the 1920s found Father Judge in search of an ecclesial shape that would retain for the developing religious an essential connection to the work of forming lay apostles for the preservation of the faith.

Two dramatic tensions shaped the conflicts of Father Judge's life during the 1920s. With his entrance onto the national Catholic stage, these two contrasts emerged clearly into view. The first pitted the improvisational spirit of the 1920s against its simultaneous forces of social, economic, and religious consolidation. The second pitted Father Judge's vision of fostering an apostolic laity against his original lay apostles' development in the direction of canonical religious life. The *Ecclesiastical Review* reached a wide clerical audience. Father Judge's 1919 "Spiritual Militia" article on the potential role of an apostolic laity gave him some initial notoriety. Though he often saw and embraced the promise of national trends in the direction of centralization and professionalization in the church, his reluctance to abandon his spiritual center in the Cenacle way made him wary of a wholesale embrace of them. His interactions with John F. Noll and with the emerging apparatus of Catholic Charities illustrate this ambivalence. But first an initial look at the birth of the brothers.

Incorporating the Brothers

New signs of the development of Father Judge's lay apostles in the direction of canonical religious life came early in 1921. In a letter to Bishop Allen of Mobile, Judge described "our young men organizing themselves into a missionary body" as the "latest phase in the Providential action which, thank God, has been so manifest in our mission." He likened their beginnings to those of the sisters, mentioning the "grade school, high school, and the beginning of a vocational school" on the old Bradley Plantation, as well as their cultivation of the "good will and confidence of the public in our extremely peculiar section of the country." At the heart of the brothers were Andrew Philips, whom he refers to in the letter as Brother Augustine, and Eugene Brennan, both of whom had come south from New Jersey in July 1916. He asked Bishop Allen for "a note of approval," which would help Philips raise money in the North, and for "permission that they be incorporated."[2]

Allen responded almost immediately in a brief letter. "You have my cordial approval for the organization of a band of Brothers at Holy Trinity Station, Cottonton, Alabama, whose purpose is to teach in agricultural and grade schools and take up charitable work in this Diocese, and if permitted by the Ordinaries, in other Dioceses of the country also." In a separate letter to Judge, Allen wrote, "I enclose letter approving, as far as I have any right to approve, of the Brotherhood at Cottonton, Alabama which will, I hope, meet with your wishes." He went on to explain that the "Holy See must give some kind of sanction to an organized work before it can advance. But as far as I can help you, I am very willing to do so." He described in some detail a work with orphans in Birmingham that he hoped the brotherhood might take up.[3] "Thank God for the good news," Judge wrote to Marie Mott Burr, now Sister Angel Guardian. "The Bishop for himself, named our city 'Holy Trinity Station.'"[4] By spring 1921, the brothers were running "a machine shop, a store and a grist mill" as well as a sawmill "turning out thousands of feet of pine." Judge placed a high "missionary value" on these enterprises, as they were the main medium of contact between the brothers, especially Philips,

2. Judge to Edward P. Allen, Orange, N.J., January 9, 192[1], AST, MF 597. This letter is dated January 9, 1920, but the date of Allen's reply and the context indicate that it should be 1921.

3. Allen to Judge, Mobile, January 22, 1921, copies of both letters preserved in the files of Rev. Thomas Lenahan, Archives of the Archdiocese of Mobile (hereafter AAM). Mobile became an archdiocese in 1980.

4. Judge to Sr. Angel Guardian Burr, Cottonton, Ala., January 26, 1921, AST, MF 4990.

and the local people of Russell County, Alabama, and Columbus, Georgia.[5]

Minutes of the provincial council meetings of the Vincentian Eastern Province indicate that around this time, Father Judge also made known to the visitor his intention to "establish a community of priests for some indefinite purpose." He requested "three priests to teach his young men" and, should that request be denied, that the visitor "allow his young men to attend classes with our students at Germantown." By this time Father Frederick J. Maune had replaced Father McHale as visitor. He served from 1919 to 1932. The provincial council unanimously disapproved both requests and advised Maune that, should the occasion arise, he inform bishops such as Bishop Allen and Cardinal Dougherty "that there is absolutely no connection between Fr. Judge's Communities and the Congregation of the Mission." This excerpt from the minutes concludes, "The V. Rev. Visitor and his Council have little confidence in Fr. Judge's fitness for the work he has undertaken and wish to disclaim all responsibility for it or connection with it."[6]

Father Judge's residence continued to be a neuralgic point in his relationship with his religious community. In fall 1922, the Vincentian superior general, Father François Verdier, visited the United States accompanied by his third assistant, Father McHale. They met with the provincial council on October 5. Among their topics of discussion was "the case of Fr. Thomas Judge, who, whilst still a member of the Community, lives outside the jurisdiction of its superiors." All his time, the minutes noted, is given to his work with the religious community of women he founded. "Fr. McHale was the only one who spoke in support, not so much of Fr. Judge, as of his work and the work of his institute. He claimed that the work had received the approbation of thirty bishops and seemed to be filling a very important need of our times." The discussion ended without final resolution. Its outcome "seemed to be that the Community should give no approbation to Fr. Judge's work and that he should be required, when in any place where there is a house of the Community, to live in that house subject to its superior."[7] The question of Father Judge's residence would recur in his relations with the American Vincentians. In 1932 it came to a head.

5. On the early work of the brothers at Cottonton, see Brediger, "Leaving All Things," 62–65.

6. Excerpt of "Minutes of Provincial Council Meeting," August 8, 1921, copy, Box 1H.17A, Folder 4, DA. The excerpts were certified against the originals by Sylvester A. Taggart, CM, visitor, August 31, 1964.

7. Excerpt of "Minutes of Provincial Council Meeting," October 5, 1922, Box 1H.17A, Folder 4, DA.

Father Judge and Monsignor John F. Noll: Clashing Visions, 1921–1922

In the spring of 1921, Father Judge sent Amy Croke, known since July 1919 as Sister Marie Baptista, to the Midwest on a fundraising trip that would also raise the profile of the work among Midwestern clergy and bishops. It was not clear, at least to her, to what extent the garb adopted by the sisters in the South was an expedient for fundraising in the North and identity in the South and to what extent it was part of a religious discipline. In any case, Father Judge wanted her to wear the garb of the Southern sisters on the trip. "There is so much difference in your dress from the Sisters," he told her. "I'm afraid it might not work out all right." He asked her ("I hope you will") to be ready with the garb by the time he returned and suggested that the sisters "could loan you a dress and trimmings."

Amy Croke/Sister Marie Baptista never made a canonical novitiate. Throughout her life, she embodied the tension in the Cenacle movement between the call to be a lay apostle and the call to canonical religious life. Croke in the garb highlighted the difference between the associates in the North and the sisters in the South in 1921. In any case, her trip was a rousing success, with Judge pronouncing it "difficult to estimate the amount of good she did," both in raising money and in publicizing the work.[8]

A significant result of Sister Baptista's trip was the temporary alliance between Father Judge and the Cenacle and Monsignor John F. Noll of Huntington, Indiana. Noll (1875–1956) was seven years Judge's junior. Like Judge, he was an accomplished ecclesiastical entrepreneur who had, for example, in imitation of Protestant practice, introduced weekly collection envelopes to Catholic parishes. As a pastor at St. Mary's Church in Huntington in 1912, he founded *Our Sunday Visitor* as an answer to the *Menace* and other anti-Catholic papers. It grew to have the widest circulation of any Catholic paper in the country.

8. Judge to Sister Marie Baptista, Philadelphia, April 28, 1921, AST, MF 11862–63; see also the fall 1921 circular letter from Father Judge, "Continuation of Summer Trip," AST, MF 5066. See also Collins, "Voice from the Past," *Holy Ghost*, June 1950, 8, and O'Bryan, *Awake the Giant*, 237. Amy Croke/Sister Marie Baptista is the central figure in O'Bryan's study. One of his book's main themes is this tension, as epitomized in Croke's life, between the call to be a lay apostle and the call to canonical religious life. "Seeds of information gathered from the fields of Cenacle tradition," O'Bryan writes, "seemingly infer Amy Marie Croke, as Sister Baptista, never quite fit the structured religious mold of the Inner Cenacle" (*Awake the Giant*, 328). He reflects most explicitly on this theme in the epilogue.

Monsignor Noll went on to become bishop of Fort Wayne, Indiana, in 1925. More committed than Father Judge to the trend toward national consolidation in the Catholic Church following upon the Great War, he helped to found the Catholic Press Association and the Legion of Decency. He was a member of the Board of Catholic Missions for twenty-five years and a member of the National Catholic Welfare Council/Conference Executive Committee.[9] The cooperation and exchange between Judge and Noll and their eventual separation highlights the distinctiveness of Father Judge's approach. Their collaboration lasted for about a year, from spring 1921, when Sister Baptista visited Huntington, until the following spring, when Judge last wrote to Noll on April 3, 1922. Both were capable priests, zealous for the faith, but their approaches to preserving and propagating it proved incompatible.

Father Judge was initially so impressed with Sister Baptista's account of her visit with Monsignor Noll that, in July 1921, he went to see Noll himself. His first visit to Noll was part of a trip he described as a six-day "swing from New York to Pittsburgh, Pittsburgh to Huntingdon [*sic*], Ind., Huntingdon to Chicago, Chicago to Rockford, Ill., Rockford back to Chicago, Chicago to Pittsburgh, Pittsburgh to Brooklyn."[10] He spent July 30 with Noll in Huntington and at the cathedral in Fort Wayne. He described their conversations as "exceedingly interesting and profitable." He was so enthused about it that on his way to Rockford he wrote a nine-point summary of "some points and views" of Noll to be a subject of "council" in the cenacles.

Noll wanted the Cenacle to come to southern Indiana, "the center of the population of the U.S.," and "start a Training School to develop vocations of young men and women for our Bros. and Sisters." As a source of revenue and an access to a national readership, Noll's mass-circulation paper would be a major resource. The school would be a joint venture among Judge and the Cenacle, Noll, and neighboring pastors. The proposal involved two hundred acres of land owned by the paper on which there would eventually be a normal school "to train our own teachers" and a hospital to "train our own nurses, men & women." He went on to explain that a board of three trustees, and not the diocese, controlled the paper. One of the three trustees would always be from the Cenacle, "a truly remarkable concession." The paper

9. On Noll, see the entry by Thomas T. McAvoy in *New Catholic Encyclopedia* (2003), 10, 410, and the entries by Owen Campion on Noll and on *Our Sunday Visitor*, in *Encyclopedia of American Catholic History*, 1052, 1079–80; see also Joseph M. White, *Worthy of the Gospel of Christ: A History of the Catholic Diocese of Fort-Wayne–South Bend* (Fort Wayne, Ind.: Diocese of Fort Wayne–South Bend, 2007), chaps. 10 and 11.

10. Judge to Sister Mary James Collins, Brooklyn, N.Y., August 3, 1921, AST, MF 5068.

would generate the donations needed "for the up keep and development of the work, building, institution, etc."

At the end of his summary, Father Judge wrote that he had "not yet been able to give this matter the prayerful consideration that it deserves, that I would wish." He instructed the recipients, "Do prayerfully think over this: read it to Cenacle for night prayer, meditate on it then hold a Council and let me know what Counsil [*sic*] says. I would let all in on this Council."[11] Noll had potential institutional resources in southern Indiana. Judge had independent and resourceful apostolic women like Sister Marie Baptista. Noll's long-term proposal never materialized.

In the meantime, however, Monsignor Noll proved a benefactor to the Cenacle. Describing Sister Baptista's spring trip in a circular letter, Father Judge identified Noll as "another well-known figure in the Church in the U.S.," whose paper "has the largest circulation of any Catholic paper in the world." He spoke of his note of thanks to Noll for his hospitality to Sr. Baptista in which he asked for help in recruiting teachers for the high school at Holy Trinity. Noll printed his note. The immediate response, which included one teacher and a priest for Holy Trinity, made a tremendous impression on Judge. "Fr. Noll, on his part also," Judge concluded, "has a desire: He wishes to place paper back of Cenacle, to welcome Brothers and Sisters; to open Schools, Colleges, etc. We cannot sufficiently thank God for the good will of these fine Churchmen [he included Bishop Muldoon of Rockford]." He urged them to keep this desire of Noll's in confidence.

With the brothers' legal incorporation and the expansion of the movement, priests for the Cenacle were much on Father Judge's mind. "So beautifully has God ordained his providence over the Cenacle," he wrote in his fall circular letter, "there has been a marvelously harmonious progression." He now looked forward to seeing "a number of generous hearted boys, young men, trained in Cenacle spirit, elevated to the Priesthood."[12] We have already seen his unsuccessful request to the Vincentian visitor regarding such training. Noll encouraged Judge's attempts, first in Philadelphia and later in Newark, to establish an "Apostolic College" or seminary high school in the North.

Father Judge returned to Huntington in late September and stayed for about a week. He gave a series of retreats at St. Mary's Church, Noll's parish, beginning on September 25, and reported to Father McHale at the end

11. July 1921, on the way to Rockford, Ill., AST, MF 5049–54.

12. "Continuation of Summer Trip," fall 1921 circular letter to Cenacles, AST, MF 5066–67.

of the year that he had started an Outer Cenacle there and that "further plans were entered into for the establishment of a training school for our work as a Western branch." While in Huntington, Judge wrote, at Noll's urging, to Monsignor Francis C. Kelley of the Catholic Extension Society to gain support for the training of young men for home missions. Judge reported to McHale that Kelley sent a telegram to Huntington urging him to come to the extension offices in Chicago "at once." Fall enrollment at St. Patrick's in Phenix City necessitated some expansion, and Judge told McHale of Noll's generosity in supporting it. "Father Noll kindly sent down the money to defray expenses of painting and roofing. He is also to put in for us one hundred extra desks. This will cost $1,000, at least."[13]

Correspondence leading up to the September retreat indicates that Father Judge was promising Noll five or six nursing sisters to begin with, cautioning that "we will have to take the time to adjust the personnel of the different mission." Noll was to start a campaign in mid-September in the *Sunday Visitor* "for young men and women to surrender two or three years of service to God, and the Appeal of our Brothers for maintenance." He enclosed copies of his correspondence with Cardinal Dougherty about an apostolic college and asked Noll to share his "Mailing List." He added that "we are sending three boys to College," as the opening of the apostolic college may be delayed. "So again, Dear Father," he concluded, "do help us out as much as you can. Depend upon it, we are going to do all we can to help you."[14] On October 23, Noll ran the brothers' appeal in the *Sunday Visitor.*[15] No nursing sisters were sent to Huntington.

Like many pastors and bishops before and after him, Monsignor Noll was taken with the apostolic energy and can-do mobility of the women known as Missionary Servants of the Most Blessed Trinity. Not only did he want to get them into southern Indiana, but, if he was going to be working with them, he was also concerned for their development. In November he wrote pressing Judge on the need for a written rule of life and questioning why there was not an age limit on who could enter. Judge thanked him for his "kind and timely advice" but did not yield on the questions of rule and age limit.

His response reveals much about how he understood the emerging reli-

13. Judge to McHale, Orange, N.J., December 3, 1921, AST, MF 5120–22; see also Judge to Rev. Msgr. Francis C. Kelley, Huntington, Ind., September 27, 1921, AST, MF 5078–79.

14. Judge to Noll, Cottonton, September 2, 1921, AST, MF 5075; Judge to Noll, Cottonton, September 1, 1921, AST, MF 5074.

15. For a copy, see AST, MF 5143.

gious community. He told Noll that constitutions, "the ends of their religious life and the good works to which they apply themselves," were already written. But the rule was as yet unwritten. "They have their rule, as the early Church had its tradition . . . they are living their rule." Since they were such a young community, "with their mission demanding such latitude, requiring such adaptability to persons and seasons and circumstances," Judge feared that borrowing "points of rule" from established communities "might make the life work of the Missionary Servants of the Most Blessed Trinity almost impossible." He asked if it might not be wiser, "while safeguarding their spiritual life, to notice the events of their day and try to guide all so that there will be harmony between their spiritual striving and the works of fraternal charity that are such a crying need today?" Rather than writing a rule for which circumstances would force changes—"I just dread the thought," he told Noll—he proposed a different approach: "to pray to the Holy Ghost in the matter that He may sweetly order all things unto His end."

He went on to describe the Cenacle practice of frequent "council" and reported on the upcoming first general assembly. Since so much discussion and prayer to the Holy Ghost had preceded this assembly, he felt confident "that the final decisions of the general assembly will be an expression of the will of God on certain matters and this decision will be a rule."

Father Judge's reluctance to fix an age limit for entrance into the women's community revealed much about a system of reckoning that Noll eventually found too impractical. He began by noting that, at a time when other communities complained of "lack of vocations, we are impressed by the number streaming towards the Cenacle." He described them as the "young and vigorous . . . the flower of the flock, 'lilies of the valley.'" He found the presence of older sisters a possible explanation for this blessing in "that these older friends of God, yes let us say even ancient friends of God, are souls very dear to Him because they have fought the good fight." Many were "hindered by the Fourth Commandment from giving themselves to God in religion." He told Noll that it was hard to refuse their gift, "for I cannot be certain that the Holy Ghost has not impelled them to offer it at the door of the Cenacle, and who am I that I should refuse?"

Most reasons for refusing them represented "a human way of deciding against them" that Father Judge feared would "shut out many spiritual reasons for taking them." This response poignantly illustrates his approach to issues that many regard as "practical." In this letter, he called it "spiritual thought." "I have many reasons," he assured Noll, "to presume that they are very dear to God, and it is not a violent stretch of spiritual thought to think that such may be sent as a benediction." In the matter of preparation for those who do catechetical work or teach in school, he reported that the sisters' emerging rule called for "a five year course of several hours a week." He concluded by appealing to the fact that the Missionary Servants were only in their beginning.[16]

In the meantime, the "tribal twenties" had erupted in Alabama. Incensed that the priest had performed a wedding joining his daughter to a Catholic, an irate Alabama father shot Father Coyle, the pastor of St. Paul's Church in Birmingham, as he sat on the rectory porch. The following Sunday, Father Judge preached at St. Patrick's in Phenix City. Even as he prayed for Father Coyle's soul, Judge eulogized him as one of the "glorious procession" of Christian martyrs. "Had it been my grace to have been at his side in that terrible moment," said Judge, "I would have as reverently sponged up his blood as the early Christians sponged up the blood of St. Lawrence, St. Agnes or any of the victorious martyrs of the church."[17] In Phenix City, the Ku Klux Klan started a campaign to intimidate local parents into taking their children out of St. Patrick's School and to threaten the sisters. Judge urged them to continue to "watch and pray" in their nocturnal adoration of the Blessed Sacrament but also to make prudent preparations and have fire extinguishers available.[18]

The situation at St. Patrick's, home to twenty sisters, occasioned Father Judge's next exchange with Monsignor Noll, who apparently wanted the sisters to leave Alabama and relocate. In his twelve-point reply, a two-page argument for the sisters staying in Alabama, Judge again thanked Noll for his "very sensible suggestions." Though he understood Noll's perspective, the Alabama mission had special features that "you will understand better when you come here." Though Judge had been to Huntington twice, this was the first mention of a visit by Noll to Alabama. Judge argued that the sisters

16. Judge to Noll, Orange, N.J., November 23, 1921, AST, MF 05101–3.

17. On Judge's sermon, see the account in the *Columbus Ledger*, August 15, 1921, from a copy in AST, MF 5141. On Father Coyle's murder, see Collins, "Voice from the Past," *Holy Ghost*, September 1950, 5. "By giving Catholics opportunity for organization and influence, the war exacerbated anti-Catholic sentiments and encouraged nativist organization"; Dumenil, "Tribal Twenties," 23.

18. "Again understand, I do not believe that this lawless and unchristian element will go to extremes but the experience of being prepared will serve many useful purposes and if they do their worst to cripple you and drive you out of town, you will be ready at least to leave with your clothes on"; Judge to My dear Children [sisters at St. Patrick's], Orange, N.J., December 3, 1921, AST, MF 9461; see Collins, "Voice from the Past," *Holy Ghost*, September 1950, 6.

had taught 1,500 children in six years and were "very deeply in the affection and respect and good-will of the towns' people." He attributed the campaign against the school to "the preachers and some of the political candidates."

Father Judge responded to Noll in the idiom of what he had earlier called "spiritual thought." Recalling the suffering and prayer that had gone into the mission in Phenix City, and addressing Noll as "Dear Monsignor," Judge wrote, "I cannot bring myself to believe it is the will of God for us to leave this place, which is to us hallowed by so many sacred memories." Finally, he urged that even if conditions in Phenix City worsened to the extent that the "blood of the martyrs may flow," this would be "no small grace." In fact, he found it "a most alluring reason for our staying, for you know the blood of the martyrs is the seed of Christianity."

In closing, Father Judge told Noll, with reference to responses from the publicity Noll had given the Cenacle in *Our Sunday Visitor*, "the letter supply is shut off." But he noted that, from those letters, they had "a most edifying priest, Fr. John F. Boyle, a remarkable male teacher, Edward Martis, three or four who are persevering in their correspondence (men) and several women."[19] As 1921 drew to a close, Judge reported in a letter to Father McHale on his cooperation with Noll as well as Cenacle expansion in the East and the Midwest.[20]

Father Judge and Monsignor Noll continued to collaborate into 1922. Noll was anxious to visit the mission in Phenix City and the plantation at Holy Trinity Station in Cottonton. Early in the year, Judge explained that, since he gave the retreat in Huntington, he had been at various tasks in the North. He had not returned to Holy Trinity even for Christmas. "I will be glad to let you know," he wrote, "when I am about to fall southwards." He also informed Noll that "the matter of which you made mention in the letter I will have put before the council." What the matter was is not clear from the context. He also reported on two conversations with Peter J. O'Callaghan, CSP, of the American Board of Catholic Missions, a program of the bishops' conference with which Noll was involved and that would centralize mission funds un-

19. Judge to Noll, Orange, N.J., December 19, 1921, AST, MF 9467–68; on Fr. Boyle, see Judge to Rt. Rev. John F. Boyle, Orange, N.J., December 19, 1921, AST, MF 9470. On Martis, whose name is sometimes spelled "Martus," see Judge to McHale, Orange, N.J., December 3, 1921, AST, MF 5120.

20. Judge to McHale, Orange, N.J., December 3, 1921, AST, MF 5120–22. Other drafts are at MF 9455–56 (dated December 1) and MF 7488. The earlier drafts were probably in the papers of different sisters to whom Judge dictated his correspondence while at Orange in early December. Together the three drafts give a fuller picture of the growth of the Cenacle during 1921.

der the control of the hierarchy, of obvious interest to Judge, but that did not get up and running until 1926.[21]

Sometime in March, Monsignor Noll finally came to Alabama. He and Father Judge traveled as far as New Orleans.[22] Noll surveyed the work and activities at both Holy Trinity and St. Patrick's in Phenix City. "The simplicity of the life won his admiration but his keen business sense made him alive to its shortcomings." Though his interest in the work "won the hearts of all," Noll remained convinced that the sisters should move out of Alabama. Upon his return, he wrote to Judge that, "unless the Holy Ghost is guiding you, I believe your Sisterhood should be established up north."[23]

Upon his return to Indiana, Noll raised three objections to Judge regarding the sisters' work in Alabama. First, he thought there were too many sisters tied up in St. Patrick's School in Phenix City. Second, he thought the Cenacle had too much land in Alabama. Third, and most important, Noll thought that too much effort and money was being expended in Alabama, where there was little hope of spreading the faith to any significant degree.

Father Judge's response begins with a report on the Klan's latest efforts to intimidate the sisters in Phenix City. In March, probably shortly after Noll's departure, flagpoles on the sisters' property were vandalized and the U.S. flag torn and left in knots on the ground. The vandals had warned the sisters in a letter to remove the crosses from the poles or stop flying the flag. Newspaper reports attributed this to the "work of ignorant persons who have been inflamed against Catholics by reading the 'Searchlight' organ of the Ku Klux Klan and other anti-Catholic publications.[24] "The midnight visit," Judge wrote to Noll," broke *in odorem suavitatis* for a national edification . . . a great wave of sympathy has spread because of the objects of this violence, the Cross, the Flag, the Sisters to whom Phoenix [*sic*] owes so much." Then he got down to business.

21. Judge to Noll, Orange, N.J., January 5, 1922, AST, MF 5163. On the American Board of Catholic Missions, see Angelyn Dries, OSF, *The Missionary Movement in American Catholic History* (Maryknoll, N.Y.: Orbis, 1998), 92–95.

22. Judge to "My dear Children," a circular letter, Cottonton, October 31, 1922, AST, MF 3740–43, recalling "a trip that Msgr. Noll and myself made last spring to New Orleans."

23. Collins, "Voice from the Past," *Holy Ghost*, September 1950, 9. All the quotations in this paragraph are from Sr. Mary James's account of Noll's visit. She doesn't reference her citation of Noll's letter.

24. "Alabama Bigots Desecrate Crosses," *Catholic Transcript*, March 23, 1922, front page, citing reports from the Columbus *Enquirer*; from a copy in AST, MF 705; see also Judge to Michael J. Slattery, Cottonton, March 23, 1922, AST, MF 5144–45. Slattery was a staffer at the National Catholic Welfare Council in Washington, D.C., who had written to Judge after the incident received some national attention.

First, he cleared up, with an entire single-spaced page explaining that only ten of the twenty sisters taught and that their average class size was forty, a "misunderstanding regarding the employment of the Sisters at Phoenix [*sic*]." "Monsignor, please God, we are building for the future," he told Noll with regard to the land. It would be the "site of the Mother House of two Communities." He reminded Noll that, five years ago, Cottonton had only one Catholic. "You saw nearly a hundred." In twenty-five or thirty years, he asked, wouldn't the clergy say "the pioneer Catholics of Holy Trinity Station were wise in their generation and that 'they builded better than they know'?"

Father Judge reserved his strongest words for his response to Noll's third point. Judge called it the "general thought or action of the Church regarding the spread of the Faith." Thinking perhaps of Blessed John Gabriel Perboyre, he reminded Noll of the example of China. "Think of the martyrs, think of the untold sums of money poured into that country to bring it to the Feet of Christ. Think of the early missionary days in our own country." Here Judge's "spiritual thought" is on full display:

> Monsignor, does it not seem a little strange to think that money or health or life itself should be considered in any work for the advancement of Christ's Kingdom? Would not the Fathers of the Church, would not the Confessors of Christ, would not the Martyrs, would not the Apostles, would not the early days of Christianity, with its story of blood, cry out against us in condemnation if we make the expenditure of a few dollars, a little lack of comfort, with absence of any present advancement, a reason for beating a retreat?[25]

He concluded with the need for prayer. The Cenacle's first historian, Sister Mary James, spoke of Noll's "keen business sense." Noll's precise response to this letter is unknown. But clearly he wanted Cenacle workers for Indiana, and Judge was not providing them. After he became bishop of Fort Wayne in 1925, Noll built a motherhouse outside of Huntington for the Missionary Catechists of Our Lady of Victory.

As collaboration between these two churchmen of the 1920s came to an

25. Judge to Noll, Cottonton, April 3, 1922, AST, MF 5189–92. In commenting on these lines and the letter's conclusion, Sister Mary James gave classic articulation to the image of Father Judge as a heroic founder. She found in this letter's conclusion his answer to critics "who could not understand the ideas, the spirit, the guiding principle which animated and literally forced him to carry on in spite of criticism and the censure of friend as well as foe. Pioneers must be valiant souls aflame with love of their mission but with wills of steel not to be swerved from their path as they see it. Thus the Holy Ghost must have guided Father Judge in these difficult days—these and later ones"; "Voice from the Past," *Holy Ghost*, September 1950, 9. Noll and later Bishop Toolen of Mobile and Archbishop Curley of Baltimore saw it differently.

end, Father Judge set his face against the national tendency in the church to "regularize, systematize, and centralize."[26] The mission in Phenix City would continue. Though both motherhouses had to move before Judge's death, Holy Trinity remained the Bethlehem of the Missionary Servants, both women and men. As Father Judge sought to respond to the church's needs, the Cenacle continued to expand in what many, sometimes including Mother Boniface, saw as a haphazard and not always financially responsible way.

Catholic Charities

Development of the National Conference of Catholic Charities

With Catholic immigrants swelling prisons and becoming likely recipients of public assistance in the late nineteenth century, the church, especially in urban centers of the Northeast and Midwest, had a strong interest in what, during the Progressive Era, was coming to be called "social welfare," especially in the care of children. Catholics performed works of mercy largely through local parish organizations such as St. Vincent de Paul Societies. For practicality and efficiency, the Progressive impulse streamlined and centralized approaches to social problems.

Jane Addams (1860–1935) symbolized scientific social work in the Progressive Era. She cofounded Hull House, a Chicago settlement house, in 1889. Its programs to Americanize Italian immigrants in Chicago's Nineteenth Ward often worked to de-Catholicize them. When in 1914 Hull House advertised a play about Giordano Bruno entitled, "The Philosopher of Nola and the Victim of the Infamy of the Catholic Church," an *America* writer denounced "The Perversion of Hull House" and asked how Jane Addams would feel if a Catholic settlement house placarded a discussion of "Hull House, the Home of Stupid Bigots, the Centre of Hatred Toward Christian Charity, the Cause of Strife Among Christian Citizens."[27] Catholics chafed at Addams's notoriety, judging her contributions minimal compared to those of both past and present Catholic women, many of whom were religious sisters.[28]

26. Dries, *Missionary Movement in American Catholic History*, 42. See Blackwell's comments on Noll's plans as not "conformable to the spirit of the Cenacle so much as it was the basis for a diocesan religious institute"; *Ecclesial People*, 108n357, relying on a 1973 interview with Sister Mary Francis Taylor.

27. "The Perversion of Hull House," *America* 10, no. 24 (March 21, 1914), 567.

28. Kathleen Sprows Cummings, *New Women of the Old Faith: Gender and American Catholicism in the Progressive Era* (Chapel Hill: University of North Carolina Press, 2009), 13, 200n24.

By the decade of the Great War, local Catholic volunteer organizations faced the professionalization of charity in social work, increased governmental regulation at various levels, and the influence of federated organizations such as community chests. Along with progressive reforms came religious campaigns to Americanize Italian immigrants. In places like East Orange, New Jersey, and Brooklyn, New York, Cenacle associates worked to thwart such campaigns.[29] The church at large responded with its own versions of professionalization and centralization. Even as Catholics adapted to these trends, they resisted by surrounding their efforts with the supernatural overtones of the name "Catholic Charities." They located themselves and their social welfare work in a long history of saints and religious, especially women, who ministered to children, the sick, and the poor.[30]

Members of the St. Vincent de Paul Societies attended the 1909 White House Conference on the Care of Dependent Children. What they saw inspired them in 1910 to begin the National Conference of Catholic Charities (NCCC), with William J. Kerby, chair of Catholic University's Sociology Department, as executive secretary. Kerby worked closely with lay volunteers, males from the St. Vincent de Paul Societies and lay women from various local charitable organizations. Catholic University's John A. Ryan, who had published *The Living Wage* in 1906, founded the *Catholic Charities Review* in 1917 and edited it until 1921. The National Conference of Catholic Charities, dedicated to incorporating the insights of professional social work into local Catholic charity organizations, held its first annual meeting at Catholic University in 1910.[31]

29. On the "Italian question" during the second decade of the twentieth century, see the ten-month debate on the topic in the pages of *America* for 1914. It began with an article by D. J. Lynch, SJ, "The Religious Condition of Italians in New York," *America* 10, no. 24 (March 21, 1914): 558–59 and ended by editorial fiat in *America* 12, no. 10 (December 19, 1914): 246. This is an unsigned editorial in *America*. The blog-like exchanges and comments, in both articles and letters to the editor, offer a thick sense of the issues in debates over the "Italian question." In addition to cultivating the faith of the immigrants and helping them to feel a part of the church, one of the editor's chief concerns as he pronounced the controversy closed was "for safeguarding them from proselytizers." The *Ecclesiastical Review* also ran a spate of articles on the Italian question. One of the best was Joseph McSorley, CSP, "The Church and the Italian Child," *Ecclesiastical Review* 48 (1913): 268–82. McSorley spoke fluent Italian and worked among the immigrants in the area around St. Paul's Church at 59th Street and 9th Avenue in Manhattan.

30. Mary Elizabeth Walsh, *The Saints and Social Work* (Silver Spring, Md.: Preservation of the Faith Press, 1937).

31. Most of the information in this section is taken from Dorothy M. Brown and Elizabeth McKeown, *The Poor Belong to Us: Catholic Charities and American Welfare* (Cambridge, Mass., and London: Harvard University Press, 1997), chap. 2, "The Larger Landscape"; see also Anne

Diocesan Catholic Charities

Between 1910 and 1916, Cardinal William O'Connell organized Boston's Catholic Charities Bureau under the direction of Fr. George P. O'Connor. Brooklyn had been organized since 1899. Diocesan charities bureaus soon appeared in other urban centers such as Pittsburgh and Philadelphia. By 1920 Missionary Servants of the Most Blessed Trinity worked in each of these bureaus under priest diocesan directors such as Fathers Francis X. Wastl in Philadelphia and O'Connor in Boston and Monsignor O'Hara in Brooklyn.[32]

By 1920, as well, Father John O'Grady (1886–1966) of Catholic University had succeeded his mentor, William J. Kerby, as executive secretary of the NCCC. He succeeded Ryan as editor of the *Catholic Charities Review* in 1921, holding both posts for the next forty years. Under O'Grady's leadership, the priest diocesan directors began to replace lay volunteers in running the NCCC.[33] Against this backdrop, Father Judge attended the annual meeting of the NCCC in Washington in September 1922. Father O'Grady and diocesan directors came to see Judge's mobile and resourceful "garb sisters" as highly desirable alternatives to, on the one hand, independent lay volunteers and organizations and, on the other, professionally trained lay Catholic social workers.

Catholic objections to professional social work were more than a question of turf. Father Wastl's experience as a Catholic chaplain at a public almshouse fueled his suspicion of "scientific" social work. He feared that its techniques allowed social workers to engage in voyeurism over the sexual behavior of their clients and gave them "an unwelcome degree of control over the lives of the poor."[34] The sisters' heroic witness to faith and charity endeared them both to the people they served in various diocesan bureaus

Simpson, "Catholic Charities USA," in *The New Dictionary of Catholic Social Thought*, ed. Judith A. Dwyer (Collegeville, Minn.: Liturgical Press, 1994), 123–24. John O'Grady, *Catholic Charities in the United States: History and Problems* (Washington, D.C.: National Conference of Catholic Charities, 1930) is a contemporary account by a participant in Catholic Charities' origin and early history; see also J. Bryan Hehir, ed., *Catholic Charities USA: 100 Years at the Intersection of Charity and Justice* (Collegeville, Minn.: Liturgical Press, 2010), especially chaps. 4 and 5, written by sisters Ann Patrick Conrad and M. Vincentia Joseph, both social workers and former Missionary Servants of the Most Blessed Trinity.

32. Gallaher, "Social Work of the Missionary Servants," especially chap. 5, on Diocesan Bureaus of Charity.

33. On O'Grady, see Thomas W. Tifft's entry in *Encyclopedia of American Catholic History*, 1079–80, and Brown and McKeown, *Poor Belong to Us*, chap. 2, esp. 64–65, 74–75, 82–83; see also Tifft, "Toward a More Humane Social Policy: The Work and Influence of Monsignor John O'Grady" (Ph.D. diss., The Catholic University of America, 1979).

34. Brown and McKeown, *Poor Belong to Us*, 74.

and to the bishops and diocesan directors. Their arrival coincided with an emerging consensus among Catholics that new social scientific methods, if joined to a supernatural perspective on human nature and ends, could be helpful in charity work.[35]

Father Judge's Critique of Professional Social Work

From years of dealing with such issues as the "Italian question," Father Judge shared Father Wastl's distrust of the "naturalism," the exclusion of supernatural motives and perspectives, characteristic of contemporary approaches to social problems. In a conference urging "purity of intention" and supernatural motives for good works, Judge invoked St. Paul's admonition, "Whether you eat or drink or whatever else you do, do it all for the glory of God (1 Cor 10:31)." He recalled Christ's indictment of the Pharisees' "hypocrisy, and cant, and snobbishness, and self-seeking." Warming to his topic, Judge warned of "some today masking under the title of social service worker." He numbered among them even "certain Catholic men and women who are really a hindrance and drag on charitable endeavor."

> It may be that they have attended a sociological school, or have taken a Correspondence Course in sociology, or have been identified in some welfare work—and because they have a diploma—one listening to their chattering would imagine they were going to reform the world. What is the basis of their effort? Their own cleverness. In whom do they trust? Themselves. What is their hope and inspiration and strength? The schools, the societies, the methods with which they have been associated. They ignore prayer. The Sacraments and other helps of religion they minimize. Supernatural light and help, it seems, has been entirely omitted in their schooling.

Such "naturalism," according to Judge, made them "harsh towards the unfortunate, unforgiving and unmerciful towards the weak." Their work cannot rise above the "level of a philanthropist, a social or welfare worker."

> These speak fluently of card systems, and bureau methods, survey, community and settlement houses, welfare work, but never do they bring a message to a poor, tired, sin distressed soul, of the hope of forgiveness. The Confessional, the Holy Communion rail, Prayer, a Saviour who has suffered and died for the miserable and Who is now waiting for the repentant sinner—all remain unmentioned.

35. Thomas E. Woods Jr., *The Church Confronts Modernity: Catholic Intellectuals and the Progressive Era* (New York: Columbia University Press, 2004), chap. 3, "Sociology and the Study of Man," esp. on scientific social work, at 68–78.

He went on to speak of those who "are keen to search" the backgrounds of their clients, "even to a remote generation" to determine they if they are "worthy" of help. Such information, "carefully indexed and stowed away," is nothing but "professional gossip, to be passed from one Social center to another." "It matters little," Judge argued, "whether the subjects are worthy or unworthy." Such "gossip" he pronounced as "hideous, a most despicable species of dishonor." "It is bad enough to patronize the poor and to insult them but to make known their misfortune seems to be extremely cruel." He urged the sisters to whom this conference was addressed to take care lest they "come under the scathing rebuke" Christ administered to the Pharisees. To be "truly godly in your good works," he commended to them St. Paul's warning to do all for the glory of God.[36]

Father Judge's critique of secular social work echoed those of many Catholics at the time. Paul Blakely, SJ, warned that the "modern social worker constitutes a greater danger to faith and morals, than godless schools or the despicable ever-present proselytizer."[37] Blakely taught at Fordham University's School of Social Service, begun in 1916. At Catholic University, William Kerby would have been less openly hostile in his remarks about modern social workers but insisted with Blakely on separating scientific methods of social work from modern naturalistic assumptions that excluded the supernatural. If Blakely and Kerby stood at either end of a spectrum of Catholic opinion on social work, Judge's tone seems closer to Blakely's. The sisters' practice seems closer to Kerby.[38]

National Catholic Charities Convention, 1922

In 1920 the NCCC annual meeting created a special section for women religious engaged in charity work.[39] In 1921 Sister Mary James Collins and

36. These citations are taken from an untitled conference whose header is, "Whether you eat or drink or whatever else you do, do it all for the glory of God." It is undated but probably from around 1921 or 1922. The word *naturalism* appears twice; see AST, MF 5290–91.

37. Paul Blakely, SJ, "The Catholic Charities and the Strong Commission," *America* 15 (May 16, 1916): 78.

38. See Woods's contrast of the "skeptical, confrontational Blakely" and the "apostle of scientific charity, William Kerby" and his simultaneous emphasis on their common agreement on the supernatural end of charity; Woods, *Church Confronts Modernity*, 82. The quote from Blakely in note 32 of this chapter is at 80.

39. Brown and McKeown, *Poor Belong to Us*, 62. They describe "religious communities of women involved in charities" as "virtually absent from Conference meetings" until the creation of this section in 1920. See also John O'Grady, *An Introduction to Social Work* (New York and London: Century, 1928), chaps. 14–15, "The Church and Social Work," esp. 313–15.

Sister Mary Francis Taylor traveled from Holy Trinity, Alabama, to Milwaukee to attend the NCCC meeting.[40] The following year, Father Judge himself attended the annual meeting in Washington, D.C. Father John Loftus, a Hartford priest who had been released by Bishop John Nilan to join the Cenacle, accompanied him. Loftus soon arrived at Holy Trinity to head the League of the Holy Ghost and begin the *Holy Ghost* magazine.[41] From Brooklyn, Judge reported to Mother Boniface that he was "astonished at the kindly reception I received on all sides. . . . I met so many eminent priests, leaders of the Charity work in the United States." The work of the Cenacle was apparently well known in Catholic Charities circles.

Among the priests Father Judge met in Washington were the Sulpician rector of Theological College, probably Anthony Vieban, SS, who invited him to stay at Theological College whenever he was in Washington; George P. O'Connor, director of Catholic Charities in Boston whom Judge had not seen in fifteen years; and John O'Grady, who was successful in interesting Judge in Negro work in Washington, D.C. Judge's subsequent travel to Brooklyn and Philadelphia suggests that he was also in contact with charities leaders from those two dioceses, as well. Judge pronounced the "two outstanding features of the Convention" to be the sections devoted to "Italian and Negro work." The former "proved to be the most enthusiastic." He commented at length on the section devoted to Negro work:

> The Negro assembly was well attended by a very representative gathering. There were a few colored Catholics evidently well instructed, one a college professor made a plea for his people's interests and a young colored school teacher, to my mind, made one of the speeches of the convention, calling upon us for equal opportunity. It seems to me that the Negro problem is going to become a burning question and if we do not solve it, great loss will come to the Church in the U.S.[42]

The well-instructed "college professor" Judge described as making "a plea for his people's interests" was probably Thomas Wyatt Turner (1877–1978), a biologist, teaching at Howard University. Since 1915 Turner had been active in the NAACP in the Baltimore-Washington region and in 1924 founded the

40. Collins, "Voice from the Past," *Holy Ghost*, June 1950, 8.

41. See Judge to Mother Boniface Keasey, Gillette, N.J., October 1, 1922, AST, MF 7547. In this letter, Judge asks Mother Boniface to arrange everything to Loftus's satisfaction for his arrival at Holy Trinity. As this letter suggests, Loftus proved a high-maintenance individual, demanding and unstable. His association with the Cenacle lasted only six years.

42. Judge to Mother Boniface Keasey, Brooklyn, September 21, 1922, AST, MF 7540–42.

Federated Colored Catholics to advocate for the rights of Black Catholics in the church.[43]

Judge reported to Mother Boniface that at the convention the Negro question was "committed to the fostering care of social workers." He wondered "how much longer the professional social worker will be in evidence in Catholic works" and hazarded the opinion that "their glory has reached its zenith." Precisely as charity workers mindful of the supernatural dimension of their work, the sisters promised a welcome alternative to the "professional social worker" for Judge, the diocesan directors he met at the conference, and other Catholic critics of professional social work.

With John O'Grady Father Judge discussed the possibility of the Cenacle coming to Washington and hit upon a plan to help with Negro work in the city. Judge told O'Grady "that the evangelization of the Negro must come from themselves." He suggested a plan to train leaders for such a work: "a half dozen of our Sisters ... training 30 or 50 young women, they being indoctrinated in Cenacle methods, start[ing] off in missionary neighborhoods, 30 more could take their place, and 30 more after them and all of these would be leaders." He envisioned the sisters in a supervisory capacity with the Negro cenacle having its own community and officers. He reported that this plan had found "high favor," especially with Archbishop Curley of Baltimore, at that time still the ordinary of Washington.[44]

To Brooklyn and Philadelphia

From the Catholic Charities convention in Washington, Father Judge traveled to Brooklyn, where he spent a week on concerns related to the Dr. White Memorial settlement at 183 Gold St. Monsignor William J. White served as the first director of Catholic Charities in Brooklyn from 1899 until his death in 1911. The house at Gold Street continued settlement work begun by Monsignor White in 1903. Lay Cenacle associates took over the work there in 1918. The house was in the Navy Yard district of Brooklyn within a few blocks of the waterfront. By the time of Judge's visit to Brooklyn in fall 1922,

43. On Turner, see Joseph Quinn's entry in *Encyclopedia of American Catholic History*, 1401–2.

44. Judge to Mother Boniface Keasey, Brooklyn, September 21, 1922, AST, MF 7540–42. Judge added that, when Archbishop Curley was in Europe, he called at the Vincentian generalate, then in Paris, and spoke "very freely" to Father McHale "of affairs in this Province of the CM's." According to Judge, Curley "spoke of our work, its necessity and the necessity of our confreres getting behind it. He said that on all sides otherwise we are getting help." Judge sent a nearly identical report of the convention to Brother Augustine; see AST, MF 718–19.

the sisters at the Dr. White Memorial ministered to children of Italian, Lithuanian, and Spanish-speaking, often Puerto Rican, immigrants who would not ordinarily be reached by parish ministry. They did home visiting and referral work, taught catechism, and sponsored a medical clinic.[45]

In the fall of 1922, Father Judge worked for increased support from the diocese for the sisters' work at the Gold Street settlement. To this end he discussed the "house report" with the diocesan director of charities, Monsignor O'Hara. In 1922 the settlement house ministered to 13,000 children. "This," he told O'Hara, "was accomplished by a few sisters and twenty or twenty-five of their friends." He was scheduled to give a retreat in Brooklyn on December 8 and hoped to recruit enough lay volunteers to increase the number of volunteers to between fifty and one hundred. He confided to Mother Boniface that he expected the settlement house sisters "to touch 100,000 children" in the coming year.[46]

Despite an impressive house report and projections for future success, Father Judge insisted to O'Hara that such work was not "the ulterior purpose of the Cenacle." Rather, they were to reach "the thousands and thousands of good-hearted souls" in the Brooklyn diocese, "leading lives of passive catholicity." The work of the Cenacle is to make them zealous and draw out their service as an agency for good. He told O'Hara "that the purpose of our Sisters is to train the work-a-day man and woman into an apostle, to cause each to be alert to the interests of the Church, to be the Church, and that here lies in a very large way the solution of all the Church's problems." He hoped that the success of the Gold Street settlement and its "prodigious volume," rather than setting records or "instituting flattering comparisons to our own work," would demonstrate what he called "a bed-rock Cenacle principle. Go to the laity. Seek the laity in your need."[47]

45. On the Dr. White Memorial settlement, see Gallaher, "Social Work of the Missionary Servants," 41–48. Monsignor O'Grady singled out the Missionary Servants as the new community "which has stood out most in Catholic settlement work in the United States," giving special attention to their work at the Dr. White Memorial Settlement House in Brooklyn. According to O'Grady in 1930, its programs included "kindergarten, summer camps, sewing clubs, mothers' clubs, working boys' clubs, and classes in industrial arts, Spanish, first aid, catechism, domestic science and home making"; O'Grady, *Catholic Charities in the United States*, 306. Another contemporary study described the sisters' social outreach work and encouragement and training of lay apostles and credited them with "using the best methods and technique of modern charity and mission science"; see John J. Harbrecht, *The Lay Apostolate: A Social Ethical Study of Parish Charity Organization for Large City Parishes* (St. Louis: B. Herder, 1929), 381.

46. Judge to Mother Boniface Keasey, Brooklyn, September 28, 1922, AST, MF 7545–46.

47. Ibid. Sister Mary Anna came in for special praise in this letter as "very much gifted by

Father Judge also reported on a "consoling council" that had proposed "a gigantic euchre to be held in an armory." He thought this would generate "a splendid mailing list." Before leaving Brooklyn, he visited Monsignor Burke of the Indian and Colored Mission Board. He told Mother Boniface that Burke had "been forty years at this work and is thoroughly impressed with the necessity of getting the negroes [*sic*] to evangelize themselves." Monsignor Burke gave him letters of introduction to three "very prominent pastors of colored parishes," where he hoped to visit and talk to parish sodalities. He enclosed notes he was working on representing "just a working idea of the Cenacle." On his way back to Holy Trinity, he stopped to see O'Grady again.

His next stop was Philadelphia, where he went to promote his Negro cenacle idea with Cardinal Dougherty, who, according to Father Judge's report to Mother Boniface, "was enraptured" with the idea and urged that Judge and Loftus return to discuss it at length. "To use your words," he wrote to Mother Boniface, "'he was lovely.'"[48] From Cardinal Dougherty, a strong Cenacle supporter, Mother Boniface had a standing invitation to move the motherhouse from Holy Trinity to Philadelphia. In October 1920, she sent four sisters to take over the Home Visiting department of the Catholic Children's Bureau in Philadelphia. Within twenty years, more than thirty sisters would be working in Philadelphia Catholic Charities.[49]

Bishop Caruana and the "Spanish Province"

At the cardinal's residence, Father Judge met Bishop George J. Caruana (1882–1951), whom he knew from Caruana's days as a pastor in Corona, Long Island, where Cenacle associates helped the Maltese priest in his work with Italian children at St. Leo's Church.[50] In 1921 Caruana became bishop of Puerto Rico. Judge called it the "largest diocese in the world." With many priests and religious having returned to Spain after the American victory in the Spanish-American War of 1898, more than two decades before, Bishop Caruana was in dire need of help in Puerto Rico. When Judge explained his

God with a sweetness and kindness of spirit, the Fruit of the Holy Ghost, Benignity, because of which she is attracting many young women to the work of the Missionary Cenacle." Sister Mary Michael and the sisters, he added, "have accomplished wonders, especially when we consider their disadvantages." His negotiations with Monsignor O'Hara had presumably "destroyed" these disadvantages and introduced a "new order."

48. Judge to Mother Boniface Keasey, Philadelphia, October 5, 1922, AST, MF 7552–53.

49. Gallaher, "Social Work of the Missionary Servants," 24, 67–71.

50. Collins, "Voice from the Past," *Holy Ghost*, December 1950, 7.

idea of the "negroes [*sic*] evangelizing themselves and the Cenacle supervising a missionary work amongst them," the bishop asked if they could "do the same thing" for him.

Knowing that yet another request for sisters might alarm her, Father Judge reported to Mother Boniface Bishop Caruana's own words:

> Your Sisters can help me and I can help them. Sooner or later they are going to get into the work of the Mexican border. For this they will need Spanish. Why not have them come down to me. They can help me start the work and at the same time they can learn Spanish.[51]

Judge asked the bishop if he wanted sisters just to begin the work or if he wanted to start a branch of the Cenacle. Caruana wanted a branch of the Cenacle. At this Judge exclaimed to Mother Boniface, "We could start a new province and this would be the Spanish province. Thank God and have prayers of thanksgiving said." By the next sentence this possibility had already been realized, as he announced to her, "Our second province is now started and this is a Spanish province."

One can only imagine the beleaguered reverend mother's response as she read that she now had a new province to staff. But Father Judge made an appeal that would be hard for her to refuse. They were "finally in foreign missions," and that "by the grace of God." "The Cenacle is living out the words of Our Lord, 'Go, and teach all nations, baptizing them in the name of the Father and of the Son and of the Holy Ghost.' It is living up to its traditions, to be zealous about an abandoned people." He described the people in the former Spanish possessions as "woefully in danger of being absolutely lost to God and to the Church."[52]

The Negro Question and Proposals for Negro Cenacles

From Philadelphia Father Judge went on to Washington, where he stayed with Monsignor O'Grady and discussed in more detail the Negro Cenacle proposal. On October 13, he wrote to Mother Boniface from "Dr. O'Grady's house," asking her to "put before the Holy Ghost the ardent wish of Cardinal Dougherty, Arch. Curley, and others that our Sisters begin a work to train negroes [*sic*] for their own evangelization." He told her that O'Grady was "very

51. Judge to Mother Boniface Keasey, Philadelphia, October 5, 1922, AST, MF 7552–54.
52. Ibid.

urgent that this work be started right away.... Do have the council. God willing, I will be home soon." If the sisters did take on this work, she would have to come to Washington to talk it over with O'Grady. Judge made clear that he had explained to O'Grady that "the work must be managed from Holy Trinity Station and *not* from the *Catholic University* and no interference from any social worker." He also told O'Grady that the "Sisters have a salary of $60 a month." This would be the sisters' work "because nobody else wants it." To Mother Boniface he concluded, "Let prayers of thanksgiving be offered that our Sisters by God's grace are being chosen for this necessary work."[53]

Father Judge traveled by train from Washington to Columbus, Georgia, and then on to Holy Trinity. He continued thinking about the "Negro question." By the end of October he had written his thoughts and circulated them as an untitled conference. Almost sixty years had passed since Emancipation. Though the memory of slavery ran deep, the majority of African Americans in 1922 had no direct experience of it. Many had fought in the Great War. This was the age of the "New Negro" and the Harlem Renaissance.

Father Judge identified the "Negro question" as "crying for notice, for prayer and help," demanding attention from both the country and the church. Of twelve million Negroes in the United States, only 285,000 were Catholic. Catholic evangelization efforts had met with little success. He noted that there were only four Catholic Negro high schools and not one college and questioned how much "equality of opportunity" there was in "existing institutions"—that is, white Catholic schools:

> The Negro is making tremendous social advances. The old plantation Negro has gone forever. There is a modern and a new type which is beginning to compare very well with its white neighbor. They are making entrance into the professions, becoming property owners, controlling banks and real estate exchanges. Some amongst them stand for great political and financial power, and Negro parents are very ambitious to give their children the best in education.

He cited from a long summary in the *New York Tribune* of the findings of the Race Relations Commission appointed by the governor of Illinois and then turned to the theme that he had talked over with John Noll in New Orleans in the spring and articulated at the Catholic Charities conference in Washington—namely, "that the whites will never solve the Negro question, that they must solve it themselves." From this he drew the conclusion—"no matter how

53. Judge to Mother Boniface Keasey, Washington, D.C., October 13, 1921, AST, MF 7550–51; emphasis in original.

startling"—that "they must have their own priesthood and their own sisterhood and, therefore, what concerns us in a very particular way, their own Apostolate and, therefore, their Inner and Outer Missionary Cenacles."

He drew support for his conclusion from Pope Benedict XV's appeal for native clergy among every people in *Maximum illud* (1919). On this question, he urged "thinking with the Church." "In the heart of the Church evidently there is not the least doubt that the Negroes are capable and should be responsible, with God's grace, of evangelizing themselves." With his project of a Negro Cenacle in mind, Father Judge found it "only reasonable that whites would start them and help them to this." Such help was "our bounden duty." "The sooner," he concluded, "this gets to the conscience of every Catholic, that in some degree he is responsible to help his colored brother, the sooner will there be a blessed consummation of a movement that will bring thousands of Negroes into the Church." The closing paragraphs of this circular expand on the proposal for a Negro cenacle that emerged from the Charities convention.[54]

Though Father Judge's proposals did involve white women working in the black community, they did not seriously challenge the hardening segregation patterns of the 1920s. In the end, such proposals failed to overcome Jim Crow. Nevertheless, in his acknowledgment of African American agency and advocacy for black priests and sisters in 1922, Judge's vision was courageous and far-sighted.[55] In 1939 Father Joachim Benson published this conference in *Preservation of the Faith* magazine under the title "The Negro Apostolate." He sent a prepublication copy to Paul Hanly Furfey, who had succeeded William Kerby as chair of the Catholic University Sociology Department. Furfey was known for his writing on and work in the black community of Washington, D.C., where he helped to found two neighborhood settlements known as Il Poverello House and Fides House. The 1922 date surprised Furfey. "It seems greatly to his credit," he wrote to Benson, "that he was concerned about Negro welfare at that remote date." He added, "My only recollection of Father Judge is a meeting which I attended with him and Msgr. O'Grady in the basement of a Negro church."[56]

54. Judge to "My dear Children," Cottonton, October 31, 1922, AST, MF 711–13; also at 3740–43.

55. On the history of African American Catholic priests in the United States, see Stephen J. Ochs, *Desegregating the Altar: The Josephites and the Struggle for Black Priests, 1871–1960* (Baton Rouge: Louisiana State University Press, 1990).

56. Furfey to Benson, Washington, D.C., May 6, 1938, carbon, The American Catholic History Research Center and University Archives, The Catholic University of America,

The meeting Furfey attended was probably an organizational meeting for the Negro Cenacle. It took place in Washington on Judge's next trip north less than two months after his circular on the Negro question. Four or five hundred attended, by Judge's count. In the presence of "several priests," he opened the meeting "in an out and out Cenacle way." The plan was "at first to rent a house, to have a few of our Sisters there and start an Outer Cenacle." Judge described the crowd as "responsive." An appeal for money to help rent a house brought in $75. "It was really touching," he wrote, "to see these poor people so eager." In their spontaneity and generosity, he compared them favorably to "an old fashioned Irish congregation." "If permitted, they will enter eagerly into the support of good works." He also reported that Mother Boniface "will visit Washington to consult with Dr. O'Grady this coming week."[57]

Back to Brooklyn

Mother Boniface was indeed on the road at this time visiting sisters and trying, in response to a threat of foreclosure on the former Mott Plantation, to raise $9,000 to pay off a delinquent loan.[58] Father Judge was in Brooklyn to give a retreat at St. James pro-Cathedral. The transition or development from a Cenacle of lay associates to one of religious sisters in what were at first private vows occurred differently in various cenacles individually, and in the South and North. The work at the Dr. White Memorial Settlement in Brooklyn represented this transition in the North. The first Cenacle associates went there in 1918 as lay women. By 1922, the settlement was staffed primarily by vowed sisters. The diocese had made no provision for a sisters' residence, salaries, or a chapel in which the Blessed Sacrament would be reserved. Judge's letters to Mother Boniface in the fall of 1922 indicate his continuing concern over this situation.[59]

Furfey-Walsh Papers, Correspondence B. Professional, Box 4, Folder—Benson, Joachim, MSSsT (1935–52); see *Preservation of the Faith* 7, no.1 (February 1939): 21–22. In 1922 Furfey would have been twenty-six years old and a student in the Sociology Department at Catholic University; see Portier, "Paul Hanly Furfey: Catholic Extremist and Supernatural Sociologist," *Josephinum Journal of Theology* 16, no. 1 (Winter–Spring 2009): 24–37. O'Grady also found Judge "far ahead of his time" on the Negro question; see Monsignor John O'Grady to Sr. Mary James Collins, Washington, July 22, 1949, as cited from AMSBT, in Blackwell, *Ecclesial People*, 99, 112n416. Collins herself, in citing this letter, compares the approaches of Judge and O'Grady; see "Voice from the Past," *Holy Ghost*, December 1950, 6.

57. Judge to "My dear Child" [Custodian at East Pittsburgh], Gold Street, Brooklyn, December 9, 1922, AST, MF 5158–59.

58. Collins, "Voice from the Past," *Holy Ghost*, December 1950, 7.

59. See Judge to Mother Boniface Keasey, Brooklyn, September 8, 1922, AST, MF 7545–46,

Bishop Charles E. McDonnell died in August 1921. Auxiliary Bishop Thomas E. Molloy (1884–1956) administered the Diocese of Brooklyn until Pope Benedict XV appointed him ordinary on November 21, 1921. During this time of transition, the priests in charge of diocesan Catholic Charities, also anxious to resolve the sisters' situation at Gold Street, had difficulty gaining access to Bishop Molloy, a man who guarded his personal privacy. At Molloy's death in 1956, Brooklyn was the largest diocese in the country, and Molloy had become a giant among the "brick and mortar" bishops of the East Coast.[60]

During his three days at the cathedral, Father Judge was able "to see and talk much to the Bishop." He gave Molloy one of the papers he had been writing during the fall and persuaded him to "view the Cenacle movement from another angle." He told the bishop that "any priest could organize this work and carry it out, provided he inspired a great devotion to the Holy Ghost in the workers, and to encourage them to frequent, at least weekly Communion." Bishop Molloy, however, preferred Cenacle workers. Father Judge reported that when he returned to the Dr. White settlement at Gold Street, he found Bishop Molloy and the sisters "chatting as old, old friends." The Spirit of God, he concluded, "has opened the diocese from beginning to end to the Cenacle."[61]

The Cenacle and Negro Work

Though Monsignor O'Grady continues to be mentioned in Father Judge's correspondence through at least March 1923, it does not seem that a Negro Cenacle in the Washington area ever materialized. "Speaking of Negro work," he wrote in summer 1924 to a priest in Chino, California, "it may please you to know that we are about to engage in a very important movement amongst the negroes [*sic*]." He went on to describe his project for training African American Catholics as lay apostles in Cenacle fashion. He asked

---

on achieving "the supreme triumph of the Brooklyn Cenacle"; Judge to Keasey, Cottonton, November 9, 1922, AST, MF 7567, on preparing Mother Boniface for a meeting with Bishop Molloy, who had been the bishop of Brooklyn less than a year. He wrote, "Probably nowhere has the Cenacle been more misunderstood and misrepresented as in Brooklyn. There is no reason not to believe that the Bishop, as a young priest, heard much that was spoken against us."

60. On Bishop Molloy, see the entry by Margaret M. Quinn, CSJ, in *Encyclopedia of American Catholic History*, 973–74.

61. Judge to My dear Child [Pittsburgh Custodian], Brooklyn, December 9, 1922, AST, MF 5158.

for prayers for this work "as it will meet with many difficulties and as you know, is absolutely necessary."[62]

October 1924 found Father Judge writing to Archbishop Curley, at that time the ordinary of both Baltimore and Washington, D.C., about property and a building near Baltimore for the kind of Negro Cenacle he had discussed with O'Grady.[63] Judge's enthusiasm for the idea of African Americans evangelizing themselves was genuine and in keeping with his basic approach of making lay apostles. But as with Washington, there was no Baltimore Negro Cenacle.

St. Peter Claver School had been in continuous existence almost from the beginnings at Holy Trinity. But here too at this time, Father Judge wanted to expand in the direction of fostering an apostolic laity among African American Catholics. In summer 1923, he wrote to Bishop Allen about a priest who had contacted him and was anxious to work among the Negroes. "We on our part," he told Bishop Allen, "are anxious to do more for the Negroes." He went on to trace the recent past at Holy Trinity. At the outset, opposition from "both the white and black preachers" rendered a too-active outreach "imprudent." "Ill will of the whites" forced St. Peter Claver to close after its first year, but it reopened the next year with assurances that it would only be for children living on the former Bradley and Patterson plantations. He went on to describe how things had changed:

> Now public sentiment has been disarmed and we have colored children coming from long distances and all our neighbors seem perfectly good willed concerning it. It seems now opportune that we begin quietly a wider missionary work amongst the Negroes. The more so as our moral and political force has grown stronger. Widespread good will has been evoked, old suspicions and distrust are disappearing, our activities are multiplying. There is an increased number of negro employes [*sic*] and new relations are springing up between ourselves and the negroes round and about Holy Trinity Station. I think we can safely open a chapel for them.

With such a chapel as well as the already existing Negro school, he emphasized to Bishop Allen how valuable it would be to have a priest devoted solely to this work. But like the Washington and Baltimore Negro Cenacles, this priest, whose work Judge conceived within the strict segregation patterns of the South in the 1920s, never materialized.[64]

62. Judge to Rev. Charles J. Creamer, Stirling, N.J., July 30, 1924, AST, MF 5712.

63. Collins, "Voice from the Past, "*Holy Ghost*, December 1951, 11.

64. Judge to Edward P. Allen, Brooklyn, June 14, 1923, copy, AST, MF 5371. The priest Judge mentioned was Rev. Thomas N. Stanton.

An Apostolic Laity

Father Judge's proposal for Negro cenacles was part of his larger vision of promoting an apostolic laity. As we have seen, Judge insisted to Monsignor O'Hara of Brooklyn that, in spite of the impressive number of children to whom the sisters at Dr. White Memorial ministered, this was not their chief purpose. Rather, their purpose was "to train the work-a-day man and woman into an apostle, to cause each to be alert for the interests of the Church, to be the Church, and that here lies in a very large way the solution of all the Church's problems." A "spiritualized and apostolic laity" would be the greatest help to Religion, and "this is the work of the Cenacle, to evoke this personal service."[65] When the National Conference of Catholic Charities held its 1923 annual convention in Philadelphia from September 9 to14, Father Judge took his message of a "spiritualized and apostolic laity" to a national audience.

In the context of the standoff between the papacy and the Italian state, and especially in response to the French laws of 1905 abrogating the Napoleonic Concordat of 1801 and radically separating church from state in France, Pope Pius X had advocated "Catholic Action" as "a very noble apostolate which includes all the works of mercy."[66] Less than a year before Father Judge's talk at the 1923 NCCC convention, Pope Pius XI provided scriptural warrant for Judge's estimate of Cenacle lay apostles' work as "almost priestly." In his first encyclical, Pius XI wrote:

> Tell your faithful children of the laity that when, united with their pastors and their bishops, they participate in the works of the apostolate, both individual and social, the end purpose of which is to make Jesus Christ better known and better loved, then they are more than ever "a chosen generation, a kingly priesthood, a holy nation, a purchased people," of whom St. Peter spoke in such laudatory terms (1 Pt 2:9).[67]

65. Judge to Mother Boniface Keasey, Brooklyn, September 28, 1922, AST, MF 7545.

66. Pius X, *Editae saepe*, May 26, 1910, §39; see also Pius X, *Il fermo proposito*, November 6, 1905, §11.

67. Pius XI, *Ubi arcano Dei*, December 23, 1922, §58. In the preface to his 1929 study of the lay apostolate, John Harbrecht identified "the revival of the Lay Apostolate" as "one of the great Apostolic works" of Pius XI. "In view of this high approval," he went on to say after citing this passage from *Ubi arcano*, "I need offer no apology for undertaking a study of the Lay Apostolate. A decade ago such an apology may have been necessary, but not to-day. In fact, the Lay Apostolate is not only an opportune topic for discussion, but it is also one of the most urgent needs of our time. Everywhere our bishops are recognizing its necessity. However, due to a lack of interpretive literature on the movement, priestly practice in America has been handicapped in organizing the Lay Apostolate." Harbrecht addressed his hefty book to this situation and

As evidenced by the long circular letter he wrote on the day Pope Benedict XV died, Father Judge's "love and invincible loyalty to Christ's vicar on earth" was strong.[68] Nevertheless, his pastoral experience was the primary driver in his advocacy of an apostolic laity. Early twentieth-century papal teaching on the lay apostolate no doubt offered general guidance and assurance that he was on the right track. But when Father Judge appeared in Philadelphia in September 1923, he spoke primarily from his conviction, based on years of experience as a missionary that long preceded Pius XI on the lay apostolate, about the laity's potential as agents for the preservation of the faith.

Father Judge had enthused about the 1922 Washington meeting's session devoted to Italian work. In 1923 he was invited to address this session. He began, however, by asking the audience's indulgence to speak more generally about principles that applied to "any work of good will for our neighbor." His brief address can be divided into five parts. First, he summarized the "gospel of charity" from the teaching of Jesus and emphasized the need to order our lives according to it with love of neighbor as "an accurate measure of our love of God." Methods that truly help our neighbor should be welcomed. But the neighbor's "spiritual needs must be served first and ever safeguarded." Judge insisted that a method or system that "shuts out the soul's interests and does not help the individual to realize the purpose of his creation, the salvation of his soul must be placed under suspicion and be considered as a menace to his welfare."

In the second part, Father Judge argued that the laity, the "general body of the faithful," was the most powerful available force "to work good for the neighbor." He likened the laity to "the scattered waters of the meadow—a vast idle flood." Like such waters, the laity represented "a tremendous power for good" that needed to be gathered and directed. As he had in 1919, Judge insisted again that "the hope of our generation lies with the faithful." The question, then, was "how to get from every work-a-day Catholic a sense of re-

---

modeled it on Mary E. Richmond's 1917 social work classic *Social Diagnosis*; Harbrecht, *Lay Apostolate*, preface, v–vi, x.

68. "There is no truer sign of a Catholic heart than a love and invincible loyalty to Christ's vicar on earth. There is no surer sign of defeat and confusion than to take sides against him. This is the incontestable working out of history, confirmed very much by events of our own day. So intensely loyal should [we] be that even if an angel were to come from heaven to enlist us in a cause excluding the pope, we should respectfully but firmly declare our allegiance to the Holy Father. This devotion to the Supreme Pontiff should be warm; it should show itself in a great affection for him and his interests; in the desire to comfort him, to help him, to strengthen him by prayer and every other means at hand"; Judge to My dear Children, Gillette, N.J., January 29, 1922, AST, MF 5165–66.

sponsibility for his neighbor . . . how to quicken the general body of the laity into missionary activity?"

Third, Father Judge warned of a danger. Instead of tapping into the great power for good of the laity, Catholics could be distracted into "creating a caste in charity workers," believing that "only those advantaged with or those having culture or easy living conditions can do good." In opposition to such a caste, Judge appealed to his life as a missionary. "It has been my experience that the people of everyday life are really great missionaries and charity workers."

He called in the fourth part for a "Catholic spirit," identifying it as "the need of the hour." Only with such a spirit could the church face the "tormenting problems wherein the faith and morals of so many are in danger." A Catholic spirit, according to Father Judge, "means nothing more than an ardent charity and living, burning, operating love of God and our neighbor." He challenged Catholic charity professionals: "Will these methods, systems, movements stretch out, gather up, and infuse into the general Catholic body a missionary spirit?" If they do not, Judge argued, they will be useless and only serve to create "a caste which may be regarded as favored or professional church workers."

Father Judge concluded by leaving a question with the audience. It was a question that the daily life and practice of the Cenacle were designed to address: how to "lead the everyday Catholic into missionary work in the providence of his every-day life?" He explained the providence of everyday life by describing each person as "a center of a particular bit of Divine Providence":

> You meet certain people, you have contact with certain persons or places, your life has a certain circumscription, God overshadowing and intervening in all. This is called your daily Providence. It is yours indeed: it does not belong to anybody else. Like the skin on your face, it is yours personally, nobody else ever had it, nobody else ever will have it.

The question was: how can Catholics be brought to realize that "in their everyday providence they are the Catholic Church"? Not only are they responsible for the church, "they should act for the Church, be vigilant for her interests, and plead her cause." He summarized his question in a form he often posed: "what can I do to make every Catholic a missionary?"[69] There is no clearer statement than this 1923 address of Father Judge's core mission of making ordinary Catholics into apostles.

69. "The Address of Father Judge before the National Conference of Catholic Charities in Philadelphia," *Holy Ghost*, October 1923, 6–8.

8

TAKING ON A MORE DEFINITE FORM 1923–1924

A Vision of the Cenacle for Vincentian Superiors

Father McHale

In 1920, when the Vincentian General Council in Paris freed Father Judge to work solely with the missionary sisters, they knew nothing of the brothers who would organize early in 1921.[1] Later in 1921, Father Judge requested Father Frederick Maune, his provincial superior, either to assign three priests to teach the Cenacle's young men in training or to allow them to attend classes at St. Vincent's Seminary. At their meeting of August 8, 1921, the provincial council "unanimously disapproved" of both of these requests. The minutes go on to record Maune's and his council's lack of confidence "in Fr. Judge's fitness for the work he has undertaken" and their "wish to disclaim all responsibility for it or connection with it."[2]

How these decisions were communicated to Father Judge is not clear. In any case, he must have been aware of the contrast between the responses to his work from the general and provincial councils. The provincial council minutes of August 8, 1921, had dismissed his proposed "Community of priests" as being "for some indefinite work." Father Judge responded by explaining it in great detail. During fall 1922, his correspondence makes fre-

1. See McHale to Judge, Paris, November 22, 1920, AST, MF 628 and 11526. The phrase "taking on a more definite form" is from Collins, "Voice from the Past," *Holy Ghost*, March 1951, 5, referring to the sisters between January 1919 and the beginning of 1923.

2. Excerpt of "Minutes of the Provincial Council Meeting," August 8, 1921, copy, Box 1H.17A, Folder 4, DA.

quent mention of "notes" or "papers" he was working on relative to the character and mission of the Missionary Servants, both women and men.

In January 1922, Judge wrote at length to Father McHale in Paris, who, since 1919, had served as third assistant to the superior general. This letter introduced McHale to the brothers and explained their beginnings. Father Judge emphasized how they had helped the sisters, that they were not attracted to the Vincentians, and that they had decided themselves "to petition the bishop for a society of their own." He described the property they had purchased with a $5,000 donation for a down payment. They made their interest payments "from the crops they are growing." Vincentian colleges would not take the young men without tuition, and he described the measures he had taken toward their education. Eugene Brennan was in his first year of philosophy at St. Mary's Seminary in La Porte, Texas. Judge hoped to have a school in the North to "begin the training of young men as missionaries and catechists for the south." He enclosed copies of his correspondence with Bishop John J. O'Connor of Newark about the possibility of such a school but, though it seemed to be implied, he did not emphasize his growing interest in having priests trained in the Cenacle spirit.[3]

Father Verdier

In fall 1922, the Vincentian superior general, Father Verdier, accompanied by his third assistant, Father McHale, made a canonical visitation of the Eastern Province.[4] On October 5, 1922, they met with the provincial council. When the case of Father Judge came up, McHale's support for Judge, at least according to the minutes, was lukewarm at best.[5] The minutes do not record that four days before this meeting, Father Judge had already seen the superior general upon his arrival in Brooklyn and at least showed him the material on the Cenacle that he had been preparing. Further, Judge strongly implied that he had shown these materials to the general on the advice of Father McHale.

"Our Superior General is in the country," an excited Father Judge announced to Mother Boniface on October 5, 1922, from Philadelphia. "He has

3. Judge to McHale, Orange, N.J., January 20, 1922, AST, MF 9481–82. Unfortunately, we do not have McHale's reply.

4. See Rybolt, *American Vincentians*, 213. Fathers Verdier, McHale, and another priest arrived in New York on October 1. After visiting both the Vincentians of the Eastern Province and the Daughters of Charity, they arrived in Chicago on October 22 and sailed back to France on November 18. For this information I am grateful to Fr. John Carven, CM.

5. Excerpt of "Minutes of the Provincial Council Meeting," October 5, 1922, copy, Box 1H.17A, Folder 4, DA.

shattered all community traditions," Judge wrote. "Never before has there been such an event." Judge reported that he learned of Father Verdier's arrival from his confrere Jeremiah Hartnett and that Hartnett's tip enabled him to join the party who met Verdier at the pier when his ship docked in Brooklyn on October 1. At this time, Judge was trying to meet with the Brooklyn priests in charge of Catholic Charities, but he does say that "I got myself to his notice and laid before him some papers, copy of which I am enclosing." He added that he was told to do this "by our good friend who is with him," presumably Patrick McHale. In view of Verdier's busy schedule, Judge told Mother Boniface, "We must esteem it a great favor that he would consider our affairs and this literature."[6] From Judge's choice of "laid before" and from his subsequent letters, it is not clear whether he actually gave the papers to Verdier or just showed them to him.

In any case, the "papers" to which Father Judge referred in this letter represented the brainstorming he had been doing on the Cenacle's work and its future, especially that of the brothers. After his return to Alabama, Judge wrote to Verdier on November 3 and again on November 7. His November 3 letter indicates that, when Judge saw the superior general in Brooklyn, he made a special petition to him and asked for some permissions. "I respectfully submit again to you," Judge wrote, "my desire to be under you directly. Secondly, I would like ample poverty permissions." He explained that, in the two years since he had been freed to work with the sisters, the Missionary Servants had supported him and "in nothing have I been a burden to the Congregation." He asked for permission to "turn over [Mass] intentions to the Cenacle," but assured the general that his masses for departed confreres would continue, along with the "monthly Mass for the departed of the two Companies, Priests and Sisters of Charity." His third request to Verdier concerned his desire that the Missionary Servants, both men and women, "will have a great devotion to St. Vincent and be animated by his spirit." "I respectfully ask," he continued, "that some copies of the different books, pamphlets, rules, Conferences of St. Vincent &c. pertaining to our Priests and Sisters of Charity be sent to me that I may circulate these amongst the Missionary Brothers and Sisters."[7]

6. Judge to Mother Boniface Keasey, Philadelphia, October 5, 1922, AST, MF 7522. Fr. Loftus accompanied Judge on this occasion. "Fr. Loftus has seen the General and, as he expressed it, 'has fixed everything up.' Just what this means," Judge wrote, "I do not know, as I was obliged to go off on some work."

7. Judge to Most Honored Father [François Verdier, CM], Cottonton, Alabama, November 3,

Judge's November 7 letter to the superior general indicates that Verdier had in the meantime communicated to Judge that his petition and request for permissions were under consideration. "Your message has reached me," Judge wrote to Verdier. "I thank you very much for your gracious consideration of my petition and the permissions." This brief letter describes eleven enclosures designed to convey the scope and spirit of the work as well as its positive reception by the bishops of the United States. The enclosures are most likely copies or expansions of the "papers" Judge told Mother Boniface he had "laid before" Verdier on October 1.[8]

Missionary Servants of the Most Blessed Trinity

The first enclosure, entitled "Missionary Servants of the Most Blessed Trinity," is a page-and-a-half description of "The Cenacle and Its Work." It begins with descriptions of "Inner" and "Outer" Cenacles, with the Inner Cenacle listed as having twenty brothers and 130 sisters. Judge devoted most of the space in the paragraph on the Inner Cenacle to the brothers. "Some of the Brothers are studying for the Priesthood." As their schools, he listed LaPorte Seminary (Texas), Kenrick Seminary (St. Louis, then run by the Vincentians) and the Ecclesiastical Schools St. Charles (Philadelphia) and Mount St. Mary's (Emmitsburg, Maryland). Then he mentioned the high school "being registered" and "*La petite séminaire*" "being opened" at Holy Trinity. The sisters' work was not mentioned.

He estimated that the Outer Cenacle numbered seven hundred associates and described their work in terms that would appear in his Catholic Charities address the following year. In addition to being encouraged to frequent Communion and devotion to the Holy Ghost, associates "are trained to be alert to the interests of the Church, in fact, in the circumstances of their every day life, to be the Church. . . . Every Catholic should be an apostle."

Next he described the five "ends of the Cenacle" in terms of devotion and prayer: devotion to the Blessed Trinity, and especially to the Holy Ghost; to the holy name of Jesus; and, recalling the Holy Agony devotion, to the sufferings of Our Lord, especially his mental sorrows; prayer, work and suffering

1922, AST, MF 5243. Judge was able to send both letters to Verdier while the latter was still in the United States.

8. Judge to Most Reverend Father, Cottonton, Feast of Blessed John Gabriel Perboyre, '22 [November 7], AST, MF 689–90. In 1922 the Feast of Blessed Perboyre was celebrated on November 7. The revision of the Roman calendar after the Second Vatican Council moved Perboyre's Feast to the date of his death, September 11, 1840.

for souls; and prayerful aid to priests. He listed seven Cenacle virtues: simplicity, prudence, humility, charity, patience, self-denial, and sacrifice. The second page added that the Cenacle's "latest development" is "the beginning of the lay apostolate amongst the negroes [*sic*], to train them to evangelize themselves through Priests, Brothers, and Sisters." He also mentioned a "crusade of prayer to the Holy Ghost through the League of the Holy Ghost," an idea Loftus had brought to the Cenacle. In a paragraph that may have been added in Philadelphia, he noted "the very latest word on the work: To-day, October 3, Bishop Caruana has asked us to start a Spanish Province."[9]

Cenacle Development

Father Judge divided the three-page second enclosure on "Cenacle Development" under eight headings: "Vocations," "Inner Cenacles," "Outer Cenacles," "Mission Schools," "Mission Retreats," "Sacramental and Mission Development," "Prospective Plan," and "Italian, Porto Rican [*sic*] and Negro Apostolates." Under "Vocations" he wrote one sentence: "These seem to be easily attracted to the Cenacle." Under the "Inner Cenacle" heading, he listed the bishops and "leaders of Catholic activity" who had asked for sisters or the establishment of what he now called the "Cenacle Lay Apostolate." The list included Cardinal Dougherty at the head, Bishop Caruana of San Juan, Archbishop Curley, Bishop Allen, Bishop Hartley of Columbus, Ohio, Bishop Hoban of Scranton, Bishop Muldoon of Rockford, Illinois, and Monsignor Noll and a committee of priests of his diocese. He also mentioned that the archbishops of Lima, Peru, and Pernambuco, Brazil, had "asked the Cenacle for help to undo the harm being done by American Baptists and Methodists."

Under "Outer Cenacles," he attached a letter from a pastor requesting the establishment of the "Cenacle Lay Apostolate" as representing the "many priests in various dioceses who are petitioning the Cenacle for help." He emphasized the need for homegrown Cenacle priests. "The need of priests, fired with the Cenacle spirit, is very essential and insistent to perpetuate the Cenacle and its works." In the number of young men already mentioned as studying for the priesthood, providence was providing.

The main topic under the heading of "Mission Schools" was "to get the Church to the child." He described St. Patrick's School in Phenix City as "one of the most extraordinary and unique mission triumphs—a school of 500 Protestant children in a country where there are no Catholics and in the

9. First enclosure, "Missionary Servants of the Most Blessed Trinity, or, The Cenacle and Its Work," AST, MF 691–92.

heart of malevolent Protestantism." The school and the work of the sisters has "Catholicized a citadel of bigotry." He referred also to the "high school" at Holy Trinity. Where there was no high school, "the Cenacle has its own."

Mission retreats were needed "to inspire work-a-day people with the missionary spirit . . . to enlighten the Catholic toiler, to encourage him and to help him to the grace of being alert for the interests of the Church." The demand for such retreats, a chief means of attracting lay apostles for the Cenacle, provided "another added reason to have priests who have been trained in the Cenacle spirit."

Under "Sacramental and Mission Development," Father Judge waxed on developments at Holy Trinity, "no longer an experiment but a worked out fact." In his idyllic description, it was "a colony . . . chartered on those words of Our Lord, 'Seek ye first the Kingdom of God and His justice, and all these things shall be added unto you.'" Here was the kind of spiritual thinking many in the church would resist:

> The question of material daily bread then became a very secondary consideration. The whole day with its works hinged on morning prayers, daily Mass and the reception of Holy Communion. Here is seen an entire people assembling around the altar of God. . . . In the evening practically the entire colony assembles again for the evening prayers and either for public or private Benediction of the Blessed Sacrament. Our people are prosperous. God is blessing the work of their hands. Their fields are returning abundant harvests; our children are protected from contagion of the cities; no malign influence can touch them; the fruits of the Holy Spirit, peace and holy joy, are very much in evidence.

Under "Prospective Plan," complete with a map, Judge outlined an ambitious vision for Catholicizing a 20,000-square-mile strategic section of the South. He described a "wedge," beginning at Holy Trinity and extending as far as Birmingham. Within it Catholic colonies would create a "Gibraltar of Catholic strength at the heart of Protestantism." The final heading was "Italian, Porto Rican and Negro Apostolates." The Cenacle's effort to spread the lay apostolate among the Italians was based on the thought that "every race should evangelize itself." They were about to add similar works in Puerto Rico and among African Americans.[10]

10. Second enclosure, "Cenacle Development," AST, MF 693–95. Around this time, Judge wrote to Mr. M. F. Ryan. He must have been a financial officer in a Chicago bank or mortgage company. Judge was trying to get a loan to finance a "farm plan" for the crops at Holy Trinity. He included a wedge-shaped map to show that the farm was "advantageously located for development and cheaper rates of transportation." "Imagine a funnel," he said to Ryan. This

Episcopal Approbation and Cenacle Plan

The third enclosure, four pages in length, listed the names of thirty-eight episcopal figures accompanied by brief descriptions of their support of and relationship to the Cenacle.[11] The "Cenacle Plan" was the fourth and briefest enclosure, a page-and-a-half outline of preventive and reclamation work centered primarily on home visiting and various programs for children and youth. It also included brief sections on "Library," having largely to do with making Catholic books and periodicals available, "Kindergarten," "Summer Outings," and "Missionary Nursing."[12] The fifth enclosure listed in the cover letter to Fr. Verdier was Judge's 1919 "Spiritual Militia" article on the need to promote an apostolic laity.

Father Judge's Vision for the Cenacle Lay Apostolate

A sixth enclosure Father Judge described as "a paper presented to Bishops on the formation of the Brothers' Cenacle." He identified the brothers in a parenthesis as "The Society for the Preservation of the Faith," the title of this enclosure. The contents indicate that it was sent to prelates such as Bishop John J. O'Connor of Newark and Cardinal Dougherty of Philadelphia in requesting "permission to start an Apostolic College in your diocese." In this paper's opening sentence, Judge offered a clear and contextual account of what he understood by the "preservation of the faith." "Because of active and multiplied evil agencies there is grave danger that loss of faith may befall many people in different parts of the United States and in foreign countries, especially those of Latin race colonization."

He described the young men banded together with Bishop Allen's permission "under the name of the Missionary Servants of the Most Blessed Trinity" as having done so "to offset, even in a humble way, this peril." He distinguished their purpose as the "Preservation of the Faith as distinct from the Propagation of the Faith" and went on to offer "the South and the West" as examples of specific parts of the United States where there is "crying need for missionary workers." These men would also "offer themselves to missions in foreign countries especially those colonized by the Latin races, for example, South America and the Philippine Islands." To "offset the ac-

map no doubt did double duty as a transportation funnel and a missionary wedge; see Judge to M. F. Ryan, Phenix City, Ala., November 6, 1922, AST, MF 5149–50.

11. Third enclosure, "Episcopal Approbation," AST, MF 696–98.

12. Fourth enclosure, "Cenacle Plan," AST, MF 699–700.

tivities of the Young Men's Christian Association," they would train men for missionary work "in places where men especially congregate." Such places included "near navy yards, ports of entry, large car barns, great industrial centers."

Under the purpose of "The Preservation of the Faith," he devoted the fourth and longest specification to the need for priests trained in the Cenacle spirit to promote and support the "Cenacle Lay Apostolate." The "Cenacle work" of the lay apostles included "the bringing of the unbaptized to the baptismal font, the delinquent sinner to confession and Holy Communion, the validating of marriages, the preserving of children from fanatical proselytizers, from perversion and seduction, and like charitable endeavor."

Such lay apostles needed "a special spirit." Father Judge described this spirit in detail and contrasted it with what he opposed. Cenacle lay apostles had to be "highly spiritualized, motived supernaturally, constantly incited to purity of intention and protected from so many material and despiritualizing influences or agencies abroad to-day under the cover of so-called 'social uplift.'" The growing demand for such workers meant a need for the kind of priests who could train them. A community of priests "would be a great utility . . . even if it had no other purpose than to evoke response from thousands of men and women throughout the United States, to train them, to encourage them, to supernaturalize them and make them constant in the work of God." He contrasted such spiritualized lay volunteers with "commercialized charity and the merely professional, salaried worker," which he described as "contradictions to the Catholic heart." These young men had banded together so that "being trained in an apostolic spirit they in turn may communicate it to others, and being filled with the Holy Ghost, the hearts of thousands of our brothers and sisters in every walk of life may be fired with holy zeal to do the work of God."[13]

The remaining five enclosures that Father Judge sent to Verdier were a newspaper clipping conveying the "strenuous missionary life of the South" and three pieces of supporting correspondence, one a typical request from a pastor, Judge's correspondence with Father O'Grady on the "Negro problem" in Washington, and what he described as a "letter of the Missionary Servants of the Blessed Trinity on the necessity of incepting a Negro Apostolate," probably the circular letter dated, in its final version, October 31, 1922.[14] The eleventh and final enclosure was the "Order of the Day."

13. Sixth enclosure, "Society for the Preservation of the Faith," AST, MF 702–3.

14. See Judge to "My dear Children," Cottonton, October 31, 1922, AST, MF 711–13; also at

The Great Depression soon rendered moot his daring, and by any account unrealistic, vision for a great Catholic wedge in the heart of the Protestant South. The name "Society for the Preservation of the Faith" would disappear. "For the Preservation of the Faith" remained a Cenacle watchword and motto. For a while in the late 1920s and 1930s it served as the name of the mission magazine of the men's community. Father Judge's hopes for Negro Cenacles, to which he devoted so much energy at this time, remained unfulfilled in his lifetime.

Nevertheless, in this great packet of pages—one might imagine Patrick McHale reading it and trying to explain it to the general council—we find Father Judge's mature vision for the lay apostolate. He saw an apostolic laity, spiritually formed and disciplined, alert to the church's interests, with a strong sense of themselves as the church in their daily circumstances, addressing the church's pressing pastoral needs. A year later he would present this vision to the Catholic Charities convention. In 1922 he saw the communities of women and men who had begun as lay apostles engaged in similar work but having as one of their chief aims the making of more lay apostles. A striking new emphasis was his insistence that making apostles would require priests trained in the Cenacle spirit.

We do not have the superior general's written response to Father Judge's petition or to his request for special permissions. But Judge's correspondence with Bishop Allen indicates that Verdier's response was a positive one. On January 3, 1923, Judge began a letter to Allen by announcing that "our Superior General's visit to the United States has been the occasion of a great change being made in my status in the Congregation of the Mission." This letter makes clear Judge's understanding that, in response to his petition and to the mass of material he had provided on the Cenacle, the Vincentian superior general had instructed him to make the Cenacle his "life's work." He continued:

> Father Verdier was much impressed by the Cenacle and its works and particularly the approbation of so many Bishops. Therefore, that I might give myself more freely to the Cenacle, I have been freed from all Provincial Superiors and subject to himself alone. I have been told not only to devote myself entirely to Cenacle interests but that this is to be my life's work. I can never thank God

---

3740–43. The correspondence with O'Grady is likely an undated, four-page, single-spaced description of the sisters' work, primarily in Phenix City but also at Holy Trinity, entitled "Missionary Efforts in the South"; see AST, MF 4186–89. The opening sentence, beginning "Seven years ago," places this document in 1922.

sufficiently for so great a trust and privilege, and feel most unworthy of it. Do pray that I will never abuse it.

Father Judge was effusive in his gratitude to the Bishop of Mobile, telling Allen that he had been the first to hear this "good news" because "I hold you as a benefactor and friend who stood by us in the weakest days of Cenacle life." The Cenacle's gratitude to the bishop was "beyond measure." But Judge, energized and reassured by what he described as "this latest development of Cenacle history which permits so much liberty and opportunity for extending our missionary activity," had more on his mind.

On the eve of his departure for Puerto Rico, he noted to Bishop Allen "the number of generous hearted young men increasing and progressing in their religious work and ecclesiastical studies." He sent a "syllabus of their work"—probably the enclosure on the Society for the Preservation of the Faith—and asked Bishop Allen to "begin the first steps of whatever is necessary for us to get Papal recognition, or let me know what we should do." He added his hope and prayer that "some day we will have a number of zealous, rugged missionaries working out of this end of your diocese, and we look to you as our father in God, to help us in this project."

He added another long paragraph thanking Bishop Allen for "the inspired foresight of a truly Apostolic Prelate." He then, with "holy joy," submitted to the bishop "a draft of our revised corporation." "You will remember," he added, "our young men formed themselves into a Community seven years ago. Since then a number have been educated in outside colleges; these now are well on their way to ordination, or are ready for advanced studies." He concluded by reminding Allen that one of the young men would be "presented next September for Major Orders."[15] This reference to Eugene Brennan, upon whom Judge rested much hope, signals his preoccupation at this time with the need for priests trained in the Cenacle spirit.

Developments at Holy Trinity

Two New Priests

By the beginning of 1923, the Missionary Servants of the Most Blessed Trinity had two new priests. Father John Loftus, formerly of the Diocese of Hartford, Connecticut, arrived at Holy Trinity in December 1922. Despite his devotion to the Holy Ghost and his passion for work among African Ameri-

15. Judge to Bishop Edward P. Allen, Cottonton, Ala., January 3, 1923, Allen Papers, AAM.

cans in the South, Loftus was an older priest, Judge's contemporary, and one who, as the beginnings of the *Holy Ghost* magazine will show, chafed under the Cenacle's pervasive deference to Father Judge's authority as founder and superior.

In February 1923 another priest arrived. "I wonder," Father Judge wrote to Patrick McHale in spring 1923, "if you remember Father Tomerlin, a young priest of the Mobile diocese. He is a Roman and one of the Bishop's most promising young men. He gave up an Italian parish and has entered."[16] Joseph Tomerlin (1890–1959), a young man of thirty-three when he arrived at Holy Trinity, a native of Birmingham, graduated from Mount St. Mary's College, Emmitsburg, Maryland, in 1912 and went to the American College at Rome. The Great War forced him from Rome, and he finished his studies at Mount St. Mary's Seminary. He served as a Navy chaplain during the Great War and was discharged in May 1919. He was a successful pastor at Eufaula, Alabama, where he rebuilt the parish church after it had been destroyed by a tornado.

As pastor at St. Joseph's Church in Ensley, Alabama, however, he angered his Italian congregation by contracting a large debt. It was after his resignation at Ensley in late February 1923 that Tomerlin went to Holy Trinity. The sisters worked at St. Joseph's in Ensley, and it was perhaps through them that Tomerlin found his way to the Cenacle.[17] Tomerlin remained a Missionary Servant from 1923 until 1932. After Mother Boniface's death in 1931, at the height of the Great Depression, Father Judge placed Tomerlin in charge of the finances. Again, he contracted a large debt, this time by trying to raise funds

16. Judge to McHale, Cottonton, Ala., May 3, 1923, AST, MF 5349. Ever the optimist, Father Judge added, "Father Boyle also is now a Missionary Servant of the Most Blessed Trinity. There are two more from the Northern diocese expected soon." Father Boyle did not last the year. The identity of the other two priests is unknown.

17. The biographical information on Fr. Joseph Tomerlin comes from his personnel file in AAM. I am grateful to Fr. Michael L. Farmer for permission to consult it. Tomerlin resurfaced in Camden, New Jersey, in 1938. Four years later, Bishop Toolen released him, and he was incardinated into the Diocese of Camden in 1942. He died in Lawrence, Massachusetts, in 1959. On Tomerlin's embattled situation at St. Joseph's in Ensley, see Tomerlin to Bishop Allen, Ensley, Ala., January 8, 1923; Sr. Cecilia to Bishop Allen, Ensley, February 13, 1923; Rev. T. M. Cassidy to Bishop Allen, Ensley, March 5, 1923, Allen Papers, AAM. In mid-February, less than two weeks before Tomerlin's departure, Sr. Cecilia described the people as "restless and unsettled." The parish men organized "a few weeks ago" and had "a committee at work planning ways and means of collecting and managing the parish finances." Father Cassidy, Tomerlin's successor as pastor, claimed that Tomerlin had alienated the people from himself as well as from the sisters, who lost support from the people because of their association with him. From these letters, it is difficult to avoid the conclusion that, though he resigned, Father Tomerlin was run out of Ensley for what amounted to financial incompetence and general pastoral ineptitude.

through gambling. With warrants out for Tomerlin's arrest in New Jersey and New York and Tomerlin nowhere to be found, Father Judge replied to a query from Bishop Toolen about Tomerlin, "he is no longer one of us."[18]

St. Joseph's School

Out from under a difficult situation at Ensley, Father Tomerlin initially flourished at Holy Trinity. He impressed Mother Boniface. "He is very active and energetic," she wrote, "and can turn his hand to anything. He has a good business head and is a past master when it comes to building, fixing automobiles, etc. He is a fine example for our boys and they have great admiration for him."[19] Brother Augustine had gone north to New Jersey in the fall. With his arrival in February, Tomerlin took over St. Joseph's, or the men's side.

Father Judge wrote to Father McHale in May that the number of vocations required a new building for the sisters. He reported on an estimate that both properties at Holy Trinity had "five million feet of A-1 oak and pine." The new building for the sisters would take "about twenty-five thousand feet." He described a "fine airy, comfortable house with an interior chapel seating three hundred and fifty."[20] As soon as school was out, Tomerlin turned his crew from farmers to "woodsmen and carpenters." "How I have listened to the tales of different woods for the cutting of lumber on the plantation," Mother Boniface wrote. "See that my coffin is made of red cedar lined with long leaf pine, handles of rosemary pine and a cross of red oak."[21] Tomerlin and his crew started harvesting lumber for the new building and renovated three other buildings.[22] But their most important project was St. Joseph's School.

For the past two years, beginning with his conversations with Monsignor Noll, Father Judge had been talking about the need for an apostolic school. It would be an essential component in his dream for priests trained in the Cenacle spirit. He had sent the two-page circular entitled, "The Society for the Preservation of the Faith," to Bishop O'Connor of Newark and Cardinal Dougherty, asking for permission to start an apostolic college in their dioceses.[23] In the first enclosure he gave to Father Verdier, he wrote in late 1922,

18. Judge to Bishop Toolen, Stirling, N.J., November 20, 1932, Toolen Papers, AAM. Tomerlin's financial dealings during the Great Depression will be treated at length later.

19. Tonra, *Led by the Spirit*, 101.

20. Judge to McHale, Cottonton, May 3, 1923, AST, MF 5349. Interestingly, in this letter, Judge does not call the new building for the sisters a "motherhouse."

21. Collins, "Voice from the Past," *Holy Ghost*, March 1951, 7.

22. Brediger, "Leaving All Things," 77.

23. "The Society for the Preservation of the Faith," AST, MF 702–3.

"This year our high school is being registered and *La Petite Séminaire* is being opened at the same time; students number thirteen."[24] Though Bishop O'Connor had given permission to have it in the Newark Diocese, the apostolic college or *petite séminarie* would be in Alabama.[25] Judge had dreamed of an apostolic college, and, during the summer and early fall of 1923, Joseph Tomerlin made it happen, not in Newark or Philadelphia, but in the fields and piney woods of rural Alabama.

By early October 1923, St. Joseph's School was ready, and Father Judge dedicated it with much ceremony on October 8. After a solemn Mass in St. Joseph's Chapel, where Judge was assisted by Fathers Loftus and Tomerlin, he "blessed the white cross atop the new building, then each of the rooms."[26] Father Judge's sermon on this occasion focused on the blessing of the cross. "It is our grace today," he proclaimed, "to exalt the Cross of Christ." "The occasion," he continued, "is the opening of a new school house, a school of advanced studies, in fact a school that will introduce young men into the sacred studies of the priesthood. The time has come for the beginning of a seminary. Our hearts are full of joy and thanksgiving."

Father Judge saw this dedication as a major step in realizing his hopes for priests trained in the Cenacle spirit. He took this occasion to review "the history of the last seven years":

> Here in this place, twenty miles from the city, ten miles from a railway station, in a virginal forest of the South, there was but one Catholic. This morning, as yesterday morning, and every morning, one hundred and twenty-five received the Blood that drenched that Cross, that Blood that washed away our sins. Here today is seen a Catholic boys' school and girls' school, a Catholic boys' high school and girls' high school, and this preparatory school for the priesthood. Here today is found an active Catholic center. Here are found the Motherhouses of two Religious Communities, the Brothers and Sisters, Missionary Servants of the Most Blessed Trinity, devoted young men and women in training for the work of Preservation of the Faith. The zeal of many bishops and priests has already found them. Many are the moving petitions coming now to this hitherto remote and unknown place, pleading with you apostolic

24. "Missionary Servants of the Most Blessed Trinity," or "The Cenacle and Its Work," AST, MF 691–92.

25. Brediger refers to a letter of September 22, 1921, in which Bishop O'Connor granted the permission Judge requested to start "a house of higher studies"; see Brediger, "Leaving All Things," 69.

26. Ibid., 78. For descriptions of the dedication, see Collins, "Voice from the Past," *Holy Ghost*, June 1951, 6–7, and Brediger, "Leaving All Things," 78–79.

men and women, pleading as the Churches long ago pleaded with St. Paul, "Pass over into Macedonia and help us" (Acts 16:9).

After drawing the crowd at Holy Trinity into the New Testament story by identifying them with the apostle himself, Father Judge waxed devotional as he recalled a familiar prayer from the stations of the cross. "Who seven years ago," he asked, "would have envisioned this spectacle; what mind could have been so daring as to conceive it? Look upon, gaze upon this exalted Cross, 'We adore Thee O Christ and we bless Thee. Because by Thy Holy Cross, Thou hast redeemed the world.'"[27]

Holy Trinity Post Office

In his sermon, Father Judge had mentioned the many petitions now coming into "this hitherto remote and unknown place." Around the same time as the dedication of St. Joseph's School, the U.S. Postal Service decided that Holy Trinity had a sufficient volume of mail for its own post office. No longer would the petitions to which Judge referred come to Holy Trinity Station, Cottonton, but to Holy Trinity, Russell County, Alabama. According to Mother Boniface, the first official Holy Trinity postmark went out on an October 5 letter to Father Judge.[28] From its opening in 1923 until it closed at the end of the 1980s, the postmaster at Holy Trinity was a Missionary Servant of the Most Blessed Trinity.

Edgar Fursman and the New Jersey Connection

Surprisingly, most of the students for this new apostolic school came from New Jersey. In spring 1923, the Missionary Servants received a gift of a former vacation property in a rural area of Connecticut called Town Hill in the Hartford Diocese. In July 1923 Sister Mary James and two other sisters went to Connecticut to take possession of "the little white house on the hilltop set in the midst of nowhere but with a beautiful view for all its isolation." Staying in a nearby vacation home on his way to Maine was Father Felix M. O'Neill (1877–1949), the pastor of St. Michael's Church in Newark, New Jersey. Father O'Neill and the sisters met by chance. He was still there when about forty lay members of the Cenacle, including Margaret Healy, began arriving

27. Father Judge's sermon on the dedication of St. Joseph's School appeared in the *Holy Ghost*, October 1923, 10.

28. Collins, "Voice from the Past," *Holy Ghost*, June 1951, 6.

for a retreat. Father O'Neill became interested in the work. Through the sisters he met Father Judge and eventually became his close friend.

Within a month, Father Judge wrote to Mother Boniface about "one of the latest friends God the Holy Ghost has sent us." "Whatever missioning out you have," he told her, "do it with this reservation, that Fr. O'Neill is to get a band of Sisters."[29] That fall O'Neill went to Holy Trinity to participate in a priests' retreat Judge organized there. A decade later, it was Father O'Neill who preached the sermon at Father Judge's funeral in the chapel at St. Vincent's Seminary in Germantown, Pennsylvania.[30]

In fall 1922 Brother Augustine Philips moved from Holy Trinity to Gillette, N.J., where the sisters had acquired a farm property in 1921 from the McGrath sisters of Brooklyn: Katherine, Belle, and Anna. All three eventually joined the community early in 1923. Katherine McGrath was a physician. Father Judge gave her the religious name of Sister Luke. Belle and Anna were called "Sisters Matthew and Mark." Later in the year, when Cardinal Dougherty and Father Wastl asked for sisters to be in charge of each department of the Children's Bureau, Sister Luke was one of those Mother Boniface sent. After 1927 she worked at Catholic Charities in Mobile and at Holy Name of Jesus Hospital in Gadsden, Alabama.[31]

Sometime after his return from Maine in the summer of 1923, Felix O'Neill surprised Augustine Philips "sweating over the Fordson tractor." O'Neill brought someone he wanted Father Judge to meet, a young man active in youth work in the Newark area. Edgar S. Fursman, known to his cadets as the "Colonel," was the leader of a Columbus Cadet Corps. Father Judge encouraged Fursman to work with Brother Augustine and bring the Columbus Cadets to Gillette for retreats. The first such retreat at Gillette took place with twenty-one boys in December 1923. Father Tomerlin gave another retreat for boys at Gillette in February 1924.

By January of 1924, Edgar Fursman had decided to become a Missionary Servant and went to Holy Trinity. As Brother Paul Anthony, he returned regularly to New Jersey and attracted a steady stream of new students to the high school and the new apostolic school. In the fall of 1924, Fursman brought

29. Judge to Mother Boniface Keasey, Gillette, N.J., August 1, 1923, AST, MF 7638.

30. Collins, "Voice from the Past," *Holy Ghost*, March 1951, 8–9; Brediger, "Leaving All Things," 80; McNutt, *Margaret: Called and Chosen*, 49.

31. See Judge to Justin McGrath, Philadelphia, March 6, 1923, AST, MF 5322. McGrath was a staffer at the National Catholic Welfare Council in Washington. Judge hoped he would publicize the entrance of three sisters, all professional women, into the Missionary Servants; see also Tonra, *Led by the Spirit*, 97, and Collins, "Voice from the Past," *Holy Ghost*, March 1951, 6, 8.

James O'Keeffe to Holy Trinity, and, at the beginning of 1925, James Norris. As Father Thomas, O'Keeffe became custodian general of the Missionary Servants of the Most Holy Trinity and has been looked upon almost as their second founder. After Father Judge's death in 1933, Norris left the Missionary Servants but went on to become a lay activist in the church. As noted in the introduction, Norris was the only layman to speak formally at the Second Vatican Council. Thomas Brediger came south in the fall of 1925. As Father Lawrence, he organized the men's archives and wrote their first histories.[32]

The *Holy Ghost* Magazine and Father Loftus

The account of Father Judge's October 8, 1923 sermon at the dedication of the new apostolic school appeared in the *Holy Ghost*, a magazine that had published its first issue at Holy Trinity the previous April under Father John Loftus. Loftus came to the Cenacle with two ideas that seemed quite compatible with Judge's vision for it. The first was to spread devotion to the Holy Ghost through what Loftus called the League of the Holy Ghost. He envisioned the magazine as the chief organ of the league. The second was to work in the Negro apostolate in the South. The magazine's beginnings gave clear signs that the relationship between Loftus and Judge would not be a happy one.

During fall 1922, Father Loftus traveled in the North with Father Judge. With Judge so often on the road, he was always concerned to have priests at Holy Trinity for daily Mass for the sisters, brothers, and students. But he did not want Loftus to arrive at Holy Trinity before everything was ready for him. The time he spent with Loftus had convinced him of how important it was that things be arranged to Loftus's satisfaction. He sent Mother Boniface a full page of instructions on how to prepare for Loftus's arrival. He urged her to have the membership register for the league ready and to give it to Loftus immediately upon his arrival, and then to make sure that office space was prepared for him. He wanted the office to "bespeak a center for this devotion to the Holy Ghost." He suggested some "appropriate phrases or prayers to the Holy Ghost" on the walls and perhaps a painting of a dove. He also wanted leaflets for the league prominently displayed. He told her that it would be a great comfort to Loftus to be able to walk into an office "that spells everywhere Holy Ghost." Speaking of Father Loftus's sacrifice in leaving his parish in Connecticut, Judge wrote:

32. Brediger, "Leaving All Things," 73–74, 88, 98, 102.

> There is a pathos about his sacrifice, think of a man of his years, of his standing in the diocese, a week or two ago, without a home, without a school, without a church, without a parish, and all for love of the Holy Ghost. Do you not see how his heart would be warmed if he walks into an office that will give a response to the love he has in his heart for the Third Person of the Adorable Trinity? Do not lose a moment on this, please.[33]

The First Cover of the *Holy Ghost*

Despite his desire to accommodate Father Loftus, Father Judge insisted that the magazine was a Cenacle project. This meant Loftus would never have complete editorial autonomy. "Either the Holy Ghost Magazine is a Cenacle enterprise or a private venture," he wrote to Mother Boniface shortly after his return from Puerto Rico in March 1923.[34] Judge spent most of the first three months of 1923 on the island. With Father Judge absent and Mother Boniface in charge at Holy Trinity, editorial problems began to surface. The magazine's first issue was due to appear at the beginning of April. By late March and Judge's return to the mainland, conflicts over the magazine had come to a head.

"The Holy Ghost magazine is in my thought and prayer," Father Judge wrote to Mother Boniface upon his return from Puerto Rico. "I am wondering will I get a copy of it before it goes to the printers," he continued. "It seems to me that I should overlook [*sic*] it. I know I asked for a copy." He feared that the contents of the magazine might be "made too ponderous."[35] As April 1 drew closer, Father Judge became a bit frantic about seeing the copy. "I am waiting so anxiously for answer to these questions which I asked in some of my previous letters," he began. Among his questions were, "Are you working in the Holy Ghost office? When will I get the magazine papers to overlook?" He repeated his concern about the tone of the articles. "It is the opinion of

33. Judge to Mother Boniface Keasey, Gillette, N.J., October 1, 1922, AST, MF 7547.

34. "If it is a Cenacle business," he continued, "it comes under the ordinary Cenacle rules ... is subject to Superiors in the Cenacle.... Now we understand it is a Cenacle enterprise, moreover, it is the mouth-piece of the Cenacle.... It is true what Father said,—that I gave the magazine over to him and put him in charge but this does not mean that I separated myself from it and divested myself from all responsibilities of its issue or manner of issue. The magazine being what we say it is, I am responsible in the first place. I am responsible to the public for the articles. All this fits into a conversation I had with Father before he came to Holy Trinity Station, that we had a Cenacle way and it was the only way we knew"; Judge to Mother Boniface Keasey, Philadelphia, March 28, 1923, AST, MF 7606.

35. Ibid., Brooklyn [March 1923], AST, MF 7588.

many that the magazine will not be a success if the style is too ponderous." He wanted "some Cenacle news," something of "a light vein," and "a story for children." He wanted the first issue to be just right and was willing to delay a week or two to get it right. "Do get this before Father," he urged Mother Boniface, "and I am writing him also."

Then Father Judge came to the chief bone of contention between Father Loftus and himself: the cover of the magazine. The cover would represent the face of the Cenacle to the public. His disagreement with Loftus over the magazine's cover offered Judge an opportunity to articulate clearly the role of the Holy Spirit in his vision of the Cenacle and its work. He sent a telegram about the cover. Loftus had set up a simple cover with only the words "Holy Ghost." Judge also wanted the words "Missionary Cenacle" and "Preservation of the Faith" on the cover. He was frustrated. "You see I haven't got a word or any idea of what is being done." He asked Mother Boniface "to suspend all your work, whatever you are doing, and get me some response in the next mail." He assured her that Loftus had "a letter in the same mail from me."[36] "I am anxious," he told Loftus, "that Cenacle and Preservation of the Faith be prominently placed on the cover." He argued for their deep inner connection to the Holy Ghost:

> We have spent years trying to educate the public into the meaning of the Cenacle and the need for the Preservation of the Faith and I am strongly of the opinion that it will please the Holy Ghost very much if in some way we will place these expressions on the front cover. Our Divine Lord Himself associated the Holy Ghost with the Cenacle. This will not crowd out some symbolical representation of the Holy Spirit as we have it. In fact the mention of the Holy Ghost will be doubly emphasized. Again it will give us a wording that none others can well copy and remove from us any suspicion of imitating title pages of other magazines.

The references to a "wording that none others can well copy" and suspicion of imitating other magazine covers suggests another dispute over rights to the term *Cenacle* that was also occupying Father Judge's attention at this time and continued into 1924. The Religious of Our Lady of the Cenacle or Cenacle Sisters, whose retreat centers were called "Cenacle Retreats," had been complaining to Father Judge, to bishops, to the apostolic delegation, and to the Vatican about what they perceived as a usurpation of their rightful name. This flap indicated that Judge's Cenacle movement was now coming to national attention in Catholic circles.

36. Ibid., Philadelphia, March 20, 1923, AST, MF 7602.

And like the disagreement with Father Loftus over the words to appear on the cover of the *Holy Ghost*, it gave Father Judge an opportunity to talk about his understanding of the term *Cenacle*. As he explained to the distinguished Paulist Walter Elliott, who had written to him on behalf of the Cenacle Sisters, "The word 'Cenacle' is scriptural and, therefore, open for all. We are very much given to it as our people have a pronounced devotion to the Holy Ghost ... and this name, attached to our mission centers, helps to keep the Holy Ghost continually before us."[37] This dispute was resolved early in 1924 by a decision of the apostolic delegate, Archbishop Pietro Fumasoni-Biondi. The Missionary Servants kept the term *Cenacle* but were to call their houses "missionary cenacles" and not "retreat cenacles." Judge's correspondence with Fumasoni-Biondi on this issue emphasizes his sense of the connection between devotion to the Holy Spirit, carried by the term *Cenacle*, and an apostolic laity.[38]

Returning to Father Judge's disagreements with Father Loftus over the magazine, Judge again brought up his worry that "if articles were too ponderous, it will not be popular." He conceded that the magazine must be "doctrinal." But "not having seen other pages, I am wondering is there any lighter vein to relieve the tension of the heavier articles." Clearly, Judge was worried that Loftus would make the magazine inaccessible to "the general Catholic public." He also instructed Loftus to omit a certain article and promised an explanation upon his return to Holy Trinity. He suggested that tongues of fire might be more appropriate than stars for the cover's representation of the gifts and fruits. With regard to Cenacle, he urged:

> I am sure that we are going to please God if we work to prevent the Cenacle and Preservation of the Faith from being submerged and to make these as outstanding as possible, for the word "Cenacle" stands not only for the place where the Blessed Mother and the Apostles met, not only for the Holy Ghost, but for devotion to the Holy Ghost and particularly that it is absolutely essential to apostolic workers. His breathing has glorified it and let us consider it as a sacred legacy that we can appropriate it for our work and mission houses.

He made a similar plea for the phrase Preservation of the Faith:

37. Judge to Elliott, Cottonton, July 22, 1923, AST, MF 5407. Elliott and the Paulists had a close relationship with the Cenacle Sisters. Joseph McSorley's notes for the many retreats he gave to the Cenacle Sisters are preserved in his papers at the Paulist Archives in Washington, D.C.

38. See Judge to His Excellency, Pietro Fumasoni-Biondi, Stirling, N.J., January 2, 1924, and Judge to Fumasoni-Biondi, Stirling, January 21, 1924, AST, MF 5658–60 and MF 5662–63; see also Judge to McHale, Stirling, August 13, 1924, AST, MF 5723–24.

> As to the wording "Preservation of the Faith," here too, we have a glorious title and one which I think if God spares us we will see become very popular and widespread within the next decade. In a certain sense we can say at present it is ours again, so that it may be made known to angels and to men that this is in a special way our vocation.[39]

Judge closed with words of encouragement for Loftus. Nevertheless, Loftus read his letter as urging that "Holy Ghost" be removed from the cover. "I cannot see," Judge wrote to Mother Boniface the next day, "how it could be interpreted from my letter that I wanted the name "Holy Ghost" taken off the magazine." He told her that he had telegraphed Loftus to that effect and that he was willing to allow the covers that had already been printed to be used. This was an "offering of peace."[40]

When the *Holy Ghost*'s first issue appeared, its cover represented a compromise, probably worked out by Mother Boniface. A large picture of Mary and the apostles gathered in the Cenacle dominated the cover. The word Cenacle did not appear. At the top of the cover in large letters was "The Holy Ghost." Nineteen stars surrounded the picture of Mary and the apostles in the upper room. Seven large stars, three at the top and four at the bottom of the picture, represented the seven gifts of the Holy Ghost. Twelve smaller stars, six on either side, represented the twelve fruits of the Holy Ghost. Below the picture in smaller letters was "Monthly Bulletin of the League."

Relations between Father Judge and Father Loftus did not improve. A few months after their disagreement about the cover, Judge reprimanded Loftus about a "new spirit" manifesting itself at Holy Trinity. It concerned the "direction of souls and the administration of the Sacrament of Penance." He accused Loftus of compelling sisters into the confessional, spreading stories about private revelations among the sisters, and "practically organizing another community for colored work." He told Loftus that "he had to choose between going off and starting his own community with the people he had trained or submitting to a 'Cenacle spirit and Cenacle practice and tradition'" that "must be supreme." He threatened to present these matters to a community assembly and have any who think they have visions from God to submit them to the bishop.[41]

39. Judge to Loftus, Brooklyn, March 27, 1923, AST, MF 5331.

40. Judge to Mother Boniface Keasey, March 28, 1923, AST, MF 7606. As Tonra remarks, "If everything he [Judge] suggested for the cover were used, it would have been crowded with information and lost its attractiveness"; Tonra, *Led by the Spirit*, 98. Tonra treats the *Holy Ghost* at 98–100.

41. Judge to Loftus, Brooklyn, June 26, 1923, AST, MF 5392–93.

Less than a year later, Father Judge sent Father Loftus a two-page critique of an article on the "Necessity of Devotion to the Holy Ghost." He feared Loftus's claim that "there are so few saints in the Church at present, might be the undoing of the Holy Ghost magazine."[42] Conflict between Judge and Loftus continued until Loftus left Holy Trinity for good in early October 1928. Loftus complained about Judge's interference in the magazine's finances and his choice of writers. "Fr. Judge," he wrote, "is of the opinion that any of 'the boys and girls' can write."[43]

As the correspondence suggests, Mother Boniface's location at Holy Trinity sometimes pressed her into service as a mediator between Father Judge and Father Loftus. With Judge's support, she also encouraged the sisters and women members of the Outer Cenacle such as Margaret Healy to write for the *Holy Ghost*.[44] Women, Judge thought, "were going to play a larger and more important part in the affairs of business and matters of everyday life, in fact almost to wrest control from men." If such women were without faith, they would "demoralize the Faith and morals of the coming generations." Judge wanted faithful women to "cross pens with a blatant and infidel womanhood." Under the supervision of the priests, he encouraged the sisters "to perfect themselves in writing." Appealing to the sisters' work in the field of social welfare, he wrote, "As they have taken precedence of others in works of charity, so that they have been for some years ahead of the general movement, so it may happen again that in advance of the action and movement of the general body of Catholic womanhood, they may invade this new world that women are creating."[45] Four years later, for example, at the urging of Mother Boniface, Dr. Margaret Healy of the Brooklyn Cenacle contributed a three-part series on "Women's Part in the History of the Early Church."[46]

42. He warned Loftus to be careful in comparing the "love of the Father and the Son and a mother's love for a child." "Do read and study carefully this analogy," he urged, "as there is danger to try to describe the mysterious relations of the Adorable Trinity from human sentiments or heart action." In the same letter, he also critiqued an article by Sr. Angel Guardian, suggesting that her background "as a live stock and poultry raiser" may account for "too much sex idea" in her article. He found terms such as "father instinct" and "mother instinct" to savor "too much of the modern school of naturalism and animalism ... too much of the cattle breeder." He advised "Catholic modesty"; see Judge to Loftus, Stirling, N.J., October 31, 1924, AST, MF 5833–34.

43. Loftus to Dear Father [Mobile Chancellor], Holy Trinity, August 21, 1928, Toolen Papers, AAM.

44. Tonra, *Led by the Spirit*, 100.

45. Judge to Fr. Boniface, OFM Cap., Cottonton, July 26, 1923, AST, MF 5411.

46. McNutt, *Margaret: Called and Chosen*, 59.

In her usual down-to-earth way, Mother Boniface best captured the magazine's importance in 1923. "We are utterly unknown to the great bulk of Catholics in this Country and to get in touch with them we need a publication. Through it we can make our wants known to them and tell them the progress of the work."[47] In its early years, by publishing such pieces as his 1923 Catholic Charities address, the magazine would prove an effective vehicle for the circulation of the details of Judge's vision for an apostolic laity. Shortly after its first issue, in an appeal to sympathetic clergy to support the magazine, Judge called the *Holy Ghost* "the latest providential manifestation of the Cenacle movement."[48] The *Holy Ghost* continued publishing until 1959.

Father Judge as a 1920s Businessman

"I thought of starting in business myself and so I am after a million names," Father Judge wrote to Sister Mary James shortly after his return from Puerto Rico in March 1923. He was talking about a mailing list for the *Holy Ghost* magazine. Mass mail advertising and sales had been going on in the United States since the mid-nineteenth century. Later in the century, Sears and other mail-order catalogs raised it to an art. In a handwritten addition to this letter, he listed eight ways to gather names. The last one was purchasing lists from "professional listers of names."[49]

For all his critique of naturalism and materialism and the technical procedures of scientific social workers—for example, card systems and surveys—Father Judge was quite taken by business and its ways, as well as by the newfangled machines of the 1920s. In this letter, he twice asked Sister James about getting an addressograph machine for the lists they would put together. But it was an "ice machine" that most caught his fancy at this time. What we might recognize as home refrigerators had been on the market since the early twentieth century. It is likely that Judge's "ice machine" had something to do with ice cream, perhaps a "continuous process freezer."[50] He worked on the ice machine project with a man he referred to in his letters as "the

47. Tonra, *Led by the Spirit*, 99.

48. Judge to Very Rev. Msgr. Luke Evers, Cottonton, May 4, 1923, AST, MF 5351. This letter offers one of the only examples of Judge citing Leo XIII's *Divinum illud*.

49. Judge to Collins, Brooklyn, March 3, 1923, AST, MF 5319–20.

50. For "History of Ice Cream," see http://inventors.about.com/od/foodrrelated inventions/a/ice_cream.htm?p=1; accessed May 15, 2009. See http://www.ideafinder.com/history/inventions/refrigerator.htm; accessed May 15, 2009, on the history of the refrigerator. General Electric had a refrigerator on the market in 1911.

Major" or the "ice cream man." In a letter to Mother Boniface, urging her to get her brother Cleve to contact the Major, Judge identified him as "Major Reveille, 217 Broadway, New York City."[51]

"My thought has been," Father Judge told Mother Boniface, "that the good God is going to place something in our hands against the day when we will have more expansion, and there will be difficulty in collecting. His providence will never fail us, if we do our part." That "something," he thought, was the ice machine. "We ought to have about $5,000," he wrote, "to safely begin the manufacture on a small scale.[52] "The ice cream man is anxious to do business."[53]

Father Judge had introduced the ice machine project to the Cenacle in a circular letter earlier in 1922 on doing the will of God. The Lord, Judge wrote, "has left us ways of finding out His blessed will." God's will is revealed in revelation and the church's doctrinal explanations of it, but also in the "circumstances of our daily lives." This is God's "Providence over us." "It is a matter of humility and prayerful delight," he went on, "to study what may be God's will toward the Cenacle." He began by considering that the Cenacle was different from other religious societies in that it had struck its roots "in a neighborhood that is positively Non-Catholic" rather than in "a kindly Catholic environment." It had none of the "encouragement and support from the faithful around them" that other societies could expect. With the continued spiritual aspiration of the Cenacle "to seek beginnings in abandoned and deserted places," this lack of local Catholic support could not be expected to change. "It seems therefore," Judge concluded, "that God will be pleased if in the development of the Cenacle there will be some feature coming out of the Cenacle that is revenue earning. What can this be?"

In such a non-Catholic and even anti-Catholic environment, Father Judge argued, business will be the main point of contact with surround-

51. Judge to Mother Boniface Keasey, Gillette, N.J., July 18, 1922, AST, MF 7527–29.

52. Ibid.

53. This sentence comes from an undated letter fragment from around this time. Judge wanted Cleve Keasey "to act for Major in handing over stock to Mason and in return receiving the Major's name assignment. The ice cream man is anxious to do business. If Steve now would throw his whole heart into this and help to get your crowd manufacturing. If friends start manufacturing, it would be well to have about $5,000." The plan seemed to involve both manufacturing and buying stock that was about to become available and that would be in the Major's name. As Judge explained, "[T]his stock could not be sold before because Major did not have assignment. These have been promised him this week." Judge's asking many blessings from our Lady of Mount Carmel suggest that the date is July 16, 1922. The identities of Mason and Steve are as unclear as the details of this business deal; see AST, MF 7513–14.

ing people. "It seems therefore a business of some kind will be an attendant feature of Cenacle activity." He pointed with delight and adoration of "God in his marvelous Providence over us" to the example of the brothers and their shops. Such shops and technical training bring the Cenacle "into the very life of the working man, sharing his toil and helping him to all those blessings guaranteed by Christian democracy." But shops, he went on to say, "cannot be kept open unless through production and the production of what is useful and reasonably profitable." "It seems then," he concluded, "the Will of God that such an article should have been procured." At this point in his study of divine providence, he introduced the ice machine. "God most wonderfully placed in the hands of our friends a machine for electrical refrigeration, or simply an electric ice machine."

Father Judge went on to explain that many such machines had been tried and failed. Then this machine came along. "That big electrical combine known as Westinghouse" had been searching for years for such a machine and unsuccessfully tried to acquire the rights to this one. "The same machine perfected," he announced, "is now in the hands of your friends, owned out-right with all the patents, foreign and domestic." This machine was about to be made public with the endorsement of Westinghouse "as their engineers have reported that it has gone above their most exacting requirements." Then, with a rather tentative conclusion, given the providential buildup, he concluded, "We beg your prayers on our good friends in this business for they may be of service later to our Brothers, even to the Sisters, and the thought comes to us in some way this affair may be of some service in our missionary undertakings."[54]

Unfortunately, in spite of this prayer, the ice machine would prove a hindrance rather than a service. Eight months later, Father Judge wrote to Mother Boniface, "The ice machine proposition is looming up very promisingly. The Major and Fr. Carroll are again writing. I do wish that you could get some word from Cleve."[55] By the time of his return from Puerto Rico in March 1923, Judge could tell Sister Mary James:

> The Major has ample money for demonstrating the ice machine. He is going on with a big New York builder this coming week and if he is successful this man

54. Judge to "My dear Children, Brooklyn, January 30, 1922, AST, MF 5171–72.

55. It was in July that Judge had first asked Mother Boniface to enlist her brother in the ice machine cause. Fr. Carroll was probably Fr. Lawrence Carroll, pastor of St. William Church in East Pittsburgh, where the sisters did nursing work; Judge to Mother Boniface Keasey, Brooklyn, September 21, 1922, AST, MF 7540–42.

> is going to place an order for 90 machines, small and from the looks of things they will be placed in many apartment houses. A new machine will have to be built. It will be the small and cheap machine.

"This brings us," Father Judge added, "to another chapter in the ice machine." The Major needed more money, and he wanted to sell "the Stirling house." Judge told him he could sell it for $7,000. "If he does," Judge joked to Sister James, "he may loan you a few dollars." In a postscript he added that the McGrath sisters were leaving for Holy Trinity in a few days. Dr. Katherine McGrath asked Judge to take over the property and gave him $4,000 "to put the ice machine going." He found Dr. McGrath's gesture "beautiful and edifying," done "with such simplicity, as if it were a few loaves of bread, wishing it to be done before she left."[56]

By the end of July 1924, Judge was trying "to close up matters with the Major." He had appealed for help, probably financial advice, to William Zeh in Chicago. Zeh, married to a former Cenacle member, had advised Judge when he was sent to help with the financial difficulties at DePaul University in 1909. He told Zeh that a "notice" had been "levied" on the Major "to deliver all papers to Gold St." Zeh had no doubt advised Judge to get from the Major a full accounting of the money the Missionary Servants had invested in his ice machine scheme:

> I have tried every way to get a statement, which I cannot. He admits he should give it and that he is not doing the right thing in not giving it. He promises to give it, promises me, promises Fr. Tomerlin and promises Sister James, as he has promised you, but none is forthcoming. I will see what can be done in this matter.[57]

Years later Bishop Toolen would invoke the ice machine fiasco as evidence that Father Judge was "most impractical" and had "no sense of the value of money." Toolen accused Judge of investing the sisters' money "in all kinds of get rich quick schemes." Toolen claimed, probably on evidence provided by Sister Gertrude, that Judge had lost $20,000 of the sisters' money on the ice machine.[58] During the apostolic visitation after Father Judge's

56. Judge to Sr. Mary James Collins, Brooklyn, March 3, 1923, AST, MF 5319–21. In July the Ku Klux Klan burned a cross at the former Torey Estate in Stirling. The property Dr. McGrath gave to Fr. Judge was in Gillette. It is not clear if this was the "Stirling house" Judge seemed willing to sell; see Judge to "Gentlemen" [Justin McGrath, NCWC Press Department], en route south, July 14, 1923, AST, MF 5472–73.

57. Judge to William Zeh, Stirling, July 30, 1924, AST, MF 5711. On Mrs. Zeh, see Judge to McHale, Orange, N.J., December 3, 1921, AST, MF 5121. On Judge and De Paul in 1909, see chap. 2.

58. Toolen to Moses E. Kiley, Mobile, January 17, 1931, AAM, Toolen Papers. Kiley was the

death, Bishop Gerald Shaughnessy also made reference to the ice machine.[59] In Judge's view, providence had sent the Major with his ice machine plans. Whether the Major was an unscrupulous speculator or someone who genuinely wanted to help Judge and got in over his head is difficult to know. That this was a very bad investment for Judge and the Cenacle is clear. But Judge and the Major did not miss by much. About two years later, Clarence Vogt of Louisville marketed the "first commercially successful continuous process freezer for ice cream."[60]

Farmer Judge: "Close Out on a Rising Market"/"Put Everything in Cotton"

As 1922 drew to a close Father Judge decided that, instead of merely supporting those who lived on it, the farm at Holy Trinity was ready to become a business venture that generated money for their work. The Missionary Servants were in the process of applying for a loan to improve the farm. Judge wrote to M. F. Ryan, a Chicago lender, describing how they had turned a "splendidly located" but run-down plantation—"a veritable jungle"—into a "smiling paradise and the most improved farmland in this section of the country." Having introduced "electrical farm implements, tractors, etc.; built up splendid pastures; put in ten miles of wiring," they were "now in a position to produce bountiful crops." He touted their farm plan as "scientific and approved by the State Agricultural College." He claimed that their past year's investment in cotton had returned 50 percent.[61] We do not know the amount of the loan Judge requested or whether Mr. Ryan approved it. This correspondence makes clear, however, that by the 1923 planting season, Judge was counting on the plantation at Holy Trinity to become a money-making operation.

---

rector of the North American College and Toolen's agent at Rome. According to Toolen, Judge had also invested in a "machine to extract oil from nuts" and a "grocery and garage business that failed" (Bro. Augustine's shop at Holy Trinity), as well as a "cotton brokerage business in New York." He cited rumors that Judge was "playing the stock market."

59. Bishop Gerald Shaughnessy, "Apostolic Visitation of the Missionary Servants of the Most Holy Trinity," September–October, 1937, typescript 15 pages, at p. 8, from a copy in AST. In addition to the ice machine, Shaughnessy also mentioned the nut machine and a "brokerage office" in New York. According to this report, Brother Augustine claimed that the patent to the ice machine had been "stolen."

60. See note 50, "History of Ice Cream."

61. Judge to M. F. Ryan, Phenix City, Ala., November 6, 1922, draft, AST, MF 5149, and Judge to M. F. Ryan, Cottonton, November 7, 1922, AST, MF 5242.

By March they had seven five-hundred-pound bales of cotton warehoused on the plantation, and it was time for a council to decide what to plant. "Mother writes that she is broke," Father Judge told Sister Mary James. As treasurer, Sister James was anxious to sell the cotton. Judge, who had been studying the market forecasts for the prices of cotton, was urging her to wait. If she couldn't, he advised her to "close out on a rising market, that is, put your selling price ahead of the market." He reminded her that, if she didn't sell the cotton, she could still, according to "new Federal credits," borrow 75 percent on the cotton in the warehouse. Here was Father Judge speculating on cotton futures.[62]

On the same day, Father Judge wrote Mother Boniface a two-page letter about cotton. After a long explanation on how to sell cotton "at a rising market," he concluded, "It looks to me that at any time there will be a runaway cotton market, which means cotton may go to any price, therefore it is wise for us to hold on if we can." After this lesson in market dynamics, he wrote, "I wish the Sisters would familiarize themselves with these conditions. It would give them a foresight and help them to forecast, for example, the planting possibilities." His final assessment: "put everything in cotton." Nevertheless, he still counseled holding on to the cotton and borrowing against it until the market went up.[63]

By October 1924, they were still holding the cotton, and Father Tomerlin wrote objecting to this as speculation. But Father Judge's reply turned speculation to thrift. "As for the cotton," he responded, "it is not gambling to refuse to throw it on the poorest and lowest month's market of the year. To hold it for a good market is thrift and a duty I owe to the labor and sweat of those who produced it."[64] Despite Judge's advice to put everything into cotton, the council must have decided otherwise, and Sister Rita planted one hundred acres of oats in the fall of 1923.[65]

In August 1923, Father Judge had told Mother Boniface that, by his calculations, they were "in debt about $60,000 throughout the province." The sisters working in Catholic Charities in various dioceses earned modest salaries, from $30 to $60 per month. There were the diocesan collections and some income from the store. At an average of 8 percent, Judge calculated

62. Judge to Sister Mary James Collins, Philadelphia, March 9, 1923, AST, MF 5324.

63. Judge to Mother Boniface Keasey, Philadelphia, March 9, 1923, AST, MF 7590–91.

64. Judge to Tomerlin, Stirling, October 29, 1924, AST, MF 5831. Tomerlin was one of those whose labor had produced the cotton.

65. Collins, "Voice from the Past," *Holy Ghost*, June 1951, 8, citing a letter from Mother Boniface.

they would need $5,000 to meet interest payments. He made no mention of farm revenue in this letter.[66]

Over the years, Father Judge would regale whoever ran the farming at Holy Trinity with his "popular science" expertise on crops, livestock, and equipment. His embrace of machines, "scientific" farming, and fundraising came along with his continuing critique of naturalism and scientific social work. As America shifted "from the creed of hard work and thrift to 'the new consumerism of the modern age,'" this ambivalence about the "modern temper" was widely shared. It is epitomized in the figure of Bruce Barton, a preacher's son turned adman, who, in 1925, entitled his wildly popular book on Jesus as the "founder of modern business," *The Man Nobody Knows*. Most revealing about Barton's book is his apologetic intent. In 1925 his book was a serious attempt to make Jesus relevant. Though Reinhold Niebuhr was appalled at seeing Christ turned into "a typical Rotarian go-getter" and a "kind of sublimated Babbitt," Americans bought it anyway. It is safe to say that Father Judge never read Barton's book, but he did share Barton's innocence in writing it and popular America's capacity to take it seriously on a grand scale.[67]

The New Motherhouse, June 11, 1924

Nothing captures Father Judge's 1920s can-do spirit better than the sisters' new motherhouse, built from Russell County pine and oak in mid-1924. Already in May 1923, Judge had reported to Father McHale on his plans for the new building.[68] Richard Ryan, a Catholic architect from Montgomery, designed it. Father Tomerlin and his crew began cutting lumber for it in the spring. St. Joseph's School temporarily distracted them from this task, but

66. Judge to Mother Boniface Keasey, Gillette, N.J., August 8, 1923, AST, MF 7640–41. As this letter indicates, the main concern in the 1920s was meeting interest payments rather than paying down the principal on the loans. See also Judge to Mother Boniface, Gillette, N.J., August 1, 1923, AST, MF 7638, which does mention "the cutting down of the mortgages."

67. On Barton's book, I have relied on Robert K. Landers's review of *The Man Everybody Knew: Bruce Barton and the Making of Modern America* (2006), by Richard M. Fried, in *Commonweal*, April 21, 2006, 24–26. Most of the phrases in quotation marks in the previous paragraph are from Landers's review. See also Bruce Barton, *The Man Nobody Knows: A Discovery of the Real Jesus* (Indianapolis: Bobbs-Merrill, 1924, 1925). Chap. 6 is entitled, "The Founder of Modern Business." Barton took the book's opening epigraph from Luke 2:49, "Wist ye not that I must be about my Father's *business*?" (Barton's italics). Landers writes that "in the first eighteen months after publication, more than a quarter million copies of the book were sold." The phrase "modern temper" is from Lynn Dumenil, *The Modern Temper: American Culture and Society in the 1920s* (New York: Hill and Wang, 1995).

68. Judge to McHale, Cottonton, May 3, 1923, AST, MF 5349.

after the dedication in October they returned to it. By this time, they had their own sawmill. It was Mother Boniface, however, who ran the operation.

"Everything going nicely, but oh, the cost. No cash," Mother Boniface wrote in November 1923. "Motherhouse going up, thirty men on it today. Johnson sawing, running $500 cash every week for Johnson and $300 for the men. But I did as I said, I paid every bill." At the end of November, her brothers, Cleve and Charlie, came for a weekend visit. "They both deal in lumber in the north," she explained, "so I was anxious to have them visit the mission to get their opinion of the lumber." Cleve and Charlie Keasey were impressed. By fall 1923 Mother Boniface could write that workers at Holy Trinity were planning the lumber for sale in the South and she was writing north to get an idea of what to charge. The new motherhouse struck her as "quite a massive structure . . . so very, very large." She wrote that they expected to have at least the chapel ready for Christmas.[69]

Traveling in the North

During October and November 1923, after the dedication of St. Joseph's School, Father Judge went north. He wanted to begin an Outer Cenacle to work with the 50,000 Italians in the neighborhoods around St. Michael's Church where Felix O'Neill was pastor. The sisters already staffed St. Michael's Center at the parish, where they worked to draw the immigrant population into the U.S. parish structure.[70] According to the detailed quantitative report Judge sent to the diocese, the success of this Outer Cenacle called attention to "the great power of the devoted laity for good, when spiritualized and encouraged."[71] He attributed this success "entirely to poor working people trained by the priest to a particular devotion to the Blessed Sacrament and the Holy Ghost."[72]

69. For the quotations from Mother Boniface, see Tonra, *Led by the Spirit*, 103–5.

70. See Gallaher, "Social Work of the Missionary Servants of the Most Blessed Trinity," where St. Michael's Center is treated in chap. 3, on settlement work.

71. Judge to Msgr. John A. Duffy, Brooklyn, July 9, 1924, AST, MF 5696, and the report at 5698. Judge claimed that between November 10, 1923, and June 30, 1924, more than 18,000 people had been brought to Sunday Mass and more than 25,000 had been instructed.

72. Judge to His Eminence John Cardinal Bonzano, Holy Trinity, October 1924, AST, MF 5819–20. A former apostolic delegate recently returned to Rome, Bonzano was already sympathetic to the Cenacle's work with Italian children. "It is sometimes said with reproach," Judge wrote, that after receiving First Communion and Confirmation, Italian children "relapse and no longer attend the Holy Sacrifice of the Mass or receive the Sacraments." Cenacle workers had not found this to be true and identified as "the most important part" of their method "to follow them up by visiting their homes and encouraging them in the practice of their faith."

During the days of preaching to begin the new Outer Cenacle at St. Michael's, Father Judge was taken ill and spent some weeks recovering at Father O'Neill's rectory. On November 10, 1923, he wrote from St. Michael's that "I am going to a hospital for treatment for two weeks." He added that he did not want this to get around. "It is nothing serious," he insisted, "but it will probably help me to avoid these inconvenient foot troubles."[73] Even while he was sick, Father Judge did not stop working.

Earlier in 1923 he had, with the cooperation of Dr. M. T. Barrett, a Philadelphia physician, started a men's cenacle there. He wrote from Newark sending his regrets to Dr. Barrett that he would have to miss a meeting of this cenacle, which he had been scheduled to attend. He urged Dr. Barrett "to effect that every Catholic will become a missionary."[74] Mother Boniface was also in the North in early December, and both she and Father Judge missed Father McHale's visit to Holy Trinity in early December. At an evening benediction of the Blessed Sacrament, McHale's talk encouraged everyone by assuring them "that the work of the Missionary Servants was of God, and that its steady development was his Providential care of the Cenacle."[75] Later in December Father Judge met Father McHale at St. Joseph's Hospital in Philadelphia.[76]

From Christmas to the Dedication of the Motherhouse

Father Judge made it back to Holy Trinity on Christmas Eve. Between Christmas and the dedication of the motherhouse scheduled for June 11, 1924, he was much on the road. At Holy Trinity, he stayed in the new motherhouse. "A suite of rooms (back of and above the sacristy), bedroom, bathroom, and office were all furnished and ready when he arrived."[77] By this time Mother Boniface had also returned. Father Judge celebrated a solemn Midnight Mass in the chapel of the new motherhouse. Fathers Loftus and Tomerlin assisted him, and eight sisters received the habit on Christmas Eve 1923.[78]

73. Judge to "My dear Child," Newark, N.J., November 10, 1923, AST, MF 5461.

74. Judge to Dr. M. T. Barrett, Newark N.J., October 21, 1923, AST, MF 5439–40. This letter articulates the spirit and purpose of Cenacle work in the same terms Judge had used in September in his Catholic Charities address. On the men's cenacle in Philadelphia, see Collins, "Voice from the Past," *Holy Ghost*, June 1951, 7, describing this as "an auspicious rebirth" of the Outer Cenacle and giving the names of some of the men involved.

75. Brediger, "Leaving All Things" (1948), 83, citing *Holy Ghost*, January 1924, 19.

76. Collins, "Voice from the Past," *Holy Ghost*, June 1951, 9.

77. Ibid., 10.

78. Ibid., 9–10, describing Christmas Eve with a citation from *Holy Ghost* and Mother

On the day after Christmas, the men, Judge, Loftus, Tomerlin, and four brothers, incorporated as an educational and charitable society in Alabama under the name Missionary Servants of the Most Blessed Trinity. Alabama law required the certificate of incorporation to be filed with the office of Russell County's probate judge within thirty days.[79]

Shortly after filing the incorporation papers, Father Judge sailed for Puerto Rico. From there, he reported to Father McHale on the new motherhouse. They had hoped to have the dedication on the Feast of the Annunciation, March 25, 1924. Building delays pushed the date forward to June 11. "I do hope that you can be present," Judge wrote to McHale. He went on to describe the new motherhouse. "The building is 250 feet long, 3 wings of 90 feet depth, two stories and all dimensions generously proportioned. The structure can easily accommodate 500."[80]

Speaking of the brothers and a "great change" in their affairs, Father Judge told Father McHale, "They will have their own garb." Two weeks later, on May 10, 1924, the men met to choose and design their religious habit. Father Judge and twenty men, including Loftus, Tomerlin, and Fursman, were present at this council, as well as Mother Boniface, Sister Mary Francis, and five other sisters. They decided on a black cassock "fairly loose fitting of wool poplin material" and a cincture "with three streamers in honor of the Blessed Trinity." They also decided on a "flap" that would "go over breast with three buttons on right in honor of the Blessed Trinity, and then hooked down to cincture." They discussed the idea of having a pictorial representation on the garb and had designs submitted. No pictorial representation was adopted. Priests would have a biretta.[81]

Boniface's description of the chapel's Christmas decorations of "holly and bamboo and long leaf pine from our own woods."

79. A copy of a three-page document, "Certificate Incorporating the Missionary Servants of the Most Blessed Trinity," is preserved in Allen Papers, AAM. It is dated December 26, 1923, and signed by Judge, Loftus, Tomerlin, Eugene Brennan, Jerome Donegan, Jerome Supple, and James McIntyre. All except Brennan wrote "MSBT" after their signatures. Judge signed as CM MSBT. Sister Mary James mentions a letter of January 17, 1924, from Judge to Judge Dudley of Seale, Alabama, with which Judge enclosed the incorporation papers to be filed at the county seat; *Holy Ghost*, September 1951, 9.

80. Judge to McHale, Holy Trinity, Ala., April 25, 1924, AST, MF 5489–91. Judge tells McHale that he had begun this letter in February in Puerto Rico but heard that McHale was "in a far off nook of the world." He hoped the letter would catch up with McHale in Philadelphia. For Mother Boniface's long description of the inside of the building, written March 13, 1924, see Collins, "Voice from the Past," *Holy Ghost*, September 1951, 9.

81. Minutes of this meeting, headed "COUNCIL, BROTHERS' CENACLE, and dated May 10, 1924, are preserved in AST, with no microfilm number.

After this May 10 meeting, Father Judge called everyone at Holy Trinity together and gave them a long talk on family spirit. He spoke at length, urging that the family spirit continue "between the Cenacles." "We have today in the Cenacle an approach to this," he said, "a very advanced approach, in our present way of living."

> It would be a pity and reason for great sorrow if this should suffer interference and decay. Think of the mutual strength you may be to one another. Think of what you do for one another. This may be so large and important a good that, indeed I hope and pray that your affairs will be as conditioned that you must depend upon one another that you cannot do without one another, that you may realize that you need one another.

He went on to spell out the obligations of custodians (local superiors) to protect and foster this family spirit. He spoke movingly of the brothers' debt to the sisters—a debt of money but also of affection. This debt of affection "will never be liquidated." Nevertheless, the brothers should feel that "this debt also they must pay off." He could foresee a future time when custodians of the brothers or sisters might "become restless about these mutual relations and wish to depart from our primitive spirit" and even from the Cenacle's peculiar works:

> I wish, therefore, the Brothers to pass it down as a tradition, that they owe their existence to the Sisters and to keep before Custodians and subjects that these poor Sisters collected what they gave by sweat and blood throughout the United States. I would not die in peace if I thought that this debt would be forgotten. Brothers, you will be the more spiritual and splendid men by having a memory and gratitude of it.

Abuses, even one or two, he acknowledged, could "shatter this beautiful relation," but not if custodians do their duty. "You are anxious to know my mind on this matter," he continued:

> You know it, but to make it the more positive and to help this holy tradition, I declare that I recognize the value of a family spirit, of a family working in the Church, of a family that with ardor will take these words from Our dear Lord's lips "Going therefore, teach ye all nations; baptizing them in the name of the Father, and of the Son, and of the Holy Ghost" (Mt 28:19).

He went on to explain why he wanted Mother Boniface and the sisters to be present at the meeting. Preserving and handing on such a family spirit would bear beautiful fruits "for the honor and glory of God and the edification of the Church." "I was, therefore, anxious," he concluded, "to have the

Sisters here today, since I knew they would not only be edified but that they would pray the more intensely for us and help foster this tradition of the family spirit."[82]

What prompted such a passionate defense of the family spirit from Father Judge on the occasion of the meeting on the men's garb? Perhaps someone had objected to the presence of Mother Boniface and six sisters at the council. From the beginning, Brothers Augustine Philips and Eugene Brennan had worked closely with the sisters. Neither could be present for this meeting. The most senior men, Loftus and Tomerlin, had not been formed in this family spirit.[83] Perhaps one or both of them objected to the natural authority, both official and informal, that Mother Boniface exercised over affairs, and especially over the money, at Holy Trinity. Loftus had complained earlier of her interference with the magazine and would complain later of her management of money. Judge's emphasis on the brothers' monetary debt to the sisters suggests that he thought on this occasion there were some who needed to be reminded of it.

Perhaps the present emphasis on the motherhouse and its great expense made some of the men feel they and their work had been put on hold. Whatever the reason, Judge spoke memorably and powerfully of a family spirit between the women and the men of the Cenacle. Within a month, the new motherhouse would be dedicated. No doubt he hoped it would be both an effect and a sign of that spirit. On June 11, 1924, the day the motherhouse was dedicated, the men received the habit they had agreed upon on May 10.

On May 31, 1924, Judge spoke at the annual Outer Cenacle meeting in Brooklyn. He returned again to the Cenacle spirit, this time dwelling on the relations between what were now called the Inner and Outer Cenacles. During the past year, he had started Outer Cenacles in Philadelphia and Newark. Building up the Outer Cenacle was much on his mind, even as he gave so much energy to the internal development of the two communities that had grown from it. "The Cenacle spirit," he urged, "came from the Holy Ghost." He told the lay apostles gathered on that Pentecost Sunday that they were called:

82. Father Judge's May 10 "Conference on Family Spirit," AST, MF 850–57; previous citations are from MF 850–54. Excerpts appear with Father Timothy Lynch's introduction in Monographs 4:81–86.

83. Later in 1924, Tomerlin would write from Holy Trinity to Judge in the North complaining of "community spite." "From the beginning," Judge replied, "there has been the best of feeling between Cenacles; Judge to Tomerlin, Stirling, October 29, 1924, AST, MF 5831.

to reservoir the spirit in your own lives, that your heart may be aflame with it; and you are to spread it, that is your mission. If you have that passion, "I want the Cenacle spirit, I want to breathe it, I want to scatter it," if we live that, then the Outer Cenacle will grow by bounds. This is the mission of the Inner Cenacle, to conserve the Cenacle Spirit. The Inner Cenacle is the sanctuary where that fire is kept.[84]

Dedication of the Motherhouse, June 11, 1924

May 27, 1924, marked the twenty-fifth anniversary of Father Judge's ordination to the priesthood. He was fifty-six years old. In 1924 the handsome, dignified, silver-haired man seated for his twenty-fifth anniversary portrait was at the height of his powers and success as a missionary. The dedication of the motherhouse on June 11 would be, in a sense, an unprecedented celebration of his life and work. Even Pope Pius XI had gotten involved. "Your Holiness has given much joy to your humble servant on this occasion of my Silver Jubilee," Judge wrote, "by imparting Your Papal Benediction to us, the Missionary Servants of the Most Blessed Trinity, and to our missionary Cenacle work."[85]

Father Judge had been in the North, drumming up support for the new work in Puerto Rico. He arrived at Holy Trinity on June 11 only a few hours before the dedication and celebration of his jubilee. Bishop Allen came from Mobile to dedicate the motherhouse and to preach at the dedication Mass. Father Judge sang a solemn high Mass, assisted by Fathers Loftus and Tomerlin. Two Vincentians served as masters of ceremonies. One of them was Father Warner Walker, the recently ordained son of Mrs. Walker, who had supported the Cenacle during the early days in Georgia and Alabama and who had given Andrew Philips $5,000 to buy the Bradley Plantation. The cablegram from Cardinal Gasparri imparting the papal blessing was read publicly.

On that day also, Fathers Judge, Loftus, and Tomerlin and eighteen brothers were formally clothed in the habit that had been agreed upon on May 10.[86] Bishop Allen confirmed a class of fifteen from the students at Holy

84. This talk is cited in Tonra, *Led by the Spirit*, 112.

85. Judge to His Holiness, Pope Pius XI, Holy Trinity, July 6, 1924[?], AST, MF 5700. Brediger cites the cablegram, dated June 11, 1924, from Cardinal Gasparri extending Pius XI's blessing: "The August Pontiff from his paternal heart sends his blessing to Reverend Thomas A. Judge on the completion of his twenty-fifth year in the priesthood and to his congregation of missionaries, wishing them all manner of success"; Brediger, "Leaving All Things," 90.

86. Brediger lists the names of all those who were clothed with the new habit; see "Leaving All Things," 90.

Trinity. He also gave, as a jubilee gift to Fr. Judge, the privilege of daily exposition of the Blessed Sacrament. Judge asked that the cabin, whitewashed in 1917 as a chapel, be preserved as it was and used for exposition. The *Holy Ghost* for July 1924 was devoted to the events of June 11, the dedication of the motherhouse, and Father Judge's jubilee. Sister Angel Guardian wrote an account of this day. In 1917, as Marie Mott Burr, she had given to the Cenacle the land on which the grand new motherhouse now stood.[87]

With amenities such as showers and electricity, and in terms of its sheer size, the motherhouse surpassed anything ever seen at Holy Trinity. On July 24, a cyclone blew part of the roof off, but Mother Boniface had it insured for tornados and cyclones, so it was soon repaired. A young woman from New Jersey who arrived at Holy Trinity for the first time in August described her first night view of the motherhouse from about a half mile away, "with the lights in the windows, and the dark sky, it looked like a huge steamer in the ocean."[88]

Continuing Expansion

With the motherhouse completed, attention shifted to the brothers' side. "The new chapel for the Brothers exteriorly is practically finished," Father Judge wrote to Brother Augustine. Also under construction were "a new dormitory for the small boys," a "priests' dining room," and a "dining room for all departments." The sisters' house was completed with other buildings under consideration: "an ice plant, cold storage house, house for the farmers and house for the working men." He announced that any young man who lived at Holy Trinity and did not wish to be a religious would live "under a mitigated rule" but have "no communications or relations with the religious body."[89] Father Tomerlin supervised all this construction, and Judge described him at this time as "very busy building."[90]

"We are going to have a hospital," Mother Boniface wrote at Thanksgiving time in 1924. On December 6, Mother Celestine of the Sisters of Divine

87. On the dedication of the motherhouse, see Tonra, *Led by the Spirit*, 112–13.

88. For Mother Boniface's eyewitness description of the cyclone, and the image of the huge steamer, see ibid., 113; see also Judge to William Zeh, Stirling, July 30, 1924, AST, MF 5711.

89. Judge to Brother Augustine Philips, Holy Trinity, September 11, 1924, AST, MF 5800. For descriptions of these buildings, see Brediger, "Leaving All Things," 94.

90. Judge to Cardinal William O'Connell, Stirling, October 4, 1924, AST, MF 5822. Judge began the letter, "Word has reached me that you will permit Father Gerald Fitzgerald to come to us." Fitzgerald (1894–1969) did not come. He joined the Congregation of the Holy Cross in 1933 and eventually founded the Servants of the Paraclete in 1947.

Providence signed Gadsden Hospital over to the Missionary Servants of the Most Blessed Trinity. Gadsden Hospital was about seven years old, with fifty beds. Mother Boniface described Gadsden as "about a seven hour drive" from Holy Trinity. "So you can see now," Mother Boniface wrote, "if you are a trained nurse, that you are in great danger."[91]

The Sisters of Divine Providence from Pittsburgh had not been able to make a go of a Catholic hospital in the Deep South. As Father Judge explained to Father McHale, they had become "a target of opposition and victims of boycott." The hospital reopened on January 1, 1925. "We changed the name, reopening it on the Feast of the Holy Name of Jesus, 1925, with many difficulties."[92] In taking on the hospital, Judge hoped "to save the Church the shame of closing a Catholic institution."[93]

Within six years, by 1931, the hospital's success led to a massive Depression-era building project resulting in a brand-new five-story Holy Name of Jesus Hospital. Looming larger on the Cenacle horizon at this time, however, was Puerto Rico. At Bishop Caruana's urging, Father Judge made his first visit there early in 1923. The first four sisters sailed for Puerto Rico on August 23, 1923. Until his death ten years later, the preservation of the faith in Puerto Rico as the gateway to Latin America remained one of the major preoccupations of Father Judge's life.

91. Tonra, *Led by the Spirit*, 117; see also Collins, "Voice from the Past," *Holy Ghost*, December 1951, 10.

92. Judge to McHale, Stirling, July 24, 1926, AST, MF 6183.

93. Judge to Fr. Henry E. Quinn, Holy Trinity, January 13, 1925, AST, MF 6192, as cited in Berry, *God's Valiant Warrior*, 86.

❖ 9

A SPANISH PROVINCE

Puerto Rico as Door to Latin America

Bishop Caruana's Invitation

"The very latest word on the work: To-day, October 3rd, Bishop Caruana has asked us to start a Spanish Province," Father Judge reported to Vincentian superior general François Verdier in November 1922. He had run into Bishop George Caruana at Cardinal Dennis Dougherty's residence in Philadelphia on October 1 and spent three days with him. He went on to say that, in working out the details, the bishop had in mind a number of "Porto Rican girls," whom he hoped "would enter the novitiate at Holy Trinity Station." He also reported that Caruana was "buying property now to make a beginning in his diocese."[1] This property would eventually become Holy Trinity Academy (El Pensionado Católico) near the University of Puerto Rico in Río Piedras.

Father Judge included Bishop Caruana among the bishops who supported the Cenacle at this time. He identified Bishop Caruana as "associated for a number of years with Cenacle work" and went on to say that, on a recent visit to Rome, Caruana had "brought the work to the attention of the authorities there." He also claimed that the Bishop of San Juan had "used his influence in the Delegate's office so that at any time we might have entrée." It was through Caruana, perhaps at the offices of the apostolic delegation in Wash-

1. "Missionary Servants of the Most Blessed Trinity, or, The Cenacle and Its Work," first enclosure, 2, with Judge to Verdier, Cottonton, November 7, 1922, AST, MF 692; see also Judge to Mother Boniface Keasey, Philadelphia, October 1, 1922, AST, MF 7552–53. In his use of "Porto Rico," Father Judge follows common usage of the time. In quotations I shall follow his practice.

ington, D.C., that Father Judge first met Archbishop Peter Benedetti, whom he wrote into the list of bishops as "Papal Delegate to Porto Rico and Cuba" and described as engaging the "Cenacle to apostolic work throughout West Indies" and "very much a friend and advocate of Cenacle."[2]

As Father Judge's references to Bishop Caruana's connections at Rome and the apostolic delegation in Washington suggest, Caruana was no ordinary parish priest. Born in Malta and the great nephew of the bishop there, he was also a sometime Vatican diplomat. He served in the Philippine Islands during the American military occupation after the Spanish-American War of 1898 and eventually became a U.S. Army chaplain. In 1910 he came to the United States and worked at St. Leo's Church in Corona, New York. There in his ministry with Italian immigrants, Caruana first encountered Father Judge and the Cenacle. He became a U.S. citizen in 1915. Caruana and Cardinal Dougherty met in the Philippines, where the latter served as a bishop from 1903 to 1915. In World War I, Caruana returned to the chaplaincy and served with the 65th Puerto Rican Infantry in Panama. Dougherty had become bishop of Philadelphia in 1917. After the war, he asked Caruana to serve as his secretary in Philadelphia. This is how Judge came to meet him at Dougherty's residence on October 1, 1922.[3]

After the Spanish-American War of 1898, the United States took possession of Puerto Rico from Spain. Like the Philippine Islands, Puerto Rico swiftly moved from a situation of church establishment to one of church-state separation. Based on Caruana's experience in the Philippines and with Puerto Rican soldiers during the Great War, Cardinal Dougherty recommended him for the vacant see of San Juan in 1921. Father Judge met him at Dougherty's residence just before he left for San Juan late in 1922. Though Judge talked to Caruana about his ideas for the Negro apostolate, he emphasized the idea of peoples evangelizing themselves. Both Caruana and Dougherty knew of Judge's success in mobilizing the laity to address the "Italian question." The immigrant Italian experience with U.S. parish structures was not unlike the situation in Puerto Rico, where U.S. churchmen were trying to impose a parish-based system on popular Puerto Rican Catholicism.

2. "Episcopal Approbation," third enclosure, 2, 3, with Judge to Verdier, Cottonton, November 7, 1922, AST, MF 697–98.

3. On Caruana and his mission to Puerto Rico, see Samuel Silva Gotay, *Catolicismo y Política en Puerto Rico Bajo España y Estados Unidos: Siglos XIX y XX* (San Juan: Universidad de Puerto Rico, 2005), 420–21. The section is entitled, "Georges Caruana, agent of the Vatican or the USA? 1921–1926." On Dougherty in the Philippines, see J. F. Connelly's entry on Dougherty in *NCE* (2003), 4:885–86.

Caruana was both a man with whom Father Judge connected as a missionary and an authoritative representative of the Vatican. And so it was at Bishop Caruana's personal urging that Judge sailed for Puerto Rico from Brooklyn in early January 1923 aboard the "Ponce." After less than a week on the island, he spoke in a circular letter of "a poverty and destitution here the likes of which I have never seen." He summed up his observations in seven brief points. "First of all, the needs of Religion are crying for notice. Secondly, any ministration will be gladly received by natives. Thirdly, there will be quick and generous response." He went on to describe the religious state of the people he had met and observed:

> The people by thousands are merely traditional Catholics, they do not know anything else, and they have not the remotest reason, save being born so, why they are Catholics. They adhere vehemently to the fact, if questioned, that this is their Religion or that they are Catholics. Fourthly, they seem to be pleasant and docile; there, to my mind, is not the least doubt but that there are numbers of possible vocations, boys and girls. Fifthly, they are bright. Sixthly, the protestants [sic] are making desperate attempts to seduce them. Seventhly, the people need industries apart from Religion, Christian education, and Cenacle work.

Under the heading "The Cenacle," he summarized "Conditions in our favor." First was the bishop, whom he described as "intensely" interested and whom he thought the priests would follow. Second, he saw "nothing of Catholic or protestant working activity corresponding to Cenacle." He described the clergy, "so few and short in resources," as "much dejected" and likely to welcome help.

He had been with the bishop at a city of 52,000 where there was only one priest. "Like congestion and spiritual destitution is all over the island." Finally, he wrote, "it would make one heart-sick to see hundreds of thousands, all Catholics at heart, growing up ignorant of the elements of our holy Religion." "Surely," he concluded, "it will please God very much, if we do something for these poor people."[4]

Father Judge did not speak Spanish. His impressions of the island were mediated through Bishop Caruana and those he met who spoke English, the language of instruction in all schools after the Spanish-American War. The five or six weeks he spent in Puerto Rico in January and February 1923 convinced him that the faith of a historically Catholic people was in grave

4. Judge to My dear Children, San Juan, Porto Rico, January 15, 1923, AST, MF 732.

danger and that the preservation of the faith in this pastoral situation required Cenacle lay apostles. He sailed back to the mainland in the company of Archbishop Peter Benedetti and immediately began a campaign to drum up support for the Cenacle's work in Puerto Rico.[5]

"Porto Rico Propaganda"

"I am commissioned," Father Judge wrote to Archbishop Patrick Hayes of New York, "to approach the Bishops and place the Porto Rico situation before them and I beg of you to give this matter some consideration as I am anxious for your thoughts." He also told Archbishop Hayes that the "Bishops of the West Indies," presumably Caruana and Benedetti, had called the sisters and brothers to "help in the formation of a native Priesthood, a native Sisterhood and a lay apostolate." He described the church in Puerto Rico as "in crisis." He found it "a thousand pities" that "vulgar American money and the conspiracy of unprincipled and untruthful preachers" was endangering a "cradle of Catholicity in the New World." The Protestants, he claimed, "are determined to make Porto Rico a headquarters for their proselytizing work in West Indies and South America and probably other Spanish speaking parts of the earth." Puerto Rico would, he feared, become a "Protestant Rome."[6]

From Philadelphia in the last two weeks of March 1923 Father Judge wrote similar letters to Monsignor Francis C. Kelley, director of the Catholic Extension Society in Chicago, and Father William F. McGinnis in New York, editor of *Truth* magazine, who had just published an article on Puerto Rico.[7] Judge used inflammatory language to describe the situation there:

> The imperative work of the moment is to save our children from the enemy in their defined purpose of making every school a Protestant center. To effect their purpose they have incepted a plan, which unless impeded, will proselyte the young people in the Normal School, who at present are all Catholics. It is of instant necessity that resistance be brought to destroy this frightful danger of perversion, otherwise these students will finish their training under the influence of these sectaries and be used by them amongst the school children

5. For Judge's lyrically prayerful reflections written from the "staunch sea going ship" on the journey back from Puerto Rico, see AST, MF 7572–74. On this first trip to Puerto Rico, see Collins, "Voice from the Past," *Holy Ghost*, March 1951, 4–5.

6. Judge to Most Rev. Patrick Hayes, DD, Philadelphia, March 23, 1923, AST, MF 764.

7. See Judge to Kelley, Philadelphia, March 18, 1923, AST, MF 9515 and Judge to McGinnis, Philadelphia, March 23, 1923, AST, MF 765.

as Protestant missionaries. If they carry their plan, will it not mean ultimately the invasion of the United States by a horde of preachers who will come from a perverted class?[8]

In each of these letters, Father Judge wrote of a "Girls' Academy" and a "Boys' High School" that would have to close if teachers could not be found. After sending out these appeals for help and advice, Judge reported to Bishop Caruana on the growth of what he called the "Porto Rican propaganda." He had also contacted the "Knights" [of Columbus] and urged Caruana to have the officers in Puerto Rico "start something" as the "Knights here promise to help them out." Msgr. Kelley had already sent a "very encouraging" reply. Judge hoped to meet with him and told Caruana that Kelley had "a very warm spot in his heart for you." By late March, Caruana had already purchased a property near the University of Puerto Rico. Judge told him that their mailing list was growing and "we will be able to take that property off your hands before many months." "Fr. Martinez," he reported, "writes me that he has about eight girls." A surprising number of sisters had already volunteered for Puerto Rico.[9]

Early in May 1923, Father Judge wrote Father McHale about developments in Puerto Rico. During the Spanish-American War, McHale was one of two Vincentian Navy chaplains from the Eastern Province who had served in Puerto Rico.[10] Judge described the property Bishop Caruana had purchased in front of the University of Puerto Rico as "beautiful and very advantageously situated for the Cenacle movement to save the young student teachers of the Island from proselytizing houses that flank this university."

He explained that the university was the only school on the island where teachers could be certified. The Protestant residence houses that "flanked" it were for Catholic students a "proximate occasion of losing their faith." Young women who lived in them during the three or four years of their studies, he concluded, would "in all probability" become Protestants. In this way, "every public school on the Island" would become "a protestant mission center." The sisters would "try to checkmate them." By May he could tell McHale that he had "interviewed several members of the hierarchy, Cardinals and oth-

8. Ibid., March 23, 1923, AST, MF 9515.

9. Judge to Caruana, Philadelphia, March 28, 1923, AST, MF 773.

10. Jaime Partsch, *La Crisis de 1898 y su impacto en los institutos de vida religiosa en Puerto Rico,* Colección Dr. Arturo Morales Carrión, Fundación Puertorriqeña de las Humanidades (2008), 48. Part of McHale's brief was to help protect the Vincentians and their property in Puerto Rico and Cuba. Partsch cites the Vincentian *Provincial Bulletin,* no. 56 (1986): 40.

ers" and found them "kindly disposed to help the movement." He mentioned cardinals O'Connell of Boston and Dougherty of Philadelphia.[11]

As part of the "extensive propaganda" he described to Caruana and McHale, Father Judge wrote an article on "Catholic Education in Porto Rico" that appeared in the June 1923 *Quarterly Bulletin of the International Federation of Catholic Alumnae*. He appealed to Catholics of the United States for men and women willing to teach in Catholic schools in Puerto Rico. The island, Judge began, has both a "glorious and sad chapter in the history of Catholicity in the New World." Within seventeen years of Christopher Columbus's first voyage, Puerto Rico had the Western Hemisphere's first bishop. "Long in advance of permanent white settlements in North America," Judge recounted, "the Holy Sacrifice of the Mass was offered daily, Holy Communion was received, the other sacraments were administered, and souls sanctified by prayerful lives, on this island in the West Indian Sea."

But by a strange providential reversal, people in the United States were now being called "to be the saviours of Catholicity in beautiful Porto Rico and the West Indies." Though Catholicity was "cradled" here, Puerto Rico has now been "invaded" by "relentless proselytizers with unprincipled methods and countless resources of American money." The ancestral faith of a people "Catholic at heart" was now at risk. "That Porto Rico may be lost to our Holy Religion,—what does this mean to you, my dear reader?" Father Judge urged those with leisure and means also to have apostolic hearts "to help the Spouse of Christ in such sorrow and calamity." Given the "spiritual destitution of Porto Rico," teachers were "the imperative necessity at the moment."

In the names of Bishop Caruana and Archbishop Benedetti, he concluded with an appeal for teachers. He announced that the Missionary Servants of the Most Blessed Trinity would "open a Mission Cenacle in Porto Rico this summer, to help offset these proselytizing evils," and he urged those willing to help to write to the sisters in Philadelphia.[12] On August 23, 1923, four sisters set sail from Brooklyn to staff El Pensionado Católico, Blessed Trinity Academy, the residence house at the University of Puerto Rico. A month later, four more left for the Virgin Islands.[13] The Cenacle's mission in Latin America had begun.

11. Judge to McHale, Cottonton, May 3, 1923, AST, MF 5349.

12. The text of Judge's article was reproduced in the *Holy Ghost*, June 1923, 10–11. The phrases in quotation marks are taken from here.

13. Collins, "Voice from the Past," *Holy Ghost*, June 1951, 5. Sister Bridget (Mother McMahon) was in charge of El Pensionado Católico in San Juan with sisters Margaret Mary, Mary Zita, and Amelia.

Puerto Rico in the 1920s: Historical Background

From 1508 to 1898

The conditions Father Judge found and described in Puerto Rico in 1923 have origins deep in the island's history. Juan Ponce de León led the Spanish settlement in Puerto Rico in 1508. The Spanish who colonized the island were part of the Companía de las Indias from the area around Seville in southern Spain. From such regions as Andalusia and Extremadura, many colonists would have been descendants of the Moors. As its name suggests, the Spanish expected the island to be rich in gold. But the gold soon petered out. Indigenous *tainos* were decimated by overwork and disease. As the easternmost island or gateway to the Caribbean region, Puerto Rico served then as a fortress and as a place where the Spanish colonists grew sugar cane. They enslaved East Africans to work the cane fields.

In 1789 John Carroll became the first bishop in what was then the territorial United States. Almost three centuries earlier, in 1511, within twenty years of Christopher Columbus's first contact in San Salvador and before the Reformation and the Council of Trent, Pope Julius II, at the request of King Ferdinand of Spain, erected the Diocese of Puerto Rico and made it suffragan to the Metropolitan See of Seville in Spain. Along with Santo Domingo and Concepción de la Vega in Hispaniola (contemporary Haiti and the Dominican Republic), Puerto Rico was indeed, as Judge claimed, the "cradle of Catholicism" in the New World. Licenciado don Alonso Manso, the first bishop of Puerto Rico, arrived on Christmas day in 1512, making Puerto Rico the first local church in the Americas to have a resident bishop.[14]

But Puerto Rico did not grow as the colonists expected, nor did the church. Colonists had to scale back elaborate original plans for the cathedral in San Juan. The church in Puerto Rico is descended from pre-Tridentine, Iberian Catholicism from southern Spain. Throughout its history, Puerto Rican Catholicism has tended to have relatively few and poorly educated clergy for the number of faithful. In keeping with its European origins, the church was centered in the city where most of the clergy were concentrated. This left few priests to serve the scattered rural population. In 1765, for example, forty-two priests lived at the cathedral and two friaries in San Juan, leaving twenty-six priests for the rest of the island. Priests from Spain tended to out-

14. Jay P. Dolan and Jaime R. Vidal, eds., *Puerto Rican and Cuban Catholics in the United States, 1900–1965* (Notre Dame, Ind., and London: University of Notre Dame Press, 1994), 15; see also http://www.arqsj.org.

number native Puerto Rican priests. During the centuries of Spanish rule in Puerto Rico, San Juan was often without a bishop for extended periods of time.

Despite the centrality of the Mass and the sacraments, and hence of the clergy, in Tridentine Catholicism, Mass attendance was not always a valid religious indicator in Puerto Rico. From the mid-seventeenth century, Puerto Rican church legislation made the obligation to attend Mass dependent on the distance one lived from a parish church. Those who lived further than six leagues from the church were obliged to attend Mass only on Christmas, Easter, Pentecost, and one of the Sundays of Lent. This legislation remained in effect until 1917.[15]

Popular Catholicism

Puerto Rican Catholics adapted to this situation of few priests and a scattered rural population by focusing on the feasts of the liturgical year and patronal feasts, especially those associated with the Blessed Virgin. There would be novenas leading up to the great feasts, festivals to celebrate them, and a great concern for the dead expressed in wakes, funeral rites, and intercessory prayers for the dead. The Virgin and her rosary were central. In helping the people through the problems of daily life, especially suffering and death, this popular Catholicism was intensely practical. Even in the absence of priests, the sacraments, and religious instruction, always there were things for people to *do*—processions, festivals, wakes, novenas, rosaries, and devotions.

Popular Catholicism at times comes into conflict with "official" theology and practice. Some scholars and commentators distinguish sharply between "popular Catholicism," or the religion of the people, and "institutional," "official," or "orthodox" Catholicism, the religion of the hierarchy. But unless one begins from a dogmatic theoretical position on the nature of popular religion and its relation to "orthodox" or official religion, such a dichotomy does not necessarily fit Puerto Rican Catholicism. In spite of minimal instruction and sacramental participation, it has been argued that the religious profile of an eighteenth-century Puerto Rican Catholic "was based exclusively on the doctrine of the Catholic Church ... the totality of his peculiar exterior manifestations were nothing more than interpretive modifications of liturgical acts or sacred cult, and in them he did not deviate

15. Dolan and Vidal, *Puerto Rican and Cuban Catholics*, 16–19.

one whit from the purest orthodoxy."[16] In addition to an array of patronal figures, priests and bishops are, after all, integral to the symbolic structure of Mediterranean Catholicism. When Father Judge came to the coastal village of Loiza or the Barrio Jiménez near El Yunque Mountain in the 1920s, he recognized the people as "traditional Catholics." They recognized him as a priest and came to call him "El Santo."[17]

The Spanish-American War and Its Effects on the Church in Puerto Rico

In a brief conflict on land and sea, lasting less than four months in the spring and summer of 1898, the United States defeated the Kingdom of Spain in what U.S. Secretary of State John Hay called "a splendid little war" and history text books call the Spanish-American War.[18] The United States was in an expansionist mood. Support for a Cuban insurrection against Spanish rule legitimated U.S. intervention, and war with Spain began in April. Fighting ended in August, and the Treaty of Paris was signed on December 10, 1898. By its terms, Spain relinquished sovereignty over Cuba. Spain "ceded" the Philippine Islands and the islands of Guam and Puerto Rico to the United States. Just months before the outbreak of the war, Spain had granted "Home Rule" (*Autonomía*) to Puerto Rico. The United States paid Spain twenty

16. Angel Lopez Cantos, *La religiosidad popular en Puerto Rico: Siglo XVIII* (San Juan: Centro de Estudios Avanzados de Puerto Rico y el Caribe, 1993), 10, as cited and translated in Reinaldo L. Roman, "On Jibaro Pentecostals and Popular Religion in Puerto Rico," Review of Nelida Agosto Cintron, *Religion y cambio social en Puerto Rico (1898–1940)* (Puerto Rico: Ediciones Huracan, 1996), in *H-LatAm* (January 1998). In dealing with Puerto Rican popular Catholicism, the question of its continuity or discontinuity with so-called official or orthodox Catholicism is both crucial and contested. The more discontinuous "popular religion" in Puerto Rico is with historic Catholicism, the less of an intrusion and American imposition Protestant Christianity appears in the island's history. If popular Catholicism and "orthodox" Catholicism are radically discontinuous, Pentecostalism and popular forms of Protestant Christianity are more easily seen as continuous with the historic popular religiosity of Puerto Rican people. The "official" Catholicism of the post-1898 American Catholic "missionaries" appears then, as we have it, for example, in Silva-Gotay's *Catolicismo y Política en Puerto Rico Bajo España y Estados Unidos*, as the intrusion and a tool for Americanization. See note 3, where Bishop Caruana must either be an agent of the United States or of the Vatican—in any case, an alien influence.

17. On the people as "traditional Catholics," see Judge to My dear Children, San Juan, Porto Rico, January 15, 1923, AST, MF 732. On Father Judge as "El Santo," see the foreword by Timothy Lynch, ST, in Judge, *Father Thomas A. Judge, C.M., Founder, The Missionary Cenacle Family*, Monographs 3, *Father Judge Teaches Ministry*, ed. Timothy Lynch, ST (Silver Spring, Md.: Archives, Missionary Servants of the Most Holy Trinity, 1983), 6.

18. On the Spanish-American War, see Jackson Lears, *Rebirth of a Nation: The Making of Modern America, 1877–1920* (New York: Harper, 2009), 207–9, quoting John Hay in a letter to Theodore Roosevelt at 207.

million dollars. And so it was that the Catholic Church in Puerto Rico came under the influence of the postwar policy of "Americanization."

The humiliation of Catholic Spain by an upstart Protestant nation offended Vatican sensibilities. The censure of Americanism in *Testem benevolentiae* followed six weeks later on January 22, 1899. The disposition of church property in the Philippines became a major concern of the Vatican. Senior American churchmen such as Archbishop John Ireland of St. Paul, Minnesota, took a leading role in these controversies. Leo XIII established a pattern by appointing the archbishop of New Orleans, Placide Louis Chapelle (1842–1905), born and educated in Europe, as chargé d'affaires for the Philippines and apostolic delegate to Puerto Rico and Cuba.

As Pius X's cardinal secretary of state (1903–14), Rafael Merry del Val (1865–1930) continued this pattern of European connections and experience in the Philippines. Son of a Spanish noble assigned to England and an English mother, Merry del Val shaped Vatican policy in Puerto Rico, preserving as much of the Puerto Rican Church's ties to Europe as possible. He made sure that the bishop of San Juan, even if from the United States, was a member of an international religious order. The bishop of San Juan continued as suffragan to a metropolitan outside the United States. Though an American territory, Puerto Rico remained ecclesiastically connected to Latin America and outside the control of American bishops on the mainland. From 1903 to 1915, a period roughly coinciding with Merry del Val's tenure as Vatican secretary of state, a young Dennis Dougherty served as a bishop in the Philippines. After his appointment to Philadelphia in 1917, the Vatican continued to rely on Dougherty in matters related to Puerto Rico. Like George Caruana, those appointed there often had connections to Dougherty and prior experience in the Philippines.[19]

The U.S. campaign to Americanize Puerto Rico exacerbated an already difficult situation for a local church with barely over a hundred priests and a population of 1.3 million, many living in extreme poverty, largely Catholic, and mostly scattered in rural areas. Except in the cities, where churches, clergy, schools, and other institutions were concentrated, the structural basis for Catholicism had never been strong. The coming of the Americans weakened it further. The majority of the Puerto Rican clergy had always been Spanish. The Spanish government paid the salary of all Catholic priests on the island. With U.S. ascendancy, most of the Spanish priests

19. On Merry del Val and Chapelle, respectively, see the entries by C. Ledré in *NCE* (2003), 9:520–21, and by H. C. Bezou in *NCE* (2003), 3:382–83.

wanted to return to Spain. Resources for training native clergy were meager. The church's property rights in Puerto Rico were not secured until a 1906 Supreme Court decision prevented the island's anti-clericals from having the new government confiscate all church buildings.[20]

Popular Catholicism after 1898, "Los Hermanos Cheos"

Despite, or perhaps because of, its institutional weakness, popular Catholicism, as described previously, was the Puerto Rican Church's strength. "The most dramatic product of Puerto Rico's vital popular religiosity was the lay organization Los Hermanos Cheos."[21] In 1902 José de los Santos Morales and José Rodríguez Medina responded similarly and independently to Protestant encroachments on rural Puerto Rican Catholicism. They wanted to form "an army of peasants and to rise in arms to defend our faith and our devotion to the Virgin."[22] With their 1904 Pacto de Cheo, they joined forces.

The name "Cheos" comes from the common nickname for men named "José." Eventually they gained ecclesiastical approval as La congregación San Juan Evangelista. The Cheos were itinerant lay preachers and catechists who traveled the mountains and *barrios* teaching the faith and defending the rosary and other Marian devotions against native Puerto Rican evangelists recently become Protestants. With the increasing emphasis of American Catholic missionaries on parish structure and centralized administration, though they left significant traces, the Cheos began to fade.[23]

When Father Judge came to the island in 1923, and for the length of his time there, the Cheos were still strong. They were his kind of people. He found their lay character, missionary zeal, devotional intensity, desire to

20. On the situation of Catholicism in Puerto Rico after 1898, see Dolan and Vidal, *Puerto Rican and Cuban Catholics in the U.S., 1900–1965*, chap. 2, "The Attempt to Americanize Puerto Rico and the Problem of Identity," especially 26–31; Silva-Gotay, *Catolicismo y Política en Puerto Rico*, 235. See also Anthony M. Stevens-Arroyo, "The Catholic Worldview in the Political Philosophy of Pedro Albizu Campos: The Death Knoll [*sic*] of Puerto Rican Insularity," *U.S. Catholic Historian* 20, no. 4 (Fall 2002): 53–73, esp. 54–60 on "Puerto Rican Catholicism in 1926"; Ana María Díaz-Stevens, "Missionizing the Missionaries: Religious Congregations of Women in Puerto Rico, 1910–1960," *U.S. Catholic Historian* 21, no. 1 (Winter 2003): 33–51, especially 40–46 on the presence of the Missionary Servants of the Most Blessed Trinity in Puerto Rico since 1923.

21. Stevens-Arroyo, "Catholic Worldview," 55.

22. David A. Badillo, *Latinos and the New Immigrant Church* (Baltimore: Johns Hopkins University Press, 2006), 46–47.

23. The standard study is R. P. Esteban Santaella, *Historia de los hermanos Cheos* (Ponce, Puerto Rico: Editorial Alfa y Omega, 1979); see also Edward L. Cleary, "In the Absence of Missionaries: Lay Preachers Who Preserved Catholicism," *International Bulletin of Missionary Research* 34, no. 2 (April 2010): 67–70.

preserve the faith, and sense of the needs of the church extremely attractive. In the fall of 1926, returning from a missionary trip to the Barrio Jiménez in the mountainous interior, Judge met a young man in a group he was instructing who belonged to Los Hermanos Cheos. He described the Cheos as a "remarkable society" of "poor illiterate country men who in lieu of Catholic priests are helping to do much to keep the people faithful to the teachings of their holy faith. These men are extraordinarily devout. They have a simple faith and piety and responsible for much good."[24]

The next month, at a Mass and celebration for the Feast of Christ the King at St. Augustine's Academy, Judge met the man he described as the "leader of the Cheos." Monsignor Torres, the administrator of the diocese, with Bishop Caruana absent, estimated that there were 80,000 Cheos and told Judge they were "in high esteem with the priests of the diocese." He was delighted to learn that they had "a very pronounced devotion to the Holy Ghost" and that they received Communion at the Mass. He said he had been trying to get in touch with them "for the last four years" and considered it providential that their leader brought a group to the celebration at St. Augustine's. "Their leader and myself," he wrote, "have become very much interested in each other. Do pray that useful developments may come out of it."[25]

Public Education: Americanization as Protestantization

Puerto Rico's new sovereign saw public education as the chief tool of Americanization. The 1898 Report of the U.S. Commission on Insular Affairs put it this way:

> The question of good citizenship and education can be more easily settled through the public schools than by any other method ... that this education should be in English we are clearly of the opinion ... Porto Rico is now and is henceforth to be a part of the American possessions and its people are to be Americans ... put an American school-house in every valley and upon every hill top in Porto Rico, and in these places the well-fitted and accomplished American school-teachers, and the cloud of ignorance will disappear as the fog before the morning sun.[26]

24. Judge, "Puerto Rican Chronicle" (1926), Monographs 3:34–35; Father Judge dictated the Puerto Rican "Chronicle" to Louise Wagner between September 12 and December 1926; see AST, MF 1172–1208.

25. Judge went on to describe "some very interesting things" he had learned about the Cheos. Clearly, he was taken with them; Judge, "Puerto Rican Chronicle," 3:43–44.

26. Insular Affairs, *Report of the U.S. Commission to the Secretary of War: Upon Investigation Made into the Civil Affairs of the Island of Porto Rico with Recommendation* (Washington, D.C.: Government Printing Office, 1898), 53, as cited by Díaz-Stevens, "Missionizing the Missionaries," 37.

In 1898 there was still something to the idea of a Protestant America. To be American was to be Protestant. Sensing Catholicism's vulnerable position on the island, Protestant denominational leaders met at New York's Riverside Church "to coordinate evangelization away from 'Romanism' without inter-Protestant competition."[27] The Puerto Rican public school became the "Trojan Horse" for missionizing the island's Catholic population. In this scheme of things, the "well-fitted and accomplished American school-teacher" might turn out to be the town's Protestant pastor's wife. By such "unofficial policies" of cooperation and favorable treatment, "Protestants turned the separation of church and state into a tool for undermining Catholic culture through the public schools." Stevens-Arroyo concludes, "It is fair to interpret these measures as means not to secularize the public schools but to *Protestantize* them."[28]

From his first days in Puerto Rico, Father Judge recognized this strategy and denounced it. Though lacking the ecumenical sensitivity of later years, his descriptions of Protestant intentions in Puerto Rico's schools are right on the mark. El Pensionado Católico, as a residence for Catholic young women at the University of Puerto Rico, was the beginning of his campaign to preserve the faith in Puerto Rico. "With their preferential option for the poor and neglected, emphasis on the role of the laity, commitment to fostering priestly and religious vocations, and strong apostolate of reclaiming Catholics back to the Church, the Trinitarians seemed a perfect fit for the Puerto Rican circumstances."[29]

Sister Bridget, Father Antonio, and the "Menu à la Porto Rican," 1924

Father Judge made his second voyage to Puerto Rico about a year after his first trip early in 1923. The church's plight there still disturbed him. Despite "magnificent opportunities for the Church on this island, " Judge wrote to Mother Boniface, "what we see here is surely not the lovely Spouse of Christ, but some distorted burlesque." With the church "shackled and

27. Stevens-Arroyo, "Catholic Worldview," 55, relying on Samuel Silva Gotay, *Protestantismo y Política en Puerto Rico: 1898–1930* (San Juan: Editorial de la Universidad de Puerto Rico, 1997), 111–19.

28. Stevens-Arroyo, "Catholic Worldview," 57, relying on Alfonso R. López, "The Principle of Separation of Church and State as Observed by the Public Schools of Puerto Rico from 1898 to 1952" (Ph.D. diss., New York University, 1971), 73.

29. Díaz-Stevens, "Missionizing the Missionaries," 40.

strangled," he likened "Religion" on the island to "a broken reed or a punctured ball without rebound." He found an "empty seminary, no vocations, a widespread distrust and contempt of God's anointed, all kinds of sectaries running all over the island, the most dangerous of whom are the spiritualists." The Protestants, he complained, "are rushing in their commercial preachers and workers from the States and letting loose numbers of apostate gospel young men and women of Porto Rico extraction who have placed the faith of their fathers at auction." A "spirit of espionage," manifest in spying and lying, helped to shackle the church in Puerto Rico.[30] This reference to "espionage" relates to Judge's assessment of a conflict he had come to resolve.

The conflict developed between the residents at El Pensionado Católico, which the sisters called "Blessed Trinity Academy," and the custodian there, Sister Bridget. At the center of this conflict was the priest who had built the pensionado and whom Bishop Caruana assigned as chaplain to the Catholic students, Antonio del Castillo, OFM, Cap.[31] Father Judge found Father Antonio concerned primarily with using the pensionado to generate revenue and neglecting his responsibility as chaplain by failing to encourage the young women residents to receive the sacraments. Judge described him as taking "all joy out of Religion by his severity and seeming indifference to the children's religious needs." Judge would later note that he had made no provision for a chapel in the pensionado.

On February 13, Father Judge wrote to Mother Boniface that Bishop Caruana had come to Río Piedras and "was closeted two hours with Sr. Bridget." According to Judge, Caruana admitted that he "made a life mistake, that he was deceived, etc."[32] "Bishop Caruana and Sister Bridget," he wrote triumphantly five days later, "have had the long sought interview [apparently this interview included Father Castillo], as a consequence, the Bishop has had a complete change of mind." He now wanted Sister Bridget to remain at Blessed Trinity Academy and Father Castillo to leave. According to Judge, Sister Bridget demonstrated that the complaints made against her by the students, with Father Castillo's encouragement, he implied, to be "a toss of lies."[33]

It appeared that the crisis was over. In a postmortem before he left to visit the sisters in the Virgin Islands, Father Judge wrote Mother Boniface, "The

30. Judge to Mother Boniface, Río Piedras, P. R., February 8, 1924, AST, MF 7671–74.

31. On Father Antonio del Castillo, see Partsch, *La crisis de 1898 y su impacto en los institutos religiosos en Puerto Rico*, 122–23, 128.

32. Judge to Mother Boniface, Río Piedras, P.R., February 13, 1924, AST, MF 7674–76.

33. Ibid., February 18, 1924, AST, MF 7678–83.

trouble seemingly began in a simple way, a discussion of food." But food was only the flashpoint for something of a culture clash between a no-nonsense New England lady, a Spanish priest, and a group of upper-class young Puerto Rican women. As this letter suggests, it involved the question of whether Sister Bridget or Father Antonio would be in charge of the pensionado's finances. Judge described Sister Bridget as now "hiring and firing and buying and saving." The previous letters suggest as well that there were differences in forms of practicing Catholicism or at least in priestly styles. When he thought the conflict had been resolved, Judge wrote, "Now as it [the trouble] ends the menu will be à la Porto Rican, the discipline will be à la American, the inspiration and management, the policy will be à la Roman Catholic.... All that remains now is to find out and weigh how many lbs. of rice we must submerge in X lbs of lard for dinner."[34]

This remark captures the ambivalence of U.S. Catholic presence in Puerto Rico and highlights the difficulty of disentangling Puerto Rican, American, and Roman Catholic. The possibility of such disentangling depends on the extent to which, in particular cases, Catholic can transcend Puerto Rican and American. At least in his early years on the island, Father Judge underestimated the difficulty. Though he would always insist on the centrality of the priesthood and the sacraments to Catholic practice, he came increasingly to appreciate the authenticity of priest-poor Puerto Rican Catholicism, especially in its more popular forms. But in 1924, one of the earliest Cenacle pioneers became a casualty of cultural and religious differences that seemed to escape him.

Mary McMahon joined the Cenacle in Connecticut in the first years of its formation after 1909 or 1910. When the Cenacle in Baltimore (ca. 1912–15) was having difficulties, Father Judge sent "Mother McMahon" as "visitor." From Baltimore she came to Alabama to help Judge in March 1916 and was in charge in the last months at Opelika in 1916 and, after June, when the school moved to Phenix City.[35] In 1923, Judge and Mother Boniface put her, now known as Sister Bridget, in charge of the sisters' first work in Puerto Rico.

The young women at the pensionado had not been consulted on the resolution of the conflict negotiated between Bishop Caruana and Sister Bridget. In addition to rice and beans, it also included replacing what Father Judge described as an "espionage system" of discipline with one based on develop-

34. Ibid., February 20, 1924, AST, MF 7684.

35. Tonra, *Led by the Spirit*, 36; see the photograph at 124.

ing the "moral sense of the children" through "weekly confession and frequent reception of Holy Communion." In a report to Father McHale, written before his trip to the Virgin Islands, he described the residents of Blessed Trinity Academy in glowing terms as "a fine class of young women . . . in fact, the representative young womanhood of the island," regarded by university faculty as "the best dressed (neatly and modestly), the best behaved, and the best standing girls in the University."[36]

But this "fine class" of Puerto Rican young women simply refused to accept what Father Judge had described as "discipline à la American" as administered by Sister Bridget. When Judge returned from the Virgin Islands in early March, the disciplinary disarray at the pensionado shocked him. The issue of "the discipline and control of the children" hit him forcefully as "an angle that even the Bishop did not until now seem to get." It seems clear from this letter that, despite Bishop Caruana's support and a "menu à la Porto Rican," the young women still did not accept Sister Bridget as the one in charge of this new system of discipline. "Sister Bridget is my problem," Father Judge wrote to Mother Boniface. "I am afraid that I must relieve her. Poor soul has worked hard, but either the work is too much for her or she has a mind so divided that she cannot follow instructions."[37] This humiliation was too much for Mary McMahon. She eventually severed her ties to the Cenacle and returned home to Connecticut.

By April Judge was reporting to Father McHale on the performance of the students in a parade celebrating the university's anniversary as a "triumph of Trinity Academy." They built a float consisting of "an enormous dove representing the Holy Ghost and seven students with shoulder badges lettering the seven gifts." Red streamers came from the dove's beak to the seven girls. Judge described it as "a piece of classic elegance." In competition with the other residences—Judge mentioned "the Masonic schools, the Protestant Union Seminary, and other houses connected with the University"—they won first prize and notice as "Trinity Academy—the gate of the University."[38]

36. Judge to McHale, Río Piedras, P.R., February 24, 1924, AST MF 5490.

37. Judge to Mother Boniface, March 4, 1924, AST, MF, 7688.

38. Judge to McHale, Holy Trinity, Ala., April 25, 1924, AST, MF 5489–90. This letter, written after his return from Puerto Rico in mid-March, is a continuation of the February 24 letter cited in note 36.

Bishop Caruana and Catholic Resurgence in Puerto Rico

In 1921 George Caruana succeeded William A. Jones, OSA, who had been bishop of San Juan since 1907. Bishop Jones had opposed Puerto Rican independence and advocated statehood for the island. He was an Americanizer and the "real builder of the American institutional church in Puerto Rico."[39] Confronted with a situation in which conformity to U.S. law changed marriage and divorce and thereby "undercut the Church's role as arbiter of family life and the sudden end of state funds that had paid the salaries of the mostly foreign Spanish clergy reduced to penury,"[40] both Jones and his predecessor, James H. Blenk, SM (1898–1907), initiated policies "in order to rebuild the Puerto Rican Church in the pattern of a successful American diocese."[41] As was the case with the young, upper-class Puerto Rican women at Blessed Trinity Academy, Puerto Rican Catholics sometimes resisted this "discipline à la American," which was not always easy to distinguish from "the inspiration and management, the policy" that Judge designated "à la Roman Catholic Church."[42]

By the early 1920s, when Father Judge arrived on the island, Americanizing, in both the political and religious life of the island since 1898, had elicited a new sense of Puerto Rican identity. Pedro Albizu Campos (1891–1965), a Puerto Rican Mason who had returned to Catholicism while a student at Harvard University, embodied this new sensibility. Though politics and Catholicism combined in a complex and volatile mix, many, both upper-class Puerto Ricans and rural peasants, came to see Catholicism as inextricably connected to their culture and sense of being an independent people. This is not to say that Protestant evangelizing had been unsuccessful. But Catholicism was on an upswing.

Despite his brief stay on the island, Bishop Caruana contributed to this new Catholic vitality by helping to "create a climate of optimism about a Catholic resurgence on the island through such decisions as changing the staff of the minor seminary in Puerto Rico from North American priests to Spanish Vincentians in 1924."[43] Caruana had never been a bishop in

39. Dolan and Vidal, *Puerto Rican and Cuban Catholics in the U.S., 1900–1965*, 42.

40. Stevens-Arroyo, "Catholic Worldview," 54–55.

41. Dolan and Vidal, *Puerto Rican and Cuban Catholics in the U.S., 1900–1965*, 42.

42. Judge to Mother Boniface, Río Piedras, P.R., February 20, 1924, AST, MF 7684.

43. Stevens-Arroyo, "Catholic Worldview," 57. Stevens-Arroyo offers other examples of

the United States and had a broader view than Blenk and Jones of how the church might be structured in Puerto Rico.

As Caruana learned during his years as parish priest in Corona, New York, Father Judge had spent a lifetime working with lay apostles on the leaky seams of the immigrant American Catholic parish structure. Judge took for granted the centrality of the sacraments and the priesthood to Catholic life. But, if anyone understood the limits of American Catholicism's parish-based immigrant subculture, it was Judge. He did not simply want to impose American-style parishes on Puerto Rican Catholics. Rather, he wanted to mobilize the laity to address the pastoral needs of the island. As Judge enthused about Negro Cenacles that day in 1922 at Cardinal Dougherty's residence, this is the spirit Caruana wanted in Puerto Rico.

And so it had been Bishop Caruana who brought Father Judge and the Missionary Servants to Puerto Rico in 1923. With Caruana behind him, Judge rode the wave of Puerto Rican Catholic resurgence in the 1920s. He was especially interested in the *campesinos* dispersed in the parish-less and priest-less countryside. In order to reach them, he hoped to tap into the resurgent sense of Catholicism among some of the upper classes. He wanted the sisters to instill a missionary spirit in the young women at Trinity Academy.

The Colegio San Agustín, or St. Augustine's Academy, figured in Father Judge's thinking almost from the beginning. He considered finding a way to keep it open as one of three key aspects of his commitment to Caruana. When no one came forward to take it on, the Missionary Servants opened it in September 1926. As we shall see, the Catholic resurgence of the 1920s is clearly an important aspect of the context for Father Judge's decision to take this work. It was, of course, an abandoned work. No one else would take it. But part of the urgency of the case came from Judge's fear of the damage its closing would do to Catholic hopes and resurgent prestige on the island.

In the meantime, Bishop Caruana spent most of 1925 as a Vatican envoy in Guatemala and Cuba. His absence from Puerto Rico created some uncertainty about the future of the Cenacle mission there. Father Judge advised Mother Boniface to postpone her first trip to the island because of Caruana's absence in Cuba and uncertainty about who the next bishop might be and whether he would want the sisters to continue there.[44] Since the chaplain at the pensionado was appointed by the bishop and responsible to the bishop,

Caruana's sense of Puerto Ricans as a distinct people. This is part of the background for his fascinating portrait of Albizu Campos.

44. Tonra, *Led by the Spirit*, 153

Caruana's absence occasioned tension at Blessed Trinity Academy between the sisters and those who claimed to represent the bishop.[45]

Father Judge caught up with Bishop Caruana while he was in the United States in September 1925 to attend the annual meeting of the bishops' conference. Caruana paid a visit to the cenacle at Gold Street in Brooklyn on September 11. By this time, Mother Boniface had withdrawn the sisters from the Virgin Islands. Caruana told Judge he would like to have fifty more sisters but would settle for seven. The next day Judge visited him in Philadelphia to settle the situation of the chaplain at Blessed Trinity Academy. "The Bishop," he reported to Mother Boniface, "was his same dear old self. He is anxious for us to start a house in Rome, in fact he is going to Rome to take it up." Judge thought that Caruana's stock at Rome was rising "first of all because of his own record, secondly because of the difficult mission work given him which he performed so successfully recently." Thirdly, Judge reported that one of Caruana's close friends had just been promoted to an important curial position. "To tell you the truth," he wrote, "if he goes to Rome, I would not be surprised if he is given some position either right away or later on."[46] Judge had not visited Puerto Rico in 1925. After his visit with Caruana, he wanted to go late in the year, but his chronic foot problems, as well as concern about Eugene Brennan's upcoming ordination, kept him in the States.[47]

Bishop Caruana's Mission to Mexico

Father Judge was correct about Bishop Caruana's future. But the bishop's new position was far from Rome and more cloak-and-dagger than curial in style. About five months after Judge met with Caruana in Philadelphia, Pope Pius XI made him a titular archbishop and appointed him apostolic delegate to the Antilles. This assignment provided diplomatic cover for a much more dangerous mission. Caruana's real assignment was to Mexico. Repression

45. See Judge to Mother Boniface, Brooklyn, September 11, 1925, AST, MF 7724–25, on the chaplain situation at Blessed Trinity Academy. It's not clear whether Father Castillo was still the chaplain. Judge says in this letter that he was going to see Caruana the next day and tell him that "that gentleman [Fr. Antonio?] is *persona non grata* to the Sisters. In fact, if we can have no one else we do not want him as chaplain." He said he was going to ask Caruana to appoint Father Joseph DeMarco as chaplain. It seems that he was successful. By 1927 Mother Boniface invited the Maltese priest to spend the summer at Holy Trinity "to arouse the interest of the young people at both Holy Trinity and St. Joseph's in the missions of the Island"; Tonra, *Led by the Spirit*, 165–66.

46. Judge to Mother Boniface, Philadelphia, September 12, 1925, AST, MF 7726.

47. Judge to Sister Claire [at Río Piedras], Stirling, December 7, 1925, AST, MF 6395.

of the church by the Mexican government under President Plutarco Elías Calles incited Catholic laity to rebel in the Cristero uprising.

In the middle of this domestic revolt, Caruana entered the country clandestinely, disguised as a Protestant minister. His mission was to help keep the Mexican bishops together and out of the civil war and to protect the archives of the Catholic Church. About a year later, on November 23, 1927, the government executed Jesuit Miguel Pro by firing squad for continuing his ministry in spite of the government ban on the church. His dying words, "*Viva Cristo Rey!*," echoed Pius XI's response to anti-clericalism in his December 11, 1925, encyclical *Quas primas*, instituting the Feast of Christ the King.[48] A decade later, with President Calles still in power, Graham Greene visited the Mexican province of Tabasco, where repression of the church was most brutal, and made it the setting for the novel *The Power and the Glory* (1939).

More fortunate than Fr. Pro or Greene's nameless "whiskey priest," Caruana was arrested within about a month of his arrival. Since he had become an American citizen, Mexico deported him to the United States, where his case made a mess for both the U.S. government and the bishops' conference.[49] On November 18, 1926, Pius XI signed his encyclical *Iniquis afflictisque*, on the persecution of the church in Mexico. It is likely that Caruana provided on-the-spot information about the condition of the church in Mexico.[50] The fate of Catholicism in Mexico loomed in Father Judge's imagination as a warning for Puerto Rico and the rest of Latin America.

Bishop Caruana never returned to Puerto Rico. The Diocese of San Juan remained vacant from 1926 until 1929 when Bishop Edwin Byrne, who had been made bishop of Ponce in 1926, was finally named bishop of San Juan. Needless to say, Caruana's absence between 1926 and 1929 was not good news for the Missionary Servants. Their presence on the island depended on Bishop Caruana's friendship for Father Judge and support of their work. After Bishop Byrne's appointment to Ponce, he also provided support. Nevertheless, Judge kept in touch with Caruana. He regarded him not only as a friend but as a personal representative of the pope in Caribbean affairs. As the papal delegate, his advice carried special weight. Bishop Caruana's approval was crucial in Father Judge's decision to take over St. Augustine's Academy in the summer of 1926.

48. For the text of *Quas primas*, see Carlen, *Papal Encyclicals*, 271–79; see, for example, §25.

49. On Caruana's mission to Mexico, see Miriam Therese O'Brien, CSJ, "Island Hopping Diplomat," *Horizontes* 39, no. 76 (1997): 117–39; Silva Gotay, *Catolicismo Política en Puerto Rico Bajo España y Estados Unidos: Siglos XIX y XX* (San Juan: Universidad de Puerto Rico, 2005), 420–21.

50. Carlen, *Papal Encyclicals*, 303–12; see, for instance, §20 on the Mexican bishops.

Soothing a Deep Wound in the Heart of the Spouse of Christ

By the beginning of June 1926, Father Judge was back in Río Piedras. As he explained to both Mother Boniface and Father McHale at this time, Bishop Caruana had asked the Missionary Servants for three things when they came to the island in 1923. The first was the introduction and spread of the "Lay Apostolate," a phrase that, thanks to Pius XI, had gained currency by 1926. Second was Trinity Academy, which the sisters had well in hand. Caruana's third request was that they do something for St. Augustine's Academy. Judge responded to Caruana's repeated pleas for St. Augustine's with his own pleas for time "to catch our breath and get through the other works we have in hand."[51] In terms of Father Judge's commitment to Bishop Caruana, St. Augustine's was the Cenacle's unfinished business in Puerto Rico. By the school year's end in spring 1926, it appeared that the academy, begun in 1920, would not reopen in the fall.

The decision to accept St. Augustine's Academy as a Cenacle work, staffed by both sisters and brothers, was made sometime after July 19, the date on which the Feast of St. Vincent de Paul was celebrated before the revision of the liturgical calendar after the Second Vatican Council. On July 22, Judge wrote McHale, "This week in the octave of St. Vincent de Paul we have started a Latin Apostolate." He enclosed a letter of support from Bishop Byrne dated July 21. On that date, Bishop Byrne authorized the sisters at the pensionado "to send out the letters to all pastors with my approval." "My dear Father Judge," Byrne wrote, "I am heart and soul with you in this grand work for I see your love for Christ's Church and souls. Anything I can do will be a pleasure for me."[52]

Father Felix O'Neill, Father Judge's close friend from Newark, had visited the island at the beginning of June. "I cannot tell you how much he has helped me," Judge wrote to Mother Boniface. "I have given Fr. O'Neill a commission," he continued, "to get in touch with Archbishop Caruana." O'Neill did not fail in this commission, and on June 22, Judge reported to Mother Boniface that the letter of support from Caruana had arrived; he enclosed a copy of it. Until he heard from Judge, Caruana apparently thought that St. Augustine's had already closed.[53]

51. Judge to Mother Boniface Keasey, Brooklyn, July 14, 1926, AST, MF 7855. The same ground is covered in Judge to McHale, Stirling, July 22, 1926, AST, MF 6046–47.

52. Judge to McHale, Stirling, July 22, 1926, as in the previous note, and Edwin V. Byrne to Judge, Ponce, July 21, 1926, AST, MF 6048.

53. Judge to Mother Boniface Keasey, Río Piedras, P.R., June 4, 1926, and June 22, 1926,

The process by which Father Judge decided to accept St. Augustine's, as revealed in his correspondence between June 4 and July 14, 1926, is significant on at least two counts. First, more than a decision, this is a rich example of how Judge went about discerning the will of God. It reveals much about how Father Judge and Mother Boniface worked together and how the virtue and vow of obedience were practiced in one fledgling U.S. religious community in 1926. Second, this correspondence clarifies in detail the substantive concerns that went into the decision.

The reasons for the decision cluster in three overlapping contexts. The first context is internal to the Cenacle—for example, St. Augustine's potential role in the development and approval of the "brothers," but most importantly, in Father Judge's terms, Cenacle "first principles" such as "to the abandoned cause." The second is the local context of Puerto Rican Catholic resurgence in the mid-1920s—for example, the impact St. Augustine's closing might have on the embattled cause of Puerto Rican Catholicism, especially in the contested area of education. The third context is that of the universal church and its plight in Latin America, highlighted at this time by the persecution in Mexico. Taking on St. Augustine's was "hastening really to soothe a deep wound in the heart of the Spouse of Christ."[54] As the weeks from June 4 to July 14 unfold in this correspondence, Judge's vision expands outward from the Cenacle to resurgent Puerto Rican Catholicism to the Latin American Church for which Puerto Rico is a microcosm. Each wider context gathers and preserves the reasoning of the more local ones.

From the Cenacle to the "Sub-Structure of the Church in the West Indies," June 4–July 14

Founded by Bishop Jones in 1920 as a minor seminary, St. Augustine's soon became a high school or *colegio* for upper-class boys. It sat on a breezy hillside overlooking Río Piedras, not far from the university and the site of Blessed Trinity Academy. "The present sorrow of the Island," Father Judge wrote to Mother Boniface on June 4, "is the closing of St. Augustine's Academy, the only accredited Catholic boys high school in Porto Rico." A "small band" of "our Bros.," in charge of discipline and joined with some of the present faculty, could make the academy "a paying proposition." In the next three pages, Judge

AST, MF 7811, 7816; 7845–47; Caruana to Judge, June 7, 1926, copy, Record no. 102.1, Box III, File 5, AMSBT.

54. Judge to Mother Boniface, Brooklyn, July 14, 1926, AST, MF 7855–58.

sketched out his plan for how this might work. Bishop Byrne was behind it. Discipline was the problem. It would take only two brothers, perhaps alternating for three-month assignments, and one priest during the school year. Most of the faculty, including two priests, could be retained. "If St. Augustine's were offered at a bargain price," he concluded, "I would favor taking it; if not then there would be the question of how we could make a beginning."[55]

Within two weeks, Father Judge's thinking, perhaps encouraged by the voices raised against closing St. Augustine's, had advanced considerably beyond the tentative and conditional proposal in his June 4 letter to Mother Boniface. His later letters indicate that she had not given a favorable response to his proposal. So on June 16, he wrote a five-page, single-spaced letter to Father Tomerlin, also at Holy Trinity. Its purpose was to excite the brothers at St. Joseph's to the possibilities of the work in Puerto Rico, especially at St. Augustine's. He began with the sisters' successes and emphasized the number of young women who had passed through Blessed Trinity Academy over the past three years. In much stronger language than he had used on June 4, he told Tomerlin that "because of what God is doing in Porto Rico and what may be done through the cooperation of our Sisters and their friends that *God is not only willing for us to take over St. Augustine's but He graciously is encouraging us to do so*" [my italics].

He repeated his verdict that the "only real problem at St. Augustine's is lack of discipline" attributable to an "almost complete lack of spiritual and sacramental training." The school, he was convinced, was losing money because of lack of discipline, and he bemoaned the fact that, rather than using spiritual means to correct the discipline problem, the decision to close it rested on purely economic grounds. In this June 16 letter, Judge began to speak of the school's fate in the discourse of 1920s Puerto Rican Catholic resurgence and tied it, as the only Catholic high school for boys, to the Catholic cause on the island. Solving the discipline problem would turn St. Augustine's into "a magnificent investment." Saving the school would contribute to "a crying reformation" and give a "foundation for a new Catholic advance." He appealed to "views of many of the enlightened Priests and many of the laity" that closing St. Augustine's would be "nothing short of a calamity." Such views would have come from both those Stevens-Arroyo designates as "Nationalist Catholics," who, like Pedro Albizu Campos, favored independence, and "Ideal Catholics" who accepted U.S. citizenship. Both associated

55. Ibid., Río Piedras, June 4, 1926, AST, MF 7811–16.

Catholicism with Puerto Rican identity.[56] While Protestants were "dazzling the Porto Rican youth" with free education at the evangelical seminary near the university, Catholics simply could not close their only secondary school for young men.

Associating Catholicism with Puerto Rican identity, whether as an independent people or as a U.S. territory, Judge took a page from local Catholic critiques of the "heavy ammunition used by protestant missionaries":

> Protestants stand for progress, ergo, protestantism is the hope of the poor and ignorant. They say, behold United States, a protestant country, powerful, rich, etc. Henry Ford, Rockefeller, Porto Rico is a Catholic country, poor, miserable, ergo, Catholicity is now [not?] progressive, Priests are reactionaries keeping you poor Porto Ricans in poverty and ignorance.

"Just think," he said to Tomerlin, "how the closing of St. Augustine's will play into their hands." Invoking the fate of Mexico, he repeated his conviction that it was God's will "for the Brothers Missionary Servants of the Most Blessed Trinity to step into the breach and to save a Catholic cause abandoned, and, help save Porto Rico from falling into the conditions that grip Mexico." For the third time in this letter, he repeated, "it seems to me to be the will of God for us to take it over and to make those sacrifices that are necessary to save it."

He urged Tomerlin to "take counsel" about this letter's contents and pray to the Holy Ghost about Puerto Rico. "Remember I wish letter discussed much and freely with Brothers." In a postscript he added eight reasons, specific to the Cenacle and particularly the brothers, why taking St. Augustine's "would be very advantageous for us." First, it would give the brothers "a status" and help them in getting canonical approval. St. Augustine's would serve as a center for missionary activities, and brothers assigned there would have opportunities for higher education. The school would generate revenue. In addition to starting a Cenacle for young men at the university, the brothers could be of service to the sisters, and the priest who accompanied them could serve Blessed Trinity Academy as chaplain. Most significantly, these inner Cenacle considerations were now gathered up into the larger context of the Catholic cause in Puerto Rico.[57]

56. Stevens-Arroyo, "Catholic Worldview," 54–60. He describes "Ideal Catholicism" as "a more conservative form of Catholicism [than Nationalist Catholicism] . . . born in Ponce among Catholic laymen from the oligarchic, blueblood families of Spanish days." Such people would have been likely to send their sons to St. Augustine's and to have lamented its closing.

57. Judge to My Dear Confrere [Joseph Tomerlin], Río Piedras, June 16, 1926, AST, MF 6160–

Between June 16 and June 22, Catholic sentiment against closing St. Augustine's picked up steam. Father Judge's June 22 letter to Mother Boniface enclosed the letter of support he had recently received from Bishop Caruana. He reported that he told Caruana that closing St. Augustine's would "cause bitter comment all over the island." "In fact," Judge wrote to Mother Boniface, "that comment now has quite a head and is growing because people are beginning to say that there is a lack of sympathy for this institution, and therefore for the Catholic cause of education, that its chief temple is going to be closed." Clearly, Mother Boniface did not share Judge's enthusiasm for taking over St. Augustine's. "It is difficult to make you realize the conditions," he wrote, "not knowing the parties concerned." Raising the rhetorical heat a notch, he called the academy "the greatest shrine that Catholic education has on the island." His efforts to save it had gained for the Missionary Servants some acclamation as "the saviours of the Catholic educational idea."[58]

Father Judge's next letter clarifies some of Mother Boniface's reservations about St. Augustine's. With no sisters to spare, she also opposed sending brothers to Puerto Rico, fearing that they were not prepared to teach and that their own education and their development as a group would suffer. "As for the Brothers," Judge wrote, "I realize what you say but, of course, there are many views of this." He insisted on the uniqueness of this opportunity. Regarding his earlier letters, he suggested, with a trace of impatience, that she "must have read those letters very hurriedly because I narrated a number of very important reasons for their coming." The brothers would not teach in the high school, but their presence would "give prestige and confidence in the school." He assured her that "up to date no negotiation has been entered into." He reminded her that Bishop Caruana, whose letter she already had, was no longer bishop of San Juan. But he added, "As Papal Delegate, of course, they will pay much attention to anything he says or advises." He urged her to reread his letters.[59]

On July 12, he sent Mother Boniface the "latest extras" on St. Augustine's. He hoped they would "explain the simple way Divine Providence is resolving the whole question." Again, he repeated, "It is difficult for me not to see that

65. Tomerlin was in charge of the brothers at Holy Trinity at this time, and the contents of the letter strongly suggest that he is the confrere addressed. See also 7834–36, a fragment of a letter, probably to Mother Boniface, which goes over these eight points in more detail.

58. Judge to Mother Boniface Keasey, Río Piedras, June 22, 1926, AST, MF 7845–47.

59. Ibid., P.R., June 29, 1926, AST, MF 7821–26.

it is the Will of God for us to undertake the work of salvaging this institution. Divine Providence graciously is simplifying the problem." Clearly, she did not yet read the signs this way. There were no qualified teachers.

Nevertheless, Father Judge insisted that "a great Catholic principal [*sic*] is at stake; that failure just now will be a calamity to the cause of Catholicity here." What he found providential was the way he and the Missionary Servants had been drawn or swept into this situation and the increasing number of good people, many clergy, who had come forward in the recent weeks urging them to step in and take St. Augustine's. "It is hard, "he told Mother Boniface, "not to hear God's voice in their appeals." With no other community to take on this work, he appealed to Cenacle "first principles." "I am thinking of our spirit to go to the abandoned. I know from first principles, it is the will of God to harken to Holy Mother Church in Her distress in Porto Rico. How can Jesus be unmindful of the distress of his Spouse and of those who succor Her for His sake?" He described a meeting with Bishop Byrne regarding the Missionary Servants and the colegio. "We practically get everything on our own terms." He made a major concession to Mother Boniface's concern about teachers. St. Augustine's would open in September only as an elementary school, with the high school division returning the following academic year.

He then launched into his final nine-point case to convince Mother Boniface that they should buy Blessed Trinity Academy. He urged her to call a council immediately and move on this proposal.[60] He saw that Trinity Academy was generating considerable revenue for the Diocese of San Juan and had been thinking about buying it from them since 1924.[61] Mother Boniface's arguments against purchasing the pensionado prevailed. She reminded Judge that they were now (1926) $190,000 in debt. "Father, do you not think it is too much for a young Community to undertake? Why not let us grow stronger in numbers, in years, and financially?"[62]

When Father Judge returned to Brooklyn on July 14, he made the case for St. Augustine's yet again to Mother Boniface in a four-page, single-spaced letter. The first two pages of this letter present a complete and elegant sum-

60. Ibid., P.R., July 12, 1926, AST, MF 7849–52.

61. See Judge to McHale, Río Piedras, P.R., June 24, 1924, AST, MF 5490. Judge to Mother Boniface, Río Piedras, P.R., June 4, 1926 AST, MF 7811–13, presents his full case for buying Trinity Academy as well as "problems and difficulties." His July 12, 1926 letter (note 60), presses for the purchase.

62. For Mother Boniface's arguments against the purchase, see Tonra, *Led by the Spirit*, 155.

mary of the arguments from his previous letters since June 4, 1926. Again he invoked the specter of Mexico. More than the question of the closing of one local school was at stake; "the substructure of the Church in the West Indies is in peril." He sent the "syllabus" and emphasized the aim: "moral training, character building, to make St. Augustine's a high grade accredited school." He had decided that sisters from Trinity Academy would do better at teaching than untrained brothers.

In response to Mother Boniface's concern for the brothers, his plan now included only one non-teaching brother, and Father Judge detailed for Mother Boniface why he thought he would "make out all right." He told her he needed five and probably six additional sisters, three for domestic work at St. Augustine's and two, or more likely three, to do the work at Trinity Academy. Puerto Rico would also need one of the priests. Coming as a new school year was about to begin, "this demand," he acknowledged, "may be distressing." He made another major gesture in the direction of Mother Boniface's reservations about lack of personnel. "I am willing, therefore," he conceded, "in case of necessity, to do this,—to close Blessed Trinity Academy, Stirling."

Finally, Father Judge gathered all this into a vision of a Latin American Church *in extremis*. This thought, he explained, had come to him the morning of July 14, "whilst offering up a Votive Mass in adoration of the Triune God." Their ready response to the church's crying need in Puerto Rico would surely bring a generous response from the Triune God. "Nowhere in the world today," he continued, "is our Holy Mother in greater suffering, in fact, not in our generation has she been in such agony as she is in Latin American countries." A generous response with confidence in God to such need "will be richly repaid." If the root of the church's present plight is "the irreligious Latin American," then the "remedy lies in Catholicizing the boys . . . to reform the grandfathers of two generations hence." St. Augustine's would be a "demonstration of Cenacle principles."

Mother Boniface must have argued that the "Brothers' cause" would be served best if they continued in the work they had begun in the South. In response, he assured her that "those who sit on the thrones of anxiety in the Church" would know and bless the brothers' work in Puerto Rico. "No, my dear child," he responded, "there is nothing that is going to help further the Brothers' cause as much as this very thing. The Church is not in distress in the South . . . there is no question of the loss of millions of Catholic souls":

> The Latin American world is another world and in that world it seems that all the solicitude of the Church today is centered. Yes, think of it, our Brothers

> and Sisters will be in the vortex and seething of it all, standard bearers for the Church, going down to the root of the trouble and applying the saving remedy, Christianizing the heart and mind and the will of the boy who is to father the generations of tomorrow.

Pius XI's *Iniquis afflictisque* did not appear until the following November, but Father Judge concluded with instructions to watch for the new encyclical on Mexico and have it read in all the cenacles. He wanted the Missionary Servants to be "amongst the first and most generous to live out its injunctions."[63]

While this letter was on its way to Holy Trinity, Mother Boniface was already responding to Father Judge's letter of July 12 from Río Piedras and his previous pleas for Puerto Rico. His next letter praised the appeal she had written for the Assumption as "very beautiful." "As for the Brothers," he continued, "I do hope you will be able to float them a while longer." He assured her that St. Augustine's would be "a revenue getter and will be a help to the Brothers." He ended this letter by acknowledging gratefully "the filial sentiments" she had expressed in her letter of July 15. "It certainly was a joy to me to receive such a letter on my return particularly after the difficulties I have had during the past two months." He concluded confidently: "Suffice it to say that we have won out in every point in the Porto Rican cause."[64]

The decision to take on the work of St. Augustine's is instructive. Though we do not have her letters to Father Judge, his side of the correspondence makes clear that, from June 4 to July 14, Mother Boniface opposed his desire to take on St. Augustine's, and, to his repeated arguments that it appeared to be the will of God (a trump card coming from someone in his position), she presented arguments for reading the signs differently. Her arguments kept Father Judge in contact with the inner Cenacle context. His thinking brought the situation in Puerto Rico and the plight of the church in Latin America into play. Eventually she deferred to the man she called "Our Father" (much to his chagrin) but, from the process leading up to her "filial" letter of July 15, there is much to learn about Father Judge's practice of "council" and about collaborative leadership in the context of practicing the virtue and vow of obedience.

She argued from lack of personnel and her genuine concern for the "Brothers' cause." She didn't think that the Missionary Servants could af-

63. Judge to Mother Boniface, Brooklyn, July 14, 1926, AST, MF 7855–58.

64. Ibid., Stirling, July 21, 1926, AST, MF 7874–75.

ford to take on St. Augustine's. Her case against buying Trinity Academy prevailed, and Judge's final plan for St. Augustine's, as well as his thinking about the Cenacle context of the decision, was shaped in dialogue with her arguments. No doubt ego, human will, and an abundance of feeling on both sides went into this correspondence, but in the end both were after what they would have called the "will of God."

Puerto Rico and the vision that emerged from the decision-making processes he went through with Mother Boniface affected Father Judge permanently. During the last five years of his life, he wrote the work of preservation of the faith in Latin America into the constitutions of both women's and men's communities.

Colegio San Agustín

On September 2, Father Judge left Brooklyn for Puerto Rico. The school year began on September 14, 1926, the Feast of the Exaltation of the Holy Cross. Presumably, for the academic year of 1926–27, St. Augustine's reopened, as Judge had announced in July, temporarily without its high school division. As Judge explained in presenting the case for taking on the school, he wanted to reach the fathers of the next generations of Catholic leaders on the island. The colegio was aimed at the sons of the Catholic upper classes, the elite of Puerto Rico and other Latin American countries. Central to this mission, the high school soon returned. Since, under the program of Americanization, instruction in all schools was in English and many teachers were Americans, the presence of the sisters and brothers on the island was not unusual, and they taught in English. The newly ordained Father Eugene Brennan played a key role at St. Augustine's.

Eugene Brennan's long-anticipated ordination to the priesthood on February 2, 1926, had been a great moment for Father Judge and the Cenacle. Judge corresponded with Mother Boniface about whether to assign Brennan to Holy Trinity or to Puerto Rico. In fall 1926, he saw Brennan's chief work as continuing, with the help of the sisters and students, the mission excursions and catechetical centers that Judge had recently begun. "There is a work here for Fr. Eugene," he told Mother Boniface as he considered Brennan for Puerto Rico, "not at Trinity Academy, not at St. Augustine's but to follow up this catechetical work to help organize it. What a beautiful work this is." He envisioned Brennan as a missionary "at the centers of a Sunday, perhaps now and again during the week," encouraging "young men and young women to give Cenacle service." He also envisioned him providing "entertainment for the University men." "You know," Judge wrote, "he is a past master in this thing himself. He doesn't need to be smart, all he needs to be is pleasant." He assured her that if Brennan came, he would have no duty at Trinity Academy, where Father DeMarco was now the chaplain, and none at St. Augustine's. "If Fr. Eugene comes, I can get away," he told Mother Boniface. He sent his letter to Brennan to her. "You are on the ground," he wrote, "you know well the needs at Holy Trinity, if you think it is a good plan, mail this letter to Fr. Eugene." If she did mail the letter, he asked her to have his passage arranged and "get him down here right away. He can help me on the big Mass [Christ the King] and I can break him in."[65]

Brennan did come in time for the Feast of Christ the King. Father Judge describes him "as making his rounds with us on the mission circuit." When he returned to the island early in 1927, Judge reported that Father Eugene had already established "twenty-five missionary centers." By March he counted 2,000 catechists for these mission centers.[66] But in addition to the catechetical work Judge hoped for, Brennan eventually became the director of St. Augustine's.[67]

By 1929 the colegio had become St. Augustine's Military Academy.[68] With Father Eugene Brennan as director, the school's military culture took center stage. A nineteen-page Spanish Catalog for the academic year 1933–34 emphasized the advantages of a military school (page 8).[69] Brennan achieved

65. Ibid., Rio Piedras, October 13, 1926, AST, MF 7912–13.

66. Berry, *God's Valiant Warrior*, 95, 96, citing Judge to Augustine Philips, January 22, 1927, and Judge to Caruana, March 3, 1927, AST, MF 1059 and 5917–19.

67. "Fr. Brennan looks very well. In fact, I never saw him look so well. He is rather quiet but it is a very amiable tranquility"; Judge to Mother Boniface, Río Piedras, P.R., November 24, 1926, AST, MF 7934–36, on Fr. Eugene's arrival. See also "Puerto Rican Chronicle," 3:60, where Judge writes, "What Caesar said of himself may be said of Father Eugene Brennan. 'Veni, Vidi, Vici.' He did not waste any stationery telling us on what boat he was coming, but we were there just the same to receive him. All agree that he looks fine, more priestly than ever." Judge joked that some of the crowd waiting for the boat may have mistaken him for the new bishop. "Some of us have not as yet recovered from our fright thinking that he was the new high priest of the diocese." As these remarks suggest, along with the comment to Mother Boniface about Brennan's not having to be smart but pleasant, there was something about Brennan that always left Judge a bit on edge, something irrepressible, unpredictable, to be deflected with humor.

68. On the history of St. Augustine's, see Partsch, *La crisis de 1898 y su impacto*, 128. Partsch cites Berry, *God's Valiant Warrior*, 173, 97. The Marianists took over St. Augustine's in 1938 and changed its name to *Colegio San José*; see Joseph Jansen, SM, *The First Seventy-Five Years: History of the Marianists in the West Indies and Colegio San José, 1938–2013*, updated by CSJ staff (Bogotá, Colombia: Argüeso Garzón Editores, 2013), chap. 1.

69. St. Augustine's Military Academy, Rio Piedras, Puerto Rico, 1933–34, 19 pp. I am grateful to Gary Banks, ST, who located this catalog in the ST Archives and translated it for me.

accreditation from the U.S. Department of Education and, under the U.S. Department of War, established an Army ROTC program. He used the military idea, complete with uniforms, rifles, and parades, to facilitate the discipline Father Judge emphasized in his summer correspondence. Students were known as cadets and wore elaborate dress uniforms modeled on those of West Point (see the pictures on pages 4 and 15 of the catalog), with simpler uniforms for daily day use. St. Augustine's Military Academy came to be known as "the West Point of the West Indies."[70]

Judge was still alive and on the island when this catalog was in preparation. His picture appears on page 11 with the student body in military uniform. He is flanked by Brother Joseph Limpert on the left and Brother Gerard Fredericks on the right, along with four unidentified sisters in white tropical garb and no hats. By 1933 Father Paul Anthony Fursman had replaced Father Eugene Brennan as director. Fursman's portrait appears prominently on page 3. The student body, listed at pages 18 and 19, included 51 students from Puerto Rico, 30 from the area around Río Piedras, and 21 from others parts of the island, 2 from areas where Judge established catechetical centers. Twelve students came from other parts of Latin America such as Venezuela, Santo Domingo, and the U.S. Virgin Islands. Most students boarded at St. Augustine's for about $500 per year.

The catalog describes the school as "completely saturated with Catholic ideas for education, which is not only a process of developing the mind, but also the evolution of character, including the mind, the heart and the will." The curriculum included a general or classical course and a scientific course. All students studied religion, military and physical training, English, and Spanish for all four years. Algebra, geometry, early European history, modern European history, and biology were required of everyone. The general course had two semesters of French, Latin, or German; the scientific course added instead two more semesters of mathematics or geometry and physics or chemistry. Each course had two electives that could be chosen from advanced offerings in the other course or advanced English, American history, geography, music, and languages (see pages 12–13).

70. Guillermo Celiá, "Cuando Puerto Rico Tenía su Pequeño West Point," *El Reportaje de la Semana* (1979): 1–3. Appearing in a group picture accompanying this article is Quentin Roosevelt, grandson of President Theodore Roosevelt, whose own military image was made in Cuba during the Spanish-American War. Quentin's father, Theodore Roosevelt III, was the governor of Puerto Rico from 1929 to 1932. Quentin Roosevelt, a day student, reportedly came to school with armed guards.

St. Augustine's as a Mission Center

Educating the sons of leading Catholic families was central to the vision for the Latin American Church spelled out in Father Judge's June and July 1926 correspondence. If, however, he had only envisioned an exclusive school for boys from well-to-do families, Father Judge would probably not have taken St. Augustine's. Like all Cenacle institutions, it had to be a center for missionary activity. Judge promised Caruana that he would establish the Cenacle lay apostolate on the island. Sisters had been training young women at Trinity Academy along these lines three years before Father Judge took on St. Augustine's. During his months in Puerto Rico from September to December 1926, Judge worked to make St. Augustine's into a center to energize the Catholic Church on the island.

With his encyclical *Quas primas* of December 11, 1925, Pius XI instituted the Feast of Christ the King, celebrated on the last Sunday in October. The inaugural feast came in 1926, and Father Judge organized a huge festival at St. Augustine's with Catholics from all over the island. It was at this celebration that Judge first made contact with the lay religious movement Los Hermanos Cheos. Father Judge described the festival Mass in "Puerto Rican Chronicle." Monsignor Torres, apostolic administrator in Bishop Caruana's absence, gave a brief address. Judge was pleased to report "nearly 100 Communions." Because of the fast from midnight, students received Communion before Mass and the sisters brought them back to the pensionado for a quick breakfast before Mass. Judge counted "sixty seminarians, eighty orphans, the Knights of Columbus in a body and two or three hundred University students." He reported that, at the end of the day, Msgr. Torres said to him, "Father, have many more such celebrations."[71]

The city of San Juan was located in the northeast coast of the island, with Río Piedras close by to the south and east. Using St. Augustine's Academy as a mission center, Father Judge directed his first missionary efforts to the east of the city in the northeast corner of the island, Loiza and Luquillo on the coast, Río Grande and Palmer further inland, and at the Barrio Jiménez at the foot of El Yunque Mountain. This hot, coastal, marshy area was part of the old sugar cane region of the island populated by the descendants of slaves. Further inland, at the base of El Yunque, the mountain's rain forest

71. For Judge's description of the Feast of Christ the King at St. Augustine's in 1926, see "Puerto Rican Chronicle," November 3, 1926, Monographs 3:41–43.

watered plentiful fruit. Judge went to areas that are to this day among the poorest and most abandoned in Puerto Rico. These missionary forays into the countryside are described in detail in the "Puerto Rican Chronicle."

On September 19, 1926, Father Judge reported to Mother Boniface on how the missionary excursions came about. He thought the boys at St. Augustine's had "taken very well to the study of doctrine." He promised those who did well in catechism "a ride out in the country, a picnic, a fiesta they call it here, and that they would be helped to gather the little boys of the neighborhood together that they might teach them catechism." He described the boys as "overjoyed." They wrote home to tell their parents. Judge turned these Sunday missionary excursions into the countryside into festive picnics that students from St. Augustine's and Blessed Trinity Academy looked forward to. Judge spread his apostolic contagion to them, and he and the sisters trained them as catechists and lay apostles.

In this same letter, Father Judge paid tribute to St. Augustine's lay teachers, "two young men and two young ladies." First among the young men was Don Agustín Hernández, whom Judge described to Mother Boniface as "a splendid young man," and though he had only just met him, with "an enthusiastic Cenacle spirit." In addition, he was "very much respected as a teacher by the students, their parents, and the people around the University." In his zeal, Hernández struck Father Judge as the "most unusual Porto Rican of his generation."[72] Hernández put himself at Judge's disposal even before classes began in the fall of 1926. Judge spoke no Spanish, and Hernández became his constant companion on these missionary junkets. Judge would talk to Hernández beforehand about what he was going to say and then pause during his presentations to the country people so that Hernández could translate. Hernández became a devoted lay apostle and true disciple of Father Judge. He tried to translate the master's enthusiasm as well as his words.[73]

Another of the young lay teachers, though he does not mention her by name in this letter, was María Cristina Vilá. She had lived with the sisters at Blessed Trinity Academy and graduated from the University of Puerto Rico in 1926. It was she who came up with the idea for the Holy Ghost float

72. Judge to Mother Boniface, Río Piedras, September 19, 1926, AST, MF 7894–97.

73. On Hernández, see Fr. Timothy Lynch's foreword to "Puerto Rican Chronicle," Monographs 3:6, and Celiá, *"Cuando Puerto Rico Tenía su Pequeño West Point,"* 3, with accompanying photograph of Hernández and a group of St. Augustine's students. As a young man, Lynch taught at St. Augustine's with Hernández and relates that Hernández thought that Judge, whom he regarded as a saint, had "cured him some years ago when his life was in danger."

that Father Judge had enthused about to McHale the previous year. After her graduation, Judge invited her to join the faculty at St. Augustine's as a Spanish teacher. In a remembrance of Father Judge, recorded forty years after the fact, she recalls riding in the car with him on Sunday missionary excursions. She eventually married and had children, but she remained a catechist and lay apostle long after Judge's death. Such apostolic young people as Hernández and Vilá energized an aging Father Judge, now fifty-eight years old. Speaking of the "Puerto Rican Chronicle," Lynch writes, "Never did Father seem so happy as he is in this narration."[74]

In one of his first mission trips from St. Augustine's into the hills at the foot of El Yunque Mountain, deep in the rural heart of Catholic Puerto Rico, Father Judge made an alarming discovery. "Our missionary beginning is very timely," he told Mother Boniface. "The Protestants are circulating a beautiful chapel car through that particular section, the machine must have cost about $10,000. They are making many converts."[75] Eventually he learned that this car belonged to the Baptists. He described it as "a magnificent piece of machinery that slips into a town and presto there is a Protestant church."[76] The chapel car was for Judge a symbolic vehicle of "sectaries making inroads on the unprotected flock," an ominous Protestant presence "hidden behind a house in a rather desolate region." He called it the "forbidden car" and "this obnoxious car."[77]

He had found the chapel car in his explorations for good locations for a catechetical center. "We have been anxiously looking for mission centers," he told Mother Boniface, "not too remote from St. Augustine's Academy, where the boys themselves can teach catechism, under supervision, to children particularly abandoned."[78] The car's presence helped him decide where the need for catechetical centers was greatest.

74. See María Cristina Vilá de Blanco, "My Memories of Father Judge," Monographs 3:8–13, and Lynch's comment in the foreword at 4.

75. Judge to Mother Boniface Keasey, Río Piedras, P.R., September 19, 1926, AST, MF 7894.

76. Judge to Florence Turner, Río Piedras, P.R., October 5, 1926, AST, MF 6090. "Puerto Rican Chronicle," October 3, 3:27–28 , describes the chapel car's "invasion" of Río Grande, a pueblo off the coast on the Río Espíritu Santo; Judge identified Río Grande as the "most abandoned *pueblo*" on the island, at 3:64.

77. "Puerto Rican Chronicle," Monographs 3:34–35.

78. Judge to Mother Boniface, Río Piedras, P.R., September 1926, AST, MF 7762.

Father Judge's Puerto Rican Legacy

In addition to its role as symbol of the danger to the faith on the island, the chapel car also fascinated Judge in its very modernity and up-to-date quality. He had called it "beautiful" and a "magnificent machine." The sight of the chapel car also set him to thinking. "What is back of their extraordinary activity?" he wondered. "Who are its masterminds that are directing it? Whence do they recruit their resources?" Though he thought the Baptists were "commercializing religion," he knew considerable resources would be required to counter their efforts. A "very prominent Catholic from Boston," Mr. Toner, came to the island from Boston University to head the Department of Finance and Commerce at the University of Puerto Rico. Through Toner, Judge hoped to reach the Knights of Columbus in the United States and get them to work with the Knights on Puerto Rico. "Mr. Toner told me he was going to interest the Knights of Columbus and the Elks of the Island, the same bodies as in the United States." It was Toner who came up with the microeconomic idea of helping Puerto Rican craftspeople to sell lace in the United States. He hoped through these contacts to raise money for "catechetical work made necessary because of the activity of the Protestants."[79]

"La Madrina": Encarnación Padilla de Armas

In addition to the Knights of Columbus, Father Judge hoped also to enlist support from the Catholic Daughters of America and the Daughters of Isabella, a female auxiliary to the Knights. Father O'Neill was chaplain to the Catholic Daughters' courts in the Newark Archdiocese. This interest in the Catholic Daughters occasions the appearance, in Judge's correspondence with Mother Boniface and in the "Chronicle," of Encarnación Padilla de Armas (ca. 1909–92). Along with Margaret Healy, Mary Elizabeth Walsh, and James Norris, Encarnación Padilla was one of the most extraordinary lay apostles and activists that Father Judge inspired.

She was seventeen and a senior in high school during the fall Father Judge spent in Puerto Rico in 1926. Of course, Father Judge loved her name. The sisters first brought this young woman to his attention. He began his September 13 letter to Mother Boniface by describing "a remarkably nice young girl with a name that is sacredly religious." Her father appears

79. Ibid., September ?, 1926, AST, MF 7762–65. Judge identifies Toner in this letter and also in "Puerto Rican Chronicle," 3:28.

throughout the "Puerto Rican Chronicle" as one of the laymen who helped Father Judge on mission trips and in other ways. Judge explained that her father was formerly well off "but is now very much reduced." Her mother was an "officer in the Catholic Daughters of America." Probably because they could no longer afford to send her to the university, and because of the trust the sisters had inspired in them, her parents entrusted her to the care of Father Judge and the sisters. Judge, of course, thought of her as a possible vocation. At the end of September, she sailed for Brooklyn and spent some time at Holy Trinity. Initially, Judge was "anxious that Incarnación [*sic*] see some of our houses and work in New Jersey and I am particularly anxious that she meet Miss Duffy, the Grand Regent of the Catholic Daughters." Judge had briefed her on what to convey to Miss Duffy. Presumably, Father O'Neill would help her make this contact.[80]

Encarnación Padilla never did become a Missionary Servant of the Most Blessed Trinity. After some years in the United States at Holy Trinity, she returned to Puerto Rico and eventually married in Cuba. Around the time of the Second World War, she found herself a single mother with a young son. In 1945 she moved to New York City. There, she eventually made contact with Jesuit Joseph Fitzpatrick, a sociologist at Fordham, well known for his work in the Puerto Rican community of New York. Fitzpatrick's brother, Vincent, was a Missionary Servant of the Most Holy Trinity. Through Joseph Fitzpatrick, she entered American Catholic history as an advocate for Puerto Rican Catholic affairs in New York and nationally, as well as city politics in New York.[81]

In 1951 Padilla de Armas told Fitzpatrick of her concern that the Archdiocese of New York was not doing enough for Puerto Rican Catholics. Fitzpatrick asked her to write a report on this situation and promised to give it to Cardinal Spellman. She gathered a group of Puerto Rican women. Their report noted that there were no priests of Puerto Rican origin in the archdiocese and insisted on the obligation of Catholic parishes to accept Puerto

80. Ibid., September 13, 1926, AST, MF 7884. In his letter of October 13, cited previously, Judge inquired if Encarnación had indeed made this contact with the Grand Regent in New Jersey. He wanted her to ask Miss Duffy to "write Mrs. Martínez Alvarez, the Grand Regent of Puerto Rico, a letter telling her to have the Catholic Daughters of the Island to get behind us." "The husbands of many of these women," he added, "are very wealthy." Whether she did make contact with Miss Duffy is not clear at this time.

81. On Padilla de Armas, see Joseph P. Fitzpatrick, SJ, *The Stranger Is Our Own: Reflections on the Journey of Puerto Rican Migrants* (Kansas City: Sheed and Ward, 1996), 8–9. Fitzpatrick calls her "my first great teacher about Puerto Rican culture"; See also Lynch, Foreword, Monographs 3: 6–7, 18, 23–24.

Ricans as ordinary members. Two years later a Spanish Catholic Action Office was established in the New York Archdiocese. In 1961, when Ivan Illich started his Center for Intercultural Documentation at Cuernavaca, Mexico, he asked Padilla de Armas to be its administrator.[82]

Padilla de Armas has been called "the first Latina to achieve national leadership" in the Catholic Church. In New York, she worked in the first national Catholic program for Spanish-speaking Catholics, training diocesan priests in Puerto Rican language and culture. She pushed for the bishops to recognize their responsibility to Puerto Ricans and helped develop the U.S. Catholic Conference's National Secretariat for the Spanish Speaking. In 1972 she chaired the planning committee for the first National Hispanic Encuentro, held in Washington, D.C.[83]

Sor Isolina Ferré and the Native Puerto Rican Missionary Servants

Ana María Díaz-Stevens has chronicled the work of the Missionary Servants of the Most Blessed Trinity in Puerto Rico, drawing attention to their novitiate at Aguadilla and their success with native Puerto Rican vocations. Among these she makes special mention of Sor Isolina Ferré (d. 2000). She was the sister of Luis A. Ferré, former governor of Puerto Rico, and aunt of novelist Rosario Ferré. "True to the Trinitarians' charism of serving the poor," writes Díaz-Stevens, "Sor Isolina gave her life to the people of her island through her commitment to the poorest areas of Ponce."[84]

The sisters' work at Blessed Trinity Academy at the University of Puerto Rico and in their other missions was the source of most of the native vocations for both women and men. Trinity Academy appears to have been a more successful work than St. Augustine's Military Academy, from which the priests and brothers were forced to withdraw in 1938. Over the years, there have been more than fifty-five Missionary Servants of the Most Blessed Trinity from Puerto Rico.[85] Of the forty-eight native Puerto Rican priests in

82. Fitzpatrick, *Stranger Is Our Own*, 9; see also Timothy Matovina, *Latino Catholicism: Transformation in America's Largest Church* (Princeton and Oxford: Princeton University Press, 2012), 49–50.

83. Vicki Ruiz and Virginia Sánchez Korrol, eds., *Latinas in the United States* (Bloomington: Indiana University Press, 2006), 620. I paraphrased the entry on Padilla de Armas. See also Matovina, *Latino Catholicism*, 76, and Mario J. Paredes, *The History of the National Encuentros: Hispanic Americans in the One Catholic Church* (New York and Mahwah, N.J.: Paulist Press, 2014), 29.

84. Ana María Díaz-Stevens, "Missionizing the Missionaries," 45. For Sor Isolina's memories of Father Judge, see Tonra, *As the Spirit Rules*, unpublished manuscript, 1988, 14–16, AMSBT.

85. Personal communication from Sister Theresa Ahern, MSBT, November 11, 2014.

1960, the religious orders had ordained only four. Two of those four, Fernando Rodríguez and Antonio Hernández Vélez, were Missionary Servants of the Most Holy Trinity. Domingo Rodríguez Zambrana, a seminarian for the Missionary Servants of the Most Holy Trinity in 1960, would go on to become the first Puerto Rican major superior of a men's religious community in the United States.[86] Thirty years after Father Judge's death, the Missionary Servants spread to Mexico and other Latin American countries.

Father Judge and the Missionary Servants in Puerto Rico, 1923–1933

Father Judge loved Puerto Rico. After his initial trip early in 1923, he sailed back to the island seven more times before his death. He went for about a month in the winter of 1924, with a side trip to see the sisters in the Virgin Islands. He didn't go to Puerto Rico in 1925 but returned in June and July 1926, and again for about four months from September to December 1926 for the reopening of Colegio San Agustín. During this period he dictated the "Puerto Rican Chronicle" to Louise Wagner. In 1927 the sisters established their novitiate for native Puerto Rican vocations at Aguadilla on the northwestern end of the island. Father Judge spent most of the first half of 1927 on the island and returned again in the fall. In the spring of 1929, he spent about a month on the island. There was no trip to Puerto Rico in 1930, but Father Judge went back in 1931, 1932, and 1933. Illness prolonged his last stay. He returned for the last time on August 10 and died about three months later. Before her own death in 1931, Mother Boniface traveled to Puerto Rico in June 1927 and again in the spring of 1929. "The natural beauty is beyond description," she reported; "Mission work wonderful. Our Father is at his best, going day and night."[87] In early November 1926 in Puerto Rico, Father Judge received word that Edward P. Allen, bishop of Mobile, had died. Bishop Allen's death marked the beginning of the final seven-year phase of Father Judge's life.

86. See Dolan and Vidal, *Puerto Rican and Cuban Catholics*, 47.

87. Tonra, *Led by the Spirit*, 165. The listing of Father Judge's trips to Puerto Rico given in this paragraph is taken from the "Itinerary of Father Judge," compiled from his collected writings by Hilary Mettes, ST, in 1973.

PART 3

TRIAL AND LOSS, 1926–1933

10

FATHER JUDGE AND BISHOP TOOLEN 1927–1930

Mobile Succession

On October 21, 1926, Bishop Edward P. Allen of Mobile died. The *Holy Ghost* magazine eulogized him as "their patron from the beginning of their work at Holy Trinity, Alabama." Mother Boniface asked that a Mass be said in every cenacle for Bishop Allen, who, she wrote, "has always been a very good friend to us. He has never refused a request from us."[1] "To Bishop Allen," Sister Mary James Collins wrote years later, "we owed great love and devotion for his kindness and wise understanding of what Father Judge was trying to do in the establishment of these new communities, so unlike the usual ones in the Church."[2]

When Bishop Allen came to Mobile in 1897, his diocese spanned the entire state and parts of Florida. The Catholics numbered only 17,000. Born in 1853 and ordained in 1881, he was a nineteenth-century churchman, a missionary bishop. He came of age before 1908, the year the Vatican removed the United States from mission status. Prior to 1908, local conciliar legislation rather than universal canon law governed the U.S. church. In 1921, four years after the promulgation of the new Code of Canon Law, Bishop Allen sent Father Judge "[a] letter approving, as far as I have any right to approve, of the Brotherhood at Cottonton, Alabama." He explained that the "Holy See must give some kind of sanction to an organized work before it can advance. But as far as I can help you, I am very willing to do

1. Tonra, *Led by the Spirit*, 158–59.
2. Collins, "Voice from the Past," *Holy Ghost*, September 1952, 7.

so."[3] Bishop Allen's careful language highlights the tentative nature of his approval.

Nearly seven months after Bishop Allen's death, on May 4, 1927, Archbishop Michael Curley of Baltimore consecrated one of his own priests, Thomas J. Toolen (1886–1976), as sixth bishop of Mobile. At the time, no one could have foreseen the tremendous impact Mobile's 1927 episcopal succession would have on Father Judge and the Missionary Cenacle. Bishop Toolen presided over Catholic consolidation in Alabama in the first half of the twentieth century. During his forty-two years as bishop, from 1927 to 1969, Toolen oversaw the building of over 700 units of new construction, including 189 churches, 112 elementary and high schools, and 23 health care facilities.[4] One of them was Holy Name of Jesus Hospital in Gadsden. Begun in 1930, amid the financial stress of the Great Depression, and dedicated on September 14, 1931, the new hospital with its half-million-dollar price tag proved a major source of tension between Bishop Toolen and Father Judge and the Missionary Servants.

Before his ordination in 1910, Bishop Toolen studied canon law for a year at the Catholic University of America. From the time of his arrival in 1927, he increasingly insisted on the regularization of the Missionary Servants' affairs and their more formal approval by the church. One could make a strong case that the time had come for such developments. Bishop Toolen held Mother Boniface, the sisters, and their work in the diocese in high regard. About the men's group, he was less enthusiastic. He tended to look on Father Judge's role as founding superior of both groups as an infringement on his own authority as ordinary. He thought of the Missionary Servants of the Most Blessed Trinity as a diocesan community who should work primarily in Alabama and not undertake new work without his approval. In these views, Bishop Toolen had the weight of church law on his side.

Neither branch of the Missionary Servants had been canonically recognized. They had come into existence under Father Judge's inspiration, at the discretion of Bishop Allen, with at least the tacit support of the Vincentian General Council and the apostolic delegate. But, as far as the Code of Canon

3. Allen to Judge, Mobile, January 22, 1921, from a copy in the papers of Rev. Thomas Lenahan, AAM. On canonical developments in the early twentieth century that led to pontifical recognition of apostolic congregations in simple vows, see Sister Deborah L. Wilson, MSBT, "To Speak with One Voice: A History of the Constitutions and Rule of Life of the Missionary Servants of the Most Blessed Trinity" (master's thesis, University of Dayton, 2006), chap. 1.

4. On Allen and Toolen, see Oscar Lipscomb's entries in *NCE* (2003), 1:295, 14:110–11.

Law was concerned, they did not formally exist as religious communities and, without Bishop Toolen's approval, never would. This canonical situation proved especially difficult in the matter of ordaining priests. Ordained in 1926, Father Eugene Brennan was technically a priest of the Diocese of Mobile. Bishop Allen released him to the Missionary Servants, making no objection when Father Judge sent him to Puerto Rico. But Bishop Toolen refused to ordain Edgar Fursman (Brother Paul Anthony) and George Mulroy (Brother Theophane) and risk having Father Judge send them out of the diocese.

In 1928 Father Judge was sixty years old. Conflicts with Bishop Toolen about how to fit the Cenacle into the church's canonical structures shape the drama of the final five years of his life. In addition to the hospital debt, which Bishop Toolen had to sign for as ordinary, the Cenacle continued to expand. By 1928 the sisters were established in Mobile; Pensacola, Florida; Greensburg, Pennsylvania; Philadelphia; Newark; Brooklyn; Stirling, New Jersey; Rockford, Illinois; Connecticut; Mississippi; and Puerto Rico. In addition to Puerto Rico, the brothers had expanded to Stirling, New Jersey, Silver Spring, Maryland, and Washington, D.C. The year also brought the painful departure of Father John Loftus, who had come to the Missionary Servants from the Diocese of Hartford in 1922, and finally, the apostolic delegate's demand for a rule by the end of the year. In the mist of conflict and difficulty, Mother Boniface proved irreplaceable, both in her ability to manage money and keep the movement from being crushed by its enormous debt and, especially, in her deep interpersonal wisdom.

Through all of this, Father Judge exhibited to a remarkable degree what St. Paul called "the fruits of the Holy Spirit." Along with Mother Boniface, he constantly urged not only that Bishop Toolen be treated with charity but that in God's providence he was the Cenacle's great benefactor. In the person of Bishop Toolen, Father Judge came face to face with acute financial savvy and the brick-and-mortar spirit of the American Catholic subculture in the first half of the twentieth century. Bishop Toolen also had a soft side that Mother Boniface never failed to touch. As much as he regarded Judge as a dangerous visionary, he had real respect for the work the sisters did in his diocese and genuine affection for them. During the years from 1928 to 1933, these ingredients came together in a volatile mix.

Puerto Rico and Cenacle Retreats, 1927

Father Judge spent Christmas at Holy Trinity; he had returned to Puerto Rico by January 22, 1927.[5] "There is no reason for us to envy the saints or apostles," he wrote after a catechetical trip in the countryside, "for these opportunities are right here today."[6] St. Augustine's Academy had reopened for the academic year 1926–27, and Judge's three-page report to Bishop Caruana, who had now been replaced as apostolic delegate to Cuba and the West Indies, indicates that the colegio was his chief concern in returning to the island. The report's opening line refers to "the magazine," presumably *El Educador Católico*, recently begun at St. Augustine's.[7] Mother Boniface's enthusiasm for Puerto Rico fell far short of his. He assured her that he would be back by March 25, but warned that he could not stay long. "I am leaving everything up in the air here." He repeated his concern that religion was dying in Puerto Rico. "There is no condition in the United States like it, absolutely none. The South is not like it. God seems to be calling us, at least in this, to be the saviors of the people of Porto Rico."[8]

Father Judge did indeed make it back to Holy Trinity for the Feast of the Annunciation. On March 29, he wrote to Monsignor Thomas Nummey asking if he could take up a collection for Puerto Rico in Nummey's parish in Richmond Hill in the Diocese of Brooklyn. Nummey got permission from Bishop Molloy, who had recently legislated against such collections, and, in early April, Father Judge collected $1,100 to take back to Puerto Rico. With the closing of Blessed Trinity Academy in Stirling, Sister Mary Rose of the Cross would be assigned to Nummey's parish, which Judge described as "positively . . . the finest exhibit of parochial work I have ever seen."[9] Within two years, Monsignor Nummey would join the Missionary Servants.

By May 1927, Father Judge was back in Puerto Rico, his sense of urgency undimmed. To Mother Boniface he described St. Augustine's educational

5. Judge to Sister Marie of the Holy Trinity, on board SS *Coamo*, January 22, 1927, AST, MF 5903–4. In hinting at difficulties among the sisters who worked in the Philadelphia Children's Bureau, this letter anticipates a blistering conference Judge gave there in July for the sisters' retreat. His stern warnings against becoming "social service workers" indicate that his views on scientific social work had not changed; see AST, MF 5980–83.

6. Judge to Sister Marie of the Holy Trinity, Río Piedras, February 22, 1927, AST, MF 5907.

7. Judge to Caruana, Río Piedras, March 3, 1927, AST, MF 5917–19.

8. Judge to Mother Boniface, Río Piedras, March 7, 1927, AST, MF 7967.

9. Judge to Mother Boniface Keasey, Stirling, April 1927, AST, MF 7969–71, describing his visit to Richmond Hill; compare Judge to Nummey, no place, March 29, 1927, AST 5922; Judge to Bishop Thomas Molloy, Stirling, April 5, 1927, AST, MF 5924–25.

work of "Catholicis[ing] the Porto Rican student or the Spanish-American youth" as "the secret of the reconstruction of Catholic life in the Spanish-American world, and the only real worthwhile remedy for Mexican troubles and any like kind of misery."[10] On June 10, 1927, Mother Boniface herself arrived on the island. She stayed for about a month, taking in the work and arranging for the sisters' native novitiate at Aguadilla. She sailed back to Brooklyn on July 4.[11]

Father Judge had left a few days before to give rounds of summer and early fall retreats. July found him at Town Hill, Connecticut, and then Philadelphia, giving a retreat to the sisters at the Children's Bureau. He attended celebrations for Father McHale's Silver Jubilee of ordination on August 14 in Germantown and August 16 in Princeton, New Jersey. From Princeton he went by train to Alabama, with a stop in Charlotte for Mass with the Benedictines. This route he dubbed the "Charlotte method."[12] He reached Holy Trinity by August 20 in time for reception of the postulants, the annual pilgrimage, and retreats. With the boys' academy closed, Stirling became a retreat center. "Thank God," he wrote to Mother Boniface, "we are having a surprisingly fine retreat—nearly forty girls." Sister Marie Baptista and Helen Mackin had brought the young women, including nurses and teachers, to Stirling over the Labor Day weekend. "This retreat work should be pushed," he concluded.[13]

Later in September, Father Judge gave a retreat for the sisters at Holy Name of Jesus Hospital. On September 14, the Feast of the Exaltation of the Holy Cross, he sent from Gadsden a beautiful conference to the brothers at Río Piedras. He told them that this feast summed up the work of the past year. In a striking demonstration of his ability to awaken the religious affections, he spoke of "heart feelings" aroused by the mystery of the incarnation. "We should love with an intense personal love anything concerning our dear Jesus.... The Mystery of the Incarnation means so much to us ... it almost seemed as if we had been invited into the privacy of the Holy Family."[14] After

10. Judge to Mother Boniface Keasey, Río Piedras, May 22, 1927, AST, MF 7998–8000. This letter summarizes the year's work in Puerto Rico. Compare Judge to Sr. Gerard [his sister], Río Piedras, May 28, 1927, AST, MF 5926, contrasting Puerto Rican and Italian work.

11. Tonra, *Led by the Spirit*, 165–66.

12. Ibid., 170 , and Judge to Mother Boniface Keasey, Philadelphia, August 14, 1927, AST, MF 8010.

13. Judge to Mother Boniface Keasey, Stirling, September 2, 1927, AST, MF 8013.

14. Judge to My dear Brothers, Gadsden, Ala., September 14, 1927, AST, MF 4202. In the same vein, see also his letter to the novices at Aguadilla, October 20, 1927, AST, MF 5996.

a brief stop at Holy Trinity, he made his way to Washington, D.C., to give a retreat at the recently acquired house of studies on Lawrence Street Northeast to the brothers studying at Catholic University.

Father Judge and Bishop Toolen Meet for the First Time

Bishop Toolen was in Baltimore in September, and Father Judge made an appointment to see him during the retreat in Washington on the morning of September 26, 1927. He reported to Mother Boniface that he found the bishop "very cordial and cooperative." He promised to help with getting money from the Extension Society and the bishops' fund for home missions. They talked about the work of the Missionary Servants in the diocese—the hoped-for charities bureaus in Mobile, Pensacola, and Eufaula. Judge described Toolen as "very much impressed with what is going on at Holy Trinity." The bishop, Judge continued, "generously admitted that we had the largest mission movement south of the Mason-Dixon Line and probably the largest home mission movement in the United States." In parentheses, Judge wrote, "I think we can count on him as a friend." But there was one ominous cause for concern.

Expecting an affirmative reply, Bishop Toolen asked if the movement had not been instituted for the South. Father Judge immediately responded in the negative. "I said 'NO,' that we had long before coming South been engaged in Italian work; and that the community came South for my convenience." Perhaps the bishop was wondering why Judge had spent half the year in Puerto Rico. In any case, Judge realized the implications of his question. "This is a very important point," he insisted, "and we must all say the same thing. It was a leading question. I suppose the inference would be that all our people should be working in the South." For the moment, Judge was spared this inference. "My answers satisfied him," he concluded. "That was the end of that."[15] But, of course, it was not.

Mother Boniface met with the bishop in Gadsden the following week. She and Father Judge had promised him sisters to begin a Catholic Charities bureau. On October 1, 1927, Sister Luke McGrath and two other sisters arrived to set up the bureau next to the bishop's residence on Government Street in Mobile. Sister Luke was a physician. Sending her from Holy Name

15. Judge to Mother Boniface Keasey, Washington, D.C., September 26, 1927, AST, MF 8025.

of Jesus Hospital to the new bureau in Mobile was surely a favor to the bishop. She spent four years at Mobile Catholic Charities until, in the fall of 1931, much to the bishop's chagrin, Mother Boniface sent her to Pittsburgh.[16]

Dr. Louis Motry Appears

"A very friendly doctor of canon law called on me during the retreat in Washington," Father Judge wrote to Mother Boniface in September 1927. It was Dr. Hubert Louis Motry (1884–1952). He had come "to felicitate me on our young men and to proffer his services." At this point, Judge hoped only that Motry might serve as liaison to Monsignor Filippo Bernardini (1884–1954), head of the Canon Law School at Catholic University, staffer at the apostolic delegation in Washington, and nephew of the cardinal secretary of state Pietro Gasparri.[17] Brother Paul Anthony Fursman was a student at Catholic University, and Judge instructed him "to explain to the friendly doctor how I am conditioned here, doing pioneer work in this ash can of the Church, trying with a few others to hold this together until we can get it fastened up to last a few years." Fursman was to bring the Puerto Rican newsletters to Motry to give to Bernardini. "I am sure that what Monsignor Bernardini gets," Judge wrote, "he will bring to the Delegation."[18]

Father Judge wanted the apostolic delegation to know about the work in Puerto Rico. "If these men could realize the terrible state of affairs on this Island, that the first thing to be done is to stop this landslide from the church, they would have a little heart for the men who are trying to do it and give them time [to catch?] their breath."[19] In the coming canonical conflicts with Bishop Toolen, Father Judge took full advantage of the "services" Motry offered. Monsignor Bernardini's role in gaining papal approval for the brothers' rule would far exceed Judge's hopes at this time.[20]

16. Tonra, *Led by the Spirit*, 172–73, 303; Collins, "Voice from the Past," *Holy Ghost*, December 1952, 8.

17. Peter D. D'Agostino, *Rome in America: Transnational Catholic Ideology from the Resorgimento to Fascism* (Chapel Hill and London: University of North Carolina Press, 2004), 218. Among his many accomplishments, between 1904 and 1917 Gasparri headed the Commission for the Recodification of Canon Law, called for by the First Vatican Council, that resulted in the 1917 code. After Bernardini's return to Rome, he was made an archbishop and in 1935 became the nuncio to Switzerland, where he served during World War II.

18. Judge to Mother Boniface, Río Piedras, December 6, 1927, AST, MF 8060.

19. Ibid.

20. In a 1963 interview, Father Turibius Mulcahy, with reference to Motry and Monsignor Bernardini encouraging Father Judge to request an indult allowing him to serve as superior of

Back to Puerto Rico

A firestorm greeted Father Judge when he returned to the Island in mid-October. The brothers at the colegio were publishing a magazine called *El Educador Católico*. Judge entitled his inaugural editorial "Religion and Education, the Divine and Useful Subjects to which the *Católico Educador* is Dedicated."[21] The brothers had reprinted an article concerning the "Pope and His Temporal Supremacy over the People of the United States." Taken from a pamphlet published in Pittsburgh in the context of Al Smith's 1928 presidential campaign, it was "approved by two Cardinals and fifteen Archbishops and Bishops" and translated into Spanish. Archbishop Caruana's successor as apostolic delegate to Cuba had become involved, along with local clergy who objected to the article, claiming that it "would be all right in the United States but would not be all right in Porto Rico."[22]

Within a week this controversy was resolved, and the magazine went to press with the article. But Father Judge learned that a good part of the problem had to do with local perceptions of Father Eugene as "undignified." His informal style offended some of the Spanish clergy. Judge referred to "that imprudent way he has of saying and working out things" and eventually concluded that Brennan's offense amounted to "just being too independent, a little imprudent and bringing himself down to the level of these frivolous girls, foolishly making himself a public entertainer." Father Judge "gave him charity," as did one of the sisters. Judge was impressed with the militarization of St. Augustine's. "It borders just on the marvelous to note the discipline and smooth action of every department." But he worried how "exercises of piety and spiritual life" could be put "on a military academy basis."[23]

---

the sisters, suggested that "this was the practice of the CUA canon law school men so that they could use such things as test cases with the Holy See"; interview with Father Turibius Mulcahy by Father David O'Connor, July 22, 1963, typescript, 1, AST.

21. AST, MF 1243–45, a single-spaced English typescript and probably the original. There is no citation for the Spanish translation that appeared in *Educador Católico*.

22. Judge to Mother Boniface, Río Piedras, October 19, 1927, AST, MF 8029.

23. Ibid., October 25, 1927, AST, MF 8032–33. This mini-theological dispute energized Judge. He appealed to Archbishop [Francis Patrick] Kenrick's tract *De ecclesia*, probably in Kenrick's *Theologica dogmatica* (1840). "All in all," he wrote, "it has opened up a very interesting question and set all of us working. It is such things as these that make good theologians."

Keeping the Ship of the Cenacle Afloat on a Sea of Debt

Money continued to be a gnawing need. Many bishops had legislated against the parish collections the sisters had done in the past. In their September 1927 meeting, Father Judge asked Bishop Toolen for his help in getting funds from national Catholic organizations. He wrote a month later thanking the bishop for his strong "letter of approbation" and seeking his help in getting support from the Paulists' Catholic Missionary Union, which funded missions to non-Catholics. Judge tried to explain that the Cenacle's outreach to Protestants was significant despite the fact that they did not do missions as such. He asked Toolen to write the union before their next meeting.

He also wrote to Cardinal Patrick Hayes of New York, seeking his help in getting funding from the Catholic Missionary Union. "We began our building work under the old system of collections. These were taken from us suddenly. The bishops referred us to the Home Mission Fund from which we received no help." This letter came to Hayes just before the bishops' annual meeting to be held in Chicago. "Columbus, Georgia is but a twenty-four-hour trip from Chicago," he told the cardinal as he offered an informal invitation to the dedication of the new buildings at Holy Trinity.[24]

The end of October brought the new Feast of Christ the King. In a circular letter, Father Judge described the celebration at the colegio. As Mass began, the band started playing, "I'll be Loving You Always." Judge described Father Eugene and the brothers as "liturgically distressed." They "squelched the musicians." The university students defended the song as meaning "loving God always." The bandleader apologized and pleaded lack of time to prepare. "It was truly a fiesta all day," Judge enthused.[25] But money woes continued to mount.

In the previous year, when arguing against taking on St. Augustine's, Mother Boniface reminded Father Judge that they were already $190,000 in debt.[26] "Debt like the sword of Damocles was ever over her," wrote Sr. Mary James in reference to 1929.[27] Father Judge's responses to Mother Boniface's letters in November 1927 indicate that she was especially conscious of the sword's presence at that time. At first he tried humor, admitting that her

24. Judge to Patrick Cardinal Hayes, Río Piedras, October 26, 1927, AST, MF 6003–4.

25. Judge to My dear Children, Río Piedras, October 30, 1927, AST, MF 8037.

26. Tonra, *Led by the Spirit*, 155.

27. Collins, "Voice from the Past," *Holy Ghost*, June 1953, 6.

"pathetic and eloquent pleas do stir me," and offering her half of the $2 million Father Delgado had promised to give him if he got it.[28]

"Now as for our debts and other troubles," Father Judge wrote six days later, "do meditate on the Divine Hand of Jesus.... Prayerfully ask that Divine Hand to help lighten your burden. Tell all to ask that Hand to touch what is sore and twisted.... We must, my dear child, leave ourselves more in the hands of God." "I think about the things you write about," he acknowledged. But he also had confidence that "our dear Lord realizes what we are trying to do for the most abandoned of the abandoned of His little ones." He would help "at the proper time." "Therefore," Judge concluded, "I am not very much worried about the debts or about Bishop this or Bishop that, or any particular canonist. All we can do is our best." With his final word on the debt, he tried to offer some more worldly encouragement: "Keep the ship of the Cenacle afloat. St. Augustine's before many months will come strong to help both Holy Trinity Academy and St. Joseph's."[29]

A few days later, Father Judge used the financial plight of Brother Augustine Philips to lighten Mother Boniface's spirits. Philips had written to Father Judge about Stirling's financial woes. In his next letter to Mother Boniface, Judge quoted at length from Philips's lament. He complained about being stuck with Sister Agnes's old bills. Father Judge made light of this by suggesting to Mother Boniface that she could send Sister Agnes back to Stirling. "See how happy everyone would be when they see her downtown." Philips went on to list his own bills. "You know my interest is $4,200 a year. My running expenses are about $500 a month. Thank God, I have been able to pay the interest but I am six months behind in the expense account and this, without revenue, is certainly trusting in Divine Providence." Philips pleaded with Judge not to cancel his trip to New Jersey. "Just now I am wondering how long this can last. When you are here, the things seem easy but when I am going it alone, it is a different proposition." Father Judge asked Mother Boniface to write to Philips, but he knew she had no money to send him.[30]

He promised Mother Boniface that, with its enrollment increasing, St. Augustine's would soon "give us a well filled pocket book." The Cenacle had

28. Judge to Mother Boniface, Río Piedras, November 16, 1927, AST, MF 8047.

29. Ibid., November 22, 1927, AST, MF 8053–54.

30. Ibid., December 6, 1927, AST, MF 8059–62. On April 19, 1926, the Diocese of Newark had taken over the Stirling property. Brother Augustine acquired the property on Long Hill Road on October 31, 1924. The Missionary Servants retained use of the property, but it was not until April 4, 1968, that they were able to buy it back from the diocese; copies of the deeds in AST.

taken over the school but did not own the building. "If we only had our own place and an opportunity to cut down our expenses, we could send some very substantial sums to you. Cheer up and keep things bobbing along for some day Porto Rico is going to put a big shoulder under the Cenacle burdens." He went on to tell her about Father Eugene's objections to a military school run by sisters. Father Judge tried to distinguish between "the work of the military academy and ordinary school class work." He knew they could not have a serious school without the sisters.[31] In the end, his faith in the colegio as a money maker would prove unfounded.

Father Judge decided to send Father Eugene temporarily back to the mainland. He wanted Brennan to find ways to sell Puerto Rican lace in the States so women laborers would get a fair price for their work and to follow up on a survey of Cenacle expenses. Affairs in Puerto Rico had distracted Judge from completing it. Brennan was also to visit Catholic college campuses to get book donations and possibly the support of the Catholic Mission Crusade.[32] The results of these efforts are unknown.

"All we can do is our best," Father Judge had told Mother Boniface with respect to the debt. Father Judge's best always included careful cultivation of those in the church who might have the wherewithal to help. One of the most important letters he wrote before leaving Puerto Rico on December 15 was to Cardinal Dennis Dougherty. Early on Dougherty had given the sisters permission to collect in Philadelphia. In 1920 he brought them to work in the Catholic Children's Bureau. Archbishop Caruana was a Dougherty protégé, and it was at the cardinal's residence that he first convinced Judge to take on the work in Puerto Rico. Later Dougherty would welcome the sisters' motherhouse to Philadelphia and bury Mother Boniface from his cathedral. It is fair to say that, among a number of others, Dennis Dougherty is the single most important reason the Cenacle did not fail after Father Judge's death.[33] Father Judge well trusted in the Divine Hand of Jesus, but he also knew just what he was doing when he wrote to Cardinal Dougherty on November 8, 1927.

31. Ibid. Father Judge's previous letter on November 27 raised the issue of finding new facilities for St. Augustine's; see AST, MF 8045.

32. Judge to Mother Boniface, Río Piedras, November 27, 1927, AST, MF 8045.

33. We have no critical biography of Cardinal Dougherty. His papers at the Philadelphia Archdiocesan Historical Research Center are "closed." I was able to see some files in which "Father Judge and the Trinitarian Sisters" are mentioned. I found nothing related to this November 8, 1927, letter. Nor did I find any related material—for example, the letter "from the Chancery," in Bishop Toolen's papers in the Mobile Archives.

Cardinal Dougherty's Support

Father Judge began with reference to a letter the sisters recently received "from the Chancery." Since Judge's letter goes on to talk about the sisters' rule, written and submitted to Bishop Allen in the early 1920s, and "papal approval" for the sisters, it is safe to conclude that the "Chancery" in question is Mobile's rather than Philadelphia's. Perhaps the letter from the chancery said the earlier rule submitted to Bishop Allen was too devotional and canonically unsatisfactory. In any case, Father Judge sought the cardinal's advice about the sisters' future "because of the rather recent beginning of their institute and the formative period they are going through."

He noted their community beginnings in 1914 and their houses "in many dioceses" as well as a "new province" in Puerto Rico with a native novitiate. He described the sisters as "anxious to seek Papal approval because of their interstate and inter-diocesan and probably international work and development. Bishop Allen of Mobile blessed and favored them very much. The rule had been committed to him before he died." He continued with a telling juxtaposition: "His successor, Bishop Toolen, has called them to work in Mobile, in fact, he has located them alongside of the episcopal residence." Even as Judge points to Bishop Toolen's approval of the work, the contrast between Bishop Allen/inter-diocesan and Bishop Toolen/Mobile is hard to miss.

The letter's next two paragraphs deal with the original rule submitted to Bishop Allen and how "doing pioneer work in abandoned places" such as Puerto Rico had prevented Father Judge from "giving much time that I would like to have put into the study of certain phases of the Sisters' organization." Clearly, something has led him to wish he had put more time in on the rule. He concludes:

> Here is my present anxiety. Many kindly disposed Bishops have given their advice on the future development and status of the Sisters. Some of this is conflicting. I am anxious, in all things, to do what is best for the interests of our Holy Religion. I feel encouraged for many reasons to put these matters before you, therefore, I will be very grateful if you will give me some broken half hours of your time when I come back to the States.[34]

According to Collins, Cardinal Dougherty did grant Father Judge's request for an interview. "That Cardinal Dougherty gave him of those 'broken half hours,' and that he aided him with wise counsel and timely sugges-

34. Judge to Dennis Cardinal Dougherty, Río Piedras, November 8, 1927, AST, MF 5933–34.

tions," she writes, "we are sure." She adds, "That he finally took the finished Rule to Rome for approval we also know, which act was only one of many for which we owe His Eminence and his memory eternal gratitude."[35] Without surrounding documents, especially the letter "from the Chancery" with which Father Judge begins, it is difficult to interpret this very careful letter to Cardinal Dougherty.

It is clear that by the end of 1927, Father Judge had some sense that the sisters' canonical status and what he called their "inter-diocesan" work was in question. Sister James *finally*, in the sentence previously cited, points to the almost five-year hiatus between this letter and Dougherty's signing of the Sister's Decree of Erection on February 20, 1932. Did Dougherty advise Judge to deal first with the brothers' rule? In any case, that is what he did, working closely with Monsignor Filippo Bernardini, assisted by Louis Motry and the apostolic delegation. In the case of the sisters' approval by Rome, Cardinal Dougherty and those associated with the apostolic delegation were definitely the key figures.

1928: A Painful Congestion of Affairs

The year 1928 began well, with Bishop Toolen coming to Holy Trinity on January 10 to dedicate the chapel and other new buildings. "Word came today," Father Judge wrote on January 18, "that the Bishop was highly edified with everything he saw at Holy Trinity"; "I went, I saw, and I am converted," were Toolen's words, as reported by Sister Luke. Father Judge went on to quote Sister Luke quoting the bishop: "Surely the finger of God is in that place. My prayer and hope is that the spirit of the place will never change. No one would ever have made me believe I would see what I saw. I am going to tell everyone about it, especially the priests that they may know what we have in Alabama."

Father Judge wrote from Gadsden, where Mother Boniface had persuaded him to check himself into the hospital. "I have been at Holy Name of Jesus Hospital observing and being observed," he wrote.[36] Writing to one of the

35. Collins, "Voice from the Past," *Holy Ghost*, December 1952, 8.

36. Judge to Sister Mary Simon, Gadsden, January 18, 1928, AST 6427. Mother Boniface herself was laboring under tremendous pressure. "What a painful experience it is to be ever recovering from the latest shock, to hope for a brief respite from care and anxiety only to feel the impact of the next shock and to realize the day has been spent in mental and conscience adjustments; in other words, to be ever stumbling under the cross and falling and getting up only to fall down again"; Judge to Sister Mary Thomas, Holy Trinity, April 17, 1928, AST, MF 6432.

brothers at Holy Trinity about their finances, he described himself as "hors de combat in consequence of an attack of an old ailment that robs me of the use of one of my feet. It may be rheumatism, but I think it is the result of over-work and nervous strain."[37]

Father Judge was now sixty years old, and his merciless schedule had begun to wear him down. "Father is perfectly healthy but not made of iron," Sister Luke reported to Mother Boniface. The doctor ordered changes in diet and lifestyle. "There is nothing to worry about," Sister Luke continued, "except the fact that Father will never learn the lesson of taking proper care of himself. I do feel that he should be sensible and give himself sufficient time to rest."[38]

January 27, 1928, found Father Judge back at Holy Trinity, Alabama, where he and Fathers Tomerlin and Loftus, along with four of the brothers, including Brothers Theophane Mulroy and Joseph Limpert, held a meeting at which they voted to incorporate officially in the state of Alabama as the Missionary Servants of the Most Holy Trinity, a seeming solidification of this name for the men.[39] By mid-February Judge was at St. Augustine's in Río Piedras for the only week he would spend in Puerto Rico during 1928. "The course of our missionary empire," he wrote to Mother Boniface, "keeps rolling on its way." Thus began a ten-page, single-spaced report on conditions on the island. "Your worries about Porto Rico are worrying me," he told her and promised not to ask for any sisters or any more money for Puerto Rico as long as she gave him "a few months down here." He told her about a new "house for the Brothers." It would cost about $25,000 to build and $200 per month to maintain. In concluding, he proclaimed "the beginning of another epoch in Cenacle life." He prayed it would "mean much to religion, to the Church, to souls, our own and to others."[40]

In an April 1928 letter to the sisters in Puerto Rico, Father Judge reported that six new brothers had entered the novitiate at Holy Trinity. One was Brother Lawrence Brediger. The big news was that Bishop Toolen had

37. Judge to Brother, Gadsden, January 12, 1928, AST, MF 6453.

38. Cited in Collins, "Voice from the Past," *Holy Ghost*, March 1953, 5. Sister James described the sixty-year-old Father Judge: "He was straight and tall, well built with no evidence of heaviness. His black hair had turned to gray but still was thick and wavy. His face showed but few lines and his deep set eyes were still keenly sharp and intensely blue."

39. Minutes of the Meeting of the Missionary Servants of the Most Holy Trinity, January 27, 1928, from a copy in AST. On the history of this name's use, see Berry, *God's Valiant Warrior*, 364n452.

40. Judge to Mother Boniface, Río Piedras, February 15, 1928, AST, MF 8065–74.

"promised us a loan of twenty-five thousand." Father Judge would continue as the "Outside Man," traveling from place to place. Later it would become clear that the bishop thought he was making this loan to the sisters. Judge went on to report $20,000 of current construction debt, presumably at Holy Trinity. The bishop's help was especially welcome because, "as our revenue comes in sporadically and fragmentarily, we find it difficult at times to allay the clamors especially of the small and persistent creditors." He also reported on the *SOS Preservation of the Faith*, the brother's mission magazine, whose first issue had come out the day Bishop Toolen dedicated the chapel. They now had 3,000 subscribers, but the cost of publication had eaten up the $8,000 in revenue that had come in since January. He also gave an excited update on the hospital, which he described as so crowded at twenty-five beds that it had to expand. Dr. Bass, one of the hospital's main physicians, was promoting the expansion, and Mother Boniface had just returned from Gadsden and a meeting with him.[41] Meeting with the doctors and Bishop Toolen about the hospital caused Mother Boniface to put off her planned trip to Puerto Rico until July.

Negotiating over Hospital Expansion

Things seemed to be going well with Bishop Toolen. On May 14, 1928, Father Judge wrote to him from East Pittsburgh on his way back from a trip to the Mayo Clinic in Rochester, Minnesota. A wildly successful cooperative venture involving the local bishop, community physicians, and Franciscan Sisters, the Mayo Clinic with its five associated hospitals struck Father Judge as a model for what they could do in Gadsden. He emphasized the role of the local bishop as "the inspiration and impulse of the enterprise."[42] On June 3, he was in Gadsden with Mother Boniface for the graduation of the first class of sister nurses. After that Father Judge went north and Mother Boniface went to Mobile to visit Bishop Toolen to seek his help in financing the hospital expansion. She had heard that a week earlier the bishop had said he thought Father Judge ought not to be involved with the sisters and prepared to ask him about that. After her June 7 meeting with Bishop Toolen, she wrote up a long account of it.

41. Judge to My dear Child, Holy Trinity, April 10, 1928, AST, MF 6431, 6461. For a fuller description of hospital plans at this stage, see Judge to Sister Mary Thomas, Holy Trinity, April 17, 1928, AST, MF 6432–33.

42. Judge to Toolen, East Pittsburgh, May 14, 1928, Toolen Papers, AAM.

Based on Dr. Herschel Bass's estimates of potential patients, Bishop Toolen found the hospital project a sound one and, based on his own estimate of the sisters' business ability, was willing to back it. But he did not have the same confidence in Father Judge. He told Mother Boniface that he had been hearing reports from Columbus that St. Joseph's was not paying its bills and from Washington that the student brothers were not paying their bills and were "running around at night." He had brought these matters up with Father Judge at their last meeting. Especially exercised about the house in Washington, he thought it a mistake to open the house of studies without a good priest in charge. Father Tomerlin was in charge. The bishop described him as a "plunger" who needed someone who could handle money to check up on him. Toolen thought the apostolic delegate might close the house of studies in Washington before classes began in the fall. The students should have been sent to a place like the Benedictine seminary in Cullmann, Alabama.

Mother Boniface insisted that what the bishop took to be the sisters' business sense owed much to the training and advice of Father Judge. She asked Bishop Toolen to sign for a loan of $100,000. He told her to get $200,000 and he would sign for it. He sent her to see John Kohn in Montgomery to secure the loan. Before she left, she pressed the issue of Father Judge's connection to the sisters. "Sure, Mother," she reported the bishop as saying, "Father Judge is your ecclesiastical superior; I would never want to interfere with his work." She concluded in triumphant overstatement, "So that is all right now; he understands, I understand, and we all understand that you are and always have been a one hundred percent businessman."[43]

While Mother Boniface was writing her report, Father Judge was in Newark, New Jersey, meeting with the recently appointed Bishop Thomas J. Walsh about the work of the Cenacle in his diocese.[44] By June 15 her account of the meeting with Bishop Toolen had reached him there. He thanked and blessed her for her "long, enlightening and very consoling letter." He said he noted a "new spirit" among the bishops he visited and, on the whole, thought

43. Tonra provides the entire text of Mother Boniface's summary of the meeting in *Led by the Spirit*, 184–87. It is hard to read this account without marveling at her many virtues and talents.

44. Father Judge sent an account of this meeting to Mother Boniface. Walsh ordered the "collecting Brothers" to leave the diocese but promised his support for the sisters' work and asked Judge for a summary of their work in the diocese; see Judge to Mother Boniface, Newark, N.J., June 13, 1928, AST, MF 8083–84.

they were "very much graced" to have Bishop Toolen. "As you say, he certainly does seem to have a heart and when he gets things from the right angle he will make the necessary adjustments." He made a terribly mistaken estimate of how Toolen would view the Cenacle in five years but promised "that in all those things you mentioned I will be pacific and long suffering." He went on to address the issue of the house of studies. He knew of three seminaries that had been closed but reported on a recent meeting with Monsignor Filippo Bernardini that left him and Father Tomerlin with the impression that "we are very much in favor with the Delegation."[45]

Around this time, after Father Judge learned about Mother Boniface's June 7 meeting with Bishop Toolen and before Toolen's reservations surfaced around June 18, Father Judge wrote a two-page report to Father McHale in Paris. "We are sailing," he began, "over uncharted waters and occasionally rasp a hidden obstruction, consequently, we have some experiences that are not on the program." He wanted to bring McHale up to date on "three developments outstanding in the general course of affairs." These were the Apostolic School at Holy Trinity, the house of studies at Catholic University, and the expansion of Holy Name of Jesus Hospital. Regarding the hospital, Judge overstated Bishop Toolen's role, reporting that "the Bishop himself is urging" the expansion. "Bishop Toolen is very much enthused and is endorsing for the Sisters' a note of $200,000."[46]

It soon became clear that Father Judge had overestimated Bishop Toolen's enthusiasm for the project. Both he and Mother Boniface knew that the bishop was leaving for Europe on June 25 and hoped to have the hospital loan settled before he left. Around June 18, Mother Boniface received a note from the bishop expressing hesitation about the project based on the number of sisters it would take to staff it.[47] Judge wrote immediately to Toolen trying to respond to his reservations. He also sent the bishop a copy of a letter he wrote to Mother Boniface on the same day. Citing the example of the Mayo Clinic and the vocations that came from St. Mary's Hospital there, he appealed to Bishop Toolen:

45. Judge to Mother Boniface, Newark, N.J., June 15, 1928, AST, MF 6511–13. Regarding the favor of the delegation and the meeting with Bernardini, he added, "More than that, our foundations, thank God, I think are deep and strong and very much according to the plan of the Church. The Preservation of the Faith and the Conservation of the Faith and our Latin work will help us."

46. Judge to McHale, no place, Feast of the Solemnity of the Sacred Heart [1928], AST, MF 1369. As best I can determine, the feast fell on June 12 in 1928, a date consistent with the letter's contents.

47. See Judge to Mother Boniface Keasey, East Pittsburgh, June 19, 1928, AST, MF 8090.

May you be our Bishop Hefferon. When the story of the Mayo Clinic is rightly known the Catholic Church is going to get the credit for founding that great medical center, and a Catholic Bishop will be honored as the patron of one of the greatest medical movements in the history of the country, if not of the world.[48]

This comparison with Bishop Hefferon and the Mayo Clinic failed to move Bishop Toolen. His brief reply is dated June 21. "I am not yet converted to the hospital idea," he wrote. "Experience shows that very few vocations come from the nurses." Despite his reservations, Bishop Toolen gave his reluctant approval. "I have told Mother that she might go ahead and I have confidence in her." He was sure Mother Boniface could "handle the proposition," but he feared the project would "hamper the work of the Sisters for years to come." The problem would not be the number of sisters required to staff it, "but the fact that they will be tied down with a heavy debt."[49]

The Apostolic Delegate Intervenes

The day before Bishop Toolen replied to Father Judge, Archbishop Pietro Fumasoni-Biondi (1872–1960), who served as apostolic delegate from 1922 to 1933, responded to Bishop Toolen's "esteemed communication of recent date concerning the Rev. Thomas A. Judge, CM and the enterprise of which he is the head." The delegate noted with pleasure that Toolen was "keeping in close touch with this work, particularly because you are responsible before the Holy See for its regularity." Fumasoni-Biondi thought the best reply to Toolen would be a copy of a letter he had recently sent to Father Judge.[50] Though Judge doesn't mention it in his correspondence, the delegate's stern letter with its strong tone of reprimand accounts for the feverish pace at which Judge worked on the brothers' rule throughout the summer and fall of 1928. The emphasis in this letter no doubt explains the order in which Judge worked on the rules, beginning first with the men and then going on to the women.

48. Judge to Toolen, East Pittsburgh, June 18, 1928, and enclosure of Judge to Mother Boniface, East Pittsburgh, June 18, 1928, Toolen Papers, AAM. See also AST, MF 8091 for letter to Mother Boniface. On the Mayo Clinic, see Sister Ellen Whelan, OSF, *The Sisters' Story: Saint Mary's Hospital—Mayo Clinic, 1889–1939* (Rochester, Minn: Mayo Foundation for Medical Education and Research, 2002).

49. Toolen to Judge, Mobile, June 21, 1928, copy, Toolen Papers, AAM.

50. Fumasoni-Biondi to Toolen, Washington, D.C., June 20, 1928, with enclosure, Toolen Papers, AAM. I found no copy of the bishop's inquiry to the delegate in Bishop Toolen's papers.

Fumasoni-Biondi began with reference to the circular letter on seminary training that he had enclosed and that had been sent to all ordinaries in the United States. It was perhaps why Bishop Toolen believed the delegate would shut down the house of studies. Father Judge seems to have received a copy of it before the June 19 date on Fumasoni-Biondi's letter.[51] The fact that Judge received this circular letter at all was an implicit recognition of the legitimacy of the Cenacle's canonically dubious programs of priestly training. The fact that the delegate began his letter with reference to it had to be a small consolation. The rest of the letter made clear that Father Judge could not take this implicit recognition for granted and that, if he did not regularize the situation as soon as possible, even this recognition would be taken away.

Archbishop Fumasoni-Biondi assured Father Judge that he was aware of and shared his predecessor's "kind interest" in the work of the Cenacle. But, he added, "I must observe that I have never seen much disposition on your part to keep me informed of the progress of the work in which you are engaged and from which it would seem much good could be expected." He reminded Judge that at their last meeting, "I suggested that your institute be given a canonical foundation." Then, in a seeming reference to Bishop Toolen's "esteemed communication of recent date," he added, "I am told, however, that up to the present your institute is not even diocesan, not having received the approval of any Ordinary in a canonical way."

The next paragraph began, "I deem it of great importance," and then described the process that occupied Father Judge for the next three and a half months. He was to work with the bishop of Mobile and secure the help of an "expert canonist" to "compile the proper Constitution of your institute and send the same to the Sacred Congregation for Religious together with the recommendations of those other Bishops in whose dioceses you may have your houses." He was to follow the same process with the "Missionary Sisters Servants of the Most Blessed Trinity, whose numbers I understand are happily increasing."

The apostolic delegate made clear that he wanted "this matter of the Constitutions" to be dealt with "without any delay." In fact, he began his

51. He makes reference to it in his response to Mother Boniface's account of her June 7 meeting with Toolen. It concluded his argument on why he didn't think the house of studies would be closed. "Above all, I received a document from the Papal Delegate that is being sent to all seminaries, no seminary but one in good standing will get it"; Judge to Mother Boniface Keasey, June 15, 1928, AST, MF 6511–13.

penultimate paragraph with that phrase. Archbishop Fumasoni-Biondi's conclusion was ominous, especially as it represented for Father Judge the will of the church's highest authority:

> If your communities, that of men and that of women, do not obtain, and this at once, a canonical approbation, at least diocesan, I shall be obliged to consider you a private person engaged in the formation of priests and of so-called religious without any authorization whatsoever. Considered as such you will be subject to the consequences of your position and your uncanonical status.[52]

After receiving Archbishop Fumasoni-Biondi's letter, Father Judge immediately arranged a meeting with him. On July 2, 1928, he reported on it from Stirling to one of brothers at the Washington house of studies. He described the interview as "most consoling and encouraging" and Fumasoni-Biondi as "extremely affable and benign; in fact, never have I had a prelate treat me so fatherly." As if answering the delegate's complaint that Judge had failed to keep him informed, he pointed out that "we left our affairs in the hands of one of his canonists [Bernardini] who has all the papers. I, therefore, did not visit the Delegation." His work "on the frontier and in the dust of the advancing Cenacle and the cataclysm of Porto Rico" left little time for such visits. Clearly, he wanted to put into circulation in Washington the reasons Fumasoni-Biondi had not heard much from him before this July 2 meeting.

"Strange to say," Father Judge wrote, "the few times I did try to make an engagement, he was away." But he had now been fully informed and "please God his welcome and kindly interest in our affairs will bring me often to the Delegation door." He asked the recipient to share the letter with the others in the house. They could all "do a great work for us in Washington, that their apostolate there is to conserve the good repute of the Brother Missionary Servants of the Most Holy Trinity. Tell all to be encouraged for the Delegate knows of the Brothers and he knows them well. Do say prayers of thanksgiving."[53] Despite the good feelings this meeting engendered, Fumasoni-Biondi's stark demand that canonical approbation be obtained "at once" and "without any delay" remained to be carried out. But there were many distractions.

52. Fumasoni-Biondi to Judge, Washington, D.C., June 19, 1928, from a copy in Toolen Papers, AAM.

53. Judge to Brother [Theophane?], Stirling, July 2, 1928, AST, MF 6436.

The Loftus Affair

Father Judge's account of the meeting was written from Stirling, where he was giving a women's retreat Sister Baptista had organized for the Outer Cenacle.[54] Other retreats in the North occupied him as he began to work on the men's rule in earnest. On July 18, 1928, Mother Boniface was finally able to go to Puerto Rico. She returned on August 5. Shortly thereafter, Father Loftus precipitated a crisis at Holy Trinity. It led to his final departure, after six years, from the Missionary Servants of the Most Holy Trinity. On August 21, Loftus wrote to Bishop Toolen's chancellor, Father Philip Cullen, accusing both Judge and Mother Boniface of misappropriating funds that belonged to the *Holy Ghost* magazine. He asked that Father Judge and Mother Boniface be ordered "not to interfere with or remove those working on the magazine and to hand over the money that they have taken so that the bills may be paid." He also reported on another building being started at Holy Trinity with a note from a Northern bank.[55]

The next day, Father Judge wrote Bishop Toolen that Father Loftus had refused his assignment to Tuscaloosa to start a Negro apostolate there. He based his refusal on a "personal arrangement" he had with the bishop. As a result of Loftus's decision, Judge told Toolen that the Missionary Servants could no longer take on the work at Tuscaloosa.[56] As Loftus had requested, Father Philip Cullen, Mobile's chancellor, sent a telegram to Holy Trinity. On August 24, Loftus wrote to Cullen complaining that Father Judge and Mother Boniface had ignored the telegram and left Holy Trinity without doing anything about it. "Mother Boniface takes the money of the *Holy Ghost* magazine, while protesting that she and Fr. Judge will do anything that the Bishop says but that nothing has been said to them."[57]

The final episode in this affair was an article on the Negro apostolate that Father Loftus had prepared for the September issue of the *Holy Ghost* but that

54. Judge to Sister Marie of the Holy Trinity, Stirling, July 4, 1928, AST 6420.

55. Loftus to Dear Father [P. Cullen], Holy Trinity, August 21, 1928, Toolen Papers, AAM. From 1926 to 1947, Father Cullen served Bishop Toolen first as chancellor and secretary, and then as secretary. According to Father Lenahan, Cullen had "adverse views on Father Judge and his community" and had told Lenahan that Toolen "would probably have them leave the diocese"; Lenahan to Toolen, Tuscaloosa, October 18, 1928, Toolen Papers, AAM.

56. Judge to Toolen, Holy Trinity, August 22, 1928, Toolen Papers, AAM; see also Thomas A. Lenahan to Toolen, Tuscaloosa, August 26, 1928, Toolen Papers, AAM. It was in Lenahan's parish that the Negro work was to begin.

57. Loftus to Dear Father [Cullen], Holy Trinity, August 24, 1928, Toolen Papers, AAM.

the sisters found inopportune to publish. Loftus left Holy Trinity on September 7, 1928. Both Father Judge and Mother Boniface traveled to Baltimore to see Bishop Toolen on the matter of the Loftus affair. After it appeared to be settled against Father Loftus, Judge received "a rather strong letter in which he [Bishop Toolen] stated that he thought he had punished too severely this very good priest, Fr. Loftus."[58] Judge responded on September 15. He tried to clarify the matter of the article and answer Loftus's various charges of "reprobate priests" and financial irresponsibility at Holy Trinity. He also responded to the bishop's claim that he had not approved *SOS for the Preservation of the Faith* as a full-blown magazine that would charge for subscriptions.[59]

On October 3, 1928, Father Loftus returned to Holy Trinity "willing and anxious to settle all differences peacefully." Mother Boniface brokered the peace between the two aggrieved priests. Only "after much persuasion" did Father Judge consent to meet with Loftus. "As a result," she reported to Bishop Toolen, "Father Loftus has settled with Father Judge and is writing you today."[60] Loftus wrote the bishop a letter in which he claimed that when earlier he told Bishop Toolen about the $5,000 note on a Northern bank, he had not meant to imply "that this money was raised under false pretenses." He said he had shown the letter to Father Judge and Mother Boniface, and both found it satisfactory.[61] The Missionary Servants returned to Loftus $1,190 that he had collected for the Negro apostolate. Father Judge wrote Bishop Toolen to expect Loftus's letter "revising his statements concerning the financing of the new building at Holy Trinity." Loftus left to start his apostolate. "As far as Holy Trinity is concerned," Father Judge wrote, "the agitation of which you wrote passes with him."[62]

This ended Father Loftus's six-year association with the Missionary Servants at Holy Trinity. In 1929 he bought a farm outside Montgomery, Alabama, and invited twenty-two African American families to live there. He died at the farm on November 14, 1933, preceding Father Judge in death by fourteen days.[63]

58. Judge to Father Sigmund, OFM, Cap., Holy Trinity, September 18, 1928, AST, MF 6438.

59. Judge to Toolen, Holy Trinity, September 15, 1928, Toolen Papers, AAM.

60. Mother Boniface to Toolen, Holy Trinity, October 3, 1928, Toolen Papers, AAM.

61. Loftus to Toolen, Holy Trinity, October 3, 1928, Toolen Papers, AAM.

62. Judge to Toolen, Holy Trinity, October 4, 1928; Mother Boniface to Toolen, Holy Trinity, October 3, 1928, Toolen Papers, AAM. On December 6, Judge wrote to two sisters who had asked about staying in touch with Loftus. He summarized his side in the dispute in a tight paragraph that concluded, "If there has been talk, he started it. If action has been taken, he forced it"; AST, MF 1300, 6446. Loftus died in 1933, two weeks before Father Judge.

63. On the farm and Loftus's death, see John P. Kohn Jr. to Bishop Toolen, Montgomery,

Finishing the Men's Rule

Father Loftus's accusations against Father Judge had created more bad feeling between Bishop Toolen and Judge and kept the latter from devoting his full attention to the rule. He spent most of the fall at Holy Trinity, where he worked on the rule and did some of the writing and editing for the *Holy Ghost*. On September 19, 1928, Mother Boniface described him as "working both day and night, just sleeps a few hours and wants to have it finished by October 1."[64]

October 1 found Father Judge still working on the rule. On October 4, the same day he wrote to Bishop Toolen closing the Loftus affair, he sent a rough draft of the rule to Archbishop Curley in Baltimore. Curley earlier offered to help with the rule. Judge expressed his gratitude, recognizing "that my mission as a frontiersman of the Church necessitates, in such specialized and sacred matters, the help of one more knowing and more conversant in these things than myself."[65] Bishop Toolen was now paying careful attention to Holy Trinity. October brought more tension with the bishop over the manner of paying off the $25,000 loan for which Toolen had signed in 1927 and an alcoholic priest who had been living at Holy Trinity.[66]

The draft Father Judge sent to Archbishop Curley was very preliminary, and at the end of October, he was still at work. He wrote to Sister Mary Simon Turner at Aguadilla apologizing that he had not written "the old fashioned conferences" to the novices. He spoke of the "painful congestion of affairs" during the past six months. "I will be so relieved when the Brothers' Rule is at least temporarily finished. It takes up practically my every free and conscious moment; in fact, I have to give so much attention to it that I am forced to be parsimonious with some of my other essential duties."[67] On October 30 he sent another revision to Archbishop Curley, who had apparently advised him to be more specific about the community's ends. Judge tended to describe them in terms of devotion to mysteries rather than in terms of specific works. "I am sending in a close mail a revision with the added chapters on the vows.

Ala., November 17, 1933, Toolen Papers, AAM. Kohn was the attorney Toolen retained to handle Loftus's estate.

64. Collins, "Voice from the Past," *Holy Ghost*, March 1953, 6.

65. Judge to Curley, Holy Trinity, October 4, 1928, AST, MF 6441.

66. Judge to Toolen, Holy Trinity, October 22, 1928, Toolen Papers, AAM.

67. Judge to Sister Mary Simon, Holy Trinity, October 29, 1928, AST 6442. On November 16, he again promised to send conferences but reminded her that he was saying much to them in the *Holy Ghost*; AST, MF 6573.

Ten pages will be the first installment as I am still working on it."[68] By December he seems to have finished. "I am in Washington about the rule," he wrote to Sister Mary Simon. "Thank God Monsignor Bernardini the canonist examined the presentation made him and he declared it correct without an emendation. Bishop Toolen reading the first page said: 'If the Brothers do all that, they will be doing wonders.'" He went on to say, "We are about to begin work on the Sisters' Rule." He thought it would not be as difficult as the brothers' rule, "because it will merely be a paraphrase and their rule adopted to the life and duties of the Sisters."[69] Next the rule went to Archbishop Fumasoni-Biondi. Two days before Christmas, Father Judge wrote to Sister James of "the favor we are receiving from the Papal Delegate and his good will and the taking over by the Church with benignity and favor the Brothers' rule."[70]

Father Judge's description of himself as a "backwoodsman pastor" during the last months of 1928 at Holy Trinity belied the crises that swirled around him. In September a hurricane hit Puerto Rico. St. Augustine's, Trinity Academy, and Aguadilla were spared, but he worried that, if parents could no longer afford St. Augustine's tuition, the Cenacle might have to withdraw.[71] November saw a new round of complaints against Father Eugene. The brothers at St. Augustine's, especially Brother John Paul, complained that he was treating them unfairly. "You know my affection and interest in you," Judge wrote to Brennan. "I hold you as a father would hold his son." For both religious and personal reasons, Judge wanted him to succeed. He insisted that success depended on cooperation among the brothers. He asked Eugene for his side of the story. In another letter the same day he told Eugene that he had granted his wish and sent Father Louis Belleau from Holy Trinity to St. Augustine's.[72] Added to this were heavy debt, the chronic

68. Judge to Curley, Holy Trinity, October 30, 1928, AST 6566. See Judge's discussion, with reference to the sisters, of the "ends of the institute" in terms of spreading devotion to the mysteries of the Holy Trinity, especially to the Holy Ghost, the mystery of the incarnation, and the mental sorrows of Jesus; Judge to Charles N. Faivre, CM, Holy Trinity, November 24, 1928, AST, MF 6575.

69. Judge to Sister Mary Simon, Brookland, Washington, D.C., December 19, 1928, AST 6584.

70. Judge to Sister Mary James, Holy Trinity, December 23, 1928, AST 6587.

71. Judge to Sr. Mary James, Holy Trinity, September 18, 1928, AST, MF 6558. The "backwoodsman pastor" designation is from Judge to Sister Emmanuel, Holy Trinity, December 29, 1928, AST, MF 6592. On December 7, he wrote a long description of the farm at Holy Trinity to Sister Mercedes Roach and emphasized how much time he had been putting in on it; AST, MF 1301.

72. Judge to My dear Eugene, Holy Trinity, November 12, 1928, and Judge to My dear Confrere, Holy Trinity, November 12, 1928, AST, MF 6570–71, 6448–50. In 1929 and 1930, two French-Canadian priests, the brothers Louis and Julius Belleau, taught at St. Joseph's.

worries that went with it, Archbishop Fumasoni-Biondi's ultimatum letter, and an up-and-down relationship with the new bishop.

A few days before Christmas at Holy Trinity in 1928, Father Judge reflected on the past year in a letter to one of the sisters whose father was ill. She had promised to pray for him.

> You know as the Cenacle goes on, our problems multiply. We have all kinds of problems.... Mother Boniface, Lord bless and keep her, and I have to do strong teamwork over anxious recurring alarms and seemingly impossible situations. We just dispose of one when up crops another. May the Triune God be blessed in his wonderful consoling and sustaining Providence. These tempests pass us, leaving the Cenacle unharmed. Sometimes we are a little worse for wear. Do pray always that we will be more humble, less in confidence of ourselves and stronger in confidence of God's goodness and mercy. Yesterday I was thinking thoughts like this. How sinful, weak, foolish and miserable I am, always messing up things, and how much I need God. Thank you therefore for the prayers.[73]

73. Judge to Sr. Pretiosa, Holy Trinity, December 22, 1928, AST, MF 6585.

11

THE GREAT DEPRESSION

1929–1930

The End of the Roaring Twenties

"Who knows," Father Judge wrote to Sister Mary Simon Turner in Aguadilla, "but fifteen years hence our novices and our Sisters may take café con leche in Porto Rico and their supper with the Sisters in the evening at Holy Trinity."[1] He was speaking of "aeroplane" travel. It was 1929, and the expansive decade of Charles Lindbergh and Babe Ruth was winding down. Crisscrossing the eastern United States by rail, sailing, and even flying to Puerto Rico and back, Father Thomas Judge was, in many ways, a dashing "streamlined" man of the 1920s.

His Cenacle movement had expanded in ways unimaginable in 1919, acquiring multiple properties from Alabama to Puerto Rico. According to financial practices of the day, such purchases involved big loans with minimal down payments and sometimes further loans to pay the interest on earlier ones, a mortgage on one property to finance the purchase of another, notes signed by third parties, and clamorous creditors in multiple states and Puerto Rico. Four years before, Sister Gertrude Ryan, the sisters' treasurer, warned Father Judge that they could not just keep borrowing but needed to generate revenue.[2] But revenue never came easy. As the country hurtled toward the Great Depression, Father Judge found himself pressed both ecclesiastically and economically.

1. Judge to Sister Mary Simon Turner, Brooklyn, March 30, 1929, AST, MF 6691.
2. Judge to Mother Boniface, Stirling, October 28, 1925, AST, MF 7755–56.

With the creation of the National Catholic War Council, progenitor of the present USCCB, the Catholic Church in the United States participated in the nationalization and consolidation that followed the Great War. In 1917, the Vatican promulgated the universal Code of Canon Law called for by the First Vatican Council in 1870. High-flying freelancers like Father Judge felt the pinch. Diocesan collections dried up. As the decade ended, Judge found himself under increasing pressure to regularize the canonical status of the two communities he founded. Even his own canonical status would be questioned. He had to squeeze the Cenacle into the available theological and canonical structures of the church. This he was more than willing to do, but it altered his vision of the Cenacle in subtle ways, draining time and energy away from the central task of forming lay apostles.

Continuing Financial Woes

The year the Great Depression began brought no end to Father Judge's worries. With Father Loftus gone, Father Brennan in Puerto Rico, and Father Tomerlin on the road, Holy Trinity had no resident priest. Confined to Holy Trinity, Judge searched for a chaplain and spent the early part of the year as the "farm overseer."[3] Financial woes continued. By the beginning of January, the interest on the $5,000 note Monsignor Neale of Meriden had signed on Judge's behalf came due. The Missionary Servants failed to pay it. Loftus, who knew Neale from his days in Connecticut, had accused Judge of securing this loan from his friend under false pretenses. Monsignor Neale was upset and disinclined to re-sign the note.

Unable to leave Holy Trinity, Father Judge sent Brother Augustine Philips to Connecticut to see Monsignor Neale and smooth things out. "Msgr. Neale was decent and generous and begged me not to fail him," Judge explained to Philips. "When I got the money, I sent it to Washington. My part, I thought, was just to get the money.... Fr. Tomerlin paid it out against the bills. No record was made of the money so that when I got anxious at the interest time, I could find nothing." Judge didn't even know the name of the bank, having left "all that to the bookkeeping department." Tomerlin had gone to see Monsignor Neale but missed him. "The complication is more intense," Judge explained, "on account of the old padre [Loftus]."

3. "You know among my other duties now I am the farm overseer"; Judge to My dear Confrere, Holy Trinity, February 24, 1929, AST, MF 1389.

Regarding Brother Augustine's own problems at St. Joseph's Shrine in Stirling, Father Judge wanted to "bring our financial affairs to some definite accounting with the diocese." "[Y]ou cannot go on as you are doing," he told Philips. "The strain must be terrible on you . . . if we are not getting the backing and the diocese fails us in its promises, I would sooner see the place closed." He spoke of the debt "hanging over Holy Trinity." Tomerlin was on the road with Brother Anthony Kelley. "I think the combination is going to give us money." He couldn't help Philips now, but he thought if they could get through the next six months, "our affairs will be more liquid all over."[4]

Brother Augustine must have had a successful fundraising trip. At the end of February, Father Judge asked him to send $7,500 to Mother Boniface, who was "strapped." Whether Philips had actually raised this money or taken another loan is not clear, but it illustrates the Cenacle practice, to which Loftus had objected, of moving money from house to house or account to account as needed.[5] Written months before the stock market crash of October 29, 1929, these letters to Bro. Augustine illustrate what Berry calls Judge's "almost maddening attitude toward money."[6] Monsignor Neale's note does not come up again, so perhaps Brother Augustine persuaded him to re-sign.

Boston Again?

January also saw the beginning of negotiations with Father George P. O'Connor, head of Catholic Charities for the Archdiocese of Boston. O'Connor wanted sisters for various forms of social work in Boston: "club work with boys and girls," providing information to young women, "family and welfare work," and assisting immigrants at the Port of Boston. He promised a new five-story building to be located in the North End. He hoped to have the building finished by the fall.[7] Negotiations dragged on into the spring. The sticking point was whether the sisters would have a chapel where the Blessed Sacrament was reserved.

Father Judge wondered how the sisters could do their work unless they were spiritual women and how they could be spiritual women without the Blessed Sacrament. He noted "a growing complaint" by the clergy "against

4. Judge to Philips, Holy Trinity, January 8, 1929, AST, MF 1372. Brother Anthony, Michael J. Kelley (1884–1950), came to Holy Trinity in 1927. He had been a cotton broker in Paducah, Kentucky.

5. Judge to Philips, Gadsden, Ala., February 27, 1929, AST, MF 1391–94.

6. Berry, *God's Valiant Warrior*, 97.

7. George P. O'Connor to Judge, Boston, January 12, 1929, copy, AST, MF 6648.

the trespass or assumption of lay charitable workers." He cited the Catholic Action maxim "Spiritual means for Spiritual things." Without the Blessed Sacrament, wouldn't people suspect that this Bureau of Charities was "too lay"?[8] By mid-April, it appeared that O'Connor had made arrangements for the chapel, and Judge came to believe that it was God's will for the sisters to go to Boston.[9] Perhaps O'Connor's new five-story building became a casualty of the fall crash, but, for whatever reason, the sisters never went to Boston.[10]

Father Judge's Canonical Status as a Vincentian

Though Father Judge was assigned to the Vincentian mission at Opelika, there is no evidence that, after 1920, he ever resided there. The nagging question of Father Judge's residence arose again in 1929. At the end of January, he wrote to his Vincentian superior general in Paris, Father Verdier, asking him "to petition the Holy See that I may be dispensed from residence in our Community houses."

With three hundred sisters, forty brothers and postulants, and sixty students in the apostolic school, Father Judge emphasized to Father Verdier how much the Cenacle had grown since his visit to the United States in fall 1922. He hoped for three more ordinations "within a year" and, writing in January, anticipated Vatican approval of the rule and Bishop Toolen's signing it. He insisted that he had not set out to found these communities. "What has been affected was done not so much by any preconceived plan for the future but rather to provide workers and maintenance for the daily problem." Providence did the rest.

Father Judge explained that he was "much occupied" at present in directing the men's community, "aspirants to the missionary Priesthood and Brotherhood," as well as the sisters. He deemed it "very necessary that I either reside with these communities or near them." This explained his request. He wanted to be "faithful to our community and at the same time not fail the generous souls who have entrusted themselves to my direction."[11]

8. Judge to O'Connor, Holy Trinity, March 14, 1929, AST, MF 6622.

9. Ibid., Brooklyn, April 6, 1929, AST, MF 6696; Holy Trinity, April 11, 1929, AST MF 6701. See also Judge to Mother Boniface Keasey, Stirling, April 9, 1929, AST, MF 8114–17, on Tomerlin in Boston to negotiate with O'Connor.

10. The sisters headed diocesan Bureaus of Charity in Philadelphia, Mobile, Birmingham, and Pensacola, but Gallaher's survey of MSBT social work makes no mention of Boston; see Gallaher, *Social Work of the Missionary Servants of the Most Blessed Trinity*, chap. 5.

11. Judge to François Verdier, CM, Holy Trinity, January 30, 1929, AST, MF 14253–54.

The Grand Conseil in Paris took up Father Judge's request in its meeting of February 11, 1929. They decided that, since Father McHale was in the United States at that time, Judge should meet with him. The council would make its decision after McHale's return to Paris.[12] Father Verdier wrote Judge that he would have to put his request before McHale. Then McHale contacted Judge, who was elated to find out that McHale was actually in the United States. "I am sending you a copy of the Superior General's letter," Judge wrote to McHale. "This letter came but a day or two ago. You see I must see you. Now don't fail me; otherwise I shall have to hop in a boat and chase you across the Atlantic."[13]

As usual, Father McHale came through. Father Judge and Mother Boniface met him in Washington on May 1. This was after the brothers' rule had been promulgated at Rome and two days after Bishop Toolen signed it, a propitious time for Judge's request. It is likely that Father McHale instructed Father Judge to make this request through the apostolic delegate to the Sacred Congregation of Religious at Rome. Mother Boniface reported that they had dinner and a long conversation afterward. "He was very nice to Father," she concluded.[14]

After Father McHale's return, Father Verdier must have written again to Father Judge. On July 4, he replied with a one-page letter in French accompanied by a "livret" summarizing the men's financial condition and promising a full report after the end of the fiscal year on August 1. Judge claimed that their financial condition had been "greatly strengthened" (*beaucoup raffermie*) since the end of the last fiscal year. He reported "that in view of the general depression, our condition is very good. We have reorganized our finances with a long-term loan of more than five years. We have our facilities at a very reasonable interest rate."[15]

Here the matter of Father Judge's relationship to the Vincentians rested until 1932, when a bishop, probably Bishop Toolen or Archbishop Curley, inquired about his canonical status.

12. "On l'engagera à communiquer son désir à M. Mac Hale, en ce moment aux États Unis. Une decision sera prise plus tard après le retour de M. Mac Hale"; Registres Du Grand Conseil, Conseil du 11 février 1929, Registre X, 613; Vincentian's General Archives, Rome, from certified copies in Box 1H.17A, Folder 4, DA.

13. Judge to McHale, Holy Trinity, March 15, 1929, AST, MF 1404. He mentioned Father Charles Wood, formerly of Charleston, whom he thought might soon join the Missionary Servants. I know of no copy of Verdier's reply to Judge.

14. Mother Boniface to Sister Catherine Marie, Washington, D.C., May 1, 1929, as cited in Tonra, *Led by the Spirit*, 207–8.

15. Judge to Verdier, Stirling, July 4, 1929, AST, MF 14255; my translation. As far as I know, neither Verdier's letter, to which this is a reply, nor the promised financial report is extant.

Developments at Holy Trinity

By mid-January 1929, Father Judge reported to Brother Augustine that Father Ignatius Klejna, "a dear old priest" from Rochester, New York, was now at Holy Trinity to help out as chaplain.[16] At the end of January Judge finally left for the North and Outer Cenacle work in Newark and Stirling. He was back in about two weeks. "We have had another flare up with our friend in Mobile," he told Brother Augustine, "but it has blown over. He came pretty near chasing our new chaplain." Bishop Toolen was upset that he hadn't heard about Klejna. "Perhaps I am somewhat to blame," Judge admitted. "He is becoming very punctilious over having papers. The day of slipping a poor fellow in and out is gone."[17] Eventually Klejna satisfied Bishop Toolen that he was a priest in good standing and decided to stay. On February 19, Judge enthused to Sister Michael, "We have a jewel of a chaplain here, Fr. Klejna, and the Sisters are enraptured with him." He found Klejna "made to order by the Holy Spirit especially for us."[18] Klejna's initial glow at Holy Trinity did not last. By the end of the year, Father Judge found himself answering serious charges Father Klejna had brought against him before Bishop Toolen.

Father Judge remained at Holy Trinity through most of March. Heavy spring rains caused flooding on the sisters' property. "The 'flats' were covered with from ten to fifteen feet of water in some places."[19] On March 16, Judge started the retreat for the postulants, who would receive their habits on March 19, the Feast of St. Joseph. Among the brothers who received the habit were Gilbert Hay, Andrew Lawrence, and Gerard Fredericks. On March 25, Joachim Benson joined them, and eight sisters entered the novitiate.[20]

The Magazines

With Father Loftus gone, Father Judge took over the editorship of the *Holy Ghost*. The February 1929 issue (6, no. 11) lists him as editor. In fall 1928, af-

16. Judge to Philips, Holy Trinity, January 16, 1929, AST, MF 1375–76; Judge to Ignatius Klejna, Holy Trinity, November 27, 1928, AST, MF 1281, in which Judge asks Klejna to come to Holy Trinity as chaplain.

17. Judge to Philips, Holy Trinity, February 19, 1929, AST, MF 1387.

18. Judge to Sister Michael Shelvy, Holy Trinity, February 19, 1929, AST, MF 6663.

19. Judge to Sister Mary James Collins, Holy Trinity, March 22, 1929, AST, MF 6623. The "flats" were the low-lying parts of the sisters' land that bordered on the Chattahoochee River.

20. Tonra, *Led by the Spirit*, 201; see the recollections of Gilbert Hay and Joachim Benson at 199 and 201, respectively.

ter Loftus's departure, Judge reminded Sister Mary Simon at the novitiate in Aguadilla that, even though he wasn't sending his usual conferences, he was saying much to them in the magazine.[21] In the October and November issues, he had a series on the sixth and seventh petitions of the Lord's Prayer, "lead us not into temptation" and "deliver us from evil." The last included meditations on Jesus' prayers in the Gospel of John and on the Man of Sorrows. In the January 1929 issue, he began a series on "The Apostles" as a particular Cenacle devotion. The first article featured a powerful description of the "apostolic spirit."[22] This series continued into the March issue, which included reflections on friendship and friendship with Jesus. He followed this with an article in the May 1929 issue on Jesus as the only teacher in an age of confusion.[23] In December, he ended a long letter to Sister Mary Thomas in Puerto Rico with a joking reference to his work with the brothers' new mission magazine. "I am now at present one of the office force at St. Joseph's," he wrote. "I have been promoted to the *SOS for the Preservation of the Faith Magazine* staff and I am also chief clerk in the appeal department."[24]

Sister Emmanuel and the Spirituality of the Child

"Please God, if I ever have the time," Father Judge wrote to Sister Marie of the Holy Trinity, "I would like to write a series of meditations on the child." "I do not think Our Lord had anything more at heart," he continued, "than to fasten the mind of His people upon the Child. The very fact that He came as a child proves this." In the early months of 1929, Father Judge's mind was much on the child. Sister Marie of the Holy Trinity worked at the Children's Bureau in Philadelphia. He told her that it was her destiny "to work for the abandoned child."[25] Days after finishing a retreat for the novices at Aguadilla, Judge estimated that "we have nearly 2,000 children directly under the care of our Sisters. Our goal is to have 25,000."[26] Providing spiritual support

21. Judge to Sister Mary Simon Turner, Holy Trinity, November 16, 1928, AST, MF 6573.

22. Judge, "The Apostles," *Holy Ghost*, January 1929, 16–18, with the description of the "apostolic spirit" at 17.

23. Judge, "Jesus the Teacher," *Holy Ghost*, May 1929, 17–18. Father Judge's contributions to the magazines are worth a study in themselves.

24. Judge to Sister Mary Thomas Champion, Holy Trinity, December 8, 1929, AST, MF 6631–32.

25. Judge to Sister Marie of the Holy Trinity, Holy Trinity, March 22, 1929, AST, MF 6613.

26. Judge to Sister Mary Simon Turner, Río Piedras, May 27, 1929, AST, MF 6714–17. See also his reply to a prospective vocation around this time. In describing the work of the Missionary Servants, the first thing he listed as a "very important feature of our work" was "to companion

to the sisters working in the children's bureaus was a likely stimulus for developing his thoughts about the child.

Sister Emmanuel Hendricks worked in the Home Finding Department of the Philadelphia Children's Bureau, where she was much beloved. She had contracted the flu and then tuberculosis and, by March 1929, was dying in St. Anthony Hospital, Woodhaven, New York. On March 13, as he prepared the postulants' retreat at Holy Trinity, since he couldn't be in New York to visit her, Father Judge wrote Sister Emmanuel an extraordinary letter. "How chummy you must be getting with all the heavenly spirits. Then, too, think what the Spirit of God is doing for your soul through your sickness. I wish I could get hold of you for one entire week and tell you all the things I want you to pray for."

Father Judge was not only consoling Sister Emmanuel in her illness, he was also completely serious about the power of the prayers of someone suffering unto death. He gave her a list of five intentions that he described as "very general," for he had "so many balls up in the air I have not much time for the typewriter." Nevertheless, it took him a page and a half (single-spaced) to detail his five intentions and provide a window on his own anxieties and prayers at this time.

First was the brothers' rule now in Rome. "What are they going to do with it over there?" he asked. "Will I be told to go on or will they give me another job?" "Now," he assured her, "the prayers apply also to the Sisters because I am working on their Rule."[27] The second intention was for the "primitive spirit, that those coming may hold to it." Preserving "the piety and self-sacrifice we see now" was much on his mind as he prepared the postulant's retreat. "I wonder will they be like you?" he asked, anticipating her protests. "If they are like you, I will be very well satisfied. I wish you could give them your smile and your willing and unmurmuring spirit."

Third, he asked her to pray for young people, "that they may be disposed to be generous with the impulses of the Holy Spirit." His fourth intention was

---

the leisure hours of youth." He asked the inquirer to give a thought to "those thousands and thousands of working boys who every year are thrown into a vortex of worldliness, impiety, and irreligion." This letter is also notable for one of Judge's first uses of the term *lay apostolate*, given currency by the writings of Pope Pius XI; Judge to Joseph Grennan, Holy Trinity, January 1929, AST, MF 6653.

27. Two months later, he wrote to Monsignor Bernardini before departing for Puerto Rico asking for a copy of the "Rule of the Sisters of Charity" [*sic*], noting that "our Sisters have many points in common with the Daughters of Charity of St. Vincent de Paul"; Judge to Bernardini, Brooklyn, AST, MF 6690, probably written around May 26, 1929.

that "peace may be in our Cenacles . . . that we may be actuated by sacrifice." "Do pray for our weaklings," he continued, "of whom I am the prince. . . . Let us pity and pursue the upset, distraught, vacillating, perturbed, hesitating, backsliding member of Cenacle life." He asked prayers for custodians (superiors).[28] Before the last intention, he wrote, "This is personal: pray for Mother and myself." He asked especially for prayers for Mother Boniface, whose burdens grew along with the work. He assured Sister Emmanuel of his own prayers for her. "Everyone loves Sister Emmanuel. It is not hard to get our Cenacle children to pray for her." He noted that he had probably given her enough to pray for "for the time being" and concluded by wishing her the graces of the season as a "promise of your own happy and glorious resurrection."[29]

Sister Emmanuel died, as she said she would, on March 25, the Feast of the Annunciation. At her funeral Mass, Father Judge preached on the verse from Matthew 25, "Amen I say to you, as long as you did it to one of these My least brethren, you did it to Me." Praising Sister Emmanuel's virtues, he exclaimed, "How beautiful must be Jesus, when a mortal enlightened by his Word, and following in his footsteps becomes so loveable." In this verse from St. Matthew, "Jesus becomes so personal. . . . He commits Himself so deliberately and absolutely." Judge identified Jesus' least brethren as the "disconsolate, the abandoned, all those whose condition is pathetic, and excites our compassion." Chief among these are abandoned children. To direct the world's attention to the abandoned child, Jesus Himself became a child:

> He came destitute. He came outraging all conventionalities, so that no child born would be needier than He. He placed the child before His Church and bade His High Priest gaze upon it. He extolled the child and delivered this startling doctrine, that unless we become as a child we cannot enter the Kingdom of Heaven.[30]

Sister Emmanuel was buried at Stirling. On March 29, Father Judge reported to Mother Boniface that he had visited the grave. This letter urged that in her visitations, in her ongoing dealings with Father Brennan, she keep before all "my view-point on Dogma, revealed truth, its necessity, its loveliness, its val-

28. On the duties of custodians, see the Memorandum at AST, MF 6727, probably written around this time.

29. Judge to Sister Emmanuel Hendricks, Holy Trinity, March 13, 1929, AST, MF 6674.

30. "Text" [no title], AST 6620–21. The contents make clear that this is Judge's sermon at Sr. Emmanuel's funeral Mass. It is a masterpiece. On Sister Emmanuel's death and funeral, see Collins, "Voice from the Past," *Holy Ghost*, June 1953, 4, and Tonra, *Led by the Spirit*, 202.

ue. What higher vocation could there be than to minister to revealed truth, to the truths Our Lord, Himself, came into the world to teach?" She was to ask if they made "these acts of Faith and other acts in the Mysteries and to carry out instructions over Saints' days." His last words: "also tell them my present teaching regarding the child."[31]

The Continuing Education of Father Eugene

After Sister Emmanuel's funeral, Mother Boniface sailed from Brooklyn for Puerto Rico, where she stayed until the end of April. On April 15, she sent a long newsletter on Cenacle work on the island. She reported that there were eighty women university students in residence at Trinity Academy and seventy-four boys at St. Augustine's. She also described in detail the missionary work done in connection with the novitiate at Aguadilla.[32]

Father Judge stayed in the North, mostly in the New York area, in Brooklyn and in Stirling and Newark, New Jersey. He started new Outer Cenacles at Monsignor Nummey's parish in Richmond Hill and at the Dr. White Memorial Settlement House on Gold Street in Brooklyn. When he got to Brooklyn, he was amazed to find Father Eugene Brennan there "at Sr. Agnes'," rather than at St. Augustine's in Puerto Rico. He told Brennan that he had "no business leaving the Island without his knowledge." "Father Eugene is to see me at the Blessed Trinity Missionary Cenacle Richmond Hill tomorrow," Judge told Mother Boniface in Puerto Rico. "I will have a long talk with him."[33]

In a few days, he reported that he had "persuaded Father Eugene to start back Thursday."[34] As Mother Boniface reported in her April 15 newsletter, Brennan made it back to Puerto Rico in time to get to Aguadilla for a Mass of thanksgiving on April 8, when three postulants received the garb at the novitiate. She credited him with an itinerary that saved time and maximized the number of places he could go. "I believe he went by boat from Puerto

31. Judge to Mother Boniface, Stirling, March 29, 1929, AST, MF 8104. This letter also talks about needing to get the specifications for the hospital and a possible contractor named "Reynolds."

32. Tonra provides text of this April 15 letter in *Led by the Spirit*, 203–6. On Judge's whereabouts at this time, see 207.

33. Judge to Mother Boniface, Philadelphia, March 31, 1929, AST, MF 8111, and ibid., Brooklyn, March 30, 1929, AST, MF 8106. Judge spent Easter in Philadelphia. Sister Agnes is probably Sister Agnes Gore.

34. Ibid., Newark, April 3, 1929, AST, MF 8112.

Rico to Cuba, and from Cuba to Florida by plane, from Florida to Holy Trinity by train, to New York by train, and back to Puerto Rico by boat."[35]

Though Mother Boniface put a good face on Brennan's trip, Father Judge had not been pleased to find him in New York. When school was over on the island, at the urging of Sister Mary Thomas at St. Augustine's, he brought Father Eugene north to help him with retreats during July and no doubt to continue mentoring him. During July he wrote enthusiastically on Brennan's progress to Sister Mary Thomas at St. Augustine's and Sister Mary Simon at Aguadilla. He told Sister Mary Thomas that Brennan was gaining both experience and confidence. "How happy you should be that he has come up here because when he gets back he will be so finished and experienced."[36] Two weeks later, he told Sister Mary Simon that they had just finished a "very successful and edifying" sisters' retreat. Father Brennan was now "much richer in retreat experience." "This gives me a great deal of joy," Judge wrote, "for he will, I feel, be of greater value to you and the Novices now."[37]

By the beginning of August, Father Brennan was back on the island. Sister Mary Thomas had written noting Father Eugene's "good disposition" and thanking Father Judge for his influence. He put it back on her. "Who was it suggested his coming up?" he asked. "Who pleaded his cause on coming up? Who put me on my good behavior towards him? Who schemed out the whole thing? Who, no doubt, went to him on the quiet and lined him up?" He told her to tell Sister Mary Thomas that "she takes the first prize; incidentally, the honors and gate receipts go to her."[38] The impulsive and mercurial Eugene Brennan was clearly a work in progress who would continue to elicit Father Judge's paternal concern.

Approval of the Brothers' Rule

On April 6, Father Judge received from Cardinal Lépicier of the Sacred Congregation of Religious the decree of erection for the Missionary Servants of the Most Holy Trinity, approved and promulgated at Rome on March 20.

35. Tonra, *Led by the Spirit*, 206. Tonra suggests that Brennan gave a retreat while he was at Holy Trinity and cites at length from Father Timothy Lynch's very favorable recollection of it. Lynch was a student at Holy Trinity in 1929.

36. Judge to Sister Mary Thomas Champion, Newark, July 9, 1929, AST, MF 6756. Father Judge also tells Sister Mary Thomas that he gave Brennan permission to get a new car, as he had put 50,000 miles on the old one.

37. Judge to Sister Mary Simon Turner, Newark, July 24, 1929, AST, MF 6764.

38. Judge to Sister Mary Thomas Champion, Holy Trinity, August 8, 1929, AST, MF 6773.

"Have prayers of thanksgiving said," he wrote to Sister Mary James, "the Brothers' Cenacle is approved. We have now our canonical life, we are now a canonical body. There is a document to be signed by the Bishop."[39] It remained for Bishop Toolen to sign the decree of erection. Father Tomerlin was in Boston, still negotiating over the Boston Charities Bureau. Mother Boniface had learned the news by cable on April 8.[40] On April 9, Father Judge told Mother Boniface that Tomerlin was on his way to Mobile to have an important document signed.[41] The decree of erection, signed by Bishop Toolen and by his secretary, Philip Cullen, is dated April 29, 1929.[42] Judge had now accomplished the first half of the task mandated by the apostolic delegate's letter of June 19, 1928. The sisters' rule still remained.

A New House of Studies

The house at Lawrence Street Northeast in Washington, D.C., was already too small for the eleven student brothers who were there studying at the Catholic University of America. More were expected for the next academic year. Father Judge's April 9 letter to Mother Boniface also mentioned a new $40,000 mortgage on Holy Trinity to finance the purchase of land for a new house of studies near Washington. The most likely holder of this mortgage was Rev. Charles Wood, formerly of the Diocese of Charleston. Judge's March 15 letter to Father McHale speaks as if Father Wood had agreed to join the community. He described Wood as "a very good priest with a fine missionary record. He brings with him a considerable sum of money. His family is quite wealthy and he himself was ordained on a patrimony [*sub titulo patrimonii*]." According to Judge, they discussed his wealth at length before he was accepted. "I told him," Judge claimed, "it was too bad he had a cent and advised him to go and get rid of it; however, he is determined to help us in some way. What this is remains to be seen." Judge reported that Wood had recently donated $100,000 to Catholic University. "Before he throws himself completely into the Cenacle, he is going to make a pilgrimage to Lourdes."[43]

Father Judge told the sisters in Puerto Rico about Father Wood. He was

39. Judge to Sister Mary James Collins, Brooklyn, April 6, 1929, AST, MF 6624.

40. Tonra, *Led by the Spirit*, 206.

41. Judge to Mother Boniface, Stirling, April 9, 1929, AST, MF 8114–17.

42. Copies of the Latin texts of Lépicier's rescript to Toolen, dated March 20, 1929, and the decree of erection signed by Bishop Toolen and dated April 29, 1929, were preserved by Father Joachim Benson, who received them from Father Judge, and are now in AST.

43. Judge to McHale, Holy Trinity, March 15, 1929, AST, MF 1404.

a priest "from a wealthy family and means will be placed at the use of the Community at a very reasonable interest."[44] A subsequent letter, probably to Father Tomerlin, inquires about the title to the property at Holy Trinity, as the wealthy priest needed it clear.[45] Father Wood never entered the Missionary Servants, but it appears that he did finance a mortgage of $40,000 on the property at Holy Trinity. On November 4, Judge asked Archbishop Curley, in whose diocese the house of studies was located, to write the Congregation of Religious to authorize the purchase of a piece of property near Catholic University.[46] Wood's mortgage was likely used to purchase the property in Silver Spring, Maryland, which Judge named "Holy Trinity Heights." Despite the expectation of a reasonable interest rate, Depression-era conditions made even this obligation difficult to meet.

Concern for the Negro Apostolate

During his time in Puerto Rico, Judge learned that, though the legacy of slavery had resulted in a racial situation somewhat different from that in the United States, there was still a "color line" and that, if the work was to succeed, the peculiar patterns of segregation on the island could not be ignored. "Be very firm in the matter of the color line," he instructed Sister Mary Simon regarding candidates for the novitiate at Aguadilla. "We cannot take any chances," he warned, "and we must be fair to the young ladies we receive."[47] Earlier he had written to Paulist John Burke, general secretary of the National Catholic Welfare Conference, about the "necessity of a colored priesthood and religious for Porto Rico."[48]

In fall 1928, Father Judge tried to send Father Loftus to the Negro parish in Tuscaloosa, which was part of Father Thomas Lenahan's pastoral responsibilities. Though Loftus never went to Tuscaloosa, the sisters did. Like Loftus, Sister Peter Claver Fahy, a native of Rome, Georgia, had come to the Cenacle with an interest in the Negro apostolate. In August 1929, Judge wrote a letter of introduction for her to an old friend, Father Joseph Smith, the vicar general of the Diocese of Cleveland. He described her as having had "a long and wide experience in Negro work."

44. Judge to Sisters in Puerto Rico, Holy Trinity, February 25, 1929, AST, MF 6669.
45. Judge to My dear Confrere [Tomerlin?], Holy Trinity, March 24, 1929, AST, MF 6688.
46. Judge to Archbishop Michael Curley, Holy Trinity, November 4, 1929, AST, MF 1449.
47. Judge to Sr. Mary Simon Turner, Brooklyn, July 1, 1929, AST, MF 6750.
48. Judge to Burke, Newark, June 30, 1929, AST, MF 6749.

"Something must be done and soon to convert the negroes [*sic*]," he told Father Smith, stressing the present need. A half century after the end of Reconstruction and a decade after the postwar migration of African Americans to the urban North had begun, Judge assessed the prospects for Catholic evangelization among African Americans with the language and attitude of Jim Crow America. "The old plantation type of negro [*sic*] is gone forever. The present negro is still simple and emotionally religious, but the generation following him is going to be worldly wise and will be trained in godless schools." He promised a future account of yet another "movement," this one to address the challenge of evangelizing the "last type."[49]

Spring 1929 found Sister Peter Claver working with Italian immigrants at St. Michael's, Father O'Neill's parish in Newark, New Jersey. In April 1929, she and Sister Carmel began working with two separated groups of African American lay Catholic women. Eventually, Sister Peter Claver received permission to make this her primary work.[50] When the two groups of lay women finally came together later in 1930, their efforts resulted in the beginnings of Our Lady Queen of the Angels Mission in Newark, the first African American congregation in Newark. For providing "the necessary link between the two black Catholic lay women's groups and the official church," Sister Peter Claver has been called "the pivotal person" in the story of Queen of Angels beginnings.[51]

Apart from the work of individuals such as Sister Peter Claver and others, the Cenacle's early involvement in the Negro apostolate failed to transcend segregation patterns of the day. Nor did it achieve the proportions of a "movement" in any meaningful sense.

Two New Cenacle Priests

With the rule approved, it was now canonically possible for priests to join the Missionary Servants and for the community to train men for the priesthood. The fall of 1929 saw two rather prominent priests enter. Monsignor

49. Judge to Rev. Joseph F. Smith, Stirling, August 29, 1929, AST, MF 6747.

50. This was perhaps the occasion for Father Judge cautioning her against being drawn into "purely social functions of the negroes." "They are indeed very ardent souls," he wrote, "however, they are likely always to introduce into their meetings racial as well as religious questions"; Judge to My dear Child [probably Sr. Peter Claver], Holy Trinity, August 10, 1929, AST, MF 6776.

51. Mary A. Ward, *A Mission for Justice: The History of the First African American Catholic Church in Newark, New Jersey* (Knoxville: University of Tennessee Press, 2002), 36.

Thomas Nummey, the pastor of Holy Child Jesus Parish in Richmond Hill, Brooklyn, came in September. Father Thomas Lenahan, pastor of St. John's Church in Tuscaloosa and Catholic chaplain at the University of Alabama, came in December. Both had worked closely with the sisters, and Nummey had known Father Judge since his early years as a pastor. Nummey was fifty-one in 1929, and Lenahan was forty-four. Neither was in particularly good health. Since neither had made a canonical novitiate with the community, until they did, they remained technically incardinated in their respective dioceses. Both Bishop Molloy of Brooklyn and Bishop Toolen released them to work outside their dioceses. Lenahan returned to Mobile in 1931, Nummey to Brooklyn in 1932.

Monsignor Nummey applied to Bishop Molloy for dimissorial letters and resigned from "parochial and diocesan charges" on September 6. He took leave of parochial and other duties at the end of the month.[52] On September 16, Judge confided to Brother James Norris that Monsignor Nummey was entering the Cenacle.[53] By the beginning of October, Nummey was at the house of studies in Washington. One of his first tasks was to deal with the purchase of the Silver Spring property that Father Tomerlin had been working on.[54] On November 21, Father Judge enthused about Nummey to Father McHale, citing "a well known Sulpician" as having declared Nummey "the model pastor of the Church in the United States." Judge expressed his surprise that Bishop Molloy had let Nummey go so easily and noted that the bishop had written Nummey "a beautiful letter." Nummey was now custodian at the Holy Trinity Missionary Cenacle in Washington. With reference no doubt to the Silver Spring property, Judge told McHale that the next time he spoke of the Washington house, it would probably be as Holy Trinity Missionary Cenacle Seminary. He promised "a very large piece of news for you in connection with the Washington House in my next letter."[55] By the beginning of January, Nummey had completed the purchase.

Monsignor Nummey's entry into the community drew notice, especially

52. Nummey to Molloy, Richmond Hill, New York, September 6, 1929; ibid., September 21, 1929, Nummey Papers, Archives of the Diocese Brooklyn.

53. Judge to Norris, Stirling, September 18, 1929, AST, MF 1431–32.

54. December 15 found Nummey at Holy Trinity to consult with Judge about the purchase. Mother Boniface visited Silver Spring and favored the property as "large enough for us to build our own college there some day, and when we get a large number of students, we will need this—we could never keep up the tuition in the University"; see Tonra, *Led by the Spirit*, 217.

55. Judge to McHale, Holy Trinity, November 21, 1929, AST, MF 1455. Father Judge identified the Sulpician as Father Vivien. Perhaps it was Anthony Vieban. In Nummey's papers, I did not see the "beautiful letter" from Bishop Molloy to Nummey to which Judge refers.

in Brooklyn. Father Judge was ecstatic, declaring Nummey "one of the most prominent priests of the East, the most honorable and high standing man in his diocese of Brooklyn." "His entrance is just a sensation," he wrote to Sister Mary Thomas. "The diocese is gasping. His poor people are stricken with grief.... I think his entrance will be a widespread edification for the whole country. We should thank God for this great grace."[56] Present at the Mass at Holy Child Jesus Parish when the announcement about Nummey's joining the Missionary Servants was made, Mother Boniface was deeply moved.[57] By October 10, Nummey had settled into the routine at Washington. "Monsignor Nummey has been properly conducted into University life," Judge told Brother James. "He is taking it very well. The Brothers like him very much. He certainly is a great edification."[58]

On the face of it, sending Monsignor Nummey to Catholic University doesn't make sense. The man was an outstanding pastor. He wanted to be a missionary. But, given the pressure Father Judge felt from both Bishop Toolen and the apostolic delegate to regularize the training of priests, sending Nummey to Catholic University made a lot of sense. During his June 7, 1928, meeting with Mother Boniface, Bishop Toolen had voiced particular concern about the house of studies in Washington. He thought it mistaken to open it without a good priest in charge. He was surprised that the apostolic delegate didn't close it.[59] In Monsignor Nummey, Father Judge had an outstanding priest.

Bishop Toolen had similar complaints about those in charge at Holy Trinity. So when Father Thomas Lenahan entered in December, with much less fanfare, he was sent to be in charge of the apostolic school at Holy Trinity. Father Judge described Lenahan to Father McHale as "a school man" with "experience in journalism." "Up to this time," he told McHale, "we have been limping along because of lack of priests." With Washington "now admirably taken care of," Lenahan would be "the principal of St. Joseph's School, Holy Trinity." "You cannot imagine what a relief this is to me," he continued, "for I

56. Judge to Sister Mary Thomas Champion, Newark, October 2, 1929, AST, MF 6629. "The Monsignor Nummey affair, please God, is going to have a far reaching effect in favor of the Cenacle and the religious life. The people in Brooklyn and the priests are flabbergasted. Pray that the Spirit of God may make use of the Monsignor's detachment for great good"; Judge to Norris, Washington, D.C., September 29, 1929, AST, MF 1433.

57. See Tonra, *Led by the Spirit*, 213, citing Mother Boniface's September 28 letter to Sister Michael.

58. Judge to Norris, Orange, N.J., October 10, 1929, AST, MF 1438–39.

59. For Mother Boniface's summary of this meeting, see Tonra, *Led by the Spirit*, 184–87.

know that the students in both institutions will be very much blessed in having these two excellent priests respectively at their heads." Judge saw Nummey and Lenahan as gifts of providence, "lifting from me a very heavy and wearing strain." He concluded, "We have passed a very biting and distracting need, the necessity of having two eminently fitted priests as superiors of our Brothers' educational institutions in the United States."[60]

On October 21, Father Lenahan wrote asking permission to enter a religious community. Bishop Toolen had brought in the Holy Ghost Fathers to take over the university parish at Tuscaloosa. Lenahan only needed someone to take over his duties at the local parish. "I shall first apply to the Trinitarians as soon as convenient to your Lordship."[61] He wrote again on November 6 to tell the bishop that Father Judge had accepted him on condition that he make a postulancy and one-year novitiate.[62]

Father Lenahan's departure from Mobile was not as peaceful as Nummey's from Brooklyn. Lenahan had written a letter to Monsignor Hackett, soon to be appointed Bishop Toolen's chancellor, explaining that his motives for joining the Missionary Servants had nothing to do with his relationship with Bishop Toolen. The bishop blamed him for breaking confidentiality. Lenahan responded that "Father Abbot [Abbot Bernard Menges, OSB, of Cullman and one of the bishop's confidants], the Chancellor, and many others have condemned me for thinking of joining the Missionary Servants. . . . So I wrote to Msgr. Hackett who was best placed to clear up any misunderstanding."[63] "The Missionary Servants," Lenahan wrote in another letter dated the same day, "although they know my weaknesses, spiritually, intellectually, physically, financially, still wish to give me a trial."[64]

60. Judge to McHale, Holy Trinity, November 21, 1929, AST, MF 1456. In this letter, he also mentions "receiving a young French Canadian priest" as a professor. This is probably Julius Belleau, whose brother Louis Judge had sent to Puerto Rico earlier in the year. On September 7, Tomerlin had written to Father Philip Cullen in Mobile asking for faculties for Julius Belleau; Toolen Papers, AAM.

61. Lenahan to Toolen, Tuscaloosa, October 21, 1929, Toolen Papers, AAM.

62. Ibid., November 6, 1929, Toolen Papers, AAM. Judge's response to Lenahan is dated November 7. He writes, "You know our life and spirit. Preservation of the Faith is our watchword and we have a predilection for the hard and tangled places in the vineyard of Christ. The abandoned missions, the abandoned soul is our search. Needless to say, this will make you a frontiersman of the Church"; Judge to Lenahan, Holy Trinity, November 7, 1929, AST, MF 1451.

63. Lenahan to Toolen, Tuscaloosa, December 6, 1929, Toolen Papers, AAM.

64. Ibid. Lenahan resigned his parish and checked into Holy Name of Jesus Hospital on the advice of his physician, Dr. Morgan, who diagnosed him as having "an acute acid condition of stomach due to nervous condition of long development." He told the bishop he wanted to join the Missionary Servants by January 1.

Apparently the bishop consented to Father Lenahan's joining the Missionary Servants. On December 12, Father Judge wrote to thank Bishop Toolen for releasing Lenahan. Probably thinking of the bishop's initial reaction to Father Klejna, he also asked for faculties for hearing the sisters' confessions for any priest in good standing in the diocese, including Nummey.[65] "Today I go to Holy Trinity to begin my novitiate Christmas," Lenahan wrote to Toolen on December 22.[66] Mother Boniface reported that Father Lenahan was at Holy Trinity to say the Midnight Mass for the brothers at Christmas.[67] Father Judge now had two exemplary priests in charge of the formation. Surely this was not lost on Bishop Toolen. And Father Judge had not sent Father Lenahan out of the diocese.

Mobile Centennial and Catholic Charities Meeting in New Orleans

The month of November brought some bright spots on the Depression-era landscape. Two occurred around the same time in mid-November. Bishop Toolen organized a celebration of the centennial of the Mobile cathedral. Both Father Judge and Mother Boniface attended. It brought a temporary relaxation of the tension between Judge and the bishop. According to Mother Boniface's long account of the celebration, Father Judge and Brother Augustine were seated at the bishop's table. Archbishop John Glennon of St. Louis gave a tribute to Bishop Allen. Bishop Boyle of Pittsburgh, one of the twenty

65. Judge to Toolen, Holy Trinity, December 12, 1929, AST, MF 6633. Apparently, until he could replace him at Tuscaloosa, the bishop had Lenahan return there from Holy Trinity every Saturday for Sunday Mass; see Tonra, *Led by the Spirit*, 213.

66. Lenahan to Toolen, Gadsden, December 22, 1929, Toolen Papers, AAM. This long letter, more than two single-spaced pages, continues Lenahan's explanation in his December 6 letter of his responses to what he perceived as unjustified criticism of the Missionary Servants by some Mobile clergy. He concluded, "Humanly speaking the work at St. Joseph's is utterly impossible but not more impossible than the Sisters' side and the Gadsden hospital a few years ago. If I can stand St. Joseph's or St. Joseph's should be successful, I would consider it a miracle and not due to our work." His next line echoed Judge: "Perhaps a fair amount of unjust criticism helps to prove the divine intervention in the work."

67. Tonra, *Led by the Spirit*, 219–20. She also reported that Father Julius Belleau said the Christmas morning Mass on the brothers' side. Mother Boniface had encouraged Lenahan in his desire to join the community. Her letters describe humorously and sympathetically his difficulties at Holy Trinity, especially with Brother James's role. After he left Holy Trinity in the spring of 1931, Bishop Toolen assigned him to Gadsden. Lenahan served the sisters heroically during the epidemic at Holy Name of Jesus Hospital in 1931. He attended Mother Boniface as chaplain during her final illness and served as the subdeacon at Father Judge's solemn Requiem Mass at Holy Trinity; ibid., 252, 258, 303, 375.

bishops present at the celebration, made the sisters' house next to the cathedral his headquarters. Their location put the sisters in the thick of the celebration.[68]

Concurrent with the celebration in Mobile was the annual Catholic Charities convention held in 1929 in New Orleans. Sisters from the Catholic Charities Bureaus in Philadelphia, Rockford, Illinois, Mobile, Ensley, Alabama, and Pensacola, Florida attended the conference. It was the fifteenth National Conference of Catholic Charities and the "first at which nuns spoke from the floor at the general sessions." Dr. John O'Grady of Catholic University was in charge and asked that one of the sisters speak. He also asked for a sister to work in the Catholic Charities Offices in Washington, but Mother Boniface had no one to spare.

Sister Mary James Collins worked at the Charities Bureau in Pensacola and attended the conference. On November 17, 1929, the New Orleans *Times Picayune* ran a feature story on "Women Religious (Who) Shatter Precedents" that highlighted the Missionary Servants. Sister Mary James must have saved it and, twenty-four years later, was able to cite extensively from it. The story portrayed the Missionary Servants, "the most modern" and "most unusual of all the groups," as completing the "tradition breaking" of St. Vincent de Paul and the Daughters of Charity. "Were you to pass them on the street you would not know them as nuns, but only as ultraconservatively dressed women." The writer was taken with "their new hats—smartly turned up affairs that many women eyed enviously." The story came with photos accompanied by the caption, "Hats of latest style worn by members of this Order of Trinity contrast with garbs of centuries ago at picturesque Religious sessions here."[69]

Bishop Byrne and the Latin American Apostolate

On November 23, Edwin V. Byrne (1891–1963), the recently appointed bishop of San Juan, visited Holy Trinity. Byrne was a Philadelphia priest and

68. Tonra cites at length from Mother Boniface's description of the Mobile Centennial celebration; ibid., 215.

69. Collins, "Voice from the Past," *Holy Ghost*, June 1953, 7. Sister Mary James doesn't say which of the sisters spoke. Mother Boniface described the new-style hat as "quite up to date, 'the latest from Paris,' ... a little felt hat, close fitting, turned up in the front, with two ends protruding." She explained it as based on the provision of the rule that they "should pattern after the style of the day, in a modest way." For her humorous account of choosing the hats in New York, see Tonra, *Led by the Spirit*, 212.

another of Cardinal Dougherty's men in Puerto Rico. He was also a major supporter of the Cenacle's work on the island. On September 18, Byrne wrote Father Judge a warm letter congratulating him on the third anniversary, on September 14, 1926, of the beginning of the brothers' work in Puerto Rico. The bishop was effusive in his praise, describing the community's "remarkable work" at St. Augustine's, Holy Trinity Academy, Aguadilla, and Coamo. Each was producing "a rich spiritual harvest" but "limited by lack of personnel and funds." Byrne pronounced the coming of the Missionary Servants to Puerto Rico as "providential." Though their work to date had been "splendid," the bishop looked forward to "a more brilliant future."[70]

Bishop Byrne stayed at Holy Trinity for three days. Amplifying on his letter, he urged that Father Brennan needed the help of more priests at St. Augustine's. He also wanted the sisters to move their Puerto Rican novices to Holy Trinity and, if that should be decided against, that they move the novitiate closer to Río Piedras.[71] From Holy Trinity Byrne traveled to Cuba, where he saw Archbishop Caruana. From Cuba he wrote to Judge, encouraging him to expand the Cenacle's work in Latin America. "It was a real joy to tell Archbishop Caruana of your splendid Bethlehem in Alabama." He had urged Caruana to visit Holy Trinity. He reported on the interest of the archbishop of Havana in the Cenacle. "Archbishop Caruana," he continued, "is delighted to know of your determination to aid Latin America. He feels that the Cenacle can do an immense work in these spiritually destitute lands."[72]

Father Judge reported to Sister Mary Thomas in Río Piedras on his conversations with Bishop Byrne at Holy Trinity. Judge told the bishop that "we had in mind for some time an Apostolate among the Latin Americans, that our end—the Preservation of the Faith—led us to consider such things." Bishop Byrne proposed as a "magnificent thing" a "Porto Rican office in New York." He urged them to "watch the boats." Judge told him about the sisters' efforts on the docks and that, despite repeated requests, they had received little support from the hierarchy. Byrne replied that the National Catholic Welfare Council was finally giving its attention to this issue. Judge expressed his skepticism about the NCWC, telling Byrne that he had "not much faith in what they were doing." Byrne wanted him to go to the docks

70. Byrne to Judge, San Juan, September 18, 1929, from a copy in the Toolen Papers, AAM.

71. From Mother Boniface's account of Byrne's visit to the sisters in Puerto Rico; see Tonra, *Led by the Spirit*, 216.

72. Judge cited a paragraph from Byrne's letter to him from Cuba, in Judge to Sister Mary Thomas Champion, December 8, 1929, AST, MF 6631.

anyway, and Judge said this would require some kind of understanding with the NCWC.[73] As with most of his efforts to align the work of the Cenacle with the NCWC, this proposal about the New York docks came to naught.[74] Something like a Puerto Rican office in New York would have to wait until after the Second Vatican Council.

Father Klejna's Charges against Father Judge

In early December, while Father Lenahan was corresponding with Bishop Toolen about joining the Missionary Servants, Mother Boniface received a letter from the bishop telling her that "very serious charges had been made against the Motherhouse at Trinity by Fr. Klejna." The bishop asked her to come and discuss these charges with him. On December 10, she told Father Klejna to leave Holy Trinity.[75] She met with the bishop in Mobile on December 21 and wrote a long account of it to Sister Miriam Lonergan, who was working in Lyons, New York, in Klejna's home diocese of Rochester. Father Judge also received a letter from the bishop. Mother Boniface reported that, after their meeting, Bishop Toolen "had written me a letter stating in writing that he meant no harm; however, let me tell you here that his letter to Father was anything but nice."[76]

On December 13, Father Judge wrote in his own hand a strong response to Bishop Toolen. He began by telling him that Mother Boniface had told Father Klejna to leave Holy Trinity. "My life has always been an open book," he protested, "and needs no defense. I have a right to my priestly reputation. Never since the day of my ordination has suspicion fallen upon it until now." He dismissed Klejna as a "suspicious and disgruntled informant." He acknowledged that Klejna's accusations were "grave," but, he objected, "you have condemned me without a hearing. As a man, as a priest, naturally I feel this."

Father Judge responded at length to two charges: first, that he was responsible for the boys missing school, and second, that he had allowed

73. Ibid.

74. See, e.g., Judge to Edwin V. O'Hara, director, Rural Life Bureau, NCWC, Newark, June 30, 1929, AST, MF 6748. "Our watchword is the abandoned missions," Judge told O'Hara, "and you know that means the rural missions"; see also Judge to John J. Burke, CSP, general secretary, NCWC, Newark, June 30, 1929, AST, MF 6749. Judge had written Burke on "the necessity of a colored priesthood and religious for Porto Rico."

75. Judge to Brother Anthony Kelley, Holy Trinity, December 11, 1929, AST, MF 1464–65. Brother Anthony was on the road trying to raise money. Father Judge told him that Father Klejna left yesterday.

76. Tonra, *Led by the Spirit*, 217–19; quotation at 219.

priests to say Mass at Holy Trinity without faculties from the bishop. A year previously, this is what the bishop had objected to about Father Klejna. "Why do you listen, Bishop," he asked, "to charges made against us without first verifying them? This you know has happened before. I ask you please, Bishop, in the name of Charity and Justice not to condemn me without a hearing." The letter closed respectfully, asking the bishop's prayers and blessing and assuring him of theirs.[77]

"I want to give my side of the story," Father Judge wrote on December 17, again in his own hand. "Judging from your last communication my attempt to explain things by letter was a failure." This letter mentioned an allegation "concerning the confessional" that he had not mentioned in his previous letter. He acknowledged the seriousness of these accusations but did not think they should be "dismissed merely with a letter." He asked Bishop Toolen for a meeting after the holidays "when we can take up these matters and get to the bottom of the various reports that have been brought to you."[78] It is not clear whether the meeting Judge requested ever took place. It is clear that, though Mother Boniface and the sisters remained in the bishop's good graces, tension between Bishop Toolen and Father Judge was high.

Money

Plans for Holy Name of Jesus Hospital at Gadsden came to a head in the summer of 1929. Of Mother Boniface at this time, Sister Mary James wrote, "The debt like the sword of Damocles was ever over her until the angel of Death came for her two years later."[79] The estimate for the cost of the new hospital was a half million dollars. Bishop Toolen had agreed to sign for the loan of $200,000 based on this figure. Now someone was telling him it would cost $750,000. Mother Boniface had to go see him in the spring. "The thought of Gadsden staggers me," she wrote. By July 22, she had the plans in hand. "It is a beautiful looking hospital," she wrote, "I wish my name was Rockefeller, Vanderbilt or Henry Ford, and I would not worry over the debt." At the end of July, she learned that Dr. Herschel Bass had withdrawn his plan to add a special wing to the hospital.[80] Amid much fanfare that included the participa-

77. Judge to Toolen, Holy Trinity, December 13, 1929, handwritten, Toolen Papers, AAM.

78. Ibid., December 17, 1929, handwritten, Toolen Papers, AAM.

79. Collins, "Voice from the Past," *Holy Ghost*, June, 1953, 6.

80. Collins, who probably knew him, described Dr. Bass: "A genius he was in his own line, but one who could not always work with others, and there were some among the Staff for whom he had great aversion"; ibid., 5–6.

tion of President Herbert Hoover, the Goodyear Rubber Company of Akron, Ohio, had just opened a new plant in Gadsden. There was a contract for their workers to use the hospital. But Goodyear shortly withdrew. Nevertheless, in August, the sisters decided to go ahead. Archbishop Glennon gave a rare permission for a collection in St. Louis in July, and Sisters Gertrude Ryan and Catherine Agnes Kuhn were in Chicago trying to raise money.[81]

Each time a note came due for the $200,000 loan for which Bishop Toolen had signed, Sister Gertrude paid the interest and part of the principal, and then had to get the bishop to endorse the new note. Her letters to him were always newsy, appropriately familiar, and solicitous of the bishop's health and circumstances. And, of course, she paid the notes on time.[82] Bishop Toolen came to think highly of Sister Gertrude's financial ability.

When the academic year began in September 1929, Father Judge sent Brother Thomas O'Keeffe to Catholic University and Brother James Norris back to Holy Trinity. It is at this time that Norris's leadership and financial responsibilities increased and his considerable ability came to the fore. Judge's correspondence with Norris begins in September 1929. Judge instructed him to keep on top of the magazine and guided him in exercising his authority without undermining Father Tomerlin's. Putting him in charge of bills and appeals, Judge told Norris to write him every day.[83]

Early in 1928, Bishop Toolen had signed a $25,000 note for the brothers. In working with the precocious Norris, Father Judge instructed him to follow Sr. Gertrude's example. On October 16, he wrote Norris that the interest on this loan was due and gave him detailed instructions for paying it. "I want the Brothers to help me as the Sisters help Mother," he told the young man. "She cannot be carrying a lot of financial minutiae around with her so Sisters Gertrude and Marie of the Precious Blood keep her informed and relieve her as much as possible not only of these items but also of looking for money." Judge assured Norris that he didn't have to worry about looking for money but should let him know when interest payments are due. "You yourself," he continued, "understand quite well how necessary it is for us to

81. On the hospital, see Tonra, *Led by the Spirit*, 208–10, with quotations from Mother Boniface at 208, 209.

82. See Sister Gertrude Ryan to Bishop Toolen, Holy Trinity, September 5, 1929, and December 7, 1929, Toolen Papers, AAM.

83. See Judge to Norris, September 16, 1929, AST, MF 1429–30; September 18, 1929, AST, MF 1431–32; and September 29, 1929, AST, MF 1433, from Stirling and Washington, D.C. The entire collection of Norris's papers is in the Archives of the University of Notre Dame. He gave AST copies of his correspondence with Father Judge.

keep our friend quiet. If we can meet right on the nose our Mobile obligation it will cover much for us." But, he warned, "if we do not, then we lose our fair name and direst things will be predicted of us." As Judge knew from experience, instead of letters, shocking wires would come. He renewed his request that Norris keep him informed and write daily.[84] By the time of the 1930 census, Norris was twenty-two years old.

With Father Judge spending much of 1929 at Holy Trinity, the fundraising that Judge told Norris he would do fell to others, including Brother Augustine, but most often to Fr. Joseph Tomerlin. Judge told Mother Boniface that in a typed letter, dictated to one of the sisters, he would refer to Tomerlin as the "Business Man."[85] The next day, he tells her that she hasn't heard from the "Business Man" because, despite his big salary, he has lost in several investments.[86]

The stock market crashed on "Black Tuesday," October 29, 1929. Its decline had been gradual. From the beginning of September to the time of the crash, the market declined by a third.[87] By the time Tomerlin left the Missionary Servants in 1932, the market was down 70 percent from its 1929 highs.[88] In 1933, 25 percent of Americans were unemployed.[89] In such a financial environment, Tomerlin was finding it very difficult to raise money. As Judge's letters to Mother Boniface at the end of March suggest, he also had trouble holding on to the money he did raise. In 1923 Tomerlin left his parish in Ensley with a considerable debt. Bishop Toolen had told Mother Boniface that Tomerlin was a "plunger" who needed someone to check on him.[90]

During his months at Holy Trinity in 1929, one of Father Judge's tasks was to organize the various appeals so that the office could keep track of the returns and properly thank benefactors. As Judge's January correspondence with Brother Augustine suggests, the "Business Man" was not very good at

84. Judge to Norris, The Catholic University of America, October 16, 1929, AST, MF 1441–44.

85. Judge to Mother Boniface, Brooklyn, March 30, 1929, AST, MF 8106. He tells her that he talked to "Joseph" and that in typed letters he would refer to him as the "Business Man."

86. Judge to Dear Mother, Philadelphia, March 31, 1929, AST, MF 8111.

87. "By mid-November some $26 billion, roughly a third of the stocks recorded in September, had evaporated"; David M. Kennedy, *Freedom from Fear: The American People in Depression and War, 1929–1945* (New York: Oxford University Press, 2005), 38.

88. Robert Sobol, *Panic on Wall Street: A History of America's Financial Disasters* (New York: Macmillan, 1968), 390.

89. Kennedy, *Freedom from Fear*, 163.

90. Tonra, *Led by the Spirit*, 185. On Judge's problems with the way Tomerlin handled money, see his letters to Mother Boniface, Brooklyn, January 23, 1926, and Newark, June 13, 1928, AST, MF 7878 and 8085.

keeping track of the money that passed through his hands. In August, Judge pleaded with him from Holy Trinity to keep him informed. "The creditors here are clamorous. How did you make out in Chicago? I wish you would drop me a line." Tied down with retreats, Judge asked Tomerlin to write once a week, "and also upon every other development."[91] By December the country's financial situation had worsened, and Judge wrote Tomerlin two letters about the community's finances. The first was mildly irritated, the second angry and exasperated.

Bishop Toolen's watchful gaze had Father Judge second-guessing himself. On December 7, he reported to Father Tomerlin that he had held up the Mobile Diocese appeals. Bishop Toolen had apparently forbidden them, but Judge wondered whether "the Bishop had overreached himself in this." He told Tomerlin he thought he remembered a statement from Pius XI that permitted missionary communities to solicit alms and donations freely. Even if he was right, Judge wondered if it would be worth challenging Toolen. He asked Tomerlin to "consult with some authority in Washington on this matter" and then to council with Nummey and the brothers so that "in humility and prayer we may get light from the Holy Ghost."

Father Judge dreaded the next accusatory communication from the bishop. He feared that the way Tomerlin was handling things could trigger another eruption from Mobile. "You see," he wrote to Tomerlin with deliberate indirection, "evidence is accumulating concerning that thing I spoke of where you were concerned. There is one thing we should do and do it at once; what you said in the office." Apparently, Tomerlin had failed to do whatever it was. "Get away," Judge continued in an agitated tone, "from all money obligation to him and have our finances so fixed that some two by four creditor will not cause a new screed." As in his earlier correspondence with Norris, Judge was intent on heading off future interventions from the bishop. Father Tomerlin was not cooperating to the fullest.

Father Judge was still looking for "that appraisal," probably attached to the title of Holy Trinity. He had written for it in November and was frustrated that he couldn't find it. He was exigent. "Cannot that magic bag of yours produce it? You know how necessary it is for us. Please get it for us. If you have it, send it down. If you have not, then can you tell me where I can get a copy." He went on to say that he couldn't find any "discarded envelopes or letters" from the last appeal, so he wouldn't be able keep track of the returns. "It is

91. Judge to My dear Confrere [Tomerlin], Holy Trinity, August 6, 1929, AST, MF 6770.

very useful," he insisted, "to know and keep track of the different appeals. It is very necessary among other things so that we may thank our benefactors." People were writing to ask if their donations had been received.[92]

By December 12, the next "new screed" from Mobile had come. After the customary salutation asking the Holy Ghost's grace and peace, Father Judge's next letter to Father Tomerlin began abruptly: "Answer the enclosed. What do you think about answering those letters the Bishop sent you?" Tomerlin had put Judge in a bad position with the bishop, and, by the end of this letter, Judge could not contain his anger. Bishop Toolen told Judge that he had twice written to Tomerlin and that the latter had not had the courtesy to reply. Father Judge assured the bishop that Tomerlin meant no discourtesy. Still, Tomerlin had not responded to the bishop's letters.

And now Bishop Toolen had sent Father Judge a letter about the Mobile appeal. He had sent it not in his own stationery but in one of the appeal envelopes with Tomerlin's name on it. At first, Judge thought a Mobile priest might be playing a joke on him. "He got the envelope somewhere," Judge wrote of the bishop, "and I imagine sent it as a reminder that he knows these appeals are circulating. None, thank God, went out." Judge was losing his patience. "Bills are coming in; for goodness sake get busy and send money down here. Jones the plumber walked in . . . made a nice speech. Fr. Tomerlin told him this and that, that lumber is costing $630." Someone else was trying to unload kitchen goods on Holy Trinity. Bishop Toolen was breathing down his neck. Finances were in bad shape. Judge was angry and upset and put considerable blame on Tomerlin for the community's financial disarray. The letter steamed to an abrupt end. "Say, Father, stop it. We cannot stand it. We sure will go broke if you keep on plunging."[93]

The day before he wrote this letter to Tomerlin, Father Judge had written to Brother Anthony Kelley, also on the road soliciting funds:

> Industry is crippled in this part of the South. Sr. Rita told me that eight men came in to her the other day looking for work. Some of the people are crying. The saw mills are shut down; the Golden Foundry and other like places closed. Birmingham is hit very hard. Industries off 60 percent.[94]

92. Ibid., December 7, 1929, AST, MF 6831.

93. Ibid., December 12, 1929, AST 6832. I have seen no record of Tomerlin's reply nor of the letters from Bishop Toolen mentioned in this correspondence. "Plunging" recalls Bishop Toolen's designation of Tomerlin as a "plunger."

94. Judge to Brother Anthony Kelley, Holy Trinity, December 11, 1929, AST, MF 1464–65. Sister Rita was the farm boss at Holy Trinity.

By Christmas Eve, Judge could report that things at St. Joseph's office were running more smoothly. The office, he had become convinced, "in a way is the brains of a work, if it is kept well, everything is in order and peaceful." With most collections having dried up, the Cenacle depended increasingly on appeals. "We depend so much on St. Joseph's office for our revenue," he wrote. He reported that the Christmas appeal had cost $1,300 to get out but had already paid for itself plus an additional $2,000 to the good with late donations still expected. He went on to describe his strategies for a good appeal. Thanking the benefactors and noting their intentions showed "not only appreciation but heart for their needs."[95]

January 2, 1930—Fire Destroys the Motherhouse

The long two-story motherhouse, completed in 1924, was the heart of what Bishop Byrne had called the Cenacle's "splendid Bethlehem in Alabama." On the evening of January 2, 1930, just after supper, it burned to the ground. The fire started in the utility building behind the center of the motherhouse. A scream came from the direction of the utility building, and then "a wall of fire-flash in the rear of the utility building followed by the crackling of wood." The fire spread quickly to the motherhouse itself. Newly waxed floors and "the beautiful Christmas trees and decorations added more fuel to the sun-seasoned pine wood."[96] A warning bell brought the neighbors, and a phone call brought the brothers from across the road. Mother Boniface evacuated the sisters. They lost all but the clothes they were wearing. Father Judge rushed to get the Blessed Sacrament from the chapel. The sisters managed to save "the money, the files, the account books, our benefactors' names ... and the file and the safe from the general offices." Two tons of coal and a fifty-gallon drum of wax stored in the cellar both exploded.

As they watched helplessly from the lawn, it took the fire only a half hour to consume the entire building. Then it appeared that the sparks might ignite the shrine, "the little chapel, the landmark of Holy Trinity."[97] Father Judge held the Blessed Sacrament at a distance for another half hour while

95. Judge to Sister Mary Thomas Champion, Holy Trinity, December 24, 1929, AST, MF 6839.

96. These quotations are from Sister Mary James's descriptions of the fire in "A Voice from the Past," *Holy Ghost*, September 1953, 3.

97. From Mother Boniface's longer description of the fire in Tonra, *Led by the Spirit*, 222, 223.

they prayed and doused the chapel roof with water. The original chapel was spared and still stands at Holy Trinity. John Burke, who was supervising the job of building the new Holy Name of Jesus Hospital, brought his family to live at Holy Trinity and had been working on improvements at the motherhouse. When it was clear that the little chapel was safe and Father Judge had placed the Blessed Sacrament there, he went to the Burkes's and Florence Burke gave him a pickled pig's foot sandwich.[98]

By morning all that remained of the motherhouse were "twisted pipes, broken plumbing fixtures and radiators."[99] Father Judge had been up all night but that morning preached a sermon in St. Joseph's Chapel taken from the words of Job: God had given and God had taken away. Blessed be the name of the Lord.[100] Two days later, he sent out a two-page circular letter on the fire. "Whether it be in abundance or destitution, whether it be in prosperity or adversity, whether it be in the flush of triumph or the dejection of contradiction and loss," he concluded, let the will of Christ be done.[101] "HOLY TRINITY IS NO MORE!" Mother Boniface wired to cenacles throughout the country.[102]

Help poured in from all sides. But now, in addition to financing the new hospital, Father Judge and Mother Boniface had to find the money to build a new motherhouse. Bishop Toolen was more than generous in his response to

98. "Our food supply was low, when he came over for coffee," recalled Florence Burke, "but I found one lone pig's foot in the refrigerator. There never was and never will be more sympathy expressed—than was expressed in that pig's foot sandwich"; Florence Conlon Burke, "Early Journal," typescript, 10. Through Mrs. Burke's friendship with Sister Gertrude, her husband, John P. Burke, took charge of the construction of Holy Name of Jesus Hospital. He brought his family to live at Holy Trinity, and they witnessed the motherhouse burn down. Mary Burke Maguire was a child of seven and received her First Communion from Father Judge at Holy Trinity. She shared with me her mother's eighty-two-page "Early Journal," which includes her memories of Holy Trinity and John Burke's account of the fire.

99. Collins, "Voice from the Past," *Holy Ghost*, September 1953, 3. "You should see," wrote John Burke, "the MELTED radiators—coils of pipe twisted like bailing wire"; "Early Journal," 11.

100. "The Lord has given and the Lord has taken away. Blessed be the name of the Lord"; Jb 1:21. Father Timothy Lynch had been a student in the chapel that morning. Years later he recalled, "Again, it was in moments of crisis that you could really see the majesty of Father Judge, another instance of the personal presence of God that seemed to be part of him"; cited in Tonra, *Led by the Spirit*, 224.

101. Judge to My dear Children, Holy Trinity, January 4, 1930, AST, MF 1484–85.

102. "All night we kept the coffee pot filled, and gave first aid to the seminarians and students from St. Joseph's, who were burned in their attempts to fight the fire. Within a few hours, Holy Trinity was but a heap of twisted iron and rubble. . . . Mother Boniface wired the various missions throughout the country—HOLY TRINITY IS NO MORE!'"; Florence Burke, "Early Journal," 10.

the fire. Early in February, he visited Holy Trinity, where the sisters were living in makeshift quarters. Mother Boniface reported that by then he had already sent in two very substantial checks. He ordered a collection to be taken up in the Mobile Diocese for the rebuilding of the motherhouse and wrote articles in both the Baltimore and Mobile diocesan papers appealing for help for the sisters.[103] Bishop Toolen, however, had serious reservations about rebuilding the motherhouse at Holy Trinity. Two years later, with the new hospital completed and the sisters' rule approved, Bishop Toolen refused to sign it, still insisting, along with his opposition to Father Judge's role as spiritual director, that the motherhouse be rebuilt in a place in Alabama other than Holy Trinity. In 1932, the sisters still had no motherhouse. The fire seemed to have smoothed their way to Philadelphia.

103. Tonra, *Led by the Spirit*, 229.

12

STRUGGLING FOR THE CENACLE'S LIFE IN THE SOUTH

January 2 to November 30, 1930

After fire destroyed the motherhouse on January 2, help poured into Holy Trinity from all sides. Bishop Toolen's response was more than generous, yet clear from the beginning that he did not favor rebuilding in a place as remote as Holy Trinity. The fire was the first of many challenges Father Judge and Mother Boniface faced during the first half of 1930. Others included the options of building a new motherhouse and a new hospital simultaneously or choosing between them, the brothers' chronic indebtedness, and the sisters' rule. Within a year, Mother Boniface could refer to the "great crisis" besetting the community. At its heart, and complicating the other issues, was the deeply conflicted relationship between Father Judge and Bishop Toolen. Bishop Toolen's genuine concern for the sisters after the fire did much to mitigate tensions, as did Mother Boniface's mediation.

A turning point occurred in May 1930. After twenty-three years, Sister Mary James still felt the sting of "that hardest cross of all, perfidy working from within."[1] In May Sister Gertrude Ryan, the procurator and a long-time member of the Cenacle, went to Bishop Toolen in confidence with very serious charges of financial impropriety against Father Judge. She felt this was her duty. By December she had complied with the bishop's request to present the charges in writing, and the bishop himself had corroborated the charges to his satisfaction. These charges confirmed his worst fears about Father

1. Collins, "Voice from the Past," *Holy Ghost*, December 1953, 4.

Judge's financial impracticality and even dishonesty. By January 1931, they had precipitated what Mother Boniface called the "great crisis." It forced the eventual removal of both motherhouses to the North, threatening the work in Alabama and the very survival of both communities.

In the Fire's Aftermath

"Though Holy Trinity is in ashes this morning through the grace of God a greater Holy Trinity will arise. It is God's work and it cannot fail." So Bishop Toolen wrote in a moving letter to Mother Boniface on the day after the fire. He enclosed a check for $250 "for use in any way you see fit."[2] Mother Boniface's long response contains the fullest available description of the fire. She asked the bishop to continue his prayers. "It seems too dreadful to be true. We are back to where we were fifteen years ago, but with this difference; we are starting all over again with a big debt. 'The Lord has given and the Lord has taken away; blessed be the name of the Lord.'" The motherhouse, she told him, was insured for $50,000, "but only $25,000 of it was fire insurance." They asked Paulist James M. Gillis to make an appeal on his WLW radio show. Bishop Toolen's brother, a Baltimore pastor, had already given them a collection at his parish on January 25.[3]

Through these and other appeals during the first half of 1930, the sisters raised thousands of dollars for relief of their circumstances and for rebuilding the motherhouse. Bishop Toolen assumed that the motherhouse would stay in Alabama and the money raised would be used for the sisters in Alabama. The financial situation was complicated by the fact that the sisters had simultaneously to raise money for the new hospital. By May Bishop Toolen came to believe that Father Judge had misappropriated these funds for other projects. His solicitude for the sisters only compounded his displeasure with Father Judge, who, he believed, had misused money meant to relieve the hardships under which the sisters were now forced to live at Holy Trinity.

The bishop's next letter to Mother Boniface in mid-January expressed sympathy for the sisters' hardships "during this cold weather." In addition to the one at St. Edward's in Baltimore, he had gotten them a collection from a pastor in Atlantic City for September. "I suppose," he wrote, "you have not

2. Toolen to Mother Boniface, Mobile, January 3, 1930, AST, MF 12968.

3. Mother Boniface to Bishop Toolen, Holy Trinity, January 7, 1930, AST, MF 12970–72. In his report on the fire to Father McHale, Father Judge estimated the sisters' losses at $125,000; see Judge to McHale, Holy Trinity, January 8, 1930, AST, MF 1497.

decided anything definite about rebuilding but I hope you are not considering another frame structure." He hoped to visit Holy Trinity "within the next few weeks."[4]

A New Hospital or a New Motherhouse?

Father Judge wrote to Mother Boniface around the same time. He was waiting for her to send a memorandum on finances he was to give Monsignor Bernardini in Washington at the beginning of the week of January 19. "The market is now at its lowest," he wrote. "Steel has not been as cheap for years." Material and labor would constitute the "major cost" of the hospital, and he raised the possibility of getting "either a gift of steel or a concession" in Pittsburgh or of ordering it at present prices. He also thought that the material and labor markets would go "still lower because business conditions are bad." He went on to hazard his opinion that "there will be no revival of industry until the labor market is liquidated. I mean by the labor market, of course, the union labor." Since the war, he continued, there had been "no real prosperity." Instead, it had been a prosperity "made up of elements of luxury, amusement, travel and all the items that concur in those different departments of diversion. The two leading members being the automobile and the radio." He was writing from Brooklyn and reported that he had been "telling the Sisters that they must decide whether it will be a new Mother House or Holy Name of Jesus Hospital. I think the hospital will carry."[5]

On the day before the collection at his brother's parish, Bishop Toolen wrote that he had heard in Mobile that the architect for the hospital "specified J and L beams which can only be obtained out of Pittsburgh." He reported a great deal of complaint in Gadsden and Birmingham about their going out of state for steel during such hard economic times. Again he sympathized with the hardships suffered by the sisters during the January cold. "I am sure," he concluded, "you will soon be able to rebuild the home that was lost."[6] Mother Boniface's letter of the same day crossed the bishop's and updated him in detail on living conditions for the sisters at Holy Trinity and prospects for upcoming collections. "We have not as yet started to think

4. Toolen to Mother Boniface, Birmingham, no date, AST, MF 12962–63. This letter was written before the collection in Baltimore on January 25, probably during the week of January 19, in response to hers of January 7.

5. Judge to Mother Boniface, Brooklyn, January 19, 1930, AST MF 8135; see also Judge to Mother Boniface, Gold Street, Brooklyn, January 20, AST, MF 8136.

6. Toolen to Mother Boniface, Mobile, January 24, 1930, AST, MF 12974.

about the future," she wrote. "We are happy to hear that you are coming to Holy Trinity, Bishop."[7]

Meanwhile, Father Judge had met with Monsignor Bernardini about the sisters' rule. He took the memorandum on finances from Mother Boniface to Washington and reported to her from Brooklyn that Bernardini had been "very much impressed" with it. "He said the Community is very good and very useful and must be saved to the Church." Rome, he assured Judge, would do whatever the bishops agree on. Bernardini thought the questions at issue in the case of the sisters' rule would be similar to the issues he had previously discussed with Father Tomerlin about the brothers' rule.[8]

By the end of January, the dilemma of rebuilding the motherhouse or going on with the hospital remained unresolved. Father Judge clearly wanted the hospital and worried that the sisters might choose the motherhouse instead. He wrote confidentially to Mother Boniface:

> The Sisters must understand that the two operations cannot go on simultaneously. They will have to be disabused of that and come flat with the choice of either one. I am wondering myself now is it wise to leave the choice to them? The Sisters in the North do not seem to understand the situation.... There is a sentiment about the building of the Motherhouse that is hard to overcome.[9]

About the same time, Mother Boniface responded to the bishop's concern that they use local steel for the hospital. Architects and the construction manager had agreed that J and L floor beams had to come from Pittsburgh, but for everything else steel mills in Birmingham and Gadsden "will have a chance to bid on the material for the new hospital." She also reported that the sisters had collected between four and five hundred dollars at his brother's parish. She was anticipating his visit.[10] Bishop Toolen wrote two days later to say he would be at Holy Trinity the following Tuesday. He enclosed two checks totaling $573.[11] Father Judge wrote from Brooklyn the same day. He was on his way to Stirling, New Jersey, to make arrangements for the sis-

7. Mother Boniface to Bishop Toolen, Holy Trinity, January 24, 1930, AST, MF 12973.

8. Judge to Mother Boniface, Gold Street, Brooklyn, January 24, 1930, AST, MF 819. Father Judge wanted to find Father Tomerlin, who had discussed these questions with Bernardini. Neither Judge nor Bernardini had a record of them. While Judge was in Brooklyn, Brother Augustine had surgery in New York.

9. Judge to Mother Boniface, Gold Street, Brooklyn, January 27, 1930, AST, MF 8143.

10. Mother Boniface to Bishop Toolen, Holy Trinity, January 29, 1930, AST, MF 12975.

11. Bishop Toolen to Mother Boniface, Mobile, January 31, 1930, AST, MF 12977. The checks came from Baltimore, $425 from his brother's parish and the rest "from the appeal that appeared in the *Catholic Review*."

ters to work in the Diocese of Newark. He reported that Father Tomerlin had surfaced and met with Monsignor Bernardini, who thought that the financial report needed to be scaled down. "The Roman authorities will wonder how a community such as ours would be so well-conditioned and possess so much."[12]

Bishop Toolen's Visit to Holy Trinity

Early in February, Bishop Toolen came to Holy Trinity. Deeply moved by what he saw, he described the motherhouse as "entirely in ruins." "The twisted pipes of the heating plant and the tall smoke stack" were all that remained. The sisters' living conditions during a particularly cold January especially concerned him. The chapel and the spirit it displayed impressed him most. He described it in detail to a friend who he hoped would be in a position to publish his letter. "I am sure that the stable of Bethlehem was no poorer or plainer than the chapel of the Trinity Sisters." They are "broken-hearted but you would never know it. They are most cheerful and their courage will carry them through. They are made out of the stuff that must have produced martyrs in the bygone ages."[13] Eventually the Catholic press widely circulated the bishop's letter. Mother Boniface sent warm thanks to the bishop for his visit. He had requested a list of what they needed for the chapel, and she enclosed it along with their best transcription of his remarks.[14]

Bishop Toolen's response included four checks and the promise of a "write up" in *Extension* magazine with its "three hundred thousand subscribers." Still taken with the chapel, he promised to send a set of "small stations" from his own chapel along with a "Holy Water Pool," "censor stand, censor and boat." Regarding the transcription, the bishop said he "just got up and said the things that came. If they enjoyed what I had to say I am more than amply repaid. I surely enjoyed my little visit to you."[15] By the end of March, the sacred objects the bishop had promised for the chapel arrived at Holy Trinity.

12. Judge to Mother Boniface, Gold Street, Brooklyn, January 31, 1930, AST, MF 8150.
13. Bishop Toolen to "My dear Vincent," Holy Trinity, no date, AST, MF 13013.
14. Mother Boniface to Bishop Toolen, Holy Trinity, February 10, 1930, AST, MF 12978.
15. Bishop Toolen to Mother Boniface, Mobile, no date, AST, MF 12979.

Bishop Toolen's "Gentle Threat" and the Decision about the Motherhouse

Bishop Toolen's undated response to Mother Boniface's of February 10 had a glaring omission. On February 12, the bishop wrote to Father Judge. He enclosed the letter he had written to Father Klejna in response to the latter's complaints about Judge and described his visit to Holy Trinity. He deemed the fire a "blessing in disguise" and added his hope that in rebuilding "you are going to consider some place nearer civilization." Then he mentioned that during his visit, "Mother ... seemed to hint that you thought of moving out of the diocese." Toolen made clear his belief that "the hand of God" was with the sisters' "marvelous work." But, if they moved, his responsibility for them would be over. No more notes would be signed or renewed. He was willing to help with the hospital, but, in the meantime, he wanted to know "just what you intend to do."[16]

On the same day, February 12, Father Judge wrote to Mother Boniface regarding the location of the motherhouse and expressing his "hesitation" about having it in Mobile. Monsignor Bernardini had been in favor of keeping the brothers' motherhouse in Mobile but during the past year had changed his mind and advised Judge to have the motherhouse "in a more friendly atmosphere ... where we would have peace." He had considered Silver Spring, Maryland, Stirling, New Jersey, and Pittsburgh, Pennsylvania. Shifting to the sisters' motherhouse, he reminded Mother Boniface of the remark she had made at the time of the fire: "Father, don't you remember having said we ought to move the Motherhouse elsewhere and I replied, 'we have so much,' now we have nothing?" With the fire, God had settled the question of moving the motherhouse but not where it would go.

Father Judge was enthusiastic for Cleveland, where the diocesan vicar general, Monsignor Smith, was an old friend and supporter. He enclosed a letter from Smith and quoted a remark he had recently made to Father Tomerlin: "I told Tommy [Judge] years ago to get out of that place. Now God sent the fire to drag him out." Though Bishop Schrembs of Cleveland could not afford to build "a million dollar Motherhouse" for the sisters, "he would be a Father to them." Father Judge didn't want to abandon Holy Trinity but at this point seemed convinced that the motherhouse must move out of the Mobile diocese.[17]

16. Toolen to Judge, Mobile, February 12, 1930, AST, MF 12979–81.

17. Judge to Mother Boniface, Stirling, February 12, 1930, AST, MF 8167–68.

Another letter to Mother Boniface on the same day included Father Judge's best attempt to "scale back" the sisters' financial report, as Bernardini had advised. "This is the best we can do," he began. As cash on hand, Judge listed $25,000 from fire insurance and another $20,000 from fire appeals. Added to the estimated real estate values of eight properties, furnishings and supplies, livestock, and farm equipment, this put the sisters' assets at $587,374. They owed $226,770 in notes payable, with most of the notes signed by Bishop Toolen. He calculated their net worth at $357,704. If she had any changes, he asked her to send them to him in Washington. He also asked her to have Brother James get copies of the two sets of incorporation papers of the brothers as Missionary Servants of the Most Blessed Trinity (1923), and Missionary Servants of the Most Holy Trinity (1928).[18]

Father Judge responded guardedly to Bishop Toolen's February 12 request to know what he intended to do about the motherhouse. He thanked the bishop for "his heartfelt sympathy and magnificent help" for the sisters, for his letter and article in the *Review*, and for his visit to Holy Trinity. Then he replied carefully:

> As for building for the Sisters or allocating them no serious thought has been given to this. Personally, I have not recovered from the shock of the fire. No plans have been made nor talked over. We wish to do God's Holy Will. We look upon the burning of the institutions as an open manifestation that God wishes us to be deeply and prayerfully concerned about the rebuilding. To build or not to build, to stay or not to stay is as God wills it. I have no will, no pleasure in all but this. I have but one settled thought; it is this, that the new building will be as fireproof as we can get it.... When the Sisters are more at leisure I will call a Council and let them decide what they want to do. Just now they are much scattered.

"Holy Trinity," he reassured Toolen, "is very dear to me and to all. The South we look upon as one of the portions of the Vineyard that the Triune God will[s] us to till." He promised the bishop that when the sisters began to deliberate in earnest, he would "place before them your generosity and kindness as reasons why the Diocese of Mobile should have first place in the affection and service." He concluded with a plea for the brothers, urging Bishop Toolen to enlist them in his work.[19] This was far from the decisive reply the bishop was hoping for.

18. Ibid., AST, MF 8170–71.

19. Judge to Toolen, Philadelphia, February 18, 1930, Toolen Papers, AAB; see also AST, MF 12983–84.

Bishop Toolen received Father Judge's letter on February 20. The next day, he wrote to Mother Boniface. The diocesan collection had amounted to $2,500. He enclosed a personal check for $1,500 and thoughtfully divided the rest of the money among the three sisters in charge of Catholic Charities in Mobile, Ensley, Alabama, and Pensacola, Florida, so they could make a contribution to the motherhouse. At the end of this letter, he mentioned without comment that he had heard from Father Judge "and he says that no thought has been given to the building as it is entirely in the hands of the Sisters."[20]

Brothers in Debt

In addition to the sisters' rule and the question of where their motherhouse would be, the brothers' indebtedness was much on Father Judge's mind as February drew to a close. Father Lenahan was anxious that he return to Holy Trinity. "I would have been back long ago," he wrote, "but the finances have me. We have a most imposing line-up of notes coming due in March."[21] In a letter of February 23, Judge listed for Brother James Norris the notes coming due in March. They totaled over $100,000. One for $20,000 was from Atonement Friars' founder Father Paul Francis Wattson's Rock of Peter Foundation. It was at 7.5 percent. The others were all at 6 percent. One loan of $10,000 was from Father Charles Woods. The rest were from banks in Washington, D.C., New Rochelle, New York, and Newton, New Jersey. At least the interest had to be paid on each of these loans in order to renew them for three to six months. In one case, an archbishop (probably Curley) had to sign. Father Tomerlin was out on the road collecting, and Father Judge was hoping that he could come up with the interest payments.[22]

Within a week, Father Judge reported to Monsignor Nummey in Washington that only five of the notes remained. Tomerlin sent him enough to pay the interest and $500 on the principal for one loan of $10,000.[23] In the meantime, Judge had written a long letter to Mother Boniface on Depression-era economics. A precarious wheat market made state banks in the South unsafe. Fearing a panic, he urged her to transfer the sisters' money to the Fed-

20. Toolen to Mother Boniface, Mobile, February 21, 1930, AST, MF 12991. She assured the bishop that warmer weather was easing the hardships that concerned him and that his letter had appeared in Catholic papers in Philadelphia, Pittsburgh, and Brooklyn; see Mother Boniface to Toolen, Holy Trinity, February 26, 1930, AST, MF 12992.

21. Judge to Lenahan, Stirling, February 27, 1930, AST, MF 1525.

22. Judge to Norris, Stirling, February 23, 1930, AST, MF 1520–21.

23. Judge to Nummey, February 27, 1930, AST, MF 1527.

eral Reserve Bank in Atlanta. "You may not remember but I spoke to you some time ago about the necessity of investing these monies." For the present, however, he was only offering a "suggestion" that she transfer the funds derived from the insurance settlement and the collections to a federal reserve bank.[24]

On March 6, Father Judge informed Brother James that "the New Rochelle note has been taken care of and has gone merrily on its way for $9,500 for three months." But, he added, "at the expiration we must pay the whole sum." He had paid the interest and some principal on two other notes. He still had to pay the bank in Newton, New Jersey, and then Father Woods and Father Paul Wattson. Monsignor William Quinn of the Propagation of the Faith office in New York promised to loan $5,000 and was helping to work out new terms with the Newton, New Jersey, bank. Judge planned to use this money for Father Woods and Father Wattson. He told Norris to keep the $5,000 to himself, as "I will be able to stretch it longer if the crowd does not know I have it." "Now," he continued, "we have to get ready for Mobile. All our money seems to be going toward the payment of notes and interest but thank God they are growing less and less each year." Over the past year, he reported, they had paid off about $4,000 with $240 interest.[25]

A Test to Prove the Will of God

On the same day, Father Judge wrote to Mother Boniface about his correspondence with Bishop Toolen. He had come to a plan of action regarding the motherhouse. She apparently had Bishop Toolen's letter of February 12, Judge's February 18 response, and then Toolen's response to that. If the sisters' motherhouse left the diocese, Bishop Toolen threatened to withhold his support from the hospital. "I am much inclined," Judge wrote, "to take up the threat of the Bishop as a test to prove the will of God in this matter. What does the Church want? The Holy Ghost is our Comfort and Light. I think it is the thought of the Delegation, if we can take Msgr. X's [Bernardini's] word as voicing it, to leave the diocese, i.e., the Mother House, the other works can remain."[26]

24. Judge to Mother Boniface, Stirling, February 23, 1930, AST, MF 8161–62.

25. Judge to Norris, Stirling, March 6, 1930, AST, MF 1531; see also Judge to Msgr. William Quinn, Stirling, March 10, 1930, AST, MF 6938.

26. Judge to Mother Boniface, Stirling, February 27, 1930, AST, MF 8175–76. I do not have a copy of Toolen's second letter, which Judge describes as "but a brief echo of the first."

On March 2, Father Judge wrote to call Bishop Toolen's bluff on his threat to withhold financing from the hospital. He wanted to separate the hospital from the issue of whether the motherhouse moved from the Diocese of Mobile. He also wanted the bishop to know that he would not be rushed into a decision on such a move. He explained that the sisters could not manage two simultaneous building projects and the practical reasons for going on with the hospital. Still insisting that he had come to no decision yet, he noted that the sentiment of the sisters seemed to "tend very strongly towards delaying the building of the Motherhouse until the Holy Name of Jesus Hospital is well under way." Then he proposed to the bishop his idea of a test: "Should this be the decision, as for financing it, the working out of this question may be just the thing that will reveal to us whether we are or are not to go on with the building of the hospital." He asked Bishop Toolen to join the Cenacle in placing this question of the hospital before St. Joseph during the month of March.[27]

Father Judge immediately sent Mother Boniface a copy of his letter to the bishop. "I can see from your letter," he wrote to her, "you are very anxious to go on with the hospital." He agreed. Mother Boniface had also made a case for staying in Alabama, in the South. He tried to address both these concerns. He reminded her of his thought to take "the Bishop's gentle threat of not financing the hospital as a test of God's Holy Will, and so let us stand." He continued, "If he refuses to finance the hospital because we will not be forced into a decision and the Sisters cannot finance it, then as far as my light goes, it is not the will of God for us to go on with this new building." He urged that her reasons for wanting to stay in the South would not be "disjointed" if the motherhouse moved. He insisted that the question for him was about the will of God in the matter of the hospital and not the "convenience, or the interest, or the plans of Bishop Toolen." He thought the bishop might turn to Mother Boniface, "as he will see from this letter there is no use in dealing with me because he cannot make me make up my mind impulsively enough for him." He assured her that, even if the motherhouse moved, "you will spend most of your year in the South." Then, of course, he sent her to St. Joseph.[28]

27. Judge to Toolen, Stirling, March 2, 1930, AST, MF 6862–63.
28. Judge to Mother Boniface, Stirling, March 2, 1930, AST, MF 8181.

A Bad Investment?

On March 6, 1930, Father Judge sent Mother Boniface "a month's interest of 6 percent on money you loaned me recently." The accompanying letter and later correspondence tell the confusing story of a financial transaction, a loan from Mother Boniface that was to come through Brother James but didn't, and a subsequent unpleasant phone conversation between Father Judge and Mother Boniface. Most of this transaction took place over the phone, so the details are difficult to sort out. The upshot seems to be that sometime in late February or early March, Mother Boniface gave Father Judge a substantial loan, he invested it at 6 percent, and he may have lost it.

None of this is mentioned in Father Judge's February correspondence about finances with Norris or Mother Boniface. The unpleasant phone conversation must have taken place sometime between Judge's March 2 letter to Mother Boniface and the March 6 letter with the interest enclosed. The March 6 letter suggests that Father Judge originally requested the money over the phone before Bishop Toolen's visit to Holy Trinity early in February but that Mother Boniface misunderstood. Judge needed the money to "restore" unidentified "burses" for which he assumed responsibility when he took over "the finances at St. Joseph's last November" from Father Tomerlin. Apparently Tomerlin had drained the burses, and Judge feared the bishop would find out about it. "I mentioned this to you over a long distance phone as I was anxious the more so because of your prospective visitor [presumably Bishop Toolen]." Judge claimed to have made three points clear in that conversation: (1) "the burse monies should be returned"; (2) "such monies must be invested"; (3) "that you would loan us the deficit." Judge thought Mother Boniface agreed to all of this over the phone.

He added that he had written to Sister Stephen and Brother James in the office at Holy Trinity, where "my plans for the burse situation engages often office conversation." Most confusing about this transaction is that the money for the loan was not to come directly from Mother Boniface but through Brother James, perhaps so it would be less clear that Father Judge had borrowed the sisters' money. When Brother James actually sent the checks, Father Judge was confirmed in his belief that Mother Boniface understood. Mother Boniface thought that Brother James had told Judge not to cash the checks. This was not clear to Father Judge, who, much to his embarrassment, did try to cash the checks.

"You left me unprotected," he wrote to Mother Boniface, "even after wiring of my distress." After the checks failed to clear, Father Judge wired Brother James, only to find "that I was left uncovered." The subsequent phone conversation was "sad and disconcerting. You seemed extremely angry and were shouting at the top of your voice." The money was for him, he had insisted, and not for Brother Augustine or anyone else. Father Judge was clearly hurt. "You must remember the things you said over the phone and inasmuch as you have not retracted any of them or said you were sorry, I suppose naturally you think the same way." He reminded her of an earlier promise to help him when he was in need. "You tell me of all the thousands you are receiving. I feel you are receiving much." She was concerned about what "they" (apparently Sister Gertrude and others) would say. "It looked to me, in your anger, that when I was in a corner you left me and cut the ground under my feet."

He assured her that the money was intact, "invested safely and profitably, not one cent has been spent or used for Brother Augustine." She could have it back on demand within 48 hours. "If you are willing to leave it with us you will receive monthly 6 percent, if not please wire me and I will have it sent South before I leave. It is here and safe, much safer than in the Southern banks where you receive 4 percent or no percent." He reminded her that he had advised her to invest the money as even "large northern banks are in a precarious position." "They" should be reminded that "when you were in a corner some time ago, Brother Augustine loaned some thousands of dollars. . . . Surely it is not pleasing to God or man to forget a thing like this." But Brother Augustine "was not the trespasser on the Sisters' fund. I am the guilty one surely 'They' should know this."[29] This letter makes clear that Father Judge received a substantial loan from the "Sisters' fund," that he invested it at 6 percent rather than banking it, and that at least some of the sisters, perhaps Sisters Gertrude and Catherine Agnes, were very reluctant to loan out money raised with Bishop Toolen's help and that they thought might go to Brother Augustine at Stirling.

Mother Boniface must have responded immediately with a "hand written, pencil, letter," to which Father Judge wrote what he called "a hurried acknowledgment."[30] The undated "hurried acknowledgment" began, "First of all, I am sorry if I hurt you." He wished he had more time to write but was

29. Judge to Mother Boniface Keasey, Stirling, March 6, 1930, AST, MF 8182–87.

30. These descriptions are from a later letter, Judge to Mother Boniface, Stirling, March 13, 1930, AST, MF 8190.

"in Washington crowded." "I cannot tell you how miserable this affair has left me." He went back over the details of the earlier letter, insisting that he had told her what he wanted to do. He found in the sisters' reluctance to loan him the money they had collected an offense against the family spirit he had spent his life cultivating. He would have said that this was a family matter and had nothing to do with bookkeeping or misappropriating funds. "When I give my word, I cannot understand attitude of Sisters. Really, I must speak about this. I do not like that spirit. Why should there be now any more than when there was but $100."[31]

A week later, on March 13, Father Judge was still upset over this incident and wrote a longer response to Mother Boniface, trying to clarify again the details of the sequence of events involved in their misunderstanding. The failed spirit he saw in the sisters' reluctance to release the money still bothered him. "Even if I asked for it suddenly, I would think that would be enough. If this is not so, I have cherished this thought for 15 yrs so please be indulgent to me if I cannot assimilate it easily." Mother Boniface had written that the Sisters "knew as well as I that you were not getting that money for yourself but for the Brothers." He denied this and chided her for hesitating to believe him. He continued to insist that "every cent of the money can be produced at this very moment. It is placed in liquid securities, that is securities, that can be converted into cash at a moment's notice."

"The money," Father Judge repeated, "was for me for a plan of mine." He went to outline a "manifestation" of the reasoning behind this plan. Canon Law required that surplus money be invested safely and prudently. He had invested the money. His work was for both communities. He could not pit one against the other. In difficult economic times he happened to "be conditioned with certain knowledge that can be capitalized for the works of Religion and urgent need in the Cenacle." Finances had been forced on him despite his resistance.

> Now since Divine Providence has put this burden on me, since so many doors are shut to us, since our mission progress has been hurt by lack of funds, the Will of God is very apparent to me, particularly since the Canons have a voice in this that I use a knowledge and experience that will be useful to the pocket book of the Lord.

He even thought that his plan would help finance the hospital. "That it is the Will of God that the Bishop have a part in this, I have my doubts, per-

31. Judge to Mother Boniface Keasey, Stirling, no date, AST, MF 8283–85.

haps, this is one reason for the fire." God, he hoped, would spare them from being "clubbed into a promise by the Bishop under a threat that he will not finance it unless we do." He assured her that "even if God calls me my plan will go through." Had they asked, he repeated, he would have returned the money. Among the brothers, only Augustine, James, and Anthony knew he had the money "and not one of them asked me for a cent."

Mother Boniface had written, "I have always tried to help but you know how I feel when those big sums are to be paid unexpectedly." Father Judge's response makes clear that the loan he invested was for a substantial amount. "The amount," he agreed, "is certainly large and imposing and proves beyond a doubt that you are offering a large help." He apologized again for "any hurt I have given you."[32] Though it manifests the reasoning behind his plan, this letter doesn't reveal what the plan entailed. A letter he wrote Mother Boniface on March 12, the previous day, suggests the plan in outline.

"Since sending interest," Father Judge began, "I have thought out a plan to amortize the amount, in a short time." The plan seemed to involve compound interest. Banks are giving the sisters 4 percent interest. But they have "a magnificent overhead of expense in running their palatial money temples." Overhead for salaries and dividends, he thought, had to come from charging excessive interest rates to borrowers or "from compounding." "Well, the sum in question is working even better than your banking friends. It is compounding in a way all of its own. Three months from now a large slab of it will be returned and these returns will be made at regular intervals and heavier payments until the cancellation." The interest payment he had sent in early March, he claimed, amounted to only ".003 percent of what had been made." He assured her that this was "secure and certain." He envisioned the compounding interest contributing significantly to financing the hospital. He reminded her that on the night of the fire he had told her that they would get $125,000 and she said that was "foolishness." Now they had $80,000, so he was "only 25 percent foolish and every day I will be less foolish." He was certain they could finance the hospital themselves "if the payments are not too heavy at first." He asked her for statements to show the amounts due as work on the hospital progressed.[33]

The letter doesn't make clear whether $80,000 was the amount of the loan in question or whether that was simply the total amount the sisters had

32. Judge to Mother Boniface, Washington, D.C., March 13, 1930, AST, MF 8190–97.
33. Ibid., Stirling, March 12, 1930, AST, MF 8188–89.

from the insurance settlement and the collections coming in for the motherhouse. It is clear that, after a memorably unpleasant exchange with him, Mother Boniface lent Judge a substantial amount of the sisters' money. He invested it in liquid securities with an unspecified rate of compound interest. In the throes of the Great Depression, this seems too good to be true.

The correspondence doesn't make clear where Father Judge invested the money. In January he had written Mother Boniface to think about the fact that "the market is now at its lowest. Steel has not been as cheap for years. If I can get to Pittsburgh, I might be able to get either a gift of steel or a concession."[34] Steel is a possibility. In any case, Father Judge insisted that the amount of the original loan could be returned on demand and that, if left as he had invested it, it would produce enough compound interest to help significantly in financing the hospital.

A later episode clarifies the amount of the loan. In May 1930, a draft of the sisters' rule was almost complete. At the end of the month, Monsignor Bernardini would take it to Rome with the sisters' formal request for a decree of praise leading to canonical erection. When Sister Gertrude Ryan heard of these developments, she went to Bishop Toolen and reported verbally on what she thought were Father Judge's financial irregularities. Father Judge and Mother Boniface had no knowledge of this visit. Sister Gertrude's assistant in raising funds for the hospital was a younger sister, Catherine Agnes Kuhn. After what she had done became known, Sister Gertrude eventually left the community in the summer of 1931. Mother Boniface expelled Sister Catherine Agnes. Early in 1932, Catherine Agnes Kuhn submitted a petition to the Holy See to have her dismissal revoked as unjust. Her petition lists the financial irregularities of which Sister Gertrude thought Father Judge was guilty. Though the petition is silent on the source of "certain knowledge" of the market Judge claimed to have, it does reveal that the amount of the March 1930 loan was $15,000 and that he invested it in "steel and general motors."[35]

34. Ibid., Washington, D.C., January 19, 1930, AST, MF 8135.

35. "In March of that year (1930), three months after the mother house at Holy Trinity, Alabama, had burned, the Founder ordered the Reverend Mother to give him $15,000 of the money collected for the rebuilding of the mother house to invest in 'steel and general motors.'" This quotation is from a copy in the Toolen Papers of a petition addressed to His Holiness Pius XI in re "Dismissal of Religious Woman from the Missionary Servants of the Most Blessed Trinity." It is typed double-spaced on legal size paper, runs to fifteen pages, and is signed by Catherine Agnes Kuhn. It is undated, but internal evidence suggests a date around the beginning of 1932. This petition will be discussed later. The previous quotation is at page 9.

Father Judge hoped the interest on this investment, "compounding in a way all its own," would contribute significantly to financing the hospital. When construction began on July 2, 1930, costs had to be financed through Bishop Toolen. Although Catherine Kuhn's petition doesn't claim that this investment was lost, I know of no evidence that the $15,000 was ever returned on demand, or that interest on it ever contributed to construction costs for Holy Name of Jesus Hospital. It appears to have been a bad investment.

Spring 1930

Mother Boniface's correspondence with Bishop Toolen indicates that donations trickled in through March and April from sources such as the Catholic Students Mission Crusade. On St. Patrick's Day, Father Judge began the eight-day retreat at Holy Trinity for postulants of both communities. On March 25, the Feast of the Annunciation, they received the garb, and the last bit of rubble from the lost motherhouse was cleared away. With his letter of April 11, Bishop Toolen enclosed a check from St. Mary's Seminary Mission Crusade. He repeated his advice not to rebuild the motherhouse at Holy Trinity. "It seems to me," he wrote, "that it would be foolish for you to rebuild on the present spot. It was all right at the beginning but to build there again will be most impracticable."[36]

Father Judge was struggling to stay ahead of his creditors. A brief one-page "Statement of Affairs," dated April 1, balances the brothers' assets and liabilities to the penny at $110,219.12.[37] On April 11, the bishop had written about the note for $25,000 for the brothers he had signed in 1928. Perhaps the payment had been late. On April 12, Judge responded, explaining that they had agreed with the bank to pay, in addition to the interest, $500 on the principal every quarter. He reminded the bishop that, since 1928, they had paid the principal down by $3,500.[38] Toolen's response of April 14 said the bank was demanding a bigger quarterly cut in the principal. He

36. Bishop Toolen to Mother Boniface, Mobile, April 11, 1930, AST, MF 13000.

37. "Statement of Affairs," April 1, 1930, Toolen Papers, AAM. In contrast to Judge's reports to Norris and Nummey back in February, this statement lists "notes payable" at only $43,091. The bishop was no doubt looking for a more detailed statement accounting for where money came from and where it went, the same kind of accounting Father Judge kept trying to get from Father Tomerlin.

38. Judge to Toolen, Holy Trinity, April 12, 1930, AST 6958. We do not have Toolen's letter to which this is a reply.

must have asked Judge for a "financial statement." Judge explained that he thought Tomerlin had provided one a year ago. He hastened to add that he had "at hand a statement up to date which I am very glad to send you."[39] This is probably how the April 1 "Financial Statement" found its way into the Toolen Papers. But this statement didn't provide the kind of accounting the bishop was looking for.

The note at Huguenot Trust in New Rochelle, New York, that Judge had renewed and "sent merrily on its way for $9,500 for three months" in late February was coming due at the end of May.[40] On April 11, he explained to Monsignor Nummey that the bank would not renew the loan and asked him if he could help get a loan of $10,000 from a Jamaica bank to pay off the Huguenot Trust loan.[41]

Becoming Canonical

Both the apostolic delegate and Bishop Toolen pressured Father Judge to regularize canonically the two religious communities he had founded. In the sisters' case, this meant submitting constitutions to Rome accompanied by letters of support from the bishops in whose dioceses they worked, and especially from the bishop of the diocese where their motherhouse was located. On April 15, Mother Boniface assured Bishop Toolen that the sisters did indeed "realize the weight of responsibility and care we are assuming in our great undertaking." She thanked him for his "suggestion on the location of the new Motherhouse," and then she asked him for a "testimonial" letter. As an example, she sent him a copy of a "testimonial" that had been sent to the brothers. "If you think you can say some such nice things about the Sisters, Bishop, will you please 'fix up' a testimonial letter for us?" Toolen answered immediately with a strong testimonial letter praising the sisters and their work "to the generous-hearted Catholics of the United States." His letter emphasized the South. "You have come as pioneers into the South, you are putting up with hardships today which I am sure no other order of Sisters in the country are called upon to suffer.... The South needs you."[42] Toolen's testimonial caught up with her in Stirling, where the renovation

39. Judge to Toolen, Stirling, April 21, 1930, Toolen Papers, AAM. We do not have Toolen's letter of April 14, to which this is a reply.

40. Judge to Norris, Stirling, March 6, 1930, AST, MF 1531.

41. Judge to Nummey, Holy Trinity, April 11, 1930, AST, MF 1546–47.

42. Mother Boniface to Bishop Toolen, no place, April 15,1930, AST, MF 13001; Toolen to Mother Boniface, Mobile, April 16, 1930, AST MF 13003.

of the chapel for the retreat center was almost complete. She thanked him "for writing us such a splendid letter" and, in answer to his earlier request, promised to send another sister to Pensacola to help Sister James.[43]

May 1930 found Father Judge hard at work on the sisters' constitutions. Dr. Louis Motry served as chaplain for the sisters at their house of studies in Washington and worked with Father Judge on the rule. In early May, both Mother Boniface and Sister Mary Francis as mistress of novices were there to consult with Motry.[44] On May 16, Father Judge wrote Brother James on their progress. Though the rule was holding him in Washington and preventing his return to Holy Trinity, he was optimistic. "We have, thank God, the very best news on it. It seems it is being very well received." Only minor changes remained. "We are asking," he added, "for two or three very big favors. One of these is to be secured only by Papal Indult." He promised to discuss them when he returned south. One of the "very big favors" requiring a papal indult was the request that Father Judge remain the sisters' spiritual director during his lifetime and that, after his death, the superior of the Missionary Servants of the Most Holy Trinity continue in this relationship. Father Judge had high praise for that "good and zealous priest," Dr. Louis Motry. "If Canon Law has the same effect on all ecclesiastical students, then it would be a good thing for all to specialize in it."[45]

While Father Judge was working with Motry on the sisters' constitutions, Mother Boniface traveled the country visiting bishops in whose dioceses the sisters worked and others who might know their work. She was collecting testimonials to accompany the constitutions when they were sent to Rome. In all, she gathered twenty-two letters. Mother Boniface dictated summaries of her visits with Cardinal Dougherty, Archbishop Curley, Bishop Boyle of Pittsburgh, Bishop Nilan of Hartford, Cardinal O'Connell of Boston, and Bishop Walsh of Newark.[46]

She stressed with each bishop the importance of their distinctive garb and asked them to recommend the indult that would allow Father Judge and

43. Mother Boniface to Bishop Toolen, Stirling, April 28, 1930, AST, MF 13004; see also Toolen to Mother Boniface, Mobile, April 21, 1930, AST, MF 13002, in which Toolen requests a sister to help Sister Mary James in the "real missionary work" of reaching the many Catholics in the "outlying districts of Pensacola."

44. Tonra, *Led by the Spirit*, 234, citing a May 9 letter of Mother Boniface to Sister Mary of the Incarnate Word, her eventual successor. "Dr. Motry," she wrote, "is more fascinated with it each day and he says he may end up joining. You know the old saying, 'many a word spoken in jest.'"

45. Judge to Norris, Washington, D.C., May 16, 1930, AST, MF 1565.

46. Tonra, *Led by the Spirit*, 234–40, for long quotations of Mother Boniface's summaries.

his successors to serve as spiritual director to the sisters. When she asked Archbishop Curley to write in favor of the indult, according to her summary, he responded, "No, never! I would not ask for him to be Spiritual Director for life over a kindergarten. I do not believe he is practical." As an example, he cited Father Judge leaving the South with only twenty-five cents in his pocket. Mother Boniface, only two months from her harrowing phone encounter with Judge, tried to explain that these were the sorts of things the saints did.[47]

A few years earlier, Archbishop Curley had signed a $10,000 note, probably to help Father Judge in acquiring the property in Silver Spring. When Father Judge discussed with Monsignor Bernardini where the brothers' motherhouse might be, if not in Mobile, Washington was the first place he mentioned. In a letter only three months before, he had written Mother Boniface, "Archbishop Curley, you know, is just an episcopal Fr. O'Neill as far as the Cenacle is concerned."[48] But Archbishop Curley had consecrated Toolen a bishop, and they were good friends. It is likely that, in addition to his own experience, Toolen's view of Judge as a financially irresponsible visionary influenced Curley's view of Judge's impracticality.

Bishop Toolen wrote a strong recommendation, dated May 13, 1930, emphasizing the importance of the distinctive garb. He made no mention of Father Judge and his successors as spiritual directors.[49] Sister Gertrude had gone to see Bishop Toolen in May, probably around this time, as it became clear to her that the rule would soon be sent to Rome. Bishop Toolen was already inclined to want to separate Father Judge from the sisters. Sister Gertrude's report decisively strengthened his resolve to do that and convinced him that Father Judge should have absolutely nothing to do with the sisters' money.

Monsignor Bernardini had to leave for a new post in Rome at the end of the school year. He left in late May or early June and wanted to take the rule and the letters with him and present them himself to the Sacred Congregation of Religious. He finally took a draft of the nearly completed constitutions and left the task of completing them to Dr. Motry. By November 5, word came from Rome that the rule was approved. Rome granted the indult, at least in part, with Father Judge as the sisters' spiritual director for life. Bishop Toolen never signed the rescript erecting the sisters as a canonical

47. Ibid., 236, for the account of her visit with Archbishop Curley.

48. Judge to Mother Boniface, Stirling, February 12, 1930, AST, MF 8167, with a reference to "our affairs being talked up" between the two bishops.

49. Bishop Toolen to Mother Boniface, Mobile, May 13, 1930, AST, MF 13005.

religious community. He simply could not agree to Father Judge as a constitutional part of their community.

Building Up the Cenacle

Even as he worked to find money to keep the brothers afloat, to finish the sisters' rule, and get them canonically regularized, Father Judge could not abandon his role as founder and spiritual father of the Cenacle. He continued to give retreats. His conferences on "Pentecostal Preparation" appeared in the April issue of the *Holy Ghost* magazine. "When, therefore," he wrote, "you have practiced examining your impulses, reforming your motives, purifying your intentions and having those God places over you pass judgment on your thoughts, strivings and emotions, you can be assured that you are acting under the impulse of the Holy Ghost."[50] No doubt in the first half of 1930 Father Judge had many opportunities to apply these words to himself.

On May 18, at St. Michael's Church in Newark, Father Felix O'Neill's parish, Father Judge spoke on the occasion of the reading of Bishop Walsh's letter on the Mount Carmel Guild, a lay charitable organization the bishop was promoting in the diocese. He spoke on the lay apostolate, a "recent thought" of Pope Pius XI's. The lay apostolate, he told them, meant that they were "privileged . . . to work for the extension of the Kingdom of our Divine Lord." It means, he continued, that "really, in the circumstances and in the Providence of your work-a-day life you are the Catholic Church."[51]

On May 28, Father Judge wrote to thank Sister Baptista for a spiritual bouquet she had sent him on the thirty-first anniversary of his priestly ordination. As he neared the end of his life, thoughts of Sister Baptista brought him back to the beginning of the work. He thanked the Triune God "that some twenty-five years ago I met a beautiful, cultured, spiritually refined, lofty-idealed young woman, nobly endowed in Faith, graced with charity and zeal for the interest of our Holy Religion." "How happy you should be," he told her, "in seeing the development of Cenacle Life. This cannot be considered independent of you whom God used as a Cornerstone on which to build the glorious temple of the Missionary Cenacle."[52]

50. Judge, "Pentecostal Preparation," *Holy Ghost*, April 1930, 11.

51. "Instruction Delivered by the Rev. Thomas A. Judge, CM, at St. Michael's Church, Newark, Sunday May 18th, 1930, on the occasion of reading the letter of Bishop Walsh of Newark concerning the Mount Carmel Guild," AST, MF 4215. A slightly different version appears as "The Lay Apostolate," *Holy Ghost*, July 1930, 16–17.

52. Judge to Sister Marie Baptista, Washington, D.C., AST, MF 1571. He went on to empha-

Financing the Hospital

On June 14, Bishop Toolen wrote to Sister Gertrude in her capacity as procurator to assure her in writing that he would "become a Co-maker with you on the note for $200,000 to be made to the Massachusetts Mutual Life Company for a loan for that amount on the new Gadsden hospital." He promised to sign the papers as soon as they were ready.[53] Three days later, he transferred at the First National Bank in Montgomery $225,000 to the account of the Missionary Servants of the Most Blessed Trinity, naming Sister M. Gertrude as Treasurer.[54] On July 2, 1930, ground was broken and construction begun for the new Holy Name of Jesus Hospital in Gadsden.

Shortly after signing over the hospital funds to the sisters, Bishop Toolen went on vacation, a sailing trip around the North Pole with a stop in Iceland. He wrote Mother Boniface twice during this trip. His first letter on July 10 from aboard the SS *Calgaric* is a newsy description of Iceland and his first sight of the midnight sun. "I am going to give you some food for thought," the second undated letter begins, "while I'm sailing around the North Pole." This letter is as serious as the previous one was light. Having undertaken "a big responsibility" by signing notes for $225,000, the bishop wanted to put his case plainly:

> I signed these notes on condition that Fr. Judge has nothing to do with the financial affairs of the Sisters. I have the greatest respect for Fr. Judge as a spiritual adviser but no respect for his judgment in financial affairs. I know that he has tried one or two times get rich quick schemes and I know also that he is heavily involved at the present time owing everyone.

He warned her against helping out Father Judge and to use money "for the purpose for which it is collected."

He advised her to think about branching out more in the South. Southern bishops, he reported, were of the opinion that the sisters only used the South for appeals and then used the money for other work. One of the reasons Southern bishops don't ask for sisters is their salaries. He urged her to pay attention to the views of Southern bishops, as they have an important

---

size how much good she had done through "personal contact," praised to her Mother Boniface's recent contacts with the bishops, and urged her to "carry on that Apostolate of visiting."

53. Bishop Toolen to Sr. Gertrude M. Ryan, Mobile, June 14, 1930, copy, Toolen Papers, AAM.

54. Bishop Toolen to First National Bank, Montgomery, Mobile, June 17, 1930, copy, Toolen Papers, AAM.

voice on the Home Mission Board. He reminded her that the Missionary Servants of the Most Blessed Trinity "exist as a Diocesan organization." As such, "you should make no move without the approval of the Bishop." He emphasized that this is what Canon Law required and complained that "the only time I have ever been consulted was when you wanted me to do something for you. You have gone ahead your own way and the Bishop has been given little consideration." He softened his conclusion but still warned, "I think you have a wonderful future but you will have to watch and pray over each step or you are likely to undo all the good done."[55]

As Bishop Toolen was writing his first letter, Father Judge was writing to Monsignor Nummey about a new property he wanted to acquire at Chesapeake Beach on Maryland's Eastern Shore. He enthused about the Eastern Shore as a mission field. He wanted to have a corporation meeting about "a new loan we are trying to arrange with Mr. Flannery."[56] By fall he was considering Father Brennan's interest in buying property for a novitiate in Puerto Rico.[57]

On November 30, about three weeks after approval of the sisters' rule, Bishop Toolen laid the cornerstone for Holy Name of Jesus Hospital in Gadsden. Father Judge preached. The January issue of the *Holy Ghost* magazine carried a full story on the laying of the cornerstone. At this time, Bishop Toolen still refused to sign the rescript that would make the Missionary Servants of the Most Blessed Trinity a canonically recognized community. The "great crisis" of which Mother Boniface spoke in January of 1931 was almost upon them.

55. Bishop Toolen to Mother Boniface, at sea, no date, AST, MF 12964–67.
56. Judge to Nummey, no place, July 10, 1930, AST, MF 6867–69.
57. Judge to Mother Boniface, Stirling, AST, MF 8230–31.

❖ 13

THE GREAT CRISIS OF 1931

In the fall of 1930, Mother Boniface invited Bishop Toolen to say Mass and preach at the cornerstone ceremony for the new hospital. Bishop Toolen replied that November 30 was the first Sunday he would be available. "I will be glad to lay the cornerstone," he wrote, "but you will have to get someone else to preach." He suggested Father Judge. "He is your founder and interested in your welfare and knows more about the development of the Order than I do and would seem to be the proper one to take care of this part of the ceremony."[1] On November 30, 1930, Bishop Toolen and Father Judge both participated in laying the cornerstone for the new Holy Name of Jesus Hospital in Gadsden. Bishop Toolen celebrated the Mass. Father Judge preached. But tension between them was mounting. When the hospital was dedicated the following September, Bishop Toolen didn't come.

Mounting Tensions between Father Judge and Bishop Toolen

By November 1930, Father Judge was temporarily winning the war of wills with Bishop Toolen. The latter's threats had yet to force a decision about the location of a rebuilt motherhouse. Though he had signed the initial notes for construction to begin in July, his threat not to finance the hospital if they moved still hung in the air. Sometime around the end of October and the beginning of November, Bishop Toolen made an unexpected visit to Holy Trinity. Mother Boniface didn't know why he had come. He appeared to be "under

1. Bishop Toolen to Mother Boniface, Mobile, October 3, 1930, AST, MF 13018.

quite a strain." The bishop was "very lovely and was grand to everybody," but still she felt "electricity in the air."[2]

On November 5, 1930, Mother Boniface announced to the sisters that Rome had approved their rule. "What a joy it must be to Father!" she wrote.[3] She told Bishop Toolen the following day and was sure to let him know that, though Father Tomerlin was collecting in the North, Father Lenahan was at Holy Trinity and Father Judge would be there soon.[4] The bishop sent his congratulations immediately but seemed surprised at the speed of the process. "You have been very fortunate in getting it through so quickly," he wrote. "It is too bad," he added, "that you have not someone to give you Mass every day."[5] He knew that, with only one priest, they could not, on a given day, have Mass on both the women's and men's sides of Holy Trinity.

Getting Brother Paul Anthony "Priested"

At this time, Father Judge was struggling to get another priest. Brother Paul Anthony Fursman had completed his fourth year of theology at the Catholic University of America, and Judge was trying to get his "ordination affair straightened out. The poor boy certainly has lots of patience and long suffering."[6] This was another point of contention between Judge and the bishop. Brother Paul Anthony had not made a canonical novitiate, and Bishop Toolen insisted that, if he ordained him, Fursman would be a priest of the Mobile Diocese and should remain in the South. Father Judge refused to agree to this condition. "Do pray that I can get Brother Paul Anthony expedited," he wrote to Mother Boniface."[7] Back in October, Father Judge had tried to get Brother Paul Anthony's dimissorial letters from the Diocese of Newark.[8]

2. Tonra, *Led by the Spirit*, 260, citing a letter of Mother Bonface to Sister James in Pensacola.

3. Ibid., citing Mother Boniface's announcement to the sisters.

4. Mother Boniface to Bishop Toolen, Holy Trinity, November 6, 1930, AST, MF 13021.

5. Bishop Toolen to Mother Boniface, Mobile, November 7, 1930, AST, MF 13022.

6. Judge to Sister Stephen Wise [?], Stirling, November 5, 1930, AST, MF 8232.

7. Judge to Mother Boniface, Holy Trinity, November 9, 1930, AST, MF 8233.

8. Judge to Msgr. John C. McClary, Stirling, October 15, 1930, AST, MF 6986; see also Judge to Mother Boniface, Stirling, October, 29, 1930, AST, MF 8230. Judge tells Mother Boniface that one of the reasons he stayed in the North was "to get a paper from the Bishop concerning Brother Paul Anthony. May the Triune God be praised, I have it. This means now we can hope for his ordination at latest, if not at Christmas, at least, by February second." Newark was Fursman's home diocese. The "paper from the Bishop" could also have been the testimonial letters that accompany dimissorials.

Dimissorial letters are the "authorization given by a bishop or other competent authority to another bishop or prelate to confer Orders ... on his subject."[9] Father Judge and Bishop Toolen went back and forth on the subject of Fursman's "proper bishop." "Divine Providence has favored us in our perplexity," he wrote to Bishop Toolen on November 26. He told Toolen that Fursman "has procured a Bishop who will ordain him" but didn't identify the bishop. He asked Toolen to send his testimonial letter to the new house of studies at Silver Spring instead of to the ordaining bishop and invited Toolen "to honor us with a visit."[10] Conflict over Fursman's ordination dragged on for the next seven months until the apostolic delegate approved a canonical solution urged by Louis Motry.

Laying the Cornerstone for Holy Name of Jesus Hospital

Amid pressing financial and canonical worries, Father Judge delivered a stirring address at the ceremonies in Gadsden on November 30, 1930. He preached on St. Peter's words in Acts 3:6, "Gold and silver I have none; but what I have, I give thee: In the name of Jesus Christ of Nazareth, arise and walk." Deep in the South, he offered a spirited apologia for naming a hospital "Holy Name of Jesus." Bishop Toolen never used this name in referring to the hospital. When it was dedicated the following September, the *Birmingham News* published an entire article on it without mentioning the hospital's name. Explaining the new hospital's name, Judge articulated a vision of the sisters' healing mission in Gadsden.

"In the name of Jesus Christ of Nazareth, arise and walk." These were St. Peter's words to the man in Acts 3, "lame from his mother's womb." "Jesus was the name invoked," said Father Judge, "the Name of God, the Name of the Son of God. Faith called on that Name. There is no other name that can work such marvels.... Be glad! Have hope! For this is the Name that is to grace this structure." Judge explained the name as "divinely becoming for we have so much to do for the sick, particularly the poor sick, therefore we

9. D. Bonner, "Dimissorial Letters," *NCE* (1967), 4:870.

10. Judge to Toolen, Stirling [?], November 26, 1930, AST, MF 6999; see also Judge to Toolen, Stirling, November 22, 1930, Toolen Papers, AAM. "I will do what I can," Father Judge tells the bishop, "toward the solution of the problem of responsibility." Since Fursman was canonically not yet a religious, this had to do with the question of the "proper bishop" to ordain him and which bishop would be ultimately responsible for him once he was ordained.

are going to call upon that Name, we are going to memorialize It for the sake of the sick and the people of this city."

Father Judge traced the healing arts in the West back "to the early days of the Catholic Church" in the third and fourth centuries, to religious men and women such as Cassiodorus, St. Benedict, and Hildegard of Bingen. It was the name of Jesus that "inspired such service and devotion to the sick" in the past, and it inspires the sisters in the present. "Reverence, faith, and love are the reasons why we exalt the Name and why we lift it above your city streets." The name of Jesus will bring hope to the sick, healing help to doctors, and blessings to the city of Gadsden. Finally, Father Judge addressed false rumors that the hospital was built to make money to send to Rome. "Blessed and praised be the Holy Name of Jesus," he concluded. "We cherish that adorable Name, we honor and exalt It, and we invoke It for you and yours."[11] After hearing this "wonderful sermon on the power of the Holy Name," Mother Boniface was "certain no one will ever question again the name of our hospital."[12]

The Sisters' Constitutions and the Troubles of December

Matters between Bishop Toolen and Father Judge came to a head in December 1930. By the end of the month, the bishop had decided that Father Judge had to be taken down. After the laying of the cornerstone in Gadsden, Father Judge returned to Holy Trinity for an eight-day retreat and then back to Gadsden for another. The sisters' constitutions had been approved in Rome, but, in order for the community to be canonically erected, Bishop Toolen had to sign the decree or form of erection. After Father Tomerlin delivered the rescript from Rome to her at Holy Trinity, Mother Boniface brought it to Bishop Toolen in mid-November at his brother's parish in Baltimore. He seemed willing to sign it but wanted to see the constitutions in final form. Rome had approved the draft that Monsignor Bernardini brought in the spring. Bernardini then advised Mother Boniface to assure the bishop that he could sign. At the laying of the cornerstone, she conveyed Bernar-

11. "Laying of the Cornerstone of the New Holy Name of Jesus Hospital, Gadsden, Alabama, November 30, 1930, Address by Reverend Thomas A. Judge, C.M.: M.S.SS.T.," *Holy Ghost*, January 1931, 16–22.

12. Tonra, *Led by the Spirit*, citing Mother Boniface's description of the event in a letter to Sister Mary Thomas Champion in Puerto Rico.

dini's assurances. Bishop Toolen asked her to get the "Form of Erection that had been used by the Brothers," bring it to Mobile, and he would sign it.[13]

On December 5, 1930, Bishop Toolen wrote Mother Boniface that he had read over "the approval granted by the Holy See." He noted that, according to this document, "the Bishop must approve the constitution." He asked her to send a copy. "It is necessary to do this not only for your own safety but for the future." He also asked for "the form that you spoke of," presumably the brothers' form or decree of erection. "Just as soon as you send me the constitution," he concluded, "I will appoint a committee here in the diocese to look it over, and, as quickly as possible, approve or make any changes that they feel necessary."[14]

After he read over the terms of the sisters' rescript, Bishop Toolen, claiming he had never received or approved the constitutions of the Missionary Servants of the Most Holy Trinity, asked Father Judge to send them. "In fact," Toolen wrote, "I do not think that the form of erection of the Missionary Servants has ever been approved by the Bishop and the rescript from Rome demands this. Si [*sic*] I would ask you to send in to me, as soon as possible, a copy of your constitution." This request confused Father Judge, who was still giving the retreat at Holy Trinity. Did the bishop mean the sisters? He reminded Toolen that he had "signed our decree of erection and also passed on our constitution." Father Cullen had signed them also and sealed them with the bishop's seal. Judge also reminded him of a remark he had made about the constitutions: "If the Brothers would do all that was in that first paragraph of the constitutions, they would do a lot." He told the bishop that the brothers' decree of erection and the constitutions were in Washington with the canonist, who was "fixing them up for a last draft." He promised to send them as soon as he got them.[15]

13. Ibid., 262–63.

14. Bishop Toolen to Mother Boniface, December 5, 1930, AST, MF 13023. Copies of the rescript from Cardinal Lépicier of the Sacred Congregation of Religious, dated March 20, 1929, and of the decree of erection for the Missionary Servants of the Most Holy Trinity, dated April 29, 1929, signed by Bishop Toolen, and witnessed by Philip Cullen, his chancellor, are preserved in AST. The latter is the form of erection that Bishop Toolen requested. Both documents are in Latin.

15. Judge to Toolen, Holy Trinity, December 7, 1930, Toolen Papers, AAM. In this letter Father Judge cites from Toolen's letter asking for the constitutions. We don't have Toolen's letter to which he is responding.

Bishop Toolen Again Refuses to Sign

Two days later, Mother Boniface arrived in Mobile as Bishop Toolen had requested. She hoped he would be ready to sign the sisters' decree of erection. She visited the bishop on December 10, 1930, bringing with her copies of the brothers' form of erection. On the same day, Father Judge wrote to Father Tomerlin, "Mother was in Mobile today. He has refused to sign the decree of erection." He added, "I have not seen her to talk with her *viva voce*, as Mother received word that her mother is dying. Lord be good to them both." By the time Judge had finished this long letter, he had received word of Bridget Keasey's death and telegraphed Tomerlin to try to attend the funeral.[16]

According to Mother Boniface's own account of the meeting, Bishop Toolen appeared conflicted. "He expressed great sympathy and sorrow before we left that he felt forced to refuse, but he just had to have the finished Constitutions, and not just the draft." During their meeting, Toolen expressed his reservations about the work in Puerto Rico. "He felt we were founded for the South and our big work would be in the South." He also expressed his view that Father Judge as spiritual director was "impractical." If the bishop was going to be responsible, "then he was going to know everything and be its guide in every way." Mother Boniface started for home immediately after her meeting with the bishop and learned of her mother's death while the train north was stopped in Nashville.[17]

It was becoming clear that Father Judge himself was the main sticking point in Bishop Toolen's refusal to sign the sisters into canonical existence. They might be forced to choose between Father Judge and staying on in Mobile. On December 17, 1930, on her way back from her mother's funeral in Butler, Pennsylvania, Mother Boniface stopped in Washington to see Monsignor Bernardini, whom she described as surprised at the bishop's refusal to sign the decree of erection without seeing the constitutions in final form. She recounted Toolen's objections to Father Judge as spiritual director for life and to rebuilding the motherhouse at Holy Trinity. She discussed with him the possibility of leaving Mobile "if the Bishop insisted on cutting off Father Judge entirely from the Community." They discussed moving to Philadelphia. Bernardini was "delighted" with the idea and told them he had suggested this to Father Judge two years before. "He thought it would take a man like Cardinal Dougherty to put it over." Mother Boniface clarified to him that

16. Judge to Tomerlin, Holy Trinity, December 10, 1930, AST, MF 6849.
17. Tonra, *Led by the Spirit*, 264–65.

it was the sisters and not Father Judge who had insisted on staying at Holy Trinity. Bernardini advised her to return to Bishop Toolen and tell him they could not give up their founder and might be forced to leave the diocese. He advised her to go at Christmas time.[18]

Bishop Toolen Threatens the Brothers with Suppression

At some point in December, probably between December 10 and 18, 1930, Sister Gertrude submitted to Bishop Toolen the written version of the charges of financial irresponsibility she had brought against Father Judge.[19] Perhaps it was this report that brought Bishop Toolen to the breaking point with Father Judge. In any case, on December 18, in a three-page burst of pent-up exasperation, Bishop Toolen exploded with a litany of canonical grievances against Father Judge that had been building up over the past two-and-a-half years.

He had come to Mobile in 1927 and found an extraordinary group of sisters with the spirit of the early martyrs, perfect for working in the South and especially in his diocese. But he had learned that they had an impractical, financially reckless founder who mismanaged their money, sent them all over the place while using the South to raise money, and, worst of all, usurped the bishop's canonical place as superior, advisor, and father protector of these exemplary women. By the final weeks of December 1930, Bishop Toolen had determined that, if Father Judge refused to comply fully with canon law, the bishop would suppress the Missionary Servants of the Most Holy Trinity.

"Perhaps you are wondering," Bishop Toolen began, "why I have not sent testimonial letters for Brother Paul Anthony and the reason is you have not sent the name of the bishop to whom these letters are to go." Unless another bishop had taken him in, Toolen reasoned, he was still Brother Paul Anthony's ordinary, and no one else could ordain him without dimissorials from him. After that opening salvo, Bishop Toolen launched into the other canonical issues he had with Father Judge.

18. Ibid., 265–66.

19. This according to the petition of Catherine Agnes Kuhn mentioned in the last chapter. The petition (11) indicates that Sister Gertrude's December report is attached as Exhibit 13, but I could not find it in the Toolen Papers. Back in July Bishop Toolen told Mother Boniface he knew of one or two "get rich quick schemes" Father Judge was involved in. Kuhn's petition provides a list of nine failed investments or "get rich quick schemes" (8–9), no doubt reflecting Sister Gertrude's report.

According to canon law, superiors should have a fixed place of residence. "Where is your fixed residence?" he demanded. "It ought to be Holy Trinity but it seems to be Newark." He accused Father Judge of violating Canon 500, no. 3, according to which he could not direct the sisters without a special apostolic indult.[20] "More of your time is spent with the Sisters than with your own men." The intent of law, the bishop argued, "is against your authority over them particularly when you teach them that you and you alone are their Superior." Rather than Judge's authority, "the Sisters are under the authority of the Bishop in whose Diocese they were established and under the Bishops in whose Diocese they work."

By Canon 500, no. 1, Bishop Toolen claimed authority to inquire into the disciplinary and financial affairs of diocesan institutes. As ordinary, he did not even have a copy of the constitutions. "I demand that you send me one at once," he steamed. The house of studies in Washington was a particular sore point with the bishop. He accused Father Judge of having started it, "as far as I know, without the consent of anyone. Surely not the consent of your Ordinary in the Diocese in which the Mother House exists."

The bishop was especially frustrated at Father Judge's failure to give him the full financial accounting for which he had repeatedly asked:

> When I ask I get a paper valuation of the farm and buildings and a general amount for debt. The money that is given by people throughout the country for the upkeep of the institutions, the money given by the faithful in the collection taken up in the churches on Sunday, the money begged by the Brothers going about has never been accounted for and God alone knows where it goes.

In these matters, Bishop Toolen accused Father Judge of being "a law to yourself above the Church." "I know," the bishop wrote, "that you are not very prompt in paying your debts." He reminded Father Judge again that, according to canon law, "money donated for one purpose cannot be alienated for another without permission. I wonder if this is adhered to."

He cited Canon 533, no. 3, to the effect that Father Judge could not engage in financial transactions valued at more than $6,000 without permis-

20. The canons Bishop Toolen cited come from Part III of the 1917 Code and have to do with congregations of religious men and women. Canon 500 concerns ecclesiastical superiors. Canon 500, no. 3, is about diocesan congregations as religious and specifically mentions the exception of the Vincentians serving as superiors of the Daughters of Charity. Canon 533, no. 3, concerns temporal goods and their administration for diocesan congregations, stipulating that every investment and every change of investment be approved by the local ordinary; see T. Lincoln Bouscaren, Adam C. Ellis, and Francis N. Korth, *Canon Law: A Text and Commentary*, 4th rev. ed. (Milwaukee: Bruce, 1963), 242, 256.

sion from the ordinary, the chapter, and the Holy See.[21] "I know," he added ominously, "that in certain cases some of these conditions have not been lived up to." The constitutions should specify the limits of the superior's discretion in such matters. "Another reason why I should have a copy of your constitution."

He returned to the issue of the house of studies in Washington, which, after questions of financial impropriety, seemed to outrage him the most. "Merely attending a theological course in a seminary or Catholic university does not satisfy the lawgiver in this important matter." There has to be an approved house of studies in which "perfect community life" is observed. Regarding the house of studies, the bishop had a raft of questions:

> Has your so-called house of studies in Washington received the ecclesiastical approval of the Ordinary of Baltimore; has it ever been subject to canonical visitation; has the society asked and obtained legal permission from the Ordinary of Mobile Diocese to erect such a house of studies; what is the manner of life there?

Because of these issues with the house of studies, the bishop explained, he had refused to ordain Missionary Servants "under the title of the Diocese of Mobile." He did not believe they could get "the spiritual and disciplinary training needed under the conditions that existed." He repeated that the "proper Bishop for Holy Orders is the Bishop of residence." In other words, without dimissorial letters from him, no other bishop could ordain Brother Paul Anthony. The testimonials Father Judge had requested were not enough.

Finally, Bishop Toolen presented Father Judge with an ultimatum: "Father Judge, the community has gone on in [a] haphazard way for years and it is about time the law of the Church was observed." If Father Judge failed to live up to the requirements of canon law, Bishop Toolen threatened "to petition Rome for suppression. I have been unable to get any cooperation or information from you, so now there must be a reckoning." With lay professors and a frequently absent superior, "the place at Trinity is most unsatisfactory." Often the boys have no morning Mass. "The whole thing has been conducted in a slipshod manner and this does not satisfy me." He emphasized the lack of community life with Fathers Judge and Tomerlin all over the country, Father Lenahan traveling in the diocese, and Father Brennan in

21. On Canon 533, no. 3, on temporal goods and their administration, see Bouscaren, Ellis, and Korth, *Canon Law*, 256.

Puerto Rico. He seemed not to know that Monsignor Nummey was in Washington. He concluded by expressing his doubt that the Missionary Servants of the Most Holy Trinity could ever fulfill the purpose for which Father Judge had founded them.

> I do not see how you are going to accomplish this aim of taking care of one abandoned mission the way you are going. Where are these missions, who is going there, how are they to be supported? The whole thing to my mind is vague and visionary. If I could see any practical use in what you are doing, I would be glad to get behind it but I do not.

He demanded a copy of the constitutions at once.[22] He copied the letter to Archbishop Pietro Fumasoni-Biondi, the apostolic delegate in Washington.

Father Judge had a deep sense of himself as a man of the church. To receive such a letter from the highest apostolic authority in his diocese, a letter accusing him of flagrant disregard for the laws of the church, must have given him considerable pause. He answered from Holy Trinity on the day after Christmas, telling the bishop that his letter "came to hand today." He briefly addressed some of Bishop Toolen's issues. He promised a financial statement after January 1 and the constitutions as soon as they came from Washington. He insisted that "Holy Trinity is never left without the Holy Sacrifice," but did not claim that both sides had Mass every day. He was trying to get two "religious men to help us out with the work of direction." In response to Bishop Toolen's threat of suppression, he wrote the following:

> Dear Bishop, whatever the Church wants is our desire. In all things we wish to conform to the Church and to Her laws. If the Church wants us to go on, we want to go on; if the Church does not, we do not, therefore as the Church wishes be it done.[23]

In the last days of 1930, Father Judge was at Holy Trinity occupied with "the writing up of the sermons I am preaching." One was his November 30 sermon at Gadsden. "It is so hard to get down to dictating these things," he wrote to Sister Mary Thomas Champion in Puerto Rico. He was explaining to her why he couldn't come to the island. "This has been a year of great blessing," he wrote, "but these blessings are bringing heavy problems, and it is some of these problems that are tying Mother and myself down."[24]

22. Toolen to Judge, Mobile, December 18, 1930, copy, Toolen Papers, AAM. This letter has been treated in detail, as it includes all of Bishop Toolen's major issues with Father Judge.

23. Judge to Toolen, Holy Trinity, December 26, 1930, Toolen Papers, AAM.

24. Judge to Sr. Mary Thomas Champion, Holy Trinity, December 27, 1930, AST, MF 7004.

The Great Crisis Unfolds—the January 7, 1931, Meeting

Bishop Toolen had also written to the apostolic delegate on December 18, 1930, enclosing his letter to Father Judge of the same day. Archbishop Fumasoni-Biondi responded on January 3, 1931. The delegate merely acknowledged receipt of the copy. He addressed Bishop Toolen's comments on the sisters and their rule, noting their "wonderful work" and the fact that Toolen had not yet signed "the rescript for their canonical establishment." The delegate wanted him to sign. "Your Lordship will, I am sure, understand," he wrote, "that the most effective way to bring them under your authority as the Ordinary of a diocesan congregation, will be to give them that canonical status which will at the same time guarantee to you the rights which you should have over them according to the canons of the Code."[25]

Meanwhile, Bishop Toolen was receiving advice from Rome not to sign. The day after his December 10 meeting with Mother Boniface, he wrote for advice to an old friend at Rome, Monsignor Moses E. Kiley, spiritual director at the North American College.[26] Kiley reported that he had "spoken several times" to Cardinal Lépicier at the Sacred Congregation for Religious, and the cardinal prefect "seems disposed to adjust the matter satisfactorily." Not knowing the details of the case, Kiley suspected that "someone must have been working on the proposition solely interested in their welfare." Fearing Bishop Toolen's canonical rights and interests had not been properly represented, Kiley advised that Toolen "not sign any document until further notice," a policy he described as "perfectly safe." Kiley promised to follow up with Lépicier, to represent Toolen's interests, and to find out why in this case the congregation was "derogating from the usual procedure followed in establishing a diocesan community." But, with reference to such possibilities as an apostolic indult, he feared what might happen if "some joker is placed

---

Sister Mary Thomas was one of Judge's accomplices in his ongoing project of forming Eugene Brennan into a Missionary Servant. Commenting on Brennan's development, Judge noted "how really softened Father Eugene is becoming."

25. Archbishop Pietro Fumasoni-Biondi to Bishop Toolen, Washington, D.C., January 3, 1931, Toolen Papers, AAM.

26. Kiley (1876–1953) and Toolen had been students together at St. Mary's Seminary in Baltimore. Kiley became bishop of Trenton in 1934 and archbishop of Milwaukee in 1940. In addition to his work at the North American College, Kiley, at this time, was also a consultor for two curial bodies having to do with the Eastern Church. For a biographical sketch, see Robert F. McNamara, *The American College in Rome, 1855–1955* (Rochester, N.Y.: Christopher Press, 1956), 765; see also 509–10, 554.

in the Constitutions or the Rescript from the Congregation. Such a thing will mean that the Bishop will have to deal with the Congregation under which these are apt to take refuge."[27]

As Monsignor Bernardini had earlier advised, Mother Boniface went to see Bishop Toolen in Baltimore on January 7. She made light of a visit she would have preferred not to make. "I just follow the mitres," she told Margaret Healy. Seeing the bishop again at this point was a "foolish trip," she thought, and she would rather have waited for the final version of the constitutions.[28] Bishop Toolen reiterated that he would not sign until he had received the final constitutions. He revealed that he had written to Rome against an apostolic indult allowing Father Judge to be spiritual director for life. In explaining his opposition to Father Judge, Bishop Toolen brought up what appear to be examples of bad investments from the Kuhn petition. Mother Boniface explained these as "business enterprises started by lay people who had come to Father Judge for advice." He had "not given one cent of Community money" to any of them. On this she insisted in the strongest terms: "I was in charge of the funds for the past fifteen years and I can give my word of honor and could take an oath that not one cent of Community money had ever been used."

Bishop Toolen claimed to have "inside information" and "had heard these charges from different people" but had no proof. The bishop insisted that he, not Father Judge, was their superior, and he thought they were founded for the South. If they left the diocese, he threatened to "write every Bishop in the Country against us." Mother Boniface responded that they could never give up Father Judge. She tried to explain "how much we owed" to him. She told the bishop that "we would stand by Father Judge, our Founder, as far as we could, unless Rome gave the order." She realized they were facing a "great crisis in our Community life." Either they give up Father Judge, whom she described as "under God … the inspiration" for "whatever good our Community had accomplished in the past," or they must move the motherhouse out of the Diocese of Mobile.

After spending hours with canon lawyers Bernardini and Motry on the constitutions, Mother Boniface at this point seemed to grasp better than the bishop the actual canonical situation of the sisters. As she had written to Sis-

27. Moses Kiley to Toolen, Rome, December 29, 1930, Toolen Papers, AAM.

28. Tonra, *Led by the Spirit*, 270–72. Mother Boniface's summary of the meeting is given at 271–72, her thoughts prior to it at 270. Subsequent quotes from Mother Boniface are from these pages.

ter Mary Francis and others at Holy Trinity only half-jokingly just before she went to see the bishop, "Now you see, after all, you are not real nuns!"[29] As their January 7 meeting wound down, Bishop Toolen reiterated that the sisters were a diocesan community and he was their superior. They could not move without his permission. "I tried to tell him," Mother Boniface wrote in her summary, "that Washington had told me that, as far as the Church was concerned, up to the present we did not exist, and whatever we had done in the past was O.K. as long as we had no trouble with an individual [bishop?]." The point Mother Boniface made to the bishop indicated the canonical path Dr. Motry, with the indispensable help of Cardinal Dougherty of Philadelphia, would take to extricate the sisters from Mobile and facilitate their move to Philadelphia. Though the men's community was already canonically erected, Motry would also use a variation on this approach to thwart what Father Judge described six months later as Toolen's "brave attempt to smash the Brothers' Community to pieces."[30]

When Mother Boniface told Father Judge the details of the meeting, she reported the same Gamaliel-like response he gave Bishop Toolen only two weeks before: "If it is God's will, the Community will go on; and if it is His Will that it break up, it is satisfactory to us, whatever is pleasing to God is our only wish." At the end of the meeting, after a heated discussion about the location of the motherhouse, Mother Boniface told Sister Mary Francis that Bishop Toolen "called a cab for me, came out to the street and paid the driver and was just as lovely as could be." Nevertheless, she ended her summary of the meeting with these words: "We left Baltimore after an interview of two hours, firmly convinced that our Community was facing a great crisis." It was now clear that the sisters would have to choose between Father Judge and Bishop Toolen.

Father Judge Responds to the Bishop

Bishop Toolen respected the sisters and their work, but he had no use for the men's community. As the drama of the sisters' canonical standing and the location of their motherhouse continued to unfold, Bishop Toolen cam-

29. Mother Boniface was not using "real nuns" in any technical canonical sense. As her subsequent remarks make clear, she meant that, until Bishop Toolen signed the rescript, they were technically not yet members of a diocesan religious congregation.

30. Judge to Mother Boniface, Washington, D.C., June 27, 1931, AST, MF 8270. The context is the apostolic delegate's acceptance of Motry's canonical argument for allowing Bishop O'Hern of Rochester to ordain Brother Paul Anthony without dimissorials from Bishop Toolen.

paigned against the brothers. Monsignor Bernardini left permanently for Rome about this time, leaving the canonical affairs of both communities in the capable hands of Louis Motry. On January 8, 1931, Father Judge sent Bishop Toolen a six-page, single-spaced response to his December 18 broadside. In the two weeks between his initial December 26 response and his longer January 8 letter, Judge no doubt consulted extensively with Motry. His January 8 letter to Bishop Toolen responded point by point to the bishop's charges in the areas of canon law, community discipline, and finances. He challenged Toolen's reading of canon law on a number of points.

First, Father Judge responded to the claim that Fursman could not be ordained without dimissorials from Bishop Toolen. After pointing out that Fursman could not technically be a Missionary Servant because he had never made a canonical novitiate, Judge made a case that testimonial letters go to the *Ordinandus* (the one to be ordained) who is to bring them to the ordaining bishop. If canon law obliged Fursman to get dimissorial letters from Bishop Toolen, Judge insisted, he would have advised Fursman to ask for them. "I must naturally realize," he wrote, "that I, in my position could not expect to teach obedience to the laws of the Church if I myself gave so flagrant an example of the opposite." This is why Fursman asked only for testimonial letters. This argument represents Motry's approach to the canonical status of both communities and their path through the "great crisis."[31]

Father Judge informed the bishop of the petition for an apostolic indult allowing him to serve as spiritual director for life. He denied that he had taught that he alone was the sisters' superior and claimed to have taken "every opportunity to teach the Community to look up to the Ordinary as their Superior." He again reminded Bishop Toolen that he had earlier offered him a copy of the constitutions.

He enclosed a financial statement, claiming to show that "the financial structure of the Missionary Servants of the Most Holy Trinity is becoming very firm." Under "Liabilities" this statement did list almost $45,000 in outstanding loans, but they were limited to the brothers' indebtedness to South-

31. Judge assured Toolen that the canons regarding the ordinary's rights to inquire into financial and disciplinary affairs (512, para. 1, no. 2; 535, para. 3) had been written into the constitutions. He challenged the bishop's reading of canons 1491–92 as applicable to religious congregations. The first two canons (512 and 535) concern respectively the bishop's right to canonical visitation of the houses of diocesan institutes and the bishop's right upon request to the "economic status of any house." Canons 1491–92 concern the bishop's right to visit institutes such as hospitals and schools conducted by diocesan religious; see Bouscaren, Ellis, and Korth, *Canon Law*, 246, 257, 798.

ern banks. Nor did they include the itemized accounting of finances that the bishop had demanded.[32] Nevertheless, he assured the bishop that "money donated for one purpose has never been alienated for another."[33]

Regarding the house of studies, he claimed to have the approval of Archbishop Curley. Father Judge followed Father Motry's line of argument. Since the community had not been canonically erected in Mobile when the house of studies was opened, the question of Bishop Toolen's permission hadn't come up. If candidates for ordination had yet to make a canonical novitiate, "questions about the suitability of their university studies would be decided by the ordaining bishop." When the members of the community became "full-fledged religious," they would comply with Canon 495, para. 1.[34] By February, this argument finally led Bishop Toolen to ask whether the community actually had any members and to renew his insistence that Father Judge find a qualified master of novices.

Father Judge appealed throughout, especially in defending conditions at Holy Trinity, to the infant stages of a young and struggling community, insisting that he had administered it "with the best of intentions." Regarding Bishop Toolen's threat of a petition to Rome for suppression of the community, he appealed to their peculiar circumstances. "Let me again reiterate," he wrote, "if the Church wishes us to go on, we want to go on; if the Church does not wish us to go on, we do not want to go on, therefore, let it be as the Church wishes."

Father Judge assured the bishop that he had made "a sincere, conscientious attempt to meet all the questions that you have placed before me." His arguments required the bishop to presume his good will, giving him the benefit of the doubt on close questions. By December, Bishop Toolen had passed the point where he was prepared to do that. What appeared to Father Judge as "highly practical" he could only see as "vague and visionary."[35]

32. From a statement of "ASSETS AND LIABILITIES," dated January 1, 1931, with "St. Joseph's School, Holy Trinity, Ala.," typed at the top; Toolen Papers, AAM.

33. He suggested that the bishop had cited the wrong canon (533, no. 3, instead of 534, §1). In the matter of amounts over $6,000, he demanded to know in what way this canon (534, §1) had been disregarded. Father Judge's response suggests that he didn't think the canons gave Bishop Toolen the right to financial information as extensive as he sought. Canons 532 through 535 concern the administration of temporal goods.

34. Canon 495, §1, concerns the foundation and suppression of religious provinces. It makes no provision for diocesan congregations to establish provinces but recommends instead they apply for pontifical status. Father Judge's point seems to be that technically they are not yet even a diocesan congregation subject to this canon; see Bouscaren, Ellis, and Korth, *Canon Law*, 238.

35. Judge to Toolen, Holy Trinity, January 8, 1931, Toolen Papers, AAM.

The Constitutions

In Rome, Monsignor Kiley learned from his conversations with Cardinal Lépicier that the sisters' rule had come to the Sacred Congregation for Religious with a petition for the indult that would allow Father Judge to serve as superior for life. "As I can gather now," he wrote, "it seems that Judge has had someone working for his interests right along and there is no one saying anything on the other side." Kiley reported telling Lépicier that he thought Judge was "trying to get the same exemption for these that the St. Vincent de Paul Sisters have who are under the Vincentians, and are really not Sisters but lay persons living in a community." He advised Toolen to "watch your step and do no signing till you are good and ready.... Just take things coolly and slowly as is done on this side."[36]

On January 13, 1931, Fathers Judge and Tomerlin visited Bishop Toolen in Mobile and brought him a copy of the men's constitutions. "We attempted an amicable and respectful conversation," Judge wrote to Monsignor Bernardini at Rome, "but we received a most ungracious reception." According to Judge, Toolen made "all kinds of unsubstantiated charges" and refused to name his sources. In addition to Father Judge, he implicated Monsignor Nummey, as well as Fathers Brennan, Tomerlin, and Lenahan. The bishop had a private meeting with Tomerlin, trying, Judge wrote, "to line him up against me" and to put Tomerlin, whom he had recently denounced as a "plunger," in charge of St. Joseph's finances. Father Judge temporarily acceded to this. The bishop also told Tomerlin that he had sent charges to Rome against Judge. This, Judge explained to Bernardini, was the reason for his letter. He made sure to tell Berdardini that Toolen had accused Tomerlin of paying the Monsignor "a fat fee" for his help.[37]

By January 15, 1931, Bishop Toolen had taken steps to get out from under the financial liabilities he had incurred on behalf of the Missionary Servants, both men and women. He sent Father Judge his initial reaction to the constitutions as claiming "all the privileges of an exempt institution." The constitutions prove that "the Bishop has never received any consideration from you." Judge could expect "nothing at all" from the bishop. Bishop Toolen insisted that his letter of approval, which Judge had cited in his last

36. Kiley to Toolen, Rome, January 12, 1931, Toolen Papers, AAM. On the indult's background, see "Petition for Indult for Men's Community to Have Jurisdiction over the Missionary Servants of the Most Blessed Trinity," document 13, Monographs 4:100–106.

37. Judge to Msgr. Filippo Bernardini, Holy Trinity, February 2, 1931, AST, MF 1694. Judge also included copies of Bishop Toolen's January 15 letter to him and his reply of January 17.

letter to the bishop, be withdrawn from the magazine. He extended the two notes he had signed for the brothers to thirty and ninety days respectively, but refused to sign any more notes. If Father Judge failed to fulfill the demands of canon law regarding novitiate, residence, and the other issues, he threatened to write to Rome. He claimed not to understand "your position on Brother Paul Anthony."[38]

Bishop Toolen wrote to Mother Boniface on the same day. His letter was softer but just as insistent on protecting his financial liability from Father Judge's future interference. Referring to their January 7 meeting in Baltimore, he told her that since then he had "given the Trinitarians serious and prayerful consideration." He had decided that he could neither consent to Father Judge as superior for life nor to the rebuilding of the motherhouse at Holy Trinity. On the question of leaving the diocese, he told her they were free to stay or go and were "not conferring a favor on the Diocese by staying in it." If they did leave, however, they would have to find someone else to assume the more than $200,000 of notes on the hospital. If they stayed, he wanted to be a cosigner on the sisters' checks. "[A] great deal of money has been spent on the house at Stirling," he wrote, "and I am not going to take chances for the same thing happening with the money that might come in from the hospital at Gadsden."[39]

The Sisters' Decisive Meeting of January 16, 1931

After her January 7 meeting with Bishop Toolen in Baltimore, both Mother Boniface and Father Judge began to suspect that the bishop's charges of financial impropriety against Judge must have come from someone inside the community. On January 16, Mother Boniface convened at Stirling a meeting of "all the Custodians [superiors] in the Northeastern region." Recent events made clear that the question now before the sisters was deeper than simply deciding between rebuilding the motherhouse and going ahead with the hospital. Now they had to decide whether to remain in Mobile without Father Judge's spiritual direction or to leave Mobile and keep Father Judge as spiritual director. They had to choose between Father Judge and Bishop Toolen. This was the "great crisis."

38. Toolen to Judge, January 15, 1931, copy, Toolen Papers, AAM.

39. Toolen to Mother Boniface, Mobile, January 15, 1931, AST, MF 13025. In this case, the bishop's concern was for money that might come in from the sale of the old hospital buildings once the new one was completed.

Of the twenty-one custodians present at the meeting on January 16, only one voted against staying with Father Judge. At this point, Mother Boniface knew that it was Sister Gertrude. When she questioned her, Sister Gertrude replied that she could not answer. Believing that Sister Gertrude could no longer perform her duties as procurator, Mother Boniface sent her to Lyons, New York, where Sister Miriam was custodian. In describing the Stirling meeting to Sister Michael in Rockford, Illinois, Mother Boniface explained that "her companion [Sr. Catherine Agnes Kuhn] had come to me last summer with many of the same charges which I now hear from Mobile. What could have been the motive for the whole thing, we cannot understand. Whatever our Mobile friend has said to the one in Lyons, he has bound her not to talk, we would judge."[40]

Back in Mobile, Bishop Toolen wrote to tell Monsignor Kiley that it was Monsignor Bernardini who "is working for them and, through Bernardini, the Delegate." He had to admit that he had signed petitions for both the men and women and had even signed the petition for the apostolic indult to have Judge as spiritual director for life, "but that was before I knew as much as I do now." He went over the "get rich quick schemes" mentioned in the Kuhn petition and charged Father Judge with teaching the sisters that the bishop had nothing to do with them. "Can you blame me for not wanting him?" he asked Kiley, "He is a CM and he has just taken the rule of the CM's. He wants to be the visitor and have complete control." The bishop reviewed his objections to the men's constitutions. "If they are going to stay in the Diocese," he fumed, "I want to know where I stand." He assured Kiley that he would not sign the sisters' decree of erection "until I know that Judge will not be appointed as their Spiritual Director." "This," he told Kiley, "is the job I am putting on you, to accomplish this for me."[41] By signing both the petition for the sisters' canonical approval and the one for the apostolic indult, however, Bishop Toolen had made Monsignor Kiley's job very difficult.

Back to the Men's Constitutions

On January 17, 1931, Father Judge replied to Bishop Toolen's first pass over the men's constitutions. He insisted that there was nothing in it "claiming that we are a Papal Institute." It is the constitution of a "Diocesan Institute." Judge invoked the authority of Bernardini, who, he reported, had

40. Tonra, *Led by the Spirit*, 275, citing at length Mother Boniface's letter to Sister Michael.

41. Toolen to Kiley, Mobile, January 17, 1931, Toolen Papers, AAM.

pronounced the constitutions "substantially correct." How could he have said this "if there can be found anything that ignores the rights of the Ordinary"? "Surely," he continued, "we can feel safe in the present instance in taking the word of so eminent an authority as Monsignor Bernardini." Father Judge correctly cited to the bishop the norms from the Sacred Congregation for Religious for approving new congregations. They specifically exclude the rights of the ordinary from mention in the constitutions.[42] Judge assured the bishop that "if there be anything in our Constitutions that is not canonical, I am anxious to correct it." He pleaded with Toolen to allow the continued use of his letter of approval in *SOS for the Preservation of the Faith*, at least for the present month's issue.[43]

In the meantime, Bishop Toolen had forwarded his recent correspondence with Judge to one of his consultors, Abbot Bernard Menges of St. Bernard Abbey in Cullman, Alabama. He wanted the abbot's opinion on Father Judge's canonical argument about Fursman's ordination and eventually on the constitutions. Menges was convinced that in this matter, Father Judge had "expert advice, more than likely from Washington." His position on the house of studies and other points "show the hand of a Canonist." Abbot Bernard concluded, "Unless there are extraordinary developments at Trinity it will be many a year before the Ordinarius of the Motherhouse has any real say-so in the ordination of their young men [except] to send the litterae testimoniales." He promised to go over the constitutions when Father Hackett (another of Toolen's consultors) finished with them. He advised the bishop to "proceed in this whole affair with great caution so as not to give the other party Canonical grounds to stand on." He suggested that Toolen keep everything relative to Judge "in writing and on file in your office."[44]

By January 26, 1931, Abbot Bernard had made his own initial pass over the constitutions. He pronounced them "vague, loose and general—all but practical to actual conditions." Eventually, Father Judge would have "to come down from his imaginary hights [*sic*], leave future possibilities of expansion to outside and distant fields completely alone, and draw up something

42. Judge referred to *Acta*, 1921, page 317; see "Normae," March 6, 1921, from the Sacred Congregation of Religious, for approving new religious congregations. Caput IV, no. 22, e, excludes "omnia ea quae respiciunt munera et officia Episcoporum"; *Acta apostolicae sedis: Commentarium officiale*, Annus XIII, vol. XIII (Rome: Typis Polyglottis Vaticanis, 1921), 317.

43. Judge to Toolen, Gadsden, January 17, 1931, Toolen Papers, AAM.

44. Abbot Bernard Menges, OSB, to Toolen, St. Bernard, Ala. [Cullman], January 18, 1931, Toolen Papers, AAM. Bishop Toolen had earlier advised Judge to send students to the abbey rather than to the Catholic University of America.

practical covering the needs of a young community struggling for existence." He promised to go over the constitutions more thoroughly and encouraged Bishop Toolen to have the sisters send their constitutions for his "examination and approval."[45]

On the same day, January 26, Bishop Toolen's letter of January 15 caught up with Mother Boniface in Washington at the sisters' new house of studies on Newton Street NE. She gladly agreed to his proposal about the checking account, acknowledging his "generosity in cooperating so strongly with us." She explained that the Stirling project had begun two years before ground was broken on the hospital and that no hospital funds had been appropriated for any other use.[46]

Cardinal Dougherty Intervenes

At the Stirling meeting on January 16, 1931, the sisters authorized Mother Boniface to consult Cardinal Dougherty on their situation. When she tried to contact the cardinal, she learned that he was on a cruise and would dock in Cuba on February 1. On January 30, Mother Boniface and Sister Mary Francis sailed from Miami for Havana. After much difficulty making themselves understood and finding a place to stay in Havana, they found a convent of Dominican sisters from Philadelphia whose superior recognized them. They got in touch with Cardinal Dougherty through Archbishop Caruana's secretary and, on February 1, 1931, the cardinal himself came straight from the boat to the Dominican convent. According to Mother Boniface's account of their visit, he gave them all the time they needed and promised that "when we had peacefully abandoned the Diocese of Mobile, he would welcome us to Philadelphia and would be happy to receive us." The cardinal also gave his sympathetic approval to Father Judge as their spiritual director. But he didn't think the Missionary Servants of the Most Holy Trinity had anyone else at present capable of being their spiritual director, and so he was against the office passing to Father Judge's successors. He told Mother Boniface to write a letter specifying what they were asking. Cardinal Dougherty would bring it to his consultors and get back to her.[47]

While Mother Boniface was in the Dominican convent waiting for Cardi-

45. Menges to Toolen, Cullman, January 26, 1931, Toolen Papers, AAM.

46. Mother Boniface to Toolen, Washington, D.C., January 26, 1931, AST, MF 13027.

47. Tonra, *Led by the Spirit*, 276–77, for Mother Boniface's summary of the meeting with Cardinal Dougherty.

nal Dougherty's ship to arrive, Bishop Toolen had written to Monsignor Kiley in Rome emphasizing his determination to separate Father Judge from the sisters. He was convinced that Judge's "principal aim" was to "have charge of their finances so he may direct and use these as he pleases. He has been doing this in the past but it is only in the last six or eight months that I have found this out." He mentioned his unsuccessful attempts to get financial statements from Judge or the sisters. Toolen had made up his mind. "This is the opportunity to straighten this thing out. If he is appointed their superior, then the hope of straightening the sisters' affairs out will be gone, so I am not going to sign anything until I am sure that he will not be the superior, or if he is the superior, that I am not responsible in any way for conditions."[48]

Cardinal Dougherty made a speedy reply to Mother Boniface's letter. The consultors approved her request, and he promised to support the petition for the indult that would make Father Judge spiritual director for life, but not to have this office pass to his successors. Mother Boniface immediately cabled this news to Monsignor Bernardini in Rome, asking, "What shall we do next?" Bernardini cabled back that he would send a letter.[49] In the meantime, Father Judge had already written Bernardini to warn that charges from Bishop Toolen would be coming to Rome. His letter and the enclosed correspondence would make clear to Bernardini that Bishop Toolen had, by implication, questioned both his competence as a canonist and his integrity.[50] When Bernardini's letter to Mother Boniface finally arrived later in February, it made clear that Toolen's change of heart within such a short space of time had confused the Sacred Congregation. They were now willing to have Cardinal Dougherty sign the decree that Bishop Toolen had refused to sign. Bernardini advised her to send the constitutions to Dougherty and ask him to inform the Sacred Congregation for Religious of his willingness to erect the sisters in his archdiocese.[51]

Bishop Toolen Demands That the Sisters Decide

By mid-February 1931 Father Judge had left for Puerto Rico, and Bishop Toolen's patience was wearing thin. On February 15, Bishop Toolen wrote in

48. Toolen to Kiley, Mobile, January 31, 1931, Toolen Papers, AAM.

49. Tonra, *Led by the Spirit*, 277–78.

50. Judge to Bernardini, Holy Trinity, February 2, 1931, AST MF 1694; see note 37.

51. Tonra, *Led by the Spirit*, 280–81, citing Mother Boniface's summary to Motry of Bernardini's letter.

his own hand a blistering letter to Mother Boniface, the harshest she had yet received from him. She surmised in a letter to Father Judge that "Sr. Gertrude must have written him about our meeting in the North."[52] The bishop had been waiting for a reply to his January 15 letter and his two nonnegotiable points: (1) Father Judge could not be spiritual director; and (2) the motherhouse would not be rebuilt at Holy Trinity. "The time has come," he commanded, "when you must make a decision." He took for granted that they would choose to leave the diocese. If they did, Toolen said he would have to write to the bishop of their new diocese and to the Sacred Congregation for Religious. He had "investigated many of the reports that came to me and I am able to prove them conclusively now." In addition, he now believed that there had been some foundation to the charges of Father Klejna he had earlier dismissed.

Bishop Toolen wanted the financing of the hospital settled so work would not be held up. "I went into it," he wrote, "because of my confidence in Sister Gertrude's business ability and if she is taken out of this work, count me out also." He accused Mother Boniface of doing Sister Gertrude "a rank injustice" in believing that she had told the Bishop "all I know about the Trinitarians." Most upsetting to Mother Boniface, he also accused her of reading his mail. He ordered her to Mobile to see him before February 26.

> The day of temporizing is past. I want action and quick action. There is no room for argument or compromise on the points I laid down. Take them or leave them and it does not matter much to me what action you take. I have tried to go along with you and you have seen fit not to want to follow; so let us settle the question one way or the other and at once.[53]

Mother Boniface answered immediately and promised to be in Mobile before the 26th.[54] She forwarded the bishop's letter to Father Judge in Puerto Rico and summarized Cardinal Dougherty's letter: "He will not ask for the Spiritual Directorship to descend, but he would ask for you." "Sister Gertrude," she reported, "is very quiet and obedient. Sister Catherine Agnes not so much so." Then she told Judge that the letter Monsignor Bernardini promised in his cable had not come yet. This explained the delay that had aroused Bishop Toolen's ire.[55]

52. Mother Boniface to Judge, Holy Trinity, February 17, 1931, AST, MF 13031.
53. Toolen to Mother Boniface, Mobile, February 15, 1931, AST, MF 13028–30.
54. Mother Boniface to Toolen, Holy Trinity, February 17, 1931, Toolen Papers, AAM.
55. Mother Boniface to Judge, Holy Trinity, February 1931, AST, MF 13032.

The harsh tone of Bishop Toolen's letter led Father Judge to speculate on what might happen to the sisters left in Alabama after the motherhouse moved. "We are dealing with a situation," he wrote, "in which not only no mercy is being shown but the methods employed against us suggest ... the strategy of thugs and unprincipled brigands." He wanted clarification on Bishop Toolen's canonical rights over the sisters in his diocese once the motherhouse was established in another diocese. Would the bishop have the right to appoint superiors or call elections? What recourse would the sisters have "supposing interference, annoyance, and aggression continue"? What is the relative authority of the ordinary in whose diocese the motherhouse is located and the "Bishops in whose diocese they merely work"? He asked Mother Boniface to seek Louis Motry's opinion on these questions.[56]

Bishop Toolen and Father Judge on the Men's Constitutions

On February 19, 1931, as if to confirm Father Judge's fears, Bishop Toolen sent an eight-page, single-spaced response to Father Judge's January 8 and January 17 defense of his conduct and the constitutions. By this time, the bishop's own team of canonists had gone over the constitutions, and he was ready to match Father Judge canon for canon.[57] The first page of his letter rehearsed familiar issues, such as Fursman's ordination and the house of studies. Bishop Toolen forbade Father Judge to give retreats in the diocese without his permission and demanded that the question of a novitiate be settled. The next seven pages went over the constitutions in detail.

By this time, the full weight of the issue about the canonical status of the Missionary Servants of the Most Holy Trinity, and the novitiate as key to resolving it, had dawned on Bishop Toolen. Regarding canonical visitation, "It might well be asked," he told Judge with a note of triumph, which "persons and institutes are there to be visited? Has the Society any Brothers with Vows? Where did they make their novitiate?" Regarding the constitutions, Toolen could "hardly believe" that they were "ever read by a canonist." Most of his comments have to do with prerogatives of the ordinary he thought were ignored. Confirming the fears Father Judge expressed to Mother Boni-

56. Judge to Mother Boniface, Río Piedras, February 18, 1931, AST, MF 8244–47.

57. A comparison of Toolen's letter with this document establishes with strong probability that the document Toolen was commenting on is an undated, forty-page draft of the "CONSTITUTIONS of the Missionary Servants of the Most Holy Trinity," AST, MF 14295–334.

face, he insisted, citing Canon 492, no. 2, that, even when diocesan congregations expanded beyond the diocese, they remained "entirely subject" to the jurisdiction of the ordinary in their original diocese. The bishop emphasized the need to simplify the lengthy document, omitting quotations, even from scripture and ascetical and mystical theology, and bringing the terminology into conformity with the language of the canons.[58]

Father Judge returned from Puerto Rico by plane on February 27, 1931. It was his first plane ride, probably urged on by Brennan. Mother Boniface had cabled asking him to meet her in Newark. Flying, he told her, was "the only way I could make the States and be in New York by Monday." Judge's reaction to flying was typically devotional. He thought of the "Sacred Heart in the Holy Eucharist residing in the Tabernacles of the churches over which we are flying, and our own Fountains of the Precious Blood." His "message from the skies" continued, "It is easy up here to cry out with David to the mountains and fields, to the streams and the sea, and all things do indeed 'Praise the Lord.'"[59]

Father Judge's unanticipated return from Puerto Rico meant that Bishop Toolen's February 19 letter was delayed in reaching him. He did not respond until around March 21, 1931, by which time he was back at Holy Trinity giving the retreats leading up to the Feast of the Annunciation. He wrote a response dated March 21 but must have received Motry's comments soon after and incorporated them into a much longer undated response written around the same time. The letter's tone is one that a subordinate might use who knows that he has the better of his superior. It combines due respect bordering on obsequy for the person and office of the bishop with complete confidence in the content. At this point, Judge thought that the Redemptorists would provide a novice master and informed Toolen of this. He also belatedly asked permission to "give the retreat over the 25th of March."

Father Judge then launched into a detailed critique of the comments on the constitutions Bishop Toolen had sent on February 19. It came complete with Latin citations of the full texts of relevant canons and directives from the Sacred Congregation for Religious. As he stressed "fundamental mistakes made in the comments on the Constitutions," he was careful through-

58. Toolen to Judge, Mobile, February 19, 1931, from a copy in the Toolen Papers, AAM. "A Brief Answer to Father Judge's Letter" is with this letter in the Toolen Papers. Either a canonical report from one of his consultors, perhaps Abbot Bernard, or the Bishop's own notes, it served as a partial basis for the February 19 letter.

59. Judge to Mother Boniface, en route, February 27, 1931, AST, MF 8243; see also Judge to Sr. Mary Thomas Champion, Holy Trinity, February [probably 28], 1931, AST, MF 7019.

out to blame these on the bishop's "informant." He cited in Latin the norm from the 1921 directives of the Sacred Congregation on excluding the rights of bishops from constitutions and distinguished the ordinary as "External Superior" of diocesan congregations from the "Internal Superiors." "I am willing to abide by every letter of the Canon Law, but I cannot permit the Constitutions to be written with the view that the Local Ordinary be also the formal Internal Superior of the Institute."

In applying canon law to a congregation such as the Missionary Servants, Father Judge distinguished between the congregation "*in fieri*" and "*in facto esse*," the former being the infant stages to which he made frequent appeal, the latter being what they would become when fully grown. He might well have been accused of interpreting the congregation as *in fieri* when it suited him, and as *in facto esse* when it did not. But even here he could claim in each case to be interpreting the law in the way that best favored the congregation bound by it, especially when one considers that Bishop Toolen had already signed off on the constitutions in 1929 and that this was, as Judge pointed out, at best a "re-approval," it is difficult to read this letter without thinking that Dr. Motry had taken Abbot Bernard to school.[60]

Mother Boniface and Bishop Toolen

In his ultimatum letter of February 15, 1931, Bishop Toolen ordered Mother Boniface to Mobile before February 26. She was waiting for the letter Monsignor Bernardini had promised so she would know how to proceed in the meeting with the bishop. It came hours before she and Sister Mary Francis were to leave for Mobile on February 24 or 25 and gave her "new heart and courage."[61] Mother Boniface described this meeting with great sympathy for Bishop Toolen, whom she respected as honest and "naturally kind-hearted." She had told him that they had to leave the diocese. He was hurt by the ingratitude he thought such a move would show. He emphasized all he had done for them, that "no Bishop in the Country had been kinder to a Community than he had been to us," putting his diocese under a $200,000 obligation. She came away from the meeting thinking that he really didn't want them to leave. "Someone works him up," she felt. But things had gone

60. Judge to Toolen, Holy Trinity, March 21, 1931, AST, MF 13532. This is the initial letter. See also Judge to Toolen, Holy Trinity, no date, AST, MF 13540–44. This is the longer canonical critique of the comments in Bishop Toolen's February 19 letter.

61. Tonra, *Led by the Spirit*, 281, citing a letter from Mother Boniface to Louis Motry.

too far, and she did not see how they could stay. "I do feel sorry for him, but I will be happy when we are erected in another Diocese. I certainly feel that it is impossible to work here."

Bishop Toolen was worried for Sister Gertrude. What would happen to her if she left the community; what if she stayed? He told Mother Boniface that they would pray over this for a week. He asked her to send Sister Gertrude to see him in Baltimore in a week, and then, after that, he would see Mother Boniface, and they would settle it. Mother Boniface agreed, but she didn't want to meet with Bishop Toolen for a final decision about the move until she talked to Father Judge. This was her reason for cabling him in Puerto Rico and why he had to fly back to get to New York in time to see her. "Sister Gertrude is to go and see him at St. Edward's and I am to go afterwards, and we are to make the settlement. Hence my reason for cabling you today. I will make no decision until it is laid before you."[62]

The meeting in Baltimore was anticlimactic. "From his attitude," Mother Boniface explained to Monsignor Bernardini, "I would judge he has softened somewhat. He will not close Holy Trinity just now, but he still intends to keep Father Judge from having any connection whatsoever with the Sisters." Bishop Toolen didn't want to lose the sisters, but, if they left, he threatened to "write every Bishop in the country." For her part, Mother Boniface was "convinced that we could never develop as Missionary Servants of the Most Blessed Trinity in the Diocese of Mobile."[63] Mother Boniface did not formally tell Bishop Toolen where the sisters' motherhouse would move until May 9, 1931, when all the details were in place. But after the Baltimore meeting on March 8 or 9, he knew the sisters would not be staying in the Diocese of Mobile.

"The Trinitarian Sisters with headquarters in the Mobile Diocese are at the present time, I think, trying to negotiate with some Bishop to take them in." So began Bishop Toolen's letter to fellow bishops warning them against Father Judge and asking them not to accept the sisters into a new diocese while Toolen's case was still pending before the Sacred Congregation for Religious. Such a premature action, he warned, "might cause embarrassment to the one that takes them in and the Sisters themselves." The letter catalogued the charges from the Kuhn petition and added more having to

62. Tonra cites at length from Mother Boniface's descriptions of this meeting. They are filled with pathos for Sister Gertrude, Sister Catherine Agnes, and for the bishop himself; see *Led by the Spirit*, 280–84.

63. Ibid., 286–87, citing Mother Boniface's March 9 letter to Monsignor Bernardini.

do with the life of the sisters. He invoked Father Tomerlin as a witness that in 1919 Father Judge had lost $20,000 of the sisters' money investing in an ice machine and that there was "too much visiting going on between the places," the brothers' and sisters' sides at Holy Trinity.[64] Mother Boniface was shaken. "We are in deep waters. Bishop Toolen has written a long letter to all the Bishops against us, or rather against Father. . . . Don't know how it will end, but it is very serious now."[65]

St. Joseph and the Spiritual Perils of the Great Crisis

On December 31, 1930, Pope Pius XI published *Casti connubii*, his encyclical on Christian marriage. Though it gives a full treatment of marriage, this encyclical is best known for its natural-law argument against contraception in terms of the rights and obligations of the married state. During the month of March, in the days leading up to St. Joseph's Feast on March 19, Father Judge masterfully personalized this encyclical and translated it into the devotional-ascetical idiom he used to inspire his followers. He read it as a word directly from the pope addressed to sisters beset by the spiritual dangers of the great crisis. He frequently counseled prayer and charity toward Bishop Toolen and Sister Gertrude as community benefactors.[66] His circular letter on *Casti connubii* didn't mention the bishop, but it spoke clearly to the circumstances in which sisters might be tempted to speak ill of him.

The pope had written about the family. His concern is deeply related to St. Joseph, "head of the Holy Family," "Patron of the Christian family," and "Saint of the hour." The most important thing to learn from him is "the lesson of charity of speech." "Let us pray during the month of St. Joseph," he urged, to be "the peace maker, and the angel of God in our houses." The peace maker says, "Oh Lord, iniquity is not in my heart, neither is it on my lips."[67]

64. Toolen to Archbishop Michael J. Curley, Mobile, March 17, 1931, Curley Papers, Box 19, T 617, AAB.

65. Tonra, *Led by the Spirit*, 289, citing Mother Boniface to Sister Mary Thomas in Río Piedras.

66. See, for example, at this time, Judge to Mother Boniface, Holy Trinity, April 4, 1931, AST, MF 8251–53.

67. Judge to My dear Children, Holy Trinity, March 16, 1931, AST, MF 7023–24.

Depression-Era Finance and Father Tomerlin's "Plunge"

"The depression is gripping all," Father Judge wrote to Mother Boniface a few weeks after Bishop Toolen sent his letter to the other U.S. bishops. Responding to such "wild and unfair charges," Judge asked, "Why should we not experience it also?" Judge thought the finances were shaping up. Father Tomerlin, he reported, had very good plans to help St. Joseph's, which Judge described as "our anxiety." Bishop Toolen had signed for a $20,000 loan with St. Joseph's as collateral and was insisting that it be paid off. On Tomerlin's authority, Judge compared the finances of the Mobile Diocese unfavorably with that of the Missionary Servants. Tomerlin was getting a loan "through a money broker" who was charging a 2 percent fee. Tomerlin was paying an insurance company 5.5 percent. Judge wondered why he couldn't just get "a letter of approval from a Bishop" and borrow directly. Bishop Toolen's letter made that unlikely. Nevertheless, Judge closed this letter with Tomerlin's assurance that "the Missionary Servants are sitting pretty."[68]

But Father Tomerlin had also been talking to Bishop Toolen. Two days later, and the day after Mother Boniface asked the bishop for his help in getting another $200,000 to complete the hospital, Father Judge had to answer the bishop's charge, based on information from Tomerlin, that the community was in bankruptcy. "Bishop, I think you must be somewhat misinformed," he wrote, "because the fact of the matter is I do not handle the money. It has been my policy from the beginning to be free from the finances and consistently I have held to this, unless circumstances called me in to assist."[69] At that moment, Tomerlin was, at Toolen's insistence, in charge of the money at St. Joseph's.

A man with a long-established weakness for spending money he didn't have, caught in the ecclesiastical crossfire between his bishop and his religious superior, Father Tomerlin found himself scuffling for loans in a hardscrabble time. To keep his head above the rising tides of debt, he played both sides. Early in March, Father Judge had sent him to try to get Archbishop Curley to re-sign for a $19,500 note that was coming due. But Bishop Toolen's allegations about Judge's financial impropriety made this unlikely. A few weeks

68. Judge to Mother Boniface, Holy Trinity, April 9, 1931, AST, MF 8251–53.

69. Judge to Toolen, Holy Trinity, April 11, 1931, Toolen Papers, AAM. Defending himself from charges that he had spoken ill of the bishop, Father Judge claimed that "instead of detracting, I have repeatedly discoursed in private and public on the virtues that I see in you."

later, Judge reported that Curley told Brother Theophane Mulroy, "Your financial conditions are in a terrible way.... Tell Fr. Judge I will not renew."[70] With Tomerlin under pressure to find money, Judge worried that he might agree to unfavorable conditions. "Be sure and do not get yourself tied up into any conditions demanded of you by the people you borrow the money from."[71]

In charge of finances at St. Joseph's, Father Tomerlin continued to spend money he didn't have and, in Father Judge's estimate, to borrow recklessly. After Judge paid $55 for a shipment of turkeys at the Fort Mitchell train station, he learned that Tomerlin's order also included "pheasants, canaries, rabbits, pigeons, etc." "Father," Judge wrote in exasperation, "I am wondering what the Bishop and the priests of the diocese will say about this." At the same time, he learned that Tomerlin had borrowed $1,400 from a man Judge considered a disreputable lender. Then Judge received a notice from Yorktown Bank of New York City on another loan of $5,000 he didn't know about. "We need money, certainly, enough to discharge our debts, but for many reasons I should know where you are getting it." "Father, really," he continued, "I am upset over this matter. Let us be sure we sign nothing unless it is correct." He wanted to talk to Tomerlin and told him he would be in Newark in a few days.[72]

By midsummer Father Judge talked about finally "getting some relief from that terrific plunge of Father Tomerlin." He referred to it as "that N.Y mess."[73] The "terrific plunge" must have taken place in the spring. Perhaps he used the New York loan for a new building at Holy Trinity. On June 29, 1931, Father Judge wrote to Monsignor Nummey that he had decided to "make the break" with Tomerlin. He enclosed a letter he had written Tomerlin, instructing Nummey to tear it up after he read it. Tomerlin would no longer be in charge of things at Holy Trinity.[74] Brother James Norris took an increasing role in finances.[75] It would be at least another year, however, before the definitive break between Father Joseph Tomerlin and the Missionary Servants of the Most Holy Trinity.

70. Judge to Mother Boniface, Holy Trinity, April 9, 1931, AST, MF 8251. "This is a reflex of what good Bishop Toolen said to you," he added. "Evidently our affairs are well talked up between them."

71. Judge to Tomerlin, March 11, Holy Trinity, March 11, 1931, AST, MF 7022.

72. Judge to Tomerlin, Holy Trinity, March 14, 1931, AST, MF 7107.

73. Judge to [probably Mother Boniface], no place, no date, AST, MF 8259. This is a letter fragment. Reference to "Fr. Bede's being here [at Holy Trinity]" dates it to sometime between the end of July when the Capuchins agreed to send Fr. Bede Hermann as novice master and his arrival sometime in August.

74. Judge to Nummey, Brookland, D.C., June 29, 1931, AST, MF 7113.

75. In May Judge sent Norris to talk to Bishop Toolen about signing for yet another loan

On June 29, Father Judge was in Washington to ask the Capuchins for a novice master. He wrote to Monsignor Nummey from the house of studies where Nummey usually resided. Nummey had gone to Cuba to see Archibishop Caruana. From his days as a pastor in Brooklyn, the monsignor was a strong supporter of what Judge now called, following Pius XI, "our Cenacle Lay Apostolate." Nummey wanted the pope to know more of this work and thought Caruana and Dougherty would be well positioned to bring it to his attention.[76] The opening line of Father Judge's letter indicates that Nummey had become sick. The financial strain was taking its toll on idealistic priests who had come to work with the Cenacle. Within a year, Monsignor Nummey returned to Brooklyn, broken in health. On May 22, 1931, Judge heard from Father Lenahan that, with the sisters leaving for Philadelphia, he had developed health problems and decided to return to his diocese. Among the many and complex reasons for his "incapacity for the work," no doubt the financial anxiety at Holy Trinity figured significantly in his decision.[77]

As he tried to persuade Bishop Toolen and Archbishop Curley to write letters in support of new loans during the spring, Father Judge wrote half-jokingly, "Now, surely these most reverend gentlemen who are anxious to get off our paper should help us to get the people who will take their names off the paper."[78] Perhaps Brother James succeeded in getting a letter from one of them, probably Curley. "Today," Judge wrote Curley on June 8, "we paid off in full our indebtedness covered by notes bearing your endorsement."[79] The next day, he explained the details of this transaction to Mother Boniface. On the promise of a larger loan from Massachusetts Mutual Insurance Company, Judge had gotten a loan of $35,000 from the Riggs Bank, which he used to pay off the notes at the Brookland Bank that had Curley's signature. From an additional loan for $10,000, he paid the interest on the discharged notes, sent $5,000 to Mobile, and used $4,000 to pay off the balance at Huguenot Trust in New Rochelle.[80]

Father Judge failed to mention the rates of interest on these loans from

and talked about sending him with Msgr. Nummey to see Archbishop Curley for a similar request; see Judge to Mother Boniface, Philadelphia, May 21, 1931, AST, MF 8255.

76. Judge to Mother Boniface, Stirling, June 13, 1931, AST, MF 8264.

77. Lenahan to Judge, Philadelphia, May 22, 1931, Toolen Papers, AAM. This letter, along with Judge's reply of May 26, also from Philadelphia, were enclosed with Lenahan to Toolen, Philadelphia, May 29, 1931, asking for reassignment in the diocese and speaking of his "incapacity for the work."

78. Judge to Mother Boniface, Philadelphia, May 21, 1931, AST, MF 8255.

79. Judge to Curley, Silver Spring, June 8, 1931, Curley Papers, Box 19, J 466, AAB.

80. Judge to Mother Boniface, Brookland, D.C., June 9, 1931, AST, MF 8260–61.

the Riggs Bank and Mass Mutual. It is not clear that they had more favorable interest rates than the loans they were used to pay off. At this point, Judge could generate no optimism about the Depression-era economy. "Circulating amongst bankers in search of help," he wrote, "I find these gentlemen very doleful. They look for no alleviation unless in the remote future." The bankers anticipated "a serious slump" in the winter of 1931–32. He recommended "study of doing two things"—"building up our income" and "retrenching where we can."[81] By fall he had begun to talk of increasing revenue through mass-mailing appeals and bonds.

Building up Income with Bonds and Appeals

Father Judge knew that, if the community's priests spent all their time and energy trying to raise money, there would be little time for the work of the congregation. Bishop Toolen was right about this. In May Judge told Brennan that he was planning to meet at Stirling with a man who might be interested in "taking over the entire finances of our Institute."[82] "Toth called with Stenzel," Judge reported in October from West Orange, New Jersey, to Brother Joachim Benson at Holy Trinity. He was impressed with their height. Both were as tall as Fursman. Fursman, along with Brothers Augustine, James, Anthony, Andrew, and Turibius, joined Judge to meet with R. S. Toth of Chicago and Werner Stenzel of New York. Together they made up R. S. Toth and Associates. The agreement between Toth and Associates and the Missionary Servants of the Most Holy Trinity is dated October 1931.[83]

Toth wanted to clean up the lists for their mass-mailing "benefactors' appeal." But he also had a "new idea," which Father Judge thought James Norris had originated. He said Will Zeh, a Chicago businessman, had made a similar proposal ten years earlier and Judge had tried to pitch it to Mother Boniface. The new plan was "to issue bonds for five years, offering, say, six

81. Judge to Mother Boniface, Stirling, June 13, 1931, AST, MF 8264–65.

82. Judge to Brennan, Stirling, May 7, 1931, AST, MF 7109.

83. Judge to Benson, West Orange, N.J., October 21, 1931, AST, MF 1811. In an interview with Father David O'Connor on July 22, 1963, Father Turibius Mulcahy recalled this fall 1931 meeting with Toth and Stenzel. He claimed not to have been in favor of the bond proposal and that James Norris "convinced Fr. Judge that the 'Toth' Financial Firm in Chicago and their representative, Werner Stenzel, could handle it." Mulcahy remembered Stenzel as "a good and honest man. There were some doubts, however, about the Toth firm." When the bonds came due between 1935 and 1939, Mulcahy was tasked with paying out a debt he recalled as $680,000; typescript of interview, AST 2. A copy of the contract is also in AST. Stenzel told Norris of his intention to separate from Toth early in 1933; see Stenzel to Norris, New York, February 23, 1933, AST.

per cent interest. These bonds are taken up [to] $10,000 or decimals down to 100." The bonds would mature after five years and could become annuity bonds. "Toth is very hopeful of realizing immediate funds for us," he wrote. The problem was "how to wobble along" until January 15, 1932, when Toth thought he could have this scheme up and running. Benson was in charge of finances at St. Joseph's now. Judge apologized for not being able to send any cash. He thought that might be a good thing, "as I do not want you to get rich. That would worry me a whole lot."[84]

"I am going from pillar to post to get money for the Brothers and, if I can, for yourself," Father Judge wrote to Mother Boniface about a week later. He was still in the North. He was hoping for a "forty thousand dollars mortgage on Washington." He admitted the rate of interest would be 10 percent, but the loan would be long-term. "The value of a thing is determined by its need and we need money very badly." Judge didn't know the exact details. Regina Armstrong, a Cenacle associate who worked for an insurance company, was managing it. This loan would get them through until January, when the bond appeal for $125,000 would be ready to go out. "Toth is taking care of this," he explained. He promised a special letter explaining the bond issue. "In the meantime," he wrote, "another appeal, really the third letter of the first appeal, went out last Tuesday and a special appeal for our good benefactors—eighteen thousand will be going out next Monday." He described this as "tri-Cenacle appeal, Holy Trinity, Alabama, Holy Trinity Hill (Stirling), and Holy Trinity Heights (Silver Spring)." Toth had apparently merged the lists and contributed some of his own to come up with 18,000 names.[85]

Father Tomerlin

Removed from his position at St. Joseph's in his home state of Alabama and supplanted as the "Business Man" by the ascendancy of Toth and Stenzel, Father Tomerlin was out on the road, increasingly marginalized from the community, and at the mercy of his own weakness as a "plunger." By late October, Bishop Toolen was writing to find out if Tomerlin had "quit." He had heard this from priests in Mobile. "I missed his page out of the magazine this past month," Toolen wrote. "I would like to know if this is true as he is a member of this Diocese of Mobile and I feel some responsibility for him." To-

84. Judge to Benson, West Orange, N.J., October 21, 1931, AST, MF 1811.

85. Judge to Mother Boniface, Brooklyn, October 29, 1931, AST, MF 8286–87. James Norris seems to have masterminded the bond issue while Stenzel continued to refine the lists.

merlin thought he had been unfairly dismissed from his position as superior at St. Joseph's. Father Judge insisted that Tomerlin had forced the decision to remove him. "I referred to the building," Judge wrote, "as one instance that he plunged into and broke his promise."[86] With Toolen's inquiry in hand, Judge had to find Tomerlin.

After five days, Father Tomerlin showed up in New Jersey, where Father Judge was to dedicate a statue of the Little Flower at Gillette on All Saints Day. Tomerlin appeared on Halloween. Judge described him as "more subdued." Tomerlin denied that he wanted to leave the community. Judge insisted that he "live and work out of a Missionary Cenacle" and went on to speak about "Outer Missionary Cenacle work, or what the Holy Father says and thinks of the lay apostolate." Tomerlin asked Judge to show him how to do this work, and Judge promised to give a mission "to demonstrate the mode of instituting a new Outer Cenacle."[87] Tomerelin was back in the fold, but his resolve would not last.

The Sisters' "Hegira" to Philadelphia

In March 1931, Father Judge gave his last retreat at Holy Trinity. Mother Boniface arrived the night of March 24. The last sixteen postulants to enter the sisters at Holy Trinity were received on March 25. The decision to go to Philadelphia was done, and Mother Boniface was working out the details with Cardinal Dougherty. Shortly after the reception of the postulants, she left Holy Trinity to look for a place in Philadelphia. At Dougherty's urging, she also consulted with Archbishop Fumasoni-Biondi in Washington. Judge also went north to request from the Capuchins a novice master for the brothers. The Redemptorist provincial in the United States had informed him that their general and his consultors had decided against lending a novice master to the Missionary Servants. With both Judge and Tomerlin gone, Father

86. Judge quotes from Bishop Toolen's letter in a postscript to Mother Boniface found in a letter fragment at AST, MF 8282. Regarding Tomerlin's removal, Judge had earlier written Mother Boniface about "our Birmingham confrere's broken promises, defaulted notes and bad checks. I just want to tell you that action was not taken one minute, not even one second too soon in getting him out of office." Judge replaced Tomerlin at St. Joseph's with Joachim Benson and reported that creditors were relieved at Benson's consistency in paying his bills; see Judge to Mother Boniface, Holy Trinity, August 27 (?), 1931, AST, MF 8276–77.

87. Judge to Mother Boniface, Stirling or Gillette, All Saints Eve '31, AST, MF 8288–89. Judge attributed Tomerlin's appearance to Sister Carmel's prayers to St. Joseph. Judge preached the next day on the "Little Way" of St. Therese. He insisted that renewal of family life was necessary for recovery from the Depression; see "Sermon Delivered at Unveiling of the Statue of the Little Flower in Gillette, N.J.," *Holy Ghost*, December 1931, 20–23.

Eugene Brennan filled in at Holy Trinity and presided at Holy Week services but left abruptly. Father Judge had to return so as not to leave Holy Trinity without a priest. Mother Boniface described him as "getting out of a sickbed" at Stirling to go.[88]

"Every moment since you left, I have been on the bridge," Father Judge wrote to Brennan on May 7. Despite the fact that Brennan had left prematurely, Judge didn't reprimand him but thanked him profusely for filling in at Holy Trinity. He told Brennan how his presence had prevented Bishop Toolen from coming down on Judge for having left Holy Trinity without a priest. "You see what a sedative you can be to an upset mind."

"This is the latest bulletin," Father Judge announced. "The Sisters have rented a house in Philadelphia. All are very much pleased from His Eminence down. The hegira begins next Monday or Tuesday."[89] The sisters had signed a six-month lease on a three-story house at 5220 Wynnefield Ave. On May 9, Mother Boniface informed Bishop Toolen of the move in a formal letter. She assured him that the sisters would be glad to continue their work in his diocese. She didn't know whether he would permit this. When she told Bishop Toolen that the sisters' "sympathy or interest for the Southern missions" would not diminish, she meant what she said. She had lived and worked in Alabama since 1916. She loved Holy Trinity and the Southern missions. She hoped their new location would enable them "to do more for the South." She disputed the charge made by Father Cullen, that they had been "disobedient." "You know, Bishop," she argued, "that we are canonically free to leave since there has been no decree of erection signed, and secondly, we have both your verbal and written permission to go." She concluded with assurances of their gratitude for all Toolen had done for them.[90]

On May 11, 1931, forty sisters, including Mother Boniface and novices and postulants, boarded the train in Columbus bound for Philadelphia. They had a passenger car to themselves for the trip. When the train stopped in Washington, Father Louis Motry and a group of sisters met them at Union Station.

88. On March 31, Father Judge wrote to Bishop Toolen from Silver Spring, thanking him for permission to give the retreat. He enclosed a letter from the Redemptorist provincial regarding a novice master. "I promise you," he wrote Toolen, "that I will indeed keep behind the matter of obtaining a Novice Master, in fact, that explains my presence in Washington at this moment"; Judge to Toolen, Silver Spring, March 31, 1931, Toolen Papers, AAM. Judge was responding to Toolen's letter of March 28, of which there is no copy in the Toolen Papers. Andrew B. Kuhn, CSsR, to Judge, Brooklyn, March 24, 1931, is filed with Judge's letter of March 31 in the Toolen Papers. On events at Holy Trinity in March, see Tonra, *Led by the Spirit*, 290–91.

89. Judge to Brennan, Holy Trinity, May 7, 1931, AST, MF 7108–10.

90. Mother Boniface to Toolen, Holy Trinity, May 9, 1931, Toolen Papers, AAM.

They arrived in Philadelphia the next afternoon. Father Judge, Brother Augustine, Monsignor Nummey, Father Lenahan, and a contingent of sisters met them at the station.

Cardinal Dougherty missed their arrival at Wynnefield Avenue but left "an immense basket of flowers" that Mother Boniface described as "the most beautiful thing I ever looked at." The cardinal returned later in the afternoon and went out of his way to welcome everyone. In his remarks, he assured the sisters that it was God's will they were there. They could be sure of that because they had not sought to move. He returned the next morning to say Mass for them and immediately gave permission for daily adoration at the motherhouse. Using one of her favorite words, Mother Boniface enthused, "I just cannot begin to tell you how lovely he was to us."[91]

The sisters at Holy Trinity, the novices and postulants, had only heard about the move a few days before it happened. Father Judge's remarks addressed their sadness and surprise at leaving Holy Trinity. "You have loved Holy Trinity, Alabama much." It would be only natural to wonder why they had to leave "that sacred place." "Because God has willed it," was his reply. "Why has He willed it? That is God's secret. As St. Paul says: 'For who hath known the mind of the Lord? Or who hath been his counsellor?' (Rom 11:34)." But they could search for the reason. He thought of Habacuc, reluctant prophet of the book of Daniel. "Looking back now over recent months, we are reminded of Habacuc, the Prophet. Habacuc was told to go from Judea to Daniel in the lion's den. 'And Habacuc said: Lord, I never saw Babylon, nor do I know the den.' And the Angel of the Lord took him by the top of his head, and carried him by the hair of his head, and set him in Babylon' (Dn 14:34–35)."

He repeated his conviction that keeping the Mother Missionary Cenacle at Holy Trinity had certainly been "up to a few months ago" God's will. "Since then, we have had reason added to reason to make us know that it was the will of God that the transfer be made." Into the striking figure of an angel-borne prophet, Father Judge's scripture-drenched imagination merged their shock and resistance at the move with the consolation that it was what God wanted. There was no mention of Bishop Toolen. It was God who had brought them Habacuc-like from Holy Trinity and set them down in Philadelphia. Who could argue with that? As the time for the Pentecost novena approached, he wished them peace.[92]

91. Mother Boniface wrote a long letter describing their trip, their arrival, and the new motherhouse for all the sisters; it is reproduced in Tonra, *Led by the Spirit*, 295–98.

92. From a transcription of Judge's remarks at Philadelphia, dated May 12, 1931, AST, MF 7111–12.

❖ 14

HOLY NAME OF JESUS HOSPITAL AND THE LAST DAYS OF MOTHER BONIFACE

Despite Bishop Toolen's warning, Cardinal Dougherty took the sisters in. The motherhouse moved from rural Alabama to Wynnefield Avenue in Philadelphia. The fate of their work in the Mobile Diocese remained uncertain. Mother Boniface faced the challenge of negotiating financial terms with a hurt and resistant Bishop Toolen that would make possible the completion of the new Holy Name of Jesus Hospital. Bishop Toolen desperately wanted Father Judge out of his hair for good. At the same time, he had no desire to be stuck with the debt on a half-completed hospital in Gadsden. His dread at this prospect gave him incentive for continuing to help the sisters finance the hospital.

The Contract with Bishop Toolen to Finance the Hospital

Construction of the new Holy Name of Jesus Hospital began in July 1930. The $250,000 in notes that Bishop Toolen had already signed financed the first phase of construction. The project's supervising engineer, John P. Burke, was the husband of Florence Conlon, a nurse who had been a Cenacle associate in New England. Sister Gertrude persuaded Burke to supervise the building project, and in June 1929 he moved his family to Holy Trinity.[1] By spring 1931, Burke had run out of funds to pay the contractors. On April 10,

1. See Florence Conlon Burke, "Early Journal," 1–5, citing the correspondence between Sister Gertrude and Burke.

Mother Boniface wrote Bishop Toolen a letter that began simply, "Would you please help us to obtain the $200,000 needed to complete our new hospital in Gadsden, Alabama?" Not counting appeals and donations, she reported an assured monthly income of $5,680. If he agreed, she promised to deposit $2,187 each month in their joint account. This amount represented the monthly interest on a debt of $450,000 for the hospital. She arrived at $2,187, she explained, by "figuring the monthly portion of the annual interest on $50,000 at 5.5 percent, $200,000 at 5.75 percent, and the new $200,000 possibly at 6 percent." She promised not to sell any of the community's holdings in Alabama without the bishop's approval unless or until the entire $450,000 had been paid off. If Toolen did approve any sales, the money would go into their joint account "to be used to decrease the principal of this indebtedness."[2]

Her request came to the bishop as he was confronting Father Judge with Father Tomerlin's claim that the men's community was in bankruptcy. Bishop Toolen felt betrayed by what he saw as the sisters' ingratitude for all he had already done for them. It was the middle of the Great Depression. He knew that no financial institution in Alabama or anywhere else was likely to lend the sisters money unless he vouched for them. He had no use for a half-completed hospital and a debt of $250,000 with his name on it. He consulted an attorney, T. R. Shannon, whom he described to Archbishop Curley as "one of the best lawyers in Mobile."[3]

On April 15, Mother Boniface and a group of sisters including Sister Gertrude, Sister Mary James, and Sister Stephen met with the bishop in Mobile at his request. Father Cullen, Monsignor Hackett, and the attorney, T. R. Shannon, were also there. Shannon was there, Mother Boniface thought, "to impress upon us the seriousness of the Gadsden problem." The bishop and his consultors now knew that Philadelphia would be the sisters' new diocese. Father Cullen accused them of disobedience, suggesting that, if Cardinal Dougherty didn't agree to Father Judge as spiritual director, the sisters would leave the church. As the meeting ended, Bishop Toolen concluded that he had done enough for them and could do no more.[4]

By the next day, however, according to Mother Boniface's account, the bishop had changed his mind. He proposed a contract, spelling out the con-

2. Mother Boniface to Bishop Toolen, April 10, 1931, AST, MF 13033.

3. Toolen to Curley, May 29, 1931, Curley Papers, Box 19, T 618, AAB.

4. Mother Boniface's account of this meeting is quoted at length in Tonra, *Led by the Spirit*, 292–93.

ditions under which he would agree to sign for the new loan. At this point, Bishop Toolen had not announced a decision about whether the sisters could stay in the diocese. It is possible that he thought that, once they moved to Philadelphia, they would reincorporate and Cardinal Dougherty would be responsible for the debt on the hospital. On April 16, T. R. Shannon sent a one-page report to Toolen, concluding that, except for two possible scenarios, he saw "no way to relieve you of liability on notes you have endorsed." Both scenarios depended on the corporation remaining in Alabama. What Toolen finally decided seems closest to Shannon's second scenario. Bishop Toolen told Archbishop Curley that it was Shannon who drew up the contract.[5]

Bishop Toolen and Mother Boniface did not reach agreement on the contract until almost six weeks after the events of April 15 and 16. In the meantime, John P. Burke needed funds for construction's next phase. On May 5, 1931, he sent Bishop Toolen "the first inspection of this job by a representative of the architects." The architect's report concluded that, regarding heating, plumbing, electrical wiring, elevator, dumbwaiter, lighting fixtures, terrazzo floors, and plastering, "everyone who has visited the job seems to be very much impressed with the looks of the building and the quality of the workmanship."[6] Nevertheless, Bishop Toolen and Mother Boniface could not agree on the terms of the contract.

On May 7, 1931, Father Judge, in a long letter to Father Eugene Brennan in Puerto Rico, expressed confidence that Toolen would sign for the additional $200,000. "Our good friend in the South seems quite willing to sign for the Holy Name of Jesus Hospital provided etc., etc., etc., be followed out. Some of these are impossible but he will sign." He described Mother Boniface "as bringing the thing to an issue." The sisters also had conditions, and he was confident that Bishop Toolen would accede to them rather than have a half-completed hospital turned over to him.[7]

5. Here is Shannon's second scenario: "make the loan on the hospital large enough to complete the same and you endorse as Security the mortgage and protect your liability by taking a mortgage from the Alabama corporation on all their property in the State or else allow the Alabama corporation to mortgage their real estate and release your liability and complete the Hospital; all of which is contingent on the corporation remaining in the State"; T. R. Shannon to Toolen, Mobile, April 16, 1931, Toolen Papers, AAM. I have been unable to find a copy of the original contract Bishop Toolen proposed to Mother Boniface on April 16.

6. J. E. Dutcher, Office Memo, Schmidt, Garden and Erikson, re. Holy Name of Jesus Hospital, enclosed with Burke to Toolen, Gadsden, May 5, 1931, Toolen Papers, AAM.

7. Judge to Brennan, Stirling, May 7, 1931, AST, MF 7109.

On May 8, 1931, Mother Boniface told Bishop Toolen that the sisters of "the Eastern and Southern corporations" were strongly inclined not to sign it. As she explained in a letter to Sister Miriam, "the contract puts Sr. Gertrude in charge of funds for ten years."[8] In other words, Sister Gertrude would be procurator for the next ten years. Without mentioning Sister Gertrude's name, Mother Boniface explained that this clause in the contract "interferes with the internal workings of the Community." The sisters found that "a guarantee in office such as the contract calls for, is unheard of in religious life and might prove detrimental to the subject and to the Community."[9]

By May 28, 1931, Bishop Toolen relented on keeping Sister Gertrude as procurator for the life of the loan. In a meeting with Mother Boniface that morning, he also relented on a clause that required all appeal money to go into their joint account. The contract also required the sisters to put $25,000 into the hospital—no doubt the amount that came in as donations after the fire. Mother Boniface explained that she only had $10,000 left, as they had to give $15,000 to Burke.[10] Instead of paying off both their Alabama notes, one in Gadsden and one in Mobile, Toolen insisted only on the Mobile note. Mother Boniface still balked at the contract's stipulation of a monthly payment on the principal. Toolen cut it to a quarterly payment, "and when the time came, if we couldn't pay it, to pay it when we could." By that afternoon, Shannon had revised the contract, and Mother Boniface had it in her hands.

Mother Boniface was "knocked out" by the contrast between the Bishop Toolen of April 15 and 16 and the Bishop Toolen of May 28, "just as lovely as you could imagine anyone could be." Amazed by the change, she attributed it all to the Holy Name. "I surely think," she told Father Judge, "that the Holy Name which is now towering over Gadsden just took care of the hospital and the whole affair, and Bishop Toolen is with us as strong today as he ever was." It was almost done. "We are to sign the papers, I mean the two corporations will, send them to him and he will wire St. Louis and send Mr. Burke the ready cash. The hospital is to go straight through without any holdup."[11]

8. Mother Boniface to Sister Miriam Lonergan, Holy Trinity, May 21, 1931, as cited by Tonra, *Led by the Spirit*, 298.

9. Mother Boniface to Bishop Toolen, Holy Trinity, May 8, 1931, Toolen Papers, AAM.

10. As Sister Mary James explained to the bishop in a letter of June 8, they had given money to Burke "from time to time as he could not wait for the loan to go through." She had sent Burke's reports to document the payments to him; see Collins to Toolen, Pensacola, June 8, 1931, AST, MF13044.

11. Tonra cites at length Mother Boniface's account of her May 28 meetings with Bishop Toolen; see *Led by the Spirit*, 300.

The next day, Bishop Toolen wrote to Archbishop Curley explaining the terms of his agreement with the sisters. Added to monthly interest payments, the quarterly payments were steep, amounting to $30,000 on the principal per year for ten years. "I have made the contract air-tight," he told Curley, "and it covers all property owned by the corporation in Alabama and the New Jersey corporation and if they are forming a corporation in Pennsylvania, where they now have their Mother-house, this corporation also." He consulted with Shannon, and they "felt this was the best solution of the problem." He expressed his relief at Monsignor Kiley's report from Rome assuring him that the Sacred Congregation for Religious would not allow the sisters to default on their debts. By May 28 the consultation with Shannon and Kiley's assurances convinced the bishop that the best way to cover his liability was to get the sisters to sign the contract. Bishop Toolen wanted desperately to be free of financial liability for the Missionary Servants. "The Sisters," he told Curley, "are taking up all notes in Alabama amounting to about $29,000."[12]

"I think you have made a good financial deal with the sisters," Archbishop Curley replied on June 1. He reported that he had seen Archbishop Fumasoni-Biondi recently but had no opportunity to bring up "the Judge situation." He told Toolen that "in your difficulties with Judge, you certainly have the sympathy of the CM's." He described the U.S. visitor, Father Maune, as "delighted" that the superior general had put Judge under Father McHale's jurisdiction. He recommended sending McHale "an outline of the situation." "I feel," he continued, "that Father McHale is friendly to Judge and in this matter has taken his cue from the present Delegate and Cardinal Bonzano."

Archbishop Curley was sure that McHale "did not understand the situation as you have it in hand." He advised Toolen against going to Rome himself—bad advice, perhaps—and thought it would be enough, regardless of what Fumasoni-Biondi might do, to send to Kiley "certified copies of the evidence you have concerning the unfitness of Judge." "After all, no matter what his [Fumasoni-Biondi's] attitude may be, he will always be subject to the decisions of the Congregation of Religious."[13] Events proved that Curley underestimated both the extent and the nature of Father Judge's support.

12. Toolen to Curley, Mobile, May 29, 1931, Curley Papers, Box 19, T 618, AAB. Mother Boniface later reported to Father McHale that "a Philadelphia lawyer said it was 'a regular Shylock contract,' although the Bishop did not hesitate to say that he was very, very sorry that the Sisters had left his Diocese"; cited by Tonra, *Led by the Spirit*, 315, from a letter written shortly after the dedication of the hospital on September 14, 1931.

13. Curley to Toolen, Baltimore, June 1, 1931, Curley Papers, Box 19, T 619, AAB.

The witness of the sisters convinced McHale, a series of apostolic delegates, Cardinal Dougherty, Motry, Bernardini, and others that Father Judge was not just another ecclesiastical-political player. From a religious perspective, he appeared to them as the genuine article. As Mother Boniface put it to the bishop in January, "Whatever good our Community has accomplished in the past we felt, under God, we owed to the inspiration of Father Judge."[14]

Delays

Financing the hospital didn't go as smoothly as the May 28, 1931, meeting led Mother Boniface to expect. On June 6, 1931, John P. Burke sent Sister Mary James the total payments due for April and May, about $47,500; $147,000 was still due on the hospital. Burke had received to date $266,000. Sister Mary James forwarded Burke's statements to Bishop Toolen.[15] After the May 28 meeting, the "spirit" of his reply proved a "great surprise" to her. On June 8, she wrote reminding the bishop of the concessions he had made on the evening of May 28 regarding their Alabama notes and the money already paid to John Burke. "I am at a loss to understand the change," she wrote, "as we certainly felt that relations between Bishop Toolen and the Missionary Servants of the Most Blessed Trinity were most amicable and that all difficulties had been adjusted to the satisfaction of each." Sister Mary James expressed her confusion. "You seemed willing to do everything to make the situation less difficult for us, and as you know we are anxious to complete the hospital as soon as possible we thought you were going to do everything to expedite matters."[16]

Bishop Toolen had raised questions about "the bookkeeper and the salaries of the Sisters in Mobile and Birmingham." Sister Mary James forwarded these to Mother Boniface, who wrote to Toolen. He responded on June 11. The sisters, he claimed, failed to send the June 1 interest payment of $2,187 stipulated in the contract. "A month's interest on the money in Montgomery is now due. I do not feel that I should go ahead and borrow the rest of the money until you have carried out this part of the contract." He insisted that the

14. From Mother Boniface's account of her January 7 meeting with Toolen, as cited in Tonra, *Led by the Spirit*, 271.

15. J. P. Burke to Sr. Mary James Collins, Gadsden, June 6, 1931, and Sr. Mary James to Toolen, Pensacola, June 6, 1931, Toolen Papers, AAM.

16. Sister Mary James Collins to Toolen, Pensacola, June 8, 1931, AST, MF 13044. I do not have Toolen's letter to which she is replying.

contract be carried out to the letter, "that interest be paid monthly and the quarterly $7,500 be sent in promptly," this latter in contrast to Mother Boniface's account of his flexibility on the quarterly payment on May 28. The additional $200,000 loan was to come from Bitting and Co. in St. Louis. Bishop Toolen told Mother Boniface that they were "sending notes down today and as soon as they are signed by you and Sr. Mary James and the conditions of the contract are carried out, the money will be forthcoming."[17]

Mother Boniface replied on June 16, 1931. By this time, preliminary steps were underway to have the money released. She told the bishop that Sister James had arrived last night with "the Bitting note" and would deposit the interest money that day. Mother Boniface was filling out the signature card for their joint account. "I note," however," she wrote, "that it says on the card in case of the death of one of the signers the right to draw on the whole account goes to the surviving party. Of course, I do not expect to die???? and then what?"[18] Toolen had the bank change the card to "Mother Boniface and Successors."

Sister Mary James returned the signed note to him on June 20, and he sent it to Bitting in St. Louis. "So I suppose," he wrote, "the money will be forthcoming in about a week." He asked how many sisters were left at Holy Trinity and what they did. He also noted that he had not seen an announcement of the move of the motherhouse.[19] Comparing Sister Mary James's business acumen unfavorably with Sister Gertrude's, he noted the "many questions that are not clear in my mind in regard to the whole transaction." He didn't know, for example, whether the sisters had actually contributed the $25,000 called for by the agreement. He asked Mother Boniface to have Sister Gertrude visit him in Baltimore after July 1.[20]

Release of the loan money dragged on through June and into July 1931. The bishop sent John Burke what he needed to pay for materials and work during April and May, but the final $200,000 was still not forthcoming.[21] On June 27, Sister Mary James asked him for the money to meet the June esti-

17. Bishop Toolen to Mother Boniface, Mobile, June 11, 1931, AST, MF 13046–47.

18. Mother Boniface to Bishop Toolen, Holy Trinity, June 16, 1931, AST, MF 13050. Mother Boniface died five months later, on November 22, 1931.

19. Bishop Toolen to Mother Boniface, Mobile, June 20, 1931, AST, MF 13052. Mother Boniface replied on June 30 explaining the work of the fifteen Sisters at Holy Trinity. She referred him to the May 22 *Philadelphia Catholic Standard and Times* for the announcement. The announcement would also appear in the July number of the *Holy Ghost*. Mother Boniface to Bishop Toolen, Newark, June 30, 1931, AST, MF 13054.

20. Bishop Toolen to Mother Boniface, Mobile, June 22, 1930, AST, MF 13053.

21. Burke to Toolen, Gadsden, June 25, Toolen Papers, AAM.

mates. "As Mr. Burke is rushing the work," she wrote hopefully, "I know he will be anxiously looking for the next installment of the loan from Bitting." She assured him the July 1 interest payments would be met.[22] Bitting and Co. had decided to sell bonds on the hospital building.[23] On July 7, Father Cullen sent Mother Boniface "a package of 265 pieces, representing a $215,000 issue of direct obligation bonds of the Bishop of Mobile and the Missionary Servants of the Most Blessed Trinity." Mother Boniface and Sister Mary James were to sign and seal them and send them to Bishop Toolen in Baltimore. "Please attend to this as soon as possible," Cullen urged, "as Bitting is rather anxious to have this whole affair straightened out at once."[24] They were not the only ones.

Sister Gertrude Takes Her Leave

On July 11, 1931, as Bishop Toolen requested, Sister Gertrude went to see him in Baltimore. Since Sister Mary James was now the procurator, Mother Boniface sent her along, too.[25] Mother Boniface traveled from Philadelphia to Baltimore the next day, probably bringing the signed bonds with her. She went to see the bishop about the opening of the hospital. He told her he wouldn't be there and they could have anybody they wanted. He also gave permission for Father Judge to give the retreat at Holy Trinity in August, but refused permission for the annual pilgrimage. Mother Boniface told the sisters at the hospital to plan for a September 14 dedication but leave open the details in case the Bishop changed his mind.[26]

At their meeting of July 11, Bishop Toolen urged Sister Gertrude to remain in the community. After a seven-hour meeting with Mother Boniface sometime around mid-July, however, she decided to leave. Mother Boniface wrote a letter of dismissal to Sister Catherine Agnes. The Sisters' Council had judged her "unable to acquire the spirit of the Community." She had until August 6 to leave.[27] Some months later Catherine Agnes Kuhn had a

22. Sister Mary James to Bishop Toolen, Philadelphia, June 27, 1931, Toolen Papers, AAM.

23. Shannon informed Father Cullen that the bonds would be legal; T. R. Shannon to Rev. Philip Cullen, Mobile, June 15, 1931, Toolen Papers, AAM.

24. Cullen to Mother Boniface, Mobile, July 7, 1931, Toolen Papers, AAM.

25. Mother Boniface to Bishop Toolen, Philadelphia, July 8, 1931, AST, MF 13058; Mother Boniface to Rev. Philip Cullen, Philadelphia, July 11, 1931, AST, MF 13057.

26. Tonra, *Led by the Spirit*, 307.

27. Ibid., 307–8, citing Mother Boniface to Sister Mary of the Precious Blood and Mother Boniface to Sister Catherine Agnes Kuhn.

petition drawn up requesting Pope Pius XI to "remove from her name the stigma of this unjust dismissal." Whether it was ever submitted to the Holy See is unclear.[28]

Completion of the Hospital in Sight

Despite plans for a September 14, 1931, dedication, by July 18 Sister Mary James still did not know if Bishop Toolen had sent the signed bonds to Bitting. They had a commitment from Massachusetts Mutual to take over the bonds from Bitting once the hospital was complete. She now knew that, since Bitting had yet to release the funds, the hospital would not be finished by August 1 and Mass Mutual would not take over. Without the funds from Bitting, they could not pay off the $15,000 loan in Atlanta that Bishop Toolen wanted liquidated according to the terms of the contract. So she had to hope that the loan could be carried for another month and that Mass Mutual would be willing to wait. "However," she wrote, with a note of desperation, "all this rests on word from Bitting, Massachusetts Mutual, and Kohn [Montgomery]." She promised to let Bishop Toolen know as soon as she heard from them. "I suppose," she added hopefully, "the bonds have gone to Bitting e'er this and we will hear from them in a few days."[29]

Bitting and Bishop Toolen must have released the money sometime later in July, and Burke was able to push the hospital through to completion by the end of August. On September 4, 1931, Sister Mary James sent the bishop

28. A copy of Kuhn's petition (fifteen typed pages, double-spaced) is preserved on legal-size paper in the Toolen Papers. It is undated, but internal evidence suggests that it was put in final form after December 1932, when the brothers' bonds were issued. The bond issue is mentioned on page 11. At least twenty-four "Exhibits" or supporting documents are referred to in the text, but I failed to locate them. A letter from a New York canonist to Bishop Toolen suggests that the petition may never have been submitted. The canonist, James P. Kelly, concluded that the dismissal was invalid because it had not been carried out at the direction of the local ordinary. But Kelly advised that Kuhn was incompetent to bring charges. This could only be done by the ordinary in whose diocese this "irregularity" took place. By August 1931, the sisters had removed to Philadelphia. Cardinal Dougherty would have to cooperate with Bishop Toolen in bringing this case to the Sacred Congregation for Religious. Referring to the supporting documents, Kelly suggested using the dismissal as "an opening wedge, and, if your Excellency would cooperate, we could bring up the irregularities rather as obiter dicta." The "irregularities" in question had to do with the allegations in the supporting documents, primarily regarding Father Judge's financial improprieties. Kelly told Bishop Toolen that he had written to Cardinal Dougherty; see James P. Kelly to Bishop Toolen, New York City, January 12, 1932, Toolen Papers, AAM. It seems unlikely that Dougherty would have cooperated in the petition. I found no correspondence in his papers indicating that he did.

29. Sister Mary James to Bishop Toolen, Philadelphia, July 18, 1931, AST, MF 13059.

a note from Mother Boniface asking him to instruct Father Cullen to release the $10,000 from the joint account "to be used on the note in Montgomery." Thanking him for his kindness in signing the note in the first place, she assured him of the sisters' prayers "even if you don't like us any more." She hoped that eventually "all these misunderstandings will be cleared up and the atmosphere will be cleared."[30]

A Brave Attempt to Smash the Brothers' Community to Pieces

"I am going to keep behind him until I force him to pay the notes, amounting to $19,000," Bishop Toolen told Archbishop Curley in May 1931. "Then I will be free from him."[31] The bishop was talking about Father Judge. Through spring and deep into summer 1931, Bishop Toolen made sure that the sisters kept to every detail of the "air-tight" May contract. At the same time, he continued his campaign to get out from under Father Judge. At the beginning of 1931, Toolen had three concerns. First, he wanted Judge to pay off the $19,000 balance on the loan he mentioned to Curley. Second, he wanted a canonical novitiate for the brothers' community. Third, he wanted to see the constitutions, which he regarded as vague and visionary. He questioned whether he had even seen them and whether he had indeed signed the brothers' decree of erection.

Finally, beneath all of this was the issue of Brother Paul Anthony's ordination. As ordinary of the diocese where their motherhouse was located, Bishop Toolen insisted that neither Fursman nor any other Missionary Servant could be ordained without dimissorial letters from him. If Father Judge were unable to get any of the brothers ordained, the issues of a canonical novitiate and the constitutions would be moot.

As early as 1929 or 1930, after Bishop Toolen had refused to advance Brother Paul Anthony to tonsure and major orders, Father Judge wrote a petition to the Sacred Congregation for Religious for a "rescript giving me faculties to issue dimissorial letters." His petition described the delay as a "serious check to the progress of this young Community." Three young men were "now awaiting the call to orders." Such a disappointing delay could "mean for us a loss of vocations to a very necessary work in the United States, that

30. Ibid., Gadsden, September 4, 1931, with enclosure from Mother Boniface, Toolen Papers, AAM.

31. Toolen to Curley, Mobile, May 29, 1931, Curley Papers, Box 19, T 618.

of the Preservation of the Faith and also the Abandoned Home Missions."[32]

Father Judge worked furiously during spring 1931 to meet Bishop Toolen's demands about the loan, the novitiate, and the constitutions. He also pursued with Father Motry the canonical case for Brother Paul Anthony's ordination without dimissorial letters from Bishop Toolen. In the early months of 1931, Judge counted on Tomerlin to raise the $19,000. By April 24, 1931, he had to report Tomerlin's failure to the bishop. "I, on my part, am now taking up the task and I will spare neither labor nor pain to accomplish it." He assured Bishop Toolen that "we will do all that we can to carry out your wishes."[33]

On May 14, 1931, a few days after the sisters had left for Philadelphia, Father Judge telegraphed Bishop Toolen, "Have succeeded in securing necessary financing negotiations being completed accordingly."[34] The next day he wrote to assure the bishop "that every cent of the current debt will be wiped out by the first of June."[35] Two weeks later Toolen told Archbishop Curley of this promise. But by June 5, 1931, Father Judge had to admit to the bishop that he didn't have the money. He hoped to have a novice master by the end of the month.[36] On June 9, Father Judge reported to Mother Boniface that he had borrowed $35,000 from the Riggs National Bank in Washington. This paid off the notes Archbishop Curley had signed. Riggs allowed him to borrow an additional $10,000, $5,000 of which he told her he sent to Mobile.[37] By the end of 1931 Judge had still not completely met Bishop Toolen's demand to liquidate the loan. In fact, he had to explain to an irate Toolen why he had paid off Curley's note on June 8 rather than Toolen's.[38]

32. It is not clear whether Father Judge ever sent this petition. It is undated but begins, "Nine years ago a group of young men petitioned me to help them to draw up a Rule to guide them in the spiritual life." At the time of its writing, one student (Paul Anthony) was in his third year of theology, another (Theophane) in his second, and a third in his first; AST, MF 7064. It was in January 1920 that Judge informed Bishop Allen that he had a group of young men who were "organizing themselves into a missionary body"; Judge to Allen, Holy Trinity, January 9, 1920, AST, MF 597.

33. Judge to Toolen, Newark, April 24, 1931, Toolen Papers, AAM.

34. Ibid., May 14, 1931, Western Union telegram, Toolen Papers, AAM.

35. Ibid., Stirling, May 15, 1931, Toolen Papers, AAM.

36. Ibid., Silver Spring, June 5, 1931, Toolen Papers, AAM.

37. Judge to Mother Boniface, Brookland, D.C., June 9, 1931, AST, MF 8260.

38. "It is true," Father Judge had to admit, "that this past year we did raise the money to pay off Archbishop Curley's note. Gladly would I have paid yours off also but the money was given conditionally"; Judge to "Your Excellency" [Bishop Toolen], no place, undated draft, AST, MF 1876.

Father Bede Hermann as Novice Master

Father Judge had more success with Bishop Toolen's demand for a novice master. In their January 13, 1931, meeting, Judge had promised that "if necessary I would go from religious house to religious house to get a novice master." He explained his dependence on the decision-making processes of the communities from whom he sought a novice master. Their provincial councils had to meet, and then they had to consult their general councils in Rome. Archbishop Fumasoni-Biondi had directed Judge to the Redemptorists, but, on March 24, they finally told him they wouldn't be able to provide a novice master. He told Bishop Toolen that it had taken "nearly two months" to get that decision. By May 15, he reported that two communities were considering his request.[39] On May 29, he wrote Mother Boniface from Philadelphia that he had to return to Washington to see one of the Capuchins, but that the letter from the U.S. Capuchins was on its way to Europe.[40] Finally, on July 28, 1931, Judge telegraphed from Stirling to Bishop Toolen in Baltimore, "Capuchin general is sending us a novice master according to letter date is coming to be arranged between Father Petrie Provincial of St. Augustine's Province and myself; do unite with us in thanking God for this great blessing."[41]

By August 16, 1931, the Capuchins had chosen Father Bede Hermann, OFM, Cap., as novice master. Father Judge wrote to welcome him and sent instructions on how to get to Holy Trinity. On the same day, he thanked the Capuchin provincial in Pittsburgh.[42] Mother Boniface knew Father Bede and played a significant role in bringing him to Holy Trinity. Bearded and diminutive, Father Bede arrived at the end of August. The first canonical novitiate of the Missionary Servants of the Most Holy Trinity began on September 8, 1931.[43] He started out with twenty-five brothers. Father Judge enthused at his "deep, sympathetic understanding of our difficulties and beginnings."[44] On

39. Judge to Toolen, Stirling, May 15, 1931, Toolen Papers, AAM.

40. Judge to Mother Boniface, Philadelphia, May 29, 1931, AST, MF 8257.

41. Judge to Toolen, July 28, 1931, Western Union telegram, Toolen Papers, AAM.

42. Judge to Bede Hermann, OFM, Cap., Philadelphia, August 16, 1931; Judge to Thomas Petrie, OFM, Cap., Philadelphia, August 16, 1931, AST, MF 1773–74. Two days after the dedication of the hospital, Judge again expressed his gratitude to Father Petrie for sending Father Bede, and for sending Father Sigmund to preach at the hospital dedication; Judge to Petrie, Holy Trinity, September 16, 1931, AST, MF 1789.

43. Tonra records Lawrence Brediger's humorous recollection of his arrival in *Led by the Spirit*, 314–15.

44. Judge to Mother Boniface, Holy Trinity, August 28, 1931, AST, MF 8276–78.

September 21, Judge reported at length to Father McHale on his efforts to find a novice master, Father Bede, and the first novitiate class.[45] On October 29, Judge told Mother Boniface that he would say a Mass of thanksgiving "tomorrow for the beautiful way in which the novitiate is running." He had heard from Father Bede the same day and described him as "so happy over the novitiate."[46]

On the constitutions, Father Judge did not fare as well. Repeatedly he assured Bishop Toolen that Monsignor Bernardini had left them in Father Motry's hands and that during the school year Motry was a very busy canonist. On June 30, he admitted to Archbishop Fumasoni-Biondi that "the signed Constitutions are not in my file." He explained that Bishop Toolen had signed the constitutions the day after a meeting with Judge and Tomerlin. Father Tomerlin had stayed behind and picked up the signed constitutions, which he brought to Washington and gave to Bernardini. Motry corroborated this. Judge promised to let the delegate know as soon as he located the signed copy of the constitutions. Fumasoni-Biondi must have requested financial reports from each of the men's Cenacles, and Judge enclosed one from St. Joseph's at Holy Trinity.[47] To Father Judge's great embarrassment, the signed constitutions failed to materialize until sometime in 1932.

Dr. Motry Saves the Day

Father Judge wrote to Archbishop Fumasoni-Biondi on June 30, three days after a long meeting with him in Washington at his offices on Biltmore Street. This June 27, 1931, meeting between Judge and the apostolic delegate represents the decisive turning point in Judge's long struggle to prevent Bishop Toolen from suppressing the Missionary Servants of the Most Holy Trinity. A month earlier, he had reported to Mother Boniface Bishop Walsh of Newark's refusal to provide dimissorial letters for Brother Paul Anthony. Though Judge claimed Fursman had lived in the Diocese of Newark since 1916, Bishop Walsh judged that, since he was from Albany and did not now reside in New Jersey, Fursman had no official domicile in his diocese.[48]

Motry and Fumasoni-Biondi were Father Judge's last hope to get Fursman ordained. "His Excellency was benignness itself," he announced to

45. Judge to McHale, Holy Trinity [?], September 21, 1931, AST, MF 7116–17.
46. Judge to Mother Boniface, Brooklyn, October 29, 1931, AST, MF 8286.
47. Judge to Fumasoni-Biondi, Holy Trinity, June 30, 1931, AST, MF 7044.
48. Judge to Mother Boniface, Philadelphia, May 29, 1931, AST, MF 8257.

Mother Boniface on May 29, 1931. "I spent three hours at the Delegation. Doctor Motry's interpretation was accepted in toto." "A letter is now on its way," he went on triumphantly, "to Bishop O'Hern with these words on it: 'His Excellency, Pietro Fumasoni-Biondi, says you can ordain the young man and incardinate him. Let him join a religious community if he wishes to and should he not take his Vows, or should he for any other reason wish to give up his Novitiate, let him then return to Rochester, for in the case of him taking residence in Rochester, you are his Bishop." Fumasoni-Biondi guaranteed that this procedure could be safely followed in the future.

Father Judge added that "Mobile came in for a great deal of consideration." A letter "had come up from the Gulf." Judge described the letter as certainly "a brave attempt to smash the Brothers' Community to pieces" but "rather mild" compared to what had been said in person to Mother Boniface and himself. "But these are all over now," he concluded. Judge had apparently been successful in answering the bishop's charges of financial impropriety. "If any impression is to be made hereafter, new things must be thought up and, please God, no new things can be said of us, or old things for that matter, if we live up to the rules and to the traditions of the Missionary Cenacle."

Father Judge heaped praise on Louis Motry, wishing they could "build a little house for him at Holy Trinity Heights." Motry's "marvelous" interpretations of canon law ensured that the Missionary Servants could survive Bishop Toolen's attempts to sink them. "He has really given a new interpretation to this section of Canon Law, and opened up procedure in cases and places where solutions were a vexatious search." Father Judge was beside himself with joy and admiration. "This solution is enough to promote a man to full Professorship and in fact, I think if a student had found this, it would have won for him the degree of Doctor."[49]

As he explained it to Father McHale almost three months later, "Bro. Paul Anthony should have been called to Orders months ago but one obstruction after another was put in his way; in fact, we are getting his ordination through on really a classic definition of Canon 969." He sent McHale a copy of Motry's solution to the case "as of Canonical interest" but emphasized, "I am not responsible for the classic though it went to the Papal Delegate over my signature." He identified Bishop John Francis O'Hern of Rochester as the "Episcopus Benevolens" who would ordain Fursman.[50]

49. Ibid., Silver Spring, June 27, 1931, AST, MF 8270–71.

50. Over the next two months, Judge corresponded with Bishop O'Hern to arrange the

Father Judge saw in the apostolic delegate's acceptance of Motry's solution to Fursman's case a sign of divine approval for the Cenacle's work. Despite Bishop Toolen's best efforts, "Holy Mother Church" had saved them. "[T]he little barque of the Cenacle," he related to McHale, "has been very much tempest tossed for the past year. . . . Every conceivable kind of questionable strategy has been used to wreck us. Holy Mother Church through the Papal Delegate, the Holy Congregation, came to our help; otherwise we might have perished."[51]

Back in May 1931, Father Eugene Brennan struggled with the uncertainty of whether an arrangement could be reached with Bishop Byrne so St. Augustine's would reopen in the fall. The bishop wanted the Missionary Servants to buy St. Augustine's. Father Judge counseled Brennan to take a lesson from the sisters' response to Bishop Toolen and their subsequent "triumph":

> Have an instinct always to get the heart beat of the Church. Keep your policy lined up to Her moods and thought. Be slow ever to oppose what the Church likes and never be caught denying what She wants. Never have an ethics or a practice that contradicts Her ideals or Her aspirations, Her ways, Her thoughts, Her sense, Her traditions, Her precepts, or Her teaching; then, shape your head always for the victor's crown. Sentire cum Ecclesia. May the Triune God be praised, from the beginning the Missionary Cenacle has tried to be true to this Church-aged tradition and I ascribe this as one reason why God has favored us so much in our tight places.[52]

Such sentiments are of a piece with, and, indeed, lend plausibility to, Father Judge's repeated insistence to Bishop Toolen that he only wanted what the church wanted. Had the apostolic delegate or the Sacred Congregation for Religious decided in Bishop Toolen's favor, Father Judge would have had no

---

September ordination and thank the bishop for "his great work of spiritual mercy"; Judge to Bishop O'Hern, no place, July 7, 1931, AST, MF 1761, and ibid., Stirling, July 21, 1931, AST, MF 1765.

51. Judge to McHale, Holy Trinity [?], September 21, 1931, AST, MF 7116–17. Judge delivered the news about Brother Paul Anthony in the context of announcing to McHale the opening of "two new chapters in Missionary Cenacle history, the transfer of the Sisters' motherhouse to Philadelphia, and the opening of the Brothers' canonical novitiate." Canon 969 in the 1917 Code of Canon Law says that "no one may be ordained for the secular clergy who in the judgment of his own Bishop is not necessary or at least useful for the churches of the diocese." It forbids bishops from ordaining more people than they can "usefully employ" in the diocese. But it does not forbid a bishop from ordaining "one of his subjects" who will later serve in another diocese. Motry's challenge seems to have been how to present Fursman as equivalent to one of Bishop O'Hern's "subjects"; see Bouscaren, Ellis, and Korth, *Canon Law: A Text and Commentary*, 433. Motry had written his JCD dissertation at Catholic University in 1922 on "Diocesan Faculties according to the Code of Canon Law."

52. Judge to Brennan, Holy Trinity, May 7, 1931, AST, MF 7108.

choice but to pack up the Cenacle's tent. He did everything in his power to make sure that would never be necessary. He had been confirmed in his belief that the church wanted the Cenacle to go on.

On the "Hay Wagon," August 1931–1933

In his letters to Father Brennan in May and Father McHale in September 1931, Father Judge described himself as being constantly "on the bridge" over the past year. Struggling to raise money during the Depression and thwart Bishop Toolen's attempts to suppress the brothers took a toll on him. He had another bout of illness. August found him at Dr. Hay's Sun and Diet Sanitarium in East Aurora, New York. "I had a hard time this time and I can thank God for having led me here," he wrote to Mother Boniface. He was hooked on colonics, an early twentieth-century diet program designed to keep the intestines clean by balancing combinations of food groups. "I really believe," he continued, "especially as you get along in years, our troubles come from too much eating, especially starchy foods and too much concentrated protein, such as meat, rather than from eating too little."[53]

Two days later Father Judge wrote to Sister Mary Francis, who was waiting for him to come to Philadelphia to give a retreat to the novices. He counseled her against discouragement, the "artifice" of the evil spirit, and to charity toward the "Big Man & the 2 others." He wished she could spend two days in East Aurora. "I feel as if I have been made over. To-day, I touched bending over the tips of my shoes with my fingers. I have not been able to do this for years. Interiorly, I am much more serene and in control of myself." He would leave in a few days "cured" and "ever so much energized.... No drugs are used. No surgery. The treatments are simple, sensible, and efficacious." He had met a bishop, two monsignors, and a reverend mother and her companion at the sanitarium. He wished that she and Mother Boniface could come and take the places vacated by the last two.[54]

A year later, in August 1932, Father Judge returned to the Sun and Diet Sanitarium. Dr. Hay wanted him to stay for two weeks. Hay warned him to stop when he felt tired and "stressed the necessity of following out the regime exactly."[55] To Sister Mary Thomas in Río Piedras, a few days after his first stay in East Aurora in 1931, he spelled out the Hay diet in detail. Hay divid-

53. Judge to Mother Boniface, East Aurora, N.Y., August 2, 1931, AST, MF 8278–79.
54. Judge to Sister Mary Francis, East Aurora, N.Y., August 4, 1931, AST, MF 7056–59.
55. Judge to Sister Mary Thomas Champion, Stirling, August 2, 1932, AST, MF 7255.

ed foods into four groups: starch (for example, bananas, potatoes, bread, rice, squash), protein (for example, meat, eggs, fish, milk), sugar (white sugar, syrups, ice cream, brown sugar preferred), and acid (citruses). The "regime" consisted in eating foods from these groups in the proper combinations. Starch and sugar could go together, as could protein and acid, but other combinations were regarded as toxic and unhealthy.[56]

Based on a popular theory according to which most diseases were caused by eating food with germ-forming bacteria that infected the intestines, Dr. Hay wanted to keep the intestines clean and prevent "autointoxication." The celebrity proponent of this approach in Father Judge's day was John Harvey Kellogg (1852–1943), whose Battle Creek Sanitarium flourished in the 1920s. The Hay diet, as Judge explained it, recalls Kellogg's categories and principles as they appear in his 1,000-page-plus *New Dietetics* (1927).[57] A near fanatical enthusiast for Dr. Hay's diet, Father Judge, over the next two years, encouraged anyone who would listen to get on the "Hay Wagon." "Now as for yourself, my dear child," he wrote to one of the sisters, "if you have those aches and pains, it is because you are chock-block full of acid. Why do you not detoxicate?"[58]

Father Judge convinced Sister Mary Thomas Champion in Río Piedras to prepare food according to the Hay "regime" and reported that Father Felix O'Neill had profited from the diet.[59] For common colds he recommended "three days fast, a citrus juice and bi-carb to get rid of that cold."[60] Some of the sisters, nurses among them, feared that he wasn't eating properly and had become too thin. After a year on the "Hay Wagon," he weighed 150 pounds. "The Sisters are scolding me all the time because I am thin," he reported to Sister Mary Thomas. He was about to make his second visit to East Aurora, where Hay pronounced him in "very good condition."[61]

56. Judge to My dear Child (a sister in Puerto Rico), Holy Trinity, August 6, 1931, AST, MF 7115. The Sister is probably Sister Mary Thomas, who prepared Judge's meals when he was in Río Piedras.

57. John Harvey Kellogg, *The New Dietetics: A Guide to Scientific Feeding in Health and Disease*, rev. ed. (Battle Creek, Mich.: Modern Medicine, 1927).

58. Judge to My dear Child, Newark, February 22, 1932, AST, MF 7153; see also Judge to Sister Mary of the Precious Blood, Río Piedras, April 7, 1932, AST, MF 7167.

59. On Fr. O'Neill, see Judge to Sister Mary John of Calvary, Newark, February 23, 1932, AST, MF 3406.

60. Judge to Sister Carmel, en route to Puerto Rico, March 1932, AST, MF 7241. There followed a lengthy pitch for the diet.

61. Judge to Sister Mary Thomas, Holy Trinity, July 18, 1932, AST, MF 7249, and Judge to My dear Child, Stirling, August 2, 1932, AST, MF 7208, and on the same day to Sister Mary Thomas, at MF 7255.

Two staunch opponents of the diet were in charge of large Cenacles where Father Judge spent a lot of time: Sister Carmel Davoren in Brooklyn and Sister Gerard Ledwidge, Judge's own sister Annie, at Wallace Street in Philadelphia. They came in for heavy proselytizing. To Sister Carmel he insisted that Puerto Rico was not to blame for his poor health. Vegetables prepared so as to have "too much concentrated protein" and the "denatured flour" in the "beautiful Jewish buns" they fed him worked "a terrible injury to our vitals." "My dear Sister Carmel," he concluded, "when are you going to provide for your children the diet that is safe and sure?"[62]

A few weeks after his first trip to East Aurora, Father Judge told Mother Boniface that he had written to Sister Gerard about Dr. Hay's sanitarium. "If she and Sr. Cecilia could go to that sanitarium and carry out the instructions, their life and usefulness would be prolonged for years and years."[63] "I am wondering," he asked about Sister Gerard some months later, "is she getting the starches and proteins mixed up in your menu.... I wonder have they got the sugars and acids mixed up."[64] To Sister Gerard herself he wrote, "I heard that many of your Sisters were sick." He laced his dietary admonitions with humor. "Sister Gerard, my dear child, when I call to see you, please do not enumerate the tribulations of your sick house. Remedy, put yourself and your Sisters in the 'Hay Wagon.' Use Dr. Hay's treatment and you will become young and beautiful."[65]

Philadelphia was also home to another sister Father Judge had converted to the Hay diet, Sister Mary de Lourdes Culhane. Before his next visit, he wanted the sisters in Philadelphia "to get straight sugars and starches, acids and proteins." He proposed "an alliance against wrong nutritive combinations ... for it irks me so much when I appear and I find that they do so much violence to nutritional values."[66] "To be candid," he told Sister Marie of the Holy Trinity on the same day, "I do have some trouble in getting the food I think I should have." He was reluctant to come to Philadelphia because he feared the sisters would provide food that would just make him sick.[67]

62. Judge to Sister Carmel, Río Piedras, April 18, 1932, AST, MF 7177.

63. Judge to Mother Boniface, Holy Trinity, August 28, 1931, AST, MF 8276.

64. Judge to a cousin at the novitiate, Holy Trinity, December 31, 1931, AST, MF 7272.

65. Judge to Sister Gerard, Río Piedras, May 26, 1932, AST, MF 7191. His sister Alice, a Daughter of Charity, recently assigned to a hospital in Maine, urged him to come there for rest. He turned her down because he did not want to offend the sisters by complaining about their poor nutritional habits; Judge to Sister Alice Judge, DC, Río Piedras, April 12, 1932, AST, MF 7246.

66. Judge to Sister de Lourdes, Holy Trinity, January 1, 1933, AST, MF 7306.

67. Judge to Sister Marie of the Holy Trinity, Holy Trinity, January 1, 1933, AST, MF 7386.

After the dedication of the hospital in September 1931, Mother Boniface described Father Judge to Father McHale as seeming well, but "much thinner." "The past two years," she continued, "have been a great strain on him, but he keeps right on going. We sometimes wonder how he stands it. There are many anxieties always regarding both Communities, and of course the financial problem is ever present."[68] Whether Dr. Hay's diet helped Father Judge to stand it for two more years or whether it hastened his decline, as some of the sisters feared, we cannot know.

The New Holy Name of Jesus Hospital Opens Its Doors

"The great day is fast approaching," Mother Boniface wrote Bishop Toolen on September 5, 1931. She still hoped he might be able to come. "We have planned to have Father Judge dedicate the building if you are not there." She told him they had chosen one of the Capuchins, Father Sigmund Kratz, to preach.[69] Two days before the dedication, the bishop responded tersely in his own hand. He had appointed a new extraordinary confessor for the sisters and promised a new hospital chaplain around October, with the sisters responsible for his annual salary of $500. "I hope," he concluded, "that you will have a big day on Monday."[70]

Monday was September 14, 1931, the Feast of the Exaltation of the Holy Cross, and it was indeed a big day. On the eve of the dedication, the Gadsden Sunday paper announced, "New $700,000 Holy Name of Jesus Hospital Is Ready for Use with Finest of Equipment." The feature story went on to describe the hospital as "one of the largest, one of the finest and one of the most modernly equipped in the country." Eight stories high with two hundred rooms, the building was "architecturally striking" in a "modern colonial" style." From the front, the white structure appeared to be five stories. The basement added another story from the back, and the towers atop the building brought it up to eight stories. Though it had 200 rooms, the hospital had only 120 beds.

68. Mother Boniface to Father McHale, September 1931, as cited in Tonra, *Led by the Spirit*, 315.

69. Mother Boniface to Bishop Toolen, Stirling, September 5, 1931, AST, MF 13061.

70. Bishop Toolen to Mother Boniface, Baltimore, September 12, 1931, AST, MF 13063. According to Canon 521, §1, of the 1917 Code of Canon Law, the local ordinary of a diocese in which a house of religious women is located is to appoint an "extraordinary confessor" who visits the house four times a year and supplements the "ordinary confessor" who visits the house every week; see *NCE* (1967), 4:144.

The article explained that during the two years before construction began, research had been done on "80 of the leading hospitals in the United States ... in order to obtain the best possible results in construction and equipment." Among the hospitals consulted was St. Mary's in Rochester, Minnesota, eventually a part of the Mayo Clinic. The Sisters of St. Francis built the hospital in 1883. In 1889, they entered into a collaborative agreement with Dr. William W. Mayo and his two sons, both surgeons. In spring 1928, Father Judge and Mother Boniface visited St. Mary's and went through the clinic for checkups. Judge described the hospital and the Mayo Clinic in enthusiastic detail to Bishop Toolen, clearly hoping the relationship there between the sisters and the doctors, inspired and encouraged by the local bishop, would become a model for Holy Name of Jesus Hospital.[71]

The chair of the Gadsden city commission opened the ceremonies at 10:00 a.m. With Bishop Toolen absent, Father Judge celebrated solemn high Mass. The hospital chapel proved too small for the throng of people, so Father Sigmund preached outside. After Mass, doctors, sisters, and hospital staff led tours through the building. At 7:30 p.m., Father Judge closed the ceremonies with a solemn benediction. Mother Boniface described his sermon to Father McHale as "straight Catholic doctrine, stressing the Holy Name and the Real Presence in the Blessed Sacrament." "Thanksgiving is the word of the day," Father Judge told his Protestant audience, "and Eucharist means thanksgiving." Beginning with St. Luke's account of the Last Supper, and moving on to the Bread of Life discourse in John 6, he explained the doctrine of Christ's Eucharistic presence as if he were letting them in "on a family secret." "The Eucharistic life," he told them, "is the secret of the Sisters' gift to Gadsden."[72]

A "distinct triumph for religion," Father Judge pronounced euphorically. "I never saw such an evident manifestation of the influence of the Holy Ghost on a crowd." According to Father Judge, 15,000 people visited the hospital on September 14 with "not a discordant note in the whole celebration." The doctors' acceptance of the hospital's name especially moved him. "It was beautiful and so soul stirring to hear the Protestant doctors pronounce in their addresses 'Holy Name of Jesus Hospital.' It seemed but a year ago an

71. Judge to Bishop Toolen, East Pittsburgh, Pa., May 14, 1928, Toolen Papers, AAM. This letter also describes visits to contractors and two medical facilities in Pittsburgh. On the relationship between the Sisters of St. Francis of Rochester, Minnesota, and the Mayo family, see Whalen, *Sisters' Story*.

72. "Sermon at Evening Services of the Dedication of the Holy Name of Jesus Hospital," *Holy Ghost*, October 1931, 19–23; see also AST, MF 1820–24.

impossibility for these men to pronounce those words. It looked as if those words would choke them."[73]

"The town has been for some time notably anti-Catholic," Mother Boniface told Father McHale, "yet there was a spirit of reverence and respect throughout the whole crowd." The local response to the new hospital delighted her. She counted it a "miracle of grace." "Facing the door in the main lobby is a life-size statue of Our Divine Savior, and strange to say, this is what attracted most of them as they entered." To Bishop Toolen she reported, "From early morning until late night steady streams of people poured into the hospital. They came to see the beautiful building and to have a share in the great event." She noted "a remarkable spirit—one could feel as it were the very breathing of the Holy Ghost in their midst. The Holy Name of Jesus has indeed worked a miracle of miracles here and no one could be so blind as not to be able to see it."[74]

Mother Boniface was proud of the hospital's up-to-date facilities and its professional standing as "a registered A-1 hospital affiliated with the American College." More important was its role as a mission center. Father Judge described the hospital as "an important and powerful missionary center" from which the sisters had "endeared themselves to all classes."[75] Mother Boniface emphasized this aspect of the hospital in her letter to Father McHale:

> Surely the Holy Name has been all powerful in this little Southern City, for the hospital is a missionary center. The work of the Sisters reaches out to the small towns and mountain districts around Gadsden. The poor people are coming to us more and more, and so often we are able to help the soul as well as the body. The Sisters visit the homes after the patients have left the hospital and the contact has been established; and we are hoping that through the new hospital we will be able to carry on a much more extensive missionary work.[76]

73. Judge to Margaret Friedenburg, Holy Trinity, October 1, 1931, AST, MF 7070. He expressed similar sentiments to Brother Augustine, who could not attend the dedication: "Gadsden is at the feet of the Sisters, also properly speaking Gadsden is clustered around the Holy Name of Jesus Hospital. . . . The debt, of course, is prodigious but debt means nothing if we have the spirit of faith"; Judge to Brother Augustine Philips, Holy Trinity, September 16, 1931, AST, MF 1790.

74. Mother Boniface to Bishop Toolen, Gadsden, September 16, 1931, Toolen Papers, AAM. With this letter, she enclosed the "clippings from the Gadsden and Birmingham papers." Her letter to Father McHale is reproduced in Tonra, *Led by the Spirit*, 315–17. A full account of the dedication appeared in the *Holy Ghost* for October 1931.

75. Judge to My dear Child, Holy Trinity, April 5, 1930, AST, MF 6952. He noted that a local Baptist preacher was "amongst their [the sisters'] most ardent advocates."

76. Tonra, *Led by the Spirit*, 317, citing Mother Boniface's post–hospital dedication letter to Father McHale.

Amid financial worries, Father Judge's thoughts turned to the Holy Name. On October 29, he wrote Mother Boniface that perhaps they had been "a little dilatory." This thought had come to him "in prayer or Mass." The hospital still had no illuminated sign with the Holy Name. "Do not forget to push them to have the illuminated sign on the building," he wrote. "Make it as ornate as possible but have it anyway ornate or not ornate."[77]

Father Paul Anthony's Ordination

Father Louis Motry on Canon 969 bore its first fruit on September 27, 1931. In the chapel at St. Bernard's Seminary in Rochester, New York, Bishop John F. O'Hern ordained Father Paul Anthony Fursman to the priesthood. "*Deo gratias!*," Judge exclaimed to Brother Joachim Benson at Holy Trinity, "The Church has another priest. We too are thankful for he will be very useful to the Missionary Cenacle."[78] After Eugene Brennan, Fursman was the Cenacle's second homegrown priest. He looked on Mother Boniface as the "Mother of my Priesthood" and, at his ordination, "with the oil still fresh on my hands," she was the first to receive Communion from his hands, even before his own mother. Father Paul Anthony said his first Mass in Rochester and his first solemn Mass at Our Lady of Good Counsel in his home diocese of Newark, home to many of the young men he recruited to Holy Trinity. Father Judge sent Fursman to Holy Trinity to be in charge of the school. With Father Bede as novice master, there would always be two priests at Holy Trinity.[79]

As Father Tomerlin moved out of the picture, Brother Joachim took over the office, the magazine, and the brothers' finances at Holy Trinity. With an assist from Brother James, who had attended the ordination, he and Brother Thomas O'Keeffe produced a special November issue of *SOS for the Preservation of the Faith* to commemorate Fursman's ordination.[80]

77. Judge to Mother Boniface, Brooklyn, October 29, 1931, AST, MF 8286.

78. Judge to Benson, Stirling, September 30, 1931, AST, MF 10806–87. Perhaps because many of his regular correspondents were at the ordination, Father Judge's letters are remarkably silent on it.

79. On Fursman's ordination, see Tonra, *Led by the Spirit*, 318–19.

80. Judge to Brother James Norris, Holy Trinity, August 31, 1931, AST, MF 1784. Father Judge was proud of their work on the magazine. On Benson's responsibilities at Holy Trinity, see Judge to Brother Augustine Philips, Newark, November 7, 1931, AST, MF 1826.

Fall 1931, Continuing Financial Woes

Despite the real joy at the hospital's dedication and Brother Paul Anthony's ordination, the Great Depression kept constant financial pressure on the Cenacle through the fall of 1931. Mother Boniface returned from the ordination to an angry letter from Bishop Toolen dated September 24, 1931. Sister Mary James had come to tell him that they could not make the September 15 interest payment. After the conciliatory May 28 meeting with Bishop Toolen, Mother Boniface had written a letter to Sister Ancilla about the meeting, no doubt expressing what she said in her summary about the bishop's flexible attitude on the interest payments. Sister Ancilla tore up the letter, but another sister, probably Sister Gertrude, took it from the trash, put it back together, and sent it to Bishop Toolen. From this letter, to which he referred in his own letter of September 24, Bishop Toolen concluded that the "double-dealing" sisters had "never intended to keep this contract."

Displeased that Mother Boniface had moved Sister Luke from Catholic Charities in Mobile to organize a Children's Bureau in Pittsburgh, the bishop accused her of taking Sister Luke away "at the crucial time of the work here in Mobile" and of "a serious lack of courtesy" in informing him of the change three weeks after he had already heard about it. Again he accused the sisters of using the South to appeal for funds they would use nationally. "My only reason for allowing Trinity to exist was that it might help you to meet the payments on the Hospital. Again, I say if these payments are not made promptly and regularly, then close Trinity and close Phoenix, stop all appeals out of Alabama and move your magazine." Before closing, he removed this condition and concluded that since the Sisters did not seem to appreciate his kindnesses to them, "I think we had better close Trinity entirely and if you so desire Phoenix, and move the magazine at once."[81]

Mother Boniface's reply ignored these threats. She knew that at bottom of Bishop Toolen's anger was the hurt, expressed again in this letter, at what he perceived as the sisters' chronic ingratitude. "Your letter surprised and grieved me.... We really wanted to tender you all honor and courtesy. We appreciate your generous assistance and help and most assuredly are grateful for what you have done, Bishop." Sister Luke's transfer, as she had previously explained, was done "with the best interests of the whole work in

81. Bishop Toolen to Mother Boniface, Mobile, September 24, 1931, AST, MF 13067; see also Mother Boniface to Bishop Toolen, Gadsden, September 16, 1931, Toolen Papers, AAM.

mind." She wanted him to know that "we are grieved over your letter. No one wants to be considered an ingrate."

Her letter of May 30 to Sister Ancilla was "but a report ... it expressed pleasure over your kindly attitude—in it there was absolutely no lack of good faith and on my part there never has been." She described the "treachery of her who stooped" down to the wastebasket as "the 'unkindest cut' of all and I am sorry to have learned about it."

Failure to make the September 15 payment "could certainly not be attributed to lack of good faith." In the "great depression from which the world in general and we with it have suffered," she pleaded for more time. "Reason, if not honor, would urge us to keep the contract, Bishop," she argued. "Think of the interest we are giving out." She concluded with a prayer that "some day Bishop Toolen will find that the hearts of the Missionary Servants of the Most Blessed Trinity are and always were 'true blue.'" She was sure to put *Gratefully* at the beginning of the customary "in the Most Blessed Trinity."[82] The sisters kept their side of Holy Trinity open as they struggled to meet the monthly interest payments.

The brothers too were squeezed hard by the Depression. The appeals of Toth and Stenzel began to show returns. By November Toth was sending $100 per week.[83] But it was not enough. At age twenty-seven, the high-strung Brother Joachim Benson had taken over the finances at Holy Trinity. Hounded by creditors, Benson needed encouragement. Father Judge administered it in a flood of fall letters that combined humor and spiritual exhortation. Back in September 1931, because of an engine room breakdown at Holy Trinity, Father Judge had asked the bishop to sign for extending the note in Mobile another month.[84]

On October 8, 1931, Judge told Benson that Bishop Toolen had been receiving notices from their creditors, including Barnes and Noble, and the First National Bank in Mobile that held the note. He cited the bishop's warning that if they failed to make a "substantial payment" on the note, "I shall ask the Bank to take proceedings against you to collect it. I do not like to do

82. Mother Boniface to Bishop Toolen, October 6, 1931, AST, MF 13069.

83. Judge to Benson, Stirling, November 5, 1931, AST, MF 10815.

84. Judge to Toolen, Holy Trinity, September 16, 1931, AST, MF 7066. On the same day, Bishop Toolen wrote to Mother Boniface demanding that she honor their contract, Father Judge thanked him for "endorsing our note." He tried to explain that "responsible people" had made promises to him but, he supposed, "these days of depression make it hard for the well-meaning to keep such promises"; Judge to Toolen, Holy Trinity, September 24, 1931, AST, MF 7065.

this but you have been promising now for about a year and it is time that something was done."[85] Within two days, Father Judge reported his optimism that Father Charles D. Wood could help them borrow the $15,000 that he had mentioned on October 8. Should they get the money, Judge instructed Benson, "Give a substantial cut to Mobile, then we have something over and above for 'the poor Brother who lives in a stew and had so many creditors he didn't know what to do.'"[86]

Brother Joachim had no money and needed to buy food for the students at Holy Trinity. He was also collecting the revenue on 100,000 copies of a booklet entitled "Confidence in God" the brothers had mailed out at the beginning of September. As restricted money, this revenue only added to his frustration. To ease Benson's worry, Father Judge tried humor. Two days before the Mobile note was due, Judge sent what he could and reported that notices from their creditors in Stirling "are not so exciting as yours. Do not think, however, that they lack sparkle and zest."[87] The next day he sent Benson some more money cobbled together from Brother Augustine and Sister Ancilla. He told him to drop Brother Augustine a note of thanks, "for if you have creditors going on high on sixteen cylinders, he has them going on twenty-four."[88] Benson had to go to Mobile on October 15, but the bank wouldn't accept the check. "I am convinced," Father Judge wrote him, "that our dear Lord is sending us these tribulations to confirm us more and more in hope and confidence."

> There are works ahead of us that are calling for men who can do violence to the Kingdom of Heaven. We do not get such power merely by reading books. Such power comes from the stinging experience of need when we are thrown back on Divine Providence. No man has a title to the Apostolic Spirit who has not affection for such a hope.[89]

Father Judge's letters to a beleaguered Benson during the fall of 1931 offers a frightening glimpse into the financial state of the Missionary Servants of the Most Holy Trinity. Father Wood failed to get the $15,000. By the end of Octo-

85. Judge to Benson, Stirling, October 8, 1931, AST, MF 1796.

86. Ibid., October 10, 1931, 1799.

87. Ibid., October 13, 1931, AST, MF 1800. On the mass mailing of the booklets, see Judge to Mother Boniface, Holy Trinity, September 1, 1931, AST, MF 8278.

88. Judge to Benson, Brooklyn, October 14, 1931, AST, MF 1805.

89. Ibid., Orange, N.J., October 21, 1931, AST, MF 1811–12; see also MF 1803. See also a moving exhortation on "the man who hoped against hope" in ibid., Stirling [?], October 25, 1931, AST, MF 1815.

ber and beginning of November 1931, Father Judge was trying to mortgage the Silver Spring property for $40,000.

On October 27, 1931, the first report of sisters with typhoid came from Gadsden. Father Judge wrote to Mother Boniface from Brooklyn two days later. "Take good care of yourself," he told her. "Do not get run down, don't lose your good disposition."[90] On All Saint's Day, November 1, 1931, Father Judge preached at the unveiling of a statue of the Little Flower in Gillette, New Jersey. In "distressful days," he wondered why "after so long a period of depression things do not lift." He looked to the family. He preached on how the "Little Way" of St. Therese could strengthen family life. In Gillette with pilgrims from Brooklyn, Margaret Healy wrote up his sermon for the *Holy Ghost*.[91]

Father Judge's last letter to Mother Boniface is dated November 10. By this time, she was quite sick with typhoid, but did not tell him. "We are just taking care of the sick and praying here," she wrote. She told him of Sister William's death, that Brother Lawrence was down with a fever, asked if he had the money for the Mobile note due November 15, and urged him to send in the text of his sermon at Gillette by November 10.[92] Having no idea how sick she was, he responded that good would come from Sister William's death and spoke much of the needs of Puerto Rico.[93]

The Last Days of Mother Boniface

Sister William Farrell, a twenty-eight-year-old nurse at Holy Name of Jesus Hospital, had, since mid-October 1931, been sick with a severe case of typhoid. Near the end of October, Mother Boniface went to Gadsden to help the sisters care for the sick. She and Sister James signed the final papers for the hospital at this time. On November 3, she sent Sister James to Philadelphia so they would not both be exposed to the fever. So far no hospital patients had contracted typhoid, only sisters and a few staff. With staff down,

90. Judge to Mother Boniface, Brooklyn, October 29, 1931, AST, MF 8286–87. On October 31, he wrote to tell her that Father Tomerlin had turned up at Gold Street in Brooklyn; see AST, MF 8288–91.

91. "Sermon Delivered at Unveiling of the Statue of the Little Flower in Gillette, N.J.," *Holy Ghost*, December, 1931, 20–24; see also AST, MF 1871, 1873–76.

92. This letter is reproduced at length in Tonra, *Led by the Spirit*, 331. In what follows, I rely on Tonra's moving account of Mother Boniface's last days and aftermath, masterfully woven from first-hand accounts, 325–56.

93. Judge to Mother Boniface, Stirling, November 10, 1931, AST, MF 8292–95.

sisters were stretched to carry on routine work at the hospital. Mother Boniface helped care for Sister William during her last week. She died on Friday, November 6. Her body was taken out through a sub-basement exit so as not to panic workers and patients. Mother Boniface accompanied the body from Gadsden to Holy Trinity, where Sister William was buried. From Holy Trinity Mother Boniface wrote her last letter to Father Judge.

In that letter she told Father Judge that she hadn't heard anything from Bishop Toolen. Mother Boniface knew that Father Lenahan, as hospital chaplain, had informed the bishop of the typhoid cases. On November 11, she dictated a letter to Bishop Toolen. She reported that three sisters and three lay staff were sick. Others had recovered or were past danger. With complications from meningitis, Sister William had had the most severe case.

> The Medical Board and the Board of Health are doing all possible to locate the germ. The consensus of opinion is that it must have been taken before we left the old hospital since it is all our own people that have been stricken. Thank God, the patients all have been safe so far. Every precaution is being taken and we have been isolating our own patients, so that the public has been protected. We are, of course, trying to keep it as quiet as possible and up to the present it has not hurt our hospital.

Mother Boniface was too weak to sign this letter. Sister Marie of the Precious Blood, her secretary, typed a postscript telling the bishop that Mother Boniface had been taken from Holy Trinity to Gadsden in an ambulance. The hospital confirmed that it was indeed typhoid. She reported "several new cases."[94] Including Mother Boniface, the list of typhoid cases grew to fourteen over the next few days, but in that time two had recovered. Having to be carried from her bed, Sister Marie reported elsewhere, was the worst part of the trip to the hospital for Mother Boniface.

On November 14, 1931, Sister Mary of the Precious Blood, the administrator in charge of the hospital, reported to the motherhouse that Mother Boniface's condition was "serious but not critical." With seventeen typhoid patients, the hospital could no longer accept new patients. Paying interest and bills would be even harder.

Father Judge was still in the North. At the end of October, he met Father McHale at Providence Hospital in Washington and took him to Silver Spring to see the brothers. He had urged Mother Boniface to come north to see

94. Mother Boniface to Bishop Toolen, Holy Trinity, November 11, 1931, AST, MF 13070. See Tonra's account of Mother Boniface's last days in *Led by the Spirit*, 333–40.

McHale.[95] On November 15, still not knowing the seriousness of her condition, he preached on the "Church as the Communion of Saints" at the opening of Queen of Angels Cenacle in Newark. Addressing an audience of young women, he included the Little Flower, St. Philomena, and St. Joan of Arc among his examples. The church is Christ's body. Helping youth, strengthening families is helping Christ. "In the ordinary providence of your daily lives," he told them, "you are the Church.... Where you are, there is the Church."[96] The sisters wanted to keep him away from the hospital and typhoid as long as possible. But by November 15, they could delay no longer, and Sister Mary of the Precious Blood wired Father Judge in Newark that the doctors had lost hope for Mother Boniface.

Father Judge asked for volunteers to help at the hospital in Gadsden. Two sister nurses volunteered, and together with Father Judge they set out from Newark for LaGuardia to get a plane south. With LaGuardia flights delayed by weather, they took a train to Richmond and chartered a plane to Gadsden the next day. Around 4:30 p.m. on November 16, they landed in a cornfield about ten miles from the hospital. Father Judge left his bag in the field, and one of the sisters returned the next day to retrieve it. By 7:00 p.m. Judge had sent a telegram to Sister Mary James, who traveled on the train with them from New York to Philadelphia, "Mother Better Marie Celeste Roof Convalescent All Improving."[97]

Between November 17 and 21, Father Judge communicated with Brother James Norris about finances and kept him abreast of Mother Boniface's condition. With cases of typhoid limited mostly to sisters, Father Judge became suspicious of foul play. Rumors were flying. "I heard tonight," he told Norris, "that [Senator Thomas] Heflin said our hospital will never open." There was talk of someone poisoning the food. In the sisters' dining room, Sister Angel Guardian was assigned exclusive access to the food after it had been prepared. Judge told Norris to look into the possibility of hiring a detective to investigate "one or two of our negro [*sic*] help" and "some white men behind them." He described the doctors as "talking very freely, even mentioning names."[98]

95. Judge to Mother Boniface, Silver Spring, October 31, 1931, AST, MF 8280–82.

96. Sermon by Father Judge on the Opening of Queen of Angels Cenacle, Newark, N.J., AST, MF 1830–39.

97. Judge to Sr. Mary James, postal telegraph, Gadsden, November 16, 1931, 7:00 p.m., AST, MF 7118. Father Judge's letter to Norris the next day reports Mother Boniface's condition in more detail and gives his account of the six-hour plane ride from Richmond to Gadsden; Judge to Norris, Gadsden, November 17, 1931, AST, MF 1840–41.

98. Judge to Norris, Gadsden, November 18, 1931, AST, MF 1842–43. By November 21,

On November 19, 1931, Father Judge began a novena to the Holy Ghost to discover the cause of the disease. "The cause of the disease remains a mystery," he told Sister Baptista, asking her to start the novena in the Outer Cenacle. The doctors agreed that the infection had started in the sisters' and nurses' dining rooms. There had been no cases in Gadsden, "and in the hospital the sickness is entirely limited to the Sisters and our personnel. Twenty-one cases have been treated. Of these six are still critically ill."[99]

On November 20, Mother Boniface seemed to rally. Her temperature went down from close to 106 to just over 102, her pulse from 150 to 112. Fully conscious, she told Father Judge he had been there too long. She wanted to know when he was leaving and why Father Eugene Brennan was there at all. During the night of November 21, Fathers Judge and Tomerlin anointed her and gave her the last rites. She died around 5:00 a.m. on the morning of November 22, 1931.

She was only forty-six years old. She succumbed, concluded Dr. Morgan, who had attended her throughout, "because she was so utterly exhausted from traveling around from place to place, so fatigued, so worn out, she had nothing with which to fight back." "I'm sorry," Father Judge told the sisters, "God's will be done." Of him as he said this, one of the sisters who was there wrote, "I never saw such a downcast sad man."[100] Later he explained that he had not expected her to die. "I did not feel her work was done. But I was wrong."[101]

Word of Mother Boniface's death reached Wynnefield Avenue while Cardinal Dougherty's chancellor, Father Furey, was preparing to say Mass for the sisters. The cardinal arrived shortly thereafter with his condolences and an offer of the Cathedral of St. Peter and St. Paul for Mother Boniface's funeral Mass. The next day came a gift from the archdiocese of a plot in Holy Sepulcher Cemetery for Mother Boniface. Father Judge described it as "quite close to the main entrance, in a very attractive spot."[102]

Father Judge reported that it might not be necessary to engage a detective. He still wanted to know what it would take to get one; Judge to Norris, Gadsden, November 21, 1931, AST, MF 1845. "Every day points to some miscreant being the source of this trouble," he wrote on the same day. "We have to be careful of our suspicions but we have the individual in mind who would know how to spread this fever and who would have the means of doing it, but just now names may not even be whispered"; Judge to My dear Brother (maybe Norris), Gadsden, November 21, 1931, AST, MF 13920.

99. Judge to Sister Marie Baptista Croke, Gadsden, November 19, 1931, AST, MF 1844[?].

100. See Tonra, *Led by the Spirit*, 339–40.

101. From a conversation with Sister Marie of the Precious Blood as cited in ibid., 348.

102. Judge to My dear Children, Philadelphia, November 29, 1931, AST, MF 1852–53.

Father Judge spent a good part of November 22 in Gadsden writing a letter to the community on Mother Boniface's death. He gave the scattered sisters the details of her death and funeral arrangements. It was a beautiful tribute that began from Psalm 116, "Precious in the sight of the Lord is the death of his saints." Mother Boniface was "the good, the strong, the wise woman of God. We have known only kindness in her and seen goodness; the fruits of her life are surely beautiful. How precious now are those numberless deeds of mercy, corporal and spiritual.... What a comforter she has been to all who came within the sweet attraction of her life!"[103]

On November 23, after a Solemn Requiem Mass at which Father Tomerlin preached, Mother Boniface's body was brought to the motherhouse in Philadelphia. At her wake, Father Judge asked Sister Mary Francis to read his letter to the assembled sisters. Mother Boniface died on a Sunday. Her funeral in the Cathedral of St. Peter and St. Paul was on a snowy November 25, the Wednesday before Thanksgiving. Cardinal Dougherty himself offered her Requiem Mass with Father Judge as deacon and Father Eugene Brennan as subdeacon. Monsignor Thomas McNally preached a sermon that Judge's circular letter described as "touchingly beautiful." McNally compared the memory of Mother Boniface to Longfellow's description of Evangeline passing through the village of Grand Pre: "When she had passed it was like the ceasing of exquisite music."[104]

At Holy Sepulcher Cemetery, Father Judge gave the final blessing and led the rosary at the grave. His reflections on the sorrowful mysteries before each decade placed the present suffering of the Missionary Cenacle inside the paradoxical gospel of the sufferings of Christ. "The lashes are laid on the backs of the Missionary Cenacles, but it was the Hand of Love." He did not shrink before the horror of the cross. "We cannot understand the reason for grief; we know it makes for reparation." Left standing by the cross, he urged them to take up their own crosses. "Remember the Cross of Christ was extolled in her life. She made much of that Cross and the Cross made much of her."[105]

Father Judge's circular letter of November 29 recounts the details of the funeral. He was especially proud that Cardinal Dougherty himself had

103. Ibid., Gadsden, November 22, 1931, AST, MF 1846; the full text appears in Tonra, *Led by the Spirit*, 341–42. Tonra includes Joachim Benson's recollection of the letter's composition, at 341.

104. Tonra includes a list of all the ecclesiastical dignitaries who came to the funeral and reproduces the text of McNally's sermon in *Led by the Spirit*, 343–45.

105. Ibid., 346–47, for the text of Judge's graveside reflections on the Sorrowful Mysteries.

sung the funeral Mass. This made it, he reported, "a Pontifical Mass of Requiem." He recalled the "young country school teacher from the hills of Western Pennsylvania" who had come to Alabama. He contrasted "a fresh faced, bright eyed young maiden kneeling devoutly in that little plantation cabin chapel in those early days" with the present, "sixteen years later, her remains lying in state in that glorious temple of God, the great Cathedral of St. Peter and St. Paul, Philadelphia."

Marveling at the providence of God, Father Judge urged the Missionary Cenacle to meditate on Mother Boniface's virtues. He reflected on her physical, mental, and spiritual perfections. Describing her preeminent virtues, he concluded, "Through a forceful nature and showing magnificent qualities of leadership and executive ability, through her sweetness and gentleness and charming simplicity she removed the friction and hurt that must often accompany discipline." Finally, he turned to the opening of Christ the King Missionary Cenacle in Jersey City and noted the "remarkable growth of the colored work" with two black Catholic congregations (Christ the King and Our Lady Queen of Angels) having been organized in the Newark Diocese in the past year. Mother Boniface's heart was "so much in this work" and he felt her presence at the opening of Christ the King.[106]

In January, Father Judge gave a talk on Mother Boniface that captures her genuineness—he called it her "simplicity"—and the self-effacing humor that gave a light touch to her every exercise of authority. "Mother Boniface never acted a part, she never staged anything; there was nothing of affectation in her. Mother Boniface was extraordinarily simple; she was extraordinarily self-effacing. Mother Boniface never set herself up, or tried to bring anyone under her sway." Comparing her to St. Vincent de Paul, he found her an example of a "law of God" found in the lives of the saints, "he who humbleth himself shall be exalted." "And the powers she had!" he exclaimed. "She was a forceful woman and yet it was all hidden. I never met anyone who was afraid of Mother Boniface; but where do we find a woman of such strength of character, such a dominant personality as Mother Boniface? You know the highest evidence of majesty is suppression of power. . . . It is not often that we find power so charitably disguised as in Mother Boniface."[107]

He wrote to both Monsignor Bernardini and Father McHale to tell them of her death. To McHale he compared her to St. Catherine of Siena. "A

106. Judge to My dear Children, Philadelphia, November 29, 1931, AST, MF 1852–53.
107. As cited in Tonra, *Led by the Spirit*, 358.

well-known ecclesiastic told me that she had the mind of a Bishop, that he gave her confidence that he would give to few, that he found her advice so helpful." He missed her. "It is so difficult to realize that she is gone," he told McHale. "She was so vital, so sunshiny, so helpful. She had a faculty it would seem of just multiplying herself. We are so used to seeing her step into some emergency that we have just accustomed ourselves to expect to meet her here or there at any time."[108]

Aftermath, 1931

In early December, he wrote two letters to Sister Mary of the Precious Blood, who was in charge of the hospital. As the typhoid epidemic wound down, doctors sent patients to the hospital again. He praised her work under the strain and urged against discouragement over possible implied criticism in the pathologist's report, which seemed to accuse Sister William of carelessness. "If anything, his tests favor the hospital," he insisted.[109] Before Christmas she sent to all the sisters a copy of the report by the Bureau of Communicable Diseases of the State Board of Health of Alabama. This report identified a "serving girl" who waited tables in the sisters' dining room as the original carrier of the typhoid germ.[110] Around the same time, he urged Brother Joachim to faith and confidence, "remember Our Lord is in the Missionary Cenacle boat."[111]

On December 7, 1931, Father Judge attended a monthly meeting of the Outer Cenacle Council in Brooklyn and confided to Sister Marie of the Precious Blood at Holy Trinity his worry about sustaining the "primitive spirit of the Outer Cenacle." He found the meeting "perfunctory," its "accumulation of brains and good will . . . a dumb oracle." He resolved to attend more of these meetings.[112]

The year 1931 marked the first Christmas at Holy Trinity without Mother Boniface. Father Judge's Christmas circular contrasted "those statuesque, dumb, lifeless things . . . placed around the little statue of the Christ Child" with "you breathing, pulsating beings," "the corps d'elite" as the "guard of

108. Judge to McHale, Holy Trinity, January 12, 1932, AST, MF 1892–93; see also Judge to Filippo Bernardini, no place, December 19, 1931, AST, MF 1861.

109. Judge to Sister Mary of the Precious Blood, Philadelphia, December 4, 1931, AST, MF 7091, and ibid., Brooklyn, December 7, 1931, AST, MF 7093.

110. See the summary of the report in Tonra, *Led by the Spirit*, 350.

111. Judge to Benson, West Orange, N.J., December 6, 1931, AST, MF 1857–58.

112. Judge to Sister Marie of the Precious Blood, Brooklyn, December 7, 1931, AST, MF 7089.

honor around the altar manger of the living Jesus in the Blessed Sacrament." They were to be "His shepherds ... filling up those valleys with good works and virtues ... straighten out your intentions, drive the natural and the creature out of them."[113]

The days after Christmas found Father Judge in Gadsden, pleased with developments at the hospital. He tried to lift Brother Joachim's spirits with a letter. "You are so engaging," he told Benson, "and you have such taking ways about you that I am going to send you all my money." Conditions at the hospital had improved. "It was like going along Fifth Avenue here today," he wrote. "It was like a triumphal march. Thank God all the Sisters are convalescent. "They have reached now that state of perfection in which they are really gay."[114]

The First General Cenacle

Father Judge accompanied the sister delegates from the South to Philadelphia for the First General Cenacle. On December 29, 1931, Mother Mary of the Incarnate Word was elected the new mother general. Her councilors were Sister Mary Francis, Sister Carmel, Sister Marie of the Precious Blood, and Sister Baptista. Sister Marie had been Mother Boniface's secretary and continued as secretary general. Sister Mary James stayed on as procurator general.

Despite the light-hearted tone in his December 27 letter to Brother Joachim, Father Judge had a lot on his mind as 1932 began. In addition to nagging creditors was the question of the status of the brothers and their motherhouse in the Diocese of Mobile. If this were not enough, Father Judge was asked, perhaps as a result of Bishop Toolen's communications with the Sacred Congregation for Religious, to clarify his status as a member of the Congregation of the Mission. These issues, especially the first, along with the work in Puerto Rico, would occupy Father Judge during the year and a half of active life left to him. He needed the strong presence of Mother Boniface, and he missed her sorely.

113. Judge to My dear Children, Holy Trinity, December 23, 1931, AST, MF 7104–6.
114. Judge to Benson, Gadsden, December 27, 1931, AST, MF 1865.

❖ 15

A WANDERING ITINERANT FOR THE LORD

1932

1932—the Longest Year

Late in December 1931, as he left Gadsden for Philadelphia, Father Judge had before him only about a year and a half of active work. In September 1932, at Holy Trinity, he described 1932 to Sister Marie of the Precious Blood as the longest year of his life.[1] "The depression is frightful that grips the country," he wrote to Father McHale in Paris as the year began. "Divine Providence is not failing us, money is coming in helping us to limp along, to, at least, discharge our debts."[2] As the Great Depression worsened, Father Judge's health continued to decline. Despite his assurances to McHale, pressure from creditors mounted.

As their own revenue continued to decrease, the sisters couldn't comply with Bishop Toolen's demand that they keep strictly to the terms of their 1931 contract on the hospital. With Bishop Toolen insisting that he had never signed the 1929 decree of erection for the brothers' community, Father Judge still had not found the original document. Brother Theophane Mulroy had finished his studies at the Catholic University of America. The first months of the year found Father Judge scrambling to get him ordained.

From June through October 1932, Father Judge tried to find a bishop who

1. In recalling this conversation, Sister Marie said she would never forget the "look of pain and loneliness in his eyes at that moment"; see Tonra, *Led by the Spirit*, 362.

2. Judge to McHale, Newark, N.J. [?], January 12, 1932, AST, MF 1892.

would accept the men's motherhouse into his diocese. Raleigh and Altoona fell through. By October, he had secured an invitation from Cleveland. In the controversy over the bond issue, Father Judge's status as a Vincentian was brought into question, and he had to satisfy the superior general in Paris. Puerto Rico continued to demand his attention. He spent from mid-March until the end of May on the island. In late September a hurricane ripped through Puerto Rico and severely damaged St. Augustine's Military Academy. He continued to juggle personnel, especially priests, to staff the community's works and allow for canonical novitiates at the same time. Weakened in health, he dealt with all of these pressing concerns without the wisdom, especially in the realm of finance, and strong support of Mother Boniface.

"In this constant shuttling from Missionary Cenacle to Missionary Cenacle," Father Judge told the new mother general, "my mail becomes like unto the burden of Atlas. It just weighs me down."[3] The new year found him trying to thank all the sisters for the Christmas greetings that had poured in. "Since Mother's death I have not found a release from the business of the Sisters' Missionary Cenacles," he wrote to another sister. "All through this long period the Brothers' affairs have been clamoring for attention, particularly their financial affairs." He hastened to add that the "spiritual affairs" of both Cenacles had never been better.[4]

$150,000 Gold Debenture Bonds at 6 Percent for Five Years

Sometime in late January the Missionary Servants of the Most Holy Trinity issued for sale $150,000 of gold debenture bonds, the first of two controversial bond issues. Bonds paid the buyer 6 percent interest semiannually and came due after five years in 1937. Father Judge had first mentioned this proposal in May 1931. In October of that year, at a meeting in Stirling, James Norris seems to have put this project together with Werner Stenzel and R. S. Toth, now working to develop the community's mailing lists. Toth's of-

3. Judge to Mother Mary of the Incarnate Word, West Orange, N.J., January 2, 1932, AST, MF 13260.

4. Judge to My dear Child, Newark, N.J., January 8, 1932, AST, MF 3610. The January correspondence is remarkable both for its volume and for its personal touch. The letters to Brother Joachim on the finances at Holy Trinity are especially striking for their personal attention to a high-strung individual and for the depth of their reflections on providence; see, for example, Judge to Benson, Newark, N.J., January 6, 1932, AST, MF 1888–89. After Mother Boniface's death, Father Judge's correspondence in general becomes more reflective and personal.

fices were in Chicago, where Norris had gone to help get out the bonds. "I am now signing the bonds," Father Judge told Joachim Benson on January 18, 1932. Having taken over as treasurer at Holy Trinity in the previous October, Benson had instituted, under Judge's instruction, a difficult policy of retrenchment. On January 18 Norris was still in Chicago, and Benson was desperate for money and the power of attorney, needing Norris's signature as the corporation's secretary, allowing Benson to function as local treasurer. "The literature [on the bonds], I guess, must be in the mail so you ought to have something soon," Judge wrote.[5]

"May the Triune God be praised," Father Judge exclaimed to Benson a month later, "it is just remarkable how the Bond Issue is coming along. Toth and Company are the most surprised of all the surprised." "How indulgent in this is the Providence of God to us," he continued. "What would we have done if this money had not come in?" He saw Mother Boniface's hand in it. He thanked Benson for implementing the policy of retrenchment at Holy Trinity and warned him against having the brothers think that money was no longer a problem. "Every cent of this is being absorbed by old debts. Then too we have a day of accounting, in fact we have two days of accounting—the interest payment day and later on the cancellation of these Bonds."[6]

As Father Judge explained to Father McHale, "The banks for the past two years have been loath to advance money, even to good customers. Within the last six months, especially, it has been difficult to get a note renewed, no matter how good the standing of the petitioner." The bond issue was a short-term solution, which he described to McHale as "doing amazingly well." He assured McHale that "we have never failed in our interest payments and have been able to make cuts on our loan principals."[7] Despite its truth, this claim was misleading. The first interest payment would not have come due until July 1, 1932. Judge insisted that the bonds were not an appeal. What would make them attractive was the 6 percent interest rate. "People are afraid of the banks," he wrote, "and are hiding their money around the house and in other unsecure places.... We are really doing these people a favor because with a generous rate of interest they are getting security at the same time on a church bond."[8]

5. Judge to Benson, Newark, January 18, 1932, AST, MF 1896, with enclosure MF 1898, authorizing Benson to sign notes as treasurer at St. Joseph's and telling him that Norris was still in Chicago.

6. Judge to Benson, Orange, N.J., ca. February 15, 1932, AST, MF 1921–22.

7. Judge to McHale, Newark, N.J. [?], February 27, 1932, AST, MF 1952.

8. Judge to Sister Marie Jean Daigle, Newark, N.J., January 18, 1932, AST, MF 7147.

The twelve-page booklet describing the bond issue made clear that the bonds were a loan to the Missionary Servants of the Most Holy Trinity. Potential buyers were urged to lend the community money "for the conduct of God's work" and "for the preservation of the faith." Backed by the community's assets, said to exceed its liabilities, the bonds were "sound and secure." The combined value of the properties at Holy Trinity, Stirling, Silver Spring, and Río Piedras was estimated at more than $400,000. The booklet included pictures of each property and accounts of the apostolic work done there. The purpose of the bond issue was "to retire current obligations and to provide working capital." The first bonds were dated January 2, 1932, coming due on January 2, 1937, with 6 percent interest payable on January 1 and July 1 of each of the five years of the life of the bonds. Perhaps Father Judge really believed he was doing the lenders a favor. The properties, however, had minimal equity. With the exception of Puerto Rico, owned by the diocese, each was mortgaged to the hilt, with their estimated value providing scant security to lenders.

The bonds were issued from Brookland Station, Washington, D.C., perhaps because both Monsignor Nummey, the community's official treasurer, and Brother James Norris, then a student at Catholic University, resided nearby in Silver Spring. Brookland Station was in Archbishop Curley's diocese. On February 11, 1932, in the *Catholic Review*, Curley published a brief statement disavowing all responsibility for the bonds. "This statement is issued," the archbishop wrote, "in view of the fact that the Rev. Thomas A. Judge, CM, Custodian-General of the above-named community has made a public appeal for funds, for which he issues 6 per cent 5-year Gold Debenture Bonds." Archbishop Curley was emphatic: "This obligation is exclusively that of Father Judge and his Community. It carries no guarantee whatsoever from the Archbishop of Baltimore."[9]

Monsignor Nummey's Departure

By this time, Monsignor Nummey had reluctantly come to share Archbishop Curley's skepticism about the safety of the bonds. Around March 1931, Father Judge lost faith in Father Tomerlin as a hopeless "plunger" and

9. Monsignor Nummey enclosed a clipping of this notice from the *Catholic Review*, along with the booklet and letter from Father Judge describing the bonds, with his letter to Bishop Molloy of Brooklyn, March 19, 1932, Nummey Papers, Archives of the Diocese of Brooklyn. The first two pages of the booklet, describing the terms of the bonds, are also found in Archbishop Curley's Papers, Box 19, J466, Archives of the Archdiocese of Baltimore.

asked Nummey to serve as treasurer. On February 2, 1931, Nummey traveled with Brother Augustine to Graymoor, New York, to seek a loan from Father Paul Wattson's Rock of Peter Foundation. The foundation's board turned down their request because the community had failed to make timely interest payments on the loan it already had. This was Monsignor Nummey's introduction to the community's finances.[10]

By the beginning of 1932, the strain of his new position had landed Monsignor Nummey in St. Agnes Hospital in Baltimore. On medical advice and after consultation with his confessor, he decided it would be best to return to the Diocese of Brooklyn. "It is with deep regret, therefore," Nummey wrote to Father Judge, "that I have to advise you that I have definitely and finally decided to withdraw from the work of the Community." Prayer and counsel had convinced Nummey that he could not "return to what I am assured would mean the loss of health again, if not indeed more serious consequences."[11] Nummey's confessor also required him "as a matter of conscience" to bring his assessment of the finances of the Missionary Servants of the Most Holy Trinity to the attention of the apostolic delegate, Archbishop Pietro Fumasoni-Biondi. Nummey reported on all this in a two and a half-page handwritten letter to Bishop Molloy of Brooklyn.

He recounted that, until Father Judge asked him a year ago to serve as community treasurer, he had "no knowledge of the Community's general financial condition." He soon learned that they were "in a very bad way," not only because of "ill-regulated overhead and over-expansion at the Mother House in Alabama," but also because of "a system of financing which instead of budgeting to balance, were balancing through increased borrowings until a crisis was reached precipitated by the depression."[12]

Monsignor Nummey was an experienced pastor, a sympathetic inside observer. His moral dilemma, a plausible response any serious Christian

10. The *Lamp*, March 1931, 70, noted the visit of Monsignor Nummey and Brother Augustine to Graymoor on February 2. On Nummey's experience seeking a loan, see Father Paul Francis Wattson, SA, to Judge, Graymoor, N.Y., May 29, 1931 (copy), and Judge to Wattson, Silver Spring, Md., June 9, 1931, Archives/Record Center of the Franciscan Friars of the Atonement–Graymoor.

11. Nummey to Judge, Baltimore, February 9, 1932, AST. Nummey enclosed a copy of a letter, also dated February 9, from his confessor, Edward A. Gilgan, SS, of Theological College at the Catholic University of America. Gilgan concluded that, after weeks of reflection and prayer on the question, he was "decidedly of the opinion that you should withdraw and return to Brooklyn your own diocese." This correspondence has no microfilm numbers.

12. Nummey to Thomas E, Molloy, Baltimore, March 19, 1932, Nummey Papers, Archives of the Diocese of Brooklyn.

might have in similar circumstances, gives both a sense of the depth of Judge's moving exhortations at this time to Benson to trust in divine providence and an appreciation for the prudential positions of Bishop Toolen and Archbishop Curley:

> Banks began calling their loans and of necessity I was forced to meet the situation by an effort of refinancing through the medium of other banks. But this gave rise to a doubt in conscience as to the morality of seeking loans on assets and resources that were predicated *ad valorem* in no small way on the hypothecation of Divine Providence. Whilst on the other hand, there was an ever present question of sufficient confidence in Divine Providence in the matter of unquestioned apostolic work.

Nummey explained that a few months of the strain of this dilemma resulted in "a serious condition of high blood pressure which, before discovery, nearly resulted in a stroke." He went on to say that he had been under treatment for this condition since July of 1931. He put the matter before his confessor. Advising an "extended sick leave," his confessor counseled that he "could not in conscience continue seeking credit where apparently only the providence of God could insure against possible jeopardy both to the investments and the credit of the church."[13]

Monsignor Nummey hoped to return to the community but with no financial responsibility. His confessor counseled him to put the matter before the apostolic delegate. Archbishop Fumasoni-Biondi decided that "Fr. Judge should be left to handle his own extrication, and that I should return to the diocese and communicate his decision to you [Bishop Molloy]." The delegate, however, asked Nummey to continue his "personal interest" in the community's work. His reason points to Father Judge's significance for the church in the United States at this time and to why he had the continuing support of the delegation. The delegate described Father Judge's work to Nummey as "the only organized movement of its kind in the church today that so completely meets the wishes of the Holy Father with reference to the Lay Apostolate."[14] Indeed, even as Nummey wrote, Father Judge and the sisters were starting an African American Outer Cenacle in Montclair, New Jersey.[15]

13. Ibid.

14. Ibid. Around this time, Judge wrote, "The Outer Cenacle movement seems to be merging into Catholic Action. What a consolation it must be to you to know that long before we heard the phrase 'Catholic Action' in the Missionary Cenacle you were working at it with your brothers and sisters"; Judge to Jerome Donegan, Brooklyn, March 9, 1932, AST, MF 1963.

15. On the Montclair Outer Cenacle, see Judge to Sister Michael Shelvy, West Orange, N.J [?], January 20, 1932, AST, MF 7131; Judge to Sister Mary Simon Turner, Newark, N.J. [?],

Since his visit to Archbishop Fumasoni-Biondi, Monsignor Nummey noted a new development: "the flotation of debenture bonds." He enclosed the booklet and letter from Father Judge, along with the clipping of Archbishop Curley's response in the *Catholic Review*. "Unfortunately," he concluded, "neither the security offered in these bonds nor the pledge made are [*sic*] justified and redeemable on the basis of current assets and resources." Despite his real difficulties with the community's financial situation, Nummey was advised by both his confessor and Fumasoni-Biondi to "predicate my leaving solely on the basis of health which is not without its embarrassment, although the physician did say that if I returned to the same strain as before, there would be a recurrence of the malady with perhaps more serious consequences."[16] Nummey's letter of resignation mentioned only reasons of health. To both Father Judge and Bishop Molloy he expressed his regret and disappointment at having to leave the community's work. To Molloy he mentioned specifically how happy he had been "training these splendid young men for the priesthood, two of whom were recently ordained."[17]

Theophane Mulroy's Ordination to the Priesthood

One of those "splendid young men" was Father Theophane Mulroy. As with Fursman's, Mulroy's ordination to the priesthood on February 21, 1932, was made possible, in spite of Bishop Toolen's opposition, when the apostolic delegate accepted Louis Motry's interpretation of Canon 969 in the 1917 Code of Canon Law. Mulroy had finished his studies at Catholic University, but, because he would be ordained ahead of his class, last-minute difficulties developed causing Father Judge added stress.

He contrasted the cases of Fursman and Mulroy, so much trouble with the former, "none at all with Bro. Theophane until this week. Then, you would imagine that half a dozen fiends got loose to tangle things up." "Thank

February 26, AST, MF 7154, describing the work at Montclair. March 4 found Father Judge at Howard University in Washington, D.C., where he found some forty Catholic students, some of whom he hoped to interest in the work at Montclair. He had sent Sister Mary Francis to Montclair to help begin the Outer Cenacle there; see Judge to Mother Mary of the Incarnate Word, Orange, N.J., March 4, 1932, AST, MF 13195. To Father McHale he elaborated on the wider context of this work in the Diocese of Newark; see Judge to McHale, Newark, N.J. [?], February 27, 1932, AST, MF 1951.

16. Nummey to Molloy, Baltimore, March 19, 1932, Nummey Papers, Archives of the Diocese of Brooklyn.

17. Ibid.

God," he concluded, "he is going to receive Diaconate Saturday morning at 7:30 and Holy Orders, Sunday, in the Church of the Assumption in New York." Bishop John J. Dunne, one of Cardinal Hayes's auxiliaries, was to ordain Mulroy.[18] But only on Thursday, February 18, was everything finally settled. "Through the great goodness of His Eminence, Cardinal Hayes, and Msgr. Carroll [his Chancellor]," Judge wrote, "we are able to have this early ordination."[19] By Friday he reported, "We have had an excruciating week to get Brother Theophane's canonical papers straightened out.... I don't know when I have gone through such experiences, beginning with last Saturday, up until yesterday.... Rest assured, it has taken a whole lot out of me."[20]

On Saturday, February 20, Father Judge wrote to Bishop John F. O'Hern of Rochester that Brother Theophane had been ordained a deacon that morning. Bishop O'Hern had given Mulroy tonsure, minor orders, and subdiaconate.[21] He wrote on the same day to Bishop Toolen, emphasizing Brother Theophane's glowing evaluations from Catholic University and promising "substantial cuts on the note" in March and a possible pay-off by mid-summer.[22]

Two days after Mulroy's ordination, Father Judge responded to Monsignor Nummey's February 9, 1932, letter of resignation. Though he was no doubt aware of what put Nummey in St. Agnes Hospital, he made no reference to community finances. He expressed his hope that Nummey's "indisposition" was "a passing phase and that you will soon be in good health." The letter's two main paragraphs heaped praise on Mulroy and effused over his ordination. "In this," Judge told Nummey, "his instructor is certainly to be commended for a thorough, practical, and edifying training."[23]

Theophane Mulroy emerges from Father Judge's correspondence as a rather shadowy figure without much shape or texture.[24] Father Judge told

18. Judge to Sister Michael Shelvy, West Orange, N.J. [?], February 16, 1932, AST, MF 7276.

19. Judge to Charles X. Walsh, West Orange, N.J., February 18, 1932, AST, MF 1925. On Thursday, February 18, they still needed certification that Mulroy had indeed made an ordination retreat. James Norris had to go to Washington with information "on this that we could not send through the mail or over the wire"; Judge to My dear Child, West Orange, N.J., February 18, 1932, AST, MF 7149.

20. Judge to Sister Mary Thomas Champion, Brooklyn, February 19, 1932, AST, MF 7150.

21. Judge to O'Hern, Brooklyn, February 20, 1932, AST, MF 1934.

22. Judge to Toolen, Brooklyn, February 20, 1932, Toolen Papers, AAM.

23. Judge to Nummey, Newark, N.J., February 23, 1932, AST, MF 1946.

24. In an interview with Father Lawrence Brediger on September 6, 1945, Brother Augustine said that Father Judge met George Mulroy through Sister Miriam's father, a policeman, who worked with a Boys Club to which Mulroy belonged.

Bishop Toolen that, after his ordination, Mulroy would remain temporarily at Catholic University to complete his M.A. Judge described him to one of the sisters as "one of those who has born the heats and burdens of the day from way back."[25] To Eugene Brennan, Judge expressed his hope that he would be able to send Father Theophane to Puerto Rico for a while. "The two of you," he noted, "have always been such good friends, I would like to have him go, for your own sake, and to give him a little bit of edification and joy."[26] By October 1932, ordained less than a year, Father Mulroy took charge of St. John's parish in Lorain, Ohio, in the Diocese of Cleveland, where Father Judge hoped to relocate the men's motherhouse.

Father Judge—Always a Vincentian

"Your recent letter at hand. Rest assured, I do wish to be with the Congregation. I am taking up the matter right away." Thus began Father Judge's February 27, 1932, letter to Father McHale.[27] The Registries of the Vincentian Grand Conseil for February 2, 1932, show that the generalate had received an inquiry from a bishop (probably Bishop Toolen) as to Father Judge's canonical status. The response was that "this confrere has not ceased to be one of us, but that, occupied of necessity with the Congregations he has founded, he has doubtless received permission from Rome to live apart from the Congregation."[28] The query in Father McHale's letter that Father Judge mentions in his own letter of February 27 probably came as a result of this February 2, 1932, discussion in the Grand Conseil.

As seen in chapter 11, Father Judge himself had already raised the question of his status as a Vincentian in January 1929 when he wrote the superior general requesting the unusual permission of living outside the community while remaining a Vincentian. At that time, he was directed to meet with Father McHale. Though no clear record of that meeting survives, the last

25. Judge to Sister Mary John of Calvary, Newark, N.J., February 23, 1932, AST, MF 3406.

26. Judge to Brennan, Newark, N.J., February 23, 1932, AST, MF 4070.

27. Judge to McHale, Newark, N.J. [?], February 27, 1932, AST, MF 1951. I don't have McHale's letter.

28. "A un évêque qui interroge sur la situation canonique de M. Judge, il sera répondu que ce confrère n'a pas cessé d'être des nôtres, mais que, [dans] la nécessité où il est de s'occuper de Congrégations dont il est le fondateur, il a sans doute obtenu de Rome la permission de vivre hors de la Compagnie"; Conseil du 1er février 1932 (Reg. XI, 203), from "Extraits Des Registres du Grand Conseil," copied at Rome, November 13, 1963, as witnessed by William M. Slattery, CM, Sup. Gen.; copies in Box 1H.17A, Folder 4, DA.

part of the Grand Conseil's response to the inquiring bishop indicates that it resulted in Father Judge being informed that this permission needed to be requested through the apostolic delegate from the Sacred Congregation for Religious at Rome. Father McHale thought that, had Judge made it, such a request would have been refused.[29] At the time of Judge's death, this issue remained providentially unresolved. From 1915 until his death, records at St. Mary's Mission House at Opelika listed him as attached to that Vincentian house.[30]

Early in June 1932 Father Judge received a request from the Vincentian superior general asking for clarification on the financial side of his work, and especially on the bonds (*emprunts*) he had recently issued. Father Verdier explained that he had received numerous inquiries about the financial affairs of the Missionary Servants of the Most Holy Trinity, some from official authorities, and wanted Judge to provide him with the information he would need to respond to these queries.[31] Judge described this letter as "very fatherly," noting that it came "after the attack on us by Archbishop Curley," and perhaps after a protest from some Vincentians in the United States. "I know," he wrote, "that some of the Vincentian Fathers were disturbed and perhaps these things accumulated and found voice in a letter of protest to Paris."[32]

Father Judge took as a providential "opportunity and a favor" this opportunity to explain the community's finances to the superior general. He promised to send a fuller account of the community's financial affairs after the end of the fiscal year on August 1. Since the end of the last fiscal year, the five-year bond issue had considerably strengthened their financial affairs. He enclosed the twelve-page booklet describing the bond issue. Having recently returned from Puerto Rico, he emphasized the work at St. Augustine's Military Academy in Río Piedras and the cooperation of Bishop Byrne of San Juan.[33] From East Aurora, New York, sometime later in July, he urged

29. "Now Father Judge never made this request of the apostolic delegate, or at least it never went to Rome. If it had gone to Rome, Father McHale believed that Rome would have refused the request"; from Brother Joachim Benson's summary of his conversation with Father McHale on May 30, 1934, at St. Vincent Church, Germantown, Pennsylvania; Typescript, 2, AST.

30. John M. Cloonan, CM, to Sylvester A. Taggart, CM, Northampton, Pa., October 16, 1958, Box 1H.17A, Folder 4, DA.

31. François Verdier to Judge, Paris, June 2, 1932, copy in Box 1H.17A, Folder 4, DA.

32. Judge to My dear Child, Stirling, November 9, 1932, AST, MF 12280. The recipient of this letter is not clear.

33. Judge to Très Honoré Père, Stirling, July 4, 1932, AST, MF 2034. This letter is in French.

James Norris, "Do work on that financial statement for France. Remember it is promised, if we do not get it over in time, it will not be so good."[34]

By August 8, 1932, the "financial statement" was ready. This brief one-page report simply enumerated the community's properties along with their acreage, the putative security for the bonds, information already available in the booklet sent in July. Father Judge thanked Father Verdier for his friendly and paternal interest in the affairs of the Missionary Servants and assured him of his willingness to provide future information that might interest the general.[35] The registry simply notes receipt by the Grand Conseil of Judge's two letters on the finances of the two communities he founded.[36] Verdier replied to the financial statements, which Judge thought had "surprised and delighted him very much," with an effusive letter of thanks.[37]

"Heartfelt [*de tout coeur*] thanks for your welcome letter," Father Verdier began, "and the consoling news you send me, the good God visibly blesses your work, thanks be to God!" Father Judge's interpretation of the letter in terms of surprise and delight is not exaggerated. "At the altar of St. Vincent," Verdier continued, "and close to his relics, I say special prayers for you and your Institute. My very dear confrere, in the name of St. Vincent, I bless you from the heart (de tout coeur) and pray you to trust in my complete devotion in Our Lord and Mary Immaculate." He signed it, "Your most devoted confrere."[38]

Father Verdier's September 6, 1932, letter indicated that Father Judge's account of the Missionary Servants of the Most Holy Trinity's finances satisfied the Grand Conseil. But the matter remained, mentioned in the meeting of February 1, 1932, of permission from Rome to live outside the congregation. Judge's February 27 reply to Father McHale, "Rest assured, I do wish to be with the Congregation. I am taking up the matter right away," as well

34. Judge to Norris, East Aurora, N.Y., July 1932, AST, MF 2051.

35. Judge to Mon Très Honoré Père, Holy Trinity, August 8, 1932, AST, MF 14158. This letter is in French.

36. Conseil du 29 août 1932 (Reg. XI, p. 237), copy in Box 1H.17A, Folder 4, DA.

37. "I am enclosing one of those letters from France and so that you may get your money's worth, I am enclosing also the French copy"; Judge to My dear Child, Stirling, November 9, 1932, AST, MF 12280.

38. "Je vous remercie de tout coeur de votre bonne lettre et des nouvelles consolantes que vous me donnez. Le bon Dieu bénit visiblement votre oeuvre: Deo Gratias! A l'autel de St. Vincent et auprès de ses reliques, je prie spécialement pour vous et votre Institut. Monsieur et très cher Confrère, je vous bénis de tout coeur au nom de St. Vincent, et vous prie de croire à mon entier dévouement en Notre-Seigneur et Marie Immaculée, Votre tout dévoué confrère. Fr. Verdier, Sup. Gen."; Verdier to Judge, Paris, September 6, 1932, Lettres des Supéreurs généreaux, Reg. No. 149 (2e Série), 31, copy in Box 1H.17A, Folder 4, DA.

as subsequent correspondence, indicate that Judge was in the process of petitioning the Sacred Congregation for Religious for permission to remain a Vincentian despite the fact that he directed the two communities of Missionary Servants that he had founded. On October 9, 1932, in the midst of negotiations to move the men's motherhouse to Cleveland, Judge wrote to McHale, who was in Germantown, asking if they could meet at the sisters' new motherhouse the next day, "there is some advice I am anxious to seek from you."[39] The advice that necessitated a special trip to Philadelphia likely had to do with an August 26 letter Judge had recently received from the Vincentian procurator general in Rome.[40]

In July 1932 Father Judge had written a petition concerning "the present status of his religious life" (*circa praesentem vitae meae religiosae*) to Cardinal Alexis Lépicier of the Sacred Congregation for Religious in Rome.[41] He recalled his life as a Vincentian for the past thirty-five years, noted the two religious institutes, one for women and one for men, founded by him, and that he still retained the office of direction and superior among the men. "And, up to this point," he went on, "I enjoy the privileges and rights of the Congregation of the Mission, and I strive to fulfill the duties of same insofar as they are compatible with my office with the above named Institutes."[42]

Father Judge's petition concluded with the request that he be allowed "to remain attached to the Congregation of the Mission for a period of up to ten years or longer should Almighty God be pleased to bless the work I have begun." He noted that his petition was being submitted "at the urging of his superiors so that the approval of the Sacred Congregation for Religious might be added to their permission."[43] Noteworthy are the facts that Judge asked only for a temporary, if indefinite, permission to live apart from the congregation and that he himself was the superior of the men's institute he

39. Judge to McHale, Cleveland, October 9, 1932, AST, MF 2114.

40. Giuseppe Scognamilli, CM, to Judge, Rome, August 26, 1932, AST, MF 14160–63. Scognamilli was the Vincentian procurator general at the Holy See, who, since the generalate was in Paris at this time, handled the congregation's business at Rome.

41. Judge to Lépicier, Holy Trinity, July 19, 1932, AST, MF 4156. The petition is in Latin and has handwritten corrections, perhaps based on the response from the procurator general.

42. "Et Congregationis Missionis adhuc praevilegiis et juribus fruor atque onera eiusdem quatenus cum munere meo apud Instituta supra dicta componi possunt, exequi nitor"; ibid.

43. "Urgentibus Superioribus meis ut eorum permissui accedat etiam Sacrae Congregationis pro Religiosis approbatio, hanc presentem petitionem Eminentiae Vestrae humillime nunc submitto, nempe ut liceat mihi et remanere subditus Congregationis Missionis atque usque ad decennium vel longius tempus, si Deo Omnipotenti placuerit opus quod incepi promovere"; ibid.

had founded. Cardinal Lépicier's staff would have been familiar with Father Judge's name, as various queries involving both women's and men's communities, along with other petitions, had been or were in the process of being submitted at this time.

Father Judge's petition would have come to the Congregation for Religious through Giuseppe Scognamelli, the Vincentian procurator general at the Holy See. With his brief August 26, 1932, letter to Judge, Scognamelli enclosed what appears to be a slightly revised text of the July 19 petition. "Would you be so kind as to return it indicating to me what response should be given to the Sacred Congregation for Religious 'pro informatione et voto.'"[44] In Scognamelli's hand, the enclosed petition includes the revisions that are handwritten on the Latin text of July 19 and is missing the second page, which would contain the last paragraph of the petition. "Nihil Obstat" is written at the top of it in a different hand. In a postscript, Scognamelli asks Judge to return the copy to avoid its becoming public ("une possible dispersion").

Asking Father Judge what response to give to the Sacred Congregation for Religious implies that Scognamelli made an inquiry there and was asked for further information. Whether Judge supplied it or ever submitted the revised petition is not clear. McHale, the apostolic delegate, or the Sacred Congregation itself could have advised him to hold off on the petition until the issue of moving the motherhouse to Cleveland, also about to be presented to the same congregation, was resolved. Questions about Father Judge's canonical status, raised by the draft petition and Scognamelli's letter, simply cannot be answered from the historical record as we have it.[45]

Pioneers in This Gold Debenture Bond Issue

"The money is still coming in on the first campaign. I would not be surprised if it would reach $50,000," Father Judge wrote to Father Eugene Bren-

44. "Ci-joint une supplique: Vous aurez la bonté de me la remettre en m'indiquant ce qu'il faut répondre a la S. Cong. Des Relig. 'pro informatione et voto'"; Scognamelli to Judge, Rome, August 26, 1932, AST, MF 14160–62.

45. A tantalizing letter suggests a favorable decision on the petition, but nothing substantive; see Judge to Lillian Moore, Holy Trinity, January 3, 1933, AST, MF 13632. Moore, at this time, put Judge's French letters into final form. Thanking her for copies recently received, Judge added, "Letter came to me the other day that is very decisive which shows that the decision will be on our side of the line." The recipient suggests that the letter he's talking about was in French rather than Latin and therefore from Paris, but this is not clear.

nan on February 23, 1932. "Another campaign has been started. We are going to send out 10,000 letters." Concerned that they meet the semi-annual interest payments, he reported that $8,000 of the bond money was invested "in first class securities." "We are pioneers in this gold debenture bond issue," he enthused. "Our friends [Toth and Stenzel] say that just as soon as the other communities hear about it, they will get busy. They want us to push the thing." He hoped they would be able to help the sisters with the hospital loan.[46]

By March 1932, Brother James Norris reported that of the $150,000 worth of gold debenture bonds issued on January 1, "we have only $11,000 left; all the rest have been reserved."[47] But things were changing fast. Bishop Toolen answered Judge's promise of February 20 to pay off the loan, cosigned by Toolen, by mid-summer with a threat to take over the loan. "I am sorry," Father Judge wrote, "I do not wish you to take over the note, so rest assured I will do all I can to make entire settlement on next payment."[48] He wrote Norris the same day, enclosing the correspondence with Bishop Toolen, and urged him to pay off the entire $10,000. He also worried about the periodic statement of financial affairs at Holy Trinity that Bishop Toolen had a canonical right to demand. Joachim Benson was in charge of this. "We must not push him too far," Judge warned Norris, "so arrange either to pay off in full or at least send $5,000 next payment, try and send the $10,000. Our helping the Sisters is hurt. We must take care of Mobile and for more reasons than the note. Please keep Bro. Joachim on that statement. Do not leave this to me."[49]

46. Judge to Brennan, Newark, N.J., February 23, 1932, AST, MF 4070: "The Brothers' financial problem is clearing. The Sisters' finances, especially the Holy Name of Jesus Hospital, are in a bad condition." The brothers had already sent $1,000 to the sisters and were considering $7,500 for the March 15 payment on the hospital loan. He outlined a plan for financial responsibility and austerity that he would put to an upcoming consultors' meeting. He was well aware that the bonds were "debt replacing debt," that a day of reckoning would come, and that austerity and retrenchment were necessary. He mentioned the possibility of refusing freshmen in September. "We must buttress the foundations of our community credit. This will cause a relief to our financial anxiety . . . and inspire people to have confidence in us." Brennan, a consultor and a fiscal conservative, would have been happy at this.

47. Judge to Norris, Río Piedras, April 1, 1932, AST, MF 1976. In his response, Judge quotes this line from Norris's letter.

48. "The note is now reduced to $10,000. A cut was made March 14 of $1,500"; Judge to Toolen, Río Piedras, March 25, 1932, AST, MF 1970.

49. Judge to Norris, Río Piedras, March 25, 1932, AST, MF 1971. "Another eruption has taken place in Mobile," he wrote the same day; "this I am afraid will prevent us from helping the Sisters as we must clean up the debt"; Judge to Mother Mary of the Incarnate Word, Río Piedras, March 25, 1932, AST, MF 13371.

By March 4, 1932, however, Brother Joachim Benson was in St. Michael's Hospital in Newark for rest, joining Tomerlin and Nummey as the latest to be broken in health or spirit or both by financial pressures. Father Judge urged him to consult with Norris about finances and finish the financial report from the hospital.[50] By March 18, Judge had returned to Puerto Rico. Again he wrote Norris about the financial report. Benson had promised it. "He wrote me that he and you had a long talk about finances, but nary a word was said about financial reports. I warn you boys that someday I'm going to get in trouble over this if you hold them off too long."[51]

On April 1 Father Judge again wrote Norris about the financial report. "It irks our friend down at the Gulf very much that we are getting money. There were several flashes in his letter that seemed ominous.... He may demand at any moment that statement. I am surprised that he has not. Should he hear of the second issue the reaction will be interesting." He told Norris that he had cabled his okay "for another gold debenture."[52] By April 7, 1932, Benson was back at his post at Holy Trinity. Judge was still waiting for the financial report. "I expect any moment, in my mail, opposition, denunciation, etc. because I have not sent it in."[53] Within two weeks, Benson finally sent in the report. "How pleased I am," Judge wrote, "with what you did and what you are trying to do and for the latest exhibit of all this in the financial statement."[54]

James Norris had clearly taken over Monsignor Nummey's role as treasurer. He seems to have had the second issue of gold debenture bonds ready in May, but the appeal letter, signed by Father Judge, was dated December 5, 1932. And that is probably when the bonds actually went on sale. The money was still going into servicing old debt. "If you find the new bond issue a little slower," Judge wrote, "you are probably experiencing the reaction to a great-

50. Judge to Benson, Orange, N.J., March 4, 1932, AST, MF 1959; Judge to Benson, Brooklyn, March 10, 1932, AST, MF 1965.

51. Judge to Norris, Río Piedras, March 18, 1932, AST, MF 1966. Father Judge wrote from bed, where an accident on the boat to Puerto Rico from Brooklyn had confined him. He wrote Norris again three days later. He warned Norris to keep him informed about the bonds and "do not loan a cent to the Sisters without a special order from me." The camp at Chesapeake Bay would be closed. He sent the name of a prospective bond buyer and, if the bonds fell off after Easter, urged advertising in the *Visitor*; ibid., March 21, 1932, AST, MF 1968–69.

52. Ibid., April 1, AST, MF 1976.

53. Judge to Benson, Río Piedras, April 7, 1932, AST, MF 1987.

54. Ibid., April 18, 1932, AST, MF 1989. Benson had another meltdown in June. Judge reprimanded him severely for "your impulsive and extraordinary trip north"; Judge to Benson, Stirling [?], ca. June 18, 1932, AST, MF 2019.

er confidence in the banks."[55] The second bond issue drew a strong response from Archbishop Curley. The December 16, 1932, issue of the *Catholic Review* published a sharply worded front-page letter, denouncing to the Catholic laity of the archdiocese an array of "religious racketeers."

Toth and Stenzel were correct in their prediction that other religious communities would jump on the gold debenture bond bandwagon. Curley's letter noted that the Discalced Carmelite Fathers of Oklahoma had advertised throughout the archdiocese their "issue of six per cent gold bonds." "Don't buy the Oklahoma bonds," Curley's letter warned:

> The same advice we give regarding the bond advertised by the "Rev. Thomas A. Judge, C.M., Superior of the Missionary Servants of the Most Holy Trinity." We have before us Father Judge's letter of December 5, 1932. It should never have been written. It is dated from Washington, D.C. We have no jurisdiction over Father Judge. We are not questioning his sincerity. We are sure he has "vision" of being able to meet his obligations. However, we do not want to see our people banking on visions. So if you are wise, leave the Oklahoma bonds and Father Judge's alone.

Archbishop Curley had lost patience with religious communities "who seem to do little else than flood the country with appeals for money," their "disgustingly pietistic prating," and "the Oklahoma sixes, the Judge gold bonds and half a hundred other offering of 'solid' securities resting on nothing." "It is time for it to stop," he concluded. "It is not helping religion." He asked pastors to make people aware of his letter and, if possible, have it read at Sunday Masses.[56]

55. At this time, the "Riggs people" and the "Propagation" had to be satisfied; Judge to Norris, Río Piedras, May 13, 1932, AST, MF 2001.

56. Michael J. Curley, archbishop of Baltimore, to the Catholic laity of the Archdiocese of Baltimore, December 15, 1932, *Catholic Review*, Friday, December 16, 1932, 1, from a copy in the Archives of the Archdiocese of Baltimore. Curley was not alone in his disgust for Depression-era religious fundraising. In 1931 the "Pilgrim" (probably Wilfred Parsons), in his "With Scrip and Staff" column in the Jesuit magazine *America*, denounced the country's burgeoning number of new religious shrines and their commercialized appeal letters. Taking a shot at one of Brother Augustine's appeals for the Shrine of St. Joseph, he noted, "The typical letter begins with a pious formula such as, 'May the grace and peace of the Holy Ghost be with us forever'"; *America* 45 (July 18, 1931): 354. For the follow-up letters, see 456, and for "An Appeal against Appeals," 408. The month after "Pilgrim's" anti-shrine rant appeared, Father Paul Wattson wrote Judge to "keep a lookout for the next issue of the *Lamp*. We have an article on Shrines in general and St. Anthony's Shrine at Graymoor in particular, in which we have a few commendatory words to say in rejoinder to a criticism which I think appeared in *America* some weeks ago relative to the campaign which Brother Augustine is conducting for St. Joseph's Shrine at Sterling, N.J. [*sic*]. I hope it will be of some slight assistance to your good

For someone who took the church and its authority as seriously as he did, Archbishop Curley's public criticism must have shaken Father Judge. Seven years before he died, Sister Mary Tonra interviewed Father Joachim Benson in Río Piedras. He recalled a story he heard from Sister Carmel Davoren. At Christmastime in 1932, shortly after Archbishop Curley's December 16 article in the *Catholic Review*, Sister Carmel came into the chapel at Gold Street in Brooklyn, probably at night, and "found him [Father Judge] flat on his face in the chapel at Gold Street, the old chapel, with the debenture bonds in his hands."[57] As he prostrated himself before the Blessed Sacrament clutching the bonds, Father Judge no doubt recalled the Agony in the Garden. It was also the position he had taken before the altar of sacrifice on the day he presented himself for ordination to the priesthood.

Puerto Rico—March to May 1932

Father Judge was anxious to get back to Puerto Rico. However, issues such as Father Theophane's ordination, the new Outer Cenacle in Orange, and the first bond issue required his attention. By the end of February, he was ready to go. He considered St. Augustine's Military Academy a signature work of the community involving formation of the next generation of lay leaders for preserving the faith in Latin America. The fate of the colegio hung in the balance as Bishop Edwin V. Byrne of San Juan, strapped for resources, pressed Father Judge to buy the school from the diocese. Under Brennan's leadership, the brothers on the island balked at this prospect. For Judge, "the needs of religion, Catholic education, etc., will guide us and throw us back confidently on the Providence of God. The institution is diocesan and if the Bishop is reasonable and [a] little bit generous, we may commit ourselves."[58]

Father Judge sailed from Brooklyn around March 10, 1932. On March 19, he explained to Bishop Byrne that he had an accident on the boat and would be confined to bed for another week. He wanted Byrne to know why he had

Community;" Wattson to Judge, Graymoor, Garrison, N.Y., August 31, 1931, copy, Wattson Papers, Archives/Record Center of the Franciscan Friars of the Atonement, Graymoor. According to Father Turibius's recollection, Father Judge told them to ignore *America*'s criticism. Perhaps he conveyed this to Wattson. In any case, there was no mention of the Shrine of St. Joseph in the *Lamp*'s next issue; see David O'Connor, ST, "Interview with Fr. Turibius Mulcahy," July 22, 1963, Typescript, 3.

57. Tonra, "Interview with Father Joachim Benson," February 5, 1974, Río Piedras, Typescript, 2, AMSBT.

58. Judge to Jerome Donegan, Brooklyn, March 9, 1932, AST, MF 1963.

not yet come to pay his respects. "The weather was very rough throughout the voyage," he explained; "as a consequence, I suffered a minor injury that produced a series of discomforts and little agonies most appropriate for personal consideration in Passion Week."[59]

To Bishop Byrne Father Judge minimized his condition, but it was more serious than he suggested and perhaps a turning point on the road to his eventual decline. He caught "a terrific cold" on the boat. He blamed this on getting away from the Hay menu. The "minor injury" he described to Bishop Byrne "disabled my elbow. I reached St. Augustine's Military Academy and practically collapsed, taken down with a champion attack of arthritis. I was badly bunged up. All I could do was lay [*sic*] in bed and study the hurt, crucified feet of Our Divine Lord and console Him."[60] "I cannot describe," he wrote from Río Piedras a year later, "what I went through a year ago in this house; in fact, I had to learn to walk all over again. Oh, what days and nights of agony!"[61]

On March 30, 1932, Father Judge wrote to Mother Mary of the Incarnate Word that Bishop Byrne had come to visit him. He hoped to be "in a condition to talk business with him in a few days." He intended to ask Bishop Byrne to hand St. Augustine's over to the Missionary Servants of the Most Holy Trinity "in consideration of what we have done, will do, and the repairs that must be made."[62] Within three days, he had prepared a five-page typed letter on his plans for St. Augustine's. As always, he thought on a big scale. If Bishop Byrne gave them the property, the old building, which needed a lot of repairs and was something of a deterrent as far as recruiting students, could eventually become an extern school.

Father Brennan had plans for "a larger, more advantaged school" that would involve a new building. Father Judge envisioned growing the student body from 60 to 200 and beginning to produce revenue. He estimated an additional $50,000 a year. Brennan put the cost of a new building at $100,000. "Should we get out that second bond issue," Judge wondered, "could we loan

59. Judge to Byrne, Río Piedras, March 19, 1932, AST, MF 12266.

60. "I thought of the little attention He received in His agony. I received comfort from these considerations, otherwise the days and nights would have become unbearable"; Judge to My dear Child, Río Piedras, March 28, 1932, AST, MF 12267.

61. "Everything here," he continued, "reminds me of how much I owe to Dr. Hay. There is so much to warn me lest I ever get away from his regimen"; Judge to Sister Mercedes Roach, Río Piedras, June 7, 1933, AST, MF 12297–98.

62. Judge to Mother Mary of the Incarnate Word, Río Piedras, March 30, 1932, AST, MF 13313.

Father Eugene $75,000?" He envisioned the new building being ready by September 1933 at the latest. They would invest the bond money with Brennan, who would pay $3,000 in interest semiannually.

"As things are," he wrote, "there is little encouragement or incentive outside the purely spiritual to carry on. This has been the leading and sustaining motive over the years and must, of course, never relinquish its prior claim to all our activities." The diocese had not really taken care of its property, and the community had put a lot of money into the building. He wanted a "fair return." The sway of the spiritual, he thought, "will be mightily helped by recognition and compensation and a fair return to reimburse the Missionary Cenacle strain and expense."[63]

One can only imagine what Bishop Toolen, Archbishop Curley, or even Mother Boniface or James Norris might have thought of this plan. "Father Eugene is conservatism itself," Father Judge wrote. "He admits in bad times he can do at least this."[64] Judge reported that he had "canvassed this matter with the Brothers" and that "it was jocosely said that if we could realize this new school idea, Father Eugene could pay off, in a few years, the whole National debt of the Missionary Servants of the Most Holy Trinity."[65] As things turned out, his own lack of financial resources, as well as a surge in "Puerto Rico for Puerto Ricans" sentiment on the island, meant that Bishop Byrne could not see his way clear to sign over the property to the Missionary Servants. Instead, the bishop pressured Father Judge to buy St. Augustine's from the diocese.[66] His grand plan never materialized. Its recklessness in the face of the Great Depression underscores the central religious importance Father Judge placed on the work in Puerto Rico.

Puerto Rico always inspired Father Judge with visions of apostolic work crying to be done. He took his ill health as a providence that caused him to stay longer and become more familiar with the pastoral needs of the island.[67] He was especially taken with needs of the children of Coamo. Despite its poverty, he described Coamo, with its historic Marian shrine, as "perhaps

63. Judge to Dear Brothers, Río Piedras, April 2, 1932, AST, MF 1980–84.

64. Ibid., MF 1984.

65. Ibid., MF 1983.

66. "Nesbit [from the San Juan chancery] is giving out over the Island that we are going to buy St. Augustine's"; Judge to Norris, Río Piedras, May 13, 1932, AST, MF 2001. In this letter, Judge was also happy to report that St. Augustine's was gaining a reputation on the Island as a place for "good Catholic boys."

67. Judge to Mother Mary of the Incarnate Word, Río Piedras, May 4, 1932, AST, MF 13298.

the best piece of Catholicity on the Island."[68] Father Judge was sick for much of his six weeks in Puerto Rico. He left the island at the end of May 1932 without settling the issue of St. Augustine's. "Really I am leaving with great sadness because of the children," he wrote, "children who are really the object of our Cenacle purpose. There are so many of them who are just abandoned and who will be lost to the Church because of the lack of means and workers."[69]

The Sisters' Decree of Erection

The decree of erection recognizing the Missionary Servants of the Most Blessed Trinity as a canonical religious congregation was dated February 20, 1932. By early March, it was probably in Cardinal Dougherty's hands, and it remained for him to sign it. But he had not yet received Rome's permission for the transfer of the sisters' motherhouse. In January Cardinal Dougherty received word from the Sacred Congregation of Religious that the apostolic delegate's office would notify him of Rome's permission for transfer of the sisters' motherhouse from Mobile to Philadelphia.[70] By February 10, he had still not received it.[71] The permission was finally sent directly from Rome with a letter dated March 7. By March 21, Dougherty had finally received it and noted it "has already been put into effect."[72]

One further complication remained. On the eve of his departure for Puerto Rico, Father Judge wrote to Mother Mary of the Incarnate Word urging her to contact Louis Motry at Catholic University. "Do try to get the letter on '*Sanatio in Radice*' [radical cleansing] from Doctor Motry, before you leave. Tell him the Cardinal is drawing up the *decretum erectionis* or, more properly, filling it in."[73] The *sanatio*, or healing, was crucial, as it would grandfather in sisters who had not made a canonical novitiate and not require them to leave their work for a canonical year. Since the community had not yet been erect-

68. Ibid., Coamo, May 7, 1932, AST, MF 13180. This letter made the case for more sisters in Coamo.

69. Judge to My dear Child, Río Piedras, May 15, 1932, AST, MF 12863. In a similar vein on the children, see Judge to Fr. William E. Hayes, Río Piedras, May 13, 1932, AST, MF 4953.

70. Msgr. Augusto Fidecicchi to Dougherty, Rome, January 19, 1932, Dennis Cardinal Dougherty Papers, 80.5303, Philadephia Archdiocesan Historical Research Center (PAHRC).

71. Dougherty to Fidecicchi, Philadelphia, February 10, 1932, Dougherty Papers, 80.5304, PAHRC.

72. Ibid., March 21, 1932, Dougherty Papers, 80.5305, PAHRC.

73. Judge to Mother Mary of the Incarnate Word, Brooklyn, March 9, 1932, AST, MF 13163–64.

ed, technically speaking, none of the sisters had made a canonical novitiate. The sanatio, in effect, recognized the novitiates sisters had already made.

Father Motry noted several difficulties with the decree of erection or with its effects. "I would suggest," he wrote, "asking His Eminence concerning the sanation of any and all invalid novitiates." Motry wanted a sanatio in radice to apply to the sisters' vows as well and include "rectification of all professions (which, thus far, have only been temporary), by repetition of vows."[74]

"Unless we can get a healing [sanatio]," Father Judge wrote to Mother Mary, "we will have an enormous amount of expense, and perhaps at times inconvenience, even embarrassment to Missionary Cenacle work" because sisters, "who have already virtually made the Novitiate," will have to leave the missions and enter the novitiate. He urged her to see Cardinal Dougherty on the sanatio. "Just study how Mother would work that," he wrote. "You know unless we get this it means that the whole world goes to Philadelphia to be enrolled."[75] Cardinal Dougherty must have gotten approval from Rome for the sanatio. By March 31, 1932, word came to Father Judge in Puerto Rico that Dougherty had signed the decree of erection. "Personally," he wrote to Dougherty, "I wish to express my sense of obligation and to state that I am very grateful for your persevering fatherly kindness to the Sisters, and, above all, for this last manifestation of your regard for them."[76]

Upon returning from Puerto Rico, Father Judge went to Philadelphia in June 1932 for the annual retreats at the new motherhouse the sisters had purchased on June 14, located at 3501 Solly Ave. in the Holmesburg section of northeast Philadelphia.[77] In September 1932, Cardinal Dougherty received from Rome the sisters' rule or constitutions, revised by Monsignor Fidecicchi and approved by the Sacred Congregation for Religious.[78] Cardinal Dough-

74. "The professions hitherto have all been made in the form of private promises. This, of course, was due to the fact that the Congregation had not developed far enough to ask for formal recognition"; H. Louis Motry, "Concerning the Decree of Erection," March 10, 1932, with Bishop Joseph Schrembs to Eugene Brennan, Cleveland, August 26, 1935, Folder 3, Box 7, Collection 63, Hubert L. Motry Papers, American Catholic History Research Center and University Archives (ACUA), The Catholic University of America.

75. Judge to Mother Mary of the Incarnate Word, Río Piedras, March 23, 1932, AST, MF 13320.

76. Judge to Cardinal Dennis Dougherty, Río Piedras, March 31, 1932, AST, MF 7237. He pronounced "a wonder of Divine Providence" the formal recognition of the sisters from such humble beginnings "seventeen years ago."

77. Tonra, *Led by the Spirit*, 361. This purchase added to the tensions with Bishop Toolen, who thought that money raised after the fire for a new motherhouse had been misappropriated and that this purchase money should have been used to service the debt on the hospital.

78. Dougherty to Fidecicchi, Philadelphia, October 25, 1932, Dougherty Papers, 80.5306,

erty granted the sanatio in radice, recognizing, as Motry urged, the sisters' novitiates and vows.[79] Father Judge remained the sisters' spiritual director. They kept their distinctive garb. However, the part of the indult naming the custodian general of the Missionary Servants of the Most Holy Trinity their spiritual director and consultor was not granted.[80] Nevertheless, the decree of erection, transfer of the motherhouse, and approval of the sisters' constitutions signaled a major victory for Father Judge in the canonical battles with Bishop Toolen. He took it as a providence and Bishop Toolen as a benefactor. Once again church authority had intervened to save the listing Cenacle boat.

A New Motherhouse for the Brothers

Raleigh, North Carolina

Father Judge's dealings with Bishop Toolen convinced him that the motherhouse of the Missionary Servants of the Most Holy Trinity had to move out of Mobile. In early June 1932, Father Tomerlin traveled to Washington to see the apostolic delegate and then to Raleigh, North Carolina, to call on Bishop William J. Hafey. On June 4, Judge wrote to thank Bishop Hafey for his "courteous reception" of Tomerlin. "I rejoice to learn," he wrote, "that you are giving our petition prayerful consideration." He wanted to assure Hafey that "the lead is not being taken by us in the present situation, we are only following the suggestions of superiors."[81]

Judge's letter to Eugene Brennan two days later clarifies the nature of Tomerlin's mission and of the petition Hafey was considering. "Bishop Hafey has been approached to receive the Mother Missionary Cenacle into his

PAHRC. The sisters sent a small check in appreciation. Dougherty explained that they were "weighed down with debts, principally on account of a hospital they founded in the Diocese of Mobile."

79. Bishop Schrembs's letter of sanation to Eugene Brennan in Motry's papers (see note 81) indicates that, if the decree allowed it, sanatio was within the competence of the ordinary where the congregation was erected.

80. The Motry Papers contain what look like Motry's undated notes for the text of a petition for a pontifical indult allowing (1) "that our religious Community may be permitted to remain subject to the jurisdiction of the Supreme Moderator of the Missionary Servants of the Most Holy Trinity, a congregation of men"; (2) that "the present Moderator of the priests, Father Judge, would be permitted to remain lifelong director of our organization"; and (3) approval for the garb. The notes emphasize that the "missionary movement" carried on by the two institutes "intensifies the Lay Apostolate so much desired by the present Supreme Pontiff." The notes elaborate on this point at some length. It appears that points 2 and 3 of this petition were granted, while the first was not; see Folder 3, Box 7, H. Louis Motry Papers, ACUA.

81. Judge to Bishop William J. Hafey, Stirling, N.J. [?], June 4, 1932, AST, MF 2008.

diocese, he listened receptively and will let us know the 20th. His consultors favor the idea very much. The Papal Delegate said he would encourage Bishop Hafey to give us his favorable decision."[82] On June 23, Judge reported to Mother Mary of the Incarnate Word that Bishop Hafey had regretfully declined to take in the motherhouse. Judge asked her to have the novices pray for a "very particular intention of mine" and told her, "I am deliberating whether to call on Pittsburgh or Cleveland or Altoona."[83]

Continuing Illness

Father Judge's main contact in Altoona was a layman, Leo P. Tiernan, most likely a banker, from the Altoona suburb of Hollidaysburg. Tiernan arranged for the community to buy land in Bellefonte, a possible site for a motherhouse, but Judge had to tell him the consultors had decided it was too expensive.[84] Father Judge wanted to get to Altoona, but when he returned from Puerto Rico, he was still too weak with "everybody waiting on me and everybody insisting that I rest."[85]

He spent most of the time in Stirling and Newark.[86] He sent regrets to Father Bede for missing the reception of new aspirants at Holy Trinity but wrote to each of the new brothers, commenting on their names. Father Eugene did the brunt of the summer retreats. Judge wrote Father Bede at Holy Trinity that "with some doctors and with other people, my health seems to be a present concern. I have to go through a few courses then I hope I will be free from these physical and health governors." Clearly failing, he hoped a visit to Dr. Hay would get him back on his feet.[87]

In addition to his other accumulating concerns, Father Judge faced another episode in the ongoing drama of Joachim Benson, who had made an

82. Judge to Brennan, Stirling, N.J. [?], June 6, 1932, AST, MF 2011. Judge hoped that, after the opening of the new motherhouse, Mother Mary of the Incarnate Word could go to Puerto Rico for two or three days in Rio Piedras and have Brennan show her Coamo, Ponce, and Aguadilla.

83. Judge to Mother Mary of the Incarnate Word, East Pittsburgh, June 23, 1932, AST, MF 13267.

84. Judge to Leo P. Tiernan, Stirling, N.J., June 28, 1932, AST, MF 2020. He instructed Brother Andrew Lawrence to keep in touch with Tiernan, whom he described as "a very good friend. Our Brothers often stay there when they are in Altoona." Tiernan had an office in downtown Altoona in the Altoona Mortgage Building; Judge to Bro. M. Andrew Lawrence, Newark, N.J. [?], July 19, 1932, AST, MF 2045.

85. Judge to Sister Marie Jean, Newark, N.J., June 9, 1932, AST, MF 7199.

86. Judge to Sister Mary Thomas, Newark, N.J., June 9, 1932, AST, MF 7201.

87. Judge to Bede Hermann, OFM Cap., Stirling, N.J. [?], June 18, 1932, AST, MF 2018.

"impulsive and extraordinary trip north." Judge worried that he could become a "murmurer" and "very much a mischief maker." "Brother," Judge wrote, "you know you are hasty, you know that you are very sensitive, you know that you are temperamental; these all make for rashness." He urged Benson to become suspicious of his impulses and seek counsel.[88] Benson's response softened Judge. "I am giving you credit for your good intentions," he wrote. He sent Bro. Augustine to Holy Trinity to relieve Benson and told him to be in Stirling for the brothers' retreat beginning on July 5. "I do think you are in need of a rest, so order the affairs of your office. Go over these with Bro. Augustine."[89] "I am still trying to get South," he wrote the next day. "Major matters hold me here and Doctor's prescriptions."[90]

By July 23, 1932, Father Judge was in East Aurora at the Sun and Diet Sanitarium. "Dr. Hay is quite consoling. If his diagnosis is correct either that famous doctor in Porto Rico exaggerated or my condition must have improved much.... Dr. Hay says I need not worry about my heart."[91] Hay assured him that "my condition is quite good, and that I am physically fit for many years yet, and if I am faithful to the regimen, my difficulties will clear up."[92] He urged Mother Mary to send "an intelligent, alert, open-minded nurse" to "go through the treatments." Convinced that "in a few years the medical profession will be generally following out Dr. Hay's prescriptions," Judge announced that Hay had "lifted from me the inhibitions placed upon me by the other doctor and nurses. He says I can go on and on until I feel fatigued, then, rest and relax." He told her that "SOS's" were coming in, especially from Father Bede, but also from the North. He would have to leave sooner than he wanted to.[93] By August 2, 1932, he was back in Stirling.

88. Judge to Benson, Stirling, N.J. [?], ca. June 18, 1932, AST, MF 2019.

89. Ibid., Stirling, June 29, 1932, AST, MF 2021.

90. "You have done good and hard work and I think you should have a rest for some days or weeks. You may not realize it but you are highly nervous. I think this is due to many things among those the strain you have been under. I wish to see you in good condition in September. Suppose that you get out of the heat of the South for a while and away from the office grind and routine." Judge wrote to say that the start of the retreat had been pushed back a day; Judge to Benson, West Orange, N.J., June 30, 1932, AST, MF 10822–25. See also Judge to Benson, East Aurora, N.Y, July 27, 1932, AST, MF 10826–29, urging Benson to return to Holy Trinity.

91. Judge to James Norris, East Aurora, N.Y., July 24, 1932, AST, MF 2047.

92. Ibid., no date, AST, MF 2051.

93. Judge to Mother Mary of the Incarnate Word, E. Aurora, N.Y., July 28, 1932, AST, MF 13303–6.

Altoona, Pennsylvania

The urgency of finding a diocese to take in the Missionary Servants of the Most Holy Trinity was pushing other concerns to the side. Father Judge sent a two-page spiritual exhortation to the brothers in Puerto Rico, expressing his regret that he could not be there for the opening of St. Augustine's.[94] In late August, Bishop John J. McCort of Altoona appeared likely to accept the motherhouse into his diocese. In western Pennsylvania, east of Johnstown and Pittsburgh, the diocese was also home to the Third Order Regular (TOR) Franciscans' St. Francis College in Loretto.

"Had a very nice day in Altoona," Father Judge reported to Brother Augustine on August 20. "Everything looks promising."[95] On August 27, he told Brother Joseph Limpert he couldn't make the opening of St. Augustine's because two bishops had invited him to stay with them. "One invitation I must accept as it is of vital interest to the Community."[96] From Holy Trinity, where he had gone for the profession of fifteen brothers who had just completed their canonical novitiate under Father Bede, he sent a list of assignments to the brothers in Puerto Rico and announced that they were opening a mission in Altoona. He quoted Bishop McCort's "thrillingly edifying" invitation: "Father, I am growing old and am not well.... When I appear before God I want to go with more good works in my diocese than when I took it over. Help me do missionary work."[97] Father Judge drafted a letter to the apostolic delegate, reporting to him on the move to Altoona.[98] On September 12, he still thought that he would be "with the Bishop of Altoona for about a week, or at least several days."[99]

94. Judge to My dear Brothers, Gadsden, Ala., August 28, 1932, AST, MF 7259–60.

95. Judge to Philips, Altoona, Pa., August 20, 1932, AST, MF 2063. Judge visited Mr. Tiernan's mother, who sent her regards to Brother Augustine. At this time, Judge was also negotiating with Capuchin superiors in Pittsburgh to extend Father Bede's stay as novice master; see Judge to Bede Hermann, OFM, Cap., Gadsden, Ala., August 22, 1932, AST, MF 2065, and Judge to Thomas Petrie, OFM, Cap., Gadsden, Ala., August 26, 1932, AST, MF 2072, a formal request to the provincial to have Father Bede continue.

96. Judge to Limpert, Gadsden, Ala., August 27, 1932, AST, MF 13496. A copy of the community letter of September 28 was enclosed with this one.

97. Judge to My dear Brothers, Holy Trinity, Ala., September 8, 1932, AST, MF 12278. McCort had been bishop of Altoona since 1920. He died four years later in 1936.

98. "It gives me joy to tell you that the Bishop of Altoona has welcomed us into his diocese. We are very happy over your thought of having a friendly Bishop [illegible] us.... Bishop McCort was exceedingly kind"; Judge to Archbishop Pietro Fumasoni-Biondi, Stirling, N.J., undated, AST, MF 2174.

99. Judge to Sister Mary of the Most Holy Agony, Stirling, N.J., September 12, 1932, AST, MF

By September 14, 1932, however, Father Judge was in Cleveland with Bishop Schrembs rather than in Altoona with Bishop McCort. "The scene is now shifted to the Cleveland Diocese," he wrote Brother Augustine. "We are petitioning for entrance here as there is more promise for the Community's future and its work."[100] Apparently the mission in Altoona was to have been what Judge described as a "school project." In hard economic times, the Franciscans at Loretto objected to another school entering the diocese. "Bishop McCort is very much for us," Judge reported to Brother Andrew, "but he does not want to hurt the feelings of the Franciscans. If they favor us he will be more than glad to let us have a school, he is so desirous to have us in the diocese, but he does not want trouble with the other Community or he does not wish to hurt them in what they think their needs and rights."[101]

Cleveland Is the Place

Father Judge's correspondence establishes that, by mid-September, he was in Cleveland. The night of September 14 he left for Washington to see the apostolic delegate, probably arriving back in Stirling on Saturday, September 17, and going to Philadelphia to preach at the opening of the Mother Missionary Cenacle on Sunday, September 18.[102] A September 20 letter to Brother Augustine clarifies this sequence. "Since I left [Holy Trinity]," Judge wrote, "I have been in Altoona and Cleveland. Cleveland is the place. Altoona is in abeyance, we cannot get enough. The Catholic population of Altoona is 150,000. Cleveland Diocese is much larger. A new batch of correspondence has been opened because of Cleveland."[103] Judge gave a long account of his visit with Bishop Schrembs of Cleveland and his chancellor, Monsignor Joseph F. Smith, Father Judge's old friend:

13553. He was trying to arrange an Outer Cenacle retreat and told Sister Mary to write him at the Cathedral Residence in Altoona.

100. Judge to Philips, Cleveland, Ohio, September 14, 1932, AST, MF 2084.

101. Judge to Brother Andrew Lawrence, Stirling, N.J., November 21, 1932, AST, MF 2128. At this time, Father Judge dispatched Brother Andrew to make peace in Altoona. Mr. Tiernan wanted to bring pressure against the Franciscans, and Judge wanted Brother Andrew to steer him in the direction of "boy work."

102. Judge to Sister Marie Anita, Stirling, N.J., September 20, 1932, AST, MF 11800. This letter establishes that he was in Cleveland on September 14 and in Philadelphia on September 18.

103. Judge to Philips, Stirling, N.J., September 20, 1932, AST, MF 2080.

> Msgr. Smith met me in his own inimitable way, made a great deal of me. I took breakfast with the Bishop, then Monsignor claimed me, took me out to the country and threw me overboard and said, "Go back to the Bishop." We arranged the petition. The Bishop was very gracious. I found myself in Washington the next day [September 15?]. I got a very nice reception from our Washington friends. I saw the high secretary [Msgr. Paul Marella?], he is just back from Rome. He told me, among other things, that our friend down on the Gulf claimed he never signed the Decretum Erectionis.[104]

This meeting most likely took place on Wednesday, September 14, 1932. Father Judge's handwritten letter to Brother Augustine of that date says, "Leaving tonight to call at Papal Delegate's office."[105] He probably visited the apostolic delegation on Biltmore Street in Washington, D.C., on Thursday afternoon or Friday morning and then returned to Stirling and began work on the "new batch of correspondence" he described to Brother Augustine on Tuesday, September 20. Two days later he wrote to Brother Joachim, "I am so shuttled about that it is difficult to state just where I will be. Please God, I will be in Philadelphia Thursday or Friday, Pittsburgh Saturday and Cleveland Monday."[106]

The "new batch of correspondence" began with a September 18, 1932, letter to Monsignor Paul Marella at the apostolic delegation. Father Judge had finally located the 1929 decree of erection for the Missionary Servants of the Most Holy Trinity that Bishop Toolen did not remember signing.[107] Marella was no doubt the "high secretary" who had just told Judge that Bishop Toolen denied signing the decree. Judge now had the satisfaction of telling Marella that he had the signed document in hand and enclosed a "photostat." "I have been in touch with two of my Consultors," he told Marella, "and talked the Cleveland matter over. As soon as I draft the letter stating our desire, I will send it to you." He also noted that on that day Cardinal Dougherty had opened and blessed the sisters' new Mother Missionary Cenacle.[108] James Norris and Theophane Mulroy were present on that occasion and were prob-

104. Ibid.

105. Ibid., Cleveland, Ohio, September 14, 1932, AST, MF 2084.

106. Judge to Benson, Stirling, N.J., September 22, 1932, AST, MF 2092.

107. Six days earlier he had written Brother James Norris about some "back rooms" at Holy Trinity. He wanted these rooms "kept under lock and key" because he had "papers there and a few books." He asked Brother Augustine to look into this. It is quite possible that this is how the missing decree of erection turned up; see Judge to Norris, Stirling, N.J., September 12, 1932, AST, MF 2083.

108. Judge to Marella, Stirling, N.J. [?], September 18, 1932, AST, MF 2086.

ably the two consultors he mentioned to Marella. The next day he wrote to the apostolic delegate, enclosing a copy of the signed and sealed decree.[109]

On that same day, September 18, 1932, Father Judge sent Bishop Joseph Schrembs a formal letter requesting to enter the diocese and transfer the motherhouse to Cleveland. He also asked permission to locate "their Apostolic School and to maintain a boarding school for boys of elementary and secondary grades."[110] Judge went on to say that the community did not wish "the care of a parish but they would like, conveniently with their Community duties, to carry on missionary activities, particularly boy work, in the diocese." He enclosed the first chapter of the constitutions to give Schrembs a sense of "the general and particular purposes of the Institute."[111]

In 1932 Bishop Schrembs (1866–1945) was two years older than Father Judge. He had been bishop of Cleveland since 1921 and had a natural affinity for the Missionary Cenacle's work with the lay apostolate and with the poor and abandoned. His long history of involvement with lay organizations went back to his days as bishop of Toledo before the Great War. During World War I, he served on the four-member administrative committee of the National Catholic War Council. After the war, his efforts in Rome were instrumental in gaining approval for the National Catholic Welfare Conference, whose Department of Lay Organizations he chaired. Deeply involved with the bishops' landmark 1919 Program of Social Reconstruction, he was committed to strong charitable and social institutions in his diocese. In 1920, he contributed significantly to the founding of the National Council of Catholic Men and the National Council of Catholic Women. Judge was more a grassroots freelancer and Schrembs more a part of the emerging national face of American Catholicism, but they were both men of the church, and Schrembs's support was genuine and strong.[112]

Equally genuine was the support of the apostolic delegate, Archbishop Pietro Fumasoni-Biondi, who, on September 22, 1932, wrote Bishop Schrembs a

109. "Negotiations are now being made for our entrance into the Cleveland Diocese. The Altoona opening is being held in abeyance"; Judge to Fumasoni-Biondi, Stirling, N.J., September 19, 1932, AST, MF 2087.

110. No doubt a similar request was made to Bishop McCort of Altoona and caused the Franciscans to object.

111. Judge to Bishop Joseph Schrembs, Holmesburg, Pa., September 19, 1932, Bishop Schrembs Papers, religious: Men, Missionary Servants of the Most Holy Trinity, 1928–38, Archives, Diocese of Cleveland (ADC).

112. On Joseph Schrembs's life, see Michael J. Hynes, *History of the Diocese of Cleveland, Origin and Growth (1847–1952)* (Cleveland: Diocese of Cleveland, 1953), chaps. 52–65; see also the article by W. H. Jurgens in *NCE* (1967), 12:1178–79.

strongly worded letter urging him to welcome Father Judge into the Diocese of Cleveland. "I feel sure," the delegate wrote, "that if you can see your way clear to do so, you will lend Father Judge the weight of your valuable assistance and I would add that I myself, so far as it lies in my power, stand ready to cooperate most willingly with Your Excellency to this end."[113] Fumasoni-Biondi told Schrembs that he had "advised Father Judge to talk over the whole matter with you frankly and sincerely, and to place himself completely in your hands without any reservation."[114] On September 26, Bishop Schrembs acknowledged Father Judge's letter of September 19. He promised to bring the petition before his consultors. "I think very highly of your work," Schrembs wrote, "and I want you to feel that we will give kindly consideration to your request."[115]

October 1932 found Father Judge in Cleveland, awaiting news of the hurricane from the brothers in Puerto Rico. He told Brother Andrew Lawrence that Bishop Schrembs had scheduled a meeting of his consultors for Thursday, October 13, at which Judge was to appear. He began a novena to the Holy Ghost and asked Brother Andrew to begin one at Stirling. Monsignor Smith was away, and Judge was anxious that he would return before this meeting.[116] He told Mother Mary about his first days in Cleveland. "Do not forget to get them up on that Novena," he reminded her. "Remember I am to face these Consultors who will have the privilege of asking me questions. Strange to say, I feel quite composed about this and rather anxious to have it over. I might not feel that way when the thing is going on. I imagine they will ask about the financial condition."[117]

Father Judge left Cleveland for Philadelphia on Sunday night, October 9, for a meeting with Father McHale at the sisters' new motherhouse on Monday afternoon, October 10.[118] He got to Newark that night and caught up with

113. Fumasoni-Biondi to Schrembs, Washington, D.C., September 22, 1932, Schrembs Papers, ADC.

114. Ibid. Regarding the work of the Cenacle, the delegate wrote, "I think all agree that his enterprise or undertaking is one which bids fair to redound to the glory of God and the good of souls and perhaps all the more for that reason does it require the benevolent interest of an Ordinary who will take to heart its welfare and give unstintedly the advice and direction which Father Judge and his associates so badly stand in need of."

115. Schrembs to Judge, Cleveland, September 26, 1932, copy, Schrembs Papers, ADC.

116. Judge to Lawrence, Cleveland, October 5, 1932, AST, MF 2108–9. He had also written to Brother Andrew on October 1 on the letterhead of the Cathedral Community House, 1115 Superior Ave., in Cleveland; see Judge to Lawrence, Cleveland, October 1, 1932, AST, MF 2105.

117. Judge to Mother Mary of the Incarnate Word, Cleveland, October 5, 1932, AST, MF 13223–26.

118. Judge to McHale, Cleveland, October 9, 1932, AST, MF 2114. It is likely that Judge made this special trip to consult with Father McHale about his status as a Vincentian.

his mail from Puerto Rico. On September 26, 1932, while Judge was deep into his negotiations with Bishop Schrembs, a hurricane slammed Puerto Rico and damaged St. Augustine's extensively.[119] He wrote Sister Mary Thomas in Puerto Rico. "You cannot imagine how much I desire to be in Puerto Rico just now," he wrote, "but for this business [Cleveland] I would be there, in fact I would have been there during the hurricane as it is only this affair that could detain me, it is so essential, I cannot get away until it is settled and I have been working on it since last August."[120] The meeting of Bishop Schrembs's consultors was Thursday. Judge left Newark for Cleveland on Tuesday night. The travel and stress of trying to transfer the motherhouse had begun to wear on him. "It is too bad that just in these trying days," he told Sister Mary Thomas, "I have been so much on trains, much more than usual, and usual is too much, or at least I feel that way."[121]

By the beginning of October, Mother Mary of the Incarnate Word was in Puerto Rico. Father Judge was glad that she could be on the island tending to the hurricane's aftermath. In her absence, the amended constitutions had been returned from Rome. Judge confessed that he had not had time "to examine them minutely or at length."[122] In addition, there was another letter from Bishop Toolen, who wanted the sisters out of his diocese. They had missed the October 1 payment to Bitting and Co. on the hospital loan.[123] "My dear Mother," Father Judge wrote, "do not worry about the financial situation." He reassured her that "every one of us concerned acted in good faith." He told her he was sending out a letter to try to get $300 more per month for the sisters.[124] "The United States Government has loaned millions and billions of dollars to distressed corporations and public works and the least that some of our church people can do is to loan us a little sympathy and patience."[125]

119. See Father Judge's compilation of excerpts from letters describing the flood and his press release, dated October 11, 1932, asking for contributions in the wake of the flood; AST, MF 2101–2 and 2116–18.

120. Judge to Sister Mary Thomas, Newark, N.J., October 11, 1932, AST, MF 7262.

121. Ibid.

122. Judge to Mother Mary of the Incarnate Word, Newark, N.J., October 11, 1932, AST, MF 13193.

123. See Sister Mary James to Bishop Toolen, Holmesburg, Pa., September 30, 1932, Toolen Papers, AAM.

124. See Judge to My dear Children, Stirling, N.J., October 31, 1932, AST, MF 2146.

125. Judge to Mother Mary of the Incarnate Word, Newark, N.J., October 11, 1932, AST, MF 13193. Mother Mary included these thoughts in a two-page handwritten response to Bishop Toolen's letter regarding the missed interest payment; see Mother Mary of the Incarnate Word to Bishop Toolen, Río Piedras, October 19, 1932, Toolen Papers, AAM. Sometime in October, Bitting and Co. brought a civil suit against the sisters in the United States District Court in

As he anticipated the meeting in Cleveland on Thursday, financial questions weighed heavily on Father Judge's mind. He mentioned this concern again in closing his letter to Mother Mary. "The business in Cleveland is coming along fine. It is keeping me busy, however, shuttling up and down the country. It is no great pleasure to be waiting on bishops and monsigniori."[126] Father Judge made it back to Cleveland the day before the meeting. Monsignor Smith had already returned. Brother Augustine's financial report arrived just in time for Judge to go over it with Smith before the meeting. "Had a long talk with him [Smith] way up to the wee hours of the morning," Judge reported to Philips. "He put it straight to me how we were to finance and keep going the Cleveland project. Believe me I was so happy to have at hand & to be able to show him the report. It came very opportunely and made a good impression."[127]

The meeting with Bishop Schrembs and his consultors took place at 10:30 a.m. "First thing of the day, I was on tip toe to be at the meeting," Father Judge reported. "The Bishop and the Consultors were very nice and easy. Friday, I am to hear results.... We will get all that we ask for 100 percent.... There is to be another Consultors' meeting Tuesday [October 18] 8:30. After that he will definitely settle everything."[128] Judge planned to go back to Philadelphia for the novices' profession and be back in Cleveland on Monday, October 17, the day before the next consultors' meeting. He asked Brother Augustine to keep the news about Cleveland confidential so that he could tell Bishop Toolen about it himself. Bishop Toolen was to come to Holy Trinity for a visitation. Judge advised Brother Augustine to be there but to have Brother Joachim answer questions about finances. "He should be in good condition by then," Judge thought. Neither of them was to act like a custodian. "One reason I am so anxious to rush the Cleveland business through," Judge concluded, "is to avoid showing our general financial statement to Bp. Toolen. It is only the Bishop of the Mother Missionary Cenacle has that right and, please God, after next Tuesday only Bishop Schrembs will have the right. Bp. Toolen will have right to see local statement but this will have no mention of bonds, etc."[129]

Pennsylvania; see J. Raymond Dyer to Bishop Toolen, St. Louis, Mo., October 26, 1932, Toolen Papers, AAM. Dyer was an attorney for Bitting and Co.

126. Judge to Mother Mary of the Incarnate Word, October 11, 1932, AST, MF 13193. "It is just too bad," he wrote to Sister Marie Jean in Puerto Rico on the same day, "that both my mail and myself at this time are so scrambled about"; Judge to Sister Marie Jean Daigle, Newark, N.J., October 11, 1932, AST, MF 7264.

127. Judge to Philips, Cleveland, October 13, 1932, AST, MF 2119.

128. Ibid.

129. Ibid.

Waiting and travel were wearing on Father Judge. "It seems I cannot plan very far ahead, and I take this constant shifting and shunting around as a penance," he wrote to Brother Joachim on October 15. Benson was at the hospital in Gadsden for a rest. "When you are looking for favors for yourself," Judge wrote, "you must be very obliging and wait on people, or rather stand around waiting for them. I have been doing nothing since I saw you but standing around waiting on Bishops, other Prelates and priests."[130] On the same day, he wrote briefly to Bishop Schrembs, perhaps in answer to a query. "No doubt, the Consultors would like to know something of my personal status." He explained that he was a Vincentian who had the superior general's permission to direct the work of the Missionary Servants. "The enclosed letter," he continued, "is very current and gives expression of his thought in the matter."[131]

On October 18, 1932, Father Judge learned from Bishop Schrembs that the consultors had consented unanimously to accept the Missionary Servants of the Most Holy Trinity into the Diocese of Cleveland. They would begin a foundation in Lorain, Ohio, "thirty miles west of Cleveland."[132] The next day he wrote to Brother Augustine at Holy Trinity with more details. The work in Lorain would be "among the Mexicans," and there would be a pastor's salary of $1,200 a year. He hoped that they would also be able to have a community of sisters and pay them a salary. "This Cleveland business has me just coming and going and turning around," he told Philips, "however, it is such an enormously big thing and it has all transpired so quickly that it is necessary for me to be on hand." It had all happened in the month since September 14, 1932. "It will take some days to get things moving," he thought. "First of all, there must be some necessary correspondence."[133] The most daunting piece of correspondence would be a letter requesting Bishop Toolen's permission for the transfer. Despite a brief handwritten draft on October 21, Father Judge had to wait another month to write that letter.[134]

On October 20, 1932, Father Judge wrote a warm letter of thanks to Bishop Schrembs. "Words fail me," he began, "in expressing the gratitude that wells

130. Judge to Benson, Cleveland, October 15, 1932, AST, MF 2123.

131. Judge to Schrembs, Cleveland, October 15, 1932, Schrembs Papers, ADC. The "current" enclosed letter is not filed with this one.

132. On October 18 Judge hand-drafted letters to both Archbishop Fumasoni-Biondi and Monsignor Marella at the apostolic delegation. Neither one was mailed, probably so that the first news of this would come to the delegation through Bishop Schrembs; see AST, MF 14024 (to Fumasoni-Biondi); AST, MF 14020–23 (to Marella).

133. Judge to Philips, Cleveland, October 19, 1932, AST, MF 2125.

134. Judge to Bishop Toolen, Cleveland, October 21, 1932, handwritten draft, AST, MF 14025.

up in my heart towards you as our great benefactor."[135] Bishop Schrembs wrote to the apostolic delegate on the same day, informing him that the consultors unanimously agreed to "the admission of Father Judge's community to the Diocese of Cleveland." Schrembs sought Fumasoni-Biondi's advice on how to proceed. He thought the transfer required the consent of Bishop Toolen, himself, and other ordinaries in dioceses where the community worked. The proper procedure, he thought, was for Judge to seek the permission of Bishop Toolen and the other bishops under whom the community worked. Nevertheless, he concluded, "Inasmuch as Your Excellency is interested in this community and is thoroughly conversant with the situation in Mobile, I should be grateful for any advice or direction you can give me in this matter."[136]

Archbishop Fumasoni-Biondi responded quickly, explaining that, in addition to Bishop Toolen's permission, "it is also necessary to have the permission of the Holy See." He advised that Father Judge write to Bishop Toolen for "the latter's written consent." He instructed Schrembs to send that letter, along with his own written consent, to him and he would forward them to the Sacred Congregation for Religious without delay. He also told Schrembs that he would write to Father Judge "today to instruct him to consult your Excellency about the proper steps to be taken in this matter."[137] On November 10, 1932, Judge, "somewhat perplexed" and "in a quandary," told James Norris that he was still waiting to hear from Bishop Schrembs. Perhaps this meant the matter had been referred to Rome.[138] They were supposed to take over the parish in a month, and he had heard nothing. On November 13 he wrote Monsignor Smith asking what he should do next.[139]

Bishop Schrembs had already written the letter on November 10. He informed Judge of what he had learned from the apostolic delegate and instructed him to write to Bishop Toolen for his consent and then forward that letter, along with Schrembs's own, to the apostolic delegate, who would for-

135. Judge to Schrembs, Cleveland, October 20, 1932, Schrembs Papers, ADC.

136. Schrembs to Fumasoni-Biondi, Cleveland, October 20, 1932, copy, Schrembs Papers, ADC.

137. Fumasoni-Biondi to Schrembs, Washington, D.C., October 27, 1932, Schrembs Papers, ADC. I have found no October 27, 1932, letter from the apostolic delegate to Father Judge in his papers.

138. Judge to Norris, Stirling, N.J., November 10, 1932, AST, MF 2134.

139. Judge to Monsignor Joseph F. Smith, Stirling, N.J., November 13, 1932, Schrembs Papers, ADC. Brother Andrew Lawrence personally delivered this letter to Monsignor Smith. Judge's note to Smith identifying Brother Andrew is also preserved in Schrembs's Papers, along with Smith's note forwarding the letter to Schrembs.

ward them on to Rome. He noted that Fumasoni-Biondi had not mentioned permission from any other bishops.[140]

"The long-looked for letter from Bishop Schrembs came in," Father Judge wrote to Sister Marie Baptista on November 18. "In fact, one came the same day from the Papal Delegate." He told her Bishop Toolen would receive his letter requesting permission to accept Bishop Schrembs's invitation by Monday.[141] When Bishop Schrembs received Judge's November 13 letter to Smith, he wrote to Judge again, also on November 18, to "set all your perplexities at ease." Schrembs thought he had already given Judge a letter "notifying you of the unanimous decision of our Diocesan Board of Consultors to accede to your petition for the establishment of your motherhouse in this diocese." But he couldn't find the copy, so he sent another, dated November 18, with the official minutes of the consultors' meeting. He also sent a telegram that read, "Lorain Parish vacated next Tuesday [November 22]. Expect Fathers to take charge at once. Letter follows."[142] Father Judge now had to make sure that he and Father Theophane made it to Lorain on time.

He still had to write to Bishop Toolen. His letter was brief, three sentences in seven lines. He told the bishop that Bishop Schrembs had invited the Missionary Servants of the Most Holy Trinity into his diocese. "I respectfully ask your permission to begin a new foundation in that diocese [Cleveland] and also to transfer the Mother Missionary Cenacle (Mother-house) to the Cleveland Diocese."[143] Father Judge wrote Bishop Toolen again the next day regarding Father Tomerlin's status. He reported that, since last spring when Toolen inquired about him, Tomerlin had "gotten himself out of touch with the Community . . . and placed himself outside of my influence as a superior." Within a year after Tomerlin preached at Mother Boniface's Solemn Mass of Requiem at Holy Name of Jesus Hospital, Father Judge disowned him. "As much as I dislike to do it, I must report him in to you and so far as the Community is concerned he is not one of us any longer."[144]

"All kinds of news is coming in, some quite sensational," Father Judge wrote to Brother Augustine on November 21, "about our roving friend from

140. Schrembs to Judge, Cleveland, November 10, 1932, copy, Schrembs Papers, ADC.

141. Judge to Sr. Marie Baptista Croke, Stirling, N.J., November 18, 1932, AST, MF 2135.

142. Schrembs to Judge, Cleveland, November 18, 1932, copies, Schrembs Papers, ADC. There are two letters dated November 18. The longer answers Judge's to Msgr. Smith on November 13; the other gives Schrembs's official approval of Judge's petition along with the consultors' minutes for the meeting of October 18. A copy of the Western Union telegram is also there.

143. Judge to Toolen, Stirling, November 19, 1932, Toolen Papers, AAM.

144. Ibid., Stirling [?], November 20, 1932, Toolen Papers, AAM.

Birmingham. When you get it, you'll understand why you got at least one telephone call concerning his whereabouts. He is, I'm afraid, in a very serious situation."[145] There was a warrant out for Fr. Tomerlin's arrest in New York, having to do with some of his financial dealings. "I would not be surprised," Judge told Father Eugene Brennan on November 28, "if the Father Tomerlin business came to a crisis before Christmas."[146] Judge wrote Tomerlin on the same day: "Numerous inquiries are coming in about your whereabouts.... You have taken yourself out of the Community and now I effectively accept your exit and say that you are out."[147]

Lorain a Land of Promise

"Father Theophane and myself are starting for Cleveland today to take possession. I think the diocese will prove to us, after all our tribulation, a land of promise."[148] On Tuesday November 22, Fathers Mulroy and Judge "took possession" of St. John's Church, 1977 E. 30th Street, in Lorain. The following Sunday was their first in Lorain. "We made a quiet entrance and faced the people for the first time yesterday," Judge told Bishop Schrembs on November 28. "We like the people. As far as we can learn, they are kindly digesting us." They had made contact with "our local clerical brethren."[149] To his sister, he described Lorain as "a Pentecostal city," gathering "races and representatives from so many different nationalities." "We were asked to take up a work among the Mexicans," he reported, "but we found we needed the *dona linguarum*."[150]

Father Theophane was in charge of the parish at Lorain, with Father Judge as his assistant. "How wonderfully the whole thing is breaking," Father Judge exclaimed. "There is no doubt about it but Lorain is going to be

145. Judge to Philips, Stirling, November 21, 1932, AST, MF 2136.

146. Judge to Brennan, Lorain or Cleveland, November 28, 1932, AST, MF 2142.

147. Judge to Tomerlin, Lorain, Oh. [?], November 28, 1932, AST, MF 2143.

148. Judge to Benson, Stirling, November 21, 1932, AST, MF 2137. He also told Benson that he expected Bishop Toolen to visit Holy Trinity on December 14 and emphasized how important it was for him to be there.

149. Judge to Schrembs, Lorain, November 28, 1932, Schrembs Papers and AST, MF 2139. Judge also explained to the bishop that his November 10 letter arrived after he had written Monsignor Smith on November 13. Schrembs replied briefly to this letter on December 2: "I am glad that the ground for your Foundation in the Cleveland Diocese has been broken and I hope that all will go well"; Schrembs Papers, ADC.

150. Judge to Sister Gerard Ledwidge, Holy Trinity, Ala., December 28, 1932, AST, MF 7270.

for us a Land of Promise."[151] Judge envisioned his role as Mulroy's assistant as temporary. Soon he hoped "to throw more responsibility on Father Theophane." At this point, Mulroy had been a priest for only about ten months. "I talked to him the other evening," Judge wrote on December 8, "and told him in a way that now we're going to throw him out into the deep and he would have to keep himself and other things afloat. I will be near at hand for a little while to steady him."

To one of the sisters who thought he was working too hard, having preached at three Masses and said two the previous Sunday, Father Judge replied that he would take it easier the next week, but he still wanted to "give the Spanish novena." "I have so many friends among the Mexicans, I really have to look out for the evening service."[152] The parish was having a novena to Our Lady of Guadalupe, to end on her feast on December 12, "and our Mexicans are coming out of their hiding places."[153] The Mexican parishioners at St. John's introduced him to Guadalupe. "Have you ever heard much about her?" he asked another sister. "I am so eager to hear more, I would do anything to get more information." Guadalupe had a new devotee. On December 27, Father Judge gave a conference on Our Lady of Guadalupe at Holy Trinity.[154]

After about three weeks, Father Judge thought his work at Lorain was done. He asked Mother Mary to "look around and see if you can put together a little Missionary Cenacle for Lorain." He envisioned "a bright future for both Missionary Cenacles in this Diocese. We are in favor and that favor will be cemented by our works. This will mean vocations and revenue."[155] He asked Brother James to "go carefully over the items for the *Catholic Directory*" and to have a council on what to call Lorain as motherhouse. When school got out at Catholic University, he asked Norris to meet him in Stirling.[156] On the next day, December 15, he was back in Stirling. He assured Sister Mary Thomas that Lorain had not crowded the needs of Puerto Rico out of his mind.[157] In the meantime, he had received "two distress calls" from Puerto

151. Judge to Brother Augustine Philips, Cleveland, November 29, 1932, AST, MF 2154.

152. Judge to My dear Child, Lorain, December 8, 1932, AST, MF 12877.

153. Judge to Philips, Lorain, December 8, 1932, AST, MF 2155.

154. Judge to Sister Clare, Holy Trinity, December 28, 1932, AST, MF 7269.

155. Judge to Mother Mary of the Incarnate Word, Lorain, December 14, 1932, AST, MF 13364.

156. Judge to Norris, Lorain, December 14, 1932, AST, MF 2165. Two days earlier, on Guadalupe's Feast, he asked Norris, "Have you ever heard of Our Lady of Guadalupe? Pray to her"; Judge to Norris, Lorain, December 12, 1932, AST, MF 2163.

157. Judge to Sr. Mary Thomas Champion, Stirling, December 20, 1932, AST, MF 7224.

Rico, "one from Father Eugene, one from Brother Joseph. They want money. They want it badly." He asked James Norris if there was anything he could do. The matter of St. Augustine's Military Academy remained unresolved from Judge's spring trip to the island. He told Norris that he was about to meet in Brooklyn with Mr. Nesbit, the lay administrator of the San Juan Diocese, to discuss St. Augustine's, but said he would try to hold off on any "consummation" until after Father Eugene had come north in January.[158] Unfortunately, Nesbit arrived on the mainland on December 16, the day Archbishop Curley's letter denouncing the "Judge bonds" appeared on the front page of the *Catholic Review*.

Bishop Toolen and the Transfer of the Motherhouse

Bishop Toolen's November 24, 1932, response to Father Judge's request for permission to transfer the men's motherhouse from Mobile to Lorain necessitated another batch of correspondence. Bishop Toolen wanted badly to be rid of Father Judge for good. This was his opportunity. "You are hereby granted the permission you request in your letter of Nov. 19," he began, "to begin a new foundation in the diocese of Cleveland and also to transfer Motherhouse to same." He followed this permission by explaining, "I understand by that you are moving out of the Diocese of Mobile entirely." This meant Holy Trinity would be "entirely closed" and the magazine would no longer be published and mailed from there. "I expect," Toolen wrote, "that you will close out entirely your work in the Diocese of Mobile."[159]

Bishop Toolen's letter was forwarded to Lorain, and Father Judge responded on December 6, 1932. The clear granting of permission gave Judge a small opening. Thanking Bishop Toolen for the permission, he went on to say, "I imagine Your Excellency must have misunderstood my letter. I did not mean that we 'are moving out of the Diocese of Mobile entirely.' It was not our intention to move the Novitiate." He explained, "It is not only useful, therefore, but essential that our young men should receive their initial training in a field in which, please God, later they will work." He described

158. Judge to Norris, Newark, N.J., December 19, 1932, AST, MF 2169. It is amazing to think that, while Norris was acting as treasurer and general troubleshooter for Father Judge, he was also a full-time student at Catholic University.

159. Toolen to Judge, Mobile, November 24, 1932, AST, MF 14028–29. Toolen responded to Judge almost immediately and wrote in his own hand. Judge noted that he had received two copies of this letter.

the work in Lorain as also "part of our plan which calls for an Apostolate among the Latin Americans." Regarding the magazine, he wrote, "Our work remaining at Holy Trinity, I would infer, in consequence, that you would kindly permit us to continue the publication of the magazine which, after all, has a message to encourage vocations for the Southland."[160]

Neither completely sure of the canonical ground, both Father Judge and Bishop Toolen danced around a bit in this correspondence. Bishop Toolen was not about to accept Judge's inference from his permission. He responded immediately on December 9. We do not have this letter, but from Judge's response on December 21, it is clear that Bishop Toolen continued to insist that the Missionary Servants of the Most Holy Trinity move out of his diocese entirely. He asked Judge to call on him to talk over these matters.[161] Judge forwarded Bishop Toolen's November 24 letter to Bishop Schrembs. "You see I was right," Schrembs wrote, "when I told you that if you moved your Motherhouse from Alabama, Bishop Toolen would insist on your leaving the diocese and giving up all work in his diocese, and leaving it forevermore." Schrembs was not sure of the extent of the work in Alabama, but he concluded, "no doubt, you will have to transfer your Novitiate." He promised that, "whatever may come, I want you to know that you have a home here and are welcome."[162]

On December 17, 1932, Father Judge wrote a long letter to Brother James Norris, enclosing "a copy of the last contribution of our big benefactor in the South." He described Bishop Toolen's December 9 letter as "quite uncanonical and to anyone of ecclesiastical sense it is surprising and shocking, because of violence to Canons, ecclesiastical procedure, courtesy and tradition in trying to get rid so summarily of a Religious Congregation." He sent Norris to the apostolic delegation with a letter for Monsignor Bernardini. He told him he would forward Toolen's letter to Bernardini separately. He only wanted Norris to convey to Bernardini "that we do not wish to leave Holy Trinity." The five reasons he gave for this would become the substance of his eventual response to Bishop Toolen four days later on December 21.

Father Judge did not believe that Bishop Toolen had the authority to move the novitiate "without the knowledge and permission of the Holy Congregation of Religious." As he put it, "the Church does not permit Religious to be

160. Judge to Toolen, Lorain, December 6, 1932, from a copy in the Schrembs Papers, ADC.

161. See ibid., December 21, 1932, AST, MF 13065–66 and 7233. Though this letter is dated from Lorain, Judge was in the East at this time.

162. Schrembs to Judge, Cleveland, December 9, 1932, copy, Schrembs Papers, ADC.

scattered as chicken are shooed away, or as vagabond itinerants are chased along the highway." In a postscript, he wrote, "The point to make with Msgr. Bernardini is, 'Msgr., can a Bishop throw out a novitiate without the permission of Rome (the Congregation of Religious)?'" He also asked Norris to try to find Louis Motry and show him Toolen's letter. "If you can get me his canonical opinion, do so." Norris was to convey to Motry that "we are now taking the offensive but cautiously." "Do pray for our good friend," Judge concluded. "Despite it all, I have great sympathy for him. It is too bad."[163]

On December 19, Norris sent Father Judge a telegram. He had not yet received Judge's December 17 letter. Perhaps they talked on the phone. "Try and find out from Doctor Motry or get a definition from some approved canonist. I prefer it not be Msgr. Bernardini." Judge summarized his plan of action: "Bishop Toolen cannot drive us out just because of an arbitrary vindictive feeling.... He has not given me any reason and even with all that we have a right to appeal to the Holy See. I do not wish to make this appeal until it is necessary, until it can be done cautiously, opportunely and canonically." He gave Norris his instructions. "Our man to locate all these things is Doctor Motry so get busy and stay in Washington until you get further orders."[164]

When Norris got back to him with Motry's counsel is not clear. In any case, Judge's "cautious offensive" began on December 21, 1932, with a carefully crafted response to Bishop Toolen's December 9 letter. He declined Toolen's invitation to call on him, noting respectfully and vaguely that "the question of our leaving the diocese of Mobile now awaits the decision of Higher Authority." He assured the bishop that, "if the Holy See wishes us to leave the Diocese of Mobile entirely, we are content, but, naturally, we should regret seeing the works we have started given up." He wanted to stay at Holy Trinity for both substantive and practical reasons: his vision for the work, the equity in the property, works already begun at Holy Trinity, and the promise of fifteen recently professed brothers. He assured Bishop Toolen of his respect and of the Missionary Cenacle's prayerful regard for him.[165]

The next day, Father Judge received the apostolic delegate's response to his letter of December 6, in which he enclosed the permissions from Bishops Schrembs and Toolen. Archbishop Fumasoni-Biondi offered "cordial congratulations on the reception accorded you by the Most Reverend Bishop of

163. Judge to Norris, Stirling, N.J., December 17, 1932, AST, MF 2167–68. The reference to Monsignor Bernardini is confusing, as he had moved to Rome the previous year.

164. Ibid., Newark, N.J., December 19, 1932, AST, MF 2169.

165. Judge to Toolen, Lorain, December 21, 1932, AST, MF 7233.

Cleveland." He reaffirmed his offer to refer this matter to the Holy See. But the matter of Bishop Toolen's understanding of his permission remained. The delegate asked Judge to "obtain from the Bishop of Mobile a simple typewritten statement to the effect that he grants permission for the transfer of the Motherhouse of your Community to the Diocese of Cleveland." This statement was to have Bishop Toolen's own signature and the diocesan seal.

Archbishop Fumasoni-Biondi, who left office and returned to Rome in March of 1933, would continue as apostolic delegate for less than three months. He advised Father Judge that "the question which the Bishop of Mobile raises in his letter of November 24th can be settled in the course of time." Indeed, it would remain unsettled at Father Judge's death less than a year later. He returned Bishop Schrembs's letter so that Judge could forward both letters to the delegation at the same time.[166] On the day after Christmas, Father Judge wrote to Archbishop Fumasoni-Biondi, turning to him "for fraternal advice in a matter that effects [*sic*] vitally the Missionary Servants of the Most Holy Trinity in Alabama." Making reference to Bishop Toolen's letters of November 24 and December 9, which he enclosed, Judge explained that "he makes very clear in his second letter of December 9th, that our houses in the Mobile Diocese are to be considered suppressed upon the removal of the Mother Missionary Cenacle from his diocese." Judge continued:

> There are so many things at stake both spiritual and material that I could not in conscience comply with the order of the Bishop without submitting the matter to Your Excellency and having due recourse to you as the representative of the Holy See. Contingently upon consultation with Your Excellency, I shall, if you think it advisable, make my recourse to the Sacred Congregation of Religious in compliance with Canon 498 of the Code of Canon Law.

In addition to his correspondence with Bishop Toolen, Judge enclosed what he described as a "recent letter from my superior general."[167] His reference to Canon 498 suggests that by this time Norris had succeeded in consulting Louis Motry.

Archbishop Fumasoni-Biondi replied on December 31. He had read care-

166. Fumasoni-Biondi to Judge, Washington, D.C., December 22, 1932, AST, MF 14031.

167. Judge to Fumasoni-Biondi, Lorain, December 26, 1932, AST, MF 14032. Though this letter is dated from Lorain, Judge was at Holy Trinity on December 26. It is likely that when Judge wrote this letter, he had yet to receive the delegate's letter of December 22. The reference to a recent letter from Verdier underlines again the question of Judge's canonical status at the end of his life.

fully the correspondence Judge enclosed and returned it. He advised that, if Judge didn't think a "personal interview" had much chance of changing Bishop Toolen's mind, "I think it would be best to lodge a recourse with the Sacred Congregation of Religious." He went on to explain what such a recourse should include:

> In such a recourse you should explain as briefly as possible and very clearly the situation as it stands to-day. You should set forth the facts in regard to your desire to transfer the Motherhouse to the Diocese of Cleveland, the consent of the Bishop of Cleveland, the correspondence that has passed between you and Bishop Toolen in the matter.

He instructed Judge to forward this recourse to the Sacred Congregation for Religious to the Delegation. From there it would be sent to Rome.[168]

By mid-February 1933, with Louis Motry's help, Judge had prepared both a "Petition for the Removal of the Motherhouse of the Missionary Servants of the Most Holy Trinity from the Diocese of Mobile, Alabama to the Diocese of Cleveland, Ohio," dated February 16, and a "Recourse of the Missionary Servants of the Most Holy Trinity to Prevent the Suppression of Their Institutions and Work by His Excellency, Most Reverend Thomas J. Toolen, D.D. Bishop of Mobile, Alabama, U.S.A.," also dated February 16.[169]

Early in February 1933, a crucial development took place that made it possible for Archbishop Fumasoni-Biondi to forward the recourse and petition to Rome with some hope of success. "It certainly is very gratifying," Father Judge wrote to Fumasoni-Biondi on February 16, "to know that you have the statement from His Excellency, the Bishop of Mobile, permitting the transfer of the Motherhouse."[170] Before he left for Rome in March, Archbishop Fumasoni-Biondi managed to obtain from Bishop Toolen the simple, unconditional written permission he had previously asked Father Judge to get. He informed Judge of this in a letter of February 10, to which Judge responded on February 16. On February 20, 1933, Judge visited Fumasoni-Biondi at

168. Fumasoni-Biondi to Judge, Washington, D.C., December 31, 1932, AST, MF 14033. On January 1, Judge responded to Fumasoni-Biondi's letter of December 22, telling him that he had written to Bishop Toolen "for the desired letter"; see Judge to Toolen, Holy Trinity, January 2, 1933, Toolen Papers, AAM, and Judge to Mother Mary of the Incarnate Word, Holy Trinity, January 5, 1933, AST, MF 13144.

169. Both documents are in English and addressed to Cardinal Alexis Lépicier of the Sacred Congregation for Religious. The two and a half-page "Recourse" is marked "draft"; the "Petition" is three pages; AST, MF 2194–96 (petition), 2191–93 (recourse). There is an Italian copy of the petition at MF 15021–23.

170. Judge to Fumasoni-Biondi, Lorain, February 16, 1933, AST, MF 2197.

the delegation in Washington, no doubt to deliver the two documents. "I feel so greatly relieved. You know I was in Washington but a few hours ago. The Papal Delegate was just gorgeous. Do you know that our briefs are finished?" "Doctor Motry was very much pleased," he added. "He said the papers are perfect. May the Spirit of God be blessed, there were very few hours given to put things together."[171]

Monsignor Kiley, Bishop Toolen's Roman agent at the North American College, thought the permission a blunder that gave Father Judge new life. "As I intimated to you in my letters," Kiley wrote, "Judge was about through and this gave him a new lease on life." Kiley thought that Archbishop Curley's December 1932 letter would tell strongly against Judge. Along with Bishop Toolen's own "Recourse" to the Sacred Congregation, Kiley supplied Cardinal Lépicier with a copy of the *Catholic Review* with Curley's letter. Kiley interpreted Toolen's February permission as a game changer. "On the face of it," he explained, "[it—the permission] makes the situation now look like this. Dougherty, Schrembs, and the Delegate, now a Cardinal back of Judge, with only yourself and the Archbishop [Curley] against him." Kiley had advised Toolen not to give his permission for the move until the question about the fate of Holy Trinity was resolved.[172] Bishop Toolen may have been a mercurial man, but he was no fool. It is interesting to think about why he might have decided to give Fumasoni-Biondi the letter of permission.[173]

On May 18, 1933, Father Judge reported to Bishop Schrembs from Puerto Rico that "affairs in reference to the Bishop of Mobile are in statu quo." He told Schrembs about the petitions he had made to the Sacred Congregation for Religious, both to transfer the motherhouse to Cleveland and to "enjoin the threatened action of His Excellency, the Bishop of Mobile." After Archbishop Fumasoni-Biondi left the delegation on March 16, Monsignor Paul Marella took care of forwarding the correspondence to Rome. "No answer has come as yet, and as soon as I have anything to report, I will let you

171. Judge to Mother Mary of the Incarnate Word, Stirling, N.J., February 21, 1933, AST, MF 13189.

172. See Moses E. Kiley to Toolen, Rome, February 28, 1933, quoting from Fumasoni-Biondi's letter to Toolen, Toolen Papers, AAM. Kiley's letter and analysis underline the key role of the permission Toolen gave Fumasoni-Biondi in February.

173. Bishop Toolen sent Fumasoni-Biondi's letter to Kiley in Rome. We do not have the letter, but Kiley quoted what the Delegate had written. "It is quite evident," Kiley wrote, "from his letter that he [Fumasoni-Biondi] knew he had no right to insist on you giving Judge permission to leave the diocese. He says: 'If Your Excellency has no objection to the transfer in question may I kindly ask you forward the desired document to me at your earliest convenience'"; Kiley to Toolen, Rome, February 28, 1933, Toolen Papers, AAM.

know."[174] Father Judge died six months after writing this letter. It was his last to Bishop Schrembs. The issue of the transfer of the motherhouse remained at his death and thereafter.

Days of Reflection at Holy Trinity

Father Judge spent the last days of 1932 at Holy Trinity—the second Christmas at Holy Trinity without Mother Boniface. Father Bede Hermann's tenure as novice master had just been extended, and the days at Holy Trinity in late December and early January gave Judge a chance to consult with him. One of Father Bede's concerns had to do with preserving the community's "primitive spirit, edification and traditions."[175] Judge wrote Mother Mary that, at the urging of Father Bede and the novices about the importance of Community history, he had charged Brother Joachim Benson with doing the chronicles. "I am giving an obedience to Brother Joachim to take this very important and sacred work in hand."[176]

A central part of the community's inspiration, spirit, and tradition had to do with what had come to be called the "Outer Cenacle." As his excitement about establishing the African American Outer Cenacle at Montclair indicates, the preservation and flourishing of the Outer Cenacle had been much on Father Judge's mind throughout 1932. In these reflective days after Christmas at Holy Trinity, as he looked back over the past decades, he was struck by how much his original vision of inviting the laity into his priestly work coincided with Pope Pius XI's promotion of the "Lay Apostolate." To a sister who had preserved memories and documents of the early days, he wrote, "Note how truly we have kept all through the years to the early Cenacle principles. Note how the Holy Father is seeking in almost the same words for the working of those principles today." He found it remarkable that, "after twenty-one years, this is the crying demand of the Church at this hour, yet remember the opposition, and how consoled we should be that truth must prevail."[177]

174. Judge to Schrembs, Río Piedras, May 18, 1933. Schrembs responded on May 24, assuring Judge that Fumasoni-Biondi's presence in Rome as a curial cardinal "and thoroughly conversant with the situation, will be a large factor in your favor"; Schrembs to Judge, Cleveland, May 24, 1933, copy, Schrembs Papers, ADC.

175. Judge to My dear Child, Holy Trinity, January 7, 1933, AST MF 7306. This sister was in charge of community history.

176. Judge to Mother Mary of the Incarnate Word, Holy Trinity [?], January 7, 1933, AST, MF 7317. No doubt this charge from Father Judge explains how Benson came to write his 1934 *The Judgments of Father Judge*.

177. Judge to My dear Child, Holy Trinity, December 27, 1932, AST, MF 7227. See also Judge

He wrote Brother Augustine to come south as soon as possible. "Catholic action is very vibrant at Holy Trinity," he reported. "Father Bede is taking quite warmly to the idea of a year's catechetical effort for the clericate." He asked Philips to "keep your ears open and see if you can get any definite expression from your clerical friends of what they understand by Catholic Action, or what they are doing about it." He continued:

> The Holy Father's principles are so clear that it is very surprising there should be so much confusion or indefiniteness about what Catholic Action means. If you remember in the Cenacle the word has been all along to the laity, "You may enter into our Priesthood there are so many things we do that you may do." The Holy Father expresses it this way. "The Participation of the Laity in the Apostolate of the Hierarchy."[178]

Crises and difficulties filled Father Judge's days in 1932. "I cannot tell you what kind of a year I have just passed since I left Puerto Rico in May of 1932," he wrote to Sister Theresa Marie in May 1933. "The story of that year, I think, will never be told."[179] Nevertheless, he was ready for 1933 to begin. "As for myself," he wrote to his sister on the day after Christmas, "I am just a wandering itinerant for the Lord, and it is so exhilarating because I don't know scarcely for the next hour just where He wants me to go, but all that in his kindly Providence will work out some way."[180] Father Judge's earlier words of encouragement to Joachim Benson at the beginning of 1932 had lent substance and thickness to such appeals to providence. He urged Benson to remember that, no matter the financial tempest, Jesus is always with us in the boat:

> It seems to me that we, living in these troublesome times when there is so much fear in the hearts of Churchmen, Statesmen, and men of affairs, that any picture or forecast come to us of the future will be one that shall demand picked men. If the logic of present events is trouble and distress to State, to Church, to our holy religion and to our country, then God has in training at present men and women of faith and courage. If, therefore, a current jam-

---

to Mother Mary of the Incarnate Word, Newark, N.J., March 7, 1932, AST MF 13355, on the need for zeal for the Outer Cenacle; to Jerome Donegan, Brooklyn, March 9, 1932, AST, MF 1963, on the merging of the Outer Cenacle into Catholic Action; Judge to Mother Mary, Holy Trinity [?], July 17, 1932, AST, MF 13165, on "to cherish and safeguard the Outer Missionary Cenacle" as "really the major purpose of their [the brothers'] Institute"; to My dear Child, Stirling, N.J., November 9, 1932, AST, MF 12280, on present vitality and importance of the Outer Cenacle.

178. Judge to Philips, Holy Trinity, December 26, 1932, AST, MF 2170–72.

179. Judge to Sister Theresa Marie, Río Piedras, May 24, 1933, AST MF 14980.

180. Judge to Sister Gerard Ledwidge, Holy Trinity, December 26, 1932, AST, MF 7270.

ming and pressure of events furnish us opportunity to qualify for such high graces, we should feel a present joy in what to many might mean fear, anxiety, and even despondency. And for you, Brother Joachim, should your present office furnish you those difficulties that would develop in you such faith and confidence, Brother Joachim, you are a picked man and be ready to speak at any time your *Te Deum*.[181]

181. Judge to Benson, Stirling [?], January 6, 1932, AST, MF 1889.

16

"LET ME REST"

1933

Nearing the End

As 1933 began, the issue of transferring the men's motherhouse from Mobile to Cleveland remained unsettled. Work on appeals to Rome concerning the transfer and Bishop Toolen's threatened suppression of the novitiate and Holy Trinity preoccupied Father Judge. The fate and ownership of the hurricane-damaged St. Augustine's Military Academy in Río Piedras remained unresolved. The sisters had to default on their interest payments on the loan for Holy Name of Jesus Hospital. Legally responsible as cosigner, Bishop Toolen seriously considered taking the sisters to court.

January through March

The last year of Father Judge's life and work divides itself into three parts. From January through March, he split time between Holy Trinity, Stirling, and Silver Spring as, with Louis Motry's faithful help, he prepared the petition, the recourse, and other supporting materials bound for the Sacred Congregation for Religious in Rome. Though Cleveland was the hoped-for site of a new motherhouse, after December 15, 1932, Judge would never set foot in that diocese again. Father Theophane remained in charge at Lorain. In addition, Judge had recalled Father Eugene Brennan from Puerto Rico and was trying to get him to make a canonical novitiate.

April through August

Father Judge spent the next five months, from April through August, in Puerto Rico. Growing Puerto Rican nationalism and his own lack of resources prevented Bishop Edwin V. Byrne from giving the St. Augustine's property outright, as Judge had hoped, to the Missionary Servants of the Most Holy Trinity. In Puerto Rico, Father Judge kept working to finance St. Augustine's Military Academy. He saw it as a central work in keeping with the community's mission and a potential revenue producer to support other works. In the absence of Father Brennan, who had been in charge at St. Augustine's since 1927, he dealt with personnel issues on the island.

August through November

In mid-August 1933, Father Judge returned from Puerto Rico in a very weak state. At the end of August, on the advice of his doctors, he checked himself into Providence Hospital in Washington, D.C., for an extended rest. He never left. His major bodily systems shut down. He died at Providence Hospital on November 23, 1933, two years and a day after Mother Boniface had died in Gadsden.

Father Eugene Brennan, Reluctant Novice

One of the most painful difficulties Father Judge faced during his last year was the vocational crisis of the community's first priest. Eugene Brennan met Father Judge at Mount Carmel Parish in Orange, New Jersey. The sixteen-year-old Brennan, a student at St. Francis Xavier Military School, a Jesuit high school in New York City, was helping Andrew Philips with a First Communion class. One of Father Judge's most dedicated early associates in the Cenacle, Mary Elizabeth Walsh, brought Philips into the work and introduced both Philips and Brennan to Father Judge. This was probably in 1914, when Judge was working on the mission band out of Springfield, Massachusetts.[1]

Mother Boniface had a tremendous impact on Brennan, and our fullest picture of him emerges from the pages of Tonra's biography of her. With Philips he went south in 1916 to help the first group of Cenacle lay associates

1. Lawrence Brediger tells this story in "In the Name of the Father," 6:54–58. The estimate of 1914 as the date is his.

at Opelika. The next year, Philips and Brennan moved to the Mott Plantation, which would become Holy Trinity. They were first called "brothers" around 1920, and by 1922 Father Judge decided to send Brennan to study for the priesthood. He studied at seminaries in Galveston, Texas, probably at Our Lady of the Angels at Niagara University, and briefly at Catholic University. On February 2, 1926, at Holy Trinity, in the chapel of the sisters' new motherhouse, Bishop Edward Allen ordained Brennan a priest of the Diocese of Mobile and assigned him to work with Father Judge. He said his first Mass in the old wood chapel at Holy Trinity. He used Father Judge's chalice, and Father Judge himself served the Mass.[2]

During Mother Boniface's last illness, despite her urgings that they leave for their own safety and the good of the Cenacle, Father Brennan stayed at the hospital with Father Judge. Brennan served as subdeacon at Mother Boniface's solemn funeral Mass. Though Andrew Philips had been called to the work first and served faithfully as Brother Augustine, Father Judge seemed to regard Brennan as the Cenacle's, and in some sense his own, first-born son. An extraordinary 1932 letter to Mother Mary, urging her to treat Brennan as Mother Boniface had, reveals something of Brennan's relationship to both Father Judge and Mother Boniface.

Father Judge was in Puerto Rico, and Father Brennan had written to Mother Mary, concerned about his health. Apparently she did not respond. Brennan took offense, and Judge took his part. "I think," Judge told her, "he feels what he considers a lack of courtesy and fraternity." He urged her to respond personally. "Father Eugene means a great deal to the work and to me personally, then, above all, he is a priest," Judge wrote. "If he has offended in anything he has written, he did it in zeal because of my condition. You mean a great deal to the work and to me. As a father, I sorrow over what seems to be a difference between two of my dearest children." He insisted that he did not want to leave Puerto Rico until he knew that she had written to Brennan. He hoped the sisters would "give him credit for his good intentions," especially "when it is known that he is my assistant."[3]

His next comments indicate the role Mother Boniface played in Brennan's life:

2. For a description of Brennan's ordination and first Mass, see Tonra, *Led by the Spirit*, 149. From the 1920 census, we know that Brennan's father was born in Ireland and his mother was from New Jersey.

3. Judge to Mother Mary of the Incarnate Word, Río Piedras, April 26, 1932, AST, MF 13307–12.

> You know Mother Boniface meant so much to him and, if you are patient and kind to him, you will mean just as much. She knew his dispositions and because of what he is and because of what he can be to me, she indulgently overlooked so much. Some of the Sisters are quite acrid [?] and critical with him. She helped him much by spoken word and letter even though at times he seemed indifferent. Her death was a terrible blow to him from which he has not recovered. Her patience and charity were well rewarded as she certainly exercised over him a very salutary influence.[4]

Father Judge went on to describe Eugene Brennan as "a dear son making a plea for his father's health, my assistant worried about his major superior, the rector of St. Augustine's Military Academy concerned about the condition of his cherished Visitor." Brennan was doing "splendid work" with St. Augustine's. "Much beloved by Brothers, Sisters, and students," he has also "gone up much in the estimation of Bishop Byrne." In view of all this, Judge thought it "would be too bad if a difference would come up that would make him think the Sisters would not cooperate."[5]

Despite Father Judge's desperately high regard for him, Father Brennan was a work in progress, a free spirit who loved horses and airplanes and, as someone who occasionally left the reservation, not entirely reliable. If Mother Mary was indeed piqued at him, perhaps it was not without reason.[6] The year before, in February and March of 1931, Judge called Brennan to Holy Trinity from Puerto Rico because of Bishop Toolen's concern for a resident priest at St. Joseph's. While Judge was still sick at Stirling, Brennan returned to Puerto Rico without permission, leaving Holy Trinity without a priest and Judge vulnerable to Bishop Toolen's criticisms at a time when he could least

4. Ibid.

5. Ibid. The letter is filled with praise for the Hay diet, which Mother Mary distrusted intensely.

6. According to Berry, Father Timothy Lynch "attributed the difficulty in large part to a great difference in personal style and temperament. Mother Mary of the Incarnate Word was from New England and very proper in her demeanor. Fr. Eugene Brennan, on the contrary, was very informal, enjoyed sports and physical activities. He was a pilot and used to enjoy taking the Sisters on airplane rides in Puerto Rico. Mother Mary of the Incarnate Word did not approve at all"; Berry, *God's Valiant Warrior*, 374n659. AST has a 1928 photograph of the legendary pilot Charles Lindbergh at St. Augustine's, where Brennan was in charge. Lynch came to Holy Trinity as a student in 1928. His picture of Brennan seems to reflect something of a young Irishman's romantic idealization of an elder brother. In apparent reference to Marlboro cigarette commercials current when he was writing, Lynch also described Brennan as giving the impression of the "real 'Man of Marlborough' [*sic*] type. He was a rugged outdoors man, someone who could ride a horse, do manly things. He was a wonderful example to us, a real he-man"; for this description by Lynch, see Tonra, *Led by the Spirit*, 206.

afford them. Judge had to return immediately.[7] Prior to his entry into the novitiate at Holy Trinity in January 1933, Brennan had gotten himself into a situation in Puerto Rico from which, Judge's correspondence with Sister Mary Thomas indicates, he wanted to extricate him. Judge made it clear to Brennan that he was not going back to Puerto Rico.[8]

As a priest of the Diocese of Mobile, Father Brennan had never made a canonical novitiate. Despite his having lived as a Cenacle missionary for at least fifteen years, canon law did not recognize him as a Missionary Servant of the Most Holy Trinity. Father Bede's first group of novices had recently made their first vows. He had just been renewed for three years. Father Judge knew that Father Bede would not be with the community forever. He wanted the community's first priest to make a canonical novitiate with Father Bede while it was still possible. Brennan balked. We do not have his side of it, but no doubt he found it insulting and unnecessary. If he was not a Missionary Servant, then what on earth could he possibly be?

Clothing of the novices was to take place on February 2, the Feast of the Purification of Mary, or what is now the Presentation of Our Lord in the Temple. By January 18, Father Eugene Brennan was in Stirling, on his way to Holy Trinity. To Brother Thomas O'Keeffe at Silver Spring, Father Judge wrote to have all the brothers pray for Father Eugene "in his coming spiritual experience." "We cannot expect to have Fr. Bede with us all the time," he continued. "It is a blessed thing for us that even at some violence Father Eugene is available for the Novitiate."[9] "It means so much to all of us," he told Brother James Norris, "to have one of our priests in the Novitiate and he is the first."[10] Judge was in Stirling working on the petition and the recourse to Rome when he "got an alarm about our 'Little Father.' Brennan had only been there one day and had brought things to a crisis." Judge thought they might work this out over the phone, but soon realized that he would have to go to Holy Trinity himself.[11]

The presenting problem was Father Eugene's dog. Though Brother Au-

7. See Mother Boniface's description of this situation as cited in Tonra, *Led by the Spirit*, 291. Father Judge's letter to him in Puerto Rico contained no reprimand but simply conveyed why it had been important for him to be there.

8. See, for example, Judge to Sister Mary Thomas, Stirling, N.J., February 9, 1933, AST, MF 7327.

9. Judge to O'Keeffe, Stirling, January 18, 1933, AST, MF 13742.

10. Judge to Norris, Stirling, January 18, 1933, AST, MF 2181.

11. Judge to My dear Child [probably Sister Marie Jean], Stirling, February 9, 1933, AST, MF 7327.

gustine got him to admit that nothing in canon law forbade a dog in the novitiate, Father Bede still refused to allow it. If he were not allowed to keep the dog, Brennan threatened to leave on the spot. At this point, Father Judge decided to go to Holy Trinity immediately. "I reached there the night of the 2nd," he reported to Sister Mary Thomas. As custodian of the sisters at St. Augustine's, she was his main confidante in matters related to the ongoing project of Father Eugene. "Dear me," Judge wrote, "what a talk to persuade him to go through with the ceremony of clothing." Brennan agreed to the clothing ceremony only if his stay in the novitiate were limited to a month. "He is teaching a class in Latin, some Liturgy in the novitiate, and works in the bindery." It was not the "duties and experiences of the novitiate" to which he objected. As Judge put it, "It is the open life that he has been leading, the authority and responsibility he possessed, etc. I told him plainly no matter what happened he was not going back to Puerto Rico." Judge thought Brennan accepted this. He talked about, when his month was up, spending some time in Lorain with Father Theophane or opening up a place on the Chesapeake property. By February 9, Judge was back in Stirling working on the documents for Rome.[12]

On February 3, 1933, Father Judge told Mother Mary that he had clothed Father Eugene but mentioned nothing about the dog and related drama. "If he perseveres," Judge wrote, "after a while I don't think he will find it difficult, but these first days will be very hard for him."[13] He wrote Sister Mary Thomas that he still hoped, if Brennan made it through the first month, "he will make it two, then perhaps, he will go through the year." He told her that it was a good thing he wasn't in Puerto Rico, "for there is reason to believe if I was, he would not be in the Novitiate."[14]

Clearly, Father Eugene was questioning his vocation. "I think he is quite discouraged about himself," Judge told Sister Mary Thomas. "For him to give up would be ignominious and he feels keenly what people would think about it. What he would do in the event he did leave came up in the course of conversation, I brought it up and I had to tell him flatly and bluntly that he was a priest and that he just could not go into secular life."[15]

12. Judge to Sister Mary Thomas, Stirling, February 9, 1933, AST, MF 7397. Judge later told Sister Mary Thomas that he either had to accept the month or "suffer the spectacle of his leaving Holy Trinity on the Feast Day of the Purification or on the days within its close shadows. If he will not stay, who can force him?"; Judge to Sister Mary Thomas, Stirling, February 21, 1933, AST, MF 7398–99.

13. Judge to Mother Mary of the Incarnate Word, Holy Trinity, February 3, 1933, AST, MF 13366.

14. Judge to Sister Mary Thomas, Stirling, February 14, 1933, AST, MF 7292.

15. Ibid., February 21, 1933, AST, MF 7398.

There was something deeper than the dog. Both Father Judge and Sister Mary Thomas knew about it. At some point, probably in early February, Judge had it out with Brennan. In a March 1 letter to Sister Mary Thomas, he referred to it as "Brother E —'s affair" and "that affair." Judge confronted him. "I got to the very bottom of *that affair* & beyond with him. Letters fell into my hands. I just uncovered his soul." Judge accused Brennan of "leading the life of a worldling, etc., etc., that he had been giving up his prayer etc., that if I did what he did and left out what he left out, I might do as he did. I told him to be honest." Judge concluded ominously, "He knows that I know. I meant for his soul's sake to abash him. I put it in the dust, it was not very sweet dust. I confounded him with evidence when he tried to evade. This, I think, helped to break him."

Though this confrontation probably occurred in early February, Father Judge didn't mention it until March 1, 1933. By this time, he felt he had done all he could. "You have done your share," he told Sister Mary Thomas; "in any case, we must leave him to God. He will ever be a reason of prayerful solicitude." Judge was adamant that Father Eugene would not return to Puerto Rico.[16] A week later, he wrote Mother Mary that he was expecting him in Stirling. "He has asked to be relieved of the Novitiate. There is some comfort in his letter as he says he may try it later, when he is better fitted for that experience."[17] Later in March, Brennan helped Judge with the sisters' retreats in Philadelphia. "Fr. Eugene gave a good part of the retreat here.... The Sisters are happy to have him in their midst, and he seems to be in good trim."[18]

Until Father Judge's death eight months later, Father Eugene split his time between Silver Spring and Stirling. In residence at Silver Spring, he was to open a place, perhaps a camp, at Chesapeake Haven and also take care of the two masses scheduled at Stirling on Sundays. Judge also wanted him to be "ready for retreat work" and to give some conferences to the brothers at Silver Spring.[19] Within a year of his failed novitiate, he assumed the position of custodian general.

16. Ibid., dated from Lorain but probably Stirling, March 1, 1933, AST, MF 7290–91.
17. Judge to Mother Mary of the Incarnate Word, Stirling, March 8, 1933, AST, MF 13401.
18. Judge to Sister Mary Thomas, Philadelphia, March 25, 1933, AST, MF 7403.
19. Judge to Brother Thomas, Río Piedras, April 12, 1933, AST, MF 13760.

On the Cenacle Bridge

On January 25, Father Judge wrote to Sister Mary Thomas, who was urging him to come to Puerto Rico. "I am forced to write a letter today that is going to close a certain series, as a consequence a certain matter will be thrown before the Roman Authorities." No doubt this was the beginning of the draft of the petition for transfer of the motherhouse. "I must also begin the compilation of another letter," he continued, "when this second letter is finished, which may take a week or two, to compose, because I must wait for material and get the mind of Church authorities." This second letter was probably the recourse to prevent Bishop Toolen's threatened suppression of the novitiate.[20] At this time, the guest room at Silver Spring was reserved for Father Motry.[21]

In explaining why he was not free to come to Puerto Rico, Father Judge used a striking series of metaphors, offering a glimpse into his soul at this time. He felt like a lone sea captain on the bridge of his ship during a triple hurricane. "You know what a hurricane is," he began. "They are terrible, but in Puerto Rico you just experience one at a time. Figuratively speaking three hurricanes and at least a baby tempest have hit the Missionary Cenacle here in the States at the same time":

> Just now we are hearing of tremendous seas on the Atlantic that are battering ships and doing great harm. During these awful nights and days of terror where do you suppose the master of the ship is and what is his concern? He is at the bridge and he is thinking of only one thing and that is of keeping the ship afloat. Figuratively again, this has been my situation for weeks. It has come down to a question of just keeping the Missionary Cenacle ship afloat.

With reference to her situation in Puerto Rico, he added, "There may be several departments and movements in that ship that need attention, but no matter how much they need it, there is only one that the master can do and that is stay on that bridge and guide his ship to safety."[22]

Father Judge traveled from Stirling to Washington on February 21, 1933, for a personal visit with Archbishop Fumasoni-Biondi before he left for Rome. Judge thought the petition and the recourse were ready.[23] "May the

20. Judge to Sister Mary Thomas Champion, Stirling, January 25, 1933, AST, MF 7393–94.

21. Judge to Brother Thomas O'Keeffe, Stirling, January 18, 1933, AST, MF 13742.

22. Judge to Sister Mary Thomas, Stirling, January 25, 1933, AST, MF 7393–94.

23. Judge to Mother Mary of the Incarnate Word, Stirling, February 21, 1933, AST, MF 13189–91.

Triune God be praised," he wrote three weeks later, "the business that has clutched me so near since my return from Puerto Rico a year ago is just ending one phase." He reported that the supporting "documents so anxiously assembled" would be ready that night and in the delegation's hands the next day. He would have been in Puerto Rico "long since only for the crisis that has been spinning itself out since last April and May."[24] The petition and recourse had to be translated from English into Latin. Not until a week later on March 22 did Judge send the twelve supporting documents to Monsignor Paul Marella at the apostolic delegation.[25]

One last difficulty remained. Father Judge had no copy of the permission for the transfer of the men's motherhouse that Fumasoni-Biondi had gotten from Bishop Toolen in February. Judge mentioned this to Marella in his March 22 letter. It was to accompany Bishop Schrembs's letter as a "companion letter." No doubt James Norris was the trusted courier who carried the documents to the delegation. "Do you not remember," Judge asked Norris, "I mentioned a letter that the Bishop was told to send and finally was forced to write?" Judge hoped that Fumasoni-Biondi had left the letter at the delegation. He instructed Norris to ask Monsignor Marella about this crucial supporting document.[26]

April 1 found him aboard the SS *Barbara* bound for San Juan.[27] Two weeks later he learned from Monsignor Marella that the petition, recourse, and supporting documents were safely on their way to Rome.[28] "I am expecting an answer to our Roman documents sometime after Easter," he wrote optimistically on April 5. With reference to asking Bishop Toolen for dimissiorial

24. Judge to Mother Mary of the Incarnate Word, Silver Spring, Md., March 14, 1933, AST, MF 13254–55. Judge also announced in this letter that "we have Father Bede for three more years. Is that not grand?"

25. Judge to Marella, Philadelphia [?], March 22, 1933, AST, MF 14038, with an accompanying list of twelve documents (MF 14039) including copies of (1) the 1929 decree of erection; letters from Bishop Toolen dated (2) December 9, 1932; (3) May 1, 1931; (4) April 3, 1931; (5) February 18, 1931; (6) November 24, 1932; (7) April 16, 1930, together with Bishop Byrne's letter of September 18, 1929; (8) April 28, 1931; (9) February 11, 1931; (10) excerpts from five circular letters (*excerpta e quinque litteris circularibus*) of Bishop Toolen; (11) undated letters of Bishop Toolen (unspecified); and (12) Bishop Schrembs's November 18, 1932, letter inviting the Missionary Servants into the Diocese of Cleveland.

26. Judge to Norris, Stirling, March 22, 1933, AST, MF 2217. This letter refers to two remaining difficulties with the Latin translations and indicates that Judge and Norris were still going over them at this time.

27. Judge to Mother Mary of the Incarnate Word, en route to Puerto Rico, April 1, 1933, AST, 13196–97.

28. Judge to Marella, Río Piedras, April 12, 1933, AST, MF 14040.

letters for an impending ordination, he concluded, "It is very important for us to await that answer."[29] It would prove to be a long wait.

Negotiating to Buy St. Augustine's Military Academy, Río Piedras

"I know you have some worry about myself," he wrote Mother Mary from the SS *Barbara*. "I am in much better condition on this trip than I was on the last, and I just feel, I am not going to collapse when I go ashore as I did a year ago." He knew "some tough problems" awaited him on the island, but, he wrote, "I have not the irritating ones that faced me a year ago and in my sickness."[30] When he got to St. Augustine's in Río Piedras, Father Judge was shocked at the extent of the damage inflicted by the "San Cipriano Hurricane." He likened it to seeing "a very dear friend" and noticing that "when he opened his mouth ... all his teeth were busted in." The administration and chapel parts of the main building had been destroyed; "the rest of the big edifice is all patched over," as if it "had been in a war zone."

Exceeding his shock at the damage wrought by the hurricane, however, was his edification at the courage and good spirit of Brother Joseph Limpert and the brothers and Sister Mary Thomas and the sisters. "It is such Christian heroes and heroines as these Brothers and Sisters," he wrote to Father Paul Anthony at Holy Trinity, "that make epochs in the world's history and periods in the flow of the Church's life." He was deeply moved and consoled. "After all this storm and stress and impact of physical and spiritual powers, I find cohesion, solidarity, courage, determination to go on, and a peace, and spirit of cooperation that is just celestial." He took it all as a "manifest of God's pleasure in the trust and confidence put in Him over the dreary years spent in resuscitating this school." He wanted Father Paul Anthony to make the brothers' work in Puerto Rico known among the students at Holy Trinity. "St. Augustine's Military Academy looks across the sea to Holy Trinity, Ala.," he wrote, "will our junior missionaries at Holy Trinity prove themselves worthy of the spirit and example shown by their elder brothers who made this foundation?"

This inspiring message was not only for the students at Holy Trinity. Judge was about to make Father Paul Anthony commandant of St. Augus-

29. Judge to Brother Thomas O'Keeffe [?], Río Piedras, April 5, 1933, AST MF 13488–89.

30. Judge to Mother Mary, en route to Puerto Rico, April 1, 1933, AST, 13196–97.

tine's Military Academy. He wanted this letter to impress vividly upon him its importance for the community and the church. "The Church is holding out to us large opportunities for good and encouraging us to go on," he wrote. "Will we fail the Church now; now, when we are better conditioned and equipped and when it is so evident that it is the will of God for us to on and on?"[31]

From Puerto Rico, Father Judge kept his hand in affairs back on the mainland. The men's community was taking shape. The recently professed brothers were at Silver Spring with Brother Thomas. Judge wrote to Brother Thomas about the farm, to Father Paul Anthony at Holy Trinity about the magazine, and to Brother Augustine at Stirling for more information than he had been sending. To Brother Andrew and Brother James, he wrote on financial affairs. Brother Joachim found himself in the doghouse again.[32]

Father Judge's main focus, during his first weeks on the island, however, was a sisters' retreat scheduled to end on Easter in mid-April.[33] He stayed in touch with Mother Mary of the Incarnate Word, repeatedly urging her to get to Cleveland lest the Cenacle be "accused of trifling," and with other sisters, who had written with concern about his health.[34] Regarding his health, he wrote, "Let me say right here I am in unusually good health; in fact, if I did not have good health, I do not know how I would have stood all that I have been through since I got off the boat." He told Sister Carmel at Gold Street in Brooklyn that he found it "amusing." People were expecting him "to have a fine rest, nothing to do but be enchanted on the Island of Enchantment." Instead, he seemed "to be covering three of the bases and the catcher's box, and I expect any time to go in and do some pitching also. I hope now you are answered on the question of my health."[35]

Now complicated by September's hurricane, the fate of St. Augustine's Military Academy was still up in the air. Father Judge went to Puerto Rico

31. Judge to Fursman, Río Piedras, April 10, 1933, AST, MF 2227–28.

32. See the remarks on Brother Joachim in Judge to Brother Theodore Jurdt, May 16, 1933, AST, MF 13420–21.

33. See, for example, Judge to Fursman, Río Piedras, April 5, 1933, AST, MF 2223–24; Judge to O'Keeffe, Río Piedras, April 5, 1933, AST, MF 13488–89; Judge to Philips, Río Piedras, April 11, 1933, AST, MF 2229–30; Judge to Brother M. Andrew Lawrence, Río Piedras, April 12, 1933, AST, MF 2231–34; Judge to Norris, Río Piedras, April 12, 1933, AST, MF 2235.

34. On Cleveland, see Judge to Mother Mary of the Incarnate Word, Río Piedras, April 9, 1933, AST, MF 13270, and ibid., April 20, 1933, AST, MF 13256.

35. Judge to Sister Carmel Davoren, Río Piedras, April 18, 1933, AST, MF 7353. Despite his separation from the community, Father Tomerlin had been having his mail sent to Gold Street, and Sister Carmel was one of Judge's main correspondents regarding Tomerlin's status.

in 1933 to settle it. While not as stressful as 1932's search for a place to transfer the men's motherhouse, the protracted negotiations with Bishop Byrne regarding St. Augustine's, without Father Eugene there to share the burden, took a big toll on Father Judge's health. It took negotiations a while to get off the ground. As with the 1932 negotiations, the chronic need for financial reports from each cenacle, consolidated by Brother James, remained. On April 9, 1933, Father Judge and Bishop Byrne had a four-hour lunch and put off discussing business until the following week. Judge found that the hurricane had given Bishop Byrne a new sense of the Cenacle spirit and a new respect for the brothers' work at St. Augustine's.[36] On April 12, Judge described to Brother Andrew his ambitious vision for St. Augustine's. It included more students, recruited with the help of alumni and Bishop Byrne, a new building, and new sources of revenue from use of the old building as a residence. He asked Brother Andrew for advice on which present novice clerical brothers would be best for the work at St. Augustine's.[37]

By April 18, 1933, Father Judge had finished the sisters' retreat, and negotiations with Bishop Byrne turned more serious. Mr. Nesbit, Byrne's lay administrator, had returned from his trip to the mainland, and Judge was in conversation with him. A financial report of assets and liabilities from Brother James was now even more crucial to negotiations, since Nesbit's arrival on the mainland had coincided with Archbishop Curley's letter in the *Catholic Review*.[38] In addition to trying to finance the purchase of St. Augustine's from the diocese, Judge was once again trying to arrange for ordinations, this time for Brothers Turibius and Ambrose, now at Silver Spring.

36. Judge to Mother Mary of the Incarnate Word, Río Piedras, April 9, 1933, AST, MF 13270; Judge to Brother Augustine, Río Piedras, April 11, 1933, AST, MF 2229–30. The subject of the difficulties with Bishop Toolen came up and, in both letters, Judge made this extraordinary observation: "This thought was stressed very much, how sorry we are for the many difficulties with Bishop Toolen, one reason particularly for Bishop Toolen's sake: that it could be said cautiously that the Missionary Cenacle could have made him one of the most outstanding prelates in the hierarchy. Flanked on either side by the Brothers and Sisters and the Outer Missionary Cenacle Alliance with its up-to-date program of Catholic Action, he would be very much advantaged in the latest phase of Catholic Endeavor and sociological action. Just think what he has lost in losing the two Mother Missionary Cenacles. Now we will be able to do that for Bishop Schrembs." Judge noted that Bishop Byrne spoke of the sisters as "my Sisters." Bishop Byrne's perhaps "cautious" agreement with this overall assessment is clearly implied.

37. Judge to Brother M. Andrew Lawrence, Río Piedras, April 12, 1933, AST, MF 2232. Mr. Bird, a Catholic sugar producer on the island, had offered bonds, issued by the diocese under Bishop Caruana, to finance the sale.

38. Judge to Norris, Río Piedras, April 19, 1933, AST, MF 2246; see also ibid., April 27, 1933, AST, MF 2248–49. By this time, Judge had decided to "deal directly with the diocese in refinancing St. Augustine's."

He delegated this to Father Theophane.[39] The threat of a major embarrassment from Father Tomerlin's reckless behavior with money still loomed. "I am wondering," Judge asked Brother James regarding bad checks, "how long J. A. T. can continue leaving those souvenirs around New York hotels."[40] He kept Father Paul Anthony abreast of the situation at St. Augustine's, "guided in Fr. Eugene's absence by that very enlightened, good and wise Brother, Joseph."[41]

On May 2, 1933, Father Judge finally met with Bishop Byrne. Albert Villa, a local architect, provided some free assessment of damages and repair costs at the colegio. Judge wanted the bishop to figure into the purchase price the in-kind contributions in losses, repairs, improvements, and labor the community had put into St. Augustine's.[42] He told the bishop that Nesbit's plan to go to a Baltimore bonding house was unacceptable. Using Villa's estimates, he tried to get St. Augustine's outright from the diocese or, at least, "that much of what the Community has put into the building out of its own revenue be considered as a conscience fund, as certainly the diocese should keep up its own property." With Byrne wanting the community to "pay the diocese off, at least whatever is decided upon," an outright transfer of the school appeared unlikely. Father Judge was to make a financial presentation to the bishop's consultors in the coming weeks. The "Puerto Rico for Puerto Ricans" movement also complicated Bishop Byrne's dealings with Judge and his American community.[43]

Though Bishop Byrne very much wanted the Missionary Servants of the Most Holy Trinity to take over St. Augustine's, it came with what Judge called a "conscience debt" of $43,000 owed to various diocesan institutions. This is what the bishop wanted the community to pay off. Against this amount, Judge posed his own conscience money. In the upcoming meeting Byrne's

39. Judge to Brother Thomas O'Keeffe, Río Piedras, April 26, 1933, AST, MF 13818–19, with an attached set of instructions in an itinerary for Father Theophane, MF 13820. By May 31, Judge had learned of the date of the two brothers' ordination to the subdiaconate; Judge to Norris, Río Piedras, May 31, 1933, AST, MF 2278.

40. Judge to Norris, Río Piedras, May 3, 1933, AST, MF 2255. A few days later, Judge received an inquiry from Father Edward Kramer at the Catholic Board for Mission Work among the Colored People asking how he planned to make good on a falsely certified check Kramer had cashed for Tomerlin in November 1932; Kramer to Judge, New York, May 9, 1933, AST, MF 2283. Judge answered on May 31 from Río Piedras that he didn't think the community should be liable for Tomerlin's debt; AST, MF 15089–90.

41. Judge to Father Paul Anthony Fursman, Río Piedras, April 28, 1933, AST, MF 2250–51.

42. Judge to Norris, Río Piedras, April 27, 1933, AST, MF 2248–49.

43. Ibid., May 3, 1933, AST, MF 2254–56.

consultors would try to work this through with the bishop and Father Judge. In preparation for the meeting, Judge began "a novena to Our Lady of Valvanera [Coamo] for our Puerto Rican problems." He did not want to see the bishop until the novena ended.[44]

"We cannot borrow money without a financial statement," he told Norris on May 15. "I saw Mr. Nesbit the other day and the subject came up again." He wanted Norris to send it before the meeting with Byrne's consultors.[45] The next day he told Norris he was still waiting for the bishop's call "to have the decisive meeting." "The proposition is pretty much the same as it was last year," he reported. "We are trying, however, to either get the place free or to have several thousands thrown off." He wanted Norris, as secretary of the corporation, to record the eventual terms in the Consultors' Minutes Book.[46]

The much-anticipated meeting finally took place on May 24, 1933, but was inconclusive. The consultors demanded concessions that Father Judge refused, claiming he had his own consultors to think about. Bishop Byrne wanted the matter settled before commencement at St. Augustine's on May 30. On Ascension Thursday, the night after the failed meeting, the bishop met with Father Judge at St. Augustine's, and they hammered out an agreement. "May the Triune God be praised," Judge wrote to James Norris the next day, "we have won out. The eventful meeting has taken place. We have everything on our own terms."

The diocese's "conscience amount" turned out to be $45,000. A reduction of $6,000 for the "conscience money" claimed by the community still left a purchase price of $39,000 to be raised or, more likely, borrowed. The bishop also agreed to include eight additional acres of land, do some landscaping that would improve the property, and obligate the diocese, should the Missionary Servants of the Most Holy Trinity leave the island, to refund what the community put into St. Augustine's over the years. He also promised help in raising the purchase price and recruiting students. In negotiating with

44. Judge to Philips, Coamo, May 10, 1933, AST, MF 4165–68. This letter is the first sign that James Norris, the seeming rock of competence upon whom Judge relied so heavily in financial matters, had also begun to crack under the burden of the community's finances. Judge made reference to Norris being "overworked" by Dr. Motry at the university and that Motry had spoken imprudently to Norris about finances, "giving so much of that depressing talk to a young student." He wondered if Motry really believed this talk, as "he is too good a man not to have a great perfection of the virtue of hope and confidence in God."

45. Judge to Norris, Río Piedras, May 15, 1933, AST, MF 2259–60. As Norris had apparently not mentioned it, Judge gave no sign that Norris was sick from overwork. His information had come from Brother Augustine.

46. Ibid., May 16, 1933, AST, MF 2265–66.

Bishop Byrne, Judge had appealed to his own consultors. Now he had to get their approval. In explaining the proposed agreement's terms to Norris, one of his own consultors and their secretary, Judge instructed him to cable the consultors' approval to him so he would have it by the end of the commencement exercises on May 30.[47]

Father Eugene Brennan was working at Chesapeake Haven and, unbeknownst to Father Judge, his consultors, or at least Norris and Brennan representing them, held a meeting there. It is possible that Brother Augustine and perhaps even Father Theophane were also present. Objections to the agreement were raised and communicated to Judge by Norris and perhaps others, as well. It is not clear whether Norris sent the cable Judge wanted before the commencement on May 30. On the day after the commencement, Judge wrote to answer his own consultors' objections—namely, that Byrne's consultors wanted to unload a damaged building on the Missionary Servants, Bishop Byrne might be replaced by a more unfriendly bishop, or that building elsewhere would be preferable to taking over a deteriorating structure. Brennan, who had worked at St. Augustine's since 1926 and whose name Judge mentions several times in this letter, is likely the main source for these objections.

Father Judge described the deal he had negotiated as "surely some bargain." He reminded Norris that "one of the strongest banks on the Island" assessed the property at $75,000. Bishop Byrne himself, rather than his consultors, was adamant that they take over the school. To offset the objection regarding a change of bishops and so that the diocese wouldn't hold the mortgage, Judge proposed "a scheme of getting money down here so that we can give the diocese $39,000 and get a quit claim and then put the property under American protection." He insisted on the value of the St. Augustine's site for carrying on their work. "Confreres twenty-five years from now," he claimed, "will bless us for going on with this proposition; and if we give it up, the same Confreres twenty-five years from now will execrate us."[48] As most often happened in community affairs, Father Judge got what he want-

47. Ibid., May 26, 1933, AST, MF 2275; see also ibid., May 24, 1933, AST, MF 2272–73. These two letters give the best available account of the negotiations for St. Augustine's between Bishop Byrne and Father Judge.

48. Ibid., May 31, 1933, AST, MF 2278–80; see also ibid., May 29, 1933, AST, MF 2276–77. This goes over some of the same ground as the May 31 letter and mentions the consultors' meeting at Chesapeake Haven. "How glad I would have been could I have walked in on you at Chesapeake," Judge wrote to Norris six days later. "That must have been a very interesting meeting"; ibid., June 6, 1933, AST, MF 2292.

ed. Within four years of Judge's death, however, the Missionary Servants of the Most Holy Trinity were forced to withdraw from St. Augustine's and hand it over to the Marianists.

Archbishop Caruana Bonds and the Reconstruction Finance Corporation

"Getting money down here" proved to be no easy task. Attempts to raise the $39,000 purchase price for St. Augustine's occupied most of Father Judge's time in Puerto Rico during the summer of 1933. Bishop Byrne wanted the community to succeed in purchasing St. Augustine's. "The Bishop is helping us to get money," Judge reported to Norris on June 6. "We can use his name and he will give us letters." Byrne put them in touch with the sugar producer Mr. Bird, whom Judge had mentioned to Brother Andrew back in April. Bird and his friends had at least $39,000 in bonds issued by Bishop George Caruana. Bird offered to give the diocese these bonds as credit for the $39,000 purchase price. "We in our turn give these men bonds on St. Augustine's over ten years." Judge found that Bird's proposal "had thrown the whole financial administration [of the diocese] into a little bit of a panic."[49]

Not surprisingly, Mr. Nesbit, the diocesan administrator, balked at this Depression-era scheme. No real money changed hands, with real debt deferred in an endless regress of bonds. Nesbit wanted to help Father Judge find other financing. He introduced Judge to a representative of the Reconstruction Finance Corporation, a government arm for disaster relief and other causes that made loans, ordinarily for "state or public enterprises." Judge submitted a proposal that emphasized "wherever we could the points where we approach a public or national institution."[50]

Father Judge spent the next week or so soliciting support for this loan. He secured letters from "high military, naval, and governmental officials" on the island, including the new governor, R. H. Gore, who, at this time, was still on the mainland. Judge wanted Norris, Brennan, and O'Keeffe to meet with Gore in Washington before he left for Puerto Rico. Norris wanted to know when he would return, but Judge explained he had to stay, cultivate sources of revenue, and raise "some large sums of cash money so that we can

49. Ibid., June 6, 1933, AST, MF 2292.

50. Ibid., June 14, 1933, AST, MF 2295. For a copy of the statement submitted to Reconstructive Finance Corporation, see AST, MF 2307–8, enclosed with Judge to Brother Anthony Kelley, Río Piedras, June 21, 1933, AST, MF 12301–2.

make a beginning ... at least enough money to insure the payroll." Father Judge thought the time was ripe, and he had to grasp it. "We have here a positive promise of receiving the money necessary for us to carry on. That money is in sight, but again we must go after it and we must give something for something. The Institution has a tremendous amount of good will over the Island." He contrasted 1933 with their beginning at St. Augustine's in 1926. "Please, God," he concluded, "I must see this thing well started." The proposal to the Reconstruction Finance Corporation went off to Washington, along with the testimonials, on June 17, 1933.[51]

Both Brother James and Mother Mary of the Incarnate Word were anxious for Father Judge's return. The sisters needed their annual retreats. Mother Mary had received a visit from Bishop Toolen's attorney, Mr. Shannon.[52] But Judge was resolute on the need to stay. After his first fundraising swing around the island on June 20, he was still convinced that St. Augustine's would prove a major source of revenue for the community's other works. To Brother Anthony, he wrote, "This institution, in God's Providence, I believe, is to bear the brunt of the Community financial shock and tide us over the difficult places.... Every strain, every sacrifice should be made to have the Community make good here." He was looking for support. "Now if our men can get this thought, this school is going to become a sensation of edification and success."[53] He wrote similarly to Brother Augustine: "This our responsible Brothers should know, that I am convinced the present very activity of the Holy Spirit is right here in Puerto Rico, in St. Augustine's ... here is the solution of St. Joseph's School." He was so sure of this that he decided Father Paul Anthony and Brother Andrew could go ahead with recruiting new students for Holy Trinity in the fall.[54]

51. Ibid., June 17, 1933, AST, MF 2297. Judge enclosed copies of some of the testimonials. He thanked Norris for a recent Dr. Hay book he had sent. "My dear Brother," he wrote, "I am convinced that Dr. Hay is on the right track and if you and I and others follow his suggestions we are going to feel better and act better, be more ready for our problems, and in the Providence of God live longer and get more out of life." Judge told Father Paul Anthony he thought he would need "between ten and fifteen thousand at the most" for the payroll; Judge to Fursman, Río Piedras, June 6, 1933, AST, MF 2290–91.

52. Judge to Mother Mary of the Incarnate Word, Río Piedras, June 18, 1933, AST, MF 13210–12.

53. Judge to Brother Anthony Kelley, Río Piedras, June 26, 1933, AST, MF 12302.

54. Judge to Brother Augustine Philips, Río Piedras, June 26, 1933, AST, MF 2309–10.

The Final Expulsion of Father Tomerlin

As he worked on financing St. Augustine's, Father Judge learned that Father Tomerlin, dismissed in 1932, wanted to return. "I am receiving confused messages, and meager," Judge wrote to Brother Augustine, "regarding Father Tomerlin's attempt to reinstate himself in the Community." He wanted the consultors to "have an emergency meeting" and go on record against Tomerlin's return.[55] Tomerlin owed almost enough money in New York to purchase St. Augustine's, and there was a warrant out for his arrest. Father Judge wanted to avoid having him arrested at Gold Street, Stirling, or any other missionary cenacle.

On June 28, Father Judge wrote Tomerlin again. Tomerlin had visited one of the sisters' cenacles, probably in Newark, asking where to find Father Judge. Judge reminded him that he had willingly separated himself from the community and that Bishop Toolen had been apprised of this. "I had, also, to protect the Community against your financial adventures. Not one cent have I received from you since December 1928, yet I know you have collected money in the name of the Community. This you have absolutely no right to do, and I protest against it." In the name of the community and himself, Father Judge "disclaim[ed] all responsibility for all your other money operations." He assured Tomerlin of his daily prayers and continuing personal charitable concern, but "as far as the Community is concerned, again I must repeat that there is no use seeking entrance or reinstatement. All that is now beyond me, and even the Community." He referred Father Tomerlin to Bishop Toolen as his ecclesiastical superior.[56]

On the same day, he wrote to both Sister Carmel at Gold Street and to Father Eugene Brennan, enclosing a copy of his letter to Tomerlin. He warned Sister Carmel that, "no matter how penitent he might become, it is too late now. We must do nothing to give the public, especially the priestly body, the impression that he is one of us." Whatever Tomerlin might say could not "destroy the records that are against him in New York City and other places." If he forced an entrance, she was to treat him "like any other trespasser."[57]

55. Ibid. A few days earlier, he had expressed the same desire for an emergency consultors' meeting on the "threatened disturbance of Father Tomerlin" to Brother Anthony; Judge to Kelley, Río Piedras, June 26, 1933, AST, MF 12301–2.

56. Judge to Tomerlin, Río Piedras, June 28, 1933, AST, MF 7360.

57. Judge to Sister Carmel Davoren, Río Piedras, June 28, 1933, AST, MF 7366. She too was urging Judge's return from Puerto Rico, and he included his optimistic thoughts on the prospects for St. Augustine's.

Father Judge took seriously the possibility that Father Tomerlin might force his way into one of the cenacles and refuse to leave. He authorized Father Brennan to "handle the situation for me." Judge thought Tomerlin might be in Newark and hoped one of the sisters could get his letter to him. But he continued to insist, "We cannot afford to allow him to give the pretense that he is associated with any of our houses." Judge then made an extraordinary suggestion to Brennan. "He is hardboiled and may have to be dealt with in a hardboiled way." He gave Brennan the name of Captain Quinn, a police captain in Newark and a friend of Brother Augustine's and his. Judge thought Quinn would have "two huskies who in civilian clothes could be conveniently nearby when you break the news to him, and who could come on the scene if he refuses to move." He advised Brennan not to tell Captain Quinn "anything about his [Tomerlin's] escapades."[58] He sent the same suggestion to Brother James Norris, adding that the two huskies might "come in at the proper time and invite an unwelcome guest for a ride to the nearest railroad station." He also reminded Norris, as the consultors' secretary, on the importance of recording "all official determinations regarding Father Tomerlin in the Minutes Books."[59] He also advised Brother Theodore, who was in charge at Stirling, on what to do if Tomerlin appeared at Holy Trinity Hill.[60]

By July 1, 1933, Father Tomerlin had received Father Judge's letter of June 28. His response, dated from a Cistercian monastery in Rhode Island, expressed shock and surprise at Judge's letter, asking if it were either just or charitable to exclude him from the community. He claimed to be responsible for thousands of dollars coming to the community. He was loyal. "I stuck with you and defended you when you were accused by authority: in fact, I faced ridicule and much more when I left diocesan work to join with you in the struggling days of the Community. My priestly services were welcome then, why not now?" He appealed to the example of Christ, who forgave St. Peter and his executioners, and to the parable of the prodigal son. He claimed to be in a ten-day retreat at the monastery and asked Judge, against his explicit instructions, to address a reply to him at Gold Street.[61]

58. Judge to Brennan, Río Piedras, June 28, 1933, AST, MF 7368.

59. Judge to Norris, Río Piedras, June 28, 1933, AST, MF 2315. "What have we got in the Minutes regarding his departure from us? The sentiments of the Consultors certainly should be strongly stressed regarding him and the necessity of him seeking other fields of labor. Now the Consultors should voice their sentiments about his not being allowed to return. It would be well to have an emergency council of the Consultors, especially those who are close together, and agitate this thing."

60. Judge to Brother Theodore, Río Piedras, June 28, 1933, AST, MF 13604.

61. Tomerlin to Judge, Valley [?] Falls, R.I., July 1, 1933, copy, AST, MF 2317.

Father Judge waited until July 14 and wrote a blistering three-page, single-spaced reply that amounted to a bill of particulars against Father Tomerlin's appeals to justice and charity. He answered Tomerlin's claim that Judge had given him permission to work at Epiphany parish in New York with a letter "from the heartbroken pastor of the Epiphany about you." "I gave you no permission to go to the race track," he retorted. Priests "in and out of New York City" were after Tomerlin, for he had borrowed or procured with bad checks. "One of your closest priest friends," Judge continued, "informed me that in N.Y. City you had established a record as a poker player."

"What do you do with a man who has the habit of being a prodigal?" Father Judge asked in response to the appeal to the prodigal son. Against Tomerlin's appeal to charity in general, Judge cited the rights and feelings of his confreres, publicly embarrassed by Tomerlin and forced to make good on his debts. "I covered you and hid you and went with you to the limit. To go farther would be to outrage charity and justice and make myself a partner in your misdeeds." Judge reminded Tomerlin that he had come to the community "in trouble with Bishop Allen" and of his record as a plunger. "I know of thousands of dollars of debt into which you have plunged us, and under which we are staggering. I know of a number of lawsuits you have brought us. I know thousands of dollars you never accounted for." He claimed that Tomerlin's "deception" in a contract, made clear in the documentation accompanying one of the lawsuits, "plunged us into another debt of $60,000." Tomerlin had violated Judge's explicit instructions to avoid the racetrack and the gamblers. "Imagine my feeling when priests would say, 'Tomerlin is a regular fellow at the track.'"

Father Judge went on to warn Father Tomerlin against having his mail sent to any cenacle and against even thinking of coming to New York City on account of "charges which, if proven, will carry a long term of years in prison." If Tomerlin wanted Judge to write, he had to provide another address. He concluded sadly. This was not the kind of letter he wanted to write, but, "in no other way, through justice and charity," could he face the situation Tomerlin had created. Older members of the community who knew Tomerlin shared this letter's sentiments. The consultors had "voted against" his return. "The whole affair has taken so much out of me," he wrote.[62]

On July 19, the Feast of St. Vincent de Paul, he again wrote Sister Carmel not to accept Tomerlin's mail at Gold Street. By this point, Tomerlin must have responded to his letter of July 14. His basic message to Tomerlin had not

62. Judge to Tomerlin, Río Piedras, July 14, 1933, AST, MF 2319; see also MF 15092–100.

changed, but his tone softened a bit. "As usual, Fr. Tomerlin is in a hurry; however, we have to indulge him some." He told her he had gotten to Tomerlin's letter "just as soon as I could. There are so many things distracting me and pulling me this way and that." He enumerated some of them for her: meetings with the new governor and the preliminary work to arrange them, "talking with architects, etc., efforts to get money, the always present community affairs, mail, etc."[63]

By mid-July 1933, these concerns had worn him down. His letters to the brothers at home became more obsessed with detail. The light touch of his humor faded. Concerned that Brother Augustine was overeating and eating improperly, he urged upon him in painful detail the Hay menu. "As for myself," he wrote, "you know, despite the terrific strain I am under and the shocks I am getting from all kinds of contradictions, I am carrying on." He had not missed saying daily Mass since his arrival in Puerto Rico. "I have a heavy day with a heavy schedule," he concluded, and he didn't want to add Brother Augustine's health to his other worries.[64]

Reestablishing St. Augustine's and the Providence of God

As July began, Father Judge had completed a swing around the island, heartened by the number of potential students and widespread support he found for St. Augustine's.[65] St. Augustine's now had an alumni association and a parent-teacher association. Governor Gore was a Catholic, and cadets from St. Augustine's had been selected to serve as honor guard at his inauguration Mass. The governor, Judge reported, was already interested in St. Augustine's, and he hoped to see him next week.[66] Gore's July 1 inauguration day began with a Mass at the cathedral in San Juan. Judge recounted Brother Gerard's description of the cadets to St. Augustine's new commandant, Father Paul Anthony: "when the Captain of the Cadets saluted with the sword,

63. Judge to Sister Carmel Davoren, Río Piedras, July 19, 1933, AST, MF 7373. By 1938 Father Tomerlin found his way to the Diocese of Camden, New Jersey. After a probation period of four years, Bishop Toolen agreed to release him, and he was incardinated into the Camden Diocese in 1942. He died in Lawrence, Massachusetts, in 1959 at the age of sixty-nine. This information is from his personnel file in AAM.

64. Judge to Brother Augustine Philips, Río Piedras, July 12, 1933, AST, MF 2334–35. Judge also expressed his displeasure with the consultors' handling of a proposed trust gift by a Mrs. Kress.

65. Judge to Father Paul Anthony Fursman, Río Piedras, June 28, 1933, AST, MF 2313–14.

66. Ibid.

the people gasped, he did it so beautifully, and then broke out into a frenzied handclapping saying 'Saint Augustine's Military Academy.'" He added proudly that the "army men themselves here say the cadets are better drilled and on parade than the soldiers." Father Paul Anthony had "better get your step good before you come down." The initial plans for the renovation of the hurricane-damaged building were ready on July 2, 1933.[67]

"We are anxious to begin," Father Judge wrote to Bishop Byrne. "Just now we are arranging all the forms of contract, planning and locating materials and workers, taking care of all preliminaries, so that as soon as the word is spoken, we can go right ahead." He also mentioned "an annoying water problem." The "word" Judge was awaiting had to do with financing, which was still not certain. He also mentioned in this letter an alternative proposal for a Jesuit school put forward by the "Spanish element." He asked Bishop Byrne to excuse him from a meeting with them that he thought would be dominated by Puerto Rican "nationalism." He described his "plan" for young men at St. Augustine's to have a "thorough academic training, a high Spanish culture, and be fitted for the English social and commercial converse they must have." Beyond academic training, "we have a moral feature in our plan and this is to develop a very high type of Puerto Rican youth, a type that will gladden the heart of the Church when she sees it operating in the home, in the professional, commercial and public life of the Island." He found the alternative proposal nationalistic, as if it had been written "in Spain and for a Spanish school."[68]

To Brother James, Father Judge explained plans for an elaborate fund-

67. Judge to Fursman, Río Piedras, July 2, 1933, AST, MF 2320. Judge recommended to Father Paul Anthony the policies laid down by Brothers Joseph and Gerard. Brother Joseph had spent five-and-a-half years at St. Augustine's. "Remember," he wrote, "Brother Joseph has carried the institution successfully under the most terrible disadvantages this past year, and he is but a humble Missionary Brother.... Bro. Joseph has been a pioneer and Bro. Gerard is his disciple. If you are humble enough to be a disciple of the two of them, you are going to make a success." He also urged him to "have a heart to heart talk with Fr. Eugene on St. Augustine's and Puerto Rican conditions."

68. Judge to Bishop Edwin V. Byrne, Río Piedras, July 3, 1933, AST, MF 7364–65. "We are Americans and Puerto Rico is an American dependency," Judge insisted. Along with "Spanish culture," he wanted "American ideals" fairly presented. On this meeting, see also Judge to Mother Mary of the Incarnate Word, Río Piedras, July 5, 1933, AST, MF 13318–19. Two weeks earlier, Brother Gerard's mother had sent Judge a newspaper clipping about a speech by an advocate of "Puerto Rico for Puerto Ricans." In sending Brother Anthony to get copies of this story, he described the speech as "a speech of a harebrained, fantastical young Puerto Rican who denounced the United States and a fellow by the name of Francisco Pagan y Fernández. He looks upon Albizu y Campos as the Gandhi of Puerto Rican youth"; Judge to Kelley, Río Piedras, June 21, 1933, AST, MF 12229–300.

raiser, a "military ball" sponsored by the Catholic Daughters of America in honor of Governor Gore. "The officers of the regular army and National Guard will be there in uniform and the Governor will walk in under the raised swords of the officers." "Much enthusiasm is being displayed," he concluded, "and we are hoping for a big success."[69]

In mid-July, Father Judge could still speak optimistically about his health. Though his stomach bothered him, he had not missed a day of saying Mass since he arrived on the island. "I am generally the first in chapel in the morning and the last to bed at night," he reported to Sister Agnes. "It is strain, I think, that takes so much out of me. For example, it would mean so much to get this work straightened out here."[70] By July 18, however, he was still waiting for construction to begin. The money for payroll and materials had yet to come through. The architect, Mr. Clar, had promised "to help us get the fifteen thousand dollars for the payroll, that he could borrow it for us." In describing the renovation plans to Brother Joseph, Judge exclaimed, "What a wonderful architect we have."[71]

No one knew how long the Reconstruction Finance Corporation would take to process the loan application. The governor promised to help with an issue of "Insular bonds." He planned to go to the States after August 1 and set the process in motion. The bonds, the governor assured Judge, "would be picked up by the banking houses at once and they would buy them in at 98. We pay 6 percent interest." On the governor's word, Father Judge told Brother James, "We have the sure promise of a hundred thousand by the end of August." The "military ball" took place on the night of July 21, 1933, with eighty couples in attendance and the money designated for the building fund.[72]

On the same day, Father Judge went over the final renovation plans with Clar and Nesbit and assured Mother Mary, "We have the certain promise of the money for the payroll and I expect when next I write you, the actual work will have begun."[73] But by July 23, the estimate of starting time had moved up two weeks. They still needed Department of Sanitation approval and $3,000 for payroll to carry the work through to the end of August, when the governor's bond money would be available. "We hope to be actually engaged in the construction work inside of two weeks."[74]

69. Judge to Norris, Río Piedras, July 2, 1933, AST, MF 2363–64.
70. Judge to Sister Agnes Gore, Río Piedras, July 12, 1933, AST, MF 12905.
71. Judge to Brother Joseph Limpert, Río Piedras, July 18, 1933, AST, MF 13513.
72. Judge to Norris, Río Piedras, July 21, 1933, AST, MF 2349.
73. Judge to Mother Mary of the Incarnate Word, Río Piedras, July 21, 1933, AST, MF 13325.
74. Judge to Brother Augustine, Río Piedras, July 23, 1933, AST, MF 2353–54. Five days

After July 23, his heavy correspondence fell off. His health must have started to fail around this time. Then came an extraordinary development. Father Judge agreed to rest. He confided to Brother Augustine on August 1 that he had seen two doctors "within a week." Both assessed his condition as generally "good," but recommended an extended period of rest, a month at the least. "Please God," Judge wrote, "I will follow their advice. The question is how can I get away?" The doctors insisted on extended rest. "Both put it on problems and work. I have not had a let-up in years so I am casting about for a place where I can lose myself for four weeks? Where is that place? Some place where people and things will not follow me, and where I can have a certain amount of comfort. Remember this is just for yourself."[75] He did not challenge the diagnosis. No talk of Dr. Hay and the menu, as there had been the previous year. Father Judge took this latest failure of his health more seriously than he had taken any previous episode.

The doctors, he told Sister Mary Thomas, "tell me in my present state the Island is not a good place for me." In the face of the payroll for the workers and delayed construction at St. Augustine's, he was prepared to take the doctors seriously. He told Sister Mary Thomas he would be at Gold Street in Brooklyn in about ten days. From there he might go to Waterville, Maine, to Sisters' Hospital, where his youngest sister Alice worked as a Daughter of Charity. He had confidence in the governor and hoped to see him once more before he left.[76]

Over the past weeks, in the midst of his other concerns, Father Judge thought about which brothers should accompany Brother Joseph to Puerto Rico to work at St. Augustine's and about arranging for their transportation, along with that of Father Paul Anthony. "We are waiting anxiously for Father Paul Anthony and his companion voyagers," he told Sr. Mary Thomas. "Thank God, I will be so relieved when he comes." He added that the governor would be going to the States soon "to try to get the loan."[77] Still, it was not clear whether construction had begun. Father Paul Anthony and Brother Joseph, along with Brothers Sebastian and Barnabas, left from Baltimore on the SS *Barbara* on August 1, 1933.[78] "It has been a gigantic task," he wrote on

later, he told Brother Theodore Jurdt that he was trying to negotiate "a loan for the workmen through the National City Bank"; Judge to Jurdt, Río Piedras, July 28, 1933, AST, MF 13550.

75. Judge to Philips, Río Piedras, August 1, 1933, AST, MF 12313–14.

76. Judge to Sister Mary Thomas, Río Piedras, August 4, 1933, AST, MF 13700–701; see also Judge to Mother Mary of the Incarnate Word, Río Piedras, August 3, 1933, AST, MF 13176.

77. Judge to Sister Mary Thomas, Río Piedras, August 4, 1933, AST, MF 13700–701.

78. Judge to Father Paul Anthony, Río Piedras, July 19, 1933, AST, MF 2347–48. In urging

August 2, "to get things moving toward the reestablishment of St. Augustine's, but thank God, things look good now."[79]

The *Barbara* landed on Sunday, August 6, 1933. His replacements had arrived. "The new Commandant of St. Augustine's Military Academy received a warm welcome. A number of the Cadets in uniform were waiting for him at the pier.... Fr. Paul Anthony is well fitted to carry on all the activities which have been inaugurated and this leaves me free for other fields."[80] Judge left it to Fursman to finish the tasks of getting the loan to pay the workers through August and dealing with Governor Gore on the insular bond issue. "I was thinking today," he wrote to Sister Carmel on August 1, "what is the best way to sweeten one's mind and to keep it serene, and the thought came to me to think on the Providence of God. What a wonderful revelation Divine Providence is to us. How marvelously does it overshadow us and guide us."[81] Father Judge was finished and prepared for what was to come.

Charity—Father Judge's Last Will and Testament

With Brother Gerard and Sister Marie of the Precious Blood accompanying him, Father Judge sailed for Brooklyn aboard the SS *Coamo* on August 10, 1933.[82] Sister Marie was the secretary general and third councilor for the sisters. Her usual place was in Philadelphia, but Mother Mary of the Incarnate Word's concern about Father Judge's health led her to assign Sister Marie as Father Judge's secretary while he was in Puerto Rico.[83] From aboard ship,

---

Fursman to make the August 1 boat rather than August 2, Judge wrote, "I need you and it is imperative that you get here at the earliest possible moment." A few days later he sent Fursman a detailed set of instructions on what to tell the new brothers on the boat as they sailed for Puerto Rico. They were not "tourists" and must have "sympathy for the people, and to close their ears to any criticism of them." They should not expect "to find things as they would be in Jersey City, New York, Chicago, Boston or Philadelphia" and avoid discussions of politics, and so on; Judge to Father Paul Anthony, Río Piedras, July 24, 1933, AST, MF 2357–58.

79. Judge to My dear Child, Río Piedras, August 2, 1933, AST, MF 7410–11.

80. Judge to My dear Child [Sister Thomas Marie?], Río Piedras, August 8, 1933, AST, MF 13964. With the departure of Father Paul Anthony, Judge had also found a Spanish priest, Father Carlos Ormaechaeo, to be in residence at Holy Trinity. He was "ensconced" there with faculties from Bishop Toolen by the time Fursman left. He described Ormaechaeo to Brother Theodore as "a very good Spanish Padre ... a gift of heaven to us ... a scientific agriculturalist"; Judge to Jurdt, Río Piedras, July 4, 1933, AST, MF 13519.

81. Judge to Sister Carmel Davoren, Río Piedras, August 1, 1933, AST, MF 7377.

82. Judge to Brother Augustine, Río Piedras, August 10, 1933, AST, MF 2365.

83. Tonra, *Led by the Spirit*, 366.

Father Judge wrote to Sister Mary Thomas, "Here is a new record. Felt sleepy after dinner. Went to bed 7:40 p.m. and slept til 8 o'clock."[84]

On Monday, August 14, they landed at Brooklyn and arrived at the Gold Street Cenacle. Sister Carmel, Mother Mary of the Incarnate Word, perhaps Sister Margaret Mary, Father Eugene, and Brother James were waiting for them there. As Sister Marie recalled, "he looked a wreck of humanity."[85] Father Judge went to lie down, and the others gathered around the kitchen table for coffee, but soon he came out, joined them around the table, and began to speak to them. "He was clear and deliberate at that talk at Gold Street," Father Gerard Fredericks recalled sixteen years later in 1949. "He gave the impression that he was aware that he might not come back again. He wanted to settle up all accounts. He wanted no antagonisms to develop and he insisted: 'If it is God's work, it will go on; if not, let God do whatever He wants with it.'"[86]

Father Judge began at the beginning with his emphasis on lay people working, as they did "going back to the time of Our Lord," for the preservation of the faith. He went over what Sister Marie described as his "aims, efforts, and work" and how he discerned about them. Good works are regularly opposed by bad people. He asked God for a sign "that his work would be opposed by good people." He urged, as he often had with reference to Bishop Toolen, that those who opposed the work be understood as "benefactors." Sister Marie likened this to Christ's plea from the cross for the forgiveness of those who had executed him. "He must have realized," she wrote, "from the way he felt that he looked a wreck of humanity and that seeing him in such a pitiable state would rouse us to considerable feeling against those who had caused it."[87]

With a reference to "the difficulties with Mobile," Father Judge made his instruction in charity specific. Bishop Toolen acted sincerely and in good conscience. "He said we needed to be disciplined," Sister Marie wrote, "and

84. Judge to Sister Mary Thomas, from SS *Coamo* at sea, August 1933, AST, MF 7407–8.

85. See Sister Marie Campbell's recollection, "Father's Last Talk at Gold Street, August 14, 1933," Monographs 2:51. "I am not too sure," Sister Marie wrote, "of who really was there." She was not sure about whether Sr. Margaret Mary was there. In his only comment on this meeting, in an unidentified fragment of his correspondence, Father Judge wrote, "Father Eugene is just superb. We had a nice gathering. I think he has changed very much for the better, thank God." Context makes clear that he is talking about the meeting in Brooklyn; AST, MF 7409.

86. These were Father Gerard's reflections upon reading Sister Marie's recollection of the talk, written sometime around 1949. Fr. Gerard's reflections appear in Campbell, "Father Judge's Last Talk at Gold Street. August 14, 1933," Monographs 2:53–54.

87. Ibid., 52.

God used the Bishop to do it." Uncharitable speech about Bishop Toolen or uncharitable thoughts against him by any of "his children" would "hurt him cruelly." Sister Marie described this as the climax and purpose of his talk. "He would not leave," she concluded, "until he had sought and pleaded for a charitable viewpoint of all that had transpired that was catalogued as hateful and unjust, he knew, in our minds." As Sister Marie recalled it, Father Judge did not speak very long.

Waterville, Maine, and Silver Spring, August 14–26

On the night of Monday, August 14, 1933, Father Judge and Brother James took a train from Grand Central Station, bound eventually for Sisters' Hospital in Waterville, Maine. Along the way, they stopped to visit Dr. Hay. Sister Alice had promised that he would have a chance to rest in Waterville. He only stayed there "for about a week," and then Brother James brought him back to Silver Spring.[88] At this time, John Baptist McCarthy was a twenty-year-old student brother. He had come to Silver Spring with Brother Thomas to help take care of Father Judge. In 1983 Father McCarthy wrote a memoir of "Father's Last Days in the Cenacle."[89] He had driven with Brother Thomas from Stirling, where he was spending the summer. They stopped at the sisters' motherhouse in Philadelphia and picked up Sister Austin, Father Judge's nurse in Puerto Rico, and Sister Catherine. Brother Thomas and Brother James planned to clear everyone else out of Holy Trinity Heights, as the cenacle at Silver Spring was called. That night Brother James arrived from Maine with Father Judge.

From Father Judge's correspondence, he and Norris left Maine on Sunday, August 20. They arrived in Silver Spring on Monday night. By Tuesday, Father McCarthy describes driving Father Judge to see Dr. Roy J. Sexton in Washington during the days for medical tests. Father Judge asked McCarthy to take dictation for his letters. When McCarthy proved incapable of that, Judge asked if Louise Wagner could come to help. She did, and Father Judge continued with his correspondence. On August 24, he described the trip to Maine:

88. Ibid., 53; see also Father Lawrence Brediger's recollection as cited in Tonra, *Led by the Spirit*, 369.

89. John Baptist McCarthy, ST, "Father's Last Days in the Cenacle," Monographs 2:64–75.

> I was really a month too late and was afraid of being caught in the cold and the damp. I reversed and had another hard trip to Holy Trinity Heights. It seemed to be a providential place, I think it was. I have heard much of Dr. Sexton from our Brothers and I have been his patient since last Tuesday [August 22]; as a consequence, I am interning in Providence Hospital, Washington, perhaps for two or three months and it is to be a rest. I never had such examinations or tests. There is nothing else to do but for me to take a rest. I am very much convinced it is the will of God.

He revealed that he had taken an extraordinary step for one who had spent the past decades trying to keep up with his mail. He would get no mail at Providence Hospital. It would be sent to Stirling. Only "very urgent" mail could come to Washington. He acknowledged that "an unpleasant feature of this would be mystery," but he continued to insist that it was "Divine Providence" requiring him to rest.[90]

Providence Hospital—Letting Go

On Friday, August 25, Father Judge wrote to thank his sister Alice "for your many kindnesses to me while I was with you." He described his medical examinations in Washington as "very thorough" and told her he expected to enter Providence Hospital the next day.[91] Father McCarthy described Father Judge on the day that Sister Austin told him Judge would enter the hospital. "I glanced at him sitting in the front seat beside me," McCarthy wrote. "His eyes were closed and he looked so very, very old. His collar stood out from his neck and just then I noticed that his trousers hung from his legs as though they were broomsticks."[92]

It was probably on Saturday, August 26, that McCarthy drove Father Judge to Providence, a Daughters of Charity hospital then located in the Capitol Hill section of Washington, between Second and Third Streets and D and E Streets SE. His letters continued for about another three weeks. On Sunday, August 27, he wrote to tell Father McHale that, on the advice of three doctors, he would remain in the hospital "for six weeks to two months." Though he did mention that he expected three brothers to be ordained in February, this was not one

90. Judge to Mother Mary of the Incarnate Word, Silver Spring, Md., August 24, 1933, AST, MF 13227. This letter is typed. He wrote similarly to Sister Carmel in Brooklyn; Judge to Sister Carmel Davoren, Silver Spring, Md., August 25, 1933, AST, MF 7415. "I am really feeling better," he told her, "than when I reached the States a week ago."

91. Judge to Sister Alice Judge, DC, Silver Spring, Md., August 25, 1933, AST, MF 7417.

92. McCarthy, "Father's Last Days in the Cenacle," 2:75.

of his usual letters to McHale keeping him informed about the community's work and progress. His brief report on the state of the community focused on the interior side. "We are enjoying great peace and seem to sense the action of the Holy Ghost in our various Missionary Cenacles." He said not a word about Puerto Rico. "It is a great joy to me," he told McHale, "that I can throw, at present, responsibilities on others."[93] This was his last letter to Father McHale.

Between this letter to Father McHale on August 27 and September 15, Father Judge wrote only a few more letters. Few concerned day-to-day operations, now far from his mind. His letters took on a more personal or pastoral cast. He had written to Bishop McCarthy of Portland, Maine, to thank him for faculties while he was in Maine and also to plead for a wayward priest, Father Fitzpatrick, who had spent time at St. Augustine's with Father Brennan.[94] He wrote a kind letter to Sister Mary James, who, despite her desire to be a missionary, continued to serve as the sisters' procurator general. He extolled her "special gift" for working in temporalities so "intimately associated" at this time in the church's history "to its spiritual progress" and spoke of the necessary role of temporalities in "our Lord's life."[95] He thanked Father Louis Motry for his help in getting dimissorial letters from the Diocese of Pittsburgh for Brother Ambrose and gave Father Paul Anthony some advice about how to proceed with the children in Puerto Rico.[96] The closest he came to the usual matter of his correspondence were two letters to Stirling regarding the proper handling of the mail.[97]

After a very brief encouraging response to a letter from one of the sisters on September 15, 1933, the author of so many, many letters fell silent for almost a month, until October 12, when he wrote to Father William Slattery, the new Vincentian visitor, sick in a Philadelphia hospital. From his own hospital bed, Father Judge made sure that his Vincentian superiors knew exactly where he was. We hear nothing more from Father Judge about urgent matters such as the petitions to Rome, the loan for St. Augustine's, or even about the three anticipated ordinations in 1934.

Father Judge's rich religious imagination returned in his final suffering

93. Judge to McHale, Washington, D.C., August 27, 1933, AST, MF 11657–58.

94. Judge to Bishop Joseph E. McCarthy, Silver Spring, Md., August 26, 1933, AST, MF 13763.

95. Judge to My dear Child [Sr. Mary James], Providence Hospital, August 29, 1933, AST, MF 7371.

96. Judge to Motry, Providence Hospital, September 10, 1933, AST, MF 13799; Judge to Fursman, Providence Hospital, September 8, 1933, AST, MF 2366–68.

97. Judge to Brother Theodore Jurdt, Silver Spring, Md., August 26, 1933, AST, MF 13933; Judge to My dear Brothers, Providence Hospital, August 29, 1933, AST, MF 13596.

to the cup of Gethsemane and the precious blood imagery of the Holy Agony devotion he had once promoted. "If I find the night long and tedious," he told Fr. Slattery, "my comfort and strength is to follow the Sacred Host and the Precious Blood as they circle daily the world." He focused on the image of the "uplifted chalice of the Precious Blood." He put Slattery and his health "in all the uplifted chalices of the Precious Blood that the Triune God may be pleased to grant you the health and vigor for your office. Do, in your charity, remember this sick Confrere."[98] Father Slattery did remember. Tonra recounts that when he got out of the hospital he came to visit Father Judge at Providence and spent about fifteen minutes with him.[99]

During Father Judge's last days at Providence Hospital, the lingering question of his canonical status lost its urgency and quietly resolved itself. Consistent with his 1933 letters to Fathers McHale and Slattery, available sources offer no evidence that Father Judge ever entertained the possibility of not being a Vincentian.[100] Nor is there any record that his Vincentian superiors wished to expel him or force him to choose between the Vincentians and the Missionary Servants. Such a directive would have had to come from the Sacred Congregation for Religious through the apostolic delegate. There is a story that someone from the office of the apostolic delegate came to Providence Hospital to get Father Judge's decision on whether he would be a Vincentian or a Missionary Servant. When the representative saw his condition, he just left.[101] Father Judge would die a Vincentian.

In the weeks before he died, Father Judge suffered from severe intestinal, chest, and back pain. He had trouble breathing and urinated frequently. At the end, he was heavily sedated to alleviate the pain.

> Hospital charts indicate that he was suffering from a very painful intestinal inflammation, treated with a variety of barbituates, including morphine and codeine. He was in severe discomfort from "irritation and inflammation in the chest cavity," necessitating the removal of up to a "quart of liquid by syringe." The doctors further diagnosed cardiovascular renal disease, causing a heart rate of 80 to 100 beats per minute, sometimes up to 110 beats.[102]

98. Judge to Rev. William M. Slattery, CM, Providence Hospital, October 12, 1933, AST, MF 7425.

99. Tonra, *Led by the Spirit*, 370.

100. See Joachim Benson's comments on Father Judge's strong attachment to the Vincentians; Sister Mary Tonra, MSBT, "Interview with Father Joachim Benson," February 5, 1974, Rio Piedras, Typescript, 35, AMSBT.

101. I have no documentary source for this story.

102. This description comes from an analysis of Father Judge's hospital charts by Sister Constance [Marie Celine] Norick, as cited from AST in Berry, *God's Valiant Warrior*, 127, 377n727.

On November 1, the doctors had removed fluid from his lungs, and he felt a little better. He dictated to his niece Grace Ledwidge, Sister Gerard's daughter and his nurse at Providence Hospital, a list of seven "Reasons Why I Think I'm Better." The list indicates that, in addition to physical weakness, he also had trouble speaking. Now he thought he was "able to exert myself a little more." The list concluded, "I still feel a weakness in helping myself personally. I no longer have convulsive stomach coughs. As a sick man, naturally I'm conscious of my own personal misery."[103]

A week later, on November 7, two weeks before he died, Father Judge still felt strong enough to dictate his final letter of "blessings and most affectionate greetings to his beloved children" of the Missionary Cenacle. He chose to compose this letter on the Feast of Vincentian martyr Blessed John Gabriel Perboyre, about whom he had written home as a young seminarian, and in whose Brooklyn chapel he had begun the Cenacle movement. This letter returned to the cup of Gethsemane, the image of the "uplifted cup filled with the Precious Blood." In the imposing sculpture depicting the Agony in the Garden that stands in the Shrine of the Holy Agony at the Basilica of St. Elizabeth Ann Seton in Emmitsburg, the angel offers to Jesus the cup he had prayed might pass from him. The depiction of the angel suggests a priest elevating the chalice at Mass. Such imagery consoled Father Judge in his own last agony. He focused on the child, the child Jesus, and the "children of the world." The Feast of Christ the King had recently passed. "When it pleases Christ the King," he concluded, "to let me come back to you all again, I shall tell you the story divine and miraculous of the uplifted cup filled with the Precious Blood. I have placed all of you in this chalice close to Jesus."[104]

On November 15, 1933, he wrote his last brief letter, more like a note and in a very weak hand. He described it as "the first personal letter I have written here." It was to Sister Mary Agnes Gore. During the previous summer, he had told her how much it would mean to him if she would come to teach at St. Augustine's. He tried to alleviate her anxieties about coming to Puerto Rico, but, in the end, she did not come. Now in November, she wrote from Newark to ask if she could come to visit him at Providence. "God bless and love you," he wrote. "You are just the same as ever to me, my dear child. Surely, you may leave and see me but all I can do is bless you. Your letter

103. List of "Reasons Why I Think I'm Feeling Better" (written by Grace Ledwidge), November 1, 1933, AST, MF 13289–90.

104. Judge to My dear Children, Providence Hospital, November 7, 1933, AST, MF 7426.

made me happy [illegible]. You are in my prayers." He wanted Sister Agnes to know that she had not disappointed him.[105]

With little correspondence and few visitors, the "mystery" Father Judge anticipated did indeed surround his stay at Providence Hospital. Accounts of his last days are, therefore, necessarily sketchy and anecdotal. Tonra recounts that Sister Thomas Francis was also on duty with Grace Ledwidge and that together they monitored his visitors.[106] In a letter to Brother Joachim on July 20, 1934, Ledwidge gave Brother Joachim her best recollection of Father Judge's last hours. The cause of death listed on his death certificate was "cerebral embolism."[107] Besides Grace Ledwidge, it is not clear if anyone else was actually in the room with him when he died. The last words she remembered him speaking to her were, "Let me rest." Then something changed, and she called for a priest immediately. Mother Mary of the Incarnate Word and Sister Mary James were nearby, as were some of the brothers from Silver Spring.[108] Father Judge died at 3:00 p.m. on November 23, 1933. If his death certificate is any indication, he had poured out his whole heart, his whole mind, and his whole strength. He had heroically carried out the two great commandments.

105. Judge to Sister Agnes Gore, Providence Hospital, November 10, 1933, AST, MF 12911; see Judge to Sister Agnes, Río Piedras, July 12, 1933, AST, MF 12905; Judge to Sister Agnes, Río Piedras, July 19, 1933, 12907; Judge to Sister Carmel, Río Piedras, August 1, 1933, AST MF 7377. Judge told Sister Carmel that Sister Agnes would not be coming to St. Augustine's and they would probably have to get one of the junior Sisters; see also Berry, *God's Valiant Warrior*, 378n729.

106. Tonra, *Led by the Spirit*, 371. See also Sister Mary Francis's moving account here of the sisters and brothers who came to donate their blood for the transfusions Father Judge needed.

107. Ibid., 129. Berry's is the fullest account of Father Judge's last days. It is based primarily on Grace Ledwidge's letter to Brother Joachim, Father Judge's death certificate, preserved in AST, and Sister Constance's notes on Father Judge's medical records, also in AST. The death certificate listed "chronic pleurisy with effusion and myocarditis" as "contributory" causes. Berry records that Father Lawrence Brediger showed the death certificate to a pathologist in 1958. The pathologist, Dr. Irving Derby, speculated that it would read, "if filled out now [1958]: cerebral thrombosis, due to generalized arteriosclerosis; contributing factor: congestive heart failure with congestive pleural effusion. [It is] not likely that it was a true myocarditis, i.e., no inflammation; simply the degenerative disease of age. It is extremely unlikely that there was any active tuberculosis present"; Berry, *God's Valiant Warrior*, 378n733.

108. See Tonra, *Led by the Spirit*, 371, and Berry, *God's Valiant Warrior*, 378n733, citing a letter of Brother Anthony Kelley to Joachim Benson, November 23, 1933, AST. Apparently, Brother Anthony and a few other brothers from Silver Spring were also nearby, and perhaps Sisters Austin and Catherine, who had come to Silver Spring with Bro. Thomas in late August. In a conversation on August 6, 2004, Sister Catherine Bernadette Mee told me that she was one of three sisters at the hospital on November 23. She said one of the sisters, a nurse, Sister Thomas Francis or Sister Austin perhaps, believing he was a saint, propped up the body and cut his hair. She said she still had a lock of his hair. Perhaps this is how James Norris got the lock of Father Judge's hair he carried with him all his life.

One of Father Eugene Brennan's first official tasks as Father Judge's vicar was to notify Bishop Schrembs and the Diocese of Cleveland of his death and funeral arrangements. He reported that Father Judge would lie in state at the sisters' Mother Missionary Cenacle in Philadelphia.[109] Bishop Schrembs responded immediately. News of Father Judge's death "had touched me deeply," he wrote. "I had learned to admire and love Father Judge and, as you know, I opened my diocese to him for the motherhouse and novitiate of the Order. . . . I hope and pray that you will not lose courage but do everything in your power to carry on along the lines which Father Judge had conceived."[110]

Cardinal Dougherty directed that, as a Vincentian, Father Judge be buried from St. Vincent's Seminary in Germantown, where he had been a student. On Wednesday morning, November 29, 1933, Cardinal Dougherty presided at the Solemn Requiem Mass, with Father Eugene as celebrant. Father Paul Anthony was the deacon and Father Theophane the subdeacon. Father Judge's old friend, Father Felix O'Neill from St. Michael's parish in Newark, preached the eulogy. Solemn requiems were also offered for Father Judge at Holy Trinity and at St. Augustine's Military Academy in Río Piedras.[111] He was laid to rest in Holy Sepulcher Cemetery in Philadelphia, beside Mother Boniface. On December 1, the Vincentian visitor, Father Slattery, wrote to tell the new superior general in Paris, Father Charles Souvay, that Father Judge had died.[112]

109. Brennan to Bishop James A. McFadden, Holmesburg, Pa., November 25, 1933, Schrembs Papers, ADC. McFadden was Bishop Schrembs's auxiliary bishop. He responded on November 29.

110. Schrembs to Brennan, Cleveland, Ohio, November 28, 1933. Father Eugene sent Bishop Schrembs a memorial card from Father Judge's funeral, and Schrembs thanked him in a brief letter; Schrembs to Brennan, Cleveland, December 14, 1933, copies, Schrembs Papers, ADC.

111. The details of Father Judge's funeral, including the full text of Father O'Neil's eulogy, are in Tonra, *Led by the Spirit*, 371–75.

112. Slattery to Charles L. Souvay, CM, Germantown, December 1, 1933, AST, MF 13992.

17

AFTER THE FOUNDERS

1933–1958

Separate Canonical Communities

In the days of Father Judge and Mother Boniface, only a rural highway separated the women's and men's communities at Holy Trinity. Father Judge died two years after Mother Boniface, leaving both men and women of the Cenacle, lay and religious, without their founders. Canonical recognition of the women's community in 1932 followed upon the men's in 1929. This, combined with the move of both motherhouses from Holy Trinity, tended to separate the two communities.

The emerging canonical structures of the universal church and the ethos of brick-and-mortar consolidation in an immigrant Catholic culture had little room for Father Judge's reimagining of St. Vincent de Paul's vision for a new place and time. Judge envisioned the Cenacle as a religious family of women religious, men religious, and lay apostles working together for the preservation of the faith. What emerged after his death were two separate religious communities with no canonical relation to one another. The women tended to remain more closely connected to the Outer Cenacle. The men's tenuous status as a struggling young community of priests and brothers separated them from both the women's community and the Outer Cenacle. These developments fractured Father Judge's vision for the Cenacle.

Missionary Servants of the Most Blessed Trinity

Under the strong leadership of Mother Mary of the Incarnate Word, as well as many other women who had known Father Judge for years, the Missionary Servants of the Most Blessed Trinity were well established at the time of his death. In keeping with the terms of their decree of erection of February 20, 1932, Cardinal Dougherty granted them a sanatio in radice, recognizing as canonical their novitiates and professions of vows. Now canonically regularized, they had more than 250 sisters and 30 foundations in the United States and Puerto Rico.

Mother Boniface was gone. Others who had long histories with Father Judge remained. Many sisters still alive in 1933 had worked alongside Father Judge as lay apostles. He had given their retreats and served as their spiritual director. Among many others, these included Sisters Marie Baptista, Miriam, and Mary Francis from New York, Mother Mary of the Incarnate Word and Sister Carmel from Meriden, Sister Marie of the Precious Blood from New Britain, and, in the Outer Cenacle, Dr. Margaret Healy of Brooklyn and Louise Wagner. Sister Mary James had begun to organize the sisters' archives. By 1949 Father Judge had become "A Voice from the Past" as Sister Mary James published the first installment of her long series on Father Judge in the *Holy Ghost*. It ran until 1954.

These women had imbibed important aspects of Father Judge's spirit: its emphasis on family among the brothers and sisters, the primacy of the love of God for apostolic work with the resultant compassion, simplicity, and rigor of life, a preference for the abandoned work, the call to make apostles of ordinary workaday people and the role of the sisters and brothers in supporting lay apostles, the passion for preserving the faith of new immigrants and of those living in Latin America, where it was under threat. But, for the most part, circumstances, along with new canonical restrictions, prevented their contact with young men in training for the Missionary Servants of the Most Holy Trinity and, in some cases, even limited their contact with the Outer Cenacle.

The Impact of the Sisters' Constitution

Despite concessions, especially regarding distinctive garb and to some extent traveling and "cloister," the newly approved constitution, distributed to the sisters in 1933, was striking for two reasons. First, its homogenizing character squeezed the Missionary Servants of the Most Blessed Trinity into emerging patterns of women's religious life in the early twentieth century, especially in terms of monastic-style rules of enclosure. Requirements in the areas of "eating, traveling, and cloister" changed the way sisters had lived and worked. The most dramatic change required that "all meals be taken in the refectory and the inclusion of the refectory within the bounds of the designated cloister." Sharing meals with "externs," or those outside the canonical bounds of the community, was prohibited, "a radical change from the family lifestyle the Missionary Servants had shared up to this point with the lay members and priests and brothers of the Missionary Cenacle Family."[1] Second, the new constitution contained no reference to Father Judge or to the Missionary Servants of the Most Holy Trinity.

Despite relatively generous concessions on garb and the broad reach of the sisters' work, the new constitution generally made the task of sustaining the founders' spirit more difficult:

> On the whole it treated the sisters as if they were generic in function and monastic in origin, as all congregations during this period were being treated. In certain key ways it did violence to the spirit and lifestyle which had formed the sisters since 1918. It severed the family connection to their spiritual brothers by removing any mention of them even in an advisory role, by removing mention of them in their prayers for the dead . . . and by imposing rules preventing them from sharing meals together.[2]

Holy Name of Jesus Hospital

When the new constitution was distributed to the sisters in 1933, the country still labored under the weight of the Great Depression. Despite their new canonical recognition, the sisters faced an overwhelming debt on the new Holy Name of Jesus Hospital. Closely connected to the ongoing conflicts between Bishop Toolen and Father Judge during the last years of his life, this issue had now found its way into courts in the United States and to the Sacred Congregation for Religious in Rome.

The issue of financing the new hospital reached the attention of the Congregation for Religious in spring 1933 when Bishop Toolen, having been sued in Mobile regarding payments on the hospital loan, raised the possibility of bringing suit against the sisters in civil court. In April 1933, a $10,000 payment on the principal of the loan for Holy Name of Jesus Hospital came due. The sisters could not pay it. They also missed an interest payment of $2,000, which they subsequently made up. Sometime in May, Bitting and Co. brought suit against Bishop Toolen because the sisters had defaulted on the payments for the loan in the form of hospital bonds for which he had signed.

1. Deborah L. Wilson, MSBT, "To Speak with One Voice, 53–54. Chapter 2 contrasts the first approved constitution with an earlier draft; see especially 51–57.

2. Ibid., 56.

This meant almost a full-year's delay before the Congregation turned its attention to the issues raised in Father Judge's two petitions.

On May 5, 1933, Bishop Toolen wrote the sisters that "it looks like you are deliberately neglecting the debt." On May 22, Sister Mary James, acknowledging his letters of May 1 and May 5, enclosed a check for the "remainder of the interest." The sisters conducted the "Catholic Bureaus" in Mobile, and Bishop Toolen had apparently threatened to give them "three months' notice." Sister Mary James expressed her sincere hope that the bureaus would remain open. "If you but knew and realized," she wrote, "the difficulties we are facing, if you but realized how heavy our burden has been during this past year, I am sure that you, with your kind heart, would never have said, 'it looks as if you are deliberately neglecting the debt.'" She concluded with these thoughts: "The responsibility which has been passed on to us is, indeed, a heavy cross, but He who permitted it to be laid upon us will, we pray, help us carry it."[3]

By June 1933, Cardinal Lépicier at the Sacred Congregation for Religious had received more Father Judge–related documentation regarding the suit against Bishop Toolen in Mobile. Bishop Toolen sent newspaper clippings about the suit to Monsignor Kiley. "I have been following the matter up," Kiley reported to the bishop, "and was told that the new Delegate was asked to look into the matter.... It generally happens that such questions are referred to the Apostolic Delegate for his opinion or for a verification of the statements made." According to Kiley, the Congregation had a copy of Bishop Toolen's contract with the sisters. Kiley told Bishop Toolen that he never would have signed the bonds. "It is too bad," he wrote, "you didn't put it up to Dougherty at the time, and let him take the blame for their debts since he never answered your letter and cares for no one except himself."

Monsignor Kiley inquired about the result of the suit against the sisters in Philadelphia and responded to Bishop Toolen's question about whether he needed permission from the Sacred Congregation for Religious to bring a civil suit against the sisters. "About permission from the Congregation," Kiley wrote, "necessity has no law." He advised Bishop Toolen to see the new apostolic delegate, Archbishop Amleto Cicognani (1883–1973), personally and suggested that he bring his contract with the sisters and Mother Boniface's letter "presenting her proposition and acknowledging what you did for them."[4]

3. Sister Mary James Collins to Bishop Toolen, Holmesburg, Pa., May 22, 1933, Toolen Papers, AAM. In this letter, Sister Mary James cites Bishop Toolen's letter of May 5.

4. Kiley to Toolen, Rome, June 14, 1933. Regarding Cicognani, Kiley wrote, "The new man is a different type, and I think much more aggressive than [Fumasoni-Biondi].... If you are

In the meantime, Bishop Toolen dispatched his attorney, T. R. Shannon, to Philadelphia to convince the sisters to agree to refinance the loan. "I think you handled Mr. Shannon very nicely," Father Judge wrote to Mother Mary of the Incarnate Word, "and met very well the strategy of our friends near the Gulf.... You did well to hesitate, to refuse, to tell that lawyer that no paper would be signed only after council in the community and with your lawyer."[5] The sisters eventually agreed to the refinance. Bishop Toolen later explained to the new apostolic delegate the outcome of Bitting's suit against him in Mobile: "The suit was dismissed when the agreement was made to refinance the loan." His explanation continued, "The sisters, when our lawyer went to Philadelphia, were loath to agree when they knew they could not meet the terms as they stood. They [*sic*] lawyer had to urge them to agree and they have paid nothing of the cost of the refinancing."[6]

With the suit against him now dropped, Bishop Toolen considered bringing his own civil suit against the sisters. On July 27, Monsignor Kiley reported Cardinal Lépicier's judgment "that recourse could be had to the civil courts for the failure to fulfill a civil contract." According to Kiley, Lépicier said there was no reason the suit could not proceed at once. Kiley concluded, "So should anyone like the Delegate raise any question, you could tell him that you were given permission by the Cardinal Prefect to protect the interests of the diocese in the civil courts in accordance with the terms of the contract entered into between the diocese and the Sisters." Kiley asked Bishop Toolen if he had seen the new delegate since his arrival in Washington. "He is quite clever, and is not at all bashful, nor afraid to take a chance."[7] As his correspondence with Archbishop Cicognani indicates, Bishop Toolen eventually decided to forego the civil suit.

In October Monsignor Kiley still had nothing to report on the hospital

in Washington at any time, I would call into see the new man and tell him you are a friend of mine." He reported that Cicognani would likely be in Washington by the end of May; Kiley to Toolen, Rome, May 13, 1933, Toolen Papers, AAM.

5. Judge to Mother Mary of the Incarnate Word, Río Piedras, June 18, 1933, AST, MF 13211.

6. Toolen to Cicognani, Mobile, Ala., January 24, 1934, Delegation File No. 7077-I, copy, Toolen Papers, AAM. Regarding this agreement, Father Judge wrote to Mother Mary: "What a current spectacle of the old fable of the monkey trying to get the cat to pull the chestnuts out of the fire. How simple, after all, that crowd must be to think that after all their legerdemain and extraordinarily surprising and painful ways of doing things that they think they can send a representative who will persuade the sisters after a little conferencing to sign their names to an agreement that their interest and suspicious strategy has inspired." Nevertheless, they did agree; Judge to Mother Mary of the Incarnate Word, Río Piedras, June 18, 1933, AST, MF 13211.

7. Kiley to Toolen, Rome, July 27, 1933, Toolen Papers, AAM.

debt. Having inquired at the Congregation for Religious, he was told "the matter was still under consideration." Cardinal Lépicier was away, and "little is done at any of the Congregations during the summer." Kiley didn't know that Father Judge was in the hospital and would die within a month. "I have been wondering just how Judge is making out with Dougherty and the Sisters," he wrote. "He will not be able to run things to his liking if Dougherty can help it." Then he added correctly, "I don't think the Congregation gave him what he asked for, to be Superior of the Sisters for another ten years."[8]

Two months after Father Judge's death, the new apostolic delegate, Archbishop Amleto Cicognani, finally addressed issues "concerning the debt on Holy Name of Jesus Hospital in Gadsden, Alabama." The delay, he explained, was due to Father Judge's death but also "to an effort to arrive at a satisfactory understanding of certain discrepancies that appear in statements made by Your Excellency and others made by the good Sisters." Cicognani enumerated three issues: (1) Bishop Toolen's "immediate cooperation in the creation of the debt"; (2) the amount paid on the debt by the sisters over the past two years; and (3) the "responsibility for the law suit which was brought against the Community in the civil court of Mobile." Cicognani now thought that detailed discussion of these issues was no longer necessary, since "Bitting and Company have refinanced the loan which Your Excellency has again signed with the Missionary Servants of the Most Holy [*sic*] Trinity."[9] "I understand," he added, "that, under the new arrangement, no payment is to be made on the principal for the next five years." Cicognani thought the new arrangement "should prove to be a relief both to the Diocese and to the Community."

The delegate considered the refinance a relief to both sides of the litigation because "although the Sisters readily admit that the debt is theirs, it seems quite certain from a *legal* point of view that the Diocese of Mobile is responsible, if not for the whole debt, at least for that part of it which was created by the sale of the bonds." While the sisters "assure me that they will do their utmost to meet the obligation," Cicognani was sure that Bishop Toolen would "consider this debt as a matter of diocesan administration." Practically, he concluded, there should be little problem. "I suppose the new arrangement has brought the obligation within reasonable limits and that, notwithstanding the present financial situation, the Community will

8. Ibid., October 21, 1933, Toolen Papers, AAM.

9. Cicognani appeared to confuse the English names of the men's and women's communities. In the Latin titles, *sanctissimae* is used for both "Blessed" and "Holy."

be able to meet it and thus avoid further expense to the Diocese of Mobile." Cicognani concluded:

> I repose much confidence in Your Excellency's paternal interest and cooperation with the members of this Community who labor in the Diocese of Mobile. It would seem that God is blessing the work of the Sisters in Gadsden: this work should redound more and more as the years go on to the good of religion in the Diocese. While the start of the Community may not have been very auspicious, I am confident that it is becoming an exemplary religious congregation and will render noble and valuable service to Holy Church.[10]

Bishop Toolen responded quickly with his side of the case. His "cooperation," he insisted, was less than "immediate" and given "only after they found it impossible to get the money any place else" and "only after they signed a contract" that they did not keep. He acknowledged that the community had indeed paid $10,000 on the principal, but pointed out their failure to pay another $10,000 that came due in April 1933. This cost the diocese $5,200 in interest. The diocese also had to bear the $3,000 cost of refinancing the loan. He pointed out that, over the past eighteen months, the diocese had to make payments on this loan amounting to over $10,000. "It certainly seems unjust," he concluded, "that we should have to pay out this money and cripple our work here in order to accommodate the Sisters of the Holy Trinity." Explaining the facts of the suit, he emphasized that "there is a grave difference of opinion as to the legal obligations of the Diocese of Mobile in this debt." But, he added, "I do not think this enters into the proposition at all. The Sisters got the money, every cent of it, to put up the hospital that belongs to them. Theirs is the debt and they are the ones that ought to pay."

The bishop then raised the specter of a lawsuit. "The Sacred Congregation of Religious," he claimed, following Kiley's advice, "gave me the right to bring them into the civil courts before you came to Washington but I hesitated about doing this because of the scandal it might cause." Then he quickly added, "On the other hand, I feel that I should take every means to protect the Diocese." He acknowledged, as he always had, that the sisters "were doing a fine missionary work." For his help in their need, "I have received mighty shabby treatment." He again raised the issue of collections "in the name of the South," implying that the money had been misappropriated. "I am not seeking anything but justice, Your Excellency," he concluded, "and I

10. Cicognani to Toolen, Washington, D.C., January 18, 1934, No. 7077-I, Toolen Papers, AAM.

am not going to let up until I get it. I am sure you can see my side of the question." He told Cicognani he would be coming north around the beginning of March and would call on him to talk this matter over.[11] Later correspondence indicates that Cicognani and Toolen met in March.

Despite Bishop Toolen's implied threat of a lawsuit against the sisters and his claim that he would not "let up," the situation with the hospital developed along the lines Archbishop Cicognani laid out in his letter of January 18, 1934. With the more immediate question of the lawsuit out of the way, the delegate turned his attention to the questions raised in the two petitions Father Judge sent to the Sacred Congregation for Religious shortly before his death: the transfer of the men's motherhouse to Cleveland and the fate of their novitiate and Holy Trinity itself.

Missionary Servants of the Most Holy Trinity

The Two Petitions

Lacking strong leadership, and much less well established at Father Judge's death than the sisters, the Missionary Servants of the Most Holy Trinity found their very existence at risk. The surprising story of their survival and rebirth cries out to be understood in Father Judge's spiritual and providential categories. A lengthy story that begins with the two petitions, it has too long been left untold.

At Father Judge's death, the two petitions Monsignor Marella sent to Rome on his behalf in March 1933 remained unanswered. Should the unresolved issue of transferring the men's motherhouse to Cleveland be approved, the recourse to prevent Bishop Toolen from suppressing Holy Trinity and the men's novitiate would still await resolution. In the meantime, Bishop Toolen sent his own recourse against Father Judge to the Sacred Congregation. Monsignor Kiley hand-delivered it to the Congregation's prefect along with a copy of the *Catholic Review* with Archbishop Curley's open letter against "Judge bonds" on the front page. The precise content of Bishop Toolen's recourse remains unknown.[12] At Father Judge's death, the three

11. Toolen to Cicognani, Mobile, Ala., January 24, 1934, No. 7077-I, copy, Toolen Papers, AAM.

12. "I gave your recourse to the Cardinal Prefect of the Congregation of Religious who said that it would be given consideration as promptly as possible.... I gave him an extra copy of the *Review* so that he would have the entire paper with the Archbishop's letter. He said he would be glad to get it since it would be evidence of what was going on in the name of religion"; Kiley to Toolen, Rome, February 28, 1933. By May Kiley reported that he had seen Cardinal Lépicier "on

questions of financing Holy Name of Jesus Hospital, the transfer of the men's motherhouse, and suppression of their novitiate in Alabama converged on the Sacred Congregation for Religious. As Monsignor Kiley predicted to Bishop Toolen, the Congregation asked the new apostolic delegate to "look into" the matters before it.[13]

On March 30, 1934, Archbishop Cicognani wrote to Bishop Schrembs regarding his agreement to accept the motherhouse of the Missionary Servants of the Most Holy Trinity into the Diocese of Cleveland. Bishop Schrembs responded on April 4. It had been almost a year since Schrembs had heard from Father Judge. He nevertheless reaffirmed his offer and noted that he had also suggested the transfer of the novitiate, "especially in view of the fact that the Bishop of Mobile was not at all well-disposed towards either Father Judge or the Community; in fact, I predicted at the time that the Bishop would likely order him and his Community out of his diocese." Since he and Father Judge originally talked, Schrembs reported, he had "heard nothing further from the late Father Judge or his Community." The bishop clearly understood the community's "critical situation": "Whatever decision may be taken in this matter, let me assure Your Excellency that if the mother-house is actually transferred to the Diocese of Cleveland, I will spare no pains to be a real father to the Community."[14]

Reassured of Bishop Schrembs's willingness to accept the Missionary Servants of the Most Holy Trinity into his diocese, Archbishop Cicognani approached Bishop Toolen. On April 18, 1934, the delegate wrote to Bishop Toolen regarding the transfer. He reminded Toolen of his February 7, 1933, letter to Archibishop Fumasoni-Biondi, decisive for the case, expressing his "unconditional consent to this project." This was the letter Monsignor Kiley thought Bishop Toolen never should have written.

Archbishop Cicognani noted that the delegation had informed the Congregation for Religious of Toolen's consent on March 29, 1933. This must have

several occasions" but learned nothing. "He [Lépicier] did say he would try to hurry the matter along, and I hope he does so"; Kiley to Toolen, Rome, May 13, 1933, Toolen Papers, AAM.

13. Kiley to Toolen, Rome, June 14, 1933, Toolen Papers, AAM.

14. Schrembs to Cicognani, Cleveland, Ohio, April 4, 1934, no. 7817-I, copy, AST. Father Judge's last letter to Bishop Schrembs is dated May 18, 1933, from Río Piedras. At that time, he informed the bishop of the status of the transfer of the motherhouse. "Petition was made to the Holy Congregation for Religious through the Apostolic Delegation for permission to transfer the Motherhouse, and also a plea to enjoin the threatened action of His Excellency the Bishop of Mobile.... No answer has come as yet, and as soon as I have anything to report, I will let you know"; Judge to Schrembs, Río Piedras, May 18, 1933, Schrembs Papers, ADC.

been the day Monsignor Marella sent Father Judge's petition, recourse, and supporting documents to Rome. The Congregation had "so far not replied to the apostolic delegation's report, either on account of the complicated nature of the report or because of the tremendous amount of business which the S. Congregation is obliged to handle." He then urged Bishop Toolen to give the struggling community, "now passing through a particularly critical period," his encouragement. If he did so "during this period of severe trial," they would eventually produce "much good." "Since the novitiate and the junior-college are in the diocese of Mobile," Cicognani continued, "it is evident that a great deal depends upon Your Excellency's apostolic zeal and paternal consideration for the struggling Institute." The bishop might be expected to exercise "prudent vigilance" to prevent premature expansion, nevertheless "the hopes engendered by the possibilities of the Institute's future labors for the Church should preclude the thought of stifling its efforts." He recalled Bishop Schrembs's positive sentiments toward the Missionary Servants of the Most Holy Trinity and Bishop Toolen's satisfaction, "from our recent conversation," with Father Bede Hermann as novice master at Holy Trinity. "Naturally, therefore," Cicognani concluded, "I turn to Your Excellency for an expression of your intentions in regard to the Missionary Servants in your diocese so that I may be in a position to report on the matter to the Sacred Congregation."[15]

Bishop Toolen responded immediately. He had indeed granted his permission for the move. "I cannot conscientiously approve of the institute," he continued, "but I have never done anything to stifle the work, as you seem to intimate." As he had done with Cicognani's predecessor, he referred the delegate to the opinions of other Southern bishops, especially Bishop Walsh of Charleston. "I can see no future in the work," he admitted. "For years they have been fooling our good Catholic people of the North and West, collecting money and squandering it in useless things." He didn't think Bishop Schrembs knew much about "what has been going on," but, "if he is willing to take them in, it is perfectly agreeable to me." He could not "approve the Society, but would not act against it." "I will keep a watchful eye on them," he concluded, "but I promise you that I will not by word or act do anything that will injure their cause. This is the most I can promise."[16] This was good enough for both Cicognani and the Sacred Congregation for Religious. No further ac-

15. Archbishop Amleto Cicognani to Toolen, Washington, D.C., April 18, 1934, no. 7975-I, Toolen Papers, AAM.

16. Toolen to Cicognani, Mobile, April 21, 1934, copy, Toolen Papers, AAM.

tion was taken on Father Judge's petition to transfer the men's motherhouse, his recourse against Bishop Toolen, or Toolen's recourse against him.

Regularizing the Missionary Servants of the Most Holy Trinity

The Missionary Servants of the Most Holy Trinity never established a motherhouse in Lorain. St. Joseph's School and the novitiate remained at Holy Trinity, Alabama. As a result of the apostolic delegate's inquiry, however, the men's community began to take steps to regularize their life as a religious congregation in the church. Around mid-June, Bishop Toolen received a letter from Father Eugene Brennan requesting "Excardination papers" for the Diocese of Cleveland.[17] After a cordial exchange of letters with Bishop Toolen's vicar general, Monsignor E. J. Hackett, Brennan received the papers he had requested, and, with Bishop Schrembs's approval, he was now incardinated into the Diocese of Cleveland.[18] Providence and the apostolic delegate had relieved Bishop Toolen of the burden of Father Judge but not on the precise terms for which he had hoped. Holy Name of Jesus Hospital, as well as Holy Trinity with its novitiate under Father Bede and apostolic school, remained.

Thanks in large part to Father Louis Motry's canonical expertise, Father Eugene Brennan was now a priest of the Diocese of Cleveland, Father Paul Anthony Fursman a priest of the Diocese of Rochester, and Father Theophane Mulroy, a priest of the Archdiocese of New York. They were assigned, or canonically on loan, so to speak, to the fledgling community. Despite Father Judge's attempt to have Brennan make a canonical novitiate with Father Bede, none of the first three priests was yet in a canonical sense a Missionary Servant of the Most Holy Trinity.

One of Father Judge's last worries before he entered Providence Hospital was getting Brother Turibius Mulcahy ordained a deacon and Brother Ambrose Metzger through the subdiaconate. From Puerto Rico he put this in the hands of Father Theophane. On a visit to St. Joseph's Seminary, Dunwoodie, New York, Father Tomerlin had attracted Mulcahy, then a student there, to the community. Having completed four years at Dunwoodie, Mulcahy went to Holy Trinity in September 1930 and made a novitiate, such as it was, before Father Bede's arrival. Brothers James Norris and Joachim Benson, both

17. Brennan to Toolen, Holy Trinity, Ala., June 10, 1934, Toolen Papers, AAM.

18. Monsignor E. J. Hackett to Brennan, Mobile, Ala., June 18, 1934, copy; Brennan to Hackett, Holy Trinity, July 26, 1934; Hackett to Brennan, Mobile, Ala., July 28, 1934, copy; Toolen Papers, AAM.

in their twenties at the time, were in charge of the novitiate. Mulcahy then went to the Catholic University of America to complete his studies and was ready for the diaconate during the fall of 1933, while Father Judge was in the hospital.[19]

Like Father Theophane Mulroy, Brother Ambrose Metzger emerges from Father Judge's correspondence as a shadowy figure. He was from the Diocese of Pittsburgh, a former Marist brother whose temporary vows had expired.[20] Mulcahy was ordained a deacon and Metzger advanced to subdiaconate while Father Judge was in Providence Hospital.[21] On the afternoon that Father Judge died, Metzger was reported to have begun the Prayers for the Dead.[22] As with Mulroy, it was through Cardinal Patrick Hayes of New York that Mulcahy was ordained and through Bishop Hugh C. Boyle of Pittsburgh that Metzger was advanced to the subdiaconate. In the canonical sense, neither Mulcahy nor Metzger were technically Missionary Servants of the Most Holy Trinity. Within a few years, both Mulroy and Metzger would be gone.[23] Father Turibius Mulcahy remained.

The Sanatio

Without a sanatio such as Cardinal Dougherty granted to the sisters, the men's community, canonically erected in 1929, had no canonically regular members except those who had completed their novitiates since the arrival of Father Bede Hermann in 1931. In 1972, when he was seventy-six years old, Father Turibius Mulcahy recalled how the canonical sanatio that helped to regularize the Missionary Servants of the Most Holy Trinity came about. "After the death of Fr. Judge," he related to Sister Mary Tonra, "I asked Dr.

19. On Father Turibius Mulcahy's life, see transcript of taped interview with Sr. Mary Tonra, MSBT, Holy Trinity Mission Seminary, Silver Spring, Md., October 4, 1972, AMSBT.

20. Louis Motry's last letter to Father Judge advised him on negotiations with the Pittsburgh chancery office regarding the "promotion of Brother Ambrose from the Order of Acolyte to Subdeaconship." Since Father Judge was in Puerto Rico at the time, Brother Turibius consulted with Motry and showed him the correspondence in the case. Motry mentions an upcoming trip of Father Theophane to Europe; Motry to Judge, Brookland, Washington, D.C., August 2, 1933, Louis Motry Papers, Box 7, Folder 3, ACUA, The Catholic University of America.

21. Mulcahy describes their visiting Father Judge, who was sedated at the time and didn't really recognize them; transcript of October 4, 1972 interview, 4.

22. Tonra, *Led by the Spirit*, 371.

23. On September 10, 1940, Father Mulroy was incardinated into the Diocese of Paterson, N.J., where he died as a monsignor on August 4, 1966. Ordained a Missionary Servant (technically for the Diocese of Cleveland), on February 13, 1934, Father Ambrose Metzger was incardinated into the Diocese of Columbus in 1948 and died November 11, 1977, at the age of 74; from personnel files in AST.

Motry of the Canon Law Department of Catholic University whether it would be possible to obtain an indult from Rome for the profession of our members who had not made a complete novitiate; some had made no novitiate at all." According to Mulcahy, Motry initially thought such a request "should not even be asked." But, as he usually did, Motry agreed to help prepare "a document seeking the perpetual vows" for the three priests and some of the community's oldest members. As Father Turibius recalled in 1972, the sanatio came from Rome in February 1936. He was off by about six months, as the reply from Rome was dated July 16, 1935. He was more than correct, however, about its significance. He described it as "a great gift because it would have been very inconvenient to have to take all of them out to make a novitiate year, or for someone who had made a novitiate to repeat the canonical novitiate."[24]

The petition for a sanation from Rome moved with astounding speed. Bishop Schrembs dated his petition to Rome May 15, 1935. The letter accompanying the more than favorable reply of the Sacred Congregation for Religious was dated July 16, 1935, and signed by Giulio Fumasoni-Biondi. Perhaps the name of this curial official helped the petition get processed in a mere two months. In any case, on August 26, 1935, less than two years after Father Judge's death, Bishop Schrembs wrote a letter to Father Eugene Brennan at Stirling. It began, "By virtue of the faculty granted to me by the Sacred Congregation of Religious in Rescript No. 4707/35, issued at Rome, July 6, 1935, I hereby sanate your succession to the Office of Superior General of the Missionary Servants of the Most Holy Trinity."[25] Bishop Schrembs went on to lay out the various effects of the sanation rescript. The Missionary Servants of the Most Holy Trinity were now on a sound canonical footing.

The documentation regarding the sanation indicates just how precarious their situation had been in terms of church law. Bishop Schrembs's petition requested "a sanation for all cases" for the Missionary Servants. He began by noting that they had been "canonically erected not long ago (1929) in the Diocese of Mobile, and subsequently (1932) transferred to the Diocese of Cleveland, on the advice (*ad monitum*)" of the apostolic delegate, and "with the consent of the bishops of Cleveland and Mobile." A recent investigation

24. Transcript of October 4, 1972, interview with Mulcahy, 8.

25. Schrembs to Brennan, Cleveland, Ohio, August 26, 1935, from a copy in the Motry Papers, Box 7, Folder 3, ACUA, The Catholic University of America. The presence of this letter in his papers indicates that Dr. Motry assisted Bishop Schrembs in preparing the petition for the *sanatio*.

of their canonical status "revealed multiple irregularities, having occurred in good faith."[26]

Perhaps because Bishop Toolen had raised the question of whether he had actually signed the decree of erection in 1929, Bishop Schrembs's petition cites the decree of April 29, 1929, in full. The petition goes on to address the issues of a canonical novitiate and the status of Father Eugene Brennan as Father Judge's successor. Bishop Schrembs notes that a novitiate was opened after the decree, "but I do not know whether it was in accord with the canons." He explained that the "four priests and two lay brothers who were the first members of the community never made a novitiate" and that the community "now numbers 150 members and does good work in different places for the good of souls." He explained further that Father Brennan had succeeded Father Judge after the latter's death "without an election and only by the will of the dying founder on 23 November 1933, as the only and best qualified candidate."[27]

There followed Bishop Schrembs's eight requests. The first asked a dispensation from canonical novitiate for "three priests and two lay brothers who were the first members of the Community and who now and for many years before the canonical erection labored with Rev. Thomas Judge." The petition doesn't name the subjects of this first and most important request. Monsignor Nummey, as well as Fathers Tomerlin and Lenahan, had already departed. The three priests referred to were no doubt Fathers Eugene Brennan, Paul Anthony Fursman, and Theophane Mulroy. Father Turibius had been ordained in 1934 after Father Judge's death. The two lay brothers mentioned in the petition are probably Brothers Augustine Philips and Joseph Limpert.[28]

The petition's second and third requests concern Father Eugene Brennan as superior. The second asks for the "ratification of his succession" on November 23, 1933, for six years until November 23, 1939. After that, he would be eligible for another six-year term as superior. The third request asks for "sanation" of Father Brennan's acts as superior between November 23, 1933, and the time when the petition will have been granted. The fourth requests "the ratification, which is probably necessary," of the transfer of the moth-

26. Bishop Joseph Schrembs to the Sacred Congregation for Religious, Cleveland, Ohio, May 15, 1935, copy, AST. The petition is in Latin; translation by Father Gary Banks, ST.

27. Ibid.

28. The 1951 *Catalogus*, the first one on record, lists Brothers Augustine Philips and Joseph Limpert as "dispensed"; AST.

erhouse from Mobile to Cleveland. It is not clear that this transfer ever took place. The fifth and sixth requests ask for "the ratification with caution of the erection of the novitiate house" and the "sanation of the vows of all religious professed in this Community." The petition also requested permission to retain Father Bede as novice master and to "approve the Constitution now in written redaction, but not yet approved." Finally Bishop Schrembs made a blanket request for the "sanation of everything that is 'sanitible' that needs sanation, so that this religious Community, so clearly founded by Divine Providence, as it appears from the fine work it has done, might be canonically erected."[29]

On June 3 the apostolic delegate, Archbishop Cicognani, forwarded Bishop Schrembs's letter to Rome, along with his own supporting letter to Cardinal Lépicier. He explained that the "Congregation is still in its initial stages and is experiencing difficulties, especially of a financial nature." But, he went on to say, "Bishop Schrembs has taken a paternal interest in this Congregation, and so I humbly ask that your Most Reverend Eminence benevolently consider the request of the Reverend Bishop of Cleveland."[30] Five weeks later, Giulio Fumasoni-Biondi responded on behalf of the Congregation for Religious, giving Bishop Schrembs the authorization for the sanations he had requested. "With pleasure," Fumasoni-Biondi wrote to Schrembs in English, "I transmit you the enclosed faculty of the Congregation of the Religious for the settlement of the Institute of the Missionary's servants [*sic*] of the Most Holy Trinity."[31] Fumasoni-Biondi's two and a half-page rescript, dated July 6, 1935, granted Bishop Schrembs faculties to sanate all that he had asked for and more, including dispensing from "impediments of age or prerequisites of profession" for the next five years.

Bishop Schrembs Implements the Sanatio

On August 26, 1935, Bishop Schrembs wrote to Father Eugene Brennan sanating his succession as superior. In virtue of his faculties for dispensing from age and profession impediments, Bishop Schrembs recognized Father Theophane Mulroy as assistant superior and Father Paul Anthony Fursman and Brother Augustine Philips as consultors. In addition, he designated Fa-

29. Ibid.

30. Cicognani to Lépicier, Washington, D.C. June 3, 1935, no. 382/35, copy, AST.

31. G. Fumasoni-Biondi to Schrembs, Rome, July 16, 1935, no. 4707/35, copy, AST. Fumasoni-Biondi's letterhead identifies him as "Spedizioniere per Affari Ecclesiastici,"—an expediter. It is not clear whether he was related to Cardinal Pietro Fumasoni-Biondi.

ther Turibius Mulcahy as consultor. Under the terms of the rescript, he authorized Brennan to admit to temporary profession without a canonical novitiate those who had spent two years in the community "under religious discipline." Those who had spent "six full years in the Community" could be dispensed from a canonical novitiate and admitted by Brennan to final profession.

"Henceforward," however, "no one will be admitted to vows without a regular canonical novitiate." Bishop Schrembs declared the "present Novitiate canonically erected and authorize you [Brennan] to retain the services of a Capuchin Father as Master of Novices for the next three years provided he has his Superior's consent." The Bishop stipulated, however, that "your Novitiate must be moved to the Diocese of Cleveland as soon as your financial condition permits." The novitiate was never moved to Cleveland. He went on to "sanate every irregularity regarding postulantship, novitiate, professions, election of officers, transferring of motherhouse, erection of your Novitiate, and all acts of officials acting in the name of the Community."[32]

Bishop Schrembs explained that what he rightly termed "this generous sanation" was being "granted by the Holy See for the complete tranquility of conscience of all the members of your Community." In a very strong statement, he went on to assure Father Eugene Brennan of both his status as legitimate superior and the broad extent of his authority:

> You are now canonically established as superior of the community of the Missionary Servants of the Most Holy Trinity. You have all the rights, privileges and obligations of Superiors, in accordance with the Code of Canon Law and your temporary Constitutions. You have a right, therefore, to admit candidates to postulantship and novitiate, profession and perpetual vows. You have a right, likewise, to issue dimissorial letters to any Bishop in communion with Rome for the Ordination of clerics.

The constitution still had to be approved and "sent to Rome as early as possible." Schrembs urged Brennan to assemble the community, "completely or by delegates," to determine whether, "after your experience under the present Constitutions, you find any changes to be recommended," and convey them to him. He explained that this "decree" would be replaced "by a more complete and formal decree later on but will be issued as of this date. Your immediate requirements demand, at least, the essential faculties be granted you at once."[33]

32. Schrembs to Brennan, Cleveland, Ohio, August 26, 1935, copy, Motry Papers, Box 7, Folder 3, ACUA, The Catholic University of America.

33. Ibid.

In view of Bishop Schrembs's "decree" of August 26, 1935, with its strong statement of Father Brennan's legitimacy as Father Judge's successor, made explicitly "for the complete tranquility of conscience of all members of your Community," it is difficult to imagine how Father Theophane could later challenge it on the basis of an earlier designation by Father Judge, to which he was the only witness. If Mulroy accepted his designation as assistant superior in this decree, it is even more difficult to imagine.[34]

1935–1937—Difficult Years for the Men's Community

Though now canonically regularized, the Missionary Servants of the Most Holy Trinity still faced overwhelming financial obligations and disarray in the wake of the deaths of Father Judge and Mother Boniface. Father Paul Anthony Fursman remained in charge at St. Augustine's. Among the priests, after Father Eugene Brennan, Fursman had the longest and closest connections to Father Judge. He came to Holy Trinity as a young man of thirty and had known both Father Judge and Mother Boniface for at least a decade. The young men he recruited to Holy Trinity who would become leaders of the community included Thomas O'Keeffe and Gerard Fredericks, the first two custodian generals, as well as Lawrence Brediger, Timothy Lynch, and James Norris.

Of Fursman, Father Gerard Fredericks said, "I knew him quite well. . . . I would put the three in the same picture, the same frame: Father Judge, Father Paul Anthony and Mother Boniface. All three had the same qualities. They related well to people. They were generous in giving of themselves."[35]

34. On this challenge, see George P. Mulroy to Thomas O'Keeffe [custodian general at the time], Philadelphia, August 23, 1958. In this witnessed and notarized letter, Mulroy claimed that, on the morning of the day Father Judge died, he and Father Brennan were visiting him in the hospital: "Father Eugene went outside for a few minutes and Father Judge told me in his absence that I, Father Theophane Mulroy, was the Vicar of the Community. He gave me instructions concerning a particular mission (Puerto Rico) to which he did not want Father Eugene to return." Mulroy continued, "It was taken for granted, since I was in Europe when Father Judge took sick, that Father Eugene because of his seniority was taking Father Judge's place. It was also taken for granted that when Father Judge died, Father Eugene was to succeed him." Mulroy's letter is dated August 23, 1958, almost twenty-two years to the day after Bishop Schrembs's letter to Father Brennan. Alas, Mulroy does not record his response, during his time in Lorain or over the intervening decades, to assumptions about Father Eugene's succession that contradicted his memory. That Father Judge conveyed to Mulroy in strong terms his wish that Brennan never return to Puerto Rico is most plausible. That he made Mulroy his successor is much less so.

35. Cited in Tonra, *Led by the Spirit*, 367.

With Father Paul Anthony's untimely death at the age of forty-three in Puerto Rico on March 8, 1936, a strong memory of the family spirit and bridge between generations of Missionary Servants of the Most Holy Trinity was lost. As did Father Gerard, Father John B. McCarthy associated Fursman closely with Father Judge and Mother Boniface and credited him as the one who "in a very large measure transmitted to these young men the Spirit he had absorbed from Fr. Judge and Mother Boniface."[36] Already on August 20, 1934, less than a year after Father Judge's death, James Norris formally resigned as secretary of the corporation and departed the community. Norris was another potential bridge to Father Judge who, in the years before his death, had entrusted Norris with the community's finances. Younger members at the time remembered Norris as "the one singled out by Father Judge" and "a favorite and a prince apparent."[37]

The promissory notes or unsecured gold debenture bonds, engineered by Norris and issued for five years on January 1, 1932, came due on January 1, 1937. Father Turibius Mulcahy recalls that Father Brennan "put me on the fund drive to replace the debenture funds that were expiring after their five year term." At the October 1931 meeting where the plan for the bonds was approved, Mulcahy had opposed the bond issue. Father Judge, however, went with Norris's judgment and regarded it as "the saving solution for the time being of the Community's financial problems." Mulcahy noted the irony in five years later finding "myself in charge of the continuation of that bond and preparation for adding annuity bonds to it. That, of course, required my traveling a great deal to people who had taken the bonds to try to urge them to change to annuity bonds."[38] Mulcahy's road trips were preceded by

36. "It was in the year 1923 that Edgar Fursman (1893–1936) met Father Judge and Mother Boniface, and it would seem that almost immediately he absorbed their Spirit. He became one with them in their cheerful love of God. I say cheerful because there was nothing gloomy, melancholy, somber, or solemn about any of the three of them. He donned a Habit that he himself helped Father and Mother design in early 1924. For the next twelve years he drew dozens of young men to Mother and Father, to the MSBTs, and it was he who in a very large measure transmitted to those young men the Spirit he had absorbed from Fr. Judge and Mother Boniface"; Father John B. McCarthy, "The Spirit," Typescript, 4 pp., May 28, 1987, AMSBT. Fursman received the habit on June 11, 1924. The military collar was his contribution to the design of the habit.

37. On the date of Norris's departure, see Kupke, "American Intervention at Rome," 235n21, citing Minutes of the Trustees of the Trinitarian [*sic*] Corporation, August 20, 1934; descriptions of Norris from Fathers Timothy Lynch and John B. McCarthy respectively, cited at 232n7–8.

38. Transcript of taped interview with Father Turibius Mulcahy by Sister Mary Tonra, MSBT, Silver Spring, Md., October 4, 1972, 5, AMSBT.

a mass mailing to the bondholders, who had been urged to accept "4 percent fifteen-year refunding debentures" in exchange for their holdings. The annuity bond program was begun in May 1932. Many people, most likely those Mulcahy was visiting, paid for them with their previous debenture bonds.[39]

With only a handful of priests, missionary or student brothers sometimes served as local custodians. As in the days of Father Judge, finding resident priests for all the cenacles continued to be a challenge. As Father Eugene Brennan had done after his return from Puerto Rico, Father Turibius Mulcahy found himself splitting time between Silver Spring and Stirling, "at the Shrine from Friday until Sunday night and in Silver Spring from Monday morning until Thursday evening."[40] In addition to staffing, the pressures of financing a large debt during the Great Depression tended to push important aspects of Father Judge's vision into the background. One of these was the lay apostolate.

From Puerto Rico in July 1933, about a month before he entered Providence Hospital, Father Judge responded to concerns about the fate of the Outer Cenacle. "How often have I said that the Brothers came into being for this major purpose," he wrote, "to cherish and give service to the Inner Cenacle and to spread the Outer Cenacle ... wait until we get the priests, and every holy throb of your heart regarding the Outer Cenacle will be satisfied."[41] Though the sisters continued to support and sustain the Outer Cenacle, Father Judge's hope for a comparable role for the brothers was rarely reflected in their training. Though Father Turibius had gone to Holy Trinity more than three years before Father Judge died, he only learned of the Outer Cenacle at Father Judge's wake. "It was at the meeting with Sr. Baptista at Fr. Judge's wake," he recalled, "that she gave me a great many of the ideals, the policies, the way of acting for those who had joined with Fr. Judge in the Outer Cenacle, later known as the Missionary Cenacle Apostolate."[42]

Father Turibius gave Outer Cenacle retreats between 1935 and 1942, and

39. Thomas O'Keeffe, ST, to Edmund A. Burke, Silver Spring, June 30, 1941, transcript, 4, AST. This letter is a detailed account to a prospective benefactor of the community's finances up to 1941.

40. Transcript of interview with Father Mulcahy, October 4, 1972, 5.

41. "The Outer Cenacle gives much evidence of life, for, first of all, if sometimes we see it decline, under a little benevolent nursing, it revives." He noted that at this time, "Divine Providence just forbids me to have the contact with the Outer Cenacle that you wish and that I would wish also, if I did not see this Providence"; Judge to My dear Child [perhaps Margaret Healy], Río Piedras, July 23, 1933, AST, 12311–12.

42. Transcript of interview with Father Mulcahy, October 4, 1972, 5.

Father Joachim worked with them in the early 1940s. Father John McCarthy claimed that he learned about the Outer Cenacle from Father Paul Anthony but that it was not emphasized in seminary training. Father Eugene understood Father Judge's idea of the Outer Cenacle, McCarthy recalled, and "went north to become involved in giving retreats to the Missionary Cenacle Apostolate. He thought that was what Father did and he was to continue in that vein. He never told any of the rest of the ... brothers about his work; just went and did it." This left "fifty or more boys in school with little or no Indoctrination in the Cenacle Idea or spirit ... they went through school with no real knowledge of the Missionary Cenacle Apostolate, the sisters, or the Cenacle spirit." As McCarthy remembered it, Fathers Francis Donohue and Lawrence Brediger promoted the Outer Cenacle. "Thomas and Gerard had it but didn't practice it. Ambrose and Theophane were like diocesan priests. These newly ordained priests knew only the abandoned missions but not the lay apostolate from the Cenacle point of view."[43]

Father McCarthy's recollections of Father Eugene Brennan reflect something of what might have been his leadership style. After two years in office, in any case, as Father Mulcahy recalled, questions had surfaced about his leadership, whether he "had the sufficient background, training, personality, and abilities to continue." According to Mulcahy, "At least one Bishop in whose diocese we had a house was in favor of an absolute change; the other Bishops were somewhat indifferent."[44] Depression-era finances as well as personnel pressures made maintaining the institute's original vision difficult. Questions about Father Eugene Brennan's leadership in such circumstances led to a 1937 Vatican call for an apostolic visitation of the Missionary Servants of the Most Holy Trinity.

Bishop Shaughnessy's Visitation, 1937–1949

Support from the Apostolic Delegation

Apart from the early and continuing support of Father Patrick McHale and the Vincentian Grand Conseil and the later support of Cardinal Dougherty of Philadelphia, the crucial factor in the survival of Father Judge's vi-

43. Interview with John Baptist McCarthy, ST, by Marie Josepha McNutt, MSBT, Margaret Healy's file, AMSBT, as cited in McNutt, *Margaret: Called and Chosen*, 110, 264n178.

44. Transcript of interview with Father Mulcahy, October 4, 1972, 9. For a lengthy defense of Father Brennan, see transcript of interview with Father Timothy Lynch, ST, by Sister Mary Tonra, MSBT, Silver Spring, Md., October 31, 1972, 8–10, AMSBT.

sion and work was the strong support of three successive apostolic delegates: Archbishops Giovanni Bonzano (1911–22), Pietro Fumasoni-Biondi (1922–33), and Amleto Cicognani (1933–58).

While some local ordinaries may have been put off by the appearance of financial and disciplinary irregularities typical of a beginning religious congregation, the apostolic delegation consistently saw a bigger picture. They assessed Father Judge and the work he inspired as responses to the pastoral needs of the church in the United States. The early Cenacle's work with Italian immigrants around the port of New York and New Jersey caught Archbishop Bonzano's attention. Archbishop George Caruana was a protégé of Cardinal Dougherty and a career Vatican diplomat. The later focus, in response to Caruana's plea, on Puerto Rico and the need to preserve the faith in the face of post–Spanish-American War Americanization could not have but pleased the Vatican.

The sisters' combination of obvious religious devotion and effective pastoral initiative, their ability to make the equivalent of "amphibious landings" into places of need from the docks of Brooklyn to the barrios of Puerto Rico, places often closed to teaching and nursing sisters in habits, endeared them to bishops wherever they worked. Much to the consternation of Bishop Toolen and Archbishop Curley, the sisters attributed all this to Father Judge. Finally, and especially during the pontificate of Pope Pius XI, the emphasis on the lay apostolate proved decisively striking to a series of apostolic delegates. Despite Monsignor Nummey's revelation of the community's overwhelming financial difficulties in 1932, Archbishop Fumasoni-Biondi clearly did not want to jeopardize a work he described to Nummey at the time as "the only organized movement of its kind in the Church today that so completely meets the wishes of the Holy Father with reference to the Lay Apostolate."[45]

Bishop Gerald Shaughnessy, SM

About four years after Father Judge's death, on August 23, 1937, Bishop Gerald Shaughnessy (1887–1950) of Seattle, Washington, received a communication from Archbishop Cicognani. It authorized him to conduct, at the request of the Holy See, a visitation of the Missionary Servants of the Most Holy Trinity. A 1909 graduate of Boston College and an experienced teacher, Shaughnessy, joined the Marist Fathers (SM) in 1916 and studied at Marist

45. Msgr. Thomas Nummey to Bishop Thomas E. Molloy, Baltimore, Md., March 19, 1932, copy, Nummey Papers, Archives of the Diocese of Brooklyn.

College at Catholic University in Washington. In 1920 Archbishop Giovanni Bonzano ordained him to the priesthood at the age of thirty-three. Shaughnessy had a Doctorate of Sacred Theology from Catholic University and taught at Marist College in Washington and at Notre Dame Seminary in New Orleans. He also preached on the Marist mission band. In the midst of his other duties, Shaughnessy also served as a member of the apostolic delegation from 1919 to 1932. When he was called to be bishop of Seattle in 1933, Archbishop Cicognani consecrated him.

Shaughnessy was well aware of the delegation's ongoing support for Father Judge's work. The question of immigrant "leakage" was as important to the Vatican and the delegation as it was to Father Judge. In 1925 Shaughnessy addressed it in his book *Has the Immigrant Kept the Faith?* He answered his title's question with a resounding affirmative.[46] Shaughnessy was known for his administrative abilities; in 1937, when Archbishop Cicognani asked him to conduct the visitation, he had recently set in order a difficult financial situation in the Diocese of Seattle.[47] He was also a vowed member of a religious community. In spite of everything that made him an excellent choice as apostolic visitor, he exhibited little sense of the men's community's relationship to the sisters or the lay apostolate, tending to treat them as a freestanding clerical congregation.

The Apostolic Visitation

Bishop Shaughnessy's visitation began on September 16, 1937, and lasted technically for more than a decade, until February 3, 1949. Within about a month, Shaughnessy had visited all six of the community's houses. At Cleveland, where he began, he found no motherhouse and no novitiate. By September 19 he was in Stirling. On September 24 and 25, he visited Holy Trinity and Mobile, Alabama. In Brother Augustine's absence, the twenty-four-year-old Brother John McCarthy was "in charge" at Holy Trinity. Father Thomas O'Keeffe, ordained in 1937, was in charge of the two-year college program, and Father Bede was still the novice master. McCarthy estimated that between the college and the novitiate, there were about thirty candidates at Holy Trinity.

Fifty years later, Father McCarthy still retained largely negative memo-

46. Sr. Joseph Miriam Blackwell, MSBT, sets Shaughnessy's work in the context of the literature about "leakage" in the 1930s when the latter returned to the topic in the pages of the *American Ecclesiastical Review* and *America*; see Blackwell, *Ecclesial People*, 75n244.

47. On Shaughnessy's life, see N. A. Weber, *NCE* (1967), 13:165.

ries of Bishop Shaughnessy. He spoke of the "awful power" invested in the visitor and his recollection that Shaughnessy came to Holy Trinity "with a frown." "I met him at the Marist House in Atlanta, Georgia," McCarthy recalled, "and drove him down to Holy Trinity, Alabama, one hundred and twenty miles, and he said not a word all the way! I don't know what he had heard about us before embarking on the Visitation . . . but I have no doubt at all that he intended to dissolve the Community." As McCarthy remembered it, Shaughnessy interviewed each member of the community privately, "starting with the youngest novice and finishing with me and Brother Augustine," and "meticulously examined our books—and never once smiled." McCarthy emphasized that they were forbidden to hold any gatherings or council meetings to discuss the visitation before Shaughnessy arrived. On September 25, 1937, McCarthy drove Shaughnessy to Mobile and dropped him at Bishop Toolen's residence on Government Street. "Though he came with a frown," McCarthy concluded, "he left with a slight smile and he was a bit more communicative en route to Mobile."[48]

From Mobile Bishop Shaughnessy proceeded to the mission for Gulf fishermen at Stella Maris Missionary Cenacle in Pensacola, Florida. He left Pensacola for San Juan on September 26. He returned to Washington and finally visited Silver Spring. Father Turibius Mulcahy was forty-one at the time of the visitation. Though he clashed with Bishop Shaughnessy before the latter's intentions became clear, he came to work closely with him. Mulcahy regarded him as "a real friend." He agreed with McCarthy that he came with the idea that the community should be dissolved. "But he came with an open mind. . . . He came as a cold, calculating New England Puritan, but in as much as he was a very pious man in his own life, and a well-trained business executive, he gave us the value of his sound advice and fatherly care and concern."[49]

Brennan failed to establish a motherhouse in the Diocese of Cleveland, and he had not moved the novitiate there. There is no evidence that the consultations on the constitutions Bishop Schrembs had instructed Brennan to hold had ever occurred. Having completed his visitation of the community's houses, Bishop Shaughnessy sent Father Brennan a letter demanding his

48. John B. McCarthy, ST, "The Spirit?" May 28, 1987, Typescript, 2–3, AMSBT.

49. Transcript of interview with Father Mulcahy, October 4, 1972, 10. Interestingly, as is often the case with oral history, both McCarthy and Mulcahy misremembered the details of the sequence of Shaughnessy's visitation, but their overall impressions were still powerfully present after many decades.

resignation as superior. It was dated October 23, 1937. The next day Bishop Shaughnessy notified Father Mulcahy that, as apostolic visitor, he was taking charge of the community. Father Turibius was named vicar for administration of ordinary affairs in December 1937. By this time, Father Brennan had already departed, having "taken the whole investigation as an attack on his character," severed contact with the community, and "made no effort to continue the exercise of his priestly office."[50]

In October 1937, Bishop Shaughessy addressed to the apostolic delegate a fifteen-page report of his visitation. Dated September–October 1937 and entitled "Apostolic Visitation of the Missionary Servants of the Most Holy Trinity," the report is divided into eight Roman-numbered sections. Shaughnessy's "General Summary of the Finances of the Institute as a Whole" reported the community's present net debt as $350,000, exclusive for the most part of the individual debts of the local houses.[51]

Bishop Shaughnessy's report presumes the strong possibility that the apostolic delegate or the Congregation for Religious on his recommendation could dissolve the community. It gave the community eight months to solicit contributions that might liquidate their debt. Shaughnessy admitted that his prohibition of their going further into debt:

> is practically equivalent to a decree of suppression since the Institute has been depending on the current principal income from the sale of bonds and acceptances of new annuities to pay interest on its outstanding obligations, to pay current principal maturities, and even to pay some of its current running expenses.[52]

Shaughnessy laid out Archbishop Cicognani's options. "Should a dissolution of the Institute be decided upon, a net debt of approximately $180,000 would have to be coped with." Additionally, interest would be owed on some

50. These quotations are from Augustine Philips to Felix O'Neill, Stirling, February 14, 1940. Brother Augustine wrote to Father O'Neill, living in retirement in St. Petersburg, Florida, pleading with him to visit Eugene Brennan, whom he described as in Coral Gables "living with some friends" from Puerto Rico. According to Philips, "Father owns a boat named 'The Truant,' which is tied up at the city docks at Coconut Grove"; from a transcription of the handwritten letter in AST. Brennan died in Miami in 1963 at age 68. He is buried at Holy Trinity.

51. Bishop Gerald Shaughnessy, SM, "Visitation of the Missionary Servants of the Most Holy Trinity," 12, AST.

52. Ibid., 13. According to this report, Mrs. Kress, a subject of Father Judge's summer 1933 correspondence from Puerto Rico with his consultors, especially James Norris, held $57,000 worth of debenture bonds and lived in "the 400 block of Park Ave." Shaughnessy described her as "a Five and Ten Store magnate," 12.

$200,000 of annuities to term, "namely to the death of the holders thereof." Shaughnessy reported that, if Cardinal Mundelein approved, Bishop William O'Brien, head of the Church Extension Society in Chicago and Father Judge's erstwhile elocution student at St. Vincent's Seminary in the 1890s, had agreed to carry this debt in the event the Missionary Servants of the Most Holy Trinity were suppressed.[53]

A Roman rescript of January 7, 1938, appointed Bishop Shaughnessy custodian general of the Missionary Servants of the Most Holy Trinity. Fathers Patrick Moore, Thomas O'Keeffe, and Joachim Benson made up his council. In July 1939, Father Thomas was appointed co-vicar with Father Turibius.[54] Shaughnessy suppressed the house at Cleveland as well as St. Augustine's in Río Piedras. The brothers "reluctantly" turned over St. Augustine's keys to the Marianists.[55] After January 1938, Bishop Shaughnessy functioned as the ex officio superior of the men's community. As his vicar, Father Turibius, with Father Thomas as his co-vicar after July, administered the day-to-day operations of the community.

Between November 1937 and the end of August 1938, Bishop Shaughnessy changed his mind about the community. Father John McCarthy thought that he recognized a "spirit" among them that McCarthy found difficult to articulate.[56] In any case, Shaughnessy's correspondence with Father Turibius indicates that, by late August 1938, the bishop believed that "the way has been fairly well cleared toward a complete rehabilitation of the Institute, for we can at least say that the opportunity is offered to you if you will be able to grasp it." Misunderstandings had arisen between the visitor and members of the community concerning what some of Shaughnessy's measures implied about Father Judge and the community.

As vicar, Father Mulcahy had voiced his confreres' frustration to Bishop Shaughnessy. Shaughnessy explained that closing Lorain was "due to the removal of the Motherhouse from the Diocese, where, in fact, it had never actually been located," and Puerto Rico "due to nothing that can be construed as a reflection on the Congregation." But regarding the latter case, he warned, "I would remark that the aftermath is unfortunately leading to

53. Ibid., 13.

54. For this information, I am grateful to Father Ralph Frisch, ST, archivist of the Missionary Servants of the Most Holy Trinity.

55. "As the story goes, the Marianists received a big box of jumbled, untagged and unidentified keys"; Jansen, *First Seventy-Five Years*, 18–19.

56. McCarthy attempts to articulate that "spirit" in his brief 1987 reflection, "The Spirit?" typescript, May 28, 1987, AMSBT.

developments, which unless they are properly handled will bring the Congregation into disrepute." Shaughnessy expressed his "charitable hope that there is enough good will among the members of the Congregation and sufficient spirit of self-sacrifice in you as the Vicar-General to effect a complete acceptance of the conditions and the opportunity laid down by the Holy See." He insisted that "only by harmonious and completely obedient acceptance of the situation will it be possible for you and me to effect the work that we may piously believe God wishes us to accomplish."[57]

By fall 1938, the community was on its way to the "complete rehabilitation" Bishop Shaughnessy envisioned. Fathers Thomas and Turibius continued as Bishop Shaughnessy's co-vicars until November 1942, when, with Bishop Shaughnessy's permission, Mulcahy returned to the army as a chaplain.[58] Father Thomas became sole vicar. In November 1945, Bishop Shaughnessy suffered a stroke and never completely recovered. During the final four years of Shaughnessy's tenure as superior, Father Thomas O'Keeffe was the de facto custodian general.

Preservation of the Faith

Bishop Shaughnessy's tenure as superior witnessed an intriguing translation of Father Judge's spirit for a new time and its integration into a larger Catholic response to the Depression. As editor, Father Joachim Benson took the magazine *Preservation of the Faith* in a new direction that included a small press called Preservation Press. Eccentric and high-strung, Benson was another potential bridge for the men's community to the spirit of Father Judge. He had come to Holy Trinity as a college graduate in 1928 and spent five years as an adult working with Father Judge. He broke under the financial pressures of his job as treasurer at Holy Trinity, questioned his vocation, returned home to Albany, and struggled mightily to understand the strangeness of Father Judge's supernatural perspective on the world. During the year before Father Judge's death, Benson moved in and out of the founder's doghouse.[59] Late in 1932, Father Judge appointed him chronicler or histo-

57. Shaughnessy to Mulcahy, Seattle[?], August 29, 1938; see also Mulcahy to Shaughnessy, Silver Spring, July 28, 1938, and Shaughnessy to Mulcahy, Seattle, August 9, 1938 AST.

58. Transcript of interview with Father Mulcahy, October 4, 1972, 9.

59. In April 1980, a year before Benson's death on April 21, 1981, journalist Paul Hendrickson interviewed him and sketched a fascinating word portrait of the seventy-six-year-old priest to go along with a transcript of his interview with Benson. Together they convey both

rian, a task more suited to his gifts as writer and editor and one he took seriously. In the year after Father Judge's death, Benson wrote *The Judgments of Father Judge* and published it with the trade publisher P. J. Kenedy and Sons in New York.[60]

Rather than a full-blown biography, *Judgments* is more a carefully crafted literary remembrance of 128 small pages. It is a young man's hagiography, tending to mystify Father Judge and portray him as something of a distant and mysterious saint. Benson was a thirty-year-old student brother in 1934, and his style sometimes betrays his youth. "Words cannot tell," he wrote, "the story of this surpliced flower of God. The beauty of the bud was concealed in the manly vase."[61] Even youthful overwriting, however, fails to obscure the essentials of Benson's authentic memory of Father Judge himself: the importance of St. Vincent de Paul's example, the emphasis on a highly spiritualized laity and the abandoned work, and, most timely for the Depression years when Benson wrote, Father Judge's response to the poor with the radical witness of the works of mercy.[62]

The book faithfully reflects Joachim Benson's struggle to relearn from Father Judge how to look at the world, to see things truly from a spiritual perspective that is impractical in a more worldly sense. This comes across most powerfully in Benson's descriptions of Father Judge's trust in divine providence. In words that recall Father Judge's patient, often humorous, responses to Benson's desperate letters during his financial difficulties as Holy Trinity's procurator, he writes of Judge ascribing faith's power to "the stinging experience of need when we are thrown back on Divine Providence."[63] For many years, Benson's *Judgments* remained the only published source for Father Judge's life. Indeed, in the *New Catholic Encyclopedia*'s second edition, published in 2004, it is the only source cited in the articles on the two communities of Missionary Servants.

In 1935, shortly after the appearance of *Judgments*, Benson took over the

---

Benson's eccentricity and his real struggle to understand Father Judge's spiritual way of looking at the world; see Hendrickson, *Seminary: A Search* (New York: Summit, 1983), 133–41.

60. "I certainly didn't like that title," Benson recalled. "I didn't want that title but the publishers wanted to sell the book and they said they had to have something in the title that connected with Fr. Judge"; transcript of taped interview with Fr. Joachim Benson, ST, by Sister Mary Tonra, MSBT, Río Piedras, Puerto Rico, February 5, 1974, 25, AMSBT.

61. Joachim V. Benson, MSSsT, *The Judgments of Father Judge* (New York: P. J. Kenedy and Sons, 1934), 94–95.

62. Ibid., 108–9.

63. Ibid., 73.

editorship of the community's six-year-old fundraising magazine, formerly known as *SOS for the Preservation of the Faith*. They dropped "SOS" from the title and moved the magazine from Holy Trinity to Silver Spring. Using his connections among the faculty at Catholic University, where he had studied, Benson turned *Preservation of the Faith* into a serious literary venture whose tables of contents read like a who's who of American Catholic intellectual life.[64] After 1937 and Bishop Shaughnessy's visitation, Benson continued to work with the full support of his superiors, Bishop Shaughnessy, Father Turibius Mulcahy, who both contributed articles, and Father Thomas O'Keeffe.[65]

Between 1937 and 1941, the magazine expanded into book publishing as Preservation Press. As editor, Benson published an extraordinary series of books in the years before the United States entered World War II. Mary Elizabeth Walsh's *The Saints and Social Work* appeared in 1937. Walsh was a Catholic University sociologist and protégé of the fiery young chair of the Sociology Department, Father Paul Hanly Furfey.[66] Father Judge called sociology "applied Christian charity."[67] Furfey wrote about "supernatural sociology."[68] Applying Furfey's sense of "supernatural sociology," Walsh made the saints the model for the kind of social work that the Missionary Servants of the Most Blessed Trinity and their lay associates had become known for in the previous decade.[69] As sociological "laboratories," Furfey and Walsh founded

64. Benson credited his initial involvement with *SOS for the Preservation of the Faith* to the instigation of Mother Boniface; see transcript of taped interview with Benson, February 5, 1974, 28. At the end of 1945, the magazine was again reconceived and Benson reassigned. In the first number of the new *Missionary Servant*, Benson wrote a farewell editorial that reviewed the history of the magazine from 1928 to 1945; see Benson, "Biography of a Magazine," *Missionary Servant* 1 (January 1946): 2–4.

65. Bishop Shaughnessy noted that, with about 5,000 subscribers, *Preservation* was considered an "asset" by the community. "It carries no advertisements; it costs about $4,500 per year and runs a deficit of between $500 and $1,000"; Shaughnessy, "Apostolic Visitation of Missionary Servants of the Most Holy Trinity," 11.

66. Walsh is not to be confused with the early Cenacle associate of the same name.

67. Judge to Dr. Margaret Healy, Holy Trinity, Ala., December 11, 1928, AST, MF 1308.

68. Paul Hanly Furfey explained his sense of "supernatural sociology" in chap. 1 of his programmatic *Fire on the Earth* (New York: Macmillan, 1936). Furfey and Walsh approached sociology and social work with a concern for the souls of the poor. See the account of Father Judge's critique of organized social work and his contrast between "organized charity and apostolic charity," in Blackwell, *Ecclesial People*, 95–103, especially at 100.

69. Furfey argued that at the end of sociological inquiry, the sociologist must recognize and even "imitate the love of the saints, a love so hot and burning that they forgot themselves entirely, died to themselves, and became totally absorbed in love of God and neighbor"; Furfey, *Three Theories of Society* (New York: Macmillan, 1937), 239.

two neighborhood houses in Washington, D.C.: Il Poverello House and Fides House. Student brothers from Silver Spring regularly volunteered at these houses.[70]

Sister Peter Claver Fahy introduced Dorothy Day, whom she had known since 1933, to the Missionary Servants of the Most Holy Trinity. In 1938, *From Union Square to Rome,* heavily edited by Benson, became Day's first book. Its chapters originally appeared as articles in the columns of *Preservation of the Faith.* "It is very easy to see how much the Missionary Servants and the Catholic Workers have in common," Benson wrote to Day after one of her first visits to Silver Spring.[71] Benson regarded the publication and promotion of Day's book as "one of my missionary activities."[72] In 1935 Furfey published a series of articles in *Preservation* on "Catholic Extremism."[73] Benson printed the articles in pamphlet form in 1937. *Catholic Extremism* was translated into French, Dutch, Spanish, and German. In 1939 Benson published *This Way to Heaven,* a guide to the spiritual life Furfey wrote for lay people. By 1941 the *Catholic Extremism* pamphlet had gone into its fourth printing. To these works by Walsh, Day, and Furfey, Benson added his own *Judgments of Father Judge* in a new printing. Together with the magazine they helped to form the literature of what Benson did not hesitate to call a "movement," a word dear to Father Judge. Furfey called it the "New Social Catholicism."[74]

Though not identical with it, Father Judge's spirit shared much with what Furfey called "Catholic Extremism" or the "New Social Catholicism." Both emphasized hands-on contact with the poor in the corporal and spiritual works of mercy. This required a certain simplicity and rigor of life that suit-

70. On the neighborhood houses as "supernaturalized settlement houses," see Paul Furfey, "House of Faith," *Preservation of the Faith* 14, no. 3 (June 1941), 5–7.

71. Benson to Day, Silver Spring, Md., October 19, 1935, Dorothy Day–Catholic Worker Papers, Series D 1, 1, Folder B41, Benson, Fr. Joachim, Letters from 1935 to 1948, Marquette University Archives. Earlier in October, Benson had told Day, "One of our men, Brother Thomas O'Keeffe, is quite interested and expects to do a thesis also on the 'CW,' though I have forgotten the exact title. He will probably stop at the 'C.W.' Office this week end. Be good to him please"; Benson to Day, Silver Spring, Md., October 5, 1935. Presumably Benson is referring to an undergraduate thesis. In conversations with Fathers Gerald Swift and Shaun McCarty, on August 15, 2003, both recalled Dorothy Day's visits to Silver Spring during their student days.

72. Benson to Furfey, Silver Spring, Md., February 10, 1939, Furfey/Walsh Papers, Correspondence, B, Professional, Box 4, Folder—Benson, Rev. Joachim, MSSsT (1935–52)," ACUA, The Catholic University of America.

73. For a discussion of the "Catholic Extremism" articles, see Portier, "Paul Hanly Furfey," 24–37.

74. Furfey's three-page letter, dated October 30, 1936, on the "New Social Catholicism" (Benson was one of its signers) appears in Joseph P. Chinnici and Angelyn Dries, eds., *Prayer and Practices in the American Catholic Community* (Maryknoll, N.Y.: Orbis, 2000), 156–59.

ed Depression-era Catholicism. Both recognized the primacy of the spiritual over the political.[75] Far from eccentric, Benson's associations with Furfey and Day during the 1930s and 1940s were based on recognition of these affinities, not only by him but by his superiors. He saw in Day and Furfey and the other social Catholics something of the way Father Judge had taught him to look at the world.

Benson would not have had to stretch far to think of Father Judge as a "Catholic extremist" in Furfey's sense. Furfey described "Catholic extremists" as "heroes of charity." Father Judge urged the Cenacle to "charity at white heat."[76] This was not "politics" in any contemporary sense of "public policy" advocacy. Rather, Catholic radicals of the 1930s offered a spiritual alternative for social reform, a spiritual alternative to the policies that had brought on the Great Depression and eventually the Second World War. A good example is the supernatural approach to social work shared by both Father Judge and Furfey and Walsh. Another is Benson's editorial policy on the war in the pages of *Preservation of the Faith*.[77]

The war changed all this and fractured the New Social Catholics. Most especially it fractured the Catholic Workers and divided them, despite their broad agreement on the primacy of the spiritual, from the other parts of the loose Catholic front that had arisen during the Depression years. Father Joachim Benson could not get on board with the Lacouture retreat that Dorothy Day embraced after 1941. He found it overly perfectionist and lacking in the "compassion of Christ."[78] Sister Peter Claver Fahy, by contrast, shared Day's enthusiasm for the retreat and was the one among those who remem-

75. In his chapter on "Cenacle Methods," Berry uses the phrase "primacy of the spiritual" to characterize one of the essential aspects of Father Judge's spirit, the idea that spiritual needs must be addressed first. Solutions to other difficulties would come from one's supernatural relationship of charity with God; see Berry, *God's Valiant Warrior*, 167–70, 184. Writing in the 1930s, Jacques Maritain defended the subordination of the temporal to the spiritual in terms of "Catholic Action"; see Maritain, *True Humanism* (New York: Charles Scribner's Sons, 1938), appendix.

76. Father Judge described the "apostolic spirit" as "charity at white heat, zeal invincible, a grace that should appeal to every Christian and to which he should attain, at least, in generous degree.... There are many gifts in the giving of the Church ... but the Church can invite souls to no higher way of living than that of the Apostolic life"; Judge, "The Apostles," *Holy Ghost*, January 1929, 17; see also AST, MF 1382.

77. On Benson's editorials, see Portier, "'Good Friday in December': World War II in the Editorials of *Preservation of the Faith* Magazine, 1939–1945," *U.S. Catholic Historian* 27, no. 2 (Spring 2009): 25–44.

78. Benson to Day, Silver Spring, Md., April 18, 1941, Dorothy Day–Catholic Worker Papers, Marquette University Archives.

bered Father Judge who remained in close contact with Day. Their correspondence, preserved at the Marquette University Archives, spans the years from 1934 to 1978.[79]

The divisions over the war and the retreat sucked all the juice out of what both Benson and Furfey had called a "movement" and tended to marginalize the survivors as economic and political "extremists" In this context, the Joachim Benson of the 1930s and early 1940s reminds all who come after him that when the memory of Father Judge crosses the great divide of World War II, something of the simplicity and rigor, the radical spiritual edge of the 1920s and 1930s, is filtered out. Postwar prosperity and consensus tended to flatten and redirect the spiritual energies produced in the crushing economic pressures about which Father Judge wrote to Brother Joachim Benson in 1932.

Refounding the Missionary Servants of the Most Holy Trinity after World War II

Father Judge's Vision Fragmented

On February 3, 1949, about sixteen months before Bishop Shaughnessy died, the Vatican decided that the Missionary Servants of the Most Holy Trinity were on sufficiently sound personnel and financial grounds to be released from more than a decade of receivership. On March 1, 1949, Archbishop Cicognani sent to Bishop Shaughnessy, with an accompanying letter, the brief Vatican rescript declaring an end to their apostolic visitation.[80] The motherhouse was now established at Silver Spring, Maryland. From the earlier days, Father Paul Anthony Fursman died in Puerto Rico on March 8, 1936. Those seemingly handpicked by Father Judge, Brennan and Norris, along with Mulroy and Metzger, were all gone. Brother Augustine died in Stirling on April 17, 1952.

A few remained who had come to know and work with Father Judge in the 1920s and early 1930s before his death: Brother Joseph Limpert, Fathers

79. On Sister Peter Claver, MSBT, see the obituary by Karen B. Lenz in the *Catholic Worker*, May 2005, 8, and the Appreciation by Dennis Coday in the *National Catholic Reporter*, January 7, 2005, 10.

80. See Cicognani to Shaughnessy, Washington, D.C., March 1, 1949, §141/37, copy, with accompanying rescript dated February 3, 1949, §4707/35, copy. Bishop Shaughnessy was incapacitated by his stroke, and Father Thomas's letter of thanks was answered by his secretary with Shaughnessy's congratulations; see O'Keeffe to Shaughnessy, Silver Spring, March 7, 1949, copy; Rev. William E. Gallagher to O'Keeffe, Seattle, Washington, March 18, 1949, AST.

Thomas O'Keeffe and Gerard Fredericks, Fathers Turibius Mulcahy, Joachim Benson, Lawrence Brediger, who began to organize the archives and keep the memory of Father Judge, Andrew Lawrence, and a few others. But at this time, most of the ordained Missionary Servants had begun as the young boys who came to study at Holy Trinity after Father Judge's death, or just before, and were ordained after 1937.[81] Except for personal, informal ties of the older members to the sisters and the Outer Cenacle, the Missionary Servants of the Most Holy Trinity appeared as a typical congregation of male religious and priests, known specifically for their work on the Southern missions. As Father John Baptist McCarthy remembered it:

> After Mother Boniface's death, because of Mother Mary of the Incarnate Word's trouble with some priests and bishops who had heard false rumors about the closeness of the men and women, she kept them all well-separated—boys' entrance, girls' entrance—"keep them over there." They [student brothers] didn't know anything about the Missionary Cenacle Apostolate; scarcely met anybody. Father Judge died in 1933. He had been busy getting the communities started. Bishop Shaughnessy didn't care anything about the Missionary Cenacle Apostolate. The big ambition was to get priests out on the missions.[82]

At the beginning of 1949, Father Thomas O'Keeffe became custodian general of the Missionary Servants of the Most Holy Trinity. Universally respected, he is sometimes spoken of as the community's second founder. After 1937 the ordination classes grew larger. As Father Gerald Swift recalled it, as soon as men were ordained, Father Thomas sent them to the Southern missions. Father Gerald, who had come to Holy Trinity in 1931 and was ordained in 1939, interpreted O'Keeffe's vision for the community as "to be southern missionaries."[83] It seems clear that emphasis on the abandoned work of the

81. Looking back at age eighty-nine on the "boys" or the little group that came through Holy Trinity between 1928 and 1935, and developments after Father Judge's death, Father Vincent Fitzpatrick felt "that Father Judge would have been scandalized at some of their attitudes and doings. Father was strict. In his absence, there was no real drive to develop virtue"; Father Gary Banks, ST, notes of personal conversation with Fr. Vincent Fitzpatrick, ST, Stirling, N.J., May 18, 24, 2005.

82. Transcript of interview with Father John Baptist McCarthy by Sister Josepha McNutt, Margaret Healy's file, AMSBT, as cited in McNutt, *Margaret: Called and Chosen*, 110, 264n178. McCarthy fails to mention the constitutional restrictions, mentioned previously, under which Mother Mary of the Incarnate Word was constrained to work.

83. According to Father Gerald, Father Thomas thought that any Missionary Servant could do any job, no training required. This led to some difficult assignments, Father Gerald recalled; from a personal conversation with Father Gerald Swift, ST, Silver Spring, Md., August 15, 2003.

Southern missions tended at this time to fragment Father Judge's spirit and vision among the men, crowding out other central aspects such as working as a missionary family with the sisters and lay associates and forming and encouraging lay apostles.

For a community desperate for legitimacy and financial stability, parishes, even abandoned Southern parishes, offered a recognized institution in the church. Even if they were not self-supporting, they generated at least some of their own revenue. Soliciting funds for the support of parishes in low-density Catholic areas of the South was likely easier than raising money for other, more innovative aspects of Father Judge's vision such as forming lay apostles. As McCarthy's observations suggest, in sending the newly ordained to the Southern missions, Father Thomas O'Keeffe was following Bishop Shaughnessy's lead. Focus on the Southern missions was an ad hoc measure that over time developed its own momentum.

Missionary Servants and Lay Apostles

That Father Thomas O'Keeffe had and understood the spirit of Father Judge there can be no doubt. Nevertheless, he was well aware that emphasis on forming and supporting lay apostles had faded among the men. In 1938, in the context of a discussion of the sisters' support of the Outer Cenacle at their second General Cenacle, Mother Mary of the Incarnate Word received from the men the following assurance: "Once we adjust ourselves, and prove our right to exist, we will be able in a far greater degree than we have ever done in the past, to participate in the common Missionary Cenacle activities planned by Father Judge."[84] As recently appointed co-vicar in the following year, Father Thomas began to deliver on this promise in an address to a general meeting of the Cenacle in Newark, New Jersey. He told the Outer Cenacle associates that, "as a result of the Outer Missionary Cenacle, the Church has been enriched by two new communities." With reference to these two communities, he went on to describe the particular work of "fostering a lay movement among the faithful" as "one of our principal works." He admonished new members that "the Outer Cenacle is not a freelance organization." One hears the clear echo of Father Judge in his words:

> It is an organization working from its beginning, under direction, in the work according to that plan, a well thought out plan—prayed over and worked out

84. Shaun McCarty, ST, "Rationale for a Common Rule," 28–29, as cited in McNutt, *Margaret: Called and Chosen*, 109, 264n176.

> thoroughly. Our work is the fostering of that movement—the spreading of it. The Communities are called the Inner Cenacle; the lay organization—the Outer Missionary Cenacle. They both make up one plan—one organization—the Missionary Cenacle whose one objective is the preservation of the faith, having the same practices, prayers and devotions.[85]

In 1941, after an agonizingly detailed account of the community's financial history in a letter to a potential benefactor, one he hoped would help him refinance the debt and who might have been interested in collateral, Father Thomas signed off, invoking the spirit of Father Judge. "We have no structures built of stone or brick or marble. Our strength lies in our man power and in the spirit that was bequeathed to us by our saintly Founder."[86]

Around the time Father Thomas became custodian general at the beginning of 1949, Father Lawrence Brediger was putting together a set of "Lecture Notes on the Early History of the Cenacle" or "Missiology Notes." In setting up the community's archives, Brediger borrowed heavily from materials Sister Mary James had gathered from the pioneer sisters who saved Father Judge's letters and transcribed his talks. The typescript of Brediger's "Missiology Notes" is less than a hundred pages. Used for teaching the younger members of the community, the "Missiology Notes" evidence Brediger's clear concern to turn the postwar direction of the community back to the integral spirit of Father Judge. He presented Father Judge as a "maker of apostles." To his students, he wrote of their vocation to be "the priestly heart of the Missionary Cenacle family" and "extensions of Father Judge." They were to be "first of all makers of apostles, not southern missionaries."[87] Rather than an "isolated men's congregation," they were "part of a religious family."[88] Despite such gestures in the direction of the religious family Father Judge envisioned, the history of the men's community tended to unfold separately from that of the sisters and the Outer Cenacle, known since 1950 as the Missionary Cenacle Apostolate.

85. Conference given by Father Thomas O'Keeffe, ST, October 29, 1939, at a general meeting, Newark, N.J., Archives MCA, uncatalogued, as cited in James P. O'Bryan, ST, *Awake the Giant*, 281, 357n749. O'Bryan's work, along with Sister Josepha McNutt's study of Dr. Margaret Healy, *Margaret: Called and Chosen* (1989), thoroughly document the central place making lay apostles had in Father Judge's vision of the Missionary Servants of the Most Holy Trinity.

86. O'Keeffe to Edmund A. Burke, Silver Spring, Md., June 30, 1941, typescript, AST.

87. Brediger, "Missiology Notes," 20–21, typescript, AST.

88. Ibid., 80.

Preservation of the Faith in Latin America

"It will be not only a Klondike in souls but I think in revenue also." This is how Father Judge described Puerto Rico to Mother Boniface in 1926.[89] The mission to preserve the faith in Latin America, with Puerto Rico understood as a gateway, was central to his vision for both communities. As superior general of the men's community, one of Bishop Shaughnessy's first acts was to close St. Augustine's. It never developed the revenue-generating potential Father Judge saw in it and was no doubt a drain on the community's resources.[90] The sisters continued to work in Puerto Rico, the Virgin Islands, and Cuba.[91] Eventually the men would return to the island. But Father Judge's vision of a larger work for the preservation of the faith in Latin America remained to be developed.

The Mission Procure Office

In their earliest days, money to finance the work of the Missionary Cenacle's two communities came from parish collections in dioceses whose bishops and pastors approved them. In a 1925 letter, Father Judge described to the "Business Man," Father Tomerlin, the procedures of the new Mission Board the bishops had established to replace collections. Given the intense competition among good works, he wondered if providence wasn't telling the community to get its own revenue.[92] The sisters already had the *Holy Ghost* magazine, and soon the brothers would have *SOS for the Preservation of the Faith*. With the help of professional fundraisers R. S. Toth and Werner Stenzel, the men used the subscription lists from the mission magazine to develop the mailing lists for their mass direct-mail appeals such as for bonds, annuities, and the Adopt a Priest Brother program. Eventually the Missionary Servants of the Most Holy Trinity became Stenzel's only client. By the 1950s, they were in a strong enough financial position to buy Stenzel's business from him and establish the Mission Procure Office.[93] Within twenty years of Father Judge's

89. Father Judge wrote this as he asked Mother Boniface for $1,200 for St. Augustine's; Judge to Mother Boniface, Newark, N.J., December 16, 1926, AST, MF 7943–44.

90. Father Judge's vision of St. Augustine's as producing lay Catholic leaders for Puerto Rico was indeed fulfilled after 1937 under the Marianists; see Jansen, *First Seventy Five Years*. After 1938 the *Colegio San Agustín* became *Colegio San José*.

91. On the sisters' work in Puerto Rico, see Díaz-Stevens, "Missionizing the Missionaries," 40–46.

92. Judge to Tomerlin, Newark, N.J., September 22, 1925, AST, MF 6367.

93. Personal conversations with Father Conrad Schmidt, ST, Silver Spring, Md., September 5, 2002, and with Father Edwin Dill, ST, Silver Spring, Md., September 10, 2002.

death, the Missionary Servants of the Most Holy Trinity had finally achieved the financial stability that eluded him during his lifetime.

A Remarkable Miracle

Father Gerard Fredericks remembered Father Judge's valedictory at Gold Street on August 14, 1933, in terms that recall Rabbi Gamaliel on the first Christians in Acts 5:38–39: "If it is God's work it will go on; if not, let God do whatever he wants with it."[94] Looking back on the work, especially between the years 1930 and 1937, it is hard to imagine how the Missionary Servants of the Most Holy Trinity did not fail, crushed by financial pressure and lost hopelessly in the labyrinth of the 1917 Code of Canon Law. "The remarkable miracle that happened to the Missionary Servants of the Most Holy Trinity," Father Joachim Benson recalled in 1974, "is that all that debt was paid off." With reference to Father Judge, he struck a note of triumph: "At the time that he was alive, they said that the Missionary Servants were going to fall apart because he was guiding it. After he was dead—it was going to fall apart because he wasn't there."[95] Always an angel-like helper appeared. At first it was Father McHale, Bishop Allen, and the apostolic delegate, then two more delegates, Cardinal Dougherty, Father Bede Hermann, Bishops Schrembs and Shaughnessy, and always the intrepid Dr. Motry passing like Theseus through the *Codex iuris canonici*. The work went on.

94. Campbell, "Father's Last Talk at Gold Street, August 14, 1933," 2:54.

95. Transcript of taped interview with Father Joachim Benson, ST, by Sister Mary Tonra, MSBT, Rio Piedras, Puerto Rico, February 5, 1974, 3, AMSBT.

EPILOGUE

Renewing the Family Spirit

Father Judge and Mother Boniface envisioned the women's and men's communities as part of one religious family. The uprooting of both motherhouses from Holy Trinity, the generic strictures of canon law for religious under the 1917 Code of Canon Law, and Bishop Shaughnessy's emphasis on Southern missions conspired to separate the two communities. Each now had its own constitution and its own history. In 1958, less than three decades after Mother Boniface and Father Judge died, both communities received approbation and recognition as pontifical rather than diocesan institutes. Nevertheless, they remained canonically separate.

In response to a plea from Pope John XXIII shortly after his election, the men's community began experimental programs in Guayaquil, Ecuador, and Giradot, Colombia. Ten years later, they opened missions in Mexico and established a formation program there. The sisters also established missions and a house of formation in Mexico. Expansion into Costa Rica and Colombia followed ten years later. Father Judge's dream of Puerto Rico as a gateway for extending his lay movement into all of Latin America was beginning to come true.

The second half of the twentieth century put both communities of Missionary Servants in a position to overcome their separate institutional histories and renew the family spirit the founders desired. The chief impetus for renewal was, of course, the Second Vatican Council (1962–65). During the council itself, in a decree dated January 20, 1964, the Vatican approved the Blessed Trinity Missionary Institute as a "pious union" in the Archdiocese of New York.[1] Under Margaret Healy's leadership, the institute pioneered ca-

1. On this, see McNutt, *Margaret: Called and Chosen*, chap.12, "Toward a Secular Institute," 224–26.

nonical space not available to the first Cenacle lay apostles. As "the only layman to participate in the debates of the Second Vatican Council," James Norris gave Father Judge's notion of "family" an international reach, describing the council as "an act of faith in the laity's capacity to animate the temporal order in a Christian spirit."[2]

A key call for renewal came from *Perfectae caritatis*, the council's decree on religious life, calling religious communities to recover "the spirit of the founder." In 1967, two years after the council, Dr. Margaret Healy addressed the general cenacle, a renewal chapter, of the Missionary Servants of the Most Holy Trinity. Looking back on fifty years as a lay apostle, she thought of Father Judge as the young priest she first met in 1912:

> From that time until today I have never ceased to marvel at what I heard and saw and felt, the lay apostolate, the sisters, the priests, and brothers all came into being—true creations as from nothing in the sense of material things but rather from something intangible—the faith, the hope and the love of a young priest who had been ordained to die. Maybe it would be more accurate to say [from] the spirit of that young priest which ignited the fires of lay apostolic action in our country.[3]

As Healy's words suggest, Vatican II inspired a Cenacle *ressourcement* represented in the works of Blackwell (1974), Tonra (1984), O'Bryan (1986), McNutt (1989), and Berry (1992). They made the founding story available to ordinary members of the Missionary Cenacle family. O'Bryan and McNutt make more than clear the central place of the Outer Cenacle or Missionary Cenacle Apostolate in the founding vision.

Returning to the founders' spirit in the long period of post-conciliar renewal, the men's and women's communities grew closer together, emphasizing their common connections as a religious family to the Missionary Cenacle Apostolate. This long process culminated in 1985 with Vatican approval of the "Common Rule of Life of the Missionary Servants of the Most Blessed Trinity and the Missionary Servants of the Most Holy Trinity."

In 1975, as both communities engaged in post-conciliar renewal and re-

2. Kupke, "American Intervention at Rome," 247–48, 250. As Kupke explains, Norris's intervention in the Aula, "World Poverty and Christian Conscience," introduced chap. 4, para. 24 of Schema XIII, which eventually became the Pastoral Constitution on the Church in the Modern World. Kupke takes Norris's description of the Council from an address on "Lay Apostolate Vocation" to the New Jersey Holy Name Society Convention, November 5, 1966, Norris Collection, University of Notre Dame Archives.

3. Healy, "Talk to S.T. Chapter," 1967, Margaret Healy file, AMSBT, as cited in McNutt, *Margaret: Called and Chosen*, 218, 271n352.

vision of their constitutions, Sister Mary Gerald Kiely, the sisters' general custodian, suggested a "joint constitution."[4] In 1982, in the midst of a near decade of dialogue and consultation on the possibility of a joint constitution, Father Stephen Quinn addressed the delegates to a pre-chapter meeting of the sisters. He spoke of "this joint effort of our branches of the Missionary Cenacle Family" as the dream of Father Judge and Mother Boniface "only partially realized in their lifetime, almost lost completely after their death." He exhorted the delegates, as they worked together on the joint document, to seize the opportunity it represented. "If we lose this opportunity," he urged, "I wonder if we shall ever again have the opportunity to speak with one voice, to articulate together that giftedness which is uniquely ours."[5]

The Sacred Congregation for Religious and Secular Institutes eventually rejected the possibility of a joint constitution. They suggested instead that the opening section of the proposed joint constitution be called a "Rule of Life," followed by separate constitutions for each community. The approved "Common Rule of Life" was dated May 26, 1985, the Feast of Pentecost. Rome now recognized, as rooted in the founding charism of Father Judge and Mother Boniface, the connection between the two communities and between them and the Missionary Cenacle Apostolate.

By the end of the twentieth century, these developments, along with the conciliar documents' emphasis on the lay apostolate and the Christian vocation in the world, put the whole Missionary Cenacle in a position to imagine how Father Judge's vision, straitened in earlier canonical structures, might translate into the more evangelical church of a new century. In the twenty-first century, what Father Judge and Mother Boniface envisioned a century ago begins to look like a religious movement, a word of which Father Judge was most fond, including women and men, laity, clergy, and religious, united in the cause of making lay apostles to work for the preservation of the faith in abandoned works and places and well-schooled in the "charity at white heat" needed for such an arduous undertaking.[6]

4. For the story of the "Common Rule's" origin, see Wilson, "To Speak with One Voice," chap. 3. Wilson relies on Sister Mary Tonra's unpublished manuscript, *As the Spirit Rules*, 1988, and Shaun McCarty, ST, *Rationale for a Common Rule of Life for the Missionary Servants of the Most Blessed Trinity and the Missionary Servants of the Most Holy Trinity*, privately distributed, 1982; both sources are in AMSBT.

5. Cited in Wilson, "To Speak," 96, from Tonra, *As the Spirit Rules*, 246.

6. See Berry, "A Study Paper: The Missionary Cenacle Family; A New Form of Consecrated Life," (January 2005), unpublished typescript, 16 pp. On Father Judge and the evangelical turn in the church, see Portier, "'Eminent Evangelist from Boston,'" 300–19.

The opening article of the 1985 Common Rule of Life begins with Father Judge on the "evangelical burning" Christ desired:

> *Our Lord had very much at heart the creating of a spirit, a missionary spirit, an evangelical burning, that would sweep over the whole world. He came to cast a fire on the earth and he willed that it would be enkindled* (Lk 12:49). The Holy Spirit has enkindled this fire in our hearts. This is our heritage: *an apostolic spirit, a Gospel spirit, a Catholic spirit*. The Missionary Cenacle spirit is *charity, charity aflame*.[7]

7. As cited in Wilson, "To Speak with One Voice," 103; appendix C gives the entire text of the Rule of Life, 103–8.

SELECTED BIBLIOGRAPHY

Archival Sources

American Catholic History Research Center and University Archives, The Catholic University of America (ACUA), Washington, D.C. The Louis Motry Papers contain correspondence with Father Judge as well as materials related to Father Judge's work on the constitutions and to canonical affairs of the Missionary Servants of the Most Holy Trinity after his death.

Archives, Archdiocese of Mobile (AAM), Mobile, Ala. The extensive papers of Bishop Allen and Bishop Toolen are indispensable sources for any study of Father Judge's life.

Archives, Diocese of Cleveland (ADC), Cleveland, Ohio. The papers of Bishop Schrembs contain correspondence related to the proposed move of the motherhouse of the Missionary Servants of the Most Holy Trinity to Cleveland, both during and after Father Judge's life.

Archives and Records Center, Friars of the Atonement, Graymoor, Garrison, N.Y. The papers of Father Paul Wattson contain a limited correspondence with Father Judge. The Atonement publication the *Lamp* is also available here.

Archives of the Missionary Servants of the Most Blessed Trinity (AMSBT), Philadelphia . This and the Archives of the Missionary Servants of the Most Holy Trinity have Father Judge's papers as well as full runs of the *Holy Ghost* and *Preservation of the Faith*. In addition, this archive has the material related to Mother Boniface upon which Tonra based her biography and extensive material related to the history of the Outer Cenacle/Missionary Cenacle Apostolate upon which O'Bryan and McNutt based their works. Both collections also contain oral histories from those who knew Father Judge.

Archives of the Missionary Servants of the Most Holy Trinity (AST), Silver Spring, Md. See Archives of the Missionary Servants of the Most Blessed Trinity.

Archives of the Roman Catholic Diocese of Brooklyn, Brooklyn, N.Y. The papers of Monsignor Thomas Nummey contain his correspondence with Father Judge and materials related to his years with the Missionary Servants of the Most Holy Trinity.

Archives of the University of Notre Dame, Notre Dame, Ind. James Norris gave his correspondence with Father Judge to AST. The full collection of his papers is housed at Notre Dame.

Associated Archives at St. Mary's Seminary and University, Archdiocese of Baltimore. Archbishop Curley's papers have his correspondence with Father Judge over the years. The Baltimore *Catholic Review* is available here.

Ducournau Archives (DA), St. Vincent Seminary, Philadelphia. Also known as the Archives of the Eastern Province of the Congregation of the Mission (Vincentians), it contains valuable material related to the early part of Father Judge's life and his background as a Vincentian priest, as well as copies of material related to Father Judge from the Vincentian General Archives in Rome.

Philadelphia Archdiocesan Historical Research Center, Philadelphia. Though closed, the papers of Cardinal Dougherty have some materials available related to the history of the Missionary Servants of the Most Blessed Trinity as well as correspondence with Bishop George Caruana related to Puerto Rico.

Provincial Archives, Daughters of Charity, Emmitsburg, Md. Materials related to the Archconfraternity of the Holy Agony are available here.

Special Collections and University Archives, Memorial Library, Marquette University, Milwaukee, Wisc. The Dorothy Day Papers contain her correspondence with Sr. Peter Claver Fahy, MSBT, and with Fr. Joachim Benson, ST.

Books and Articles

Abelly, Louis. *La vie du Vénérable Serviteur de Dieu, Vincent de Paul.* 3 vols. Paris: 1664, 1891.

———. *The Life of the Venerable Servant of God Vincent de Paul.* Translated by William Quinn, FSC. Introduction by Stafford Poole, CM. New Rochelle, N.Y.: New City Press, 1993.

Alberigo, Giuseppe, and Joseph Komonchak, eds. *History of Vatican II.* Vol 4. Maryknoll, N.Y.: Orbis; Leuven: Peeters, 2003.

Allen, Frederick Lewis. *Only Yesterday: An Informal History of the 1920s.* San Francisco: Harper and Row, 1964. Originally published in 1931.

Anderson, Floyd, ed. *Council Daybook, Vatican II, Session 3, September 14 –November 21, 1964.* Washington, D.C.: National Catholic Welfare Conference, 2005. Originally published in 1964.

Badillo, David A. *Latinos and the New Immigrant Church.* Baltimore: Johns Hopkins University Press, 2006.

Balthasar, Hans Urs von. "Theology and Sanctity." In *Word and Redemption: Essays in Theology.* Vol. 2. Translated by A. V. Littledale, in cooperation with Alexander Dru. Montreal: Palms, 1965.

Barnes, Margaret Anne. *The Tragedy and the Triumph of Phenix City, Alabama.* Macon, Ga.: Mercer University Press, 2005.

Barry, John M. *The Great Influenza: The Story of the Greatest Pandemic in History.* New York: Penguin, 2005.

Barton, Bruce. *The Man Nobody Knows: A Discovery of the Real Jesus*. Indianapolis: Bobbs-Merrill, 1924, 1925.

Benson, Joachim V., MSSsT. *The Judgments of Father Judge*. New York: P. J. Kenedy and Sons, 1934.

——. "Biography of a Magazine." *Missionary Servant* 1 (January 1946): 2–4.

Berry, Dennis M., ST. "A Comparative Study of the Spiritual Theologies of Saint Vincent de Paul and Father Thomas A. Judge, CM." Ph.D. diss., Washington University, St. Louis, 1989.

——. *God's Valiant Warrior.* Holy Trinity, Ala.: Missionary Cenacle Press, 1992.

Bireley, Robert. *The Refashioning of Catholicism, 1450–1700: A Reassessment of the Counter-Reformation*. Washington, D.C.: The Catholic University of America Press, 1999.

Blackwell, Joseph Miriam, MSBT. *Ecclesial People: A Study of the Life and Times of Thomas Augustine Judge, CM*. Holy Trinity, Ala.: Missionary Cenacle Press, 1984.

Blakely, Paul, SJ. "The Catholic Charities and the Strong Commission." *America* 15 (May 16, 1916): 78.

Bouscaren, T. Lincoln, Adam C. Ellis, and Francis N. Korth. *Canon Law: A Text and Commentary*. 4th rev. ed. Milwaukee: Bruce, 1963.

Brediger, Lawrence, ST, ed. *Father Judge Anthology*. Silver Spring, Md.: Archives of the Missionary Servants of the Most Holy Trinity, 1961.

Brediger, Lawrence, ST. "Leaving All Things: A History of the Beginnings of the Cenacle in the South." unpublished manuscript, 1948. Archives of the Missionary Servants of the Most Holy Trinity.

——. "In the Name of the Father and of the Son and of the Holy Ghost." In Judge, *Father Thomas A. Judge, C.M.*, Monographs 6. 1985.

Brown, Dorothy M., and Elizabeth McKeown. *The Poor Belong to Us: Catholic Charities and American Welfare*. Cambridge, Mass., and London: Harvard University Press, 1997.

Campbell, Marie of the Precious Blood, MSBT. "Father's Last Talk at Gold Street, August 14, 1933." In *Father Thomas A. Judge, C.M.*, Monographs 2. 1983.

Carlen, Claudia, IHM. *The Papal Encyclicals*. 5 vols. Raleigh, N.C.: McGrath, 1981.

Carven, John W., CM. "Son of St. Vincent." *Vincentian Heritage* 6, no. 2 (1985): 241–46.

Celiá, Guillermo. "Cuando Puerto Rico Tenía su Pequeño West Point." *El Reportaje de la Semana* (1979): 1–3.

Chinnici, Joseph P., OFM, ed. *Devotion to the Holy Spirit in American Catholicism*. New York and Mahwah, N.J.: Paulist Press, 1985.

Chinnici, Joseph P., and Angelyn Dries, eds. *Prayer and Practices in the American Catholic Community*. Maryknoll, N.Y.: Orbis, 2000.

Cleary, Edward L. "In the Absence of Missionaries: Lay Preachers Who Preserved Catholicism." *International Bulletin of Missionary Research* 34, no. 2 (April 2010): 67–70.

Collet, Pierre. *Life of St. Vincent De Paul, Founder of the Congregation of the Mission and of the Sisters of Charity*. Translated by a Catholic clergyman. Baltimore: John Murphy, 1878.

Collins, Mary James, MSBT. "A Voice from the Past." *Holy Ghost,* March 1949–June 1954.

Coste, Pierre, CM. *Grand saint du grand siècle: Monsieur Vincent.* 3 vols. Paris: Gabalda, 1932.

Cummings, Kathleen Sprows. *New Women of the Old Faith: Gender and American Catholicism in the Progressive Era.* Chapel Hill: University of North Carolina Press, 2009.

D'Agostino, Peter D. *Rome in America: Transnational Catholic Ideology from the Resorgimento to Fascism.* Chapel Hill and London: University of North Carolina Press, 2004.

Daniel-Rops, Henri. *Monsieur Vincent: The Story of St. Vincent de Paul.* Translated by Julie Kernan. New York: Hawthorn, 1961.

——. *The Church in the Seventeenth Century.* New York: E. P. Dutton, 1963.

Day, Dorothy. *From Union Square to Rome.* Silver Spring, Md.: Preservation of the Faith Press, 1939.

de Lubac, Henri. *The Mystery of the Supernatural.* Translated by Rosemary Sheed, with an Introduction by David L. Schindler. New York: Crossroad Herder, 1998. Originally publishd in 1965.

de Paul, Vincent. *Conférences de S. Vincent de Paul aux Filles de la Charité.* Edited by Jean-Baptiste Pémartin, CM. 2 vols. Paris: Pillet et DuMoulin, 1881.

——. *Correspondence, Conferences, Documents.* Vol. 2, *Conferences.* Translated and edited by Marie Poole, DC. Newly translated, edited, and annotated from the 1925 edition by Pierre Coste, CM. Hyde Park, N.Y.: New City Press, 2008.

Deville, Raymond. *The French School of Spirituality: An Introduction and Reader.* Translated by Agnes Cunningham, SSCM. Pittsburgh: Duquesne University Press, 1994.

Díaz-Stevens, Ana María. "Missionizing the Missionaries: Religious Congregations of Women in Puerto Rico, 1910–1960." *U.S. Catholic Historian* 21, no. 1 (Winter 2003): 33–51.

Dodin, André, CM. "De l'uniformité," 5 novembre 1657. In *Conférences de S. Vincent de Paul aux Filles de la Charité,* edited by Jean-Baptiste Pémartin, CM, 2:295. Paris: Pillet et DuMoulin, 1881.

——. *Vincent de Paul and Charity: A Contemporary Portrait of His Life and Apostolic Spirit.* Translated by Jean Marie Smith and Dennis Saunders. Edited by Hugh O'Donnell, CM, and Marjorie Gale Hornstein. New Rochelle, N.Y.: New City Press, 1993.

Dolan, Jay P. *Catholic Revivalism: The American Experience, 1830–1900.* Notre Dame, Ind., and London: University of Notre Dame Press, 1978.

——. *The American Catholic Experience: A History from Colonial Times to the Present.* Garden City, N.Y.: Doubleday, 1985.

Dolan, Jay P., and Jaime R. Vidal, eds. *Puerto Rican and Cuban Catholics in the United States, 1900–1965.* Notre Dame, Ind., and London: University of Notre Dame Press, 1994.

Dolan, Timothy M. "'Hence We Cheerfully Sent One Who Should Represent Our Person': A Century of Papal Representation in the United States." *U.S. Catholic Historian* 12, no. 2 (Spring 1994): 1–26.

Dries, Angelyn, OSF. *The Missionary Movement in American Catholic History*. Maryknoll, N.Y.: Orbis, 1998.

Dumenil, Lynn. "The Tribal Twenties: 'Assimilated' Catholics' Response to Anti-Catholicism in the 1920s." *Journal of American Ethnic History* 11, no. 1 (Fall 1991): 21–49.

———. *The Modern Temper: American Culture and Society in the 1920s*. New York: Hill and Wang, 1995.

Ellis, John Tracy. *The Life of James Cardinal Gibbons, Archbishop of Baltimore, 1834–1921*. 2 vols. Westminster, Md.: Christian Classics, 1987. Originally published in 1952.

Fitzpatrick, Joseph P., SJ. *The Stranger Is Our Own: Reflections on the Journey of Puerto Rican Migrants*. Kansas City: Sheed and Ward, 1996.

Flynt, Wayne. *Poor but Proud: Alabama's Poor Whites*. Tuscaloosa and London: University of Alabama Press, 1989.

Furfey, Paul Hanly. *Fire on the Earth*. New York: Macmillan, 1936.

———. *Three Theories of Society*. New York: Macmillan, 1937.

———. "House of Faith." *Preservation of the Faith* 14, no. 3 (June 1941): 5–7.

Gallaher, Margaret Alacoque, MSBT. "The Social Work of the Missionary Servants of the Most Blessed Trinity, from the Year 1909 Up to and Including the Year 1940." Master's thesis, Fordham University School of Social Service, 1942.

Handlin, Oscar. *The Uprooted*. Boston: Little Brown, 1951.

———. *Boston's Immigrants*. New York: Atheneum, 1971.

Harbrecht, John J. *The Lay Apostolate: A Social Ethical Study of Parish Charity Organization of Large City Parishes*. St. Louis: B. Herder, 1929.

Hardon, John A., SJ. "Historical Antecedents of St. Pius X's Decree on Frequent Communion." *Theological Studies* 16 (1955): 493–532.

Hehir, J. Bryan, ed. *Catholic Charities USA: 100 Years at the Intersection of Charity and Justice*. Collegeville, Minn.: Liturgical Press, 2010.

Hendrickson, Paul. *Seminary: A Search*. New York: Summit, 1983.

Higham, John. *Strangers in the Land: Patterns of American Nativism, 1860–1925*. New Brunswick, N.J.: Rutgers University Press, 1955.

Hill, Joseph A. *Women in Gainful Occupations, 1890–1920*. Census Monographs 9. Westport, Conn.: Greenwood Press, 1978. This work was originally published by the U.S. Government Printing Office in 1929.

Hynes, Michael J. *History of the Diocese of Cleveland, Origin and Growth (1847–1952)*. Cleveland: Diocese of Cleveland, 1953.

Jansen, Joseph, SM. *The First Seventy-Five Years: History of the Marianists in the West Indies and Colegio San José*. Updated by CSJ staff. Bogotá, Colombia: Argüeso Garzón Editores, 2013.

Judge, Thomas A., CM. "The Lay Apostolate in the South." *Catholic Convert*, September 1918, 4–5, 18.

———. "A Spiritual Militia." *Ecclesiastical Review* 61, no. 3 (September 1919): 276–85.

———. "Catholic Education in Porto Rico." *Holy Ghost*, June 1923, 10–11.

———. "The Address of Father Judge before the National Council of Catholic Charities in Philadelphia." *Holy Ghost*, October 1923, 6–8.

———. "Sermon on the Dedication of St. Joseph's School." *Holy Ghost*, October 1923, 9–10.

———. "The Apostles." *Holy Ghost*, January 1929, 16–18.

———. "Jesus the Teacher." *Holy Ghost*, May 1929, 17–18.

———. "Pentecostal Preparation." *Holy Ghost*, April 1930, 1–5, 11.

———. "The Lay Apostolate." *Holy Ghost*, July 1930, 16–17.

———. "Laying of the Cornerstone of the New Holy Name of Jesus Hospital, Gadsden, Alabama, November 30, 1910, Address by Reverend Thomas A. Judge, C.M.; M.S.Ss.T." *Holy Ghost*, January 1931, 16–22.

———. "Sermon Delivered at the Unveiling of the Statue of the Little Flower in Gillette, N.J." *Holy Ghost*, December 1931, 20–23.

———. "Sermon at Evening Services of the Dedication of the Holy Name of Jesus Hospital." *Holy Ghost*, October 1931, 19–24.

———. "The Negro Apostolate" (1922). *Preservation of the Faith* 7, no. 1 (February 1939): 21–22.

———. "The Puerto Rican Chronicle" (1926). In Judge, *Father Thomas A. Judge, C.M.*, Monographs 3. 1983.

———. *Father Thomas A. Judge, C.M., Founder, The Missionary Cenacle Family*. Edited by Timothy Lynch, ST. Silver Spring, Md.: The Archives, Missionary Servants of the Most Holy Trinity, 1983–85: Monographs 2, *Early Days and Final Days* (1983); Monographs 3, *Father Judge Teaches Ministry* (1983); Monographs 4, *The Writings of Father Judge: Key Documents* (1984); Monographs 5, *The Grace of Our Founder, 1974* (1984); and Monographs 6, *Father Judge and the Missionary Cenacle* (1985).

———. "The Annunciation Novena–March 1912." In Judge, *Father Thomas A. Judge, C.M.*, Monographs 4 and 5. 1984.

Kellogg, John Harvey. *The New Dietetics: A Guide to Scientific Feeding in Health and Disease*. Rev. ed. Battle Creek, Mich.: Modern Medicine, 1927.

Kennedy, David M. *Freedom from Fear: The American People in Depression and War, 1929–1945*. New York: Oxford University Press, 2005.

Kolata, Gina. *Flu: The Story of the Great Influenza Pandemic of 1918 and the Search for the Virus That Caused It*. New York: Touchstone and Simon and Schuster, 2001. First published in 1999.

Komonchak, Jospeh A. "The Enlightenment and the Construction of Modern Roman Catholicism." In *Annual of the Catholic Commission on Intellectual and Cultural Affairs (CCICA)* (1985): 31–59.

Kupke, Raymond J. "James J. Norris: An American Catholic Life." Ph.D. diss.,The Catholic University of America, 1995.

———. "An American Intervention at Rome: Father Judge and James Norris at Vatican II." In *Building the Church in America: Studies in Honor of Monsignor Robert F. Trisco on the Occasion of his Seventieth Birthday*, edited by Joseph C. Linck, CO, and Raymond

Kupke, 230–51. Washington, D.C.: The Catholic University of America Press, 1999.

Lafarge, John, SJ. *The Manner Is Ordinary*. New York: Harcourt, Brace, 1954.

Landers, Robert K. Review of *The Man Everybody Knew: Bruce Barton and the Making of Modern America*, by Richard M. Fried. In *Commonweal*, April 21, 2006, 24–26.

Lears, Jackson. *Rebirth of a Nation: The Making of Modern America, 1877–1920*. New York: Harper, 2009.

Ledwidge, Sr. Mary Gerard, MSBT, and the Ledwidge Sisters. "Life with Father Judge." In Judge, *Father Thomas A. Judge, CM*, Monographs 2. 1983.

Lonergan, Sr. Miriam, MSBT. "The Alabama Adventure." In *Father Thomas A. Judge, C.M.*,Monographs 2. 1983.

López, Alfonso R. "The Principle of Separation of Church and State as Observed by the Public Schools of Puerto Rico from 1898 to 1952." Ph.D. diss., New York University, 1971.

Lopez Cantos, Angel. *La religiosidad popular en Puerto Rico: Siglo XVIII*. San Juan: Centro de Estudios Avanzados de Puerto Rico y el Caribe, 1993.

Lyles, John. *Images of America: Phenix City*. Charleston, S.C: Arcadia, 2010.

Lynch, D. J., SJ. "The Religious Condition of the Italians in New York." *America* 10, no. 24 (December 21, 1914): 558–59.

Maritain, Jacques. *True Humanism*. New York: Charles Scribner's Sons, 1938.

Matovina, Timothy. *Latino Catholicism: Transformation in America's Largest Church*. Princeton and Oxford: Princeton University Press, 2012.

McCarthy, John Baptist, ST. "Father's Last Days in the Cenacle." In Judge, *Father Thomas A. Judge, C.M.*, Monographs 2. 1983.

McKeown, Elizabeth. *War and Welfare: American Catholics and World War I*. New York: Garland, 1988.

McNamara, Robert F. *The American College in Rome, 1855–1955*. Rochester, N.Y.: Christopher Press, 1956.

McNicholas, John T., OP. "The Need of American Priests for the Italian Missions." *Ecclesiastical Review* 39 (1908): 677–87.

McNutt, Marie Josepha, MSBT. *Margaret: Called and Chosen; A Life of Margaret Mary Healy, Ph.D., A Pioneer Cenacle Lay Missionary*. Holy Trinity, Ala.: Missionary Cenacle Press, 1989.

McSorley, Joseph, CSP. "Devotion to the Holy Spirit." *Catholic World* 71 (June 1900): 290–304.

——. "The Church and the Italian Child." *Ecclesiastical Review* 48 (1913): 268–82.

Meagher, Timothy J. *Inventing Irish America: Generation, Class, and Ethnic Identity in a New England City, 1880–1928*. Notre Dame: University of Notre Dame Press, 2001.

Miller, William D. *Dorothy Day: A Biography*. San Francisco: Harper and Row, 1982.

Moore, Lucy. *Anything Goes: A Biography of the Roaring Twenties*. New York: Overlook Press, 2010.

Newman, John Henry. *An Essay in Aid of a Grammar of Assent*. London: Longmans, Green, 1870.

Nordstrom, Justin. *Danger on the Doorstep: Anti- Catholicism and American Print Culture in the Progressive Era*. Notre Dame, Ind.: University of Notre Dame Press, 2006.

O'Brien, Miriam Therese, CSJ. "Island Hopping Diplomat." *Horizontes* 39, no. 76 (1997): 117–39.

O'Bryan, James P., ST. *Awake the Giant: A History of the Missionary Cenacle Apostolate*. Holy Trinity, Ala.: Missionary Cenacle Press, 1986.

Ochs, Stephen J. *Desegregating the Altar: The Josephites and the Struggle for Black Priests, 1871–1960*. Baton Rouge: Louisiana State University Press, 1990.

O'Grady, John. *An Introduction to Social Work*. New York: Century, 1928.

———. *Catholic Charities in the United States: History and Problems*. Washington, D.C.: National Conference of Catholic Charities, 1930.

O'Toole, James M. *Militant and Triumphant: William Henry O'Connell and the Catholic Church in Boston, 1859–1944*. Notre Dame, Ind.: University of Notre Dame Press, 1992.

Paredes, Mario J. *The History of the National Encuentros: Hispanic Americans in the One Catholic Church*. New York and Mahwah, N.J.: Paulist Press, 2014.

Partsch, Jaime. *La crisis de 1898 y su impacto en los institutos de vida religiosa en Puerto Rico*. Colección Dr. Arturo Morales Carrión, Fundación Puertorriqueña de las Humanidades, 2008.

Poole, Stafford, CM. "The Educational Apostolate: Colleges, Universities, and Secondary Schools." In *The American Vincentians: A Popular History of the Congregation of the Mission in the United States, 1815–1987*, edited by John E. Rybolt, CM, 291–346. Brooklyn, N.Y.: New City Press, 1988.

Portier, William L. "*Père Just*'s Hero-Martyr Secularized: John R. Slattery's Passage from Self-Sacrifice to 'Honest Manhood.'" *U.S. Catholic Historian* 17, no. 2 (Spring 1999): 31–47.

———. "'The Eminent Evangelist from Boston': Father Thomas A. Judge as an Evangelical Catholic." *Communio* 30 (Summer 2003): 300–19.

———. "'Good Friday in December': World War II in the Editorials of *Preservation of the Faith* Magazine, 1939–1945." *U.S. Catholic Historian* 27, no. 2 (Spring 2009): 25–44.

———. "Paul Hanly Furfey: Catholic Extremist and Supernatural Sociologist." *Josephinum Journal of Theology* 16, no. 1 (Winter/Spring 2009): 24–37.

Powers, Felicitas, RSM. "Prejudice, Journalism, and the Catholic Laymen's Association." *U.S. Catholic Historian* 8, no. 3 (Fall 1989): 201–14.

Pyne, Tricia T. *Faith in the Mountains: A History of the Diocese of Wheeling-Charleston, 1850–2000*. Strasbourg, France: Éditions du Signe, 2000.

Roche, Maurice A., CM. *St. Vincent de Paul and the Formation of Clerics*. Fribourg, Switzerland: University Press, 1964.

Ruiz, Vicki, and Virginia Sánchez Korrol, eds. *Latinas in the United States*. Bloomington, Ind.: Indiana University Press, 2006.

Rybolt, John E., CM. "Parish Apostolate: New Opportunities in the Local Church." In *The American Vincentians: A Popular History of the Congregation of the Mission in the*

United States, 1815–1987, edited by John E. Rybolt, CM, 229–89. Brooklyn, N.Y.: New City Press, 1988.

Rynne, Xavier [Francis X. Murphy, CSsR]. *Vatican Council II*. Maryknoll, N.Y.: Orbis, 1999). First published in 1968.

Sanders, James W. "Catholics and the School Question in Boston: The Cardinal O'Connell Years." In *Catholic Boston: Studies in Religion and Community, 1870–1970*, edited by Robert E. Sullivan and James M. O'Toole, 121–69. Boston: Roman Catholic Archbishop of Boston, 1985.

Santaella, R. P. Esteban. *Historia de los Hermanos Cheos*. Ponce, Puerto Rico: Editorial Alfa y Omega, 1979.

Shaughnessy, Gerald. *Has the Immigrant Kept the Faith?* New York: Macmillan, 1925.

Silva Gotay, Samuel. *Protestantismo y Política en Puerto Rico: 1898–1930*. San Juan: Editorial de la Universidad de Puerto Rico, 1997.

———. *Catolicismo y Política en Puerto Rico Bajo España y Estados Unidos: Siglos XIX y XX*. San Juan: Universidad de Puerto Rico, 2005.

Slawson, Douglas. "'To Bring Glad Tidings to the Poor': Vincentian Parish Missions in the United States." In *The American Vincentians: A Popular History of the Congregation of the Mission in the United States, 1815–1987*, edited by John E. Rybolt, CM, 163–227. Brooklyn, N.Y.: New City Press, 1988.

Sobol, Robert. *Panic on Wall Street: A History of America's Financial Disasters*. New York: Macmillan, 1968.

Stevens-Arroyo, Anthony M. "The Catholic Worldview in the Political Philosophy of Pedro Albizu Campos: The Death Knoll [*sic*] of Puerto Rican Insularity." *U.S. Catholic Historian* 20, no. 4 (Fall 2002): 53–73.

Sussman, Warren I. *Culture as History: The Transformation of American Society in the Twentieth Century*. New York: Pantheon, 1973.

Swanton, John Reed. *Early History of the Creek Indians and Their Neighbors*. Smithsonian Institution. Bureau of American Ethnology. Bulletin 73. Washington, D.C.: Government Printing Office, 1922.

Tanner, Norman P., SJ, ed. *Decrees of the Ecumenical Councils*. Vol. 2. London: Sheed and Ward; Washington, D.C.: Georgetown University Press, 1990.

Tentler, Leslie Woodcock. *Wage-Earning Women, Industrial Work and Family Life in the United States, 1900–1930*. New York: Oxford University Press, 1979.

Thompson, William M., ed. *Bérulle and the French School: Selected Writings*. Translated by Lowell M. Glendon, SS. Preface by Susan A. Muto. Classics of Western Spirituality. New York and Mahwah, N.J.: Paulist Press, 1989.

Tifft, Thomas W. "Toward a More Humane Social Policy: The Work and Influence of Monsignor John O'Grady." Ph.D. diss., The Catholic University of America, 1979.

Tonra, Mary, MSBT. *Led by the Spirit: A Biography of Mother Boniface Keasey, MSBT*. New York: Gardner, 1984.

Tucker, Margaret. "Catholic Settlement Work: An Analysis." *Catholic Charities Review* 2, no. 10 (December 1918): 304–8; *Catholic Charities Review* 3, no. 1 (January 1919): 18–21.

Van Doren, Mark. *The Travels of William Bartram*. New York: Dover, 1955. Originally published in 1928.

Vilá de Blanco, María Cristina. "My Memories of Father Judge." In Judge, *Father Thomas A. Judge, C.M.*, Monographs 3. 1983.

Walsh, Mary Elizabeth. *The Saints and Social Work*. Silver Spring, Md.: Preservation of the Faith Press, 1937.

Ward, Mary A. *A Mission for Justice: The History of the First African American Catholic Church in Newark, New Jersey*. Knoxville: University of Tennessee Press, 2002.

Whelan, Ellen, OSF. *The Sisters' Story: St. Mary's Hospital–Mayo Clinic, 1889–1939*. Rochester, Minn.: Mayo Foundation for Medical Education and Research, 2002.

White, Joseph M. *Worthy of the Gospel of Christ: A History of the Catholic Diocese of Fort Wayne–South Bend*. Fort Wayne, Ind.: Diocese of Fort Wayne–South Bend, 2007.

Wilson, Deborah L., MSBT. "To Speak with One Voice: A History of the Constitutions and Rule of Life of the Missionary Servants of the Most Blessed Trinity." Master's thesis, University of Dayton, 2006.

Woods, Thomas E., Jr. *The Church Confronts Modernity: Catholic Intellectuals and the Progressive Era*. New York: Columbia University Press, 2004.

Woodward, C. Vann. *Tom Watson, Agrarian Rebel*. New York: Oxford University Press, 1963. First published in 1938.

INDEX

Every Catholic an Apostle: A Life of Thomas A. Judge, CM, 1868–1933 was designed in Mrs Eaves with Mr Eaves Sans display and composed by Kachergis Book Design of Pittsboro, North Carolina. It was printed on 60-pound Natures Book Natural and bound by Thomson-Shore of Dexter, Michigan.